INTRODUCTION TO CRIMINAL EVIDENCE

Other books by Jon R. Waltz

The Trial of Jack Ruby (1965) (with John Kaplan)
Cases and Materials on Evidence (1965; 8th ed. 1994) (with Roger C. Park)
Principles of Evidence and Proof (1965; 2nd ed. 1972) (with David W. Louisell and John Kaplan)
Medical Jurisprudence (1971) (with Fred E. Inbau)
The Federal Rules of Evidence: An Analysis (1972; 2d ed. 1975)
Basic Materials on Criminal Evidence (1980) (with John Kaplan)
Law and Medicine (1980) (with Walter J. Wadlington and Roger B. Dworkin)
Evidence: Making the Record (1982) (with John Kaplan)
Criminal Prosecution in the PRC and the USA: A Comparative Study (1995) (with He Jiahong)

FOURTH EDITION

INTRODUCTION TO CRIMINAL EVIDENCE

JON R. WALTZ

Edna B. and Ednyfed H. Williams Memorial Professor of Law, Northwestern University School of Law, and Lecturer in Medical Jurisprudence, Northwestern University Medical School, Chicago

Nelson-Hall Publishers/Chicago

Library of Congress Cataloging-in Publication Data

Waltz, Jon R.
Introduction to criminal evidence / Jon R. Waltz -- 4th ed.
p. cm.
Includes bibliographical references and index.
ISBN 0-8304-1479-7 (pbk.)
1. Evidence, Criminal--United States. I. Title.
KF9660.W32 1997
345.73'06--dc21
96-47174
CIP

Cover painting: "X" by Susie Levin

Manufactured in the United States of America

10 9 8 7 6 5 4 3 2 1

TM The paper used in this book meets the minimum requirements of American National Standard for Information Sciences—Permanence of Paper for Printed Library Materials, ANSI Z39.48-1984.

for RE
my good right arm

Contents

Preface

This book describes, in a sensible degree of detail, all of the important rules of evidence. As the book's title indicates, the emphasis is on the applicability of those rules in criminal matters. Even so, the book provides an overview of the evidentiary principles applicable in civil litigation as well.

After identifying the sources of evidence law, a description of the adversary trial process sets the backdrop for a discussion that ranges across the gamut of evidence rules. Relevance, the most pervasive of evidence concepts, and hearsay, perhaps the most technically challenging rule, are explored. Techniques used by trial lawyers to attack the credibility of court witnesses—so-called impeachment—are detailed. Then there is in-depth analysis of the most weighty constitutional principles, such as unlawful search and seizure and the privilege against self-incrimination. Here the reader encounters *Miranda* and other significant Supreme Court decisions and is plunged into the continuing controversy over the proper scope of the rule excluding evidence unlawfully obtained. Testimonial privileges, such as those shielding communications between lawyer and client, husband and wife, informant and law enforcer, are dissected. The evidentiary status of confessions, identification procedures, scientific investigation techniques, and expert testimony is described. Throughout the book are clear-cut examples and blocks of trial testimony that illustrate the operation of the rules of evidence in a real-world setting. In short, *Criminal Evidence* presents a broad-ranging discussion aimed at providing the reader with a solid grounding in evidence law.

I have tried to write this book in plain English. For a lawyer, that is easier said than done. Like the people encountered by Gulliver in his travels, we have "a peculiar cant and jargon of [our] own." Sometimes we seem capable of talking only to each other.

I have wanted to reach a larger audience; one made up of nonlawyers as well as lawyers—the undergraduate, the law student, the law enforcement trainee, the interested layperson. Furthermore, I have wanted to demonstrate that even between fullfledged lawyers the language of the law ought to be concise and direct. And so the discussion in this book will not be shrouded in lawyers' jargon or, if occasionally for some defensible reason it is (one defensible reason is that the reader will want to know some of the jargon), the legalisms will be explained in an understandable way.

In other words, I'll try to remember the instructive story about Prime Minister Arthur Balfour, who is supposed to have silenced a critic in the House of Commons by shouting in exasperation, "I know that! I am talking English, not law."

The organization of the book tracks that of the Federal Rules of Evidence, a codification of evidence rules that has been widely adopted. It is now so important at the federal and state levels that for the first time its text is reprinted in full as an appendix to this edition.

Jon R. Waltz

Chicago, Illinois
April 15, 1996

CHAPTER ONE

Published Sources of Law

While this book will not be loaded down with technical footnotes of the sort whose only real purpose is to suggest the author's vast learning, it will give the source of most of the judicial opinions, court rules, statutes, and the like that are discussed in the text. For this reason, and because the readers of this book may occasionally wish to locate and read cited materials in full, we begin with a brief explanation of the source of law in general and evidentiary rules in particular and of the way in which these sources are identified for reference purposes.

A. The Sources of Law in General

Legislatures, Agencies, Courts

The literature of the law is gigantic, filling huge libraries. This is because in this country law is generated in such a wide variety of ways. It might be much simpler if laws were handed down periodically by a dictator or an absolute monarch, but our kind of democracy trades harsh and unpredictable simplicity for broad concepts of fairness. And so law does not come in the form of autocratic edicts having a single source. Instead, law comes from elected and appointed judges who are hedged about by long-standing traditions of justice and who are overseen by appellate courts which are not reluctant to reverse incorrect lower court decisions. It also comes from state legislatures and city councils, from Congress and from state and federal agencies and commissions. Legislative bodies enact statutes and ordinances; at a less lofty level, agencies and commissions, authorized by legislatures to do so, draw up rules and regulations. Courts interpret statutes, ordinances, rules, and regulations if their meaning is unclear and enforce them when they are applicable to a given situation.

But legislative and administrative bodies cannot pass laws and draft regulations to channel every aspect of human behavior or to govern every question of evidence and courtroom procedure. Some legal principles are threshed out in courtrooms during trials. These principles, some of them downright ancient, make up the great body of the so-called *common law*—

Legal literature is usually found in specialized law libraries.

law declared by judges operating in areas not controlled by statutes, ordinances, and governmental regulations. In many jurisdictions, the law of evidence, for example, is mostly common law—judge-made law.

The Literature of the Law

This process of law-making has produced a monumental literature. First there are the sources of basic law: the innumerable statutes, ordinances, administrative regulations, and judicial opinions. All federal and state statutes and regulations, all county and municipal ordinances, and all but the most insignificant judicial opinions are published in full, officially or unofficially, in one place or another and frequently in several. Lawyers and judges refer to published statutes, court opinions, and the like as *primary authority,* since they, and they alone, constitute fundamental "law" to which citizens must adhere and which courts must enforce. Then there is a great mass of secondary authority that explains and interprets the primary sources of law: encyclopedias, treatises (such as this one), dictionaries, law reviews published by students at the nation's top law schools and other legal periodicals, and so on—and on and on. Finally, there are elaborate indexes, digests, and citators that aid lawyers and courts in locating relevant primary and secondary legal authorities.

Law Libraries

The publications described above are usually available only in specialized legal libraries and in the offices of those who deal regularly with the law. Law schools maintain the largest law libraries. City, county, and state legal organizations (bar associations) also maintain libraries of legal publications as a service primarily to their members. Nonlawyers, however, can usually get permission to make at least limited use of law school and bar association collections.

Courthouses contain law libraries, but these are mainly for the use of the judges and their law clerks and for members of prosecutorial staffs and other government lawyers and often are not open to others. The same is true of the law libraries maintained by some governmental departments such as the United States Department of Justice and the state's attorneys general. Law firms and single practitioners of the law invariably have their own law libraries, occasionally of a highly specialized sort reflecting the restricted nature of their law practice, but they tend not to encourage browsing by outsiders. Public libraries and undergraduate university libraries do not have extensive collections of law books, but some of the larger institutions may have the statutory codes and municipal ordinances of the state in which they are located, as well as some explanatory texts.

Finally, law enforcement agencies usually issue books or manuals containing criminal statutes and ordinances to their personnel.

B. Methods of Publishing Court Opinions

Court Reports

Judicial opinions are printed in books called *reports* or *reporters.* For many years there was no organized method for the publication—the reporting—of American court decisions. The job was left to private court reporters and publishers. The result was a hodgepodge of separate publications that made it difficult to locate the sources of law. Today the situation is different and much improved. The volumes of what is called the National Reporter System include all of the decisions of the highest state courts. This system of reports also includes the decisions of intermediate state appellate courts. And it publishes the opinions of federal courts, including the Supreme Court of the United States. Computer technology is making decisional law even more readily available.

Except in connection with opinions of the U.S. Supreme Court, when we will rely on the Court's own official publications, this book will refer the reader to the volumes of the largely unofficial but highly accurate National Reporter System.

C. Methods of Citing Published Court Opinions

Legal Citations

A typical citation to a state court decision will look like this: *People* v. *Miller,* 238 N.E.2d 407 (S. Ct. Ill. 1968). "People" and "Miller" are the names of the parties to this reported criminal case: the People, represented by the state's attorney, are prosecuting the defendant, Miller. The intervening "v." stands for *versus,* which, translated from the Latin, simply means "against"—*People* against *Miller.* The initial number, 238, refers to the volume in the reporter series. The "N.E." refers to the geographical region covered by the reporter series; "2d" indicates that this system of regional judicial reports has gone into a second series of volumes, the preceding series having been denominated simply "N.E."

Other phases of the National Reporter System reprint decisions from the Pacific region (Pac. and P.2d), Northwestern (N.W. and N.W.2d), Southwestern (S.W. and S.W.2d), Atlantic (Atl. and A.2d), Southeastern (S.E. and S.E.2d), and Southern (So. and So.2d). Separate series are published for New York (N.Y.S. and N.Y.S.2d) and California (Cal. Rptr.).

The number 407 in our citation to the case of *People* v. *Miller* refers to the page of volume 238 of the N.E.2d series on which the opinion in that case begins. Within the parentheses in the citation to *People* v. *Miller* are the name of the court handing down the decision—here, the Supreme Court of Illinois—and the year in which the decision was announced, 1968.

Citations to federal cases are similar in appearance. *United States* v. *Harris*, 403 U.S. 573 (1971), refers to a decision in volume 403 of the official series that reports decisions of the Supreme Court of the United States. (Occasionally in this book it will be necessary, in connection with very recent opinions, to cite to an unofficial Supreme Court reporting system because the opinion has not yet been officially published by the Court. Such a citation will look like this: *Florida* v. *Riley*, ______ U.S. ______, 109 S.Ct. 693 (1989).) *United States* v. *McCann*, 465 F.2d 147 (5th Cir. 1972), would lead the legal researcher to a volume in the second federal series that reports decisions of the United States Courts of Appeal. *United States* v. *England*, 348 F. Supp. 851 (W.D.Mo. 1971), identifies an opinion written by a federal trial judge sitting on the United States District Court for the Western District of Missouri.

Where a case is too ancient to have been included in the official U.S. Supreme Court reports or in the National Reporter System, we cite the available series of official or private reporters: *Slater* v. *Baker*, 60 Barb. 488 (S.Ct. N.Y. 1871), for example, is a citation to an opinion of a New York trial court rendered prior to commencement of the National Reporter System. "Barb." refers to Barber, who was a private court reporter.

For a much more complete and detailed description of legal sources and methods of citation, the interested reader is directed to an outstanding reference work: *How to Find the Law*, edited by law librarian William R. Roalfe.

D. The Sources of the Law of Evidence

Case Law and Codes

Not so many years ago it would have been reasonably accurate to say that almost all evidentiary rules are judge-made; in other words, they are a product of the common law. There had been a few efforts to pull together all the different rules of evidence and codify them in statutes or codes but they met with little success. The *Uniform Rules of Evidence*, drafted by the Commissioners on Uniform State Laws and published in 1954, exerted some influence on courts but was formally adopted in only a few states. An earlier effort to codify the rules of evidence, the American Law Institute's 1942 *Model Code of Evidence*, was not adopted in any state.

Today, however, California, after years of research and debate by its Law Revision Commission, has adopted in statutory form a complete and in some ways innovative Evidence Code and in mid-1975 the Federal Rules of Evidence, a more or less complete evidence code, went into effect. Many of the states have adopted or are considering the adoption of evidence codes modeled along the lines of the California and the federal codes.

These efforts to develop codes of evidence are, in the main, just that: they are attempts to catalog in one place the evidentiary principles that have long been firmly settled in our courts. Only occasionally do the evidence codes break new ground.

What this means is that judges, lawyers, and law enforcement agents must now have a grasp not only of the emerging evidentiary codes but also of the case law, the prior judicial decisions. An understanding of these opinions will carry with it an understanding of the new codes. Of course, it will also bring an understanding of the governing evidentiary principles in those jurisdictions that have not yet adopted codifications of the rules of evidence.

Accordingly, the ensuing analysis will be drawn from, and will make reference to, both the case law and the codes.

But first we must consider the trial process and the classifications of evidence.

CHAPTER TWO

The Trial Process and Classifications of Evidence

A. Adversary Trial System

Most knowledgeable observers would agree that the Anglo-American adversary trial system is a thing of wonder. One wonders whether it is properly designed to reach its announced goal, the ascertainment of relevant truth. Beyond that, one wonders how it ever works at all.

"Set the Parties Fighting"

There is nothing very scientific about the process of litigation. As one highly experienced trial lawyer, who believed in being frank, once described it, "The way we administer justice is by an adversary proceeding, which is to say, we set the parties fighting." Professor Robert E. Keeton of the Harvard Law School has said it less dramatically: "A trial is a competition of inconsistent versions of facts and theories of law." Defying all precepts of scientific fact-finding, the trial system actually works quite well. Adversariness seems to be the best method yet devised for forcing the truth into the open.

Some Distinctive Characteristics

A few distinctive characteristics of the adversary trial system stand out. In the main, cases are prosecuted by the parties through their legal representatives. Criminal cases are prepared and prosecuted by an elected or appointed representative of the people; they are defended by lawyers retained by the accused or, if the accused is without funds (indigent), by counsel—often a member of a public defender office—appointed by the trial court. These lawyers, guided by a judge, control the content and flow of the evidence.

And the litigation process is, at least theoretically, two-sided, not one-sided, in the sense that each party has an equal opportunity to investigate the case and present his or her side of it at trial through evidence and argument. (Although each side has an equal *opportunity* to do this, the accused may not possess equal *means* of doing so. Ordinarily, the prosecution—well financed and with large support staffs—has a genuine advantage in the investigation and preparation of cases.)

B. The Role of the Trial Judge

Umpire or Arbiter

The trial judge in an American jury case serves only as a sort of umpire. He or she applies the procedural rules to the lawyers and explains the substantive principles of law to the jurors, but generally the jurors, and they alone, decide what facts have been established beyond a reasonable doubt by the evidence.

In other words, the judge is the arbiter of the law; the jurors are the arbiters of the facts. The jurors, in reaching their verdict, apply to the facts, as found by them, the law as it is explained to them by the judge in his or her instructions (sometimes called the judge's "charge" to the jury). Of course, if trial by jury has been waived, the trial judge herself will find the facts and apply the law to them in what is referred to as a *bench trial.*

C. The Role of Legal Counsel

The Stage Managers

When a criminal case goes to trial, the parties, through their legal representatives, produce the evidence that the jurors are to consider in reaching their verdict. Trial lawyers are like producers and stage managers. Except in a few special situations, the trial judge has no power to tell the parties what evidence to produce or to produce any him- or herself, and the jurors never have any such power. (Occasionally the court may itself appoint and call to the witness stand one or more impartial experts; for example, a psychiatrist in a case involving an insanity defense.)

Although at first blush it may seem strange that the parties, through their lawyers, are free to decide what evidence the jury will hear and see, free to decide how the trial will be staged, the workings of the adversary trial system usually ensure that what one side suppresses the other will triumphantly produce—with the result that the first side will probably introduce it initially rather than be charged with hiding relevant information. This process of smoking out the evidence would prove ineffective if one side were unaware of favorable evidence in the possession of the opposite side. In times

In a jury trial the judge's role is to be the arbiter of law, not facts.

past, criminal defendants were often at a distinct disadvantage in this respect because there were few procedures by which they could discover the prosecution's evidence. This disadvantage is gradually being remedied by new rules of criminal procedure that give the accused greater access to the prosecution's evidence.

D. Questions of Law and Questions of Fact

The outcome of criminal trials is determined by propositions of law (What are the elements of first-degree homicide?) and questions of fact (Did the accused, with premeditation, kill someone?). In most criminal cases, fact-questions have the greatest impact on the trial's outcome. The rules of evidence govern what materials can be used by a fact-finder in resolving these fact-questions.

E. Two Crucial Questions about Evidence

There are two principal questions about evidence that have to be answered. First, what matters and what materials should be *admitted* into evidence for the jury to consider? Secondly, what *use* can properly be made by the jurors of those matters and materials that are ruled admissible?

Almost all of the rules of evidence relate to the first of these two questions. That is, most of the rules of evidence relate to the problem of what shall be received in evidence—the problem of *admissibility.*

The second question—what *use* should be made of matters and materials admitted into evidence—is an important one, but no very effective means exist to control the way a jury deals with items of admitted evidence. For example, in a criminal case a judge may instruct the jurors that certain evidence, perhaps a prior inconsistent statement, is admissible only for the purpose of casting doubt on (impeaching) a witness's credibility and not as substantive evidence affirmatively proving any element of the alleged offense. Consciously or unconsciously, however, the jurors may nonetheless use the evidence as substantive proof of *guilt.*

F. The Problem of Admissibility

"Admissibility" is a decision as to what matters and materials the jury will be permitted to hear, see, read, and perhaps even touch or smell. Two principal areas of concern influence the admissibility problem.

Time Consumption

First of all, there is concern about time consumption. A narrowing of the matters to be considered during a litigation is vital; otherwise, trials would go on forever. The rules of evidence, in other words, are a concession to the mortality of humankind. A criminal case would go on for an unbearable length of time if there were no reasonably restrictive evidentiary principles putting outer bounds on the sheer amount of evidence to be admitted.

Protection of the Jury

Second, and of even more pressing concern, is the supposed need to protect lay jurors from improper or inappropriate influences. Most of the complexities of our rules of evidence are a direct product of the system that uses laypeople—the jury—as fact-finders. The assumption is that inexperienced fact-finders must be carefully shielded from misleading or prejudicial influences that might induce them to arrive at an incorrect verdict. The crucial question is, What can we safely let lay jurors see and hear? The importance of this question is borne out by the fact that many evidentiary problems are the result of attempts by flamboyant trial lawyers to score points with the lay jury by adopting methods of advocacy that would probably not have much impact on an experienced trial judge who was acting as the trier of the facts in a bench trial.

G. The Basic Types of Evidence

Two Fundamental Types

There are two fundamental types, as distinguished from forms, of evidence: *direct* evidence and *indirect* or *circumstantial* evidence.

Direct Evidence

Direct evidence proves a fact-proposition directly rather than by an inferential process. It goes directly, in one step, to a material issue in the case.

> EXAMPLE:
> "I saw the accused pull a revolver from his belt and shoot the man standing behind him at the bar three times."

Direct evidence is often referred to as "eyewitness" evidence. This is putting it too simply, however. Direct evidence is the product of a person's sensory perception and most people, but not all, have five senses: sight, touch, taste, smell, and hearing. The person who observed the accused person pulling a revolver from his belt was giving direct eyewitness testimony. Had he also testified, "I heard three shots," he would have provided an example of what could be termed direct "ear-witness" testimony. The person who testifies, "It smelled like smoke," is a "nose-witness," and the person who testifies, "I felt his wrist and got no pulse," is a "touch-witness." "It tasted like bitter almonds," is, of course, an example of direct evidence based on the witness's sense of taste.

Indirect or Circumstantial Evidence

Standing in contrast to direct evidence is indirect or circumstantial evidence. Circumstantial evidence depends on *inference* for its relationship to the fact-proposition to be proved. In other words, it does not prove that proposition directly; it is indirect evidence. It is evidence of a subsidiary, even collateral, fact from which, alone or in conjunction with a cluster of other facts, the existence of an ultimate fact-proposition can be inferred by the fact-finder. This simply is a way of saying that one fact or a group of them may imply the existence of yet another fact.

> EXAMPLE:
> Bushmat and Stitz are observed going into a room that has only one means of entry and exit, a door. That door is locked behind them. A loud "bang," coming from inside the room, is heard by persons standing outside the door. The door is then broken down. Bushmat

is observed standing over the prostrate body of Stitz, who has a bleeding circular wound in his forehead. Bushmat is holding a revolver in his hand. There is one spent cartridge, still warm, in the chamber.

All of this is circumstantial evidence that Bushmat shot Stitz in the head. It is not direct evidence that he did so since no one actually saw Bushmat shoot Stitz.

Circumstantial evidence is frequently far more persuasive than direct evidence, as the example above demonstrates. Were Bushmat to announce, "I have not shot Stitz and nothing else unusual has occurred here," his statement would constitute direct evidence, since Bushmat is the only living eyewitness to what happened in the locked room. Jurors, however, not being nitwits, are likely to give greater weight to the circumstantial inferences generated by the surrounding circumstances. (But be careful; circumstantial evidence is not always what it seems to be. Maybe Stitz committed suicide and Bushmat was foolish enough to pick up the gun. The jurors will want to hear more facts.)

Most of the evidentiary rules concerning relevance, and most of the exclusionary rules of evidence that will be discussed later, relate to circumstantial evidence, since this type of evidence raises the most problems of reliability and the like. Direct evidence, such as eyewitness narratives, is almost invariably admissible so long as it is relevant to the issues in the case being tried. (Under some circumstances, however, a trial court will give jurors a cautionary instruction regarding the possible unreliability of direct, eyewitness testimony. See, e.g., *State* v. *Long,* 721 p.2d 483 (Utah 1986).)

H. The Three Basic Forms of Evidence

The two fundamental types of evidence (direct and circumstantial) come in three basic forms: *testimonial, tangible,* and *judicially noticed* evidence.

Testimonial Evidence

Testimonial evidence is oral testimony given by a witness in court, under oath or solemn affirmation, from the witness stand, or it may occasionally be by way of sworn pretrial written deposition.

Tangible Evidence

The phrase "tangible evidence" refers to the physical exhibits in a case. Exhibits—all manner of tangible things—can be offered into evidence for the fact-finder's consideration if they bear upon the issues in the case.

There are two basic sorts of tangible evidence. First there is so-called *real evidence.* This is the "real thing" in the case—the actual murder weapon, the allegedly forged check, the heroin allegedly sold to an undercover agent.

Secondly, there is *demonstrative evidence.* This is not the real thing. It is a visual and sometimes audio-visual aid for the fact-finder, such as a model or mockup of the crime scene, a diagram, or an anatomical model. Chapter 19 is devoted to this kind of evidence.

Judicial Notice

Third, there is the phenomenon known as *judicial notice.* Some matters, because they are subject to common knowledge in the community or to certain verification through reference to some highly reliable source such as a calendar or a medical treatise, need not be proved in the usual manner. Instead, a trial judge will take judicial notice of them and instruct the jurors to take them as fully established in the case without any necessity of formal proof through witnesses or exhibits. In this sense, judicial notice, which will be discussed in detail in chapter 14, is a form of evidence.

I. Admissibility Again

Sometimes television dramas give a fairly accurate picture of the complicated workings of the law. On television, and in mystery novels, one hears such invariably successful trial lawyers as Perry Mason say, "Object, Your Honor. Irrelevant, immaterial, incompetent!" The fact is that this classic objection, known to trial lawyers as the "Three I's," pretty well summarizes the entire body of evidentiary rules.

To be properly receivable for the fact-finder's consideration, evidence must be probative of a material issue in the case and otherwise competent under the rules of evidence. Every item of evidence offered at trial must pass the tests of materiality, probativeness, and competency.

Materiality

In assessing admissibility it is first necessary to ask, To what issue does the offered evidence go? What is the issue? Is that issue, whatever it may be, a material one in the case, made so by the wording of the charge against the accused, the rulings of the trial court, and the stipulations of the prosecutor and the defense counsel? If the issue to which the offered evidence goes is not a material one in the case, the evidence will be excluded on objection by opposing counsel.

EXAMPLE:
Evidence pertaining to the way the accused treats his mother-in-law probably goes to no material issue in an arson prosecution.

Probativeness

If the issue to which the offered evidence goes is a material one in the case, it next becomes necessary to ask, Is the offered evidence probative of that issue? That is, does the evidence tend to establish the material point? Does it tend to make the point more probably true, or untrue, than would be the case without that evidence? If the answer to the question of probativeness is in the affirmative, the relevance question has been answered, since materiality and probativeness, taken together, add up to relevance. Relevance, in other words, can be defined as a tendency to prove a fact-proposition properly provable in the case.

> EXAMPLE:
> The fact that the accused stole some candy bars from a corner drugstore when he was a schoolboy is not probative of his guilt of grand larceny twenty years later.

Competency

If the entire two-part relevancy question can be answered in the affirmative, it will then be necessary to inquire, Is the offered evidence nonetheless incompetent—that is, inadmissible—because of some special exclusionary rule of law? To answer this third and last question, one must have a working knowledge of the entire body of evidentiary rules.

Evidence may be probative of a material issue and still be excluded by some special rule because the particular type of evidence is thought to be generally unreliable (for example, hearsay evidence); unjustifiably disruptive of trial procedure (for example, surprise evidence as to which advance notice must be given under some special rule—alibi evidence, for instance); too overwhelmingly probative, that is, evidence whose unfairly prejudicial impact far outweighs its substantive value (for example, relevant but horrendously prejudicial or inflammatory evidence, ranging from an excessively gruesome photograph of a dead body to the testimony of a qualified mathematician expert that the odds are a billion to one that the accused was the perpetrator of the crime charged against him); contrary to policies favoring confidentiality in order to encourage certain sorts of relationships (for example, the testimonial privileges, such as attorney-client, physician-patient, husband-wife); or violative of some constitutional doctrine (for example, principles pertaining to self-incrimination or unlawful search and seizure).

J. The Weight of Evidence

Even though evidence has been ruled admissible by the trial judge, it is for the jury to decide what if any weight to give to it. Being the finders of facts, the jurors are entitled to assess the persuasiveness or believability of evidence. They can give it no weight at all if its believability is suspect, or they can give it full weight where it is persuasive and uncontradicted.

> EXAMPLE:
> The accused's wife takes the stand in his behalf and testifies that her husband was with her during the entire night on which he is charged with having committed a gas station robbery. However, on cross-examination and through other witnesses the prosecutor brings out the fact that on the night in question the accused's wife had been out of town. Under these circumstances the jury would undoubtedly give no weight to the testimony of the accused's wife, having also in mind that she is interested in the outcome of the trial. Had the witness's testimony not been so thoroughly impeached, the jury might have accorded it full weight.

K. The Structure of a Criminal Trial

This is a book about evidence, the testimony and other materials that are offered by the prosecution and the defense for the jury's consideration during a criminal trial. A courtroom trial, therefore, provides the framework—the context—for our subject. Before getting into the rules of evidence, then, we had better provide a blueprint of a criminal proceeding.

The Sixth Amendment Guarantee of Jury Trial

Who says that a person accused of criminal conduct should get a full-blown jury trial? Our Founding Fathers said it, in some detail. They wrote it into the nation's charter, the Constitution of the United States. The Sixth Amendment to the Constitution, employing a verb that many defendants would reject as inappropriate to their situation, guarantees, at least in cases in which the penalty includes imprisonment for more than six months, that "the accused shall enjoy the right to a speedy and public trial." What the drafters of this part of the Bill of Rights meant by their use of the verb "enjoy" was that in America a criminal accused is *entitled* to a prompt and public trial. While the accused may not enjoy it (in the sense of finding it pleasurable), he or she is likely to agree that a trial, convened without unjustifiable delay and not carried out in secret, is better than a midnight lynching.

The Sixth Amendment lays down additional requirements. A trial must take place before an impartial (unbiased) jury. The accused must be informed of the exact nature of the charge against him, so that he knows what he is up against and can prepare his defense. At his trial the accused is entitled to be confronted, face-to-face, by the witnesses against him so that his defense counsel can cross-examine them and the jurors can see and hear them. And

An appeals court reviews the trial process.

the accused is empowered, by means of subpoenas (a type of court order), to compel witnesses to appear in court and give testimony that may be helpful to the defense. Finally, the Sixth Amendment makes it clear that an accused is entitled to have the assistance of a defense lawyer.

Arrest

Of course, the criminal justice process begins long before the trial that is described in the Sixth Amendment. An incident triggers an investigation by law enforcement agents. The investigation produces a suspect and an official decision to arrest him/her. The decision to arrest is backed by an *information* (a charge filed in court by a prosecutor) or an *indictment* (handed down by a grand jury). The arrest, depending on the circumstances, may be accomplished with or without a formal arrest warrant.

Arrest means that the suspect is taken into custody. He or she will then be "booked," which simply means that the arresting agency will make a record of the suspect's name and address, the name of the arresting officer, the date and time of the arrest, the charge, and the suspect's physical description. At this time the accused will be fingerprinted and photographed.

Arraignment

Of course, the accused may be released from custody shortly after being booked if a decision is made to dismiss the charge against him, perhaps because a prosecutor who has been consulted thinks the evidence is weak or incomplete. Otherwise, the arresting agency must without delay present the accused before a magistrate or judge. This will be the accused's first contact with the judicial system. It is called an *arraignment,* a term drawn from the French word meaning "to speak." Most of the speaking will be done by the magistrate or judge, who will advise the accused of the charge against him and inform him of his rights—particularly of his right to be represented by a lawyer. If the accused is too poor to retain private legal counsel a public defender will be assigned to assist him.

If the charge is a minor one, a petty misdemeanor, the accused's plea ("Guilty," "Not Guilty," "No Contest") can be accepted at the arraignment. If the charge is a more substantial one, such as a felony, a plea will not be taken at this time; the matter will be set for a *preliminary hearing* and, typically, the accused will be permitted to make bail. The making of bail, usually involving the posting of a cash bond, is intended to guarantee that the accused will show up for all future proceedings. If the accused makes bail he/she will be set free pending the preliminary hearing.

Preliminary Hearing

At the preliminary hearing it is determined by a judge whether there are reasonable grounds for believing that a crime has been committed and that the accused was the perpetrator. If both questions are answered in the affirmative, the accused will be "bound over" for trial or, in some jurisdictions, such as Kentucky, bound over for a grand jury unless he enters a "guilty" or "no contest" plea. He can again be released on bail; if he has been unable to post bond he will be remanded to jail to await trial.

Pretrial Motions

During the period between arrest and trial there may be a flurry of activity by defense counsel, often taking the form of motions made before a judge. The defense may move to dismiss the accusation on the ground that it is technically defective. In a case that has attracted a great deal of prejudicial local publicity, the defense may move for a change of venue, which means a change of the place of trial to a locality in which there has not been saturating publicity.

The defense may move to suppress (exclude) evidence that it believes is inadmissible. For example, it may move to suppress a confession that it claims was coerced or obtained without advising the accused of his right to remain silent and to be represented by counsel. The defense may also seek to exclude items of tangible evidence that it contends were secured by means of an unreasonable search and seizure, which would be violative of the Constitution's Fourth Amendment. It may even seek to obtain advance rulings that specified evidence is inadmissible under principles found not in the Constitution but in codes of evidence or prior judicial decisions.

Counsel for the defendant will also take pretrial steps to learn what the prosecution's evidence is expected to be, and will demand a list of the witnesses that the prosecutor intends to call to the stand at trial. The prosecution, in fairness, will be expected to reveal its evidence quite freely, and this is especially true if it has come into possession of evidence that is favorable to the defendant.

An Outline of the Trial Process

A criminal trial is a tightly structured procedure and passes through a number of stages that can be outlined as follows:

1. Selection of the jury.
2. Opening statements to the jury by the prosecutor and the defense counsel.
3. The prosecution's case-in-chief against the defendant.
4. The defendant's case-in-chief.
5. The prosecution's rebuttal, and perhaps evidence from the defendant to counter the prosecution's rebuttal evidence.
6. Closing argument to the jury by the prosecutor and the defense counsel.
7. The judge's instructions to the jury.
8. Deliberation and verdict by the jury.
9. Sentencing.

Jury Selection

The first in-court aspect of a criminal trial is jury selection. Typically, the process goes this way: a panel of prospective jurors is brought into the courtroom; perhaps twenty in an ordinary case, more in a case in which, perhaps because of heavy pretrial publicity, a large number of potential jurors are likely to be excused from service because they have already formed an unshakable opinion about the defendant's guilt or innocence.

These persons, whose names were drawn at random from voter registration rolls, have already been screened to some extent, usually by means of a printed questionnaire that was mailed to them. The questionnaire probes for basic disqualifications that are laid down by statute: is the person under twenty-one years of age, is she an alien, is he a convicted felon, is she incapable of understanding English, is he/she in poor health?—and so on. No one who has given an affirmative answer to any of these basic questions will be called for jury duty.

Up to twelve prospective jurors are placed in the jury box. What they are about to undergo is called the *voir dire,* a Norman French term meaning "to tell the truth." The prospective jurors now take an oath to do just that. The questioning of them is about to begin.

Jury Commissioners randomly selecting capsules containing the names of potential jurors.

At one time the *voir dire* questioning was conducted almost exclusively by the lawyers—the prosecutor and the defense counsel—who sometimes abused the process. They realized all too well that the *voir dire* presented their one and only chance during the trial to speak directly to the jurors as individuals. Consequently, each attorney strove to ingratiate himself with the jury, to impress individual jurors with the force and charm of his or her personality in order to win the jurors to his side. Lawyers also used the jury-picking process to explain their case at the earliest juncture; through the artful framing of questions they acquainted the jurors with their main contentions of law and fact. Many times implications contained in *voir dire* questions could be used by clever counsel to substitute for real evidence. Finally, selection of the jury could be made to serve a powerful tactical purpose by requiring panel members to promise that they would judge the case in one light or another. They might be asked such questions as "Will you disregard the fact that the defendant is divorced?" or that he has a record of prior, unrelated crimes or is a member of a particular racial or ethnic group? When the case came to a close and the lawyer was delivering his closing argument, he could then argue that the jurors should do this or that not only because it was *right* but also because they had solemnly *promised* during the *voir dire* to do so. Not much wonder, then, that jury selection came to be one of the principal battlegrounds in the trial of a criminal matter, in some cases consuming more time than the ensuing trial itself. And not much wonder, either, that today the *voir dire* questioning in many courts is conducted by the trial judge and not by the lawyers.

The trial judge, relying in part on questions that have been submitted to her in writing by counsel, will concentrate on what, in theory, is the only legitimate function of the *voir dire*: development of sufficient information upon which to select qualified, impartial jurors. After the questioning each juror may be accepted or excused by the two sides. Two kinds of challenges are recognized in American trial courts—the *challenge for cause* and the *peremptory challenge.* The former must be based on a specific, recognized ground, be it statutory or the result of past judicial rulings, while the latter, as its name "peremptory" implies, can usually be for good reason, bad reason, or no reason at all, provided only that the limited number of such challenges allotted each side has not been used up. (And the Supreme Court has held that peremptory challenges can never be employed in a deliberately discriminatory way to purge a jury of members of a racial minority.)

The recognized grounds for challenging a potential juror for cause are numerous. She may be subject to challenge because, although qualified in general, she is automatically presumed to be biased either because of a relationship to the defendant or to one of the attorneys. Undoubtedly the largest target of challenges for cause are those jurors who, because they are biased or hold some fixed notion, cannot fairly judge the case before them. On this point the applicable Texas statute is representative. It provides for a challenge for cause if "there is established in the mind of the juror such a conclusion as to the guilt or innocence of the defendant as will influence him in his action in finding a verdict." The Texas statute goes on to provide that where a prospective juror admits to an opinion as to the guilt or innocence of the defendant but "states that he feels able, notwithstanding such opinion, to render an impartial verdict upon the law and the evidence, the court if satisfied that he is impartial and will render such verdict may in its discretion admit him as competent to serve in such as case." (But you can be pretty sure that one side or the other will expend a peremptory challenge to get rid of such a juror.)

In theory, an unlimited number of challenges for cause can be granted, depending only on the presence of a specified ground. In fact, however, many of the grounds will be revealed only if the prospective juror is willing to admit to the type of bias which most people are eager to hide. Taking this into account, the law also allows each side a set number of peremptory challenges that can be employed on the merest hunch or suspicion of prejudice. But, as is common in the law, a guarantee intended to protect one side or the other from unfairness can readily be converted into a means of gaining a tactical advantage. The peremptory challenge has become something other than a device to secure an unprejudiced jury; it is now generally regarded as a method of obtaining jurors who are most likely to be biased in one's favor. It is in this context that a vast body of folklore has been generated concerning the behavior of jurors—some of it quite ridiculous. Silly or not, however, many criminal lawyers adhere almost religiously to an elaborate system of stereotypes in determining what sorts of jurors should be peremptorily challenged and what sorts should be retained. Defense lawyers have long surmised that Irish, Italians, Jews, Eastern Europeans, and African-Americans make good jurors for their side in criminal cases. Where the juror identifies with a group that at one time or another in American history has been the underdog, he/she supposedly tends to have sympathy for an accused. Americans of English, German, and Scandinavian extraction, on the other hand, are favored by the prosecution since they are thought—again in an empirical vacuum—to be more willing to administer justice untempered by mercy. Occupational groups also occupy an important position in lawyers' folklore. Bankers, stock brokers, and low-rank white-collar workers are regarded as good prosecution jurors, while union members, artists, musicians, salespersons, and taxi drivers are thought to lean toward the defense. Myriad other rules are bandied about. It is sometimes said that, for the defense, young jurors tend to be better than the elderly, women better than men, poor better than rich, married better than single. A substantial part of the questioning of prospective jurors is regularly directed to finding out in which pigeonhole of the folklore they fit.

Of course, not all trial practitioners have abiding faith in this jury folklore. Every experienced prosecutor has his anecdote about the wealthy, elderly, bachelor Swedish banker who held out for acquittal; many a defense attorney has seen her client's cause lost at the hands of a young, married black juror of moderate means. Although the social scientists keep trying, it is difficult to get really reliable information on the behavior of jurors. One of the most careful and promising efforts to discover what happens in the jury room, by obtaining a judge's permission and then "bugging" a jury's deliberations, created such an outrage that Congress promptly made it a federal crime.

In trials that are likely to be lengthy, a few extra jurors ("alternates") are usually selected, just in case one or more jurors are lost during the trial due to illness, hardship, even death. In any event, when the questioning is over and all available challenges have been exercised, the acceptable panel that remains is sworn to well and truly try the case. In important cases that are likely to generate coverage by the news media, the jury may be sequestered in quarters provided by the court at the end of each trial day in order to insulate it from outside influence.

Opening Statements

At the very outset of a trial the lawyers are permitted to make opening statements to the jury that they have just selected. These are not arguments; argumentation must await the end of the trial. They are, or should be, straightforward recitations of what each side expects its evidence will be and what it will show. The prosecution, because it brought the charge and has the burden of proving it, is the first to address the jurors. Defense counsel can then make an opening statement or it can be reserved until the beginning of the defendant's case, when the defense lawyer has had a chance to hear the prosecution's evidence and gauge its effect. Since this is not argumentation, the prosecution is not permitted to make a rebuttal or closing statement following the defense's opening statement.

This is how an opening statement will sound:

> BY THE PROSECUTOR: Ladies and gentlemen of the jury, at this time I, as the prosecutor, am permitted to make to you what is called an opening statement. What I am about to say to you is not itself evidence in this case—what we lawyers say is never evidence. Evidence comes from witnesses and exhibits in the case.
>
> And it is not supposed to be an argument, either. We are not trying to get you to make up your minds about this case even before the first witness has been called to the stand to give testimony. Keep an open mind until you have heard all the evidence.
>
> An opening statement is simply intended to outline for you what we expect our evidence will show. The idea is, and I hope it's correct, that this will be helpful to you. The evidence is introduced

> in bits and pieces, some testimony from a witness and then an exhibit such as the murder weapon, then another witness, and so on. It has to be this way. We can only do one thing at a time during a trial, you see, and so you can't get the big picture all at once.
>
> Think of this as a preview. I am just going to give you a preview of what the prosecution expects its evidence to be, and then the defense will have an opportunity to tell you what it thinks its evidence will show. We hope that this will help you to follow the evidence as it is admitted for your consideration.
>
> I first take you to the night of April 4, 1990. We expect the evidence to show that at about 6:30 on the evening of that day, Clyde Bushmat was driving home from work in his car.
>
> We further expect the evidence to show that he was northbound on the Outer Drive. . . .

In this fashion the prosecutor and the defense counsel sketch the picture—the mosaic—that each hopes his or her evidence will reveal. The evidence is often described in chronological sequence. Counsel will speak in a rather general way; she will not attempt a word-for-word description of expected testimony, lest the jury read some significance into a slight variation in the words that eventually come from the witness' mouth. It is sometimes said that in opening statements the lawyers tell the jurors *what* the evidence will show, not *how* it will show it.

After the opening statements have been made, the moment that brings butterflies to the stomach of the most experienced trial lawyer has arrived. That moment is announced when the judge says, "Call your first witness, Mr. Prosecutor." (All other witnesses will have been excluded from the courtroom to prevent them from listening to each other testify, which might result in the convenient altering of testimony.) It is now time for the prosecutor to make good on his opening statement by presenting the People's case-in-chief.

The Prosecution's Case-in-Chief

The prosecutor will have issued subpoenas to all or most of its witnesses in order to ensure that they come to court at the specified time to give their testimony. (A subpoena can also require the witness to bring tangible evidence with her, such as documents or records.) During the prosecution's case-in-chief it must present evidence—testimony and exhibits—that support every legal element of the crime charged.

The elements of a crime are set forth in public laws (statutes), where the penalty for committing the crime will also be found. For example, the elements of the crime of larceny (theft) consist of (1) taking (2) and carrying away (3) personal property (4) from another person's possession (5) with a specific intent to steal it. The prosecution, to carry its burden of proof, must produce admissible evidence calculated to establish all five of these elements beyond a reasonable doubt. (If the charge is grand larceny, as distinguished from petty larceny, the prosecution will also have to prove that the property had a value in excess of the amount set forth in the statute covering grand larceny.)

When a witness is called to the stand the prosecutor asks him/her non-leading questions aimed at eliciting relevant facts within the witness' personal knowledge. This is called *direct examination,* in contrast to the more freewheeling *cross-examination* of the same witness that will be conducted by defense counsel immediately following the direct. The prosecution may also use the witness to identify tangible evidence (exhibits) such as the murder weapon, a letter, a photograph. Objections to the admissibility of evidence can be made by defense counsel, based on the rules that will be described in this book, and the trial judge will rule on them, sustaining them or overruling them.

We will describe in detail the process of examining witnesses and dealing with exhibits in the next chapter.

When the prosecutor believes that he/she has introduced sufficient evidence to support all elements of the charge, she will announce that "The prosecution rests" or "The prosecution rests its case," which simply means that she has completed the process of evidence-offering. The prosecution's case-in-chief has now concluded.

Defense Motion for Dismissal of the Charge

At this point the defense will move to dismiss the charge if it believes that the evidence as to any essential element of the charge is insufficient to justify a conviction. It may argue that as to some element there has been a total absence of proof. ("There has been no proof of criminal intent, your Honor. The prosecution's evidence fails to establish an intent to steal the coat from the checkroom. It was just a mistake.") Or the defense may contend that the prosecution's evidence was just not weighty enough to convince any rational juror beyond a reasonable doubt. (This motion is sometimes called a motion for a *directed verdict of acquittal* since, if it is granted, the jury is ordered by the judge to render a verdict of Not Guilty.) If the defense's motion is denied, it will now present the defense's case-in-chief.

The Defense's Case-in-Chief

Just as the prosecution summoned witnesses and produced exhibits, the defense will call people to testify on direct on behalf of the accused and will introduce relevant exhibits. However, the accused himself may invoke his Fifth Amendment privilege against self-incrimination and stay off the witness stand, thereby avoiding cross-examination by the prosecutor, who will not even be allowed to comment on the accused's failure to testify.

The prosecution is entitled to cross-examine the defense witnesses; as in the prosecution's case-in-chief, there may then be redirect by defense counsel and recross by the prosecutor until all relevant evidence has been extracted from the witnesses. Objections to the admissibility of testimony and exhibits, and rulings on those objections, will again be heard.

After presenting all of its evidence, the defense will signal the end of its case-in-chief by "resting."

Rebuttal Evidence

The prosecution will now be accorded an opportunity to produce evidence rebutting—countering, contradicting—the defense's evidence. This opportunity is especially important where the defense has gone beyond flat denial ("It never happened!") and has injected some sort of affirmative defense or legal justification into the case, as when it presents alibi evidence ("The defendant was with me in Los Angeles when this crime in New York went down.") or a claim of self-defense ("True, I shot him, but only after he came at me with a knife!"). Of course, the defense will then be given a chance to counter the prosecution's rebuttal efforts.

When both sides have finally rested it will be time for the lawyers' *closing arguments* (summations) and the trial judge's *instructions* (charge) to the jury regarding the applicable law. In most jurisdictions the arguments come first, followed by the judge's charge to the jury; in a few jurisdictions the sequence is the other way around.

There will first have been a conference, in the judge's chambers, during which the prosecution and defense will have been given a chance to tell the judge what legal principles they think he/she should explain to the jurors during the charge. (The lawyers will want this conference to precede their summations so that they can confidently refer to the contents of the judge's charge when they address the jury.) For example, the prosecutor may request that the judge's charge describe the difference between direct and circumstantial evidence; defense counsel is sure to want a charge that stresses the presumption of innocence and the beyond-a-reasonable-doubt standard of proof. The judge, of course, will have her own ideas about what should be included in the charge. The charge in its final form will be hammered out and reduced to writing. Any objections to its content will be made and ruled upon at this time.

Closing Arguments to the Jury

Unlike opening statements, the summations of the evidence at the end of a criminal case are argumentative, sometimes intensely so. Counsel for both sides are now at the last and perhaps most important stage of the proceedings. In those cases where the skill of counsel can make the difference, it is the closing argument more often than any other single stage of a case that determines who wins and who loses.

This is not to suggest that criminal cases are often won by flamboyant oratory and mock tears. Modern-day jurors, who have been brought up on a diet of Perry Mason and *L.A. Law,* are too sophisticated to be moved by the techniques that contributed to the success of yesteryear's great advocates. But, as we mentioned earlier in this chapter, a trial is a patchwork of bits and pieces of evidence. A jury may not appreciate the significance of many of these individual evidentiary scraps until they have been pieced together by a skillful advocate. Often the crux of the case will be one key answer on cross-examination which the astute trial lawyer did not emphasize at the time for fear the hostile witness would recognize its importance and change his testimony on the spot. Once it is in the record, the unguarded remark can be read to the jury during closing argument and its full significance revealed. In this sense it is frequently said that the closing argument reveals for the first time the method by which one side or the other has already won the case.

Although the day of flaming oratory is pretty much past, this is not to say that closing arguments are emotionless lectures. In a serious criminal case, where the jury's decision is especially likely to depend on its collective emotional response to the justice—the rightness—of the matter, a properly pitched argument may constitute the turning point. Logic, to be palatable, may require the lubrication not only of appealing organization and presentation but of emotion and drama as well.

The judge will have told the lawyers how much time each of them can have for argumentation. It is invariably less than they would like to have: an hour, let us say, for the prosecutor's "opening close," an hour and a half for the defense counsel's closing argument, and half an hour for the prosecutor's "closing close." (Since this *is* argument, the prosecution—which has not only the burden of proof but also the burden of persuasion—is allowed to present a rebuttal argument.) The arguments must be based on the evidence that was admitted into the record of the trial; no reference can be made to evidence that, upon objection, was excluded by the trial judge. Inflammatory arguments, appealing to prejudice and other base instincts, will not be tolerated. In fact, objections are rarely heard during the lawyers' summations. Both sides know that their arguments to the jury, even though forcefully presented, must be both accurate and fair.

The Judge's Instructions to the Jury

The trial judge will now deliver to the jurors her instructions on the law. An explanation of the law is essential since the jurors must not only decide what facts have been proved to their satisfaction but also must apply the pertinent principles of law to those facts in reaching their verdict.

The jurors will be told to elect one of their members to chair their deliberations. The elements of the offense or offenses will be described. The jury will be told that it cannot convict unless it finds, as matters of fact beyond any reasonable doubt, that each and every element has been established by the prosecution. In some cases it will also be necessary for the trial judge to explain the legal components of an affirmative defense that has been raised by the accused, such as self-defense or insanity.

Deliberation and Verdict by the Jury

Following the judge's instructions, the jurors will be taken to their deliberation room. Exhibits that have been admitted into evidence will be provided to them for their review.

A unanimous verdict is required for conviction or acquittal in a criminal case. If the jurors cannot agree on a verdict the result is what lawyers inelegantly refer to as a "hung" jury. This sort of deadlock will produce a *mistrial,* which in turn will result in the ordering of a new trial for the accused unless the prosecution, discouraged, decides at this point to drop the charges.

If the accused is found not guilty, he is discharged—he goes free—and as a consequence of the constitutional concept of double jeopardy, which prohibits the prosecution from trying a defendant over and over again until it finally secures a conviction, he cannot ever again be tried on the same charge.

If the accused is convicted, the defense will move the court to grant him a new trial. This motion will be based on assertions that prejudicial errors occurred during the trial. Typically, it will be argued that the trial judge erroneously admitted or excluded significant evidence—in other words, that he or she failed to understand the rules of evidence that we will be explaining in this book. Less commonly, it may be suggested that the judge gave incorrect instructions on the law to the jury. Even less commonly, it may be contended that the trial judge or the prosecutor engaged in misconduct that prejudiced the accused's right to a fair trial. For example, it might be demonstrated that the judge improperly took over the questioning of witnesses or engaged in secret and harmful communications with the jurors; the prosecutor might be charged with coercing false testimony or with making a grossly inflammatory and baseless closing argument.

If the defendant's motion for a new trial is granted, the jury's verdict will be set aside and a second trial ordered. If the motion is denied, as it usually is, the judge will set a date for the defendant's sentencing.

Sentencing

There will be a delay, usually quite brief, between verdict and sentence because the judge will ask the court's probation department to conduct a presentence investigation. The resulting probation officer's report to the sentencing judge will contain information, not brought out during the trial, about the defendant's character and past conduct. The judge can take this information, be it favorable or unfavorable, into account in arriving at an appropriate sentence. Criminal sentences run the gamut from probation (the defendant is not imprisoned but his conduct is supervised for a period of time by a probation officer and he/she may be required to perform some sort of public service as a condition of probation) to imprisonment or death.

After the defendant's sentence is handed down, activity at the trial level ends. The defendant's only recourse lies in appeal to reviewing (appellate) courts in an effort to have his conviction reversed on the basis of the errors that were cited in defense counsel's motion for a new trial. If the cited errors involve important and unresolved constitutional issues, the defendant's appeal may go all the way to the Supreme Court of the United States.

Having broadly sketched the structure of a criminal trial, we will next describe, in greater detail, the manner in which the lawyers and the trial judge deal with evidence as the trial of a criminal case proceeds. In other words, we will go from the structure of a trial to its mechanics.

CHAPTER THREE

The Trial Record

A. The Function of the Trial Record

In the last chapter the trial process and the different classifications of evidence were discussed. The present chapter considers in somewhat greater detail the mechanics of a trial.

This is a book on criminal evidence and will not range much into purely procedural areas. Those areas are better left for exploration in books devoted exclusively to criminal procedure. Still, it is possible to isolate and focus on those aspects of criminal trial procedure that bear directly on the introduction of evidence. That is what this chapter does. A basic familiarity with the mechanics of evidence-offering at trial will make it easier for the reader to understand the body of rules governing the admissibility and permissible uses of evidence. In other words, before asking whether particular types of evidence are admissible, we must first ask and answer the question, How do lawyers go about offering and, for that matter, objecting to evidence? This involves what lawyers and judges refer to as the making or, in their most optimistic moments, the "perfection" of the trial record.

Every experienced prosecutor and defense attorney realizes as he or she begins a criminal case that his cause may not be victorious at the trial level and that his client, either the state, when permitted, or the accused, may wish to appeal to a higher court if, in counsel's opinion, legal errors occurring during the trial brought about the unhappy outcome. An experienced trial lawyer understands, therefore, that he or she must be able to show an appellate court exactly what happened during the trial and perhaps also at any important pretrial and out-of-court hearings.

It follows that counsel must accomplish two different things at once as he goes about the trial of a case. First of all, he must make every proper effort to win at the trial level. Essentially, this means that he must, with the aid of evidence and argument, persuade the fact-finder of the rightness of his case. Second, because no lawyer can ever be absolutely positive of success at the trial level, counsel must do all that's possible to produce a record of the trial that will demonstrate to a reviewing court that justice did not prevail in the lower court.

A complete and understandable trial record is vital to an appeal. An appellate court can neither speculate about what happened during the trial nor accept on blind faith the lawyers' uncorroborated narration of events in the lower court. An appellate court can act only on the formal written record of the trial which has been officially transmitted to it by the trial court's clerk.

B. The Contents of a Trial Record

The trial record in almost any serious criminal case, assembled and bound into one or more volumes after the trial concludes, is made up of all the basic papers in the case (indictment, motions, supporting legal briefs, orders of the trial judge, proposed jury instructions, everything). The formal trial record also contains what in some jurisdictions is called the "Report of Proceedings." This is the word-for-word transcript of any on-the-record proceedings in the case. There will be the actual trial transcript—the typewritten recordation of all the words that were spoken by the trial's participants (judge, jurors, prosecutor, defense counsel, witnesses, and possibly others). There will also be a verbatim transcript from any on-the-record pretrial or out-of-court hearings.

Attached to the back of the trial transcript, or in the final volumes of an especially lengthy record, will be all but the most bulky exhibits that were identified and offered in evidence at the trial, whether or not they were actually received.

The trial record, then, has three parts: (1) the *paperwork* of the case, (2) the word-for-word *transcript* of hearings and trial testimony, and (3) the tangible *exhibits* which the parties marked for identification and offered into evidence. Only in minor cases, or where counsel have agreed to an abbreviated record, is there less.

C. How the Trial Record Is Made

The active participants in a criminal trial—the judge and the lawyers—literally "make" the trial record. They go about it almost as though they were dictating a nonfiction book, or the script for a documentary movie, to an especially competent secretary. They produce the trial record, in other words, with the aid of that most important of courtroom personnel, the court reporter. The court reporter has numerous responsibilities during the trial, by far the most crucial of which is the accurate taking down, with high-speed shorthand or by mechanical means, of everything that is said by the participants in the trial. The reporter will take down not only the testimony of the witnesses but also the objections and arguments of the lawyers and the comments, rulings, and jury instructions of the judge. The reporter will usually also have the job of putting identifying markings on exhibits at the request of the lawyer offering them and may have the practical responsibility for taking care of the exhibits when they are not in use during the trial.

Throughout a trial the judge and the lawyers are working with the court reporter in a joint effort that generates a complete record of the trial. Competent judges and lawyers, and knowledgeable witnesses, are therefore constantly aware of the court reporter and his (or her) importance.

The making of a trial record consists in large part of offering evidence for the fact-finder's consideration. The evidence will be in the form of oral testimony, exhibits, and perhaps also of matters subject to judicial notice.

The customary method of offering oral testimony into evidence is by counsel's direct examination or cross-examination of a witness who has been called to the stand to testify on oath or solemn affirmation. (Occasionally oral testimony can also be offered in the form of a written pretrial deposition or a transcript of testimony previously recorded in a pretrial hearing or another case.)

A tangible exhibit is usually introduced through a witness who "sponsors" it; that is, through a witness who can identify or authenticate the item and reveal its relevance to some material issue in the proceeding. After laying this necessary foundation, examining counsel will say something like, "Your Honor, we now offer into evidence what has previously been marked Prosecution Exhibit No. 7 for Identification." At this point opposing counsel can object and the trial judge will rule on the offer, either receiving the exhibit (holding it admissible) or rejecting it (holding it inadmissible.)

D. Examination of Witnesses

The Question-and-Answer Method

In most European countries a witness in a criminal case stands up and delivers a long and sometimes rambling narrative concerning everything he or she knows about the case. The approach to the examination of witnesses is different under American law. Here, all witnesses give their testimony through the question-and-answer method. We require the witness to provide his or her answers in reply to relatively pointed questions propounded by examining counsel. This method permits opposing counsel, who has been forewarned by the question that the jury may be about to hear inadmissible evidence, to object in time to prevent receipt of the damaging answer.

An attorney cross-examines actress Lana Turner during her daughter's trial for the murder of Johnny Stompanato.

EXAMPLE:

Q: Mr. Bushmat, isn't it a fact that at the age of fifteen years you were charged with the crime of shoplifting?

BY OPPOSING COUNSEL: Object, Your Honor, irrelevant.

THE COURT: Sustained. What he did as a teenager is in no way probative of the charge against him now. That was twelve years ago.

In Anglo-American law the lawyers not only must proceed by question and answer, but they also must use certain *forms* of questions. The restrictions are much more rigorous on the side calling the witness to the stand. The examination of one's own witness (direct examination as contrasted with cross-examination) is governed by a number of special rules, the most familiar one being the rule against "leading" questions.

The Rule Against "Leading" Questions

A leading question is one that strongly suggests its own answer to the witness. A typical leading question in an assault and battery case would be this one, put by defense counsel to his or her client: "You never touched the man, isn't that a fact?" The accused may answer, "Yes, that's true. I never touched him," but it is the examining lawyer's version of the story that the jurors hear. This form of questioning, at least when it goes to the very heart of the case, is, with a few exceptions, objectionable on direct examination. The accused is the examining lawyer's own witness and is undoubtedly highly suggestible; he might accept false suggestions contained in leading questions. The point is that although questions on direct examination can point the witness to a particular subject of inquiry, they should be reasonably balanced and neutral.

The rule against leading questions cannot be avoided by the use of gimmick questions. Some lawyers seem to think that they have only to begin a question with "Did you or did you not . . . ?" or "What is the fact as to whether or not . . . ?" in order to avoid a successful objection from opposing counsel. However, "Did you or did you not hear the man say, 'I just murdered my own son'?" is a leading question, despite the seemingly neutral alternatives offered in the prefatory, "Did you or did you not . . . ?" It is probably mildly leading to inquire, "And then did you hear the man say anything"? but the question is probably allowable to suggest the desired field of inquiry: what was *said* rather than what was *done* next. The following is an example of a completely nonleading approach:

EXAMPLE:
Q: What, if anything, occurred next?
A: The man screamed, "I've just murdered my own son!"

And every trial lawyer knows the all-time favorite nonleading question, which may leave a witness totally confused: "Q: Directing your attention to April 1, 1990, I'll ask you whether anything unusual took place?"

Exceptions to the Rule Against Leading Questions

There are a number of situations in which leading questions are allowed, even on direct examination.

1. Leading questions are permitted on preliminary or threshold matters that do not go directly to the heart of the case.

EXAMPLE:
Q: And you are employed by the Ace Tool Company, I believe?
A: Yes, sir, that's right

2. Leading questions can properly be used to provide a transition or bridge from one field of inquiry to another.

EXAMPLE:

Q: Now, Mr. Lishniss, drawing your attention to the day in question, were you still in the employ of Ace Tool Company?
A: Yes, I was.

3. An adverse or hostile witness can be asked leading questions since there is little danger that such a witness would accept a false suggestion contained in a leading question.
4. Leading questions are permitted during direct examination when a witness gives surprise answers. Surprise is most commonly demonstrated to a court's satisfaction when a witness's direct testimony is sharply at odds with a previous statement or with his testimony at a preliminary hearing or grand jury proceeding. Examining counsel is not, however, free to call a potentially adverse witness to the stand in the blind hope that his testimony will be helpful and then, when it proves not to be, begin to lead and discredit him.
5. Leading questions are allowed on direct examination of a witness of limited understanding, such as an adult of low mentality, a foreigner who is having difficulty with the English language, or a child.
6. Leading questions can be put to a witness whose recollection has been exhausted but who apparently has additional relevant information. In other words, it is sometimes proper to refresh a witness's recollection by means of a leading question where the answer appears to be on the tip of his tongue.

EXAMPLE:

Q: Are you able to remember the names of any other persons who were present at the meeting to which you have referred?
A: No, I can't. I'm certain that there were some others there, but I just can't seem to come up with their names now.
Q: You have exhausted your recollection of those who were present?
A: Yes, I'm afraid so. I just have a temporary mental block.
Q: Would it ring any bells if I suggested to you that Mr. Morton P. Lishniss also attended that meeting?
A: You're right! I remember now. Lishniss was there, too.

Some judges would require that counsel request permission of the court before asking a leading question of the type seen in the example above. Immediately after drawing the response that began "Yes, I am afraid so," counsel would inquire of the trial judge, "Your Honor, may I now put a leading question to the witness? His present recollection is temporarily exhausted, but he has indicated that he has additional knowledge. We would like to ask a leading question in order to jog his memory." Under the circumstances indicated in the example, the lawyer's request would undoubtedly be granted.

7. Hypothetical questions of the sort commonly put to expert witnesses are intensely leading, up to a point, but they are permissible as a means of supplying the factual basis for the expert's opinion.

EXAMPLE:

Q: Dr. Ziff, I am going to ask you to assume that all of the facts which I am about to describe to you are true and then I will ask you for your opinion with respect to those facts. First, please assume that the deceased was a male who on April 1, 1989, was forty-three years of age. Assume further that on that day he . . . [Examining counsel supplies additional data, the truth of which is to be assumed by the expert witness.]

Now, assuming all of these facts to be true, do you have an opinion, based upon a reasonable degree of medical certainty, as to the cause of death?

A: Yes, I do.

Q: What is that opinion, Doctor?

A: [The witness testifies to his opinion.]

The Rule Against Compound and Otherwise Confusing Questions

In making the testimonial record on either direct or cross-examination, examining counsel are required to avoid using questions that will unjustifiably confuse or mislead the witness. The principal offender is the double-barreled or compound question, which may leave everyone in the courtroom baffled. Such questions almost always result in ambiguous or incomplete answers.

EXAMPLE:

Q: Tell the court and jury where you were and whether at that time you were conversing with Mr. Lishniss—what was his first name?—and, if so, tell them what that conversation concerned.

A: Right. He said his first name was Morton, and . . . I have forgotten the rest of your question.

BY EXAMINING COUNSEL: Will the court reporter please read the question back?

THE COURT: It might be better to ask him one question at a time, counsel. Why don't you just put another question?

Particularly on direct examination, questions by counsel are expected to be brief, clear, and phrased in reasonably simple terms. For example, experienced trial counsel will avoid the use of negatives in their questions because they cause confusion.

EXAMPLE:
Q: The fact is, you don't know whether Lishniss was there, do you?
A: Yes.
THE COURT: Wait just a minute. Does the witness mean, "Yes, I know," "Yes, it is true that I don't know," or "Yes, Lishniss was there"?

Questions Assuming an Unproved Fact

The trial record cannot properly be made with questions that assume the existence of facts that have neither been proved nor conceded. The classic example under this heading is, When did you stop beating your wife?, there having been no evidence that the defendant ever *started* to do so. Nonexistent evidence cannot be supplied, either on direct or cross-examination, by means of "loaded" questions, since counsel is not permitted to testify.

Expert Witnesses

The direct examination of an expert witness will differ somewhat from that of ordinary fact-witnesses. This is true because of the operation of the so-called opinion rule, which will be discussed in chapter 17.

Generally speaking, witnesses are required to testify only about facts of which they have *direct knowledge.* They are not permitted to express opinions and beliefs about subjects on which any reasonably knowledgeable lay juror could form a correct conclusion. And the ordinary witness is not free to unburden himself of opinions and beliefs on matters that are beyond his or her competence.

On the other hand, experts of one sort and another—for example, firearms identification witnesses—are permitted to state their opinions on relevant matters so long as a proper foundation, revealing their special qualifications, has been laid.

The Rule against Impeaching One's Own Witness

It once would have been generally accurate to say that a lawyer cannot seek to discredit a witness that he himself has summoned to the witness stand to testify on behalf of his client. In a very real sense counsel was required to vouch for the veracity, the credibility, of any witnesses he or she called to the stand, even though those witnesses might prove to be hostile. Out of this antique notion grew the rule against impeaching one's own witnesses.

Today, there are ever-increasing exceptions to this rule. Witnesses who give surprise testimony can be cross-examined by the side that called them and, as would be anticipated, witnesses who prove to be hostile in their answers can usually be cross-examined and impeached by the side calling them.

The most recent evidence codes, such as the Federal Rules of Evidence, Rule 607, permit counsel to impeach the credibility of *any* witness. And a 1973 Supreme Court decision gives strong support for this approach in criminal cases.

Chambers v. *Mississippi,* 410 U.S. 284 (1973), was a murder case. After Leon Chambers was arrested for the killing of a policeman, another person, Gable McDonald, made but later repudiated a written confession, and on three separate occasions—each time to a different friend—McDonald orally admitted the killing. At his trial, Chambers called McDonald to the stand when the prosecution failed to do so. Through McDonald the defense laid the foundation for receipt of his written confession and, after its formal admission into evidence, it was read to the jury. The State, on cross-examination, brought out the fact that McDonald had repudiated this confession. On the State's cross-examination McDonald further testified that he had not shot the dead policeman and that he had falsely confessed to the crime as part of a scheme to sue for false imprisonment.

At the conclusion of the State's cross-examination, defendant Chambers's counsel sought permission to cross-examine McDonald as an adverse witness, impeaching his veracity in the process. Both the trial judge and the Mississippi Supreme Court ruled that Chambers's counsel was not entitled to adopt this approach. (He was also precluded from introducing the testimony of the three witnesses to whom McDonald had confessed.)

The Supreme Court of the United States reversed Chambers's conviction, in part because of its disapproval of the rule against impeaching one's own witness. Justice Powell, in an opinion from which only Justice Rehnquist dissented, said that "Whatever validity the 'voucher' rule may have once enjoyed . . . , it bears little present relationship to the realities of the criminal process." In modern trials, Powell observed, criminal defendants are rarely able to select their witnesses: they must take them where they find them. In this case McDonald's testimony was unquestionably damaging to the accused who called him to the stand. Justice Powell, and the Supreme Court's majority, concluded that "The availability of the right to confront and to cross-examine those who give damaging testimony against the accused has never been held to depend on whether the witness was initially put on the stand by the accused or by the State." The Court rejected the notion that the right of confrontation "may be governed by that technicality. . . . The 'voucher' rule, as applied in this case, plainly interfered with Chambers's right to defend against the State's charges."

E. Cross-Examination of Witnesses

Cross-Examination as a Matter of Right

Cross-examination of the opposing side's witnesses is a matter of right. Thus if a witness dies or otherwise becomes unavailable as a witness before cross-examination of him has been concluded, a trial judge can strike his direct testimony and instruct the jury to disregard it.

Restrictions on Cross-Examination

As was suggested earlier in this chapter, cross-examination is a much more flexible method of questioning than direct examination. It is surrounded by far fewer restrictive rules than is direct examination.

The most significant restrictions on cross-examination—and they are in the process of fading away—have to do with limitations on the scope of cross-examination. In some jurisdictions the permissible scope of cross-examination has been more or less restricted to the subject matters covered during the witness's direct examination. For example, §773 of the California Evidence Code contains this limitation. Rule 611(b) of the Federal Rules of Evidence is to like effect: "Cross-examination should be limited to the subject matter of the direct examination and matters affecting the credibility of the witness."

Traditional limitations on the scope of cross-examination have never applied to inquiries that affect a witness's credibility.

The Purposes of Cross-Examination

The purposes of cross-examination are numerous. On one level, cross-examination may do no more than clarify, supplement, or qualify the direct testimony of a not very damaging witness. However, cross-examination is usually employed in a much more aggressive way. In an effort to weaken or demolish the witness's direct testimony, the cross-examiner's questions may challenge the sources of the witness's knowledge and attack his or her perception and memory. The cross-examiner may also try to demonstrate the witness's inability to describe events accurately and consistently. Cross-examination can be employed to extract admissions that undermine the witness's direct testimony. Furthermore, as will be considered in depth in chapter 7, cross-examination can be employed to cast doubt on the witness's truthfulness. This is called *impeachment.*

It is enough at this point to say that a witness's credibility can be put in doubt (impeached) by cross-questions revealing an interest or partisanship, the existence of a prejudice or bias, which could lead him to misinterpret the facts or to twist them. For example, cross-examination can be used to demonstrate that a witness is related to or friendly with the accused or for some other reason hostile to the prosecution.

A witness can also be impeached, on a somewhat different level, by cross-questions showing that he has made prior out-of-court statements that are inconsistent with the answers he gave during his in-court direct examination. Occasionally a witness can also be impeached, on yet another level, by evidence of serious criminal convictions or prior bad conduct tending to cast doubt on his current reliability as a witness.

It follows from this thumbnail sketch that lawyers are free to use leading questions on cross-examination. It is almost impossible to conduct an impeaching cross-examination without asking leading questions. However, this does not mean that excessively argumentative or badgering cross-questions will be permitted by a trial judge. It is one thing for a prosecuting attorney to inquire, in an altogether leading way, "Isn't it a fact that you have been a close friend and business associate of the defendant for many years?" It is quite another thing, upon getting an unsatisfactory answer, heatedly to ask, "Do you really expect the jury to believe that?" The first question is proper on cross-examination, there being little risk that the opposing side's witness will blindly accept the suggestion built into the leading question and give the prosecutor a favorable but false answer. The second question is improper on either direct or cross-examination. It is unduly argumentative and contributes nothing of value to the trial record.

As was indicated earlier, questions assuming unproved facts ("loaded questions"), compound and otherwise confusing questions are no more permissible on cross-examination than on direct examination.

F. Introducing Tangible Evidence

Standing in contrast to testimonial evidence is tangible evidence, the physical exhibits in a case. Tangible evidence may be a murder weapon, a writing such as a ransom note, the seized heroin, the scar on a witness's face.

Putting writings to one side for a moment, because special rules surround them, it can be said that there are two basic types of tangible evidence: (1) *real* evidence, and (2) *demonstrative* evidence. Just as one must qualify oral testimony for admission into evidence by showing that the witness has direct knowledge of relevant facts, one must also qualify items of tangible evidence for receipt into evidence.

Real Evidence

This, as we have said before, is "the real thing"—the actual murder weapon, not a mere example of a weapon of the type said to have been used in the alleged crime. Real evidence can be *direct* evidence, offered to establish facts about the thing itself, such as the extent of the victim's disfigurement as a consequence of an observable facial scar. Real evidence can also be *circumstantial,* as when facts about an object are offered as the basis for an inference that some other fact is true. For example, rust inside a metal container implies the prior presence of moisture in the container.

The trial procedure in connection with real evidence is often quite elaborate, depending on the nature of the particular exhibit. (It is usually easier to get a one-page letter into evidence than an alleged draft evader's complete Selective Service file, consisting of numerous separate records made by different persons at different times in different places for different reasons.) In general, there are six foundational steps, all of them important.

1. *Marking the Exhibit for Identification.* In order to produce a trial record that will be comprehensible and efficient to work with later on, counsel will cause real evidence to be marked or tagged for identification. The marking or tagging is ordinarily done by the court reporter. Thereafter, during his examination of witnesses, counsel will carefully refer to the exhibit by its identifying number or letter. Still later, when someone reads the typewritten trial transcript, counsel's questions and the witness's testimony can readily be connected with the marked exhibits that are bound into the formal record.

With competent trial counsel the matter of marking exhibits for identification becomes virtually automatic. When a trial lawyer picks something up from counsel table with the intention of introducing it in evidence, he or she will first go to the court reporter and request him to mark it in numerical or alphabetical sequence. Counsel will then subside into silence, since the court reporter, having only two hands, cannot take down counsel's comments or continued questions to a witness while at the same time marking the exhibit for identification. After the exhibit has been marked, counsel will as a matter of courtesy show the exhibit to the trial judge and opposing counsel unless they have already seen it or, in the case of a writing, chart, diagram, map, or the like, been provided with copies.

Step Number 1, then, works as follows:

OFFERING COUNSEL [having picked up a letter from the counsel table]: I now ask that the court reporter mark this for identification. If I remember correctly, this would be Prosecution Exhibit 10.

COURT REPORTER [marking the exhibit]: Yes, this is going to be Prosecution's 10.

OFFERING COUNSEL: Your Honor, I think we provided you with a Xerox copy of this letter. It is dated April 1, 1989, on the defendant's business letterhead.

THE COURT: Yes, I have got it here.

OFFERING COUNSEL [addressing defense counsel]: And we gave you a copy, too, didn't we?

DEFENSE COUNSEL: Yes, we have our copy. Of course, we reserve our right to object to its introduction when the time comes.

OFFERING COUNSEL: Certainly.

2. *Laying the Foundation.* In the absence of an agreement with opposing counsel (in lawyers' jargon, a *stipulation*) that the exhibit is admissible, it will next be necessary for offering counsel to lay the foundation for

admission of the item of real evidence. This is accomplished through e or more witnesses who "sponsor" the exhibit, identifying (authenticati) it and showing its relevance to the issues in the case. Essentially, this involv s testimony that the exhibit is "the real thing," "the genuine article."

Step Number 2 will proceed in this way:

OFFERING COUNSEL: Officer Krupke, I hand you what has been marked Prosecution Exhibit No. 5 for Identification and ask you if you recognize it?

A: Yes, I know what it is.

Q: What is it?

A: That is the length of lead pipe that I found next to the victim's body that night.

Q: By "that" you are indicating Prosecution Exhibit Number 5?

A: Yes, sir.

Q: How do you happen to know that Prosecution Exhibit Number 5 is the same piece of lead pipe that you saw that night?

A: At that time, I scratched the date and my initials on it right here [indicating].

If the witness, unlike the police officer in the preceding example, is unable to identify the exhibit to the exclusion of all similar objects, the chain of custody without any hearsay links must be traced in order to establish that the exhibit is "the genuine article." This means that there will be a series of witnesses summoned to the stand, each one accounting for the period during which the exhibit was in his or her custody. In this manner, each link in the chain of custody is forged and it is demonstrated that the exhibit is in fact "the real thing." The process is exemplified by the case of *United States* v. *Cardenas,* 864 F.2d 1528 (10th Cir. 1989). At the accused's trial for cocaine possession with intent to distribute, the prosecution introduced a plastic sack of cocaine said to have been seized from the accused's automobile. Officer Garcia testified that he found the sack in a paper bag under the car's front seat and handed it to Officer Gunter. Garcia had accompanied Gunter to the police station, where Officer Mares assisted Gunter in tagging and sealing the sack in an evidence bag. Gunter then took the evidence bag to the third floor evidence room where an evidence technician accepted it. The accused objected that the prosecution's chain of custody was defective because Gunter did not testify. The Tenth Circuit rejected this contention, saying that "There is no rule that the prosecution must produce *all* persons who had custody of the evidence to testify at trial" (court's emphasis). The testimony of Garcia, Mares, and the evidence technician accounted for the whereabouts of the cocaine except for Gunter's trip to the evidence room. Given the brevity of the period during which Gunter was alone with the sack, together with the fact that it had been tagged and sealed, there was no significant break in the chain of custody.

If the condition of the object is important, the sponsoring witness must be in a position to testify that its condition has not changed in any significant way since the pertinent time.

Finally, it should be mentioned here that the trial record has not been adequately developed when the instrumentality of an alleged crime has not been linked both to the crime and to the accused.

3. *Offering Exhibits into Evidence.* The third procedural step involves offering the tangible exhibit into evidence once the necessary foundation has been laid. Step Number 3, although sometimes neglected by inexperienced counsel, is a purely mechanical one:

> OFFERING COUNSEL: Your Honor, we now offer into evidence, as Prosecution Exhibit Number 5, what was previously marked as Prosecution Exhibit Number 5 for Identification.
>
> THE COURT: Hearing no objection, it will be received as Prosecution Exhibit Number 5.

4. *Obtaining an Express Ruling on the Record.* In the example above the trial judge made a prompt and explicit ruling on the lawyer's offer of Prosecution Exhibit Number 5. Occasionally, however, lawyers find it necessary to request the judge to make an express ruling. A trial judge's silence in the face of an offer will not necessarily be taken, on appeal, as an acceptance of the offered evidence.

5. *A Precautionary Measure.* Exceptionally cautious lawyers, having secured a ruling admitting an exhibit into evidence, foreclose any possible future confusion by requesting the court reporter to cross out the words "for Identification" in the exhibit mark, thereby making it doubly clear that the exhibit was received in evidence by the trial judge.

6. *Showing or Reading the Exhibit to the Jury.* Now, for the first time, offering counsel is free to show the exhibit to the jury, or, in the case of written material, to read it to them or direct the sponsoring witness to read it to them. As a matter of courtroom protocol, express permission to do so is usually requested of the trial judge.

> OFFERING COUNSEL: Your Honor, may we now hand the exhibit, Prosecution's Number 5, to the jurors for their examination?
>
> THE COURT: You may.

Counsel will put no new questions to the witness on the stand until all of the members of the jury have had a chance to inspect the exhibit that has been handed to them.

So-called *testimonial exhibits,* such as a pretrial deposition that has been put in evidence, usually must be read into the record (in the jurors' hearing, of course) since most courts will not allow this kind of exhibit to be taken by the jurors to their deliberation room for examination along with the other tangible exhibits in the case. It is thought that giving such a testimonial exhibit to the jurors might unduly underscore an isolated block of testimony during their deliberations. Offering counsel can read the exhibit into the record himself or, in the case of a deposition or prior recorded testimony, he can put someone in the witness chair to read the deponent's or witness's answers in response to counsel's reading of the questions contained in the deposition or transcript.

G. Demonstrative Evidence

Demonstrative evidence, once again, is *not* "the genuine article" or "the real thing." Instead, it is tangible material used for illustrative or explanatory purposes only. It is a visual or audio-visual aid, such as a drawing, a model, or a film. Evidence that is demonstrative only is not ordinarily offered into evidence in the way real evidence is, and it thus does not go with the jury into its deliberation room at the trial's conclusion. This does not mean, however, that there is no foundation-laying procedure, no making of the trial record, in connection with demonstrative evidence.

Two Types of Demonstrative Evidence

There are two basic types of demonstrative evidence. First, there is *selected* demonstrative evidence, such as handwriting specimens or exemplars used as standards of comparison by a handwriting expert in, for example, forgery cases. Second, there is *prepared* or *reproduced* demonstrative evidence (understandably, lawyers tend to avoid the term "manufactured"), such as a model of a murder room or a free-hand sketch of it.

It is in connection with prepared or reproduced demonstrative material that there is the greatest risk of intended or unintended distortion. Perhaps the model is not built to scale; the diagram shortens or elongates distances; the filmed reenactment of the crime is inaccurate. The law seeks to minimize these risks of distortion by requiring certain testimonial assurances of accuracy. These assurances are part of the foundation, part of the trial record that must be made, as a precondition to the use of demonstrative materials in the criminal courtroom.

Elements of the Foundation for Demonstrative Materials

There are two essential foundational elements for demonstrative material. First of all, it is again true, just as it is with real evidence, that conditions shown by the exhibit must not be substantially different from those that existed at the time of the occurrence in question. If conceded variations in condition are irrelevant, they must at least be accounted for, as, for example, in connection with a photograph of the site of the offense charged against the accused.

Second, there must be testimony by a knowledgeable person that the demonstrative exhibit is a "true and fair representation" of what it purports to show. Thus a person familiar with the scene depicted in a photograph—it need not be the photographer—can lay the testimonial foundation for use of the photograph as an item of demonstrative material. In connection with motion pictures, there must be testimony from a knowledgeable witness that the film has not been improperly edited by means of splicing. (See chapter 19 for further discussion of demonstrative evidence.)

H. Writings

The significance of writings as evidence often depends on their *authorship*. Accordingly, it frequently is essential to prove authorship. Is the proffered writing actually what it purports to be on its face, a ransom note composed and written by the accused? A writing, in other words, is not admissible until its *authenticity* has been satisfactorily demonstrated. Its genuineness must be demonstrated to the trial judge, as a preliminary matter, before the jurors can consider it. It cannot be read or shown to the jury until the proper foundation has been laid and the writing has been formally received in evidence by the trial judge.

A writing can be authenticated in a wide variety of ways. The most obvious way is by direct evidence, which can be either the identifying testimony of the writing's author or the testimony of someone who observed the writing being made. Of course, writings can also be proved circumstantially. The methods of authenticating writings will be discussed in detail in chapter 16.

I. Objections to Evidence

The Parties' Responsibility for Making Objections

The rules of evidence can be made to function properly only if a party which contends that opposing counsel's question is impermissible or that certain evidence should be excluded promptly informs the trial judge, who is the umpire of the case, of the contention and the reasons underlying it. The initiative in making evidentiary objections lies with the parties, speaking through their lawyers, and not with the trial judge. This is simply an example of party responsibility in the adversary trial process.

It is a responsibility willingly assumed by competent trial lawyers, who dislike few things more than an overreaching trial judge's usurpation of the litigator's duty to decide which objections, perhaps for purely strategic or tactical reasons, he or she will forego. It is therefore unusual, although it would hardly be without precedent, to hear a judge exclude evidence to which counsel has not raised an objection. A competent judge will do this only when the proffered evidence is not only technically inadmissible but also potentially prejudicial, or where he or she is preserving the rights of an absent and unrepresented holder of a testimonial privilege.

Occasionally, however, there is encountered the sort of judge who, perhaps because he is himself a frustrated prosecutor or defense lawyer, will interrupt testimony to inquire of one silent side, "Did I hear an objection?" With almost equal frequency one will hear an attorney for that side reply, with a tinge of irritation in his voice, "You did not, Your Honor." Counsel, for reasons of his own, has made a deliberate decision to forego any objection.

Some Reasons for Dispensing with Available Evidentiary Objections

No trial lawyer makes every evidentiary objection that may technically be possible. There are many reasons for this. (1) Trial counsel neither needs nor wishes to complain about every leading question posed by opposing counsel, since the use of leading questions as to unimportant preliminary topics speeds up the examination of witnesses, which is usually advantageous to all concerned. (2) Counsel may permit a questionable objection to pass because he or she does not wish to run the risk of underscoring hurtful testimony. (3) Counsel may forego an available objection in order to avoid giving the jurors the impression that he or she is excessively obstructive or distrusts their judgment. (4) Frequently counsel abandons an objection because the evidence offered by the other side, although arguably inadmissible, in some way favors his side's position. (5) And sometimes counsel remains silent because the opposing side's offer of objectionable evidence "opens the door" for more important evidence that the silent side hopes to offer later on the very same subject.

Objections Made Only for Effect

Objections that are directed to nothing more than the form of the question (for example, leading) are as often as not made simply for their effect on the jury.

EXAMPLE:

OPPOSING COUNSEL: We've been extremely patient, Your Honor, but the jury might like to hear a little more testimony from the witness and a little less from defense counsel. This is all leading, Your Honor, and, much as we hate to interrupt, we have to object to it.

THE COURT: The objection will be sustained. Try not to put all the answers in the witness's mouth, counsel.

Of course, the use of objections as an excuse to make speeches for the jury's benefit is ethically questionable, just as is the use of objections solely for the purpose of interrupting the flow of a damaging examination or to coach a witness who is having difficulty weathering an effective cross-examination. The making of objections for improper purposes can bring an embarrassing warning from the bench.

It is the practice of an increasing number of trial judges to require that any argumentation in support of an objection be made in a conference at the bench, out of the jury's hearing. Objecting counsel inquires, "May we approach the bench?" If the judge is willing to hear argument on the objection, he will permit counsel to engage in a whispered presentation and may even adjourn to his chambers if the arguments seem likely to be lengthy.

The Time for Objections

Since the duty to make legitimate objections is lodged with counsel, and not the trial judge, failure to make a timely objection in proper form to an offer of evidence will operate to waive (to forever abandon) any possible basis of complaint about its receipt. "Let them speak now or forever hold their peace" is as applicable at trials as it is at weddings.

An objection to evidence must be made as soon as its basis becomes apparent. Counsel is not free to sit on his hands, gambling that an opposing witness will give a favorable answer or at least a harmless one, and then object when the answer proves to be damaging. The judge is likely to react to the tardy objection with a terse, "Asked and answered, counsel. You weren't fast enough on your feet, I'm afraid."

Ordinarily examining counsel's question will by its own wording reveal that it calls for inadmissible testimony. Opposing counsel must make an effort to interpose his or her objection before the witness answers.

EXAMPLE:

Q: Young man, were you ever adjudged a juvenile delinquent?

OPPOSING COUNSEL: Oh, Your Honor, we strenuously object to that. Counsel knows that's an improper question.

THE COURT: The objection is sustained and the witness will not answer the question. Ladies and gentlemen of the jury, disregard the question completely.

Of course, it is not always possible for a lawyer neatly to insert his or her objection between the question and the response. For one thing, the witness may answer too quickly. All that opposing counsel can do in this situation is announce his objection as soon as possible, adding a two-part request that the witness's answer be stricken from the record and that the judge instruct the jury to disregard it. (If the objection is sustained, the witness's answer is not actually physically removed from the record; it remains in the record for consideration by a reviewing court if, on appeal, the trial judge's ruling is assigned as error.)

Occasionally an apparently unobjectionable question brings out an inadmissible answer. Here, obviously, counsel—be it examining counsel or opposing counsel—cannot phrase his objection until the impropriety of the witness's answer emerges. Perhaps the witness's answer is unresponsive to the question, with the result that the examining lawyer is entitled to object to the testimony. He or she will make what is often referred to as an after-objection.

EXAMPLE:

Q: Did you observe the defendant run out of the bank?

A: Yes, and he appeared to be holding a pistol in his right hand and a large paper sack in his left hand.

BY EXAMINING COUNSEL: We object to everything after the word "Yes" and ask that it be stricken, Your Honor. We also request that you instruct the jurors to disregard everything except the answer "Yes" as being unresponsive to the question.

THE COURT: The objection is sustained and the jury is so instructed.

It is usually said that only the examining lawyer, and not the lawyer on the other side, is entitled to object to an answer whose only impropriety is its lack of responsiveness. To put it another way, examining counsel is free to "adopt" an unresponsive but favorable answer. He adopts it either by expressly stating that he does or by the even more simple expedient of withholding any objection to it. The opposing lawyer, not being the author of the question, lacks the standing to object to an unresponsive answer unless by chance it is excludable on some evidentiary ground over and beyond unresponsiveness; for example, the witness's answer is not only unresponsive but also in violation of the rule against hearsay evidence. Here are two examples of correct rulings by a trial judge:

DEFENSE COUNSEL: Did you observe the defendant coming out of the bank?

A: Yes, and he appeared to have nothing in his hands.

THE PROSECUTING ATTORNEY: Objection, unresponsive after the word "Yes."

DEFENSE COUNSEL: We adopt the entire answer.

THE COURT: The objection is overruled.

The result will be different if the witness's answer is varied slightly.

DEFENSE COUNSEL: Did you observe the defendant coming out of the bank?
A: No, I didn't, but a man standing beside me did and he said that the man was not carrying anything in his hands.
THE PROSECUTING ATTORNEY: Object. Unresponsive and hearsay, Your Honor.
DEFENSE COUNSEL: We adopt the entire answer.
THE COURT: The objection is sustained on the ground of the rule against hearsay.

From time to time the inadmissibility of testimony does not become clear until long after it has actually been received in evidence. This happens where it is revealed only after probing cross-examination that a witness's responses to direct examination were based on hearsay rather than direct knowledge. In this situation opposing counsel will move to strike all of the witness's testimony and ask that the jurors be instructed to disregard it.

This can also happen in instances of so-called conditional relevance. When one side fails to "tie up" or "connect up" conditionally relevant evidence with other evidence that renders the earlier evidence relevant, a renewed objection to the earlier evidence will be sustained, it will be stricken, and the jury, on objecting counsel's request, will be ordered to disregard it in their deliberations.

Objecting to Tangible Evidence

Objections to tangible evidence (exhibits) will ordinarily be made at the time the exhibit is formally offered into evidence. Offering counsel is entitled first to attempt the laying of the necessary evidentiary foundation. This counsel will do, as we have seen, through one or more "sponsoring" witnesses who must be capable of identifying and otherwise authenticating the exhibit. Objections interjected before offering counsel has had a chance to lay the foundation for an exhibit would usually be premature. Certainly an objection made at the time an exhibit is marked by the court reporter for identification would be premature in all but the most extraordinary circumstances.

EXAMPLE:
Q: Will you give the Court and jury your name in full, please?
A: Irene Stitz.
Q: And where do you reside, Ms. Stitz?
A: At 42 West Melrose Street in Chicago, Illinois.
Q: What is your current occupation, Ms. Stitz?

Copyright © 1984 Louvass-Nagy. *Trial Diplomacy Journal.*

A: I am the Records Librarian at Roosevelt Memorial Hospital here in the city.

Q: Would you briefly describe your duties as a records librarian?

A: [Witness details her duties.]

Q: Thank you very much. Now, in response to a subpoena issued to you by the Office of the State's Attorney, have you brought anything with you to court today?

A: Yes, sir, I have.

Q: What have you brought?

A: I have with me the records of Roosevelt Memorial Hospital pertaining to a patient named Clyde Bushmat.

BY DEFENSE COUNSEL: Object, Your Honor.

THE COURT: Overruled. You may proceed, Mr. Prosecutor.

Q: Thank you, Your Honor. Would you hand that folder to me, please? [Witness hands folder to examining counsel.]

BY OFFERING COUNSEL: There appear to be twenty pages or pieces of paper in the folder that the witness has just handed to me. I ask that the court reporter mark each separate page, front and back. What number have we reached with our exhibits at this point, Shirley?

BY THE COURT REPORTER: This would begin with number 9.

BY OFFERING COUNSEL: Then we can commence with 9-A. [Court reporter marks the group exhibit.]

Q: Ms. Stitz, I hand you what has been marked Prosecution's Group Exhibit 9-A on the front and 9-B on the reverse, and I ask you what it is?

BY DEFENSE COUNSEL: Objection, Your Honor.

BY OFFERING COUNSEL: I haven't offered this exhibit yet, Your Honor. I've just barely gotten its various parts marked for identification so that I can lay the foundation. May I have an opportunity to lay the proper foundation? I believe I can do it through the witness. Then I'll offer it and counsel for the defense can then make any objection he may have.

THE COURT: The objection will be overruled. You're jumping the gun, counsel. Wait until the exhibits are offered.

Q: Read my last question back, please? [Court reporter complies and the direct examination of the witness proceeds.]

Of course, an early objection, in advance of the formal offer, is appropriate if improper use of an exhibit is being made. For example, if examining counsel displays the exhibit, such as a diagram, to the jurors in advance of its receipt in evidence, or if he requests the sponsoring witness to read a written exhibit to the jurors before it has been received in evidence, an objection to counsel's conduct will be sustained.

EXAMPLE:

BY THE COURT REPORTER [reading the last question to the witness]: "Ms. Stitz, I hand you what has been marked Prosecution's Group Exhibit 9-A on the front and 9-B on the reverse, and I ask you what it is?"

BY OFFERING COUNSEL: Can you answer the question now, Ms. Stitz?

A: Yes, it is the admission sheet pertaining to Mr. Clyde Bushmat's admission to Roosevelt Memorial Hospital.

Q: Would you just read the first eight lines of that to the jury, please?

BY DEFENSE COUNSEL: If the Court please, we object to any reading of this exhibit. He isn't doing what he said he would a moment ago. He hasn't laid a proper foundation for its admission and he hasn't offered it in evidence. It can't be read to the jury yet.

THE COURT: The objection is sustained. Lay your foundation, Mr. Prosecutor. Then we'll see whether any of this can be read to the jury.

Specificity of Objections

The question arises: How specific must evidentiary objections be? Is it enough for counsel to stand up and say nothing more than "Object, Your

Honor"? Is something more meaningful accomplished where a lawyer, after the time-honored fashion of Perry Mason and other trial lawyers whose practice is limited to television serials, leaps up and dramatically shouts "Object, Your Honor. Irrelevant, incompetent, and immaterial!"? Or must counsel be quite specific? "Object, Your Honor. It's hearsay." Or, "Object, this is all subject to the husband-wife privilege."

A reading of the great mass of court opinions dealing with specificity *versus* generality in the phrasing of objections indicates that the bare announcement that "I object" is insufficient and that even the slightly more elaborate "Three I's" are a useless ritual except perhaps to preserve the fundamental question of relevance.

The lesson of the decided cases to lawyers is that an objection must be accompanied by a reasonably specific description of the legal grounds for it. The idea is that the trial judge, no matter how expert, should not be expected to recognize instantly the particular evidence rules applicable to the testimony and exhibits being offered in a given case. The prosecution and defense lawyers have been analyzing the case and preparing it for trial; hopefully, they have had enough time to get a firm grip on its evidentiary problems. The burden should be on them to reveal the bases for their in-court objections since the judge will be less closely familiar with the details of the case.

The concept of adversariness is at work here, too. It is up to the opposing lawyers, and not the judge, not only to make objections but to support them with legally sound reasons.

In making objections the trial lawyer will have three aims in mind, two of them being directly involved with what has been described as the "making" of the trial record. First, counsel is trying to familiarize the trial judge with the rule or rules of evidence that authorize the objection and the exclusion of the challenged evidence. Second, by being reasonably explicit in describing the bases of his objection, counsel is preserving a record for possible appeal in case the judge overrules his objection. Third, and this is the reverse of the same coin, counsel is making a record that will *support* the trial judge on appeal if he or she *sustains* counsel's objection.

All of the rules regarding the required form of evidentiary objections are weighted in favor of the trial judge. If a general objection is made by defense counsel and overruled, reviewing courts will not reverse a conviction unless a valid basis for the objection is perfectly clear. And the rules also aid the trial judge when he has *sustained* a general objection. On appeal the trial judge's action will be upheld if there was *any* ground on which the evidence could properly have been excluded. It is assumed that the trial judge had the right reason in mind when he excluded the evidence. In short, a trial court will usually be upheld on review whether it has sustained or overruled a general objection.

Where a *specific* objection ("Object, hearsay") has been erroneously overruled, the record will support a reversal on appeal if the evidence was of a prejudicial sort. If a specific objection is properly sustained, there obviously has been no prejudicial error. If the ground of objection specified by court and counsel is invalid but there existed another and valid but undisclosed basis for the objection, the rule again favors the trial judge and, indirectly, the objecting lawyer. The rule makes good sense. It would be pretty silly to reverse the trial court, and return the case to it for a new trial, for having excluded the evidence on the wrong ground, only to have the trial court exclude it for the *right* reason the second time around. In other words, "right ruling, wrong reason" will not lead to reversal on appeal.

The Necessity for Repeating Evidentiary Objections

Where one side, through one or more witnesses, repeatedly offers similar evidence which opposing counsel believes is inadmissible, a new objection must be made each time the evidence is offered unless the trial judge permits a single statement of objection to stand as a continuing objection to the entire line of questioning or category of evidence.

If counsel's initial objection to a string of similar evidence is overruled, the trial court will often permit a continuing objection, sometimes also referred to as a standing objection, in order to conserve time and to save opposing counsel from seeming unduly obstructive in the eyes of the jury.

EXAMPLE:

BY THE PROSECUTING ATTORNEY: Isn't it a fact that years ago you were arrested for stealing a quantity of cigarettes from a warehouse in Fort Wayne, Indiana?

BY DEFENSE COUNSEL: We object to this, Your Honor. He's asking about an arrest and only a conviction could possibly be admissible. Anyway, it's much too remote to be probative.

THE COURT: I'm inclined to let him inquire about this to show a pattern of conduct.

BY DEFENSE COUNSEL: May we have a standing objection to questions about arrests on this man's record, as distinguishable from convictions?

THE COURT: You may.

The failure to object to inadmissible evidence does not foreclose counsel from successfully objecting to his adversary's subsequent efforts to introduce more of the same. Some lawyers, desiring to avoid an excessive number of objections, will wait until it becomes unavoidably clear that a type of evidence is potentially damaging before objecting to it. The conscious waiver of objection to the earlier evidence does not operate as a waiver as to later offers of similar evidence. For example, the fact that counsel permitted some hearsay to come in on a particular subject does not preclude him or her from objecting to later offers of hearsay on the same subject.

Obtaining a Ruling

As was indicated earlier, the trial record in connection with an objection to evidence has not been effectively made until a ruling by the trial judge has been obtained. It is objecting counsel's job to secure an express ruling. This is vital to appellate reviews since a trial judge's silence is not considered tantamount to an overruling of the objection. In the heat of trial the judge may neglect to make an explicit, audible ruling; indeed, he may not have heard the objection. If the matter is of any importance, objecting counsel can properly interrupt to forestall the witness from answering the challenged question and can request an on-the-record ruling from the trial judge.

> EXAMPLE:
> Q: What did your friend tell you about the shooting?
> BY OPPOSING COUNSEL: Object, Your Honor, the question calls for hearsay.
> BY EXAMINING COUNSEL: Well, it's entirely relevant.
> OPPOSING COUNSEL: That may be, but it's still hearsay.
> THE WITNESS: She told me . . .
> OPPOSING COUNSEL [addressing first the witness and then the judge]: Just a minute, sir. Your Honor, we would appreciate your admonishing the witness not to respond to the question until Your Honor has ruled. And we would very much appreciate having a ruling on our hearsay objection.
> THE COURT: The witness will not answer the question. The objection is sustained. The question clearly calls for hearsay.

Exceptions

There was a time when, in many jurisdictions, it was necessary for counsel to get an express exception on the record to those evidentiary rulings of the trial court that counsel considered erroneous. This is rarely required today. No longer does one hear the final sentence of the following exchange:

> OPPOSING COUNSEL: Object, Your Honor, irrelevant.
> THE COURT: Overruled, counsel.
> OPPOSING COUNSEL: Please note our exception to Your Honor's ruling.

All that is required today in most jurisdictions is the making of an objection and the presentation of counsel's reasoning. Of course, it will later be necessary to set forth in a motion for new trial any assignments of legal error that are based on objections made by counsel during the trial.

J. Offers of Proof

Offer of Proof as Distinguished from Offer of Evidence

The so-called offer of proof is something quite different from the typical offer of testimonial or tangible evidence about which we have been talking. The necessity for an offer of proof is most commonly encountered during the examination of a witness on the stand. Examining counsel puts a question to the witness in order to elicit testimony. He may value the anticipated testimony for its own sake or because it lays the identifying or authenticating foundation for the introduction of an exhibit. Opposing counsel, for reasons drawn from the rules of evidence, makes a timely objection to counsel's question. The objection is sustained. Examining counsel, either before or after the trial court's ruling on the objection, must make an offer of proof unless he is willing to concede the merit of opposing counsel's objection.

The offer of proof can be a very simple affair: examining counsel puts a question to the witness, opposing counsel's objection to the question is sustained by the trial judge, and examining counsel, to perfect the record for possible appeal, states to the judge, "Your Honor, through this witness we offer to prove. . . ."

The Two Purposes of an Offer of Proof

The offer of proof has two legitimate purposes: (1) If properly made, it permits the trial court to make a fully informed and, hopefully, correct ruling on the pending objection. (2) If the ruling is against the side offering the evidence and is arguably erroneous, an adequate offer of proof is usually essential to preserve the point for posttrial review. Point (2) is simply one way of saying that the offer of proof is an aspect of making the trial record. In the absence of an explicit offer of proof an appellate court often would have no way of knowing whether or not the trial court's evidentiary ruling was correct. Of equal importance, the appellate court would have no sure way of knowing whether the loss of the excluded evidence was prejudicial to the offering side's case. A reviewing court cannot weigh the importance of rejected evidence without knowing what that evidence would have been. An offer of proof discloses what the excluded evidence would have been.

Three Ways to Make an Offer of Proof

There are three basic methods for making an offer of proof during the course of a witness's oral testimony. These three methods can be labeled (1) the tangible offer, (2) the witness offer, and (3) the lawyer offer.

Tangible Offer

The offer of tangible proof is easy. Any lawyer who knows how to mark for identification, authenticate, and offer into evidence an item of tangible evidence knows, almost automatically, how to make an offer of proof of the exhibit's nature or contents if his offer of it is rejected upon opposing counsel's objection. The lawyer offering the rejected exhibit need only hand it to the court reporter for insertion in the trial record. Or, if the item happens to be a writing, such as a letter, counsel might also, out of the jurors' hearing, read it into the trial record at the very time of its exclusion, thereby ensuring its consideration in proper context by a reviewing court.

Unlike received exhibits, rejected tangible evidence will not be given to the jury. It will, however, find its way into the record on appeal, along with all other offered exhibits whether received or rejected. Offering counsel's only additional task may be to state for the record the purpose of the rejected evidence, if there is any possibility that its intended function is unclear.

Witness Offer

The witness offer is even easier than the tangible offer. When an objection has been made to a question posed to a witness and an exclusionary ruling is made by the judge, examining counsel can make his offer of proof through the witness. He simply proceeds with his examination of the witness, employing the standard question-and-answer method, and the witness's recorded answers, ordinarily taken outside the jurors' hearing, comprise the offer of proof.

As with tangible offers, counsel's only additional obligation may be to explain the relevance of the offered testimony more completely than he or she did at the point of opposing counsel's successful objection to it.

Lawyer Offer

Where it appears that a question in appropriate form was posed during the direct examination of a witness on the stand and that, on objection by opposing counsel, the trial court excluded the answer, examining counsel's offer of proof may simply consist of a statement to the court at the time of its ruling, and on the record, revealing what the witness's answer would have been. Counsel's statement for the record will include any additional information essential to show that the described answer would be material and otherwise admissible. His statement will also be aimed at showing that the response would benefit his client in some way.

As was previously indicated, the so-called lawyer offer may not be much more complicated than "Your Honor, the witness, were he [she] permitted to answer the last question, would have testified [to such-and-such]."

This third type of offer of proof, the lawyer offer, is not favored by many judges. Most judges prefer a methodical question-and-answer approach because it makes it easier for opposing counsel to frame specific objections to the offer. Perhaps it also reflects a persistent distrust of lawyers, the fear being that the unethical lawyer will invent a favorable answer in describing in his own words what the witness's response would have been.

A possible safeguard against an untruthful lawyer offer lies in the witness's ability—especially after inquiry by a skeptical trial judge or opposing counsel—to contradict the offer, pointing out that in fact his answer would be a different one. Of course, this assumes a witness who is sufficiently honest to take exception to counsel's narrative.

Making Offers of Proof Outside the Jurors' Hearing

Trial judges will usually require that counsel present his offer of proof in such a way that although the court, opposing counsel, the witness, and the court reporter can hear it, the jurors cannot. A trial judge has the right to insist that offers of proof be made out of the jurors' hearing. A judge is not invariably required to exercise this authority, however. Whether an offer of proof will be presented outside the jurors' hearing is a question addressed to the trial judge's discretion.

It would be a waste of time were a trial court to send the jury out of the courtroom during every offer of proof made during a trial, because many lawyer offers that follow an objection are one brief sentence in length. Furthermore, the content of brief offers of proof may be altogether harmless.

CHAPTER FOUR

A Return to Relevance

The concept of relevance was touched upon in chapter 2 in connection with the admissibility of evidence. It was said there that relevance is a combination of (1) materiality and (2) probativeness. If the offered item of evidence is probative of (tends to establish) a material issue in the case, it is relevant. Now we can delve more deeply into the notion of relevance.

Despite the seeming simplicity of our two-step definition, relevance is a concept that is difficult to define in a really helpful way. Relevance is easier to recognize than it is to describe. It is reminiscent of U.S. Supreme Court Justice Potter Stewart's remark about obscenity: "I can't define it, but I know it when I see it."

A. Definitions and Tests of Evidence

Impact on the Probabilities

Relevance, in the sense of probativeness, has to do with the ability of evidence to prove or disprove a material issue. Relevance has to do with the probabilities of a situation. If we say that relevance has to do with the tendency of evidence to render a fact-issue more probably true, or untrue, than it would have been without the particular evidence, we are talking about probabilities. Will the offered evidence make the existence of a proposition (material fact-issue) probable (or *not* probable?) If it will, it has probative force and is therefore relevant.

To put it another way, the question is, Will the offered evidence *help* the fact-finder?

Relevance and Circumstantial Evidence

Relevance problems, as was suggested in chapter 2 when the basic types of evidence—direct and circumstantial—were being examined, arise in connection with circumstantial evidence, since direct evidence of a material fact-issue is invariably relevant (probative) and will be ruled admissible unless it runs afoul of some special exclusionary rule such as a testimonial privilege.

Relevance Involves Content, Not Form

Relevance relates to the *content* or *substance* of evidence, not the *form* or *manner* in which the evidence is offered. Relevance, in other words, is concerned with the *subject matter* of evidence, not with how it is offered. For example, an objection based on the rule against hearsay goes to the *form* of the evidence; the evidence is being offered in the form of hearsay.

It can be said, as a general principle, that all relevant evidence is admissible if it is offered in an unobjectionable form and manner and does not violate some special exclusionary rule such as a privilege.

Tests of Relevance

Are there any tests that can be used to detect relevance? In chapter 2 the key questions were given:

1. What is the offered evidence being used to prove? (What is the issue?)
2. Is this a material issue in the case?
3. Is the offered evidence probative of (does it tend to establish) that issue?

Courts probably decide most relevance questions on the basis of (1) a "feeling" about the offered evidence, and (2) settled judicial precedent or codified rules, if there are any. Judges sometimes have a feeling about evidence, an intuitive reaction to it, that is based on their experience, common sense, and knowledge of the way the world turns. Their problem with relevance questions is greatly eased, of course, if they can find a decided case by another court in which similar or identical evidence was ruled either relevant or irrelevant. Recourse to prior judicial precedent and to codifications of it is always reassuring to judges.

Although there are few real tests for relevance, there are some significant warning signals.

Whenever in a trial one becomes aware that testimony is being brought out, or exhibits are offered, that relate to a *time*, a *person*, or an *event* other than the time, the persons, or the events directly involved in the case that is being tried, one becomes acutely sensitive to the relevance problem.

Remoteness in time can be particularly important. A circumstance that would be relevant if it happened in close time-proximity to the event in question is irrelevant if instead it was greatly removed in time from the event in question.

EXAMPLE:
To establish value of personal property, proof that similar items sold on the open market for $1,000 during the year in which the alleged larceny took place would be *relevant.* Proof that similar items sold for $1,000 twenty years earlier would be *irrelevant.*

Relevance and the State of Humankind's Knowledge

Relevance is sometimes dependent upon humankind's increasing knowledge and expertise in specialized fields. There was a day when firearms identification evidence—so-called ballistics evidence—was considered irrelevant, even preposterous. Nowadays judicial notice of its general validity will be taken. Our knowledge has expanded enough to give us faith in such evidence. We have similar faith in the reliability of radar equipment, blood-alcohol testing equipment and, in some jurisdictions, so-called voiceprints. So far, few courts have had sufficient faith in the reliability of polygraph tests (the "lie detector").

Probability Theory

Although it is true that the concept of relevance poses a question about how *probable* it is that a given proposition is true (or untrue), the actual use in court of statistical probability theories can be dangerous. A notorious California criminal case, *People* v. *Trujillo and Woodmansee,* is illustrative.

This was a murder case in which the victim had been killed by a bullet fired from a weapon that had five characteristics: (1) .38 caliber, (2) right-hand rifling, (3) a misaligned cylinder that gave the bullet a shaved edge, (4) five lands and grooves, and (5) it was a revolver. One of the accused had such a gun. In his closing argument to the jury the prosecuting attorney suggested that (1) because seven calibers of guns are manufactured, there was, conservatively speaking, 1 chance in 5 that a given gun would fire a .38 caliber bullet; (2) the chances are 1 in 2 that a gun will have righthand rather than lefthand rifling; (3) the chances are 1 in 5 that a gun's cylinder will be misaligned so as to cause a shaving of the bullet; (4) the chances are 1 in 4 that a gun will have five lands and grooves; and (5) the chances are 1 in 2 that a gun will be a revolver rather than an automatic.

The prosecuting attorney, using the "product rule" of elementary probability theory, multiplied these probabilities and announced that the chances were 1 in 400 (1 x 5 is 5; 2 x 5 is 10; 5 x 10 is 50; 4 x 50 is 200; 2 x 200 is 400) that a given gun would possess all of the described characteristics. This was done to suggest to the jurors that it was extremely unlikely (improbable) that the similarity between the characteristics of the accused's gun and the fired bullet were merely coincidental. But the prosecutor's argument had two basic flaws.

1. The assumptions on which the prosecuting attorney's estimates of the probabilities of the characteristics occurring were based were inaccurate. There is no valid reason to assume, without proof, that one-fifth of all guns are .38 caliber; there is also no reason to assume that half of all guns manufactured have righthand rifling.
2. The factors mentioned in the prosecutor's closing argument were not independent. Even if half of the guns manufactured have righthand rifling and one-fifth of them are of .38 caliber, it could be that all or most .38 caliber guns have righthand rifling. If *dependent* factors are treated as *independent,* they are being multiplied *twice* and the resulting odds are improperly inflated.

Another widely publicized California case, *People* v. *Collins,* reported at 438 P.2d 33 (S. Ct. Cal. 1968), also underscores the difficulties inherent in the use of probability theory in trials. A witness observed a blond woman with her hair in a ponytail running from the scene of a mugging in San Pedro, California. The witness testified that the women entered a yellow automobile driven by a black man with a beard. The defendants, a married couple, fit these descriptions. The prosecutor, backed by the testimony of an expert witness, calculated that the probability of a couple selected at random fitting this description was 1 in 12 million.

The California Supreme Court reversed the Collinses' conviction, holding that the prosecutor's argument had been improper. The court picked out numerous defects in his approach to probability theory.

In the first place, the assumed probabilities against the various components of the witness's description were mostly speculative. It is extremely difficult to secure accurate information about the probabilities of particular physical characteristics.

Furthermore, the factors multiplied into the 1:12 million probability were probably not independent. For example, experience reveals that black men frequently date white women and those who do are often bearded.

Finally, in criminal cases one must always consider the possibility of misobservation or of a deliberate frame-up. These two possibilities are entirely unrelated to the prosecutor's elaborate probability calculations and undermine them seriously.

B. Recurring Relevance Problems

Even though there are virtually no "rules" of relevance other than those discussed in the preceding section (basically, Does the evidence help?), a few relevance problems have been encountered by courts so frequently that judicial attitudes toward them have crystallized and can be predicted.

"Motion denied. Counsel's taste in clothes is not grounds for dismissal..."

Testing for relevance becomes a slightly more complex process in these recurring situations. The inquiry now becomes, Is the possible helpfulness of the evidence outweighed by its potential for improper prejudice? This somewhat more complicated test is reflected in Rule 403 of the Federal Rules of Evidence, under which a judge is free to exclude relevant evidence if its probative value is substantially outweighed by the danger of unfair prejudice, of confusion of the issues in the case, or of misleading the jury.

Character Evidence

Some of the most frequently recurring relevance problems have to do with character evidence. The general rule is that evidence of a person's character, or of a particular character trait (for example, a violent streak), is not relevant to prove that on a particular occasion the person acted in conformity with it. "Once a thief, always a thief" is not a recognized legal principle.

As is usually true of general rules, however, there are some important exceptions to the rule against the use of character evidence.

Accused's Character

The accused in a criminal case can introduce evidence of his own good character. This is sometimes called "putting one's character in issue." Then, because the accused has thereby "opened the door," the prosecution can introduce rebuttal evidence to show the accused's bad character.

A 1948 Supreme Court decision, *Michelson* v. *United States,* 335 U.S. 469, provides an example. There the accused, charged with having bribed a federal revenue agent, put up an entrapment defense. He called five witnesses who testified to his good reputation for honesty and truthfulness. In cross-examining four of these character witnesses, the prosecuting attorney asked whether each witness had heard of the accused's arrest almost thirty years earlier for receiving stolen goods. The Supreme Court held that this was permissible as a method of testing the extent of the character witnesses' knowledge of the accused's true reputation. The evidence was not, however, usable by the jurors to establish that the accused was guilty of the charge against him.

Sometimes it is possible to put the accused's character for a specific trait in issue in the indictment against him. It is then permissible to prove that character trait as an essential *element* of the crime charged.

> EXAMPLE:
> In *Carbo* v. *United States,* 314 F.2d 718 (9th Cir. 1963), a well-known gangster was charged in the indictment with having used his evil reputation as a weapon for extortion. This paved the way for proof of his reputation by the prosecution at trial.

Victim's Character

To support a defense, the accused in a criminal case is sometimes permitted to introduce evidence of his alleged victim's character. For example, to support a claim of self-defense, the accused may introduce evidence that the alleged victim had a violent character. This is done to raise an inference that the victim was the first aggressor.

Special protection has recently sprung up around the background of one sort of witness, the person who has allegedly been subjected to the crime of rape or sexual assault. In times past the complainant in a rape or sexual assault case was often subjected to an embarrassing cross-examination concerning his or her past sexual conduct with persons other than the accused. (The reference to "*his* or her" is not an exaggerated effort to maintain the gender neutrality of this text. Men, straight or gay, are subject to sexual violation, especially in a prison environment. It should be added, however, that in most jurisdictions the rape statutes have not themselves been made gender neutral; the charge against a person accused of sexually attacking a male will be called criminal sexual assault or sodomy rather than rape.)

Defense counsel who engaged in demeaning cross-examinations in rape or sexual assault cases attempted to justify their approach on one or both of two counts, insisting that it was relevant to consent, which is a defense to a charge of rape or sexual assault, or claiming that it somehow went to the veracity of the complaining witness. The fact that courts freely permitted such attacks on cross-examination made many victims reluctant to report rape and to press charges. Occasionally it may also have resulted in unjust verdicts of acquittal on the mistaken or chauvinistic notion that the complainant had "asked for it" or "deserved what he/she got."

In an era of increased sensitivity to the rights of women, Congress and almost all of the state legislatures have enacted statutes that strive to limit the use of prior sexual conduct evidence in rape and sexual assault cases. Some of these statutes are extremely simple in design, perhaps too simple. In a few sentences they virtually prohibit inquiry on cross-examination into sexual activities by the complainant with anyone other than the accused. The announced reasoning behind these statutes is that the complainant's past consensual behavior with the *accused* is arguably relevant to the issue of consent on the occasion of the claimed assault, while evidence of the complainant's reputation and specific evidence that the complainant previously consented to sexual intercourse with some *other* person is not. In this sense the statutes are a reaffirmation of American law's distaste for so-called propensity evidence. Just as "Once a thief, always a thief" is bad law, "Once willing, forever willing" is, too.

Despite the trend mentioned above, the influential Federal Rules of Evidence, in their original form, perpetuated the generalization that a criminal defendant could introduce reputation testimony concerning a victim's character, and prior acts evidence, in order to raise an inference that on the occasion in question the victim had acted in conformity with the indicated character trait. Thus under Federal Rule of Evidence 404(a) (2) it was permissible for a rape defendant who claimed consent to introduce evidence of the prosecutrix's reputation for promiscuity, the implication being that she had consented to sexual intercourse with the defendant. The analogy—hardly a perfect one—was to the murder defendant who claimed self-defense and was allowed to show the deceased's reputation for violence to suggest that he had been the first aggressor; that is, that he "started it." It had also been suggested in some judicial opinions that evidence of reputation and of past sexual behavior could be used to attack an alleged rape victim's testimonial credibility, although the relationship between consensual sexual activity and truth-telling was not always explained with much precision.

In 1978 a so-called rape shield provision was added to the Federal Rules of Evidence by Congress as Rule 412. (Privacy Protection for Rape Victims Act of 1978, Pub. L. 95-540, 92 Stat. 2046.) Far from being a simply worded, unqualified prohibition, Rule 412—which overrides Rule 404(a) (2) in rape cases—was drafted in dizzyingly complex form. Its operative provisions are these:

> (a) Notwithstanding any other provision of law, in a criminal case in which a person is accused of rape or of assault with intent to commit rape, reputation or opinion evidence of the past sexual behavior of an alleged victim of such rape or assault is not admissible.
>
> (b) Notwithstanding any other provision of law, in a criminal case in which a person is accused of rape or of assault with intent to commit rape, evidence of a victim's past sexual behavior other than reputation or opinion evidence is also not admissible, unless such evidence other than reputation or opinion evidence is—
>
> (1) admitted in accordance with subdivisions (c)(1) and (c)(2) and is constitutionally required to be admitted; or
>
> (2) admitted in accordance with subdivision (c) and is evidence of—
>
> (A) past sexual behavior with persons other than the accused, offered by the accused upon the issue of whether the accused was or was not, with respect to the alleged victim, the source of semen or injury; or
>
> (B) past sexual behavior with the accused and is offered by the accused upon the issue of whether the alleged victim consented to the sexual behavior with respect to which rape or assault is alleged.

The rule goes on to provide for a special procedure to be followed when a rape defendant proposes to offer evidence of the complainant's past sexual conduct:

> (c) (1) If the person accused of committing rape or assault with intent to commit rape intends to offer under subdivision (b) evidence of specific instances of the alleged victim's past sexual behavior, the accused shall make a written motion to offer such evidence not later than fifteen days before the date on which the trial in which such evidence is to be offered is scheduled to begin, except that the court may allow the motion to be made at a later date, including during trial, if the court determines either that the evidence is newly discovered and could not have been obtained earlier through the exercise of due diligence or that the issue to which such evidence relates has newly arisen in the case. Any motion made under this paragraph shall be served on all other parties and on the alleged victim.
>
> (2) The motion described in paragraph (1) shall be accompanied by a written offer of proof. If the court determines that the offer of proof contains evidence described in subdivision (b), the court shall order a hearing in chambers to determine if such evidence is admissible. At

such hearing the parties may call witnesses, including the alleged victim, and offer relevant evidence. Notwithstanding subdivision (b) of rule 104, if the relevancy of the evidence which the accused seeks to offer in the trial depends upon the fulfillment of a condition of fact, the court, at the hearing in chambers or at a subsequent hearing in chambers scheduled for such purpose, shall accept evidence on the issue of whether such condition of fact is fulfilled and shall determine such issue.

(3) If the court determines on the basis of the hearing described in paragraph (2) that the evidence which the accused seeks to offer is relevant and that the probative value of such evidence outweighs the danger of unfair prejudice, such evidence shall be admissible in the trial to the extent an order made by the court specifies evidence which may be offered and areas with respect to which the alleged victim may be examined or cross-examined.

(d) For purposes of this rule, the term "past sexual behavior" means sexual behavior other than the sexual behavior with respect to which rape or assault with intent to commit rape is alleged.

If we pull the federal statute apart we can see that—

a. *Reputation* or *opinion* evidence concerning an alleged rape victim's past sexual conduct is *never* admissible;
b. Evidence of an alleged rape victim's prior *specific sexual acts* are *generally* not admissible, with several important exceptions.

The first exception, seen in subdivision (b)(1), applies if the evidence of past conduct is "constitutionally required to be admitted." This is a safeguard not always found in state rape shield statutes, probably because it was considered superfluous. It preserves the due process right of a criminal defendant to present any valid defense he may have. (Presumably, courts would preserve the right with or without a statutory admonition.) A statute that unreasonably limited a criminal defendant's ability to present relevant exculpatory evidence would be unconstitutional as applied to that defendant. On the defensive issue of consent in a rape case, for example, it might violate notions of due process to prevent the defendant from introducing evidence that the complainant was a prostitute; it might also be constitutionally impermissible to block the defendant from demonstrating that the complainant had a specific motive, rooted in past sexual misconduct, to testify falsely against the defendant. (See, e.g., *Olden* v. *Kentucky*, ______ U.S. ______, 109 S.Ct. 480 (1988); *Chambers* v. *Mississippi*, 410 U.S. 284 (1973).)

The second exception to the general rule prohibiting evidence of past sexual behavior, found in subdivision (b)(2)(A) of Rule 412, allows evidence that the defendant was not the source of semen that was discovered in the course of investigation or examination, or that the defendant did not inflict injuries suffered by the complainant. This is simply a long way of saying that the defendant is permitted to prove that someone else raped the complainant.

Finally, under subdivision (b)(2)(B) of the federal rule, the accused can introduce evidence of his own past sexual relationship with the complainant. Although not conclusive, this would go to the issue of consent.

The rape shield statutes, with their general proscription of evidence of "past sexual behavior," pose a problem of definition. How should the quoted phrase be interpreted? It could be read to cover all manner of activities, ranging from "sexy" attire to nude dancing.

One important question that remains is whether a rape shield statute precludes a rape or sexual assault defendant from introducing evidence of the complainant's sexual conduct with other persons in an effort to cast doubt on her trial testimony. As was mentioned earlier, prior to the enactment of these statutes it was suggested by some courts that this would be a legitimate use of so-called sexual history evidence. In 1990 the issue was addressed by the Illinois Supreme Court. In *People* v. *Sandoval* the Court upheld Illinois' rape shield law and concluded that it barred the defendant from using evidence of sexual conduct with others to contradict the complainant's in-court testimony. In *Sandoval* the complainant had testified that she had never engaged in a deviate form of sexual intercourse with anyone other than the defendant. She had also testified that the alleged sexual assault had led her to stop dating. The trial judge refused to let the defense call a witness who would testify that he had engaged in deviate sexual intercourse with the complainant prior to the defendant's alleged assault. The judge also refused to allow the defense to introduce evidence that the complainant had been "hanging all over" a man in a bar the week leading up to the defendant's trial. These rulings were affirmed by the Illinois Supreme Court. It noted that "prior sexual history is irrelevant" under the rape shield statutes, adding that "[T]he witness may not be impeached on irrelevant or collateral matters." The court seems not to have considered the possibility that prior sexual history might be irrelevant as to consent but powerfully relevant as to credibility.

When all is said and done, it may be that the rape shield statutes are simply a strong reminder that evidence of a rape or assault complainant's past sexual conduct must be relevant to a legitimate issue (identity of the attacker, consent, veracity) and not productive of unfair prejudice. That, of course, may well be justification enough for their enactment.

Witness's Character

The character of an ordinary witness, as distinguished from the accused or his victim, can be delved into if it bears on his or her veracity. It can be attacked or supported (once it has been attacked) by reputation or opinion evidence.

EXAMPLE A:

[Some preliminary questions omitted.]

BY THE PROSECUTING ATTORNEY: What is your occupation, Mr. Ziff?

A: I am the president of the Second National Bank here in town.

Q: How long have you held that position, sir?

A: For thirteen years.

Q: What was your occupation before that?

A: Vice-president of the bank, and before that, trust officer. I've been with the same bank for twenty-three years.

Q: And how long have you lived here in Central City?

A: I was born here. I've lived here almost forty-five years.

Q: Do you know the community well?

A: I hope to tell you I do. A banker has to. I think I probably know everybody in this town by his first name.

Q: Mr. Ziff, yesterday the defense in this case called a witness by the name of Clyde Bushmat, who gave the defendant an alibi for the day that is important to us in this case. I will ask you whether you know Clyde Bushmat?

A: I know him.

Q: For how long?

A: Approximately fifteen years.

Q: I'll also ask you whether or not you are familiar with his reputation in the community of Central City for truth and veracity?

A: I know his reputation.

Q: And what is his reputation for truthfulness and veracity?

A: It is very bad. He cannot be trusted to tell the truth.

BY THE PROSECUTING ATTORNEY: Your witness.

EXAMPLE B:

[Preliminary questions omitted.]

BY DEFENSE COUNSEL: Reverend Goodheart, do you know Mr. Bushmat's reputation in this community for being a truthful person?

A: Yes, I do.

Q: What is it?

A: It is excellent.

These two examples show how a witness's character can both be attacked and then supported by reputation evidence, but they also reveal the almost impossible task confronting jurors when conflicting character evidence is given by equally or almost equally respectable witnesses. In the examples the two character witnesses would probably cancel each other out in the minds of reasonable jurors.

A witness's character can also be attacked by proof of conviction (not simply an arrest) of a crime if it was a felony (defined as being any offense punishable by death or imprisonment in excess of one year) or if it involved dishonesty or the making of a false statement and is not so remote in time as to lack probative weight.

Proof of Other Crimes or Specific Bad Acts

As a general rule, evidence of other crimes or specific bad acts is not receivable in evidence to establish a person's character for the purpose of showing that he or she acted in conformity with that character on a given occasion.

> EXAMPLE:
> Proof that Bushmat was convicted of shoplifting fifteen years ago is not relevant to prove a current charge of larceny.

However, evidence of the accused's other crimes or evil deeds may be admissible for numerous *other* purposes. In general, these other purposes fall into the categories of plan, purpose, motive, identity, opportunity, preparation, knowledge, the absence of mistake or accident on the accused's part, and impeachment of credibility.

1. *Prior Crimes or Bad Acts as Part of a Scheme or Conspiracy.* Evidence of prior crimes or other bad conduct can be offered to demonstrate the existence of an on-going conspiracy or scheme of which the offense charged against the accused is but one part or aspect. The existence of a larger plot is relevant to show motive, which in turn is circumstantial evidence of the doing of the act charged. Proof of a larger scheme may also serve to establish the accused's intent and perhaps even his identity as the perpetrator of the crime.

2. *Motive, Opportunity, Preparation.* Evidence of specific prior criminal acts, unrelated to any conspiratorial scheme, can be used to reveal motive, opportunity, and preparation for the current crime. It has sometimes been said that the motive for a crime is immaterial, but experienced criminal investigators know that this is incorrect. True, motive is not itself a technical element of any crime. As a practical matter, however, proof of motive may be relevant, inferentially, to some other fact-issue that *does* constitute an element of a crime. For example, proof of powerful motive may tend to *identify* the perpetrator of a crime.

> EXAMPLE:
> Bushmat murdered Fred Stitz. He then murdered Ms. Stitz when he discovered that she was an eyewitness to the killing of her husband.

> Bushmat also murdered the Stitz's daughter when she discovered her mother's body. At Bushmat's trial for the murder of the elder Ms. Stitz, the other killings will be admissible to show motive. (The killing of the daughter also qualifies as an implied admission of guilt. See 7, below.)

A warning is in order: prior misconduct is usually at its most questionable when it is employed to suggest motive. This is true in part because the legitimate role of motive evidence is frequently unclear and not carefully analyzed; it is often used by prosecutors and courts as a grab-bag term. It is also true because this brand of evidence usually requires a far lengthier and more dubious chain of untested inferences than any other type of misconduct evidence. The risk inherent in some motive evidence is that its injection into a case will induce the jurors to engage in groundless speculation and to succumb to inappropriate prejudices and biases. Supreme Court Justice Benjamin Cardozo put it in chillingly simple terms: it can, he said, be a "peril to the innocent."

3. *Modus Operandi.* It is permissible for the prosecution to prove the commission of other crimes and bad acts by the accused where they are so similar in method as to qualify as *modus operandi* (method of operation). In other words, the accused's methods of criminal operation are like a signature. Proof of *modus operandi* is relevant when the crime currently charged against the accused was accomplished in precisely the same fashion.

> EXAMPLE:
> The accused is charged with having molested a child after enticing it into an automobile with a promise of "a wonderful magic show at my house." The prosecution will be permitted to establish that the accused had five times in the fairly recent past employed the same method of enticing children into his car before assaulting them sexually.

4. *Absence of Accident or Mistake.* It is allowable to show similar acts by the accused in order to demonstrate that the acts for which he is currently on trial were not accidental or unintentional.

> EXAMPLE A:
> Bushmat is charged with the theft of a coin purse. The prosecution's theory is that Bushmat, posing as a supermarket customer standing close to the purse's owner, took it from her shopping bag. Bushmat insists that he found the coin purse on the floor and, thinking it had been lost, was on his way to the store's Lost and Found Department. Testimony by a store detective that he had observed Bushmat remove a coin purse from another customer's shopping bag would be admissible in evidence.

EXAMPLE B:
Bushmat shot Fred Stitz three times in the space of a month. The first two shootings are relevant to show that the third one was no mistake.

EXAMPLE C:
Similarly, accident seems an unlikely explanation where a series of deaths by poisoning have occurred in the same family.

5. *Deviate Passion.* Evidence of prior conduct can be used to demonstrate a passion or propensity for having unlawful sexual relations with the victim involved in the current prosecution.

The idea is that at least some perverted or abnormal sexual conduct is in and of itself so extraordinary that earlier acts of the same kind by the accused with the same person are probative that he is the one guilty of the acts described in the current charge.

EXAMPLE:
The accused is charged with the statutory rape of one of his daughters. The prosecution will be allowed to show prior incidents of sexual intercourse by the accused with the daughter.

In times past it was widely thought that evidence of similar sex with persons other than the current victim was impermissible. However, some recent cases and, especially, legislative enactments, suggest that such evidence may be admissible where its probative worth appears to be substantial. Thus, to vary the example given above, it might be permissible today for the prosecution to show that the accused had previously been convicted of statutory rape of a second daughter.

The trend mentioned above is clearly discernible in legislation. Recently the Congress enacted rules making evidence of similar prior sexual offenses admissible in cases charging the defendant with sexual assault or child molestation (Fed.R.Evid. 413–414.) It remains to be seen whether the states will adopt similar rules.

6. *Impeachment.* If the accused takes the witness stand in his own behalf, his credibility can be impeached by proof of his previous conviction for one or more serious crimes. This method of attacking credibility is considered in greater detail in chapter 7.

7. *Tacit Admission.* The criminal conduct of an accused occasionally constitutes an implied admission, as when the conduct was calculated to obstruct justice or effect an escape from punishment.

EXAMPLE A:
Proof that Bushmat murdered the only eyewitness to his killing of Stitz would be admissible in his prosecution for the murder of Stitz. [And see 2 above.]

EXAMPLE B:
Similarly, Bushmat's theft of a getaway car would probably be ruled admissible.

Methods of Proving Character

There are three basic methods of proving character: (1) It can be accomplished through proof of *reputation* in the pertinent community. (2) It can be shown through *opinion* evidence; for example, an employer's opinion as to the honesty of an employee. (3) On cross-examination of reputation and opinion witnesses of the sort referred to in (1) and (2), inquiry into pertinent specific instances of conduct is permissible to cast light on the witnesses' knowledge of the character of the person in question.

Unconsummated Offers to Plead Guilty; Withdrawn Pleas of Guilty; Nolo Contendere

An offer to plead guilty, never actually consummated, is not receivable in evidence to prove the commission of a crime. The same is true of withdrawn pleas of guilty. Of course, a criminal accused can withdraw a guilty plea only upon a showing to the trial judge that it would be unfair to hold him to his plea. It is thought that if for some reason it is unfair to hold him to the plea, it is equally unfair to permit the prosecution to introduce the withdrawn plea against him as proof of his guilt. And a plea of *nolo contendere* (no contest) is not admissible to establish the commission of an offense covered by the plea.

CHAPTER FIVE

The Rule Against Hearsay

A. Definitions of Hearsay

Common Law Definitions

The broadest common law (judge-made, as distinguished from statutory) definition of hearsay evidence is: An oral or written assertion, or nonverbal conduct that carries with it a conscious or unconscious assertion, made or carried on by someone other than a witness who is testifying at a trial or hearing, which is offered in evidence to establish the truth of the matter asserted.

The Evidence Codes

Some recent evidence codes, most notably the Federal Rules of Evidence and the California Evidence Code, define hearsay evidence more narrowly. For example, Rule 801 of the Federal Rules excludes from the operation of the hearsay rule (1) nonassertive conduct, (2) certain types of prior statements by a witness, (3) admissions made by an opposing party, and (4) statements of co-conspirators.

For the time being, our discussion will be based on the broad common law definition of hearsay rather than upon the recent codes.

Types of Hearsay

Under the common law definition given above, hearsay can be (1) oral, (2) written, or (3) by conduct; that is, actions.

A Three-Part Process

Hearsay evidence unfolds in a three-part process: (1) An assertion (or action—conduct—that *translates* into an assertion, such as pointing at someone to identify him), that assertion (or action) having been (2) made or done by someone other than a testifying witness on the stand (in other words, by an *out-of-court declarant* or *actor*), which is (3) offered in evidence to prove the *truth* of the matter asserted.

In view of the third step in this process—the evidence is being offered to establish the *truth* of the matter asserted—a crucial question by which to test an out-of-court declaration is, To what *issue* is the evidence directed?

> EXAMPLE:
> The witness on the stand testifies, in response to counsel's questioning, "On April 2, 1989, the accused said to me, 'Yesterday I was in New Orleans.'" If the *issue* is whether the accused was in New Orleans on April 1, 1989, (that is, if the accused's out-of-court declaration is being offered to prove the *truth* of the assertion contained in it), the testimony is classic hearsay.
>
> On the other hand, it is not hearsay if the issue is whether on April 2, 1989, the accused was capable of *talking*.

Hearsay as Belief

It may be helpful to think of hearsay as being *belief* translated into either *words* (spoken or written) or *actions*. Testimony as to these words or actions by an out-of-court declarant or actor is offered in evidence at trial, through some other witness, to prove the *truth* of the underlying belief.

Thus the hearsay process works this way: A witness on the stand testifies: "Bushmat told me the automobile was going 90 miles an hour." In other words, Bushmat—the out-of-court declarant—*said* the car was going 90 miles an hour, which indicates that he really *believed* that it was going 90 miles an hour. And, so the hearsay process goes, if Bushmat believed that the car was going 90 miles an hour, it is probably *true* that it was going 90 miles an hour. Bushmat's *belief* about something he thought he perceived in the outside world (a speeding automobile) was translated by him into *words* ("The automobile was going 90 miles an hour."). A witness in court is asked to repeat Bushmat's words as evidence that the car was in fact going 90 miles an hour (Bushmat's out-of-court words are being offered to prove the *truth* of what they asserted). And the factfinder is called upon to believe what Bushmat professed to believe. This may be pretty much a call to accept Bushmat's belief as a matter of blind faith. How does the factfinder know that Bushmat's apparent belief is worthy of credence?

Now we come to the risks involved in receiving hearsay evidence. The difficulty is that, in the example given above, the validity of Bushmat's belief, and thus of his verbalization of it, depends on a number of unknown factors.

1. The validity of Bushmat's belief depends on how good his eyesight was, on how close he was to the car, on whether visibility was in any way obstructed, on how good Bushmat was at estimating the speed of rapidly moving objects. In short, the validity of the out-of-court declarant's belief depends on the level of his *perception.*
2. The validity of Bushmat's stated belief was dependent on how good his *memory* of the event was at the time he spoke about it.
3. It also depends on whether Bushmat had any motivation to lie about the speed of the automobile. That is to say, the validity of his out-of-court declaration depends on Bushmat's *veracity* or *sincerity.*
4. Finally, the worth of Bushmat's belief depends on how effective he was at communicating to others precisely what he meant. This can be termed the problem of *articulateness.* (Did he say "90" or "19"?)

To put it another way, underlying the general rule against admission of hearsay evidence are serious concerns about the *reliability* of this type of evidence.

Putting it yet another way, the law is concerned about opposing counsel's inability to *test* the reliability of hearsay evidence, since the declarant or actor is not on the witness stand in court at the time of his declaration or act. The person on the witness stand, reporting what he heard Bushmat say, is a mere conduit or pipeline for the out-of-court declarant's words or acts. And, in effect, the person on the stand is insulating, shielding, the out-of-court declarant from cross-examination by opposing counsel.

An Absurd Example: The Toadlike Witness

An absurd but helpful example of classic hearsay involves an overly innovative trial lawyer's method of dealing with a crucial eyewitness who presents a poor appearance and probably would make a bad impression on the jury. (The witness is absolutely toadlike in appearance, nervous, and inarticulate.) Let us suppose that the prosecution has such a witness. The prosecuting attorney could solve the problem by telling the toadlike witness, "When you come to the courthouse don't go anywhere near the courtroom. Go directly to the basement and wait there. Let no one see you." On the witness stand the prosecutor would place the most attractive and articulate person he or she can find, despite the fact that this person knows nothing about the facts of the case and thus cannot be cross-examined about them. The prosecutor, in examining this attractive witness, will say, "Down in the basement you will find a man who was an eyewitness to the events involved in this matter.

"The jury will disregard the witness's last remark."

Drawing by Lorenz; © 1982 The New Yorker Magazine, Inc. Also reprinted in *Trial Diplomacy Journal.*

I'm going to give you some questions to ask him. Go to the basement, ask my questions of the eyewitness, and then come back up here and tell the jury what the eyewitness's answers were."

This approach would be an effective way to keep the jurors from seeing the repulsive eyewitness. It would also be an effective way to prevent defense counsel from using cross-examination to test the perception, memory, veracity, and articulateness of the only witness whose perception, memory, veracity, and articulateness really count—the eyewitness in the cellar. Needless to say, it is abundantly clear that this imaginative maneuver would run afoul of the rule against hearsay evidence. The unsworn words (assertions) of the out-of-court declarant (the toadlike witness in the basement) are being offered in court to prove their truth.

Summary

To summarize, underlying the rule against hearsay evidence are serious worries about the worth of such evidence, since (1) it was not under oath or solemn affirmation, and (2) it was not subject to cross-examination to test for the presence of hearsay risks or dangers. Opposing counsel was deprived of the opportunity to test the perception, memory, veracity, and articulateness of the out-of-court declarant, or actor, upon whose reliability the worth of the in-court testimony depends.

An Example Drawn from a Celebrated Case

The most important example of classic hearsay to be found in the report of an actual case is that of Sir Walter Raleigh. It was Raleigh's case that led to the formulation of the rule against hearsay evidence. On the basis of two out-of-court statements, Raleigh was charged with treason. The first statement was by Lord Cobham. It was to the effect that Raleigh had joined with Cobham in a conspiracy to overthrow Queen Elizabeth I. The second statement was by a Portuguese gentleman as reported to the tribunal by a British ship's pilot. It was to the effect that Raleigh had expressed an intention of cutting King James's throat. The prosecution used both of these out-of-court declarations to prove the truth of the assertions contained in them. Thus both statements were hearsay. Raleigh asked for, but was not given, an opportunity to confront and cross-examine Lord Cobham. Disgust with the result in Raleigh's case resulted, in the latter part of the seventeenth century, in the rule against hearsay.

Assertive and Nonassertive Conduct as Hearsay

The common law definition of hearsay is broad enough to embrace *conduct* as well as spoken or written words. In fact, the common law rule against hearsay covers two types of out-of-court conduct: assertive and nonassertive.

1. *Assertive conduct* is conduct that is consciously *intended* as an assertion; for example, pointing at someone or something for identifying purposes, or nodding one's head to indicate "yes" or "no." Here, action is simply substituted for words. The conduct is hearsay, just as would be the words.

EXAMPLE:
BY THE PROSECUTING ATTORNEY: Officer Krupke, what did you do next?
A: We arranged for a lineup and I told the little girl to point out the person who had molested her if she saw him in the lineup.
Q: What did she do, if anything?
A: She pointed to the third man from the left, the defendant in this case.
BY DEFENSE COUNSEL: Object, Your Honor. Hearsay by conduct.
THE COURT: The objection is sustained. The jury will disregard the witness's last answer in its entirety.

2. *Nonassertive conduct* is conduct which was *not* consciously intended as a direct assertion concerning an issue in the case but which nonetheless can be translated into such an assertion by a process of inference. That is, the out-of-court conduct carries with it an implied assertion concerning a material issue.

At common law, but not under some of the new evidence codes, nonassertive conduct violates the rule against hearsay, just as does assertive conduct (finger-pointing).

The landmark example of nonassertive conduct as hearsay is an old English case in which the issue was whether the maker of a will, one Marsden, was mentally competent. The person (a stableboy) to whom Marsden's will left everything sought to introduce three letters which had been addressed to Marsden and which requested him to perform acts that only a sane person could do. The letter-writers, in other words, had *treated* Marsden as a mentally competent person.

The English court refused to admit the letters on the ground that they were hearsay. The letters did not directly and consciously *assert* the matter in issue, Marsden's mental condition. Nevertheless, by implication they did show that the letter-writers *believed* Marsden to be mentally competent. The writing of the letters was nonassertive conduct and, under the common law, this is hearsay.

Another example of nonassertive conduct as hearsay can be found in a famous closing argument for the prosecution made by Daniel Webster. The accused in the case was tied to the alleged murder through one Crowninshield, who had recently killed himself. If Crowninshield's involvement in the murder could not be established, there would be no independent evidence linking the accused to the homicide. Webster skillfully tried to demonstrate that Crowninshield's suicide was nonassertive conduct attesting a guilty conscience. His suicide was asserted to be a natural consequence of his having been the killer. However, at common law this would be considered hearsay. (And of course prosecutor Webster did not take into account other possible explanations for Crowninshield's suicide—he was a terminal cancer patient, or had had a tragic love affair. Webster neatly sidestepped the relevance problem.)

Nonassertive Conduct Under the Evidence Codes

Section 1200(a) of the influential California Evidence Code states that "'hearsay evidence' is evidence of a *statement* . . ." (italics added). Section 225 of that code states that "'statement' means (a) oral or written verbal expression or (b) nonverbal conduct of a person *intended by him as a substitute for oral or written verbal expression*" (italics added). Thus nonassertive conduct is not hearsay under California's Evidence Code. Rule 801 of the Federal Rules of Evidence is to the same effect. Clearly, the modern trend is to treat only deliberately assertive words or actions as hearsay.

B. Out-of-Court Declarations That Are Not Subject to the Rule Against Hearsay

Declarations as "Verbal Acts"

Sometimes an out-of-court declaration is offered in evidence not to prove its truth but because the fact that the declaration was *made* possesses importance; the very act of making the verbal declaration is a significant fact.

More specifically, out-of-court declarations are sometimes admitted in evidence to show their effect, their impact, on a hearer or reader of them, regardless of their truth or falsity.

A good example is *Subramanian* v. *Public Prosecutor,* 100 Solicitor's Jour. 566 (Privy Council 1956), a criminal prosecution that took place in Malaya in 1956. During an uprising in that country the accused was captured by the British. He had in his possession some live ammunition, which was in violation of British law. At his trial the accused sought to testify that earlier he had been taken prisoner by Communist terrorists who had threatened to kill him unless he took up arms against the British. The trial judge ruled that this was hearsay, but on appeal he was reversed. The threats to which the accused testified were not offered to establish their *truth*—that is, the terrorists would in fact kill the accused if he did not rebel—but instead were offered to show that the accused had acted under duress in the *belief* that he would be executed if he did not obey. The issue was the effect of the threat on the hearer of it, not the content or substance of it.

An example that is closer home would be a police officer's testimony that he or she had been told by a reliable informant that a crime was in progress at a described location, offered on the issue of probable cause for arrest.

Out-of-Court Declarations as "Legally Operative Facts"

Occasionally, because of the operation of the law, out-of-court declarations have significant legal consequences in and of themselves, without regard to their "truth." The making of such legally consequential statements is a legally operative fact and testimony about them will not be excluded as hearsay.

> EXAMPLE:
> Bushmat is charged with offering a bribe to Lishniss, a public official. Testimony by Stitz that he overheard Bushmat say to Lishniss, "I'll give you $25,000 if you'll see to it that my company gets the street paving contract" is not violative of the hearsay rule. The words spoken were the words of bribery. The words *constituted* the offense charged

and thus were legally operative. Crimes that are committed by means of words—extortion is another illustration—can *only* be established through proof of the words used, just as in a civil case a contract or a defamatory speech can be established only by showing the words that were used.

C. The State of Mind Issue

Is It Hearsay?

Sometimes the out-of-court declaration amounts to a report by the out-of-court declarant of his state of mind at the time of the incident in question. Perhaps he has said uncomplimentary things about Bushmat, such as, "Bushmat is a thief." If the issue in the case is whether or not Bushmat is in fact a thief, the quoted out-of-court declaration is clearly inadmissible hearsay right out of the classic mold. But perhaps the issue is whether or not the out-of-court declarant was, at the time he spoke, fond of Bushmat. If he were fond of him, he probably would not go around calling him a thief. And even if what he said about Bushmat was false, the out-of-court declarant's having said it would nonetheless indicate that he was not fond of Bushmat.

Absence of Hearsay Risks

Statements of this sort, aimed at establishing the declarant's state of mind (affection, hate, love), are usually admissible in evidence even in jurisdictions that would exclude nonassertive conduct. This is because the most powerful of the hearsay dangers are likely to be absent. There is no *perception* problem where state of mind is an issue since the out-of-court declarant ought to know perfectly well what his or her own existing state of mind is. Furthermore, the evidence is being used solely to prove internal state of mind, not to establish the truth of observations about the external world. ("Bushmat is a thief," offered to show that the speaker does not like Bushmat [internal state of mind], not to prove that Bushmat really *is* a thief [an observation about the external world].) This again suggests the lack of any perception problem. The declarant has spoken only of what is inside his own head.

There is little risk of a *memory* problem where the issue is the out-of-court declarant's state of mind as of the time he spoke. It is hard to forget an existing state of mind.

There is also little risk of a *veracity* problem in the usual situation since there is not much likelihood that the out-of-court declarant was trying in an exceptionally clever way to mislead people into thinking he disliked Bushmat. Most people who wanted to accomplish that end would simply announce, "I hate Bushmat."

The Possibility of a Bluff

Nevertheless, some evidence that might at first glance seem to reflect a state of mind is excluded by courts because of its inherently suspicious character. The most famous example is found in an English case, *Corke* v. *Corke and Cooke,* [1958] 1 All Eng. Rep. 224 (Ct. App.), decided in 1958. Mrs. Corke was found with a lodger, Cooke, in his bedroom. Mr. Corke sued for divorce on grounds of adultery. The husband contended on appeal that a hearing commissioner made a mistake in receiving evidence that Mrs. Corke, soon after she was discovered, had called a doctor and asked him to administer tests to herself and Cooke to determine whether they had engaged in sexual intercourse recently. The doctor had refused to come to the Corke home. The issue was whether Mrs. Corke's request should be received to show her innocent state of mind.

The English court held that Mrs. Corke's request was hearsay evidence and inadmissible. Her request could be read as a proclamation of innocence; it could also be regarded as nonassertive conduct indicative of her state of mind. The trouble is that her request could have been a carefully calculated bluff. The law is reluctant to let a defendant manufacture his own evidence in this fashion.

It is because of cases like *Corke* v. *Corke and Cooke* that a criminal accused's loudly voiced requests for a lie detector test are not admissible in evidence as proof of innocence. Many criminals are sufficiently conversant with the law to know that the results of polygraph tests are not admissible in evidence. A demand for a test, which the accused may fail, may thus not be a very risky bluff on his part.

D. Nonhuman Evidence

Is It Hearsay?

Does it violate the rule against hearsay when a police witness on the stand testifies that radar equipment "said" that the defendant was driving his automobile at 90 miles an hour? Is violence done to the rule when a meter reader testifies that the parking meter "said" the defendant's allotted time had expired? What if the computer printout "said" that Clyde Bushmat had no bank balance at the time when he was drawing checks with wild abandon? Are these machines all out-of-court declarants within the meaning of the common law hearsay rule?

On the theory that machines, unlike humans, lack a conscious motivation to tell lies, and because the operation (including the accuracy and reliability) of machines can be explained by human witnesses who are then subject to probing cross-examination by opposing counsel, the law permits so-called nonhuman hearsay. (See chapter 18.)

"Old Boston"

Curiously enough, one of the judicial opinions most frequently cited in support of the admissibility of nonhuman evidence involved not a machine but a bloodhound. In *Buck* v. *State,* 138 P.2d 115 (S. Ct. Okl. 1943), the defendant objected, on hearsay grounds, to evidence that a bloodhound named "Old Boston" had followed a scent from the scene of the crime to him. However, the evidence was held to be admissible if an adequate foundation, revealing the dog's training and talent, was first laid.

If Old Boston's case seems antiquated, it should be remembered that it is perfectly good support for the admissibility of evidence concerning dogs trained to sniff out such illicit substances as marijuana.

In *City of Webster Groves* v. *Quick,* 323 S.W.2d 286 (Mo. App. 1959), radar equipment's recordation of an automobile's speed was held not to be in violation of the rule against hearsay.

E. "Straight from the Horse's Mouth"

Everyone has heard the phrase that supposedly originated with a bookie who was supremely confident of his tips on the races because he got his information "straight from the horse's mouth." The bookie did not realize it, but the readers of this volume comprehend that he was also giving a pretty good description of the hearsay rule's demands. Criminal cases cannot be made on gossip and secondhand accounts of what happened. The law of evidence has a strong preference for witnesses who can testify from personal knowledge based on direct observation, not "I was told it happened this way," but "I saw the whole thing and this is the way it happened."

In view of the hearsay rule, the competent criminal investigator will always endeavor to get his or her information "straight from the horse's mouth." If the investigator turns up someone who says, "I heard it from Clyde Bushmat, who tells me he was present at the time and that Lishniss shot Stitz last Saturday night," he is on his way to some usable evidence, but he is only on the way. He has not gotten to the right witness yet. The witness he needs is Bushmat, who apparently has some direct knowledge. Bushmat's account will not be secondhand; if he really was present at the shooting of Stitz he can testify from personal knowledge. Armed with a comprehension of the rule against hearsay evidence, the criminal investigator will search for Bushmat.

Any time a knowledgeable law enforcement agent hears someone say to him, "I was told . . .," he knows that the hearsay rule is probably involved and that he should locate the person who did the telling. The agent will know that courtroom testimony beginning with "I was told . . ." will be excluded from evidence—unless, of course, one of the numerous *exemptions* from or *exceptions* to the hearsay rule comes into play. We now move to an analysis of the principal exceptions to the rule against hearsay.

CHAPTER SIX

Exceptions to the Rule Against Hearsay

In the past the law of evidence did not give trial judges much leeway or flexibility in dealing with hearsay evidence. Hearsay, as we have seen, was defined rather rigidly at common law. However, some evidence that qualifies technically as hearsay under the common law definition given in chapter 5 is nonetheless quite reliable and helpful. Some hearsay is *good* hearsay, maybe even *great,* because of certain surrounding guarantees of reliability that make up for the absence of oath and cross-examination.

Accordingly, the law has developed a number of exceptions to the rule against hearsay. Those exceptions that are important in the trial of criminal cases will be discussed in this chapter.

A. Previously Recorded Testimony

Reasons for the Exception

The recorded testimony of a witness, given at an earlier proceeding, is hearsay; it is a statement by an out-of-court declarant (out of the *present* court, that is) and it is being offered to prove the truth of its assertions.

> EXAMPLE:
> A criminal case is tried and results in a conviction; the accused appeals; a new trial is ordered; between the first and the second, a witness has died; at the second trial, the court reporter from the first trial is called to the stand to read the deceased witness's previously recorded direct and cross-examination. This is permissible under the present exception to the hearsay rule.

It makes sense to have an exception to the hearsay rule for previously recorded testimony because (1) the out-of-court declarant (he/she is an out-of-court declarant in relation to the *second* court) is now unavailable to testify; (2) his previously recorded testimony was under oath or solemn affirmation; (3) his prior testimony was recorded with great accuracy by a trained court reporter; (4) it is being used against a party that has already had an opportunity to cross-examine the witness (or possibly it is being used against the party that originally *called* the witness); and (5) the previous examination in its entirety can be introduced into evidence at the second proceeding.

Requirements of the Exception

The hearsay exception for previously recorded testimony has four basic requirements or conditions:

1. As suggested above, the previously recorded testimony must have been given under oath or solemn affirmation.
2. The testimony at the previous proceeding must have been given at the instance of or against a party which had a chance to develop the testimony by direct, cross, or re-direct examination with motive and interest similar to those of the party against whom the prior testimony is now offered.
3. Both of the proceedings must have involved substantially the same issues, thereby ensuring that the examination at the first proceeding was relevant to the issues in the second proceeding.
4. The particular witness's testimony must be unavailable at the time his/her previously recorded testimony is offered in evidence.

The Meaning of "Unavailable"

Unavailability as a witness, mentioned in the last paragraph, is not nowadays strictly limited to *physical* unavailability. The term embraces a number of situations in which the declarant (1) is exempted from testifying by a ruling of the trial judge on the ground of testimonial privilege, as when a witness, having testified in the first proceeding, claims the privilege against self-incrimination at the second proceeding; (2) persists in refusing to testify concerning the subject matter of his prior testimony despite an order of the trial judge to do so; (3) claims failure of memory as to the subject matter of his prior testimony; (4) is unable to be present or to testify because of death, physical or mental illness or infirmity; or (5) is absent from the proceeding and the proponent of his previous testimony has been unable to procure his attendance by subpoena or other reasonable means.

Of course, a declarant is not unavailable as a witness if his refusal to testify, claim of lack of memory, inability to testify, or absence from the hearing is due to the connivance of the proponent of his previously recorded testimony for the purpose of preventing the witness from attending the second proceeding or testifying in it. (Remember the absolutely toadlike witness, sent to the courthouse basement.)

B. Dying Declarations

Reasons for the Exception

At common law the hearsay exception for dying declarations is limited to murder cases in which the out-of-court declarant has named his killer or described specific details of the homicide.

It has been thought, rightly or wrongly, that dying declarations have intrinsic assurances of trustworthiness, making cross-examination unnecessary. The notion is that a person who is in the process of dying, and knows it, will be truthful immediately before departing to meet his Maker. (Of course, the validity of this hearsay exception is open to some debate. What about the person who is not deeply religious? What of the person who, as his last act, seeks revenge by falsely naming a lifelong enemy as his killer? How reliable is the perception and memory of a person who is dying?)

Requirements of the Exception

The common law version of the dying declaration exception has six fundamental requirements:

1. The out-of-court declarant must have been the murder *victim,* not a third person (such as someone *confessing* to the murder).
2. The victim must have been *conscious of impending death* at the time of his or her declaration. The victim must have been aware that death was both *near* and *certain.*
3. The victim must have been in a position to have *direct and accurate knowledge* of the fact-assertions contained in his dying declaration.
4. The victim's statement must have been related to the *immediate cause* of his or her impending death, not to matters more remote in time.
5. The victim's statement must have been about *facts,* not opinions or guesses. "I think Bushmat shot me," would not be admissible under this hearsay exception.
6. The declarant must in fact be *deceased* at the time his declaration is offered in evidence.

EXAMPLE:

BY THE PROSECUTING ATTORNEY: Officer Krupke, you say that you accompanied the victim to the hospital in the ambulance that was dispatched?

A: Yes, sir, I did.
Q: Was anyone present in the back of the ambulance besides you and the victim?
A: Yes, there was a Dr. Faust who had come out in the ambulance.
Q: Did any conversation take place between Dr. Faust and the victim?
A: Yes.
Q: Tell us about it, please.
BY DEFENSE COUNSEL: May we have a standing objection to this line of questioning, Your Honor, at least until the necessary foundation has been laid?
THE COURT: Yes, we'll see what comes out.
BY THE PROSECUTING ATTORNEY: You may answer the last question, Officer Krupke. What was said?
A: The victim, Mr. Bushmat, kept moaning and asking for a priest. He said he wanted the last rites. Dr. Faust looked at the wound and said to Mr. Bushmat that there wasn't going to be time to get a priest, that Bushmat was dying. The doctor said that if there was anything Bushmat wanted to get off his chest, now was the time to do it.
Q: Did Bushmat say anything after that?
DEFENSE COUNSEL: Well, we object, Your Honor.
THE COURT: Overruled.
BY THE PROSECUTING ATTORNEY: You may answer.
A: Yes, Bushmat said he was sorry for the way he had wasted his life, gambling, running up debts, borrowing from juice loan operators, abandoning his family. And then he said, "Doc, Charlie 'The Pipe' Connor got me. I owed him money. He hit me with a section of lead pipe. He hit me too hard, huh?" And then Bushmat just went limp all over and didn't talk any more—ever.

Dying Declarations Under the Evidence Codes

Under Rule 804(b)(3) of the Federal Rules of Evidence, the dying declaration exception is extended to civil cases; it is no longer limited to murder cases. Furthermore, the victim need not be dead at the time his declaration is offered in evidence. He must, however, be unavailable in one or more of the ways listed in section VI.A., above. To the same effect is Section 1242 of the California Evidence Code.

C. Admissions

An Important Exception

The exception to the hearsay rule that permits the receipt in evidence of a party's admissions is an important one because it is encountered in both civil and criminal litigation with great frequency. On the civil side, personal injury lawsuits (to name only one type of case) are often based in large part on the defendant's pretrial admissions of negligent conduct.

EXAMPLE:

BY THE PLAINTIFF'S COUNSEL [examining an occurrence witness]: What happened next?

A: The driver of the truck jumped down out of his cab, ran over to plaintiff and said to him, "I'm sorry about this. I was looking for a lighted cigarette I'd dropped and I wasn't watching where I was going."

And many a criminal case involves admissions made by the accused prior to trial. They may have been made in casual conversation or in response to interrogation by the police or by a member of the prosecutor's staff. (A confession achieved by means of a properly conducted interrogation is simply a special type of evidentiary admission for purposes of the present hearsay exception.)

EXAMPLE A:

BY THE PROSECUTING ATTORNEY [examining an alleged accomplice of the accused who has turned State's evidence]: When the defendant Bushmat came back to his car where you say you were waiting, did he say anything?

A: Yes, he did.

Q: What did he say to you?

A: He said, "Sam was in the garage. I shot him twice. I got him good. Sam won't be talking to any grand jury."

EXAMPLE B:

BY THE PROSECUTING ATTORNEY [examining a police interrogator]: Officer, during the course of this interrogation session, did the accused make any kind of statement to you?

A: Yes, sir, he did.

BY DEFENSE COUNSEL: Your Honor, we object to anything further at this time. We'll ask for the usual hearing, out of the presence of the jury.

THE COURT: We will be in recess for half an hour. [Trial judge holds a hearing on admissibility. Was the accused's statement voluntary? Was he given the *Miranda* warnings? Court will resume after the judge makes a preliminary ruling that the statement is admissible.]

Q: Was the accused's statement reduced to writing?

A: It was.

Q: [The prosecuting attorney poses additional foundation questions, leading to the eventual receipt in evidence of the accused's signed incriminating statement.]

It may seem odd that an accused's own statements are considered to be hearsay. Certainly it would be a strange spectacle to see defense counsel object, on hearsay grounds, to receipt in evidence of an admission made by the accused himself. How can the accused object to his own statement? Can he complain that he was not under oath at the time he spoke? Can he argue that he had no opportunity to cross-examine himself? The fact is that the accused's admission or confession is usually categorized as hearsay for no more weighty reason than that it was an out-of-court declaration. It is therefore not surprising that the Federal Rules of Evidence do not treat admissions as hearsay at all and that state jurisdictions have a clear-cut hearsay exception for such statements.

Constitutional Requirements Considered Elsewhere

For the moment we are discussing only the requirements of the admissions exception to the rule against hearsay. Reserved for special consideration in a separate chapter—chapter 11—are the various *constitutional* safeguards surrounding confessions and admissions.

Reasons for the Admissions Exception to the Hearsay Rule

The theory underlying the admissions exception is that if a person's statement is offered in evidence against him, he can hardly complain that he had no chance to cross-examine *himself.* Such an argument would be absurd. He can, if he chooses, deny having made the statement or he can try to explain it away, but the statement will be received in evidence nonetheless.

Elements of the Admissions Exception

The present exception involves any statement or conduct made or carried on by the accused prior to trial which, at the time of trial, is against his interests. (Note that this exception is applicable to statements by a party, the accused, in contrast to the hearsay exception for so-called declarations against interest by nonparties. See D, below.)

1. The accused's statement need not have been against interest (that is, inculpatory) at the time it was *made*; it need only be incriminating as of the time of trial.
2. Lack of *personal knowledge* does not necessarily exclude a party's admissions. For example, the president of the defendant corporation

said, "My company has carefully investigated the matter and all of the reports indicate that we have been polluting the river."

3. A statement in the form of an *opinion,* as distinguished from a hard fact, is not necessarily excludable under this exception. For example, the president of the defendant corporation said, "Our dumping of all that oil into the river was negligent."

Judicial and Extrajudicial Admissions

There are three types of admissions: (1) *formal judicial admissions,* (2) *informal judicial admissions,* and (3) *extrajudicial admissions.*

Formal judicial admissions—for example, those contained in stipulations of trial counsel—are *conclusive*; informal judicial admissions made during courtroom testimony are *not* conclusive and can be denied, explained, or rebutted by other evidence; extra-judicial admissions—for example, evidentiary admissions made in conversation or in pre-trial statements—are *not* conclusive and can be denied, explained, or rebutted by other evidence.

Implied Admissions

As is true of hearsay in general, not all admissions are verbal statements. Admissions can be *inferred* from conduct or the absence of conduct.

EXAMPLE A:
Silence in the face of a charge to which a person would normally respond were it untrue. (But see chapter 8, discussing the possible applicability of the privilege against self-incrimination.)

EXAMPLE B:
Failure to call a witness or produce tangible evidence at trial can be taken as admission that the witness or exhibit would be damaging. Before this inference can properly be drawn, however, it must be shown that the witness or exhibit was more readily available to the side against whom the unfavorable inference is to be drawn.

Although it is true, as suggested in Example (a), above, that admissions can be inferred from conduct such as silence in the face of an accusation, a person under arrest has no obligation to reply to an accusation and, consequently, no inference can be drawn from his failure to do so.

Misconduct constituting an effort to obstruct justice, such as attempting to bribe a prosecution witness, may give rise to an implied admission of guilt. A frequently cited opinion in support of this proposition is *Nowack* v. *Metropolitan Street Railway Company,* 60 N.E. 32 (Ct. App. N.Y. 1901), a civil case. *Nowack* was a personal injury action in which the plaintiff offered to prove that an agent of the defendant railway, employed to talk with the occurrence witnesses, had attempted to bribe one of them. The New York Court of Appeals held that this testimony was receivable against the defendant. The theory is that the procuring of false evidence is an implied admission that one's case is either weak or nonexistent. (Note that *Nowack* also poses a problem of an admission by an *agent.* The question whether the implied admission of an agent is binding on his principal will be considered next.)

Admissions by an Agent

Where an accused (the principal) has expressly authorized someone else to speak for him, admissions made by that person (agent) will, by a well-recognized extension of the admissions exception to the hearsay rule, be admissible against the accused.

> EXAMPLE:
> Bushmat's lawyer (agent) writes a letter to a stockbroker on Bushmat's behalf, telling the broker to transfer specified shares of stock to Bushmat's daughter and adding, "The purpose of this transfer is the avoidance of inheritance taxes." This admission by the lawyer-agent is receivable against the client-principal, Bushmat.

Admissions by a Co-Conspirator

The law has developed a presumption that things said by a conspirator during the conspiracy and in furtherance of its goals are authorized by his co-conspirators. This makes the statements receivable in evidence against the other conspirators under the admissions exception to the hearsay rule. Just as the words of one business partner, uttered in pursuance of the partnership business, are binding on all of the partners, the words of one criminal conspirator are binding on his cohorts. The law regards conspirators as partners in crime, so to speak.

> EXAMPLE:
> BY THE PROSECUTING ATTORNEY: What, if anything, did the defendant Bushmat say to you?
> A: He said, "Why don't you join up with our counterfeiting ring? We've already got Lishniss with us."
> [This testimony is admissible against not only Bushmat but against Lishniss as well, if other conditions, described below, are met.]

The co-conspirator aspect of the admissions exception has a complicated array of requirements:

1. By way of preliminary foundation, there must be evidence of the *existence* of a conspiracy. The trial court, in determining preliminarily whether a conspiracy existed, is free to examine—among other things—the co-conspirator statements in question. However, the Supreme Court has not yet decided whether the co-conspirator statements *alone* would invariably be sufficient to support a finding that a conspiracy existed.
2. There must be evidence that the out-of-court declarant was a *member* of the conspiracy.
3. There must be evidence that the declarant's statement was made *during the course of and in furtherance of the conspiracy's purposes.*
4. There must be evidence that the accused against whom the declaration is offered was a *member* of the conspiracy at the time of the making of the declaration. The trial judge determines the accused's membership in the alleged conspiracy as a fact-question preliminary to the admissibility of his co-conspirator's declaration. While the evidence of membership must be strong to support the judge's ruling of admissibility, it does not have to be proved beyond a reasonable doubt.
5. Proof of the accused's membership in the alleged conspiracy must be *independent* of the out-of-court declaration. It cannot be based upon the out-of-court declaration of the co-conspirator. As indicated in (4), this independent evidence must be strong.

D. Declarations Against Interest

Reasons Underlying the Exception

The rationale behind the hearsay exception for so-called declarations against interest is different from that underlying the admissions exception, considered in the last section.

The admissions exception is grounded on the idea that a party who assertedly made a statement cannot sensibly argue that he had no opportunity at the time to cross-examine himself. The declaration against interest exception is grounded on the notion that people do not go about saying potentially harmful things about their own interests unless they are true.

Distinctions Between Party Admissions and Nonparty Declarations Against Interest

There are a number of distinctions to be drawn between admissions and declarations against interest.

1. *Party Admission; Nonparty Declarations.* In the first place, the admissions exception is applicable to the out-of-court declarations of

parties to litigation. The declaration against interest exception applies to *nonparties.*

2. *Restricted Admissibility of Admissions.* It follows logically from what was said above about the reasons underlying these exceptions that an admission is receivable in evidence *only against the party who made it,* while a declaration against interest is receivable *against anyone to whom it is relevant.*
3. *The Unavailability Requirement.* A declaration against interest is not admissible in evidence unless it can be demonstrated that the out-of-court declarant is *unavailable* as a witness. This is *not* true of a party admission.
4. *The Personal Knowledge Requirement.* For the declaration against interest exception to be admissible, it must be shown that the declarant had *personal knowledge* of the facts involved in his declaration. This is *not* true of the admissions exception.
5. *Knowledge That the Declaration Is Against the Declarant's Interest.* Under the declaration against interest exception, the out-of-court declarant must be shown to have known, *at the time he made his declaration,* that the making of it was contrary to his best interests. This is not the case with party admissions.

Elements of a Nonparty Declaration Against Interests

As will be at least partly apparent from the foregoing discussion, a declaration against interest at common law was an out-of-court statement

1. Against the declarant's *proprietary* or *pecuniary* interest (*proprietary* pertains to one's interest in property; *pecuniary* refers to one's financial interests) or other important interest;
2. *When made* (and the declarant then knew that it was against his interests);
3. Based on *personal knowledge* and expressed in terms of *facts,* not conjecture or opinion;
4. Made by a declarant who had *no overriding motive to lie*; and
5. Who is *unavailable* to be produced as a witness at the trial or hearing.

EXAMPLE A:
McGraw v. *Horn,* 183 N.E.2d 206 (Ind. App. 1962) ("proprietary or pecuniary interest" narrowly defined to *exclude* declarant's statement that he had failed to yield the right of way).

EXAMPLE B:
People v. *Spriggs,* 389 P.2d 377 (S. Ct. Cal. 1964) (California holds that declaration against *penal* interest qualifies under this exception; i.e., a statement exposing the speaker to criminal prosecution).

EXAMPLE C:
United States v. *Dovico,* 261 F.Supp. 862, *aff'd.,* 380 F.2d 325 (2d Cir. 1967) (declaration against "social interest"—holding one's self up to ridicule, scorn, vilification, etc., is *not* admissible as a declaration against interest).

EXAMPLE D:
Demasi v. *Whitney Trust & Savings Bank,* 176 So. 703 (La. App. 1937) (declaration had both self-serving and disserving—favorable and unfavorable—aspects; court concluded, on balance, that declaration was motivated by its self-serving aspects and therefore was *not* admissible as a declaration against interest).

Declarations against Penal Interest and the Chambers and Williamson Decisions

In *Chambers* v. *Mississippi,* 410 U.S. 284 (1973), the Supreme Court examined two Mississippi common law evidentiary rules to determine whether their joint application deprived the accused of due process of law in his trial. One of the rules was that the side calling a witness to the stand cannot attack the credibility of (impeach) that witness. The other rule, pertinent here, was one excluding declarations against penal interest (as being violative of the hearsay rule).

Leon Chambers was found guilty of murdering a policeman. At trial he put forward two interrelated defenses. First, he claimed that he had not shot the policeman. Second, he contended that another person, one Gable McDonald, had killed the officer. McDonald had confessed to the crime prior to Chambers's trial, but then had repudiated his confession. Chambers's claim that McDonald was the killer was corroborated at trial by two witnesses.

Chambers's second defense was frustrated at trial in two ways. The trial judge refused Chambers's request that he be permitted to call McDonald as a witness but then cross-examine him as an adverse or hostile witness; the judge cited the rule against attacking the credibility of one's own witness. And the trial judge excluded the testimony of three of McDonald's friends to whom he had admitted the crime; here the judge cited the Mississippi rule that declarations against penal interest, as distinguished from pecuniary or proprietary interests, are not admissible in evidence.

It was in *Donnelly* v. *United States,* 228 U.S. 243 (1913), that the Supreme Court had held that declarations against penal interest (in this instance, an out-of-court confession by a person other than the accused) were inadmissible as hearsay. In the circumstances of the *Chambers* case, however, the Court, breaking with its *Donnelly* holding, placed the trustworthiness of declarations against penal interest on a par with declarations against proprietary or pecuniary interests. Several facts in Chambers's case stood out in sharp relief, justifying the Court's decision. All of McDonald's admissions had been made to close friends and within a day of the murder. Each of his admissions was corroborated by other evidence. The admissions were quite obviously against McDonald's interests; he assuredly had nothing to gain by making them. Finally, McDonald himself was in the courtroom and was subject to cross-examination by the prosecutor.

In its disapproval of the older rule excluding declarations against penal interest, the Court aligned itself with a growing number of evidentiary codes and judicial decisions. (See Federal Rule of Evidence 804(b)(3), and see, *e.g., United States* v. *Candoli* 870 F.2d 49b (9th Cir. 1989).)

While a great deal of judicial attention has been paid to the use of declarations against penal interest to exculpate the defendant, the fact is that such statements have been offered in evidence by the prosecution where they have included statements inculpating the defendant. This involved a sort of hybrid statement, partly damaging to the speaker but in some aspect inculpating the defendant as well. A typical example would be, "I did take part in the robbery but I just drove the getaway car. Fred Stitz had the gun and did the actual robbery." The beginning of this statement is self-incriminating; the second part of it inculpates Fred Stitz. In times past the prosecution could offer the entire statement as part of its case against Stitz.

Prosecutorial use of a third person's declaration against penal interest has now been sharply limited by the U.S. Supreme Court's opinion in *Williamson* v. *United States*—U.S. ______, 114 S.Ct. 2431 (1994), in which a majority of the Court held that a declaration against penal interest is admissible only when it is exclusively self-inculpating. As Justice Sandra Day O'Connor put it, the pertinent rule "does not allow admission of non-self-inculpatory statements, even if they are made within a broader narrative that is generally self-inculpatory." Needless to say, a third person's exclusively self-incriminating statement will not ordinarily be helpful in the prosecution's case against someone other than the speaker. "I did the robbery," an exclusively self-inculpatory declaration, hardly helps the prosecution in its case against someone else.

Why would the Court so severely limit the use of self-incriminating statements that include statements inculpating another? The answer betrays a degree of cynicism on the Justices' part. They view such statements as being highly suspect because they may have been made to shift blame to another or to curry favor with the police and prosecutors.

E. State of Mind (Mental or Emotional State)

Reasons for the State of Mind Exception

In our discussion of the hearsay rule itself, we considered the situation in which a man says, "I hate Bushmat." It was suggested that such a directly assertive out-of-court declaration would be hearsay evidence if the issue were whether the declarant disliked Bushmat. It was also stated that a more oblique statement, such as "Bushmat is a thief," might simply be circumstantial evidence of a certain lack of affection, admissible without hearsay problems.

To make certain that *all* such evidence is rendered admissible, the law of evidence has produced a hearsay exception for declarations of existing states of mind. The reasoning behind this exception is, once again, that two of the principal hearsay dangers are absent: There is neither a *perception* nor a *memory* problem in connection with the declarant's then-existing state of mind. (There may, of course, be a *veracity* problem from time to time.)

Sheer necessity plays a role in this hearsay exception. When a person's state of mind is in issue, there is no very good way to prove it *except* by that person's statements about it.

Requirements of the Exception

A person's out-of-court declarations regarding his or her then-existing state of mind (mental or emotional state) are admissible in evidence when (1) there is an issue in the case concerning the person's state of mind at a particular point in time, and (2) his or her declarations with respect to it were made under conditions evidencing sincerity (that is, the absence of any motivation to falsify or mislead.)

EXAMPLE A:
Irene Stitz, shortly before her death by poisoning, was heard to say, "What a wonderful year this is going to be! I'm so happy. Fred and I have the perfect marriage, even after all these years." Evidence that these statements were made by the deceased would be admissible to negate suicide on her part. Such a joyous state of mind is inconsistent with suicidal intent.

EXAMPLE B:
"I've fallen head over heels in love with Charlie. Who needs Fred?" These statements would be admissible to show that the declarant's affections had been alienated.

F. State of Mind

Reasons for the Exception

In Section D, above, we considered out-of-court declarations of a person's then-existing state of mind, offered in evidence because his or her mental condition as of the time of his/her declaration was an issue in the case. An out-of-court declaration may also be receivable to evidence a then-existing *intent* to do something in the future. Although the inference will sometimes be a weak one, this evidence is admissible as circumstantial proof that the declarant thereafter accomplished the intended act. The somewhat arguable theory is that people, more often than not, do what they say they intend to do.

Requirements of the Exception

The hearsay exception for declarations of intent has two basic elements:

1. The declaration of intent must be *forward*-looking, not *backward*-looking. That is, the declaration must reflect an intent to engage in future conduct and not be a mere recollection of past events.

EXAMPLE A:
Mutual Life Insurance Company of New York v. *Hillmon,* 145 US. 285 (1892), is the leading case involving forward-looking intent. The issue in the *Hillman* case was whether one Walters had gone to Colorado at a particular time. Letters written by Walters to his sister and fiancée, expressing an intent to leave Kansas and go to Colorado, were ruled admissible in evidence to show that Walters did in fact go to Colorado.

EXAMPLE B:
Shepard v. *United States,* 290 U.S. 96 (1933), provides an example of an impermissible recollection of a past event. Mrs. Shepard, as she lay dying, asked a nurse to bring her a bottle of whiskey from a closet. Mrs. Shepard smelled its contents (it contained bichloride of mercury, which is a poison) and then announced, "Dr. Shepard has poisoned me!" Receipt of this statement in evidence was error. The statement, said Mr. Justice Benjamin Cardozo, "looks backward," not forward as in *Hillmon.* If backward-looking declarations, which really are statements of recollection, were held to be admissible, the hearsay rule would be destroyed. (Note that Mrs. Shepard's statement involved both a perception and a memory problem, while Walters' letters, in *Hillmon,* did not.)

2. The declaration of intent is admissible only to evidence the probability that the *declarant* engaged in particular conduct. It cannot be used in an effort to show that *someone else* engaged in particular conduct. This is simply another manifestation of the concept that state of mind is an internalized thing and cannot be employed to convey an out-of-court declarant's observations regarding the world *outside* his head, the external world.

EXAMPLE:
In *People* v. *Alcalde,* 148 P.2d 627 (S. Ct. Cal. 1944), the accused was convicted of murdering a woman friend. At trial a declaration by his alleged victim, "I'm going out with Frank tonight," was received against him to show access, opportunity. The California Supreme Court affirmed Alcalde's conviction, but the distinguished Justice Roger Traynor vigorously dissented, correctly pointing out that the woman's statement did not come within the *Hillmon* principle. It was something more than a simple declaration of the woman's future intent; it purported to state what Frank was intending to do, as well. Thus the statement involved an externalized observation, an observation about the outside world, and violated the rule against hearsay. (The result might have been different had the victim said, "I am going to Frank's apartment tonight." Then it would have been a statement of the declarant's intent exclusively, placing her within the accused's reach.)

G. Excited Utterances

Scope of the Exception

There is a long-established hearsay exception for out-of-court declarations relating to a startling event made while the declarant was under the stress of excitement caused by the event. These declarations are usually referred to as *excited utterances* or *spontaneous exclamations*. It is the spontaneity of such statements that is supposed to guarantee their trustworthiness.

Participation by the out-of-court declarant in the startling event is not necessary. Merely observing a startling event, such as a homicide, may be enough to provoke an excited outburst.

The words of excited utterance itself can be used to establish that the observed event was a startling one. Independent evidence that the event was startling is not essential, although usually some additional circumstantial evidence will be available. The words of the exclamation can also be used to show that the declarant adequately *observed* the startling event, *unless* the declarant was an unidentified bystander.

Applicability in Rape and Other Sex Offense Prosecutions

The excited utterance exception has special application in rape cases and in other cases involving sex offenses. Evidence that the victim made a so-called "fresh" (prompt) complaint is admissible. The only requirement is that the complaint must have been made without undue delay. The complaint can include details of the crime and the identity of the offender.

EXAMPLE:

BY THE PROSECUTING ATTORNEY: Drawing your attention to the night of April 1, 1989, Ms. Stitz, I will ask you whether anything unusual occurred?

A: Yes.

Q: What was it?

A: At about ten-thirty there was a pounding on the back door, which we keep locked. I opened the door and there was our daughter, Melody. The minute I opened the door she screamed, "I've been raped by the newsboy!" Her dress was all torn, her face was puffy and red, she was out of breath, and she was crying, but three times she screamed it, "I've been raped by the newsboy!"

H. Declarations of Present Sense Impression

Unexcited Utterances

If an excited statement is admissible, why not a calm contemporaneous description of something that the speaker is observing? Excitement, arguably, is some indication of veracity (that is, lack of premeditation) if not necessarily of accuracy; spontaneity and contemporaneity of statement, calmly expressed, also suggests trustworthiness. And so the Federal Rules of Evidence and some state evidence codes and judicial decisions have adopted a separate hearsay exception for out-of-court statements made by a person while perceiving an unexciting event or condition and which describe or explain it. This is generally referred to as the exception for statements of present sense impression. (Fed.R.Evid. 803(1); see Waltz, *The Present Sense Impression Exception to the Rule Against Hearsay: Origins and Attributes,* 66 Iowa L. Rev. 869 (1981).)

EXAMPLE:

Clyde Bushmat is charged with the murder of Fred Stitz, his business associate. The prosecution offers the testimony of Irene Stitz, Fred's spouse: "On the afternoon that he was killed I spoke on the telephone with my husband, Fred, at his office. I could hear a knock, like a knock on the office door. Fred said, 'Hold on, there's someone at the door.' I heard Fred talking with someone in the background, a man, but I couldn't make out what they were saying. Then Fred came back on the line and said, 'Bushmat just came in and we need to settle our argument. I'll call back in a while.' That was the last time I talked with Fred."

The testimony of Irene regarding husband Fred's out-of-court state ments will be received through the present sense impression exception. (See *Booth* v. *State*, 508 A.2d 976 (Ct. App. Md. 1986).)

Most jurisdictions that recognize the present sense impression exception require that the out-of-court statement have been made at the very time the speaker was perceiving the event that his/her words describe or explain. This is to assure the spontaneity and accuracy of the statement: it was unpremeditated and made before memory could fade. The federal rule expands this somewhat, admitting statements made while the declarant was perceiving an event or condition "or immediately thereafter." Still, even under the federal rule the time-lapse must have been negligible. This is evidenced by the fact that the Congress rejected a proposed additional hearsay exception for statements of "recent" sense impression, indicating its insistence on a minimal time-lapse between perception and descriptive statement.

As with the excited utterance exception previously discussed, there is no requirement that the maker of a declaration of present sense impression be available as an in-court witness or even identified, so long as there are adequate indications that he/she had firsthand knowledge. And there is no unvarying requirement that the accuracy of the declaration be corroborated by other evidence, although such corroboration will obviously enhance the declaration's evidentiary force.

EXAMPLE:
The driver of a car, upon being passed by another car, says to her passenger, "That guy must be drunk. Look at the way he's weaving on the road." This statement is reported on the witness stand by the passenger, who also observed the erratic course of the other car and thus can corroborate the out-of-court declaration to which he has testified. Here there is a strong case for admissibility under the present sense impression exception. (See the leading case of *Houston Oxygen Co. v. Davis,* 161 S.W.2d 474 (S. Ct. Tex. 1942).)

I. Physical Condition

Reasons for the Exception

Out-of-court statements concerning then-existing bodily conditions — symptoms, pain, and the like — are thought to have some built-in guarantees of reliability. Often such declarations are truly spontaneous: "Oh, my aching back!" They appear to be especially reliable when made to a treating physician. If the declarant knows that the physician is going to treat him, he is unlikely to give the physician deliberately incorrect information; the joke could prove to be on the patient. Furthermore, the patient is likely to believe that the physician knows a great deal about physical conditions. It is arguable, therefore, that the patient will not supply false data since the physician will only discover its falsity after possibly painful and costly tests. Finally, the physician's expertise is available to corroborate the accuracy of the out-of-court declarant's statements concerning his physical condition.

The hearsay risks are at a minimum here. There is no perception problem since the declarant is relating what he or she feels at the time. There is no memory problem where the declaration relates to present symptoms. And there is probably no great veracity problem, for the reasons already suggested.

Statements Made to a Nonphysician

Statements concerning present (then-existent) bodily condition are usually received in evidence no matter to whom they are made. They need not have been made to a treating physician; they may have been made to a spouse, to other relatives, to a friend, to a co-worker on the job, to a paramedic, to a nurse, or to a hospital roommate. The declaration can relate to symptomology, including the existence of pain. Past symptoms are excluded.

Statements Made to a Physician

Statements concerning bodily condition may be made to a treating physician or to one whose assignment is only to examine the patient and render a diagnostic opinion.

1. *Statements to a Treating Physician.* Statements of present bodily condition to a treating physician—one who is going to diagnose the patient's problem and prescribe treatment for it—are admissible in evidence to prove the existence of the condition and are generally considered weightier than such statements made to a nontreating physician. Some courts, but not all of them, will exclude declarations about past bodily condition as proof of the existence of that condition. However, all courts will permit receipt of declarations of past symptoms, made to a treating physician, to show the basis for the physician's opinion (diagnosis, prognosis).

> EXAMPLE:
>
> In *Ritter* v. *Coca Cola Co. (Kenosha-Racine) Inc.,* 128 N.W.2d 439 (S. Ct. Wis. 1964), the plaintiff, who had discovered a mouse in her bottle of Coca Cola, consulted a psychiatrist *after* having consulted her lawyer. The psychiatrist treated the plaintiff and testified, over objection, that she had sustained psychological injury. The psychiatrist's testimony was ruled admissible.
>
> The Wisconsin Supreme Court said that intrinsic guarantees of trustworthiness apply when treatment was at least part of the reason for consulting a physician. There was enough evidence that the plaintiff had not consulted the psychiatrist solely to secure his expert testimony.

2. *Statements to a Nontreating Physician.* Many courts hold that a nontreating physician's testimony about his patient's narration of present bodily condition is not admissible as proof that the condition actually existed. Such statements can come in only indirectly, where the nontreating physician relied on them in making a diagnosis or prognosis and they help to explain that diagnosis or prognosis.

A minority of courts will permit a nontreating physician—one who has been retained solely to provide an expert opinion and perhaps thereafter to testify in court—to testify only as to objective facts clinically observable to him. The nontreating physician, in other words, cannot testify as to declarations by the patient as to subjective matters, such as pain.

EXAMPLE A:
In *Gonzales* v. *Hodson,* 420 P.2d 813 (S. Ct. Idaho), a neuropsychiatrist's report was excluded because the consultation had been exclusively for the purposes of getting the neuropsychiatrist's testimony for trial.

EXAMPLE B:
In *Davidson* v. *Cornell,* 30 N.E. 573 (Ct. App. N.Y. 1892), a personal injury case, the plaintiff, just before trial, was examined by a nontreating physician. Plaintiff, mostly in response to questions by the physician, described his physical sensations and abilities—mainly sexual—during the fifteen months between his injury and the physician's examination. The physician's testimony was ruled inadmissible, the New York court saying that declarations of physical condition are receivable only if made to a *treating* physician about *present* conditions.

The new evidence codes make no distinction between statements made to treating physicians and those made to nontreating physicians. Under these codes the jurors are permitted to decide what weight to accord such statements. This is the trend of the future.

Finally, it should be emphasized that involuntary indications of pain, such as groans or grimaces, are not subject to the hearsay rule at all. Anyone who hears them or sees them and then testifies about them is simply giving direct eyewitness or ear-witness testimony.

J. Prior Identification

Elements of the Exception

In a number of jurisdictions, testimony as to prior identification of an accused or of some other person as one who participated in a crime is admissible if two basic conditions are met:

1. The out-of-court statement of identification must have been made at a time when the crime or other occurrence was *reasonably fresh in the declarant's memory.*
2. The evidence of the out-of-court statement of identification can only be offered *after the witness has testified on the stand* that he made the identification and that it was a true reflection of his opinion at the time he made it. In short, the witness must be available for cross-examination.

Prior identifications, having been made closer to the time the witness first observed the person identified, are probably more *trustworthy* than later in-court identifications.

EXAMPLE A:
In *People* v. *Gould,* 354 P.2d 865 (S. Ct. Cal. 1960), Gould and Marudas were charged with second degree burglary. Mrs. Fenwick, the victim, had identified photographs of both men at the police station. Gould admitted his guilt but did not implicate Marudas. Marudas denied his involvement. When asked where he was on the day of the crime, Marudas said, "I don't know, but by the time I get to court I will have four or five people to place me where I want to be." At trial, Mrs. Fenwick was unable to identify either defendant positively but testified to the fact that she had made prior identifications from photographs. The admission in evidence of her prior identification of Gould was upheld by a reviewing court. Marudas appealed on the question whether Mrs. Fenwick's prior identification was sufficient in the absence of any other evidence linking him to the crime to support a conviction. The California court held that it was not; additional evidence would be required. Had Mrs. Fenwick positively identified Marudas while she was on the stand, her testimony would undoubtedly have been sufficient to support a conviction.

EXAMPLE B:
In *United States* v. *DeSisto,* 329 F.2d 929 (2d Cir. 1964), the accused was charged with hijacking. His conviction was reversed on appeal and at his second trial the driver of the hijacked truck, on direct examination, identified DeSisto as the hijacker. On cross-examination, however, the witness became unsure of his identification after being shown the accused's tattooed arms. The witness said that he had gotten a good look at the hijacker's arms and had observed no tattoos. On re-direct examination the witness was asked by the prosecutor whether he had not previously identified the accused, five days after the crime, in a line-up at FBI headquarters during which DeSisto's tattooed arms were exposed, and also on two other occasions.

The witness responded that he had made all three of these earlier identifications. The re-direct examination and the witness's response to it were held admissible.

K. Past Recollection Recorded

Reasons for the Exception

In order to understand the principle of past recollection recorded as an exception to the rule against hearsay, it is important to recognize that there are only three ways a witness can recall (recollect) the things about which he is called upon to give testimony.

1. The witness whose memory is intact can simply rely on his recollection of the matters about which he is to testify. He gives eyewitness (or ear-witness, etc.) testimony from memory. This is called *simple recollection.*
2. Leading questions can be posed to a witness whose present recollection has been temporarily exhausted but who apparently has additional information of a relevant sort. Memoranda and other aids, such as a copy of a police accident report, may also be used to refresh the witness's present recollection. This is called *present recollection revived.*
3. If the witness has no present recollection, refreshed or otherwise, concerning the matter in question, a writing prepared by him or under his immediate supervision and known by him to have been correct when made can be introduced in evidence. This is called *past recollection recorded.*

The rationale behind the hearsay exception for past recollection recorded is that a writing which dates from a time when the witness's recollection was fresh is more trustworthy than his memory at the time of trial could possibly be.

Elements of the Exception

Past recollection recorded is defined as:

1. A memorandum or record concerning a matter about which a witness *once had knowledge,*
2. But about which the witness now has *insufficient recollection* to allow him to testify *fully* and *accurately,* which is
3. Shown to have been made when the matter was *fresh in the witness's memory* and to reflect the witness's knowledge correctly. It may be enough if the witness can testify that it was his or her *habit* to record such matters accurately and contemporaneously.

Some courts hold that the memorandum or record of recollection can itself be introduced in evidence after having been properly marked and identified. The majority of courts and the modern evidence codes, however, hold that the memorandum or record can only be read into the trial record, thus putting it on a par with the oral testimony in the case.

It is not necessary that the memorandum or record have been made during the course of a business or other regularly conducted activity.

EXAMPLE A:
In *Kinsey* v. *State,* P.2d 1141 (S. Ct. Ariz. 1937), a court reporter's shorthand notes of an accused's incriminating statement were held to be admissible as past recollection recorded.

EXAMPLE B:
In *Shimabukuro* v. *Nagayama,* 140 F.2d 13 (D.C. Cir. 1944), 384 entries on nine sheets of scrap paper were admissible as evidence of sums loaned to the defendant.

L. Business Records

Background of and Reasons for the Business Records Exception

Under a centuries-old rule a creditor, because he was a party to the suit, was barred from testifying against his debtor, with the consequence that the debtor might escape his obligation to pay altogether unless the law devised some special mechanism for proving the debt. It came up with the shopbook rule, which permitted the creditor to introduce his shopbooks—for example, a ledger—to establish the debt.

The old shopbook rule was an imperfect one because it was so narrowly restricted in its operation. It pertained only to cash sales; it applied only where the creditor kept his own records and there was no bookkeeper who could be called as a witness; the shopbooks had to be kept in the regular course of the creditor's business and the creditor's reputation for making accurate entries had to be demonstrated.

The narrow common law shopbook doctrine gradually gave way to a broader and more flexible common law business records doctrine. Even this doctrine had problems, however, because it required the testimony of every person who had anything to do with the preparation of the particular business record.

The common law business records doctrine has now largely been supplanted by business records statutes and rules. It is the function of these statutes and rules to conform the law of evidence to modern-day business realities. Many presentday businesses and other regularly conducted activities are sufficiently complex that it would be both difficult and time-consuming to call to the witness stand each and every employee who took part in the preparation of the organization's records. Furthermore, routine records, upon which organizations so heavily rely, are quite likely to be accurate and reliable. This is so because the best interests of the persons preparing them are tied to their correctness, since business decisions will be based on an assumption of their accuracy. The employee who persistently generates inaccurate records gets fired.

Requirements of Modern Business Records, Statutes, and Codes

Quoted below is Section 374-a of the New York Practice Act, which is a typical state business records provision:

> Any writing or record, whether in the form of an entry in a book or otherwise, made as a memorandum or record of any act, transaction, occurrence or event, shall be admissible in evidence in proof of said act, transaction, occurrence or event, if the trial judge shall find that it was made in the regular course of any business, and that it was the regular course of such business to make such memorandum or record at the time of such act, transaction, occurrence or event, or within a reasonable time thereafter. All other circumstances of the making of such writing or record, including lack of personal knowledge by the entrant or maker, may be shown to affect its weight, but they shall not affect its admissibility. The term business shall include business, profession, occupation and calling of every kind.

A close reading of this and other state and federal business records provisions reveals six requirements of the hearsay exception for business records.

1. The record of an act, transaction, occurrence, or event must have been some form of *writing,* at least in the broadest sense of that term. It can be a memorandum, report, record, or data compilation such as a computer print-out. Theoretically, however, there is no such thing as an *oral* business record.
2. The record must have been made during the *regular course* of a *business, profession, occupation,* or *calling.*
3. It must have been the *custom* of the business, profession, occupation, or calling, to make such records.
4. It must have been the custom of the business, etc., to make such records *at the time of the act, transaction, occurrence,* or *event* recorded, or within *a reasonable amount of time thereafter,* while the entrant's memory was still fresh.
5. The subject matter of the entries in the record must have been within the *personal knowledge* of the maker of the entry or have been based on the reports of others who *themselves* possessed personal knowledge and had a *duty to the business* to report such knowledge to the entrant.

6. The record must be *identified* and *authenticated* as being what it purports to be. Under modern business records statutes and rules, this is usually a simple task. The usual practice is to call a witness who is the custodian of the particular business's records. Modern business records provisions eliminate the common law requirement calling, or accounting for the failure to call, all participants in the making of a record. Thus, for example, Rule 803(6) of the Federal Rules of Evidence provides that the necessary foundation testimony can be supplied by "the custodian or other qualified witness." Large organizations, such as banks, utility companies, and hospitals, employ persons whose sole responsibilities are as custodians of the organization's records.

The Johnson *v.* Lutz *Interpretation*

The most significant judicial opinion regarding business records is the one in *Johnson* v. *Lutz*, 170 NE.517 (Ct. App. N.Y. 1930). This case concerned a wrongful death action, a civil suit, during which the defendant offered in evidence the accident investigation report of a police officer. The report contained the statements of bystanders. The police officer, who had not himself been present at the time of the accident, had filed his report at the station house. The report was held to be inadmissible.

The New York Court of Appeals remarked that the policeman's report was made from "hearsay statements of third persons who happened to be present at the scene." It was not even clear that these persons were not passing along information that *they* had received from others.

After recounting the history of the shopbook rule and the law's efforts to align the rules of evidence with the realities of the commercial world, the court stated that the New York business records statute, which we quoted above, was "never intended to apply to a situation like that in the case at bar." In a burst of judicial legislation which did some violence to the express language of the statute, the court declared that it applied only where "the record was made as a part of the duty of the person making it, or on information imparted by persons who were under a duty to impart such information." The statute, the court continued, "was not intended to permit the receipt in evidence of entries based upon voluntary hearsay statements made by third persons not engaged in the business or under any duty in relation thereto." Since the bystanders were not engaged in the "business, profession, occupation, or calling" of law enforcement, their statements were not admissible under the New York statute.

The *Johnson* v. *Lutz* interpretation has been widely adopted. If the writing in question was made during the regular course of a business and any informational sources relied upon by the maker had an occupational duty toward the particular business or other type of organization, the business records exception to the hearsay rule will result in admission of the writing. If the informational sources—the inputs, so to speak—had *no* occupational duty toward the particular business or other type of organization, their statements, included in a record, will not be admissible under the present hearsay exception alone. On the other hand, such statements may be admissible in a two-phase process, the first phase of which involves use of the business records exception and the second phase of which involves recourse to some other hearsay exception.

The Two-Phase Approach

Phase 1: The business records exception is used as a *vehicle* for getting an alleged statement *into the courtroom.* The making of a statement itself is an "act, transaction, occurrence or event" within the meaning of the business records exception. A business employee has made a record of that act. That record can be used to establish the bare fact that a statement was *made.*

Phase 2: So far, however, all that has been shown is an *act*—the making of a statement. Because of the impact of the *Johnson* v. *Lutz* interpretation, the content of that statement has not yet been shown to be admissible in evidence. But perhaps the statement's content is admissible under some *other* exception to the hearsay rule. Perhaps, for example, the statement constitutes an admission by a party. Perhaps the police officer has included in his accident investigation report the admission by one driver in an automobile accident that he was not paying attention to his driving and was over the center line at the point of impact. This statement would be receivable in evidence to establish its truth because it constitutes an admission under the party-admission exception to the hearsay rule. The police accident report functions as a sort of conduit; it is like a witness on the stand who testifies to having heard an out-of-court admission by the defendant.

The two-phase approach described above is supported by one of the leading cases in the field of business records, *Yates* v. *Bair Transport, Inc.,* 249 F.Supp. 681 (S.D.N.Y. 1965). In this case, a personal injury plaintiff offered in evidence a police department blotter which reported statements that were damaging to the defendant's case. The policeman who made the blotter entries had not done a good job. It could not be determined from the blotter whether the statements had been made by the plaintiff or by the defendant; if they were made by the defendant they were damaging admissions, but if the plaintiff made them they were merely self-serving hearsay. The statements were held to be inadmissible for this reason: the police blotter was ambiguous. The court stated, however, that if the speaker had been identified the blotter would have been admissible to show that a statement had been made by him. It having been shown that a statement was made, the substance or content of the statement could then be received in evidence if it fell within some additional exception to the hearsay rule. In other words, if the blotter had established that the statements considered in it had been made by the defendant rather than the plaintiff they would have been admissible under the party-admissions exception to the hearsay rule.

Diagnostic and "Opinion" Entries

A few jurisdictions refuse to include in the business records exception records containing diagnostic and other "opinion" entries.

> EXAMPLE:
> *New York Life Insurance Company* v. *Taylor,* 147 F.2d 297 (D.C. Cir. 1945), in which a psychiatrist's reports suggesting suicidal tendencies on the part of the patient, included amongst the patient's hospital records, were held inadmissible.

However, the more recent cases and the modern evidence codes repudiate such cases as *New York Life Insurance Company* v. *Taylor,* above, and permit the offering of diagnostic and "opinion" entries.

> EXAMPLE A:
> *People* v. *Kohlmier,* 31 N.E.2d 490 (Ct. App. N.Y. 1940), in which it was held that a hospital record containing a physician's observation of the defendant and his diagnosis of manic-depressive insanity constituted a business record and was receivable in evidence to support an insanity defense.

> EXAMPLE B:
> Rule 803(6) of the Federal Rules of Evidence would permit the admission of diagnostic entries and other "opinion" evidence.

Entries Recording Illegal Activities

The business records exception can apply to recordations of unlawful activities. For example, in *United States* v. *McPartlin,* 595 F.2d 1321 (7th Cir. 1979), diaries or appointment calendars kept by a corporate official and recording bribes paid to city officials were held admissible as business records.

Entries Unrelated to the Particular Business or Activity

To qualify for admission under the business records exception, the information entered in a record must relate to the particular business or activity.

> EXAMPLE:
> *Williams* v. *Alexander,* 129 NE.2d 417 (Ct. App. N.Y. 1955), a civil case in which defendant offered a hospital record that quoted plaintiff's

description of the cause of an automobile collision involved in the lawsuit. These entries substantiated the defendant's version of the accident. They were ruled inadmissible. The court stated that the detailed description of the accident, entered in the hospital records by a physician, could not properly be said to have entered in the regular course of hospital business. It *would* be in the regular course of hospital business to note the fact that plaintiff had been struck by a car, but it was unnecessary for therapeutic purposes to go into additional detail.

There was an impressive dissent in this case, reflecting the fairly widespread split of judicial authority on entries of this type. Furthermore, the New York court could have concluded that the entries in *Williams* v. *Alexander* constituted party-admissions, receivable under the two-phase approach previously described in this chapter.

Computerized Business Records

All manner of activities, from businesses to agencies of law enforcement, are to an ever-increasing degree computerizing their records. Computerized records come within the reasoning underlying the business records exception, which involves alignment of the law of evidence with modern recordkeeping procedures. The decided cases recognize this fact.

For example, in *King* v. *State for the Use and Benefit of Murdock Acceptance Corporation,* 222 So.2d 393 (S. Ct. Miss. 1969), computer printouts showed the balance due on six conditional sales contracts. They were held to be admissible. The Mississippi court held that print-out sheets of business records stored in electronic computing equipment are admissible without the necessity of identifying, locating, and producing as witnesses the persons who made the entries in the regular course of business if it is shown (1) that the electronic computing equipment is recognized as standard equipment, (2) that the entries are made in the regular course of business at or reasonably near the time of the happening of the event record, and (3) the foundation testimony satisfies the trial judge that the sources of information and the computer methodology were such as to indicate the trustworthiness of the computer output.

Oral Business Records

It was previously stated that, theoretically, under the present business records statutes and rules there can be no such thing as an oral business record. However, the admissibility of oral business reports is a logical extension of these provisions and one reported case has gone this far. In *Gerald* v. *Champlin,* 37 A.2d 155 (S. Ct. N.H. 1944), the question was whether a foreman's oral report to his employer, which, had it been in writing, would have qualified as a business record under the business records exception, was admissible. The New Hampshire court held that it was. The analogy to a written business record was considered sufficiently strong.

Absence of an Entry in Business Records

The omission of a matter from a record which ordinarily would mention such a matter has generally been considered satisfactory evidence of the nonexistence of the matter. Although it is somewhat awkward to think of the *absence* of any statement as hearsay, some decisions have done so. Modern evidence codes settle the controversy by expressly providing for admissibility, thereby easing the sometimes difficult task of proving a negative.

EXAMPLE:
In *United States* v. *DeGeorgia,* 420 F.2d 889 (9th Cir. 1969), evidence that a car rental agency's records showed no rental or lease activity in connection with a particular vehicle was admissible as tending to prove that the accused, in whose possession it was discovered, had stolen it.

M. Public Records

Scope of the Exception

There is a hearsay exception for records, reports, statements, or data compilations of public agencies or officials which set forth the activities of the agency or official or matters observed by them pursuant to a duty imposed by law. This exception will permit receipt against the prosecution, but not against the accused (who is entitled to confront the witnesses against him), of findings of fact resulting from an investigation made under a grant of legislative authority unless the circumstances of the investigation suggest a lack of trustworthiness.

The guarantee of reliability underlying this exception is one that some may conclude is not invariably impressive. It is based on the assumption that a public official will perform his/her duties properly and that the records he generated will be more reliable than the official's own recollection.

The public records exception permits the admission of records of matters observed, such as U.S. Weather Bureau records. In some jurisdictions it also permits the receipt of evaluative reports, such as the director of prisons' certificate that a convict has been examined and found probably mentally incompetent at the time of trial.

Guidelines

In assessing the trustworthiness of evaluative reports under this exception, courts usually employ four guidelines:

1. The investigation backing up the report must have been conducted *promptly.*

2. The special *skills* and *experience* of the persons conducting the investigation will be weighed.
3. The question whether a *hearing* should have been held will be considered.
4. Questions of *motivation* will be explored. For example, was the report prepared with a criminal prosecution specifically in mind?

In federal courts the exception relating to public records rather than the private business records exception, Rule 803(6), is generally said to govern law enforcement investigative reports. (See, for example, *United States* v. *Oates*, 560 F.2d 45 (2d Cir. 1977).) And Federal Rule of Evidence 803(8), dealing with public records, *prohibits* the introduction in criminal cases of reports of "matters observed by police officers and other law enforcement personnel." Furthermore, law enforcement reports that include "factual findings resulting from an investigation made pursuant to authority granted by law" cannot be used *against* a criminal accused, although they can be offered *by* the accused if they are advantageous to him. These prohibitions were intended to prevent the prosecution from making its case on the basis of law enforcement agents' hearsay reports of their contemporaneous observation of criminal activity. Accordingly, the prohibitions of 803(8) have been held inapplicable to the prosecution's use of reports by law enforcement personnel that contain routine recordations of fact, such as listings of serial numbers on seized weapons (*United States* v. *Grady*, 544 F.2d 598 (2d Cir. 1976)), or license plate numbers on automobiles crossing a border (*United States* v. *Orozco*, 590 F.2d 789 (9th Cir. 1979)).

N. Miscellaneous Exceptions to the Hearsay Rule

We have not discussed all of the recognized exceptions to the hearsay rule since a number of them are rarely encountered in criminal cases. For the sake of comprehensiveness, however, it should be mentioned that there are also exceptions to the rule against hearsay covering the following types of evidence:

1. *Commercial and Scientific Publications.* Certain commercial and scientific publications are receivable in evidence under an exception to the hearsay rule. This exception's coverage differs from jurisdiction to jurisdiction, but in general it can be said to cover tabulations, lists, directories, and other published compilations generally relied upon by the public or by persons in particular occupations; scientific treatises; books of history; scholarly works on the arts; atlases; and market quotations.
2. *Vital Statistics.* There is an exception for records or data compilations of births, deaths, and marriages, where the report of them was made to some public office pursuant to the requirements of the law, such as a public health law.

3. *Family History.* A hearsay exception has been developed for statements relating to family history—births, deaths, marriages, ancestry, and the like—contained in the regularly kept records of a religious organization, such as a church.
4. *Marriage Certificates and the Like.* There is an exception for marriage, baptismal, and similar certificates, when made by a member of the clergy, public official, or other person authorized to perform the act certified and purporting to have been issued more or less contemporaneously with the act.
5. *Family Records.* There is a hearsay exception for statements in a family record such as a genealogy, family Bible, engravings on tombstones, and the like, when they are offered to prove birth, marriage, divorce, or other similar fact of family history.
6. *"Ancient" Documents.* "Ancient" documents are covered by a hearsay exception. An "ancient" document is usually defined as one that is more than twenty years old and whose authenticity is demonstrated in the evidence.
7. *Reputation Regarding Family History.* There is an exception permitting proof of reputation among members of a person's family by blood or, sometimes, by marriage, concerning that person's birth, marriage, divorce, death, legitimacy, relationship by blood or marriage, ancestry, or similar fact about the person's personal or family history.
8. *Reputations as to Character.* A long-settled exception to the hearsay rule provides for proof of a person's character, where relevant and otherwise admissible, by reputation testimony.

CHAPTER SEVEN

Impeachment of Witnesses' Credibility

In chapter 3, which was devoted to a general description of the making of the trial record, the major distinctions between direct examination by one side of its own witnesses and the cross-examination of those witnesses by the opposing side were outlined. It was stated in chapter 3 that an important purpose of cross-examination is to diminish the examined witness's credibility or veracity in the eyes of the jurors. This process is commonly called *impeachment.* Impeachment can also be accomplished with evidence other than the witness's responses to cross-questions; it can be accomplished with what is called *extrinsic evidence.*

A. Levels of Impeachment: Methods

Three Levels of Impeachment

The impeachment of witnesses can be carried on at three different levels.

1. *Bias, Prejudice.* A witness's credibility can be attacked by questions that reveal a *bias* or *prejudice* that might lead him to falsify or twist the facts.
2. *Prior Inconsistent Statements.* A witness can be impeached by a demonstration that he or she has made prior out-of-court statements that are inconsistent with the responses the witness gave during his direct examination at trial. (Of course, *internal* contradictions in a witness's direct testimony can always be brought out, too.)

3. *Ciminal Convictions and Prior Bad Acts.* A witness can also be impeached by evidence of serious prior criminal convictions or previous bad acts tending to cast doubt on his veracity.

Methods of Impeachment

There are two basic procedures for impeaching the credibility of trial witnesses: (1) cross-examination, already mentioned, and (2) introduction of other evidence extrinsic to the witness's answers on cross-examination, also mentioned above.

B. Impeachment During Cross-Examination

Six Impeachment Techniques on Cross-Examination

There are six principal impeachment techniques used by trial counsel in cross-xamining witnesses on the stand. They involve the following: (1) sensory eficiencies; (2) the character of the witness; (3) the witness's psychiatric ondition; (4) the witness's previous conviction of a serious crime; (5) the existence of prior inconsistent statements by the witness; and (6) interest or bias on the part of the witness.

1. *Sensory Deficiencies.* The most basic sort of impeaching cross-examination reveals sensory deficiencies on the part of the witness. This is simply a demonstration of the fact that the witness was not in a position because of certain deficiencies in his senses (poor eyesight, obscured vision, poor hearing, and the like) to see, hear, smell, touch, or taste what he testified about on his direct examination. Although usually developed by means of cross-examination, the existence of sensory deficiencies on a witness's part may also be shown by extrinsic evidence; that is, through the testimony of other witnesses who have knowledge of his or her sensory deficiencies.

EXAMPLE:

BY DEFENSE COUNSEL [cross-examining a prosecution witness]: Ms. Stitz, you gave us on your direct examination just now a detailed description of a person you say ran out of the service station on the evening of April 1, 1989. You described the color of his jacket and his cap. You had the color of his hair. You even said there was a badge of some sort on the front of his cap. And, among other details, you described his complexion as being "ruddy," didn't you?

A: I sure did.

Q: Incidentally, I said "evening" a moment ago, but actually it was almost eleven o'clock at night, wasn't it?

A: Yes.

Q: Now I notice that you are not wearing eyeglasses, Ms. Stitz. Do you usually wear eyeglasses?

A: No, I do not.
Q: Have you ever worn them, Ms. Stitz, to correct poor vision?
A: Never, never.
Q: You're quite sure you weren't wearing corrective eyeglasses on the night of April 1, 1989?
A: Absolutely sure.
Q: Then let me ask you another question. Has an ophthalmologist or optometrist ever recommended, after an eye test, that you wear eyeglasses to correct impaired vision?
A: No, sir.
Q: Is it not a fact that an optometrist had strongly urged you, as recently as February, 1989, to wear corrective lenses?
A: That is not true.
Q: You're sure?
A: Certain.
Q: No further questions at this time, Your Honor.

. . .

BY DEFENSE COUNSEL [in the defense's case-in-chief]: I call to the stand Dr. Harvey L. Ziff. [Witness is sworn.]

. . .

Q: What is your occupation or profession, sir?
A: I am an optometrist with offices in the Hillston Building.

. . .

Q: What does an optometrist do?
A: We examine eyes for defects and faults of refraction and we prescribe corrective lenses.
Q: Were you an optometrist during the years 1988 to 1989?
A: I was. I have been an optometrist for thirteen years.
Q: During those two years, 1988 and 1989, did you ever have occasion to see Ms. Fred Stitz? You may consult any office records that you have brought with you to refresh your recollection.
A: Yes, I saw Ms. Fred Stitz, 3730 North Lake Shore Drive, twice in 1988 and once in 1989.
Q: When was the last time you saw her in 1989?
A: I saw her on February 13, 1989, at 4:00 P.M.
Q: What did you do for Ms. Stitz at that time?
A: I gave her a standard eye test, just as I had on her two previous visits.
Q: Did Ms. Stitz have any complaints about her vision in February of 1989?
A: Yes. She complained of blurred vision, especially when reading. She also complained of eye strain and headaches.

"Your Honor, I have a rebuttal witness."

Drawing by Levin; ©1988. The New Yorker Magazine, Inc.

Q: Did you make any recommendation to Ms. Stitz as a consequence of the symptoms she described to you and the results of her eye test?
A: Yes, I did. I recommended that she begin wearing corrective lenses. Q: Without corrective lenses, how much of the eye chart could Ms. Stitz read?
A: She could read only the first three lines, and of course the first line is the big "E."
Q: She got the "E" all right, did she?
A: Yes, she managed that one, and two more lines.
Q: To your knowledge, did Ms. Stitz obtain the corrective lenses that you prescribed?
A: Not from me she didn't. She said she was too young to start wearing glasses. She said she'd rather give up reading than start wearing glasses.
Q: Did you make any response to this?
A: Yes, I told her it would not just be a matter of giving up reading. I told her she could expect to fall down a lot. [Laughter.]
THE COURT: Order in the courtroom.

Q: Sir, do you have an office card for Ms. Stitz that reflects the results of her eye tests and your prescription of corrective lenses.

A: Yes, I have it right here.

Q: Would you please hand it to me? [Witness complies and the card is marked for identification, authenticated as a business record or past recollection recorded, and offered in evidence. Examining counsel would undoubtedly ask additional questions of the witness, bringing out the full extent of impairment of Ms. Stitz's vision in early 1989.]

2. *Criminal Convictions and Previous Bad Acts.* In some jurisdictions, but not all, cross-examination can be used to bring out a witness's bad character for purposes of demonstrating that his testimony is not trustworthy. The English rule has always been that a cross-examiner is free to impeach a witness by asking him about specific instances of prior bad conduct supposedly illuminating his character. The majority rule in this country is different. Few American jurisdictions have allowed inquiry into specific instances of prior bad conduct unless they resulted in a felony conviction or have independent relevance to material issues in the case being tried.

However, some American jurisdictions follow the English rule described above and permit cross-questions concerning specific instances of prior bad conduct and this would appear to be the trend of the future.

EXAMPLE:

People v. *Sorge,* 93 NE.2d 637 (Ct. App. N.Y. 1950), involved a charge of criminal abortion. The prosecuting attorney, on cross examination, asked the accused about prior abortions committed or observed by her. This was held to be proper examination. The court said that "Defendant, like any other witness, may be 'interrogated upon cross examination in regard to any vicious or criminal act of his life' that has bearing upon his credibility as a witness."

Rule 608(b) of the Federal Rules of Evidence provides that specific instances of a witness's conduct, for the purpose of attacking the witness's credibility, can be inquired into on cross-examination of the witness himself or on cross-examination of a witness who testifies to his character for truthfulness or untruthfulness.

EXAMPLE:

BY THE PROSECUTING ATTORNEY: Sir, you said a minute ago, during your direct examination by defense counsel, that you are closely familiar with the defendant's reputation in the community for honesty and truthfulness, did you not?

A: That's what I said.

Q: And I believe you said you'd known him well for almost thirteen years and that you knew him to be a man of impeccable character?
A: That's right.
Q: Well, Mr. Barbie, let me ask whether when you gave that testimony you were aware of the fact that in 1981 the defendant was accused of having embezzled $1,500 from his employer, the First Federal Savings and Loan Company of Stone Valley, and that he repaid the money to avoid prosecution?
A: I never knew anything like that.
Q: And did you or did you not know that in 1975 the defendant was charged with passing a worthless check in the amount of $1,000, also in Stone Valley, and made restitution?
A: I didn't know anything about that, either.
Q: Your knowledge of the defendant's background and character seems to have a few holes in it, doesn't it?
A: Well, yes, if those things are true.
Q: You don't hear the defense objecting to these questions, do you?
A: Nope.
Q: If you knew that the defendant had been convicted of passing a bad check and of embezzlement, would it tend to change your opinion of his character for honesty and truthfulness?
A: Of course.

In marked contrast to the Federal Rules of Evidence, which would permit the foregoing type of cross-examination, Section 787 of the California Evidence Code makes evidence of prior bad conduct inadmissible for impeachment purposes.

The Rule against Collateral Impeachment

In that minority of American jurisdictions which permit impeachment by prior bad conduct the cross-examiner is bound by the answers he or she gets from the witness; a denial by the witness ends the matter—except for a possible perjury prosecution. In other words, acknowledgment of the previous bad conduct must be obtained from the witness who is undergoing the impeaching cross-examination. Extrinsic evidence of the asserted prior bad conduct cannot be offered against the witness who has denied the commission of them unless evidence of the acts would be receivable on some independent ground.

EXAMPLE A:

In *State* v. *Oswalt*, 381 P.2d 617 (S. Ct. Wash. 1963), the defendant was charged with robbery and burglary committed in Seattle. He offered testimony, through a Portland, Oregon, restaurant owner, that he had been in the witness's restaurant on the night of the alleged crimes. On cross-examination the prosecuting attorney asked the witness whether defendant had not been in his restaurant every day for the past few months and the witness replied that he had. The prosecutor then called a rebuttal witness who stated that the accused had been in Seattle for a few days within the past few months (not on the day of the crimes). The rebuttal witness's testimony was ruled inadmissible. The prosecutor's approach was said to be an improper effort to impeach a witness (the restaurant owner) with extrinsic evidence (the rebuttal witness's testimony) as to a collateral or peripheral matter (whether the accused had been in the witness's restaurant every day for the past few months).

The test of collateralness was put this way: "Could the [impeach ing] fact . . . have been shown in evidence for any purpose independently of the contradiction?" If not, the fact is collateral to the issues in the case and cannot be proved by any evidence other than the witness's admission that it is true.

EXAMPLE B:
In *United States* v. *Pugliese,* 153 F.2d 497 (2d Cir. 1945), defense counsel asked a prosecution witness on cross-examination whether she had ever been in a mental institution. The witness denied that she had. Defense counsel thereafter introduced no evidence contradicting the witness's denial; he simply let the innuendo hang in the air. The rule against collateral impeachment would not have prohibited him from doing so, however. Insanity, unlike prior bad conduct, is strongly relevant to credibility and is in no way collateral. The prosecuting attorney in Pugliese could properly have put defense counsel on the witness stand and brought out the fact that he had no evidence that the prosecution's witness had ever been institutionalized for mental illness.

Opinion and Reputation Evidence

Opinion and reputation evidence concerning a person's character for truth and veracity is admissible for impeachment purposes; character evidence as to general immorality is not.

EXAMPLE:
In *State* v. *Williams,* 87 S.W.2d 175 (S. Ct. Mo. 1935), the defendant was charged with murder; his defense was self-defense. The defendant took the stand; thereafter the State produced a number of witnesses who testified that the accused's reputation for "morality" was poor. The Missouri Supreme Court held that this was improper. Only character evidence having to do with the trait of untruthfulness, or veracity, could be used in evidence.

Most jurisdictions require that the inquiry relate to general reputation in the community or among the witness's associates, not to personal opinion based on specific incidents.

A party to a case cannot prove the good reputation of his witness for truth and veracity unless and until it has been attacked by the opposing side.

3. *Psychological Condition.* A showing of psychological condition (for example, insanity), as suggested in *United States* v. *Pugliese,* discussed above, can be made through cross-examination of the witness whose impeachment is sought. (It can also be accomplished through extrinsic, nonprivileged evidence, such as the testimony of nonmedical personnel attached to a mental institution, who may have observed bizarre conduct on the part of the witness.)

Harsh as it sometimes may seem, other psychological conditions, such as drug addiction or alcoholism, can be brought out to diminish the witness's trustworthiness.

EXAMPLE A:

BY THE PROSECUTING ATTORNEY: Mr. Jones, you are a heroin addict, are you not?

A: Yes, sir, I am.

Q: And have been for many years, isn't that so?

A: Yes.

Q: Have you had a fix today?

A: Yes, just before I came in here.

Q: So you were under the influence of an injection of heroin during your direct examination by defense counsel this morning?

A: Yeah.

Q: In times past has the accused in this case assisted you in getting heroin, in getting a fix?

A: Sometimes, yeah.

Q: And do you think he might help you again in the future if he doesn't go to prison on this charge?

A: He might, sure.

Q: Have you ever lied to get dope?

A: Sure I have.

Q: Would you lie under oath in order to get a fix?

A: If I needed one bad enough, sure.

Q: Now, I draw your attention to the evening of April 1, 1989, Mr. Jones . . . [Fearful of posing one question too many, the prosecuting attorney now turns to a different subject.]

EXAMPLE B:

BY DEFENSE COUNSEL: Mr. Lishniss, you have stated in the most positive terms that Mr. Bushmat, the defendant in the case, is the man you observed run into Hoeland's Bar and throw a fire bomb, have you not?

A: That's what I said.
Q: Mr. Lishniss, isn't it a fact that on the night in question you were heavily intoxicated?
A: No, it's not a fact.
Q: You are an alcoholic, are you not, Mr. Lishniss?
A: I wouldn't say that.
Q: Have you ever been treated for chronic alcoholism?
A: Well, yes. The family did that to me.
Q: How long ago were you treated for chronic alcoholism?
A: Up until about six months ago.
Q: Do you drink now?
A: Yes.
Q: About how much do you drink in an average day?
A: Oh, maybe a pint or a little more.
Q: Bourbon, Scotch, what?
A: Anything I can get.
Q: Had you anything to drink on the night of April 1, 1989?
A: Practically nothing to speak of.
Q: How long had you been in Hoeland's Bar before you saw the defendant come in?
A: Maybe two hours. Barney the bartender would know.
Q: And during those two hours you had "practically nothing to speak of"?
A: Right.
Q: What were you, a man who currently drinks a pint or more a day of anything he can get his hands on, doing in that bar for two hours?
A: Well, talking, watching the TV, taking a little drink now and then.
Q: As much as a pint?
A: I don't recall.
Q: Could you have drunk as much as a pint of alcohol during that two-hour period?
A: Maybe. I don't keep count.
Q: You don't keep count of how much you drink?
A: No.
Q: And you say you're not an alcoholic?
A: Right.
Q: Have you ever been arrested for public drunkenness?
BY THE PROSECUTING ATTORNEY: Object, Your Honor. What relevance does this have? He doesn't even specify a date.
BY DEFENSE COUNSEL: Oh, I ll withdraw the question.

4. *Prior Felony Convictions.* As a general rule, evidence of a prior felony conviction is admissible to impeach a witness's credibility. This rule

finds its roots in the old English principle, long since abandoned both in England and America, that a felon was wholly incompetent to give testimony in court because felons were unworthy of belief.

The types of felony convictions usable to impeach a witness vary somewhat from jurisdiction to jurisdiction. For example, some states allow only proof of felonies that involve moral turpitude, such as perjury. A few jurisdictions will even permit proof of a misdemeanor conviction if it involved moral turpitude.

The bare *fact* of the prior felony conviction is all that can be inquired into; the cross-examiner is not allowed to dig into the details of the previous offense on the ground that this would often be unduly time-consuming and might generate unfair prejudice against the witness.

If the witness denies that he was previously convicted, the conviction can then be proved by means of other evidence, such as a certified copy of the judgment of conviction.

EXAMPLE:

BY THE PROSECUTING ATTORNEY: Mr. Lishniss, the defense counsel didn't go into your background in much detail. I'd like to ask you a question or two about your past history.

Mr. Lishniss, isn't it a fact that in April of 1989 you were convicted in Dade County, Florida, of perjury?

A: Yes, that's a fact. And I served some time.

Q: How much time?

A: I was sentenced to a year and a day but I got out in eight months.

Q: The perjury, the lying under oath, was committed before a jury, was it not?

A: That's what they said.

Q: What was it that you lied about?

BY DEFENSE COUNSEL: We object, Your Honor. He's getting into the details now and that's improper. We can't retry this witness's Florida case in the middle of our case.

THE COURT: I would ordinarily allow examining counsel some leeway where the prior conviction was for perjury. Here, however, the witness has readily admitted the conviction and I think that's all you're entitled to, Mr. Prosecutor. Let's not get bogged down in all the details. You've brought out the fact that he was convicted of lying under oath in front of a jury. Go on to something else now.

BY THE PROSECUTING ATTORNEY: Very well, Your Honor.

In *United States* v. *Escobedo,* 430 F.2d 14 (7th Cir. 1970), the question arose whether the accused in a criminal case is to be treated like an ordinary witness in connection with impeachment based on previous convictions. The United States Court of Appeals for the Seventh Circuit held that an accused is no different from an ordinary witness in this respect. Escobedo had been charged with possession of marijuana. He claimed that proof of a prior narcotics conviction would be used by the jury to infer his guilt of the present charge and not simply to undermine his credibility. The Seventh Circuit, adhering to the traditional rule, approved the method of impeachment nonetheless.

5. *Prior Inconsistent Statements.* A witness, including an accused in a criminal case who takes the stand and testifies generally in his own behalf, can be impeached through a showing that he made one or more pretrial statements that were inconsistent with (contradictory of) his testimony at trial.

Before evidence of a prior inconsistent statement can be offered in evidence, the witness must be examined about the making of it.

Oral Statement

If the prior statement was oral, the witness must be asked whether he ever made such a statement at a described time and place and in the presence of specified persons.

EXAMPLE:

BY THE PROSECUTING ATTORNEY: It was your direct testimony, was it not, that you saw the defendant Bushmat in the Club 88 at about midnight on April 1, 1989?

A: Yes, that's correct.

Q: And I believe you further testified that to your certain knowledge he remained in the Club 88 until closing time, which was approximately 4:00 A.M.?

A: That's right.

Q: Have you ever told anyone a different story?

A: No.

Q: Specifically, did you ever tell anyone that you hadn't seen Bushmat in over three years but that you owed him a favor and would give him an alibi for April the 1st?

A: No, sir.

Q: Do you happen to know George M. Wacker, Mr. Lishniss?

A: Yes, I know him.

Q: Did you ever tell him that you in fact had not seen the defendant Bushmat on the night of the first and the morning of the second of April 1989?

A: No, sir.

Q: Do you know where the bar called the Bloch House is located?

A: Yes. It's at 421 Melrose Street.

Q: Have you ever met George Wacker there?

A: Yes.
Q: Did you meet him at the Bloch House on March 13 of this year?
A: I can't remember whether I did or not. I might have. I don't know.
Q: Is it a fact that on March 19 you met Wacker at the Bloch House and told him that you were providing a phony alibi for Bushmat?
A: I wouldn't have said that.
Q: And wasn't Milton Morton present when you told Wacker that you were giving Bushmat an alibi?
A: I never told Wacker anything like that.
Q: Mr. Lishniss, I think you should know that the State will call George Wacker and Milton Morton to the stand in this case.
A: So what?
Q: Do you still say to the court and jury that you never told George Wacker, in the presence of Milton Morton, that you were going to give the defendant in this case an alibi? Do you say it with a realization that we have laws against perjury in this state?
A: Sure I say it.
Q: Very well.

. . .

[On rebuttal, after the defense has rested its case, the prosecution can call the two impeaching witnesses to the stand and prove the making of the prior inconsistent oral statement.]

BY THE PROSECUTING ATTORNEY: Give us your name, please.
A: George M. Wacker
Q: Where do you reside?
A: At 1360 North Sandburg Terrace, here in the city.
Q: What is your occupation?
A: I'm a television repairman.
Q: Do you know Morton P. Lishniss?
A: Yes, I'm sorry to say.
Q: How long have you known him?
A: Oh, five or six years, I guess.
Q: I direct your attention to March 13 of this year, at around five in the afternoon, and ask you whether you saw Morton P. Lishniss then?
A: Yes, I did.
Q: Where did you see him?
A: At a place called The Bloch House on Melrose.
Q: That's a bar or tavern?
A: Yes.
Q: Was anyone else present at the time I mentioned?
A: Yes, Milton Morton, my assistant, was along.
Q: Did you have a conversation with Morton P. Lishniss at this bar called The Bloch House?

A: I did.
Q: Was any reference to this case made by Mr. Lishniss?
A: Yes.
Q: What did he say about this case?
A: He said an old buddy, Clyde Bushmat, was going on trial for a killing that happened at about 12:30 on the night of April 1, 1989. And he said he owed Bushmat a big favor for something Bushmat had done years before. Mort said he was going to give Bushmat an alibi for April 1, although actually he hadn't seen Bushmat in a long time. Lishniss told me that he was going to say that he had seen Bushmat at the Club 88 between midnight and 4:00 A.M.

[The prosecuting attorney will engage in the same kind of examination of Milton Morton.]

It should be emphasized here, and it will be mentioned again later, that the calling of the impeaching witnesses, Wacker and Morton, would not have been proper had the witness Lishniss conceded on the stand that he had made the claimed prior inconsistent statement to them. A prior inconsistent statement can be proved up through other witnesses only where the witness whose impeachment is sought has flatly denied making the statement or has been equivocal about it. Otherwise the cross-examiner would be proving the prior inconsistent statement twice, which is arguably overkill.

Written Statement

If the prior inconsistent statement was a written, signed one, the witness whose impeachment is sought must be asked whether he ever signed such a statement.

EXAMPLE:

BY THE DEFENSE COUNSEL: Mr. Stitz, on your direct examination just now, you testified that you saw the defendant Bushmat run out of the alley and that he was wearing a cap pulled down low over his face, didn't you?
A: That was my testimony, yes.
Q: Have you ever made a statement about this case to anyone from my law firm?
A: Not to my knowledge.
Q: You don't remember a young lawyer named Beckley coming to your house about a month ago and asking you about this case?
A: I remember that.
Q: Did you talk with Beckley?
A: Yes.

BY DEFENSE COUNSEL [to the court reporter]: Would you mark this single sheet of paper Defendant's Exhibit Number 13 for identification. [Court reporter complies.] Thank you.

Q: I hand you Defendant's Exhibit Number 13 for Identification and ask that you look at it. [In many jurisdictions it is necessary to let the witness look at his prior written statement before any additional cross-questions are put to him; in other jurisdictions this need not be done.]

A: I'm looking at it.

Q: Does your signature appear on Defendant's 13?

A: Yes, at the bottom.

Q: Did you sign it on the date that appears on it?

A: Yes.

Q: Is Defendant's 13 in the same form and condition as it was when you signed it?

A: It appears to be.

Q: Have any changes or alterations been made to the statement?

A: No, I don't think so.

Q: Does Defendant's 13 constitute your true and correct statement?

A: I guess it does.

Q: Then I will ask you whether or not on April 1 of this year you did not make the following statement: "This man ran out of the alley wearing a green jacket. He had on brown pants. He wore nothing on his head. I think he might have been wearing glasses." You made that statement, didn't you?

A: I remember the cap now.

Q: But in your written statement to Mr. Beckley, given very shortly after the incident in question, you specifically and quite positively stated, "He wore nothing on his head," did you not?

A: Yes, but I now remember the cap.

Q: Are you one of those rare people whose memory gets sharper and sharper as more and more time passes?

A: Well, no.

Q: Your memory was probably clearer and more accurate at the time you made your statement to Mr. Beckley, don't you think?

A: Maybe.

It should be emphasized that it would be improper to call impeaching witnesses to the stand—Wacker and Morton in the first example, lawyer Beckley in the second one—if the witness whose impeachment is sought has conceded on the stand that he made the claimed prior inconsistent statement to them. A prior inconsistent statement, whether written or oral, can be proved up through other witnesses only where the witness whose impeachment is sought has flatly denied making the statement or has been equivocal about it ("I'm not sure"). The prior inconsistent statement can be read into the record in the jury's hearing, but it cannot then also be proved through other witnesses. This would be proving the prior statement twice, which would be overdoing it; it would be what in the trial lawyer's parlance is termed *cumulative* evidence. The witness's confession that he made the prior inconsistent statement is all that cross-examining counsel is entitled to.

EXAMPLE A:

BY THE PROSECURING ATTORNEY: This morning, during your direct examination by defense counsel, you said that you had never in your life met Clyde Bushmat. I now ask you whether you recall having talked with Detective Arnold Wilson about this matter on April 1, 1989?

A: Yes, I recall that I talked with him.

Q: And did you not tell Detective Wilson that you have known Clyde Bushmat ever since you were in the Army together during the Korean conflict?

A: Well, yes, I did.

[The witness having admitted making a prior inconsistent statement, the prosecuting attorney will not be permitted to call Detective Wilson to the stand to testify to the making of the same statement. The witness's admission is all that the prosecution is entitled to; Detective Wilson's testimony would prove the prior inconsistent statement *twice,* which might be unfair.]

EXAMPLE B:

BY THE PROSECURING ATTORNEY: When you were under direct examination by your own lawyer, you said that you have never owned a rifle in your life. I want to ask you, sir, whether you recall having made a written statement about this case at the time of your arrest?

A: I made a statement to the arresting officer, yes.

Q: Did you make it of your own free will, with knowledge of your right to remain silent and of your right to legal counsel? [As we saw in chapter 3, this question is not legally important where the pretrial statement is being used only to impeach the witness, but it may be impressive to the jury that the pretrial statement was made voluntarily by the witness and with his eyes wide open.]

A: I knew what I was doing.

BY THE PROSECUTING ATTORNEY: I'll ask the court reporter to make this prosecution Exhibit Number 14 for Identification. [Court reporter complies.]

Q: I will now hand to you what has been marked Prosecution Exhibit Number 14 for Identification and ask you whether it is the written statement that you gave to Detective Arnold Wilson on April 1, 1989.

A: Yes, it is.
Q: How do you know it is your statement?
A: I recognize what I said and I recognize my signature on it at the bottom.
Q: Very well. I now ask you whether in that statement, marked as Prosecution's Number 14, you did not say, and I am quoting, "I have owned quite a number of rifles in my time but I don't go around murdering people with them"?
A: That's what I said.
Q: Thank you, that's all. [Having read the written statement into the record, the prosecuting attorney will not be permitted to offer the actual written statement into evidence since, once again, this would be akin to proving the same thing twice. He has read the statement into the record, so it stands on a par with other testimony in the case; if he introduced the written statement as well, the jury would be entitled to take it to their deliberation room to read and this might unduly emphasize one item of testimonial evidence over all the rest of the testimony in the case.]

If the witness whose impeachment is sought denies having made the prior statement, or is equivocal, extrinsic evidence of his making of the statement can be introduced, as was done in the first of the preceding series of examples. If the statement was in writing, the writing can be produced, marked for identification, and, after having been authenticated, offered into evidence. There are a number of ways in which such a writing can be authenticated. Although the process of authenticating writings is discussed in detail in chapter 16, some examples are given here.

EXAMPLE A:
BY THE PROSECUTING ATTORNEY: You deny ever having given a written statement to Officer Krupke?
A: I never gave him no statement.
Q: Handing you what has been marked Prosecution Exhibit 12, I ask you whether your signature appears on it?
A: Well, yes.
Q: Where does it appear?
A: At the bottom of the page.
Q: Is any other part of the statement in your handwriting?
A: Yes.
Q: What part?
A: The part just above my signature.
Q: And what does it say, just above your signature and in your own handwriting?
A: It says, "I have read the foregoing and it is true to the best of my knowledge."

Q: Do your initials appear anywhere on Prosecution's Number 12?
A: Yes, they do.
Q: Where?
A: The cop spelled rifle wrong. He spelled it "rifel." He corrected it and then I initialed the correction.
Q: So although the main part of this statement was written down in Officer Krupke's handwriting, you initialed a misspelled word right in the middle of it?
A: True.
BY THE PROSECUTING ATTORNEY: Your Honor, we offer into evidence what has been marked Prosecution Exhibit Number 12 for Identification.
BY DEFENSE COUNSEL: Object, Your Honor. Insufficient foundation.
THE COURT: Well, counsel, he says he signed it and you have some other things in his own handwriting on it. I think the jury is entitled to consider whether his signature and these other things would appear on a written statement that he didn't make. I'll overrule your objection. The exhibit is received in evidence.
BY THE PROSECUTING ATTORNEY: May I read it to the jury now, Your Honor?
THE COURT: You can read it into the record. You cannot offer it physically.
BY THE PROSECUTING ATTORNEY: I understand, Your Honor. I'll just read it aloud so that both the jurors and the court reporter can get it.

EXAMPLE B:

BY THE PROSECUTING ATTORNEY: Your Honor, we call as our next witness Ronald Krupke. [Witness is given the oath.]
Q: What is your name?
A: Ronald Krupke. [Other preliminary questions are posed.]

. . .

Q: And after the warnings regarding his legal rights that you have described, did the accused make any statement to you?
A: He did.
Q: In what form?
A: He made an oral statement, which I wrote down on a pad that I had with me. He signed it. He also wrote on it, "I have read the foregoing and it is true to the best of my knowledge." He initialed a spelling mistake.
Q: Had he or had he not been given an opportunity to read the statement before he signed it?
A: Oh, yes. He read it over with great care. It took him about five minutes.

Q: Officer Krupke, I'm handing you what has been marked Prosecution's Exhibit 12 and I will ask you whether you know what it is?
A: I know what it is.
Q: What is it?
A: This is the statement that I took from the accused in this case, Clyde Bushmat, on the afternoon of April 1, 1989.
BY THE PROSECUTING ATTORNEY: [The offer of the exhibit into evidence is made.]

If the accused in the examples above refused to identify the signature and other handwriting as his and if Officer Krupke were not available to identify the exhibit, the prosecuting attorney might find it necessary to rely on a handwriting expert or a witness who is familiar with the accused's handwriting to authenticate the statement. The use of handwriting experts and other witnesses to authenticate questioned writings is considered in chapter 18.

Hearsay Rule Not Involved

Introduction of a prior inconsistent statement does not violate the rule against hearsay, discussed in chapter 5, because the statement is being offered not to prove the truth of assertions contained in it but to undermine the witness's credibility. Furthermore, some jurisdictions now hold that prior inconsistent statements made by a witness are in no event within the hearsay rule. For example, Section 1235 of the California Evidence Code permits the jurors to weigh the substance of prior inconsistent statements against the substance of in-court testimony. This means that the prior inconsistent statements are being used as evidence of their truth and not simply to impeach the witness's credibility. Rule 613 of the Federal Rules of Evidence, read in conjunction with Rule 801(d)(2), achieves approximately the same result as Section 1235 of the California Evidence Code by defining certain prior statements of witnesses and party-admissions as not being within the definition of hearsay. The result of this is that they are admissible to prove the truth of their assertions. The California approach was held to be constitutionally permissible in California v. Green, 399 U.S. 149 (1970). This development makes the taking of statements in criminal cases all the more important.

6. *Bias, Interest, Prejudice.* The sixth and final impeachment technique on cross-examination involves bias, interest, or prejudice on the part of the witness whose veracity is to be attacked. Proof of bias and the like is always relevant to credibility and can be inquired into thoroughly. This can run the gamut from showing that the accused's solitary alibi witness is his devoted wife to demonstrating that the witness on the stand has been bribed by the side whose cause his testimony favors.

Thus it can be brought out that an accomplice who has turned "State's evidence" was granted immunity from prosecution or promised a reduced sentence as a *quid pro quo* for testimony advantageous to the prosecution. Less dramatic circumstances can be revealed. Perhaps the defendant's witnesses can all be shown to be his relatives or close friends. Or perhaps—and this will be more difficult for the criminal investigator to develop—the defendant's witnesses, such as alibi witnesses, are persons over whom the defendant has some sort of hold. He has threatened them, or gotten others to threaten them, with bodily harm unless they testify in his favor. Threats to the witness's loved ones can be shown, as can threats to destroy the witness's business or reputation. Promises of a monetary or other type of reward for favorable testimony can be brought out.

Sometimes defense counsel, lacking anything more solid, will bear down on the fact that the proseuction's key witness has been housed in a good hotel, wined and dined, and supported financially pending and during the trial.

EXAMPLE:

BY THE PROSECUTING ATTORNEY: Let s get this straight, Ms. Adams. You state, as I understand it, that the accused was with you during all of the night in question?

A. That's correct.

Q: It is a fact, is it not, that you have been living with the accused, although not married to him, for the past five years?

A: That's true. But we're going to get married sometime. He's promised me.

Q: That is your hope, is it?

A: Yes.

Q: You won't be able to get married if he goes to jail on this charge, will you?

A: No. Maybe I could wait for him.

Q: And the fact also is that the accused has been and is now your sole source of financial support, isn't that so?

A: Yes.

Q: And he could not continue to support you if he goes to prison, could he?

A: I guess not. They don't earn much in there.

Q: You have everything to gain if Charlie is acquitted and everything to lose if he is convicted, is that not correct?

A: Yes, but I'm not lying.

Q: Can you give the court and jury the name of any person who saw you and Charlie together on the night in question?

A: No.

It is proper to ask expert witnesses, such as a psychiatrist who has supported an insanity defense, whether he is being paid a fee for his testimony, although a carefully coached expert will usually sidestep this sort of cross-examination fairly artfully.

EXAMPLE:

BY THE PROSECUTING ATTORNEY: Doctor Faust, is the defendant or his lawyer paying you a sum of money to testify here today?

A: I wouldn't put it that way. I'm not being paid for my testimony. I do expect to be compensated for the time spent in my examination of the defendant and in the preparation of my report. And I expect to be compensated, at a reasonable level, for my time away from the office.

Of course, if in the example given above the prosecutor plunges ahead and asks how much the psychiatrist expects to be compensated for his time and the witness replies, "Two thousand dollars a day," the jurors may be inclined to believe that his opinion has been more than slightly affected by his handsome fee.

C. Impeachment by Means of Extrinsic Evidence

Limitations and Purposes

By and large it is accurate to say that whenever a party can properly introduce extrinsic evidence to impeach a witness he can properly cross-examine the witness to the same effect. However, this rule of thumb does not invariably operate in reverse. There are some situations in which a court will permit cross-examination but will not allow extrinsic evidence. This happens when proposed extrinsic evidence is only marginally relevant. Courts are acutely aware that the putting in of extrinsic impeaching evidence is more time-consuming than cross-examination and that it poses a greater risk of distracting the jurors from the main issues in the case.

When permitted, the introduction of extrinsic evidence, as contrasted with cross-examination of a witness on the stand to impeach him directly, has two primary purposes: (1) to dispute or to demonstrate the incorrectness of the witness's testimony, or (2) to demonstrate something about the witness himself, such as that he has a bad reputation among his associates for truth and veracity.

Examples of the proper use of extrinsic evidence to impeach a witness inevitably came up during the preceding discussion of cross-examination as the principal impeachment tool. Six impeachment techniques on cross-examination were mentioned. Extrinsic proof is permissible in connection with five of those techniques. Proof through witnesses other than the witness whose impeachment is sought can be introduced:

1. To demonstrate the existence of sensory deficiencies on the witness's part (for example, by calling the optometrist who prescribed corrective lenses);
2. To show the witness's psychiatric condition (for example, by evidence, not subject to a testimonial privilege protecting confidentiality, that the witness is a pathological liar);
3. To establish the witness's prior conviction of a serious crime (for example, by introducing a certified copy of the judgment of conviction, obtained from the court in which the witness was tried);
4. To establish the making of a prior inconsistent oral or written statement, where the witness to be impeached has denied the making of it, denied its accuracy, or has equivocated (for example, by calling the police officer, the police station stenographer, the court reporter who heard and perhaps also took down and later transcribed the statement); and
5. To show bias, interest, or prejudice on the part of the witness (for example, by putting in extrinsic evidence that a prosecution witness holds a long-standing grudge against the accused.)

The Collateral Impeachment Rule Again

It will be recalled that the rule against collateral impeachment blocks the use of much extrinsic evidence. This rule, enforced in those jurisdictions that permit the use of prior bad conduct to impeach a witness, dictates that acknowledgment of the prior conduct must come from the witness himself. The cross-examiner can forcefully repeat his question about the asserted prior conduct, and he can try through cross-examination to break the witness down, but if the witness persists in denying the prior conduct the cross-examiner is not allowed to produce extrinsic evidence of it.

The book GREAT TRIALS OF FAMOUS LAWYERS contains as good an explanation of the collateral impeachment rule as any:

> . . . if a lady takes the stand and testifies that the defendant stole her purse, you can call witnesses to show that she never had a purse, or that she was in Chicago at the time, or anything else to show that the purse was not stolen. But if you want to prove that she is no lady you must prove it out of her own mouth. You may have a dozen witnesses to show that she ran a gambling house, or tortured stray cats, or engaged in any number of activities that are not looked upon with approbation, but if she denies them (and you must ask her) that is the end of it.

EXAMPLE:

BY THE PROSECUTING ATTORNEY: Mr. Lishniss, is it not a fact that in the years 1984 and 1985 you failed to file any income returns whatever?

A: That's a lie. I filed in both of those years. I always pay my income taxes. I'm as good a citizen as the next guy.

Q: Mr. Lishniss, do I understand you correctly? These things are subject to verification. You filed no federal or state income tax returns in either 1984 or 1985, isn't that true?

A: That is not true. I filed.

Q: Would you care to produce those returns in court, sir?

BY DEFENSE COUNSEL: Oh, he's not obligated to do anything of the kind, Your Honor. He's testified under oath that he filed in those years. This is cross-examination by innuendo. We're running afoul of the rule against collateral impeachment here, Your Honor, and we object.

THE COURT: Well, I sustain the objection to the extent that it goes to the last question. You may proceed.

BY THE PROSECUTING ATTORNEY: Will you authorize us to examine your tax records at the offices of the Internal Revenue Service?

BY DEFENSE COUNSEL: Same objection.

THE COURT: It will be sustained.

BY THE PROSECUTING ATTORNEY: I have no further questions of this witness at this time, Your Honor.

. . .

BY THE PROSECUTING ATTORNEY: [during a conference out of the jurors hearing, occurring during the prosecution's rebuttal of the defense's case-in-chief]: Your Honor, we next propose to call to the stand Mr. George Nett, who is a representative of the Internal Revenue Service. He will testify that the Service has no record that Morton P. Lishniss filed an income tax return in either 1984 or 1985.

BY DEFENSE COUNSEL: Your Honor, this would fly in the face of the rule against collateral impeachment. It opens up a whole new tangent. What do we do now, have a trial within a trial to decide this witness's tax liability? Right in the middle of a complex murder case? If this is an offer of proof, we object to it.

THE COURT: I am treating this as an offer of proof and it is going to be rejected. You can't put on extrinsic evidence. He said he filed in 1984 and 1985 and you're bound by his answer. Tell your witness to go back to his office.

BY THE PROSECUTING ATTORNEY: Might I respectfully suggest that there may be a perjury prosecution of this witness, Your Honor?

THE COURT: That's your business. You're the U.S. Attorney. Have his testimony typed up. But the perjury prosecution is your only recourse against this witness. I won't let you call the IRS agent and further confuse the issues in this case.

D. Proof of the Making of a Prior Consistent Statement

The General Rule against Proof of Prior Consistent Statements

In dealing with methods of impeachment we have discussed the introduction of evidence that the witness on the stand has made prior inconsistent oral or written statements. We now consider the question whether it is ever proper for the side that called the witness to introduce evidence that he or she has made prior consistent statements; that is, earlier statements that were in accord with his or her direct testimony at trial.

The general rule is that the credibility of a witness's direct testimony cannot be shored up by reference during the direct testimony to prior consistent statements made by the witness. This would be self-serving and cumulative. Furthermore, it would in a very real way be premature since the witness's direct testimony has not yet been challenged in any way. There is no call to corroborate direct testimony the truthfulness of which has in no way been attacked by the opposing side.

However, the rule is different where the truthfulness of a witness's direct testimony has been attacked on cross-examination. It thereafter is permissible for the side calling the witness to establish that the witness has made prior statements that were consistent with his or her in-court testimony, thus suggesting that the witness's direct testimony was not made up of recently concocted falsehoods.

The Barmore *Rule*

The leading case here is *Barmore* v. *Safety Casualty Co.*, 363 S.W.2d 355 (Tex. Civ. App. 1962). The plaintiff in this civil case sued to obtain benefits under a workmen's compensation statute. Counsel for the defendant contended that the plaintiff's injury claim was a "recent fabrication," an invention on his part, and asked him on cross-examination whether he had reported his injury to any of the people he talked with immediately after the alleged accident. The plaintiff's responses to this questioning were mostly negative; he thought he might have mentioned his injury to one person. The plaintiff thereafter tried to introduce the testimony of his wife to the effect that on the morning after the accident he had told her about his claimed injury. The trial court excluded her testimony but was reversed on appeal for having done so.

The *Barmore* case holds that where a charge of recent fabrication is made on the basis of prior inconsistent statements ("Your earlier statements were different, so your current story must be false"), it is relevant to show that the witness made a consistent statement before or contemporaneously with the making of the assertedly inconsistent statements. In order to make the evidence pertinent to the recent fabrication issue, it is usually also essential to demonstrate in some degree that the prior consistent statement was made before any motive to fabricate, to lie, arose.

EXAMPLE:
People v. *Neely,* 329 P.2d 357 (Cal. App. 1958), murder prosecution in which accomplice testified for State, connecting co-defendant to crimes charged; two written statements made by accomplice to police officers immediately after the crime but before any formal charges had been made, both of them consistent with his trial testimony, *held,* admissible to rebut defense counsel's suggestion that accomplice's implicating of co-defendant was a recently contrived statement.

The U.S. Supreme Court has adopted the condition suggested in *Barmore.* The Justices agree that prior consistent statements can be offered to rebut a charge, made during cross-examination, that the witness' testimony was a tissue of recently invented falsehoods. However, they have insisted that the prior consistent statement must have been made *before* there arose any ulterior motive to make it. (*Tome* v. *United States,* ______ U.S. ______, 115 S. Ct. 696 (1995).)

CHAPTER EIGHT

The Constitutional Privilege against Compulsory Self-Incrimination

A. The Fifth Amendment

A number of provisions of the United States Constitution create privileges and exclusionary rules that prevent the use in criminal prosecutions of certain sorts of incriminating evidence. Perhaps the most important of these constitutional privileges is the Fifth Amendment privilege against compulsory self-incrimination. In succeeding chapters other constitutional privileges and exclusionary rules will be explained: (1) the rules which exclude identification evidence resulting from improper pretrial identification confrontations; (2) rules which exclude improperly obtained confessions and admissions; and (3) rules excluding the fruits of an unlawful search and seizure. In later chapters we will also discuss a number of testimonial privileges that do not rise to a constitutional level but which have their origin in statutes and judicial opinions: (1) the attorney-client privilege; (2) the physician-patient privilege; (3) the psychotherapist-patient privilege; (4) the husband-wife privilege; (5) the clergy-penitent privilege; (6) the journalist's source privilege; (7) the privilege surrounding a person's political vote; (8) military and state secrets; and (9) the informer's privilege.

The Fifth Amendment to the federal Constitution reads in pertinent part as follows:

> No person . . . shall be compelled in any criminal case to be a witness against himself.

If restricted to its literal meaning (assuring a person that he cannot be forced to testify against himself once he has been put on trial on a criminal charge), the Fifth Amendment would not be very effective; the accused might *already* have been compelled to give enough evidence against himself not only to support the bringing of the criminal charge against him but also to support his conviction. Accordingly, the decided cases and some of the evidence codes extend the privilege against self-incrimination well beyond the literal language of the Fifth Amendment.

B. The Privilege against Compulsory Self-Incrimination under the Decided Cases and the Codes

The privilege against forced self-incrimination as worked out in the decisional law and in some of the evidence codes has two branches: there is a defendant privilege and there is a witness privilege.

1. *The Defendant Privilege.* A *defendant* cannot be compelled to testify in a criminal case. He cannot even be compelled to be sworn and take the witness stand. In other words, he cannot be forced to invoke the privilege in front of the jury. Furthermore, one defendant cannot require a co-defendant to testify in a criminal case.
2. *The Witness Privilege.* In a civil action a *party,* and in either a civil action or a criminal case a *nonparty witness,* can be compelled to take the stand, but once on the stand he can then invoke the privilege against self-incrimination when and if potentially incriminating questions are asked of him.

Scope of the Privilege

The risk protected against by the privilege against self-incrimination is the danger that what one says will be used as evidence in a criminal prosecution or in an action for a penalty or a forfeiture. For the privilege to be applicable, the risk of criminal prosecution must be *real* and *substantial.*

EXAMPLE A:

In *Rogers* v. *United States,* 340 U.S. 367 (1951), Mrs. Rogers, the treasurer of the Denver Communist party, was summoned before a federal grand jury. After testifying about the office she held and that she did not currently have certain records, she was asked to provide the name of the person who now held the records. Mrs. Rogers refused to reveal this name. The District Court turned her over to a federal marshall, told her to discuss the matter with her lawyer and to appear in court the following morning.

On the following day Mrs. Rogers again refused to reveal the name. On the previous day she had said that she did not want to put anyone else through the "ordeal" that she was experiencing; on the following morning she for the first time specifically invoked the privilege against self-incrimination. She was held in contempt of court.

The Supreme Court held that Mrs. Rogers had waived the privilege by not claiming it on the preceding day.

More importantly, a majority of the justices in *Rogers* held that Mrs. Rogers could not have successfully invoked the privilege the first time because she had already given incriminating answers. Having exposed herself to prosecution by giving these earlier answers, she could not argue that *more* testimony would subject her to a danger of prosecution. The damage was already done.

The Court laid down a test in response to the argument that the accused was being required to subject herself to an increased risk of prosecution. Having given incriminating testimony, a witness is precluded from claiming the privilege as to later questions unless the answers would add significantly to the risk of prosecution.

EXAMPLE B:

In *Reina* v. *United States,* 364 U.S. 507 (1960), it was held that a grand jury witness who has been granted immunity from state and federal prosecution cannot successfully invoke the privilege against self-incrimination.

Because the risk protected against by the privilege is the danger of *criminal* prosecution, the witness privilege, described above, does not apply to essentially noncriminal situations.

EXAMPLE:

California v. *Byers,* 402 U.S. 424 (1971), posed the question whether a statute that requires the operator of a motor vehicle involved in an accident to stop and leave his name and address violates the privilege against self-incrimination. The Supreme Court held that it does not. The Court drew a sharp distinction between the sort of disclosure requirement that operates in a basically noncriminal context where self-reporting is crucial to some enforcement program, on the one hand, and, on the other, those reporting requirements that compel disclosure in an essentially criminal area, such as the gambling tax laws. Giving one's name and address after an automobile accident is no more testimonially incriminating than appearing in a police lineup or giving a blood sample.

Applicability of the Privilege to the States

The Fifth Amendment privilege against compelled self-incrimination is applicable to the states, which must follow federal standards for its application.

It was in *Malloy* v. *Hogan,* 378 U.S. 1 (1964), that the Supreme Court held that the privilege was applicable, through the due process requirements of the Fourteenth Amendment, to the several states. In *Malloy,* the petitioner had previously been found guilty of a gambling charge. After he had served his sentence he was called before a referee who was conducting an inquiry into gambling activities. When asked questions about events surrounding his conviction, the petitioner refused to answer "on the grounds it may tend to incriminate me." The state court which had appointed the referee sentenced the petitioner for contempt of court.

The Supreme Court reversed the lower court, saying that answers to the questions put to the petitioner about persons with whom he had been involved "might furnish a link in a chain of evidence sufficient to connect [him] with a more recent crime for which he might still be prosecuted."

The Court held not only that the Fifth Amendment privilege was binding on state courts as well as on the federal courts but also that the states must follow the federal standard in enforcing the privilege. The Court described the federal standard as follows:

> The privilege afforded not only extends to answers that would in themselves support a conviction . . . but likewise embraces those which would furnish a link in the chain of evidence needed to prosecute.

Malloy, in its recognition of the importance of answers that supply investigative leads, forces judges to determine what constitutes an initial link in a chain of prosecutorial evidence.

Proceedings in Which the Privilege Can Be Invoked; the Miranda *Rule*

The privilege against compelled self-incrimination is available at every level of governmental investigation. It can be invoked in courts, before legislative committees, before grand juries, at coroners' inquests. And the privilege now extends well beyond situations of "legal" compulsion and includes extralegal compulsion by law enforcement agents during interrogation of suspects.

The well-known and frequently criticized case of *Miranda* v. *Arizona,* 384 U.S. 436 (1966), exemplifies the process of expanding the privilege against forced self-incrimination far beyond the explicit wording of the Fifth Amendment. *Miranda* holds that the privilege is available to persons undergoing police interrogation. It brings the privilege to the station house.

The Supreme Court's opinion in *Miranda* recognized the unreality of the argument that the police lack any *legal* authority to compel answers to questions—for example, the police do not have the contempt power that judges do—and that therefore the privilege against compelled self-incrimination is irrelevant to police interrogation. In fact, as the Supreme Court's review of police practices demonstrates, the custodial environment of the station house and sophisticated interrogation methods contribute to the undeniable ability of the police to get many suspects to talk.

Miranda adopts the position that many people will forfeit their right against self-incrimination at the station house, long before they ever see the inside of a courtroom, if the privilege is not safeguarded at pretrial stages. The Supreme Court's opinion lists the applicable safeguards:

1. Prior to any questioning, the suspect must be warned (a) that he has a right to remain silent, (b) that any statement he does make can be used against him, and (c) that he has a right to have a lawyer, either privately retained or judicially appointed, present at the questioning. (The suspect need not, however, be advised of the nature of the charge against him. *Colorado* v. *Spring,* 479 U.S. 564 (1987).)
2. Any waiver (abandonment) by the suspect of the rights listed in the foregoing warning must be made "knowingly and intelligently." And, of course, it must be voluntary.
3. If the suspect "indicates in any manner" a desire for the presence of a lawyer at any stage of the interrogation, the questioning must immediately be interrupted until a lawyer can be obtained.
4. If the suspect "indicates in any manner that he does not wish to be interrogated," the questioning will not begin or, if it has already been commenced, it will halt, even though the suspect may already have given incriminating information, until the suspect has consulted legal counsel and has consented to further questioning.

It follows from all of this that a suspect's post-arrest, post-*Miranda* silence cannot be referred to at trial in an effort to cast doubt on his exculpatory testimony. It would be unfair to promise an arrested person that his silence will not be used against him and then break that promise by using his silence to impeach his trial testimony (*Wainwright* v. *Greenfield,* 474 U.S. 284 (1986); *Doyle* v. *Ohio,* 426 U.S. 610 (1976)).

The "Public Safety" Exception to the Miranda *Rule*

In *New York* v. *Quarles*, 467 U.S. 649 (1984), the Supreme Court developed a narrow but nonetheless significant exception to its *Miranda* rule: the "public safety" exception, aimed at protecting the safety of police officers and the general public.

Quarles had been charged in a New York state court with criminal possession of a weapon. The record showed that a woman had approached two police officers who were on road patrol and told them that she had just been raped. She described her attacker, who she said had just entered a nearby supermarket and was carrying a gun. While one of the officers radioed for assistance, the other—Officer Kraft—entered the store and

Interrogation Warnings to Persons in Police Custody

The following warnings must be given to the subject before the interrogation begins:

1. "You have the right to remain silent and refuse to answer questions." Do you understand? *Subject replied* ______.
2. "Anything you do say may be used against you in a court of law." Do you understand? *Subject replied* ______.
3. You have the right to consult an attorney before speaking to the police and to have an attorney present during any questioning now or in the future." Do you understand? *Subject replied* ______.
4. "If you cannot afford an attorney, one will be provided for you without cost." Do you understand? *Subject replied* ______.
5. "If you do not have an attorney available, you have the right to remain silent until you have had an opportunity to consult with one." Do you understand? *Subject replied* ______.
6. "Now that I have advised you of your rights, are you willing to answer questions without an attorney present?" Do you understand? *Subject replied* ______.

The *Miranda* warnings. *(UPI)*

spotted the defendant, who matched the woman's description. Quarles ran toward the back of the store and Kraft briefly lost sight of him. Upon regaining sight of the suspect, Kraft ordered him to stop and to put his hands over his head. He then frisked the suspect and discovered that he was wearing an empty shoulder holster. After handcuffing Quarles, Kraft—without giving the *Miranda* warnings—asked him where the gun was. The defendant nodded toward some empty cartons and said "The gun is over there." Kraft then retrieved the gun, formally arrested Quarles, and for the first time read him his *Miranda* rights. The trial court excluded the defendant's statement and the gun itself; it also excluded Quarles' subsequent statements to the police on the ground that they were tainted by Officer Kraft's *Miranda* violation. An appellate court agreed but the Supreme Court reversed. It created a "public safety" or "exigency" exception to its *Miranda* rule. Application of the exception was not made to depend on the subjective motivation of the police officer in questioning a suspect. The Court's majority said, "Whatever the motivation of individual officers in such a situation, we do not believe that the doctrinal underpinnings of *Miranda* require that it be applied in all its rigor to a situation in which police officers ask questions reasonably prompted by a concern for the public safety."

The Use of Improperly Obtained Statements for Impeachment Purposes

Another important watering down of the *Miranda* rule took place in the case of *Harris* v. *New York,* 401 U.S. 222 (1971). The accused had been charged with possession of heroin. *Before* being given the *Miranda* warnings discussed above, but *after* having been arrested, he had said to police that he was only an intermediary between an undercover agent and the actual narcotics pusher.

At his trial the accused took the witness stand and testified that he sold baking powder to the undercover agent in order to cheat him. To impeach the credibility of this story by the accused (whose post-arrest statements were admittedly unavailable to establish his *guilt* because of the absence of any *Miranda* warnings), the prosecution offered his prior inconsistent statements about having been a mere intermediary. The accused was convicted.

The Supreme Court's majority in *Harris* held that, despite *Miranda,* the admission of the prior statements for impeachment purposes was

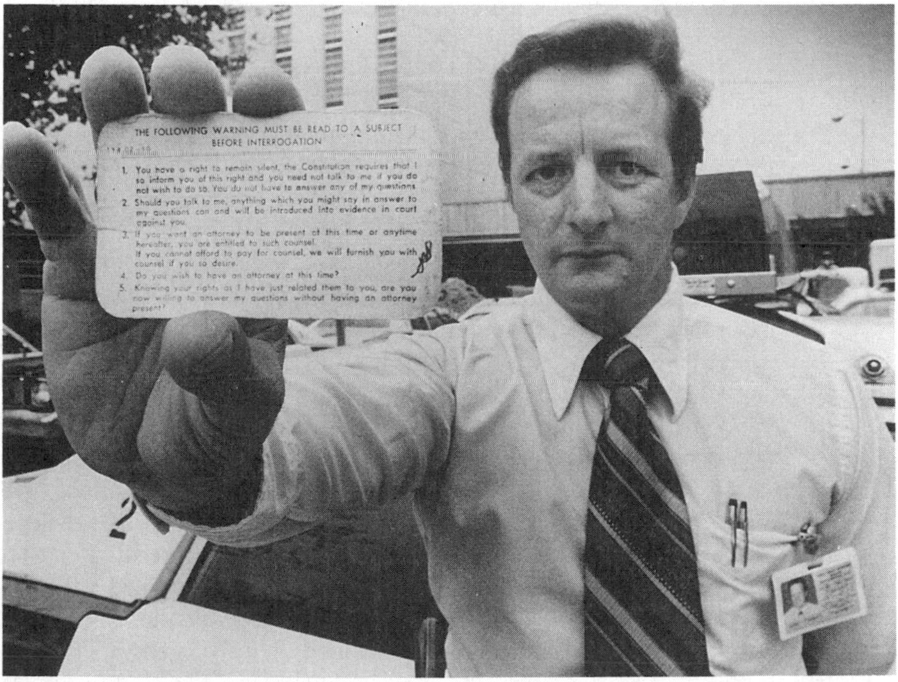

The *Miranda* card, which law officers must read to any person being taken into custody.

permissible. Any suggestion to the contrary in the *Miranda* opinion was to be disregarded since the evidence in *Miranda* had been used to prove *guilt,* not simply to impeach veracity. The Court pointed to its earlier decision in *Walder* v. *United States,* 347 U.S. 62 (1954), in which it had said, "It is one thing to say that the Government cannot make an affirmative use of evidence unlawfully obtained. It is quite another to say that the defendant can turn the illegal method by which evidence . . . was obtained to his own advantage, and provide himself with a shield against contradiction of his untruths." (The holding in *Harris,* in other words, is a narrow one. This was emphasized by the Court in 1990 in *James* v. *Illinois* (not yet officially published), in which it refused to permit an accused's illegally obtained statements to be used to contradict the trial testimony of defense witnesses *other than* the accused himself.)

The decision in *Harris* should not inspire law enforcement agents to disregard the *Miranda* safeguards. Failure to give the *Miranda* warnings will still make subsequent inculpatory statements inadmissible to prove guilt, unless the Supreme Court expressly overrules *Miranda* or Congress finds a constitutional way to nullify it. Under *Harris,* all that can be salvaged if the *Miranda* warnings are omitted is the later impeaching value of any post-arrest statements made by the accused if he changes his story at trial. (For additional discussion of *Miranda,* see chapter 11, relating to confessions.)

The Privilege Is Restricted to Communicative Evidence

The privilege against compulsory self-incrimination shields only evidence of a *testimonial* or *communicative* nature. It is not applicable where a person's *body* constitutes or is the source of real or physical evidence.

> EXAMPLE:
> In *Schmerber* v. *California,* 384 U.S. 757 (1966), the accused, who had been involved in an automobile accident, was arrested at a hospital where he was being treated for his injuries. He was charged with driving while intoxicated.
>
> While at the hospital, the police instructed a physician to take a blood sample from defendant Schmerber and it was from this sample that it was determined that he was intoxicated. Schmerber claimed that the taking and analyzing of the blood sample violated his privilege against self-incrimination. The Supreme Court disagreed.
>
> In *Schmerber* the Supreme Court was again concerned with the scope of the privilege against compulsory self-incrimination. The question now was the subject matter to which the privilege is applicable. The evidence (the report of chemical analysis of the blood sample) was distinctly incriminating but it did not constitute and was not based on *testimony* from the defendant. They took his blood, not his words.

> The privilege against self-incrimination had always been thought to apply only to communicative evidence against one's self.
>
> The question posed by *Schmerber,* essentially, was whether a person's body could properly be used against him, over his opposition. The majority of the justices held that the privilege is not applicable if a person's body itself constitutes or is the source of physical evidence.

This means that it is permissible for police investigators to require a suspect to write or speak for identification, to stand, to assume a stance, to walk, or to make a particular gesture. *Schmerber* also authorizes the police to take fingerprints, "mug" photographs, hair samples, breath specimens, fingernail scrapings, and objects concealed in body cavities. The reasoning of the *Schmerber* opinion also authorizes police to remove the suspect's clothing in order to search for concealed items such as stolen property and narcotics. The suspect can be required to try on articles of clothing for size, and the police can inspect his body for cuts, abrasions, scars, tattoos, and the like. Finally, *Schmerber* provides ample judicial authority for requiring a suspect to appear in a lineup for identification purposes.

On the other hand, neither *Schmerber* nor any other decided case authorizes forced submission to a polygraph (lie detector) test since the nontestimonial physical evidence (the subject's physiological responses to the testing process) is meaningless unless correlated with the oral communications to which they are related.

Although a suspect's privilege against self-incrimination is not violated by requiring him to participate in a police lineup, a post-indictment lineup identification will be excluded from evidence at trial if the accused is deprived of desired legal counsel at this crucial juncture. The Supreme Court announced the requirement that legal counsel be permitted at a post-indictment police lineup in *United States* v. *Wade,* 385 U.S. 811 (1967). The requirement was intended to combat the rigging or "loading" of police lineups. For a more detailed discussion of pretrial identification confrontations, see chapter 9, below.

Application of the Privilege to Corporations and Unincorporated Associations

The privilege against compelled self-incrimination is a personal one, applicable only to natural persons. It does not extend to artificial entities such as corporations and unincorporated associations (for example, a trade union).

Furthermore, the privilege is not available to an agent of such organizations where the agent is seeking to invoke the privilege on behalf of the organization. And if the evidence called for is a corporation's or an association's records, an agent who is the custodian of them cannot invoke the privilege on his own behalf even though the records may incriminate him, since they are not his personal and private records.

EXAMPLE:
The defendant in *Curcio* v. *United States,* 354 U.S. 118 (1957), was subpoenaed to testify before a grand jury and to bring with him the books of a phantom trade union. Curcio, the custodian of the books, failed to produce them. He was then asked for their whereabouts but refused to answer, invoking the privilege against self-incrimination. For his failure to answer, but not for his failure to produce the books, Curcio was sentenced for criminal contempt. The Supreme Court reversed, however, holding that the privilege applied to Curcio's oral testimony.

Curcio could properly have been held in contempt for his failure to produce the union's records, even though their production might have incriminated him. A record's custodian, acting as the representative of others, cannot invoke a personal privilege to protect his principals. To put it another way, if Curcio were to be prosecuted as a result of information contained in the union's records which he was forced to produce, it would be as though he were being convicted on the "testimony" of the union, not on his own testimony. If Curcio were to be prosecuted on the basis of his own oral testimony, his conviction would be based on his own testimony and his personal privilege against self-incrimination would be applicable. (See also *Braswell* v. *United States,* 487 U.S. 99 (1988).)

Application of the Privilege to Required Reports

A serious question exists concerning the extent to which the government can compel a person to prepare, produce, or permit inspection of records regarding the person's activities and thereafter offer the records, or evidence to which they led, against him. The leading case is *Shapiro* v. *United States,* 335 U.S. 1 (1948), involving records required under the Emergency Price Control Act of 1942. The Court held that these required records were subject to an exception to the privilege against self-incrimination; their production could be required without a grant of immunity from prosecution.

The required reports exception has three bases:

1. The purposes of the government's demand for records must be essentially regulatory rather than prosecutorial.
2. The required records must be of a sort which the regulated person has customarily kept.
3. The records must have assumed "public aspects" which make them similar to public documents, such as a schedule of approved public utility rates.

Shapiro's required reports exception to the rule of privilege is not applicable, the Supreme Court later held, in areas that are "permeated with criminal statutes" and where the government's investigation is aimed at "a highly selective group inherently suspect of criminal activities." And so it has been held that officers of the Communist party would not be compelled to file a registration statement for the party under the Subversive Activities Control Act, that persons could not be required to register or pay an occupational tax under the federal wagering tax laws, and that persons could not be required by statute to register regulated firearms. (An amended version of the National Firearms Act has been upheld by the Supreme Court; it places the registration requirement on the manufacturer or importer of firearms, not on the purchaser.)

Indirectly Compelled Testimony

Self-incriminating statements are not always compelled directly; there are more subtle, indirect pressures that may induce a person to give damaging evidence against himself. Indirectly compelled testimony is fully as subject to an exclusionary rule as directly compelled testimony.

> EXAMPLE:
> A police officer is called before a grand jury looking into claims of police corruption. He is advised of his Fifth Amendment privilege and of the possible consequences of giving testimony. He is also advised that police department rules require that he be discharged if he relies on the Fifth Amendment. Not wishing to lose his job, the police officer testifies. Later he is indicted and his grand jury testimony is offered against him at trial. The testimony will be excluded as having been obtained in violation of his Fifth Amendment rights. The coercion was indirect but potent.

Inapplicability of the Privilege to One Who Has Been Granted Immunity from Prosecution

The privilege against forced self-incrimination cannot be claimed by a person who has been granted immunity from the use of the compelled testimony and any evidence derived from the compelled testimony (so-called "use and derivative use" immunity, as distinguished from immunity from prosecution for crimes to which the compelled testimony relates—so-called "transactional" immunity).

> EXAMPLE:
> In *Kastigar* v. *United States,* 406 U.S. 441 (1972), the Supreme Court was called upon to decide whether testimony can be compelled by

granting immunity from the use of the compelled testimony and evidence derived from the compelled testimony ("use and derivative use" immunity) or whether it is necessary for the government to grant immunity from prosecution for offenses to which the compelled testimony relates ("transactional" immunity).

The Court concluded that "use and derivative use" immunity leaves both the witness and the prosecution in substantially the same position they would be in had the witness claimed the Fifth Amendment privilege. The Court said, "The immunity therefore is co-extensive with the privilege and suffices to supplant it."

The Risk of Incrimination under the Laws of Another Jurisdiction

When one state grants immunity to prosecution under its laws to a person from whom it desires self-incriminating evidence there often remains the risk of prosecution under the laws of some other jurisdiction. It breaks down this way: (1) a witness in one state may claim a risk of prosecution under the laws of another state; (2) a witness in a state or federal court may claim a risk of prosecution under the laws of some foreign country; (3) a witness in federal court claims a risk of prosecution under the laws of one or more states; or (4) a witness in a state court claims a risk of prosecution under federal law. For many years a majority of courts held that the privilege against self-incrimination protected a person only against incrimination under the laws of the sovereign seeking that person's damaging evidence. More recently, however, the U.S. Supreme Court has taken a different attitude.

In *Murphy* v. *Waterfront Commission of New York Harbor,* 378 U.S. 52 (1960), Murphy had been summoned as a witness before a commissioner and was granted immunity from prosecution by the states of New York and New Jersey. Murphy claimed the Fifth Amendment anyway, claiming that his answers might expose him to federal prosecution. He was cited for contempt. The rule was said to be that a witness granted immunity by the jurisdiction calling for his testimony could not claim the privilege even though his answers might lay him open to prosecution in some other jurisdiction. The Supreme Court disapproved of this rule, holding that it was untenable because of the requirement, laid down in *Malloy* v. *Hogan,* previously discussed in this chapter, that all jurisdictions must respect the Fifth Amendment privilege and follow the federal standard for its enforcement.

The Supreme Court reached a compromise rule. States will be permitted to compel answers from witnesses in state inquiries if adequate immunity is granted under state law. The federal government will then be precluded from using the witness's responses against him. Under *Murphy* the federal government would have the burden of demonstrating in any later federal prosecution of the witness that it "had an independent, legitimate source for the disputed evidence" before it could properly prosecute the witness or offer the evidence against him.

Presumably the *Murphy* rule will also apply where the witness's answers would subject him to prosecution in another state.

Waiver of the Privilege against Self-Incrimination

1. An *accused* waives the defendant privilege by electing to take the stand and testifying unrestrictedly. This was decided by the United States Supreme Court in *Johnson* v. *United States,* 318 U.S. 189 (1943), a tax evasion case in which the accused took the stand to testify on his own behalf.
2. A *witness* who voluntarily makes partial disclosure of incriminating facts waives the privilege and can be compelled to testify to additional facts unless the additional responses would add significantly to the risk of prosecution.

Privileged Matter Disclosed Under Compulsion or Without Opportunity to Invoke the Privilege

Evidence of a statement or other disclosure of privileged matter is not admissible against the holder of the privilege if the disclosure was made without any opportunity to assert the privilege or was compelled by mistake.

EXAMPLE:
In *Ellis* v. *United States,* 416 F.2d 791 (D.C. Cir. 1969), one Izzard, after consultation with legal counsel, waived his privilege before a grand jury and gave testimony against his companions. At the trial of the companions Izzard was required, over objection, to testify against them and they were convicted.

On appeal it was held that, in the absence of a special statute, a federal judge has no authority to compel testimony by giving immunity to a witness. However, an immunity would nonetheless flow from an erroneous denial of the privilege. Furthermore, an accused has standing to challenge, as erroneous, the denial of another person's privilege against self-incrimination. In *Ellis,* however, Izzard's privilege had been waived by his testimony before the grand jury.

Comment on the Inferences from Failure to Testify

As a general rule, neither the prosecution nor the trial judge can comment on the accused's failure to testify and the fact-finder cannot properly draw an inference of guilt from such failure.

EXAMPLE A:
In *Grunewald* v. *United States,* 353 U.S. 391 (1957), the accused claimed the privilege against self-incrimination before a grand jury but then testified as to the same matters, in a way consistent with his innocence, at trial. On cross-examination, the prosecuting attorney sought to impeach his credibility by asking about his reliance on the Fifth Amendment before the grand jury. This was held by the Supreme Court to be improper; the prosecutor's questions were calculated to demonstrate consciousness of guilt and the privilege protects a witness from this.

EXAMPLE B:
In *Griffin* v. *California,* 380 U.S. 609 (1965), the accused had been charged with first-degree homicide. Under a California rule of law, both the trial judge and the prosecuting attorney were free to comment on an accused's failure to explain or deny evidence introduced in the case which he could reasonably be expected to have knowledge about. Moreover, the jury could take this failure as tending to establish the truth of the evidence.

The accused did not take the stand, and the prosecutor in *Griffin* remarked on his failure to explain certain facts. The Supreme Court held that this was improper. Comment on the accused's assertion of the privilege against self-incrimination for the purpose of showing his guilt is in violation of the Constitution.

The real problem in *Griffin* was that California's rule served to discourage defendants from exercising their constitutional privilege since they knew that their silence could be held against them. Procedural rules that operate to deter an accused from relying on the Fifth Amendment are unconstitutional.

Despite the decision in *Griffin* v. *California,* above, it is permissible for a prosecutor to point out to a jury in closing argument that "The State's case is uncontroverted," or "No evidence to contradict the State's case has been introduced."

The Impact of the Privilege on Pretrial Discovery of Evidence in Criminal Cases

A party to a civil case is entitled to learn virtually everything there is to know about his adversary's case. The term *pretrial discovery* is applied to this process. It refers to formal investigatory methods, authorized by enforceable procedural rules and available to the parties only after a lawsuit has been commenced. In the civil practice, as distinguished from the field of criminal litigation, the following pretrial discovery devices are typical:

1. *Written Interrogatories to Parties.* A party to a civil suit can require any adverse party to answer, in writing and under oath, relevant written questions served on him or her. Written interrogatories are usually used to get detailed information which the answering party must obtain from records in his or her possession or control.

2. *Oral Depositions.* Parties and nonparty witnesses alike can be required, by means of a subpoena, to come to legal counsel's office for deposition purposes in a civil case. Counsel will ask questions orally, much as he would at trial, and the questions and answers, given under oath, will be taken down and transcribed by a court reporter. In this way, counsel gets desired information from the witness. Furthermore, the transcription of the witness's deposition testimony will rise to haunt him at trial if he then tries to shift his story in any significant way.

3. *Motions for the Production of Documents and the Like.* A party to a civil case can obtain a court order requiring an opposing party to produce relevant documents and objects for inspection, testing, copying, or photographing.

4. *Physical and Mental Examinations.* In any civil lawsuit in which the mental or physical condition of a party is in dispute, the court can order him (or her) to submit to a mental or physical examination by a qualified physician or psychiatrist.

5. *Requests for Admission of Facts.* A party to a civil lawsuit can serve a request on his or her opponent for a formal admission of relevant facts set forth in the request, including such matters as the genuineness of writings. If the opposing party refuses the requested admission and the side requesting it later establishes the truth of the disputed matter, the adverse party can be required to pay the expenses involved in proving the matter.

From this brief outline of available procedures it can be sensed that there is almost no limit to the ability of parties to civil litigation to smoke out the facts of a case. No such liberality in pretrial discovery procedures exists on the criminal side of most American courthouses. Some jurisdictions will permit the prosecution and the defense to obtain a court order requiring the other side to produce the names, addresses, and the gist of the expected testimony of its witnesses. A large number of jurisdictions will order the production of witnesses' prior written statement for impeachment purposes. But the most important criminal discovery development came in a 1966 amendment to Rule 16 of the Federal Rules of Criminal Procedure.

Under this amendment to the rules governing federal prosecutions, a trial judge can give the accused discovery of confessions or statements which he himself made, including his testimony before a grand jury. A judge can also permit an accused to obtain the results of tests and examinations made by the prosecution. After a demonstration of need and reasonableness, the accused may also be granted discovery with respect to "books, papers, documents, tangible objects, buildings or places." An order of this sort can be conditioned upon the accused's letting the prosecution have discovery of "scientific or medical reports, books, papers, documents, [and] tangible objects" that are in the accused's possession and which he plans to use at trial.

Criminal discovery rules generally favor the accused. They are not a two-way street. The reason for this is plain enough. The giving of discovery rights to the prosecution in criminal cases raises serious Fifth Amendment questions. It has been argued that forcing the defendant to cooperate in any fashion with the making of the case against him would conflict with his Fifth Amendment privilege. By and large, however, this argument has not impressed the courts, which hold that privilege does not come into play unless the conduct compelled is of a testimonial nature.

The leading judicial decision in this somewhat confused area is *Jones* v. *Superior Court of Nevada County,* 372 P.2d 919 (S. Ct. Calif. 1962). Jones was charged with rape. He asked the trial court for a continuance, saying that he needed more time to produce medical evidence in support of his claim that he had been rendered impotent by injuries suffered in 1953 and 1954. The State, alerted to Jones's defense, then demanded production of the names and addresses of any physicians who would be called by the defense to testify about the defendant's injuries, the names and addresses of any physicians who had treated the defendant prior to trial, any reports pertaining to the defendant's injuries and his asserted impotence, and any relevant X-rays.

The State's discovery effort in *Jones* would have given rise to an implied representation by the defendant that the materials he produced were the materials that the State had demanded. To this extent the compelled conduct would be testimonial in nature. It is as though the prosecution were to demand that defense counsel produce for inspection "the murder weapon used by the defendant in this case." Were the defense to produce a knife in response to this request, an inference of a distinctly testimonial and incriminating nature would arise. In *Jones* the State sought even more. It sought not merely the production of described materials of which the prosecution was already aware. It also attempted to use the defendant's knowledge to discover whether other suspected evidence was in existence. This would have significantly increased the testimonial aspect of the compelled production.

In *Jones* the California Supreme Court ruled that discovery could properly be allowed only as to (1) the names and addresses of witnesses the defendant intended to call to the witness stand at trial and (2) reports and X-rays that he planned to offer in support of his impotence defense. This, the court said, would not require Jones to reveal anything that he was not already planning to reveal. Anything more would force the accused to disclose his knowledge of possible evidence. The court held that this would be violative of the accused's Fifth Amendment privilege.

Whether discovery procedures in criminal cases will ever closely parallel those presently available in civil suits and whether discovery in criminal cases will ever become a two-way street depends on the degree to which courts are willing to erode interests usually thought to be shielded by the Fifth Amendment. If the erosion is counterbalanced by an increase in the amount of pretrial discovery available to criminal defendants, courts can be expected to move toward more nearly parallel discovery procedures since they make for more accurate fact-finding in trials.

CHAPTER NINE

Exclusion of Identification Evidence Resulting from Improper Identification Confrontations

A. Factual Background of the Exclusionary Rules

The Nature and Characteristics of Pretrial Identification Confrontations

Often in criminal matters an eyewitness to the offense is requested by law enforcement agents to identify a suspect. One or more of three basic identification procedures will be employed:

1. *A lineup.* The suspect is presented for observation by the eyewitness in a group, usually of three persons or more.
2. *A showup.* The suspect is presented alone.
3. *A photograph.* The suspect is presented to the eyewitness in photographs. A single photograph may be displayed, or the suspect's photograph may be included in a group of photographs of other persons. The photograph of the suspect may show him alone or in a group shot.

If the eyewitness identifies the suspect as having been the perpetrator of the alleged crime, he or she will usually be asked at the time of trial to make an in-court identification.

EXAMPLE:

BY THE PROSECUTING ATTORNEY: Ms. Stitz, you have described the events on the night of April 1, 1989. I now ask you whether you see in this courtroom the man you have described as being your attacker?

A: I see him.

Q: Would you point him out to the court and jury, please. Don't be nervous.

A: There he is. [Indicating.] He is sitting at the table right behind Mr. Ryan.

BY THE PROSECUTING ATTORNEY: Let the record reflect that the witness has pointed to and identified the accused in this case, Clyde Bushmat.

Q: Lest there be any question about it, Ms. Stitz, would you please step down off the witness stand and go over and touch the man whom you have identified on the shoulder. [Witness complies.]

BY THE PROSECUTING ATTORNEY: Let the record further reflect that in response to counsel's request the witness stepped down and placed her hand on the left shoulder of the accused in this case, Clyde Bushmat. Thank you, Ms. Stitz.

In many jurisdictions an eyewitness can also be asked whether he or she made a pretrial identification of the accused in the case. Thus the foregoing example could be extended in the following fashion:

BY THE PROSECUTING ATTORNEY: Now, let me ask you another question, Ms. Stitz. Have you ever on any occasion previous to today identified anyone as having been the man who assaulted you?

A: Yes, sir, I did.

Q: On how many occasions?

A: One.

Q: Would you tell us about it, please.

A: Well, the police had what they called a lineup. I was called down to the Markham Avenue Police Station and they had me sit in a sort of auditorium. There was a lighted platform and the sergeant marched five men onto it. They asked me if I saw the man who had attacked me last April and I said that I did. They asked me to point him out and I pointed my finger at him. He was the second man from the left.

Q: And who was the man that you pointed out in the police lineup?

A: The same man I have identified here today.

Beyond doubt, eyewitness identification testimony of this sort is usually damning unless defense counsel can somehow cast doubt on its worth. Because of the high impact of eyewitness identification testimony, the Supreme Court has stated that pretrial identification procedures constitute a critical stage of the criminal prosecution effort. This conclusion reflected the Court's recognition of the potential for prejudice inherent in procedures which it thought were "peculiarly riddled with innumerable dangers and variable factors which might seriously, even critically, derogate from a fair trial." (*Stovall* v. *Denno,* 388 U.S. 293 (1967).) Obviously, a mistaken identification of a suspect could be disastrous to an innocent person; on the identification testimony of one witness alone the suspect could be consigned to a lifetime in prison or even execution. This is not an idle concern. Data assembled and evaluated by the Supreme Court of the United States has demonstrated the hazards to suspects of unfair practices in identification procedures. The following are some lineup examples that impressed the justices:

1. Everyone in the lineup except the suspect was known to the identifying witness;
2. Other participants in the lineup were grossly dissimilar in appearance to the suspect;
3. Only the suspect was required to wear distinctive clothing of a type that the culprit allegedly wore;
4. The witness was told by the police that the culprit had been caught, after which the suspect was brought before the witness alone or is viewed in jail;
5. The suspect was pointed out to the witness by police officers before or during the lineup;
6. The participants in the lineup were asked to try on an article of clothing that would fit only the suspect;
7. The suspect was the only Oriental in the lineup;
8. The suspect, known to be a youth, was placed in a lineup with five other men, all of whom were over forty years of age.

Other researchers have catalogued numerous cases of misidentification by one or more eyewitnesses, resulting in later convictions of innocent persons. Probably the most famous of these disturbing catalogues is Edmund Borchard's CONVICTING THE INNOCENT.

B. The Emergence of Exclusionary Rules

Three Leading Cases

In a series of three cases decided in 1967 the Supreme Court recognized the "dangers inherent in eyewitness identification and the suggestibility inherent in the context of the pretrial identification." It was the Court's belief that a suggestive identification procedure could result in misidentification. Because it is human nature to adhere to first impressions, a misidentification made during a pretrial identification procedure is likely to cast the die, to crystallize the witness's opinion; he is likely to make the same misidentification at trial.

In two of its three 1967 decisions the Supreme Court held that a post-indictment, pretrial identification procedure is a critical stage of the prosecution effort. Denial of legal counsel at this crucial stage, the Court ruled, would violate the Constitution's Sixth Amendment, which provides that "in all criminal prosecutions, the accused shall enjoy the right . . . to have the assistance of counsel for his defense." The Court believed that the availability of counsel would go far toward avoiding prejudice to a suspect stemming from suggestive identification procedures and would assist counsel in mounting a meaningful cross-examination of eyewitnesses at the time of trial. The two cases referred to are *United States* v. *Wade*, 388 U.S. 218 (1967), and *Gilbert* v. *California*, 388 U.S. 263 (1967). *Wade* involved a federal bank robbery prosecution in which a post-indictment lineup was conducted without notice to the accused's appointed lawyer; *Gilbert* was virtually identical to *Wade* except that it involved a state prosecution for aggravated robbery and murder. Again the Court held that evidence resulting from a pretrial lineup is to be excluded at trial if the accused was deprived of counsel at the earlier juncture.

The third case in this trilogy was *Stovall* v. *Denno*, 388 U.S. 293 (1967). In this case the victim had been hospitalized with multiple stab wounds. The accused was taken to the hospital in handcuffs. At the bedside of the victim, whose survival was in doubt, the accused, who was the only black person in the room, was identified by the victim as having been her assailant. The identification was made after a police officer asked the victim whether this "was the man" and after the accused, at a police officer's request, had repeated a number of words for voice identification purposes. The accused contended that this one-to-one confrontation was unfair, and therefore in violation of the Fourteenth Amendment's Due Process Clause, because it strongly suggested to the victim-witness that he was the one suspected of having committed the crime.

Stovall v. *Denno*, it will be seen, presented both a factual picture and an issue different from those presented in *Wade* and *Gilbert*. The latter two cases involved lineups and the Sixth Amendment right to counsel. In *Stovall* the identification procedure was more in the nature of a showup and the Fourteenth Amendment was relied on by the accused. The Supreme Court was willing to recognize the Due Process Clause of this Amendment as a ground of challenge. If the identification procedure "was so unnecessarily suggestive and conducive to irreparable mistaken identification," due process would have been denied to the accused. The Court made it clear that the "totality of circumstances" in every case would have to be taken into account.

C. The Dual Approach of *Wade* and *Gilbert*

The *Wade* and *Gilbert* cases set up a dual approach:

1. A pretrial, postindictment identification made during the course of a procedure in which the suspect's right to counsel or to due process of law was denied will be inadmissible at trial, since in these situa-

tions the identification was "the direct result of the illegal lineup 'come at by exploitation of [the primary] illegality."

2. An in-court identification of the suspect at trial, following an improper pretrial, postindictment identification, will also be inadmissible under *Wade* and *Gilbert* unless the prosecution can establish by clear and convincing evidence that the in-court identification either (a) had an origin wholly *independent* of the improper pretrial confrontation or (b) constituted harmless error in light of all the other incriminating evidence against the accused.

D. *Wade* and *Gilbert* Undercut

The Kirby *Decision*

Despite the fact that the Supreme Court in both *Wade* and *Gilbert* was careful to refer only to pretrial identification procedures occurring *after* an accused's indictment, most lower courts thereafter held that the *Wade-Gilbert* right to counsel doctrine was also applicable to preindictment identification procedures. With the change in the Court's makeup brought about by President Richard M. Nixon's appointments, this approach has been condemned and the *Wade-Gilbert* right to counsel doctrine has been so sharply restricted as to be of no large importance today. The clarification of *Wade's* and *Gilbert's* scope came in *Kirby* v. *Illinois,* 406 U.S. 682, decided in 1972. The facts were these: Thomas Kirby and Ralph Bean were convicted of robbery. The evidence against them included a preindictment showup identification made at a police station at a time when the two men had no legal counsel. Kirby and Bean had been walking along Madison Street in Chicago on the day of their arrest. They were stopped by two policemen and asked to produce identification. At trial one of the policemen testified that the men were stopped because Kirby resembled a wanted man whose picture was on a bulletin in his cruiser. When Kirby opened his billfold, this policeman observed traveler's checks made out to one "Willie Shard." The two men were arrested and taken to police headquarters when Kirby was unable to give a satisfactory explanation for his possession of the traveler's checks. At headquarters the policemen learned that a man named Willie Shard had been a robbery victim two days earlier. They sent for Shard. When he entered the room in which Kirby and Bean were being held, he identified them as the men who robbed him. Only the two suspects and the two policemen were in the room at the time of Shard's identification. At no time had Kirby and Bean been advised of their legal right to counsel.

Kirby and Bean were tried and convicted of robbery after a motion to suppress Shard's identification failed. Bean's conviction was reversed on appeal, but Kirby's was upheld by the Court of Appeals. The Supreme Court then agreed to consider the question whether there is a right to counsel at preindictment identification confrontations.

In a five to four decision, the Court declined to extend the *Wade-Gilbert* right to counsel doctrine to preindictment confrontations. It held that the Sixth Amendment's guarantee of counsel becomes operative only after the beginning of formal criminal proceedings by way of formal charge, arraignment, preliminary hearing, information, or indictment. (The *Miranda* right to counsel case, discussed in chapter 8, had no application to *Kirby; Miranda* is limited to protection of Fifth Amendment self-incrimination rights, an area not involved in *Kirby*.)

The Supreme Court apparently agreed with widespread criticism of the idea that lawyers should be present at lineups. This criticism has had numerous bases. It is difficult to obtain a lawyer for prompt on-the-scene identification efforts or for witnesses' examination of photographs at a time when the suspect is not in custody. Furthermore, it has been argued that a lawyer's presence does not eliminate the potential risks of unfairness that pretrial identification procedures may pose. A lawyer at a lineup can only take the passive role of observer. If the police wish to coach a witness privately, no lawyer can stop them. Not being trained psychologists, most lawyers are poorly equipped to detect more subtle influences that may lead to an identification. Lineup observation is a time-consuming police task that requires few if any legal skills. Finally, it is possible that the presence of a lawyer at a lineup will make witnesses reluctant to participate. They may fear that the defense lawyer will tell their names to the suspect or his associates, leading to retaliatory measures.

The *Kirby* holding was consistent with Section 3502 of the 1968 Omnibus Crime Control and Safe Streets Act: "The testimony of a witness that he saw the accused commit or participate in the commission of a crime for which the accused is being tried shall be admissible in evidence in a criminal prosecution in any [federal] trial court . . ." It was also consistent with a pre-*Wade* remark made by a man who was then a federal Court of Appeals judge. In *Williams* v. *United States,* 345 U.S. 733 (D.C. Cir. 1965), Judge Warren E. Burger, who was to be the Chief Justice of the United States by the time *Kirby* was decided, said that the accused's claim that his right to counsel had been violated by the absence of a lawyer at a police lineup was a "Disneyland" contention. Judge Burger thought that such arguments were being made by court-appointed lawyers who feared that they would be maligned by their clients if they did not raise every conceivable argument on their behalf. The judge felt that court-appointed defense counsel should "be entirely free to withdraw [from a case] rather than be compelled to advance absurd and nonsensical contentions on pain of a vicious attack from the jailhouse."

Since most pretrial identification procedures occur prior to indictment, the *Wade* and *Gilbert* decisions are no longer of much significance. From now on the crucial question will be the one inspired by *Stovall* v. *Denno.* That is, the key question will be whether any due process violations occurred at pretrial identification confrontations, not whether the suspect was allowed to have legal counsel present. In *United States* v. *Ash* (413 U.S.300) (1973), the Supreme Court unequivocally refused to extend the right of counsel to photographic displays conducted for purposes of witness identification. Whether or not the accused is in custody or the photographic display takes place after indictment, the Court decided that the right to counsel applies only when the physical presence of the accused himself is required. The Court thought that the photographic identification process is not so inherently subject to improper manipulation as to require the protective presence of legal counsel.

In 1988 the Supreme Court held, in *United States* v. *Owens,* ______ U.S. ______, 109 S. Ct. 2419, that testimony about an out-of-court identification by a declarant who later suffered a loss of memory violated neither the rule against hearsay nor the accused's rights of confrontation and cross-examination. (See Fed.R.Evid. 801(d)(1).)

E. *Stovall's* Due Process Approach

Fairness as the Key

The *Stovall* opinion concentrates not on the right to counsel at pretrial identification procedures but on the fair conduct of such procedures within the Fourteenth Amendment's meaning. By analogy, the dual approach of *Wade* and *Gilbert*, described above, will be applied to violations of due process under *Stovall.*

Unfortunately, but perhaps inevitably, *Stovall* does not provide any very helpful guidelines for the proper conduct of pretrial identification procedures. However, a survey of post-*Stovall* decisions permits some generalizations and some concrete examples.

Showups: a Dangerous Technique

The presentation of a suspect alone, a so-called showup as distinguished from a lineup, has been dubbed by one commentator "the most grossly suggestive identification procedure now or ever used by the police." (WALL, EYEWITNESS IDENTIFICATION IN CRIMINAL CASES 28 (1965).) In the *Wade* case the justices said that it would be difficult for them "to imagine a situation more clearly conveying the suggestion to the witnesses that the one presented is believed guilty by the police."

The message is clear. Showup procedures are likely to be considered unduly suggestive and thus violative of the Due Process Clause. Wherever possible, they should be avoided.

Courts are likely to approve of the showup method only when:

1. Compelling circumstances, such as those noted in *Stovall,* dictated the use of a showup rather than some more satisfactory alternative procedure;
2. "Fresh" identification and efficient law enforcement required an on-the-scene identification, as when the accused was rapidly apprehended and promptly returned to the scene of the crime; and
3. Extrinsic factors establish the accuracy of the showup identification.

However, since most judges are reluctant to scrap eyewitness identification evidence, courts with frequency find the existence of one or more of these bases for salvaging showup evidence.

EXAMPLE A:
In *Bates* v. *United States,* 405 F.2d 1104 (D.C. Cir. 1968), a housebreaker was apprehended within half an hour after the crime. He was returned to the scene and was identified by his victim as he sat alone in a patrol wagon. Judge (later Chief Justice) Burger said that "police action in returning the suspect to the vicinity of the crime for immediate identification . . . fosters the desirable objectives of fresh, accurate identification which in some instances may lead to immediate release of an innocent suspect and at the time enable the police to resume the search for the fleeing culprit while the trail is still fresh." Considering the "totality of the circumstances," any prejudice to the accused through the suggestive on-the-scene showup was outweighed by the freshness of the identification and the need for efficient criminal investigation methods.

EXAMPLE B:
In *Caruso* v. *United States,* 406 F.2d 558 (2d Cir. 1969), *cert. denied,* 396 U.S. 868 (1969), the accused was apprehended within fifteen minutes and returned to the scene of a bank robbery. The police required him to put on a ski hood that had been left at the scene. Three witnesses then identified him. Noting that even without the ski hood the suspect was distinctively garbed, the U.S. Court of Appeals held that this confrontation was neither suggestive nor conducive to misidentification because the confrontation took place so soon after the crime. It also held that requiring the suspect to wear the ski hood did not violate due process.

EXAMPLE C:
In *Young* v. *United States,* 407 F.2d 720 (D.C. Cir.), *cert. denied,* 394 U.S. 1007 (1969), the accused was apprehended and returned to the

scene within a few minutes of a robbery. The victim could not identify the suspect until the suspect had put on his own hat, sunglasses, and trench coat. The court said that "obliging appellant [the accused] to don his own apparel did not make the resulting identification less reliable; indeed, in the circumstances it is doubtful whether a reliable identification could have been made in the absence of the robber's distinctive accouterments."

Occasionally police do overreach sufficiently in the showup situation to convince the court that there has been a violation of due process of law. One especially flagrant example will make the point.

EXAMPLE:
In *State* v. *Cooper,* N.E.2d 653 (Comm. Pleas Ohio 1968), the police took four of the five eyewitnesses in a cruiser to "identify Mr. Cooper." The accused was presented to the group after the police had informed the witnesses that they "thought they have the right man." When two witnesses failed to make an identification, the suspect was required to put on glasses and a hat which were the fruits of an illegal search and seizure. All of the witnesses subsequently made a positive identification of the accused. Two of the victims then gave statements at police headquarters after again viewing the suspect in hat, glasses, and trench coat.

An Ohio judge said, "Each of the five things the police did would in and of itself be grossly suggestive and likely to result in a mistake. Together their effect is crushing and in this case not a single one of them was at all necessary to accomplish any legitimate police purpose."

Lineups

There is nothing inherently unfair about the lineup method of pretrial identification confrontation. Only if those conducting a lineup overreach themselves in an unfair effort to induce a positive identification will there be due process problems. A properly conducted lineup will withstand the closest judicial scrutiny. It is possible to describe the ideal lineup:

1. It would involve at least half a dozen participants.
2. These six or more persons would closely resemble each other in:
   (a) height
   (b) physical characteristics; and
   (c) attire.
3. All of the lineup participants would be presented to the witnesses simultaneously.
4. No undue attention would be drawn to any particular lineup participant.

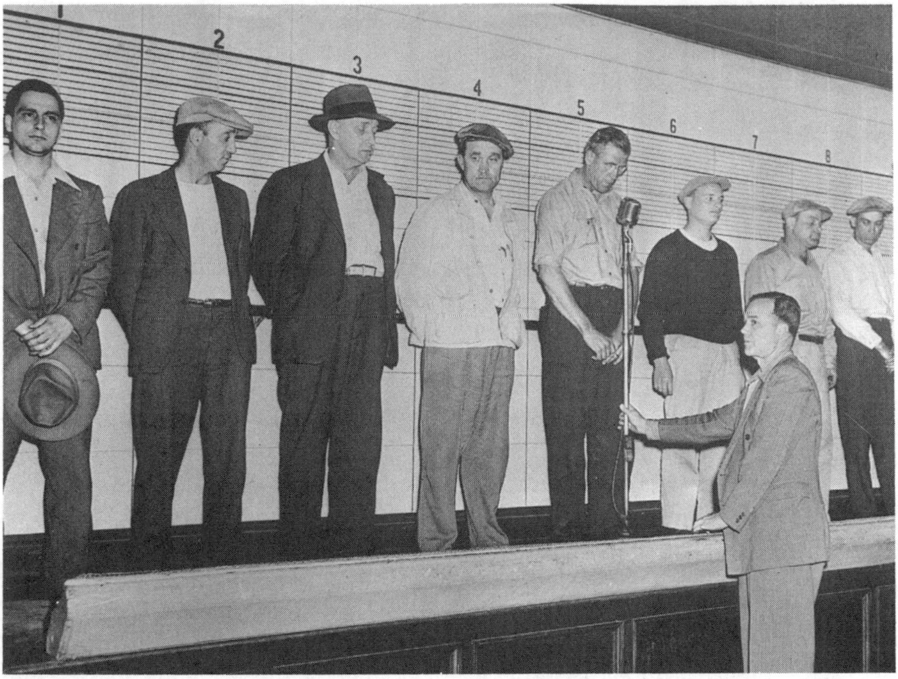

A police lineup from the early 1940s. Because a line-up identification can be highly incriminating, there are numerous restrictions on their use.

5. Witnesses would be allowed to request that the participants repeat a bodily movement or words used by the criminal, but all lineup participants, not just one of them, would be asked to comply with the request unless the witness specifically directs his or her request to a particular participant.
6. If there is more than one witness, each would convey his reactions to the police while separated from the other witnesses, thus avoiding being influenced by the opinions of the others.
7. The witnesses would be told that the question to be answered is not, "Which lineup member is the criminal?" but instead "Is the criminal in the lineup?"

By way of contrast, the following practices have been judicially condemned:

1. *Pre-Lineup Suggestion.* Prior to the formal lineup the witnesses are subjected to suggestions by means of statements made by policemen ("We think you'll find your man in this lineup."), photographs ("Here's a picture of your man."), a pre-lineup confrontation ("There's your

man, standing over there by the water cooler."), or multiple lineup confrontations in each of which the only repeater is the suspect.

2. *Lineup Suggestions.* The composition of the lineup itself and the conduct of participants in it may be unduly suggestive. The suspect may stand out from the other lineup members by reason of physical features and characteristics (height, scars, age, hair color, mustache, beard, etc.), race (the suspect is the only Hispanic participant in the lineup), or police suggestion (police officer tells one lineup member to step closer to the witnesses, "So they can get a better look at you, Charlie").

F. The Admissibility of In-Court Identification Following an Improper Pretrial Identification Confrontation

The Lingering Taint

An improper pretrial identification confrontation between a suspect and a witness may taint any subsequent in-court identification by that same witness and make it inadmissible as evidence. The notion is that an unduly suggestive or otherwise unfair identification procedure will cause any resulting identification, no matter how badly mistaken, to become firmly fixed—crystallized—in the witness's mind, with the consequence that he will simply parrot his identification, or misidentification, at the time of trial without really taking a new look at the accused. This does not mean, however, that every in-court identification that was preceded by an improper out-of-court identification will be excluded from evidence. Plainly, the Supreme Court has rejected a rigid rule of exclusion for unnecessarily suggestive identification procedures. Instead, it has opted for a balancing test based on the reliability of the identification procedure viewed against the "totality of the circumstances." (*Mason* v. *Brathwaite,* 432 U.S. 98 (1977).) Weighing the reliability of an identification procedure against its suggestiveness requires consideration of five factors earlier listed by the Court in *Neil* v. *Biggers,* 409 U.S. 188 (1972): (1) the opportunity of the identifying witness to observe the suspect at the time of the alleged crime; (2) the level of the witness's attention at that time; (3) the accuracy of any earlier description by the witness; (4) the degree of the witness's credibility at the time of the challenged identification confrontation; and (5) the time-lapse between crime and confrontation. Suggestiveness, standing alone, will not preclude admission of an identification that appears nonetheless to be reliable. (See, for example, *United States* v. *Leonardi,* 623 F.2d 746 (2d Cir. 1980) (photo spread may have been suggestive, but in-court identification was reliable by *Biggers* standards).)

Independent Source of Identification

An in-court identification will be received in evidence if the prosecution can establish that its witness's identification is traceable not to an improper pretrial identification procedure but rather to some independent origin. Courts have attached weight to a variety of factual situations in trying to decide whether such an independent source existed. Some of the more important recurring fact-pictures have been these:

1. *Length of Opportunity for Observation of the Criminal.* The length of time during which the eyewitness was able to observe the criminal at the time of the offense is the most commonly encountered evidentiary factor. If the witness had a lengthy opportunity to observe the criminal, courts are likely to conclude that his or her in-court identification is traceable to the time of the crime rather than to an improper later confrontation; the shorter the period of observation, the more likely courts are to decide that the witness's in-court identification was produced by the antecedent improper confrontation.

> EXAMPLE:
> In *People* v. *Ballot,* 233 N.E.2d 103 (Ct. App. N.Y. 1967), an in-court identification was excluded from evidence because the chance for observation at the time of the offense was minimal. The court stated that the victim had observed the robber "but for a few minutes during a frightening and upsetting episode." Because of this, the court concluded, "We cannot say . . . that . . . the in-court identification was not predicated, at least in part, upon the earlier grossly and unnecessarily suggestive showup in the police station a year after the crime had been committed."

As might be expected, courts take a fairly flexible view of what is a "short" and what is a "long" period of observation on the part of an eyewitness. For example, in *Hill* v. *State,* 252 A.2d 259 (Md. App. 1969), the court decided that, under the prevailing circumstances, eighteen seconds was a sufficient observation-span to support the reliability of an in-court identification.

2. *The Speed with Which the Pretrial Identification Was Made.* If a pretrial identification was made positively and without hesitation, courts have inferred that there was instant recognition by the witness, traceable to his observation of the crime and not to the suggestiveness of the identification confrontation. (On the other hand, one court has suggested that hesitation in making an identification may indicate that the witness is endeavoring to be absolutely fair and certain.)

3. *Length of Time Between the Crime and the Pretrial Identification.* Subsequent to the *Stovall* decision, some lower courts have considered the length of time elapsing between the crime and the pretrial identification to be significant. If the length of time was brief, courts have been more willing to conclude that the pretrial identification was a product of the witness's observation of the crime, not the assertedly suggestive identification

confrontation. Again, courts have taken a flexible attitude. By way of example, in *Lucas* v. *State,* 44 S.W.2d 638 (Tex. Crim. App. 1969), the court held that two months was a "short" time lapse.

In *United States* v. *Crews,* 445 U.S. 463 (1980), the Supreme Court held that an otherwise valid pretrial identification is admissible even though the accused's custody at the time was unlawful. In *Crews* the accused had been unlawfully arrested. He was then identified by his victim at both a photographic procedure and a lineup. The trial court suppressed these identifications as the fruits of an illegal arrest, but the Supreme Court reversed because the identifications had had a source, a foundation, independent of the unlawful custody. The identifier had formed a mental picture of the suspect during the crime; this was an "independent recollection" untainted by the illegal arrest and the identifier's subsequent opportunities to observe the accused. (See also *United States* v. *Flenory,* 619 F.2d 301 (3d Cir. 1980).)

Harmless Error

Occasionally, but not often, courts have used the doctrine of *harmless error* to salvage a conviction based on a tainted in-court identification. In other words, the reviewing court holds that receipt of the in-court identification testimony was legally erroneous—a mistake on the part of the trial judge—but that its receipt did not harm the accused.

There are two bases on which an appellate court can conclude that the receipt of a tainted in-court identification was harmless (nonprejudicial) error:

1. The appellate court may conclude that the accused was not prejudiced by the in-court identification testimony because the witness could have identified him irrespective of any improper pretrial identification confrontation. In fact, this is simply a version of the independent source doctrine that was described earlier in this chapter.
2. Sometimes a reviewing court will conclude that admission of a tainted in-court identification was harmless error because the prosecution's other evidence of the defendant's guilt, even though perhaps largely circumstantial, was overwhelming.

G. Efforts to Draft Standards Regulating Pretrial Identification Practices

The Clark County, Nevada, Approach

A set of regulations drawn up jointly by the district attorney and the public defender of Clark County, Nevada, has attracted favorable reactions. It provides a useful checklist for police lineups:

1. No lineup identification should be held without discussing the legal advisability of such lineup with the office of the district attorney.
2. No lineup should be held without a member of the district attorney's office being present.
3. No lineup should be held without a member of the public defender's office (or privately retained counsel, if any) being present.
4. Insofar as possible, all persons in a lineup should be of the same general age, racial and physical characteristics (including dress).
5. Should any body movement, gesture, or verbal statement be necessary, this should also be done uniformly and repeated only at the express request of the person attempting to make identification.
6. The customary lineup photograph should be taken, developed as soon as possible and a copy of such photograph made available immediately to the public defender's office.
7. If more than one person is called to view a lineup, the persons should not be allowed, before the completion of all witnesses' attempted identification, to discuss among themselves any facet of their view of the lineup or the result of their conclusions regarding the same.
8. All witnesses who are to view the lineup should be prevented from seeing the suspect in custody and in particular in handcuffs, or in any manner that would indicate to the witness the identity of the suspect in question.
9. All efforts should be made to prevent a witness from viewing any photographs of the suspect prior to giving the lineup.
10. All conversation between the police officer and prospective witnesses should be restricted to only indispensable discussion. In all cases nothing should be said to the witness to suggest suspect is standing in the particular lineup.
11. Should there be any more than one witness, only one witness at a time should be present in the room where the lineup is conducted.
12. There should be a minimum of persons present in the room where the lineup is conducted, and a suggested group would be the law enforcement officer conducting the lineup, a representative of the public defender's office and an investigator of that office if requested by the public defender.
13. The lineup report prepared by the law enforcement agency conducting the lineup should be prepared in sufficient number of copies to make a copy available, at the lineup, to the public defender.
14. Each witness, as he appears in the room where the lineup is conducted, should be handed a form for use in the identification. Explanation for the use of the form is self-explanatory and a sample copy is attached hereto. This form should be signed by the witness, by a representative

of the public defender's office, and by the law enforcement officer conducting the lineup.

15. A copy of this identification form should be given to the public defender's office at the completion of the viewing of the lineup by each individual witness.

The American Law Institute Approach

The prestigious American Law Institute has tried its hand at drafting a proposed statute to govern pretrial identification procedures. The Institute's proposal reads as follows:

1. Restrictions on Identification. No law enforcement officer shall conduct a lineup or otherwise attempt, by having a witness view or hear the voice of an arrested person, to secure the identification of an arrested person as a person involved in crime unless such identification procedure is authorized by this section.
2. Presence of Counsel or Other Witness. An identification procedure is authorized by this section if:
   a. counsel for the arrested person is present or has consented thereto;
   b. counsel for the arrested person has received reasonable notice and opportunity to be present at such procedure, but refuses or fails to be present;
   c. counsel for the arrested person designates some other person to be present at such procedure, and such other person is given a reasonable opportunity to be present;
   d. the arrested person is unable to obtain counsel to represent him at such identification procedure and there is present a lawyer specifically designated [in accordance with prescribed procedures], who shall represent such person at the identification procedure;
   e. the arrested person, having been informed of his right to be represented by counsel as provided in this section, waives such representation, *provided* that the arrested person may designate some other person to be present, and such other person must be given notice and a reasonable opportunity to be present at such procedure; or
   f. awaiting the presence of counsel or such other person as the arrested person or his counsel designates is likely to prejudice the possibility of making an identification.
3. Required Procedures: Regulations. An identification procedure is authorized by this section only if there has been compliance with regu-

lations, to be issued pursuant to Section 1.03 [of Tentative Draft No. 1], setting forth procedures designed to insure

a. that identifications will not be erroneous or otherwise prejudice the rights of the arrested person; and

b. that written, sound and visual records, and disinterested testimony, will be available so far as necessary to verify the conditions under which such identification procedures were conducted.

CHAPTER TEN

Unreasonable Searches and Seizures of Evidence; Evidentiary Protection of the Right to Privacy

A. The Constitutional Background

The Fourth Amendment to the U.S. Constitution

The Fourth Amendment to the federal Constitution, dealing with searches for and the seizure of evidence, reads as follows:

> The right of the people to be secure in their persons, houses, papers and effects, against unreasonable searches and seizures, shall not be violated, and no Warrants shall issue, but upon probable cause, supported by Oath or affirmation, and particularly describing the place to be searched, and the persons or things to be seized.

Pre-1914 Background

Neither the common law nor early constitutional law contained any rule requiring the exclusion at trial of evidence that had been obtained improperly by law enforcement agents. To paraphrase Justice Benjamin Cardozo, the courts were unwilling to let a guilty man go free merely because the police had blundered. Furthermore, judges were reluctant to detour away from the main issues of a criminal case to explore the collateral and sometimes complicated question of the legality of the evidence-gathering methods of the police. A change in these attitudes came in 1914.

Emergence of an Exclusionary Rule in the Federal Cases

In *Weeks* v. *United States,* 232 U.S. 383, decided in 1914, the U.S. Supreme Court held that evidence obtained in violation of the Fourth Amendment was not admissible in federal criminal cases. If there were no exclusionary rule, said the Court, "the protection of the Fourth Amendment . . . might as well be stricken from the Constitution." The Court would not "affirm by judicial decision a manifest neglect if not an open defiance of the . . . Constitution." The Court would back up the commands of the Fourth Amendment with a rule that any evidence obtained in violation of those commands would be inadmissible at trial.

Applicability of the Exclusionary Rule to State Proceedings

At first the Supreme court was unwilling to apply the *Weeks* exclusionary rule to the states. In *Wolf* v. *Colorado,* 338 U.S. 25 (1949), the Court, although not backing away from its holding in *Weeks* that the Fourth Amendment barred the use of evidence obtained through an illegal search and seizure, decided that the *Weeks* exclusionary rule would not be imposed upon the states, at least at that time. However, in 1961 the Court did an about-face and ruled that the *Weeks* rule of exclusion would henceforth be applicable to state criminal proceedings.

The Court's reversal of position came about in *Mapp* v. *Ohio,* 367 U.S. 643 (1961). The defendant, Ms. Mapp, was charged with possession of obscene materials. The Supreme Court of Ohio upheld her conviction while explicitly observing that her conviction had been "based primarily upon the introduction in evidence of lewd and lascivious books and pictures unlawfully seized during an unlawful search of defendant's home." The Ohio court, justifiably pointing to the U.S. Supreme Court's decision in *Wolf* v. *Colorado,* said that the State was not prevented from using unconstitutionally seized evidence against defendant Mapp.

But the Supreme Court reversed the Ohio court. It first drew attention to its decision in *Weeks* v. *United States,* in which it had for the first time declared that in a *federal* prosecution the Fourth Amendment prevented the use of evidence obtained by means of an unlawful search and seizure. It then stated that *Wolf* v. *Colorado,* which declined to extend the *Weeks* exclusionary rule to the states, had been based on "factual grounds." The principal factual ground was that in 1949, before the *Wolf* decision, almost two-thirds of the states were opposed to the use of an exclusionary rule as a penalty for illegal searches and seizures. By the time of *Mapp,* however, more than half of the states that had considered the question had adopted an exclusionary rule of the *Weeks* type, even though under *Wolf* they were not obligated to do so. The California Supreme Court had announced that an exclusionary rule patterned after *Weeks* was vital because other remedies—for example, civil suits against lawless policemen—had failed to secure compliance with constitutional prohibitions against unreasonable searches and seizures of evidence.

Accordingly, the U.S. Supreme Court in *Mapp* concluded that the most crucial factual consideration underlying *Wolf* was no longer controlling. It spoke now of a "right to privacy free from unreasonable state intrusion." And it held that this right of privacy, derived from the language of the Fourth Amendment, was applicable to the states through the Fourteenth Amendment's Due Process Clause. Finally, it held that this right of privacy was enforceable against states by the sanction of a *Weeks*-type exclusionary rule. If you do not get your evidence in the right way, then you cannot use it against the accused, the Court said.

The potency of the expectation of privacy rationale was reconfirmed by the Supreme Court's ruling that random vehicle registration and license checks are an unreasonable invasion of privacy. (*Delaware* v. *Prouse,* 440 U.S. 648 (1979).)

Policy Bases of the Exclusionary Rule

The Supreme Court's *Mapp* opinion makes it quite plain that the primary function of the exclusionary rule is to "police the police" by removing any incentive to violate the Fourth Amendment. This has not saved the rule from severe criticism, however. In the first place, it has been suggested that an exclusionary rule is not an especially effective tool for enforcing constitutional requirements. Some law enforcement agents may simply be unaware of the Fourth Amendment's demands. And a few, fully aware of those demands, may be willing to ignore them and to lie about having ignored them.

Even if it be assumed that the exclusionary rule serves its policing purpose, it has often been argued that it does so at too great a cost in the loss of probative evidence of criminal guilt. Does an exclusionary rule create a proper balance between individual and social interests? It can result in freedom for a menace to society. That undeserved freedom may stem from the blundering of a single law enforcement agent. No matter how competently other members of a criminal investigation team accomplish their work, one officer can bestow immunity on a guilty person by illegally obtaining a damning item of evidence. Among other things, this places a premium on compliance with the rules of the chase. There are those who argue that what is more important is the capturing and immobilizing of dangerous criminals.

Lastly, it is sometimes contended that there are better and less costly ways to enforce the requirements of the Fourth Amendment. Although civil liability to the victims of police misconduct is not a completely realistic suggestion, criminal prosecution of policemen who abuse the rights of suspects can be a potent deterrent. And as the President's Task Force on the Police pointed out in 1967, the best answer may lie in the careful working out of internal police standards and enforcement procedures.

Despite the arguments against it, the exclusionary rule is still with us. It is still with us mainly because judges take a moral position that the use of tainted evidence would suggest that the courts were turning their backs on the Constitution. Because the exclusionary rule still has vitality, all law enforcement agents must have a firm grasp of the Fourth Amendment's requirements.

B. Proceedings in Which the Exclusionary Rule Can Be Invoked

Criminal Proceedings

Before getting into the details of the Fourth Amendment's requirements, consideration should be given to the range of proceedings, criminal and civil, to which the *Weeks* exclusionary rule may be applicable.

It is perfectly clear that the rule excluding improperly obtained evidence is applicable at the trial of a criminal case. On the other hand, its applicability to the pretrial stages of a criminal matter is doubtful. It is generally held that the *Weeks* rule is not available to an accused at a preliminary hearing, although there are a few decided cases to the contrary. It has also been ruled that a grand jury indictment is not invalidated because improperly obtained evidence was considered by the jurors during their deliberations. From this, and from the practical difficulty an accused would have in trying to make an effective objection at the grand jury stage (there being neither defense counsel nor a judge present in the grand jury room), it was long assumed that the exclusionary rule had little or no influence on grand jury proceedings. Then, in early 1974, the Supreme court confirmed the longstanding assumption. In *United States* v. *Calandra,* 414 U.S. 338 (1974), the Court limited the application of the exclusionary rules to trials only. Specifically, it held that the exclusionary rule was not applicable to grand jury proceedings. Justice Lewis F. Powell wrote that the Fourth Amendment does not require the "adoption of every proposal that might deter police misconduct." Besides, he said, extending the exclusionary rule to grand jury proceedings "would deter only police investigation consciously directed toward the discovery of evidence solely for use in grand jury investigation." The *Calandra* opinion reversed a federal Court of Appeals decision holding that the Fourth Amendment barred a grand jury from forcing a witness to answer questions that were based upon illegally seized evidence. The case involved John Calandra, whose Cleveland, Ohio, tool company had been searched in 1970 by federal agents with a warrant to search for gambling equipment. No gambling devices were found, but the agents discovered records evidencing a loan shark operation. When Calandra was summoned before a grand jury, he refused to answer questions about the records and moved to suppress the evidence on the grounds that the search exceeded the scope of the warrant.

In his *Calandra* opinion Justice Powell pointed out that grand jury questions based on unlawfully obtained evidence "involve no independent governmental invasion of one's person, house, papers, or effects, but rather the usual abridgement of personal privacy common to all grand jury questioning." Since illegally obtained evidence is still not admissible at trial, Justice Powell felt that the *Calandra* ruling left intact an adequate deterrent to overreaching police conduct.

Moving to the post-trial period, a number of courts have held that the *Weeks* rule will not prevent improperly seized evidence from being considered by a judge when sentencing a convicted defendant. The Court of Appeals for the Ninth Circuit held, in the widely followed case of *United States* v. *Winsett,* 518 F.2d 51 (9th Cir. 1975), that the rule is inapplicable at a probation revocation hearing. Other federal courts have held the rule inapplicable at parole revocation hearings. The rationale for many of these decisions is that the post-trial period is too far removed from the work-a-day practices of law enforcement agents to have any appreciable deterrent effect on their possibly unlawful conduct.

Civil Cases

The exclusionary rule has been held applicable in certain sorts of civil cases that are at least vaguely criminal in nature, so-called quasi-criminal actions. Thus the rule has been claimed successfully in civil proceedings for narcotics addict commitment, in proceedings to oust a judge from the bench, in proceedings to declare the forfeiture of a motor vehicle used to transport untaxed liquor, and in liquor license cancellation proceedings. These proceedings may not be precisely criminal in nature but in them the State is using the improperly obtained evidence in much the same way, and for much the same purposes, as it uses it in truly criminal proceedings. If such evidence cannot be introduced in a criminal proceeding, the policies underlying the *Weeks* doctrine generally dictate that it cannot be used in other proceedings to which the State is a party and where the goal is penalization of the defendant.

However, one Supreme Court decision, *United States* v. *Janis,* 428 U.S. 433 (1976), brings into question the continued viability of the exclusionary rule in quasi-criminal cases. The case involved Max Janis, who was under investigation by the Los Angeles police for bookmaking. Law enforcement agents seized Janis' wagering records pursuant to a warrant. Later, one of the officers turned the records over to the IRS, which assessed Janis for wagering excise taxes. At his state criminal trial, Janis successfully challenged the initial search and the gambling records were excluded, so the issue facing the U.S. Supreme Court was whether the evidence upon which the IRS assessment was based should be excluded from a civil tax proceeding. A majority of the Supreme Court ignored the close relationship between enforcement of federal tax laws and state gambling laws. Specifically, the Court held that the exclusionary rule should be extended to forbid the use, in the civil proceeding of one sovereign, of evidence illegally seized by criminal law enforcement agents of another sovereign. This holding is important as a revival of the "silver platter" doctrine in civil cases. But it also signals a strong predilection on the part of the Court to limit application of the exclusionary rule to purely criminal cases.

Few courts have confronted the situation in which a private individual, in a case in which the government is not a party, makes use of evidence improperly obtained by law enforcement agents. The tendency is to conclude that the exclusionary rule has no application. However, there are some cases like *Lebel* v. *Swincicki,* 93 N.W.2d 281 (S. Ct. Mich. 1958), in which it was held that blood taken from the defendant by a policeman in violation of the state constitution was not admissible in a civil damage action arising out of a traffic accident.

There is also confusion about whether the *Weeks* rule should apply where a private individual has himself obtained evidence improperly and used it in a lawsuit to which the government is not a party. It would seem strange were a private individual to have a right to seize evidence in a way prohibited to agents of law enforcement. On the other hand, it might be argued that the state has not deprived anyone of due process, within the Fourteenth Amendment's meaning, where the challenged evidence was seized by a private person in a case in which the state had no real interest. The answer to this contention is that there is sufficient state action where the evidence is employed in a private lawsuit that culminates in a judgment that is judicially enforceable. And the policies underlying the *Weeks* rule favor application of the exclusionary rule in this situation.

C. Applicability of the Exclusionary Rule to Evidence Improperly Obtained by State Agents and Used in a Federal Criminal Proceeding

Occasionally state law enforcement agents obtain evidence illegally and turn it over to federal prosecutors for use in a federal criminal action. In *Elkins* v. *United States,* 364 U.S. 206 (1960), the Supreme Court decided that the exclusionary rule was applicable to unlawfully obtained evidence given to federal prosecutors on a "silver platter" by state agents.

All that is left for consideration, then, is the status of evidence that has been improperly obtained by private persons and turned over to the prosecution for use in a criminal case. It might seem to follow from the *Elkins* decision that the exclusionary rule would be applicable to privately obtained evidence that is offered in a criminal prosecution, but the courts have taken a different view.

D. Applicability of the Exclusionary Rule to Evidence Improperly Obtained by Private Persons and Used in a Criminal Proceeding

The *Elkins* case notwithstanding, state and federal courts alike have said that evidence obtained by private persons is admissible against an accused in a criminal case even though it was secured by means which would be violative of the Fourth Amendment had law enforcement agents used them.

EXAMPLE A:
In *Burdeau* v. *McDowell,* 256 U.S. 465 (1921), the defendant moved to suppress evidence which private persons had stolen from him and turned over to an assistant attorney general. The Supreme Court reversed the order of suppression, saying that the Fourth Amendment was intended only as a limitation on the activities of a sovereign authority. (See also *United States* v. *Jacobsen,* 466 U.S. 109 (1984).)

EXAMPLE B:
In *United States* v. *Andrews,* 618 F.2d 646 (10th cir. 1980), an airline employee searched a suspicious airfreight package, discovering cocaine. Exclusionary rule inapplicable.

EXAMPLE C:
In *Coolidge* v. *New Hampshire,* 403 U.S. 443 (1971), murder suspect's wife, on her own initiative, searched for her husband's guns and clothing and brought them to the police station. Exclusionary rule inapplicable.

While it is plain that the exclusionary rule does not apply where the questioned search or seizure is conducted solely by a private individual, participation by law enforcement agents complicates the situation. Generally, if a law enforcement agent joins in an illegal private search or if the private individual perpetrates a lawless search at the behest of an officer, evidence discovered will be excluded.

EXAMPLE:
In *State* v. *Boynton,* 574 P.2d 1330 (S. Ct. Ha. 1978), an informant was actively recruited and paid by police to secure information about drugs. His illegal intrusion by climbing a fence constituted an unreasonable search by the government, and the evidence secured was inadmissible.

E. The Meaning of "Searches and Seizures"

Definitions

What the Fourth Amendment protects citizens against is "searches and seizures" that are "unreasonable." The content of a term like "unreasonable" is a genuine riddle. Before attacking that riddle, however, it is essential as a threshold matter to figure out what is meant by the phrase "searches and seizures" in order fully to describe the legal obligations of law enforcement agents. This is more easily said than done because the Fourth Amendment today applies to the broadest imaginable range of fact-situations that a law enforcement agent can encounter. But some generalizations, at least, are possible.

Privacy

At the outset it must be said that the philosophy behind the Fourth Amendment is that American citizens are entitled to reasonable expectations of privacy. The Supreme Court has viewed the amendment in this light.

The Meaning of "Searches"

A search has two basic elements, one *mental* and one *physical*.

1. *The Mental Element.* A search is obviously an exploration or quest; thus in *Weeks* v. *United States*, 232 U.S. 383 (1914), the Supreme court said that "a search ordinarily implies a quest by an officer of the law." But a search involving no additional intent on the law officer's part would hardly seem offensive to the Fourth Amendment. An additional mental element must be involved. That mental element is the intent on the law officer's part to seize (take possession of) the object of his search.
2. *The Physical Element.* From the foregoing it becomes plain that the physical component of a search consists of some action on the law officer's part aimed at affecting the seizure in a way that impinges on a person's reasonable expectation of privacy regarding the object of the search.

A search of constitutional dimensions occurs when governmental action impinges on an individual's legitimate expectation of privacy. Included within this definition are activities which range from physical entry to electronic surveillance; from the use of marijuana-sniffing dogs to the employment of high-powered telescopes. Indeed, the investigating officer may not even be looking for evidence of a crime. But if his activities place him in violation of an individual's legitimate expectation of privacy, he is "searching" in the constitutional sense and is thus bound by the Fourth Amendment's warrant requirement.

Of course, the rub to all this is the phrase "legitimate expectation of privacy." Initially, it should be observed that these "expectations" define the scope of the Fourth Amendment's protection. In *Katz* v. *United States,* 389 U.S. 347 (1967), a case which involved warrantless electronic surveillance of a public telephone booth, the U.S. Supreme Court said that "the Fourth Amendment protects people, not places. What a person knowingly exposes to the public, even in his own home or office is not a subject of Fourth Amendment protection. But what he seeks to preserve as private, even in an area accessible to the public, may be constitutionally protected." Justice Harlan, in his concurring opinion, formulated the now widely accepted test for determining where the privacy line is drawn between citizens and their government: "There is a two-fold requirement," he said, "first that a person have exhibited an actual (subjective) expectation of privacy and, second that the expectation be one society is prepared to recognize as reasonable/legitimate." The Court further concluded that Mr. Katz reasonably/legitimately relied on the privacy of the telephone booth.

There is no actual (subjective) expectation of privacy and hence no Fourth Amendment protection where a person conveys information to third parties who, in turn, give it to law enforcement officials. In this vein, the Supreme Court has held there is no legitimate expectation of privacy regarding bank records (*U.S.* v. *Miller,* 425 U.S. 435 (1975)), or the numbers one dials into a telephone system (*Smith* v. *Maryland,* 442 U.S. 735 (1979)), because the employees of the bank and the telephone company have access to that information. People assume the risk that they will turn their records over to the police. Similarly, we exhibit no expectation of privacy when we conduct our affairs within the sight or earshot of others.

However, Justice Harlan's *Katz* test also requires that expectations of privacy be reasonable/legitimate. In making this assessment, the Supreme Court has considered a number of factors. Of importance, first, is whether the individual claiming protection of the Fourth Amendment took normal precautions to maintain his or her privacy.

EXAMPLE A:
In *United States* v. *Chadwick,* 433 U.S. 1 (1977), the defendants placed marijuana inside a double-locked footlocker, manifesting an expectation that the contents would remain free from public scrutiny.

EXAMPLE B:
In *Arkansas* v. *Sanders,* 442 U.S. 753 (1979), the Court concluded that while other areas of a taxi could be searched pursuant to a lawful stop, a closed suitcase in the car's trunk could not be opened without a warrant.

Second, the Court has examined the way a person has used a location to determine whether the Fourth Amendment should protect his or her expectations of privacy.

EXAMPLE:
In *Jones* v. *United States,* 362 U.S. 257 (1960), the Court found that the defendant had a Fourth Amendment privacy interest in an apartment in which he had slept and in which he kept his clothing.

Third, areas of Fourth Amendment privacy are sometimes defined by the Court through reference to history.

EXAMPLE:
In *United States* v. *Chadwick,* 433 U.S. 1, 8 (1977), the Court said: "Although the searches and seizures which . . . were foremost in the minds of the Framers, were those involving invasions of the home, it would be a mistake to conclude . . . that the Warrant Clause was therefore intended to guard only against intrusions into the home."

And, fourth, the Court has recognized that a property right in the area searched or the item seized can give rise to a reasonable expectation of privacy.

EXAMPLE:
In *Rakas* v. *Illinois,* 439 U.S. 128 (1978), the defendants asserted neither a property or possessory interest in the automobile which was searched, nor an interest in the property seized. The Court concluded that for these reasons the defendants established no reasonable expectation of privacy.

The Meaning of "Seizures"

A seizure is the actual exercise of dominion over the object—the taking of control over it by the law enforcement agent.

It is natural to think of seizure as being the exertion of control in the sense of physical custody, but this is not necessarily accurate. A tangible item—a gun, a knife, a section of lead pipe, an ax—is, of course, subject to a physical taking. But what about acts or events that are not ordinarily subject to easy visual observation? Is action undertaken with the intent to observe this sort of conduct a "search" and is the ultimate observation a "seizure"? So the courts have often held. Thus a vice squad member's observations of homosexual conduct through a vent in the ceiling of a restroom may be inadmissible in evidence.

The significance of the privacy concept, previously mentioned, can be discerned here. If the conduct or object is in plain view, no "search" is involved; observation of the conduct or object could hardly be avoided. Of course, whether something is truly in plain view can be subject to debate. The answer depends a good bit on what people could reasonably expect under the circumstances.

EXAMPLE A:
Tangible items are left on the seat of a parked automobile at night. They can be observed from outside the car by a policeman who shines a flashlight into the vehicle. There would seem to be no expectation that these items would be immune from official observation. The "plain view" doctrine would apply; visualizing the items is not an unreasonable search and seizure.

EXAMPLE B:
The occupants of a motel room leave the front door ajar, with the result that persons in the public parking lot can readily overhear conversations inside the motel room. There could have been no genuine expectation of privacy here and so there has been no unlawful search.

EXAMPLE C:
Photographs of an unenclosed yard, made from the public sidewalk, are immune to a claim of illegal search and seizure.

EXAMPLE D:
Defendant places the butt of a marijuana cigarette in a hotel ashtray. The ashtray and its contents are thereafter removed by a maid in the course of her normal duties. Retrieval of the butt by narcotics agents is not an illegal search and seizure, although it would have been if accomplished without warrant prior to the maid's removal of the ashtray from the hotel room. Anyone who leaves a joint in a hotel ashtray is seemingly unconcerned about privacy.

EXAMPLE E:
A fleeing suspect hurls a pistol from his automobile. Policemen who take possession of the weapon have not done so pursuant to a "search and seizure."

Related to the "plain view" doctrine is the "open fields" doctrine, which again has its roots in a privacy concept. Under the "open fields" doctrine, no right to privacy, and thus no Fourth Amendment protection, attaches to objects and activities that can easily be observed from a vantage point in the open fields. (See, e.g., *Oliver* v. *United States*, 466 U.S. 170 (1984).)

Sometimes the search and seizure process is complex, having a number of separate stages, each of which must be analyzed. A good example is *State* v. *Elkins*, 422 P.2d 250 (S. Ct. Ore. 1966). The accused was arrested for drunkenness. The arresting officer looked in the accused's shirt pocket and found an unlabeled bottle that contained several different kinds of pills and capsules. The officer took custody of the bottle and had the pills and capsules chemically analyzed. Some were found to be methadone. When this brief fact-situation is sifted, four separate stages emerge: two searches and two seizures. (1) The arresting officer's taking of the accused into custody was a *seizure* of his person. (2) The examination of the accused's shirt pocket was a *search.* (3) Taking custody of the bottle and its contents was a second *seizure.* (4) The chemical testing of the pills and capsules from the bottle was a second *search.* The propriety of each of these four stages would have to be considered separately by a court.

F. The Reasonableness Requirement; The General Requirement of a Search Warrant

The Meaning of "Reasonableness"

The Fourth Amendment does not decree that people shall be completely free from searches and seizures. Police work would collapse if criminal investigators could never search for and seize incriminating evidence. All that the Fourth Amendment requires is that searches and seizures be conducted in a reasonable way.

The second part of the Fourth Amendment declares that "no Warrants shall issue, but upon probable cause, supported by Oath or affirmation." It might therefore be argued that no search and seizure is ever reasonable unless it is carried on pursuant to a search warrant, issued on "probable cause, supported by Oath or affirmation." The courts have avoided this narrow construction, however. It has been recognized that the Fourth Amendment provides for flexibility and does not lay down a single, precise standard of reasonableness. One thing can safely be said: it has been the position of the Supreme Court that the Fourth Amendment reflects a powerful preference for reliance on search warrants based upon probable cause.

Justice Robert H. Jackson of the U.S. Supreme Court once tried to explain why there should be recourse to search warrants:

> The point of the Fourth Amendment, which is often not grasped by zealous officers, is not that it denies law enforcement the support of the usual inferences which reasonable men draw from evidence. Its protection consists in requiring that those inferences [*i.e.,* that probable cause exists] be drawn by a neutral and detached magistrate instead of being judged by the officer engaged in the often competitive enterprise of ferreting out crime . . . When

the right of privacy must reasonably yield to the right of search is, as a rule, to be decided by a judicial officer, not by a policeman or government enforcement agent. (*Johnson* v. *United States*, 333 U.S. 10 (1948).)

Justice Jackson's explanation may seem to be a touch on the naive side. It assumed that magistrates really are "neutral and detached." More importantly, it assumed that they are equipped to and will conduct a careful study of the probable cause evidence. Actually, the justice's assumptions have been borne out by field research conducted by the American Bar Foundation. In a report released in 1967 the Bar Foundation said that "With rare exceptions, magistrates do read and carefully consider the evidence presented by law enforcement officers requesting a search warrant . . . rather than relying totally on the police and prosecutor." (TIFFANY, MCINTYRE & ROTENBERG, DETECTION OF CRIME 119 (1967).)

Procedural Aspects of the General Warrant Requirement

As all competent law enforcement officers know, there are important procedural requirements in connection with the issuance of a search warrant.

1. *The Issuing Judicial Officer.* As has been indicated, the application for a search warrant must be made to an appropriate judicial officer. (*Sandwich* v. *Tampa,* 407 U.S. 342 (1972).)

EXAMPLE:
In *Lo-Ji Sales* v. *New York*, 442 U.S. 319 (1979), a town justice issued an open-ended warrant to seize obscene materials and then participated in the search, identifying as he went what was obscene and what, in his view, was not. The Supreme Court held that he had not acted as a neutral and detached magistrate.

The power to issue warrants is regulated by statute, and if a judicial officer exceeds his or her statutory authority, the warrant he or she issues will be invalid. For one example, a justice of the peace may be prohibited by statute from issuing warrants for certain types of property (e.g., narcotics) in certain places (e.g., a house). Another example: municipal judges usually lack the power to issue a warrant that is to be executed outside the city limits. If both federal and state law enforcement agents take part in a warrant application, the issuing magistrate must conform to the restrictions imposed by the laws of *both* jurisdictions, federal and state. The rule is different where there has not been a joint application.

EXAMPLE:
In *State* v. *Davis,* 251 A.2d 394 (S. Ct. R.I. 1969), federal agents seized property under a warrant which they, without state participation, had

obtained and which was valid under federal law. The seized property was admissible in a state prosecution even though the federal warrant did not conform to the requirements of a special state statute.

2. *The Application.* A search warrant is sought by means of a formal application. It may be done with a printed form, but that form, when filled out, must contain sufficient information to support the request for a warrant. This means, as the Supreme Court said in *Aguilar* v. *Texas,* 378 U.S. 108 (1964), that it must give the magistrate enough information to enable him to decide for himself whether probable cause has been established. It is not enough for the applicant to say in an affidavit that he believes the facts set forth in the application because they are based on "reliable information."

Applications for a search warrant must be sworn to on oath, or be upon solemn affirmation. Telephoning a warrant request in and swearing to its accuracy later will not be countenanced. (*United States* v. *Shorter,* 600 F.2d 585 (6th Cir. 1979).) The warrant request must describe (1) the place to be searched, (2) the matters to be seized, (3) the person having custody of the property, if it is to be taken from his or her control, and (4) the nature of the underlying criminal offense.

All of this need not be set out in the warrant application itself; affidavits (i.e., sworn statements) can be attached to the application or the sworn testimony of witnesses can be produced for the magistrate's consideration. The application need not employ the fancy and esoteric language of lawyers. Since applications for warrants are usually prepared by law enforcement officers, who are not always steeped in the use of legalese and other obscure tongues, warrant applications can use understandable, nontechnical language. Unless an application is accompanied by affidavits or testimony, however, it must speak in terms of facts and not consist of a parade of unsupported conclusions and speculations.

3. *The Necessary Showing.* As has been indicated previously, the application's purpose is to demonstrate to an issuing judicial officer that there is probable cause for believing that a crime has taken place and that a search would result in the seizure of incriminating evidence of that fact. The data relied upon for this showing must be set forth either in the application itself or in supporting affidavits and/or testimony.

If the police officer-applicant was an eyewitness to the alleged offense, he can offer his own affidavit and it will undoubtedly support issuance of a search warrant. The affidavit of a victim or of any other eyewitness would also suffice. The accused's confession, if properly obtained, would be enough.

The applicant for a warrant can also present hearsay evidence if it is of the sort that justifies reliance. He must ordinarily identify the source of the hearsay—the out-of-court declarant—and may be required to establish his reliability. The number of hearsay links cannot be endless: where one police officer swore that another officer had told him that an informant had said that the accused possessed narcotics, the probable cause evidence was inadequate.

The police informer presents a special problem. Here it is *always* essential to establish the informant's reliability. The applicable guidelines were laid down by the Supreme Court in *Spinelli* v. *United States,* 393 U.S. 410 (1969). Five allegations had been made in an application for a search warrant: (1) On four of five days of surveillance the subject had traveled from Illinois into St. Louis, Missouri, between 11:00 A.M. and 12:15 P.M. and had parked his automobile near a particular apartment house; (2) on one of these days the subject had been followed farther and had been observed to enter an apartment in the building; (3) a check of telephone company records revealed that the apartment was not listed in the subject's name and that it contained two telephones with particular numbers assigned to them; (4) the surveillance subject was "known to . . . federal law enforcement agents as a bookmaker, an associate of bookmakers, a gambler, and an associate of gamblers"; and (5) the FBI had been told by a "confidential reliable informant" that the subject was operating a handbook and was taking bets over telephones having numbers identical to those listed on telephone company records as being assigned to the two telephones in the apartment to which the subject had been going.

The issue in *Spinelli* was whether these allegations amounted to probable cause to believe that the apartment contained items that were subject to seizure. To put it another way, the issue was whether there was probable cause to believe that the apartment was being used for bookmaking.

The Supreme Court engaged in a two-part analysis. (1) It first inquired whether the informant's tip would in and of itself constitute probable cause. To answer this question, reference to another Supreme Court case, *Aguilar* v. *Texas, 378 U.S. 108 (1964),* was necessary. In *Aguilar* it was decided that an informant's tip must be accompanied by (a) "some of the underlying circumstances on which the informant based his conclusions" and (b) some basis for concluding either that the informant was generally credible or that his information in the particular instance was reliable. Corroboration of some of the tipster's information might be sufficient to satisfy the latter requirement, and the level of detail contained in the tip might be enough to suggest that the information was reliable. (2) Secondly, the Court said that the informer's tip, although insufficient when taken by itself, might constitute probable cause when considered with other information in the hands of the police.

On the facts presented to it in *Spinelli,* the Supreme court concluded that the warrant application was inadequate. There was no proof aside from the agent's naked assertion that the informant was reliable. There was insufficient corroboration or detail to overcome this defect. Furthermore, even when considered along with the other evidence set out in the warrant application, the tip in *Spinelli* did not add up to probable cause.

In deciding whether there is sufficient detail and corroboration to lend credence to an informer's tip, the Supreme Court in *Spinelli* looked to its earlier opinion in *Draper* v. *United States,* 358 U.S. 307 (1959). There the informant had relayed information that the subject had gone to Chicago the day before and would return to Denver by train with three ounces of heroin on one or another of two specified mornings. The informant described in some detail the clothing that the subject would be wearing, the suitcase that he would be carrying, and his peculiar way of walking. Police officers met the Chicago-Denver train on the two mornings. On the second morning they saw a man get off the train whose clothing, luggage, and walk corresponded to the informant's description. The Supreme Court said that the detail of the informant's report was enough to support its reliability. In addition, the informant's report was corroborated by the police officer's observation of the subject, with the consequence that "it was perfectly clear that probable cause had been established."

The only difficulty with all of this is that the detail and the corroboration in *Spinelli* would seem to many to be just as impressive as it was in *Draper.* The upshot is that there is only one safe generalization: "probable cause" in informer cases and in other cases cannot be defined with precision. The more evidence there is, the more corroboration of it there is, the more likely it is that the existence of probable cause will be found.

Under *Spinelli,* the corroborating information can be hearsay evidence or it can be the direct product of a police officer's own investigative efforts. One court has said that the testimony of a grand jury witness, summarized by a police officer, is adequate corroboration within the rule laid down in *Spinelli.*

In *Illinois* v. *Gates,* 462 U.S. 213 (1983), the Supreme Court emphasized that *Aguilar* and *Spinelli* should not be read as calling for a rigid test. It stated that the elements of the two-pronged test discernible in those cases—the informant's basis of knowledge and his/her veracity—should be understood simply as closely intertwined issues that may illuminate the common-sense, practical question whether there is probable cause to believe that evidence or contraband is located in a particular place. The task of the warrant-issuing magistrate is to decide whether, given the "totality of the circumstances" set forth in the police affidavit, there is a "fair probability" that evidence of a crime, or contraband, will be found in a particular place.

Neither *Spinelli* nor *Gates* does violence to the somewhat shaky holding in *McCray* v. *Illinois,* 386 U.S. 300 (1967), discussed in chapter 12, which deals, among other things, with the informer's privilege. *Spinelli,* in other words, suggests that in testing the propriety of search warrants (or, for that matter, arrests), only the credibility or reliability and not the identity of an informer need have been disclosed. The matter is undoubtedly within the discretion of the issuing judicial officer, such as a magistrate, who can direct that an informer's identity be revealed if she feels the need for doing so.

The application for a search warrant must set forth the date on which the information supporting it was obtained, since there must not be an undue time lag between the events described and the making of the warrant application. A finding of probable cause is defective if the information on which it was based was stale. The courts have indicated that information gets stale within a fairly short period of time.

EXAMPLES:
Ashley v. *State,* 241 N.E.2d 264 (S. Ct. Ind. 1968) (delay from October 3 to October 11); *State* v. *Ingram,* 445 P.2d 503 (S. Ct. Ore. 1968) (1 month); *State* v. *Scheidemann,* 448 P.2d 458 (S. Ct. Ore. 1968) (34 days); *Durham* v. *United States,* 403 F.2d 190 (9th Cir. 1968) (4 months).

On the other hand, a mistake of fact on the part of the applying officer will not necessarily invalidate a search warrant. The accused would have to show intentional falsification or reckless disregard for the truth. Proof of negligence or innocent mistake is not enough. Furthermore, the accused has the burden of demonstrating that the incorrect statement of the officer was crucial to the finding of probable cause. (*Franks* v. *Delaware,* 438 U.S. 154 (1978).)

4. *Issuance of the Warrant.* The issuing judicial officer must have sufficient information in front of him to convince a reasonable person that probable cause exists. He has some allowable discretion in assessing the evidence and reviewing courts are not often likely to do much more than see whether the magistrate followed required procedures. The fact that a magistrate has discretion means that he must *exercise* it. If a reviewing court has reason to believe that the magistrate simply rubber-stamped a police officer's application, the warrant will be held invalid. In order to challenge the validity of a search warrant, the accused is entitled to take the issuing magistrate's sworn testimony to show what evidence he considered. (The magistrate's thought processes in issuing the warrant cannot be explored, however.)

Statutes or rules usually require that the issuing magistrate sign the warrant. This task cannot properly be delegated to a clerk.

For a long time it was thought that search warrants could not properly be issued for "mere evidence," as distinguished from the instrumentalities of crime (e.g., a murder weapon), the fruits of a crime (e.g., stolen goods), and contraband (e.g., illegal narcotics). However, in *Warden* v. *Hayden,* 387 U.S. 294 (1967), the Supreme Court made it clear that search warrants can be issued to obtain evidentiary matters so long as there is some connection between the items and the asserted criminal conduct and there is a pertinent statute or rule permitting evidence searches. (If the local statute or rule *prohibits* evidence searches, its terms control; *Hayden* simply provided a go-ahead sign by delineating how far such a statute or rule can go.)

When issued, a search warrant must contain a particularized description of the place to be searched and the matters to be seized. General searches are constitutionally impermissible; that is what the Fourth Amendment is all about.

EXAMPLE:
In *Stanford* v. *Texas,* 379 U.S. 476 (1965), the Supreme Court said it was sufficiently precise for a search warrant to describe the matters to be seized as being "books, records, pamphlets, cards, receipts, lists, memoranda, pictures, recordings and other written instruments concerning the Communist Party of Texas, and the operations of the Communist Party of Texas."

Sometimes it is not feasible to be quite so precise about individual items. At least where the materials to be seized are not potentially subject to free speech claims based on the First Amendment (as was the case in *Stanford* v. *Texas,* in the example above), a more generalized description of a class of materials may be permissible.

EXAMPLE:
In *James* v. *United States*, 416 F.2d 467 (5th Cir. 1969), it was enough to describe the items to be seized as "gambling paraphernalia, including but not limited to dice, crap tables, wires, magnets. . . . "

5. *Execution of Search Warrants.* Most statutes provide that the serving (execution) of search warrants can be done only by law enforcement officers. Rarely do civilians take part in the process unless they are simply assisting a law officer who is present at the time.

Warrants, once issued, must be served promptly lest probable cause fade with the passage of time. Warrants have been declared void because the force of the underlying probable cause determination has been diluted by delay. Furthermore, some search warrants contain a built-in time limit (e.g., they speak of "immediate search") and some relevant statutes and rules contain time limitations (e.g., Rule 41(c), Federal Rules of Criminal Procedure: " . . . to search, within a specified period of time not to exceed 10 days . . . ").

The service of search warrants is commonly restricted to the daylight hours unless nocturnal service is explicit or some emergency dictates nighttime execution to avoid the destruction or loss of evidence.

It is ordinarily required that officers executing a search warrant announce their identity as law enforcement officers, that they have a search warrant, and that they intend to execute it. These requirements can be avoided only if the three-part announcement will inspire resistance or destruction of the evidence. The evidence of an emergency situation must be substantial.

Compliance with the announcement requirement must be genuine. It is not proper for law officers to shout the announcement while at the same time smashing down the door. If, after the announcement has been made, the officers hear significant noises from within, such as the sound of someone scurrying about or, in narcotics cases, the repeated flushing of a toilet, forceful entry can be made immediately in an effort to prevent the destruction of vital evidence.

6. *Extent of the Search.* It is not altogether clear whether law officers are free to seize evidence not specified in their search warrant. In 1927 the Supreme Court held that nothing could be taken unless it was mentioned in the warrant. The basis of this holding was the Fourth Amendment's prohibition of purely exploratory or general searches. However, lower courts have tried to generate some exceptions applicable to contraband and the fruits of criminal behavior. One of these courts, the influential California Supreme Court, has said that contraband not specified in the warrant must either be in plain view or come into view while the described items are being searched for by the executing law officers.

A warrant to search premises is not authority to search persons on those premises. However, if an offense is committed in the executing officer's presence or if what he observes on the premises gives him probable cause for a felony arrest, an arrest can be accomplished on the spot and then a search can be conducted. (See section H, below, on searches and seizures incident to arrest.)

G. Exceptions to the General Requirement of a Search Warrant

The Six Main Exceptions

There are a number of exceptions to the general proposition that a search and seizure independent of an arrest are reasonable only if conducted under the authority of a valid warrant. The six most important exceptions involve: (1) emergency situation; (2) searches of vehicles; (3) "hot pursuit" of a dangerous suspect; (4) searches of things that are in official custody; (5) the "plain view" doctrine; and (6) border searches.

As the reader considers these exceptions, he or she will wish to ask whether they form a consistent doctrinal framework that law enforcement agents are likely to find helpful as they confront myriad and subtly variant search and seizure problems. Such astute observers of criminal procedure as Virginia's Professor Stephen A. Saltzburg have suggested that the Supreme Court has needlessly complicated the exceptions, drawing ever more intricate and confusing lines of demarcation. (Saltzburg, *The Flow and Ebb of Constitutional Criminal Procedure in the Warren and Burger Courts,* 69

Georgetown Law Jour. 151, 183 (1980).) As the expanding network of exceptions is considered, the reader might consider a possible alternative approach: a general rule allowing warrantless searches and seizures on a showing (1) of probable cause that a crime had been perpetrated, (2) of need for swift action, and (3) that the law enforcement personnel took the least intrusive means of maintaining the *status quo* until a magistrate could authorize further action. (See also the proposal of Professor John Kaplan in *The Limits of the Exclusionary Rule,* 26 Stanford Law Rev. 1027, 1050–1052 (1974), reprinted in KAPLAN & WALTZ, BASIC MATERIALS ON CRIMINAL EVIDENCE 500–502 (1980).)

1. *Emergency Situations.* Intrusions into private homes to make a warrantless arrest are ordinarily unlawful (*Payton* v. *New York*, 445 U.S. 573 (1980)) and therefore provide no support for a search and seizure. However, it is vital that law officers be free, within reasonable bounds, to engage in warrantless activity when it gives promise of preventing harm to persons or property or the destruction of incriminating evidence.

A useful example of the "cry for help" type of case is *State* v. *Hunt,* 406 P.2d 208 (Ariz. App. 1965), in which a servant reported to law enforcement agents that she had discovered her employer's little girl tied up in a furnace room with her bloody head under a hot water heater. The responding officer insisted that he be permitted to accompany the mother to the furnace room. His conduct was approved by the Arizona court, which said that he "had not only the lawful *right* [court's italics], but the lawful duty to enter the premises, investigate, and take the child into custody if necessary, with or without a search warrant. . . ."

The exigent circumstances exception may apply to searches conducted during or after a fire. In *Michigan* v. *Tyler,* 436 U.S. 499 (1978), police and fire officials reentered a building five hours after a fire in it had been put out, and again three weeks later. The first reentry was upheld by the Supreme Court, which pointed to the officers' need to pursue their arson investigation and salvage relevant evidence. The second set of reentries, three weeks after the blaze, was disapproved by the Court since these reentries "were clearly detached from the initial exigency and warrantless entry." Of course, the result might be altogether different where the law enforcement officer entered a building to seize evidence of a crime *unrelated* to suspected arson since this would not constitute a "mere extension" of the firefighters' original investigation. (*United States* v. *Hoffman,* 607 F.2d 280 (9th Cir. 1979).) (*Hoffman* involved a search for a sawed-off shotgun. The judicial reaction might be different where the officer had reason to fear the destruction of important evidence, for example, volatile chemicals. See *United States* v. *Calabrass,* 607 F.2d 559 (2d Cir. 1979), *cert. denied,* 446 U.S. 940 (1980).) An example of the exception as it applies where evidence might be lost or destroyed is found in *Schmerber* v. *California,* 384 U.S. 757 (1966), in which the Supreme Court approved the conduct of a law officer in conducting a blood test when he had probable cause to believe that the subject had been driving while under the influence of alcohol. The defendant argued that the officer should have gotten a search warrant first. The court observed that alcohol is quite quickly eliminated from the blood, with the consequence that time is of the essence when conducting blood-alcohol tests. The officer, confronted by a situation threatening loss of vital evidence, had properly gone ahead without a warrant. Perhaps a more typical example of this aspect of the exception came up in *Boyden* v. *United States*, 363 F.2d 551, *cert. denied,* 385 U.S. 978 (6th Cir. 1966). In that case it was held that the warrantless search of an automobile damaged in an accident was permissible since leaking gasoline and a hot engine posed a danger of fire that would destroy the car's contents. What this branch of the exception comes down to is that a warrant is not necessary where the police have a reasonable fear that taking time to secure a warrant would jeopardize the success of the intended search. (See also *Welsh* v. *Wisconsin,* 466 U.S. 740 (1984).)

2. *Searches of Vehicles.* This exception is sometimes called the *Carroll* exception because it can be traced back to *Carroll* v. *United States,* 267 U.S. 132 (1925). In *Carroll* the Supreme Court upheld the searching of a moving car where law officers had reasonable grounds for believing that it contained contraband.

There are two underlying reasons for the *Carroll* exception. (1) The subject of the search was an automobile, not a dwelling. The fourth Amendment's requirements are less demanding as soon as one gets away from the notion that a person's home is his castle. (2) An automobile might be driven beyond the officer's jurisdiction before he could get a search warrant. Here one gets overtones of the exception which permits law officers to prevent the loss or destruction of incriminating evidence.

The *Carroll* exception was extended somewhat in later cases, beginning with *Chambers* v. *Maroney,* 399 U.S. 42 (1970). The facts in *Chambers* were these: Chambers and three other men were arrested late one night while they sat in an automobile. The police had probable cause for believing that the four men had been involved in a gas station robbery and that the weapon used in the crime, together with the proceeds of the robbery, were in the car. The automobile was taken to the police station where, the next morning, it was searched without a warrant. The gun and the loot were discovered inside.

Chambers argued the car had been immobile at the time of the search since he and his companions were then under arrest. He contended that there was an exception to the general warrant requirement only if the vehicle had been moving. The Supreme Court was unimpressed. It said, first, that the police had probable cause to search the car when they arrested Chambers, so probable cause still obtained in the morning. Second, the vehicle was operable even after the accused's arrest. This meant law enforcement officers should have either the power to render it completely immobile until a search warrant could be secured or the power to conduct a warrantless search of it.

Under the facts in *Chambers*, law enforcement officers can search an automobile back at the station if circumstances—darkness, for example—make an immediate search impractical. But the Supreme Court has taken this one step further. In *Texas* v. *White*, 423 U.S. 67 (1975), the Court upheld the warrantless search of an automobile at the station even though an immediate search was entirely feasible. The Court's opinion read *Chambers* as holding that probable cause to search, once established, will justify a later warrantless search regardless of the circumstances.

The full significance of *Chambers* remains clouded, however. It is clouded by the subsequent Supreme court cases of *Coolidge* v. *New Hampshire*, 403 U.S. 443 (1971) and *Cardwell* v. *Lewis*, 417 U.S. 583 (1974). Both cases involved the warrantless search of non-moving vehicles, a situation typically less threatened by exigent circumstances than a vehicle search on the highway. And both cases demonstrate how difficult it is to interpret some Supreme Court decisions.

In *Coolidge*, police investigators in a homicide case went to the accused's house to arrest him and to search his car under the authority of what was later ruled to be an invalid search warrant. After arresting Coolidge, the officers made his wife leave the house. About two and a half hours after Coolidge's arrest they took his parked car to police headquarters. Two days later the vehicle was searched; almost a year later it was searched again; fourteen months after the arrest it was searched a third time. Vacuum cleaner sweepings obtained during these searches were introduced at trial and contributed to Coolidge's conviction.

Justice Potter Stewart, writing an opinion fully concurred in by only three other members of the nine-member Supreme Court, rejected the claim that this had been a justifiable warrantless search under the authority of Chambers. Justice Stewart's opinion would restrict the vehicle exception to those critical situations that demanded immediate action, making it impractical to pause long enough to obtain a search warrant. Stewart explained away the *Chambers* case. He said it stood for nothing more than that a warrantless search on the open highway that would have been valid under the earlier *Carroll* case could be postponed by the police and made later at the police station. Justice Stewart did not accept the argument that the mobility of a motor vehicle justifies warrantless searches. Furthermore, neither Coolidge nor his wife had access to Coolidge's automobile, and so the *Carroll* case itself was said by the justice to be inapplicable.

Justice Harlan wrote a separate opinion. He refused to concur in that part of Stewart's opinion which limited the Court's *Chambers* opinion. Harlan did agree, however, that a warrantless search is reasonable only if there are critical—"exigent"—circumstances requiring quick action. Justice White, joined by Chief Justice Burger, filed an opinion in which he seemed to agree with Justice Stewart's reading of *Chambers.* Justices Black and Blackmun dissented, believing that the searches in *Coolidge* had all been reasonable under *Chambers.*

The situation in *Cardwell* v. *Lewis, supra,* resembles in many ways the facts in *Coolidge.* Lewis, a murder suspect, came to the police station to answer questions. After being formally arrested later in that day, Lewis turned over to police his car keys and parking lot claim check. His car was towed to a police impoundment lot, where a warrantless inspection of the outside of the car revealed that a tire matched the cast of an impression taken at the scene of the crime and that paint samples taken from his car were similar to foreign paint on the fender of the victim's car.

As in *Coolidge,* the Supreme Court could marshall only a plurality opinion. In *Cardwell,* though, the Court validated the questioned police conduct. Justice Blackmun distanced his opinion from the *Coolidge* case, focusing on the lesser intrusion in *Cardwell* and the fact that the car had been towed from a public lot, not a private driveway. Justice Blackmun then compared the circumstances in *Cardwell* to those in *Chambers* v. *Maroney.* "That the car in *Chambers* was seized after being stopped on a highway, whereas Lewis' car was seized from a public parking lot has little, if any, constitutional significance. The same arguments and considerations of exigency, immobilization on the spot, and posting a guard obtain."

Because of the hodgepodge of opinions in *Coolidge* and *Cardwell,* the scope of the vehicle exception to the general warrant requirement has not been altogether clear. In mid-1982 the Supreme Court made a strong effort, in an opinion by Justice John Paul Stevens, to clarify the patchwork of rules relating to warrantless searches of automobiles and their contents. In *United States* v. *Ross,* 456 U.S. 798 (1982), the Court ruled that when law enforcement agents have probable cause to believe that an automobile is transporting contraband they can search for it wherever it might be concealed, even in a closed container as to which there might exist an expectation of privacy. As Justice Stevens pointed out, the holding in *Ross* does not mean that the police are entirely unfettered in vehicle searches. In the first place, they cannot undertake contraband searches of vehicles absent evidence that would justify the issuance of a search warrant, even though they are not required to obtain a magistrate's advance approval. Secondly, they can only search places and things that could conceal the item for which they are searching; if, for example, a van is believed to be transporting illegal immigrants, police would not be justified in undertaking a warrantless search of the glove compartment. (See also *United States* v. *Villamonte-Marquez,* 462 U.S. 579 (1983) (boarding of vessel by customs officers held reasonable).)

3. *"Hot Pursuit."* The term "hot pursuit," often used in international affairs to justify over-the-border flights by military aircraft chasing enemy planes, can accurately be employed to label a third exception to the general

requirement of a valid search warrant. The law would be genuinely foolish were it to require that police officers pause in their pursuit of a fleeing criminal in order to apply for and obtain a search warrant; the criminal would be long gone by the time the officers had gotten their warrant. This commonsense proposition was recognized by the Supreme Court in *Warden* v. *Hayden,* 387 U.S. 294 (1967). In that case police officers had been told by eyewitnesses that an armed robber had gone into a particular house. The officers immediately entered the house, searched for the robber, and found him along with his weapons. Not too surprisingly, the Court held that this warrantless search was reasonable. "The Fourth Amendment," it said, "does not require police officers to delay in the course of their investigation if to do so would gravely endanger their lives or the lives of others." Giving factual content to the term "reasonable," the Court said, "Speed here was essential, and only a thorough search of the house for persons and weapons could have insured that [defendant] Hayden was the only man present and that the police had control of all weapons which could be used against them or to effect an escape." The court in *Hayden* made it clear that it was not viewing the search as one made incident to arrest, in which case the officers' search could not properly have extended much beyond the defendant's person. The Court ruled that a "hot pursuit" search could extend beyond the limited area that could be searched incident to an arrest. This, too, makes sense, especially where the search is for concealed weapons that could be used against the investigating officers and others.

Of course, once again it could be said that the exception under consideration is actually a particularized application of the first exception discussed in this chapter—the exception covering emergency or "exigent" situations.

4. *Searches of Things That Are in Official Custody.* This is another exception the exact scope of which is not perfectly clear. Its beginnings can be found in the case of *Cooper* v. *California,* 386 U.S. 58 (1967). Defendant Cooper's automobile had been seized by police and subjected to a forfeiture proceeding on the ground that it had been used to transport illegal narcotics. A warrantless search of the car was conducted a week after the seizure. The Supreme Court held that the search was reasonable since the police were obliged to keep the car in official custody until the forfeiture proceedings were over. The Court emphasized that the search was "closely related to the reason [Cooper] was arrested, the reason his car had been impounded, and the reason it was being retained."

The *Cooper* opinion should be considered a rather narrow one. It does not apply to every situation in which law enforcement agents find themselves in lawful possession of another's property. That this is so can be inferred from a case that came down just one year after *Cooper.* In *Dyke* v. *Taylor Implement Manufacturing Co.,* 391 U.S. 216 (1968), the arrestee's automobile had not been formally impounded; it had been brought to the police station as a favor to the arrestee. Furthermore, there was no indication that the search of the automobile was in any way related to the reason that the arrestee had been taken into custody. The Supreme Court concluded that the facts were significantly different from those considered in *Cooper* and held that the search, in the absence of a warrant, was improper.

Some lower federal courts have considered what degree of official custody is sufficient to activate the *Cooper* principle. In *Brett* v. *United States,* 412 F. 2d 401 (5th Cir. 1969), the court held that the warrantless search of an arrestee's clothing three days after it had been placed in a property bag was unlawful; the level of custody was insufficient. By way of contrast, it was held in *United States* v. *Kucinich,* 404 F. 2d 262 (6th Cir. 1968), that police seizure of a stolen automobile on behalf of its owner will bring *Cooper* into play, validating a warrantless search.

A variation on the theme of searches of things in official custody is the *inventory search.* These are not considered criminal searches and thus are not governed by the Fourth Amendment's warrant and probable cause requirements. The leading case in this area is *South Dakota* v. *Opperman,* 428 U.S. 364 (1976). Defendant Opperman parked his car illegally in downtown Vermillion, South Dakota, and police officers towed it to a city impound lot. There they inventoried the contents of the car according to standard procedure. In the glove compartment they discovered a plastic bag of marijuana. At his trial for possession of the drug, Opperman sought to exclude its admission into evidence on the theory that the inventory search contravened the Fourth Amendment. The Supreme Court did not accept Opperman's argument. They upheld the search as reasonable, saying that "inventories pursuant to standard police practices are reasonable," even when conducted without probable cause or a warrant. The rationale for these standard police inventories may be either to protect the owner's property or to protect police from property claims or potential danger.

About all that can safely be said is that a warrantless search can be undertaken when an item of evidence is in official police custody as the consequence of a formal seizure that gives the police a right of possession that is not merely temporary. The *Cooper* decision, in other words, probably cannot be pushed much beyond its own special facts, involving the formal impounding of property. Additionally, the reason for the search, and its scope, must be directly related to the justification for seizing the property in the first place. Seizure for one purpose will not support a sweeping warrantless search for some other purpose.

5. *The "Plain View" Doctrine.* This principle, along with the closely related "open fields" doctrine, was briefly mentioned earlier in this chapter when the Fourth Amendment right of privacy was examined. From the plurality opinion in *Coolidge* v. *New Hampshire,* 403 U.S. 443 (1971), it is possible to extract three conditions attaching to the plain view exception. This first of these is a requirement that the searching officer have had a

prior, independent justification for being physically in a position to observe the seized evidence.

EXAMPLE:
Plain view seizure of chemicals and drug equipment left in a burning building was justified because DEA agent had been summoned by police to dispose of hazardous chemicals. (*United States* v. *Callabrass,* 607 F.2d 559 (2d Cir. 1979), *cert. denied,* 446 U.S. 940 (1980). Compare *United States* v. *Hoffman,* 607 F.2d 280 (9th Cir. 1979).)

The second condition laid down in *Coolidge, supra,* is that the seizing officer must have immediately recognized the seized items as evidence; in other words, it must have been immediately apparent to the officer that the seized materials constituted evidence. This condition is supposed to foreclose exploratory searches.

EXAMPLE:
Open envelope in plain view on dashboard during traffic stop revealed a return address to a state agency and treasury checks payable to someone other than driver; officer recognized something "amiss"; seizure upheld. (*United States* v. *Druckett,* 583 F.2d 1309 (5th Cir. 178); see also *Texas* v. *Brown,* 460 U.S. 730 (1982).)

The third *Coolidge* condition was that the seizing officer's discovery of the evidence must have been inadvertent. This requirement has now been abandoned by the Court.

The Supreme Court has also decided a number of cases involving aerial surveillance. In *Dow Chemical Co.* v. *United States,* 476 U.S. 227 (1986), an industrial complex had been surveilled from an airplane. The Court held that no search was involved since the complex was "open to the view and observation of persons in aircraft lawfully in the public airspace immediately above or sufficiently near the area for the reach of cameras." (See also *California* v. *Ciraolo,* 476 U.S. 207 (1986) (aerial observation of marijuana cultivation); *Florida* v. *Riley,* ______ U.S. ______, 109 S.Ct. 693 (1989) (observation from helicopter flying at lawful altitude).)

Border Searches

A specific statute, 19 U.S.C.A. §482, enacted in 1789, empowers customs officials at the border to halt and examine persons, baggage, and vehicles entering the United States. In a narcotics case upholding this statute the Supreme Court has said that "the detention of a traveler at the border, beyond the scope of routine customs search and inspection, is justified at its inception if customs agents, considering all the facts surrounding the traveler and her trip, reasonably suspect that the traveler is smuggling contraband in her alimentary canal" (*United States* v. *Montoya de Hernandez*, 473 U.S. 531 (1985)).

A number of Supreme Court decisions have dealt with the legality of warrantless stops and searches away from the actual border. In *Almeida-Sanchez* v. *United States*, 413 U.S. 266 (1973), the Court held that warrantless searches by roving patrols of the Immigration Service (INS) violate the Fourth Amendment. Writing the majority opinion, Justice Stewart could find no support for such searches in the Court's administrative inspection decisions or its automobile search rulings. The power of roving patrols of INS agents to stop a car briefly and question the driver and passengers about their citizenship was, however, upheld two years later in *United States* v. *Brignoni-Ponce*, 422 U.S. 873 (1975). But such a stop can be made only if the agents are aware of specific, articulable facts, together with rational inferences drawn therefrom, reasonably warranting suspicion that the vehicles contain illegal aliens. Finally, in *United States* v. *Martinez-Fuerte*, 428 U.S. 543 (1976), the Court validated brief stops at permanent checkpoints away from the border even in the absence of individualized suspicion.

H. Searches and Seizures Incident to the Seizure (Arrest) of Persons

Searches Incident to Arrest

Thus far the discussion in this chapter has centered on searches for and seizures of things, objects, independent of the seizure of any person. The Fourth Amendment, by its very language, applies also to seizures of persons. And if the seizure (arrest) of a person is unreasonable, incriminating evidence obtained from him at the time will be excluded at trial. The exclusionary rule which is the subject of this chapter applies to this kind of evidence just as surely as it applies to objects searched for and seized during investigatory activity that is independent of any arrest activity.

There is one important difference between the independent search and seizure situation and the arrest situation. In connection with the independent search and seizure situation, there is a general requirement that a search warrant first be obtained. Except in certain situations of an emergency nature, the reasonableness of an independent search and seizure depends on whether a valid search warrant was secured. There is no such general requirement of a warrant in connection with the seizure (arrest) of *persons*. There are a number of situations in which a police officer can lawfully effect an arrest without a warrant, and a warrantless search of the arrestee's immediate vicinity will then be constitutionally permissible.

In late 1973, in *United States* v. *Robinson*, 414 U.S. 218, after comprehensive consideration of the issue, the Supreme Court reconfirmed what it termed "the traditional and unqualified authority of the arresting officer to search the arrestee's person" when the purpose of the arrest was to take the arrestee into custody. The Court, with Justice Rehnquist writing the majority opinion, said that this authority has two branches: "The first is that a search may be made of the *person* [Court's italics] of the arrestee by virtue of the lawful arrest. The second is that a search may be made of the area within the control of the arrestee."

In *Robinson* the Supreme Court flatly rejected a lower federal court's ruling that a police officer, even after his lawful custodial arrest of a suspect, must restrict himself to a limited "frisk" of the outer clothing in a search for weapons. The Court explained the rationale of its *Robinson* opinion in clearcut terms:

> The authority to search the person incident to a lawful custodial arrest, while based upon the need to disarm and to discover evidence, does not depend on what a court may later decide was the probability in a particular arrest situation that weapons or evidence would in fact be found upon the person of the suspect. A custodial arrest of a suspect based on probable cause is a reasonable intrusion under the Fourth Amendment; that intrusion being lawful, a search incident to the arrest requires no additional justification. It is the fact of the lawful arrest which establishes the authority to search, and we hold that in the case of a lawful custodial arrest a full search of the person is not only an exception to the warrant requirement of the Fourth Amendment, but is also a "reasonable" search under that Amendment.

The holding in *Robinson* seems consistent with the Supreme Court's earlier decision in *Chimel* v. *California,* 395 U.S. 752 (1969), in which it described the scope of a search incident to lawful arrest as being restricted to the arrestee's "person and the area 'within his immediate control' "—construing that phrase to mean the area from which he might gain possession of a weapon or destructible evidence.

EXAMPLE A:
Because they have probable cause to believe that Bushmat is guilty of selling illegal narcotics, police officers arrest him on the street. As an incident of that arrest, the officers can search Bushmat's person for narcotics and weapons.

EXAMPLE B:
Example A, above, is now altered slightly. Bushmat is arrested in his automobile. The arresting officers can properly search at least those areas of the car, such as the glove compartment and the area beneath the driver's seat, that are within Bushmat's easy reach.

EXAMPLE C:
Again the basic example is altered slightly: Bushmat is arrested in the living room of his apartment. The arresting officers search the

bathroom and find narcotics hidden in a toothbrush container. The search of the bathroom is probably illegal since that room was beyond the arrestee's reach.

EXAMPLE D:
A variation: Police officers effecting a lawful arrest of a criminal suspect in his home can conduct a protective "sweep" of other parts of the residence if they have a reasonable belief, based on specific and articulable facts, that the area to be searched harbors a person posing a danger to those on the arrest scene.

EXAMPLE E:
A final alteration: Bushmat is arrested in the living room of his home and taken immediately to the police station. Later the arresting officers return to search the living room. While this area was, at the time of the arrest, within Bushmat's immediate control, the later search is illegal because a search incident to arrest must be conducted contemporaneously with the arrest.

The existence of a valid arrest warrant for one person will not support a search of the dwelling of another person, not named in the arrest warrant, when the subject of the warrant is not found in the dwelling. In *Steagald* v. *United States,* 101 S. Ct. 1642 (1981), law enforcement agents had an arrest warrant for one Ricky Lyons. They found defendant Steagald, but not Lyons, at the residence described in the arrest warrant. They proceeded to search the Steagald residence, found a quantity of cocaine, and arrested Steagald. The Supreme Court held that the arrest warrant for the absent Lyons did not justify a search of the Steagald house; the agents were obligated to obtain a search warrant.

The Meaning of "Arrest"

In a criminal case an *arrest* is the taking of a person into custody for the purpose of bringing him or her before a court or appropriate official to answer a charge of criminal activity. An arrest can be effected by words joined with physical touching or seizure, or by oral statements alone—a simple "You're under arrest"—if the arrestee is thereby put in fear of force and submits. Of course, not every detention is an arrest in the technical sense of the term. A merchant who halts a suspected shoplifter with no intention of turning him over to the police or prosecuting him in court may be *imprisoning* the subject but he is not *arresting* him.

Warrantless Arrests

A law enforcement agent can lawfully make an arrest without a warrant when he has probable cause to believe that a felony has been or is being committed by the person or persons to be arrested. Under the common law, the rule is different in connection with misdemeanor arrests. At common law (that is, under cases decided in the absence of any applicable statute), neither a peace officer nor a private person can arrest without warrant for a misdemeanor even when it is committed in his presence. Furthermore, the later securing of a warrant will not render lawful any seizure of the person occurring prior to its issuance. This common law rule still governs the police in about a dozen states. The common law rule relating to misdemeanor arrests has been modified at least partially by statute in many states. These statutes empower peace officers to arrest for misdemeanors without a warrant in some situations. Thus in more than half the states a warrantless misdemeanor arrest is valid if the offense was committed in the arresting officer's presence. A few states are more liberal, allowing a peace officer to arrest without a warrant where a misdemeanor has been committed outside his presence if he has reasonable grounds to believe that the person to be arrested is guilty.

The Preference for Arrests Pursuant to Warrant

Although warrantless arrests can be lawful, many courts have expressed a preference for arrests made under warrant. As the Supreme Court said in *Beck* v. *Ohio*, 379 U.S. 89 (1964), "An arrest without a warrant bypasses the safeguards provided by an objective predetermination of probable cause, and substitutes instead the far less reliable procedure of an after-the-event justification for the arrest . . . , too likely to be subtly influenced by the familiar shortcomings of hindsight judgment." While an arrest made pursuant to a warrant is presumed to have been based on probable cause, the prosecution must come forward with proof of probable cause in cases of warrantless arrest.

I. Stop and Frisk

The Terry *Case*

The controversial stop-and-frisk procedure was considered by the Supreme Court in *Terry* v. *Ohio*, 392 U.S. 1 (1968). The Court held that the procedure is constitutionally justifiable whenever a reasonable person in the position of the police officer would believe that stopping and frisking a person was essential to the preservation of his own safety or that of others. It should be noticed that the Court spoke in terms of reasonable belief, not probable cause. The *Terry* ruling was a cautious and narrow one, however. The Court was unwilling to extend its ruling to include frisking for the purpose of obtaining evidence or frustrating the destruction of it. Under *Terry,* a police officer could properly do only that which is minimally necessary to ascertain whether the suspect has a weapon and to relieve him of it.

EXAMPLE:
In *Sibron* v. *New York,* 392 U.S. 40 (1968), the arresting officer engaged in no preliminary frisking for weapons. Instead, he plunged his hand into the suspect's pocket and found a packet of narcotics. The Supreme Court said that "The search was not reasonably limited in scope to the accomplishment of the only goal which might conceivably have justified its inception—the protection of the officer by disarming a potentially dangerous man." (Compare *Michigan* v. *Long,* 463 U.S. 1032 (1983) (protective search of suspect's automobile approved.)

Some states have adopted stop-and-frisk statutes. By way of illustration, New York's stop-and-frisk law allows a policeman to halt and frisk when he has reason to suspect that a person has committed, is committing, or is about to commit a felony or serious misdemeanor and that the police-

A policewoman frisks a suspect while her partner covers her. No warrant is needed for officers to ensure their own safety by searching for weapons.

man is in danger of life or limb. The policeman can search only for weapons; the stop-and-frisk statute, for example, will not support a search for narcotics. His action must be based upon reasonable inferences from the fact-situation confronting him; it cannot be grounded on vague hunches or baseless suspicions.

J. Detention for Field Interrogation, Fingerprinting, and the Like

An Open Question

In *Terry* v. *Ohio,* discussed in the preceding section, the Supreme Court deliberately left open the question whether, in the absence of probable cause, the detention of a person for field interrogation is constitutionally allowable. (Field interrogation of limited duration for the purpose of gathering information does not constitute an arrest, though it may be a "seizure" in the constitutional sense.) After the *Terry* decision the Supreme Court at first only hinted at an answer. Within the special context of a border search, the Court held in *United States* v. *Brignoni-Ponce,* 422 U.S. 873 (1975), that roving border patrols could stop and investigate an automobile if they "reasonably suspected" that the car contained illegal aliens. But this decision, like *Terry* decision, is a narrow one, restricted to border situations. The Court's attitude toward more typical encounters between citizens and law enforcement officers arises in many cases, but often only in the form of what lawyers and judges refer to as *dicta*: language that is not necessary to the decision of the case at hand and which therefore does not carry full weight as judicial precedent. An example of this is a statement by the Court in the case of *Brown* v. *Texas,* 443 U.S. 47, 51 (1979):

> We have recognized that in some circumstances an officer may detain a suspect briefly for questioning although he does not have "probable cause" to believe that the suspect is involved in criminal activity, as is required for traditional arrest. However, we have required the officers to have a reasonable suspicion, based on objective facts, that the individual is involved in criminal activity.

So there was some indication that a *Terry*-type stop might soon be sanctioned even where the officer does not fear the subject is armed.

Lower courts, however, were not timid. In a number of cases these courts have approved the brief detention of suspicious persons on less than probable cause for interrogation regarding their activities. While these courts have not insisted upon the existence of probable cause to believe a crime has been or is about to be committed, some objective basis for interrogation must be evident or the seizure involved in a field interrogation will be considered unreasonable.

EXAMPLE A:
In *United States* v. *Fallis,* 414 F.2d 772 (9th Cir. 1969), a police officer halted the car of a person who answered the physical description of a wanted robber and engaged in a cursory inquiry. This was proper.

EXAMPLE B:
In *State* v. *DeMasi,* 419 A.2d 285 (1980), police officers stopped a heavily laden car they saw cruising an industrial area late at night after the backseat passenger glanced back at them. The Supreme Court of Rhode Island invalidated this action because the circumstances leading to the stop did not amount to "reasonable suspicion" that criminal activity was afoot.

EXAMPLE C:
The subject was a stranger to the neighborhood, he was poorly dressed, and was walking slowly in the rain at night. No thefts or other crimes in the area had been reported. On these facts it was held, in *United States* v. *Hostetter,* 295 F. Supp. 1312 (D. Del. 1969), that investigational detention was unjustified.

In 1985 the Supreme Court again addressed the field interrogation issue and, in so doing, cleared the air somewhat. In *United States* v. *Hensley,* 469 U.S. 221, the Court extended the *Terry* doctrine. The facts were these: Following an armed robbery in the Cincinnati suburb of St. Bernard, a St. Bernard police officer, on the basis of information obtained from an informant that Hensley had driven the getaway car, issued a "wanted flyer" or bulletin to other police departments in the area. The flyer stated that Hensley was wanted for investigation of the robbery; it described him, gave the date and location of the robbery, and asked the other departments to pick him up and hold him for the St. Bernard police. On the basis of the flyer, police officers in Covington, Kentucky, near Cincinnati, stopped an automobile that the suspect was driving. One of the officers recognized a passenger in the car as a convicted felon and, upon observing a revolver butt protruding from underneath the passenger's seat, arrested the passenger. After a search of the car uncovered other handguns, Hensley was also arrested. He was indicted on the federal charge of being a convicted felon in possession of firearms.

Hensley moved to suppress the handguns from evidence on the ground that the Covington police had stopped him in violation of the Fourth Amendment and the principles announced in *Terry.* The trial court rejected the motion but was reversed by a Court of Appeals, which held that the stop of Hensley's car was improper because the crime being investigated was not ongoing and the "wanted flyer" was insufficient to create a reasonable suspicion that Hensley had committed a crime. The Supreme Court reversed

"Follow my finger with your eye." An officer tests a driver at a Sobriety Checkpoint in California.

the Court of Appeals. Where police have been unable to locate a person suspected of involvement in a crime, said the Court, the ability briefly to stop him, ask questions, or check identification in the absence of probable cause promotes the strong government interest in solving crimes and bringing offenders to justice. Furthermore, restraining police action until probable cause is determined would not only hinder the investigation but might enable the suspect to flee and remain at large. Still, the Court spoke cautiously:

> We need not and do not decide today whether *Terry* stops to investigate all past crimes, however serious, are permitted. It is enough to say that, if police have a reasonable suspicion, grounded in specific and articulable facts, that a person they encounter was involved in or is wanted in connection with a completed felony, then a *Terry* stop may be made to investigate that suspicion.

The Court concluded that the Covington police officers' reliance on a "wanted flyer" was reasonable. And evidence uncovered in the course of the stop is admissible if the police who *issued* the flyer possessed a reasonable suspicion justifying a stop.

Whether a standard even lower than reasonable suspicion will be recognized is a question that is certain to be raised in future cases involving checkpoint systems. For example, some law enforcement agencies have instituted so-called sobriety checkpoint operations. Motorists passing through a particular fixed location are briefly detained to permit police to look for signs of intoxication. The states are likely to argue that the constitutionality of these operations can be upheld under the Supreme Court's border checkpoint decisions; opposing counsel are sure to insist that no standard lower than reasonable suspicion will suffice.

Detention for Fingerprinting

In *Davis* v. *Mississippi*, 394 U.S. 721 (1969), coming just a year after *Terry*, the Supreme Court said that it was at least "arguable" that detention of a suspect on less than probable cause for purposes of fingerprinting him would be justifiable. The Court noted that fingerprint comparison is a "reliable and effective crime-solving tool" and that detention for fingerprinting purposes involves no very radical intrusion upon a person's privacy. A clear-cut ruling on this issue has not yet been made by the Court. The suggestion contained in *Davis* came in the form of what lawyers and judges refer to as *dicta:* language that is not necessary to the decision of the case at hand and which therefore does not carry full weight as judicial precedent.

Required Production of Voice and Handwriting Exemplars

In two 1973 opinions the Supreme Court turned down claims that voice and handwriting specimens, not subject to any Fifth Amendment privileges claim, could not be subpoenaed by a grand jury without a preliminary showing of reasonableness. (*United States* v. *Dionisio*, 410 U.S. 1 (1973); *United States* v. *Mara*, 410 U.S. 19 (1973).) The Court stated that the giving of an exemplar, like the provision of fingerprint impressions, is not a serious infringement of personal freedom and privacy. For example, the intrusion is minimal when compared with that involved in a frisk, particularly when a subpoena is served. The subject thus gets advance notice and can obtain legal counsel if he wishes.

The Court did not absolutely foreclose a challenge to a subpoena on the ground of unreasonableness. However, it is fairly clear that a witness would have to make a strong showing of unreasonableness in order to have a subpoena quashed: in *Dionisio* the Court upheld subpoenas to twenty persons for voice comparison with recorded conversations.

K. Searches Pursuant to Consent

The Lawfulness of Consensual Searches

A search to which the subject has freely consented is a lawful search. The prosecution will have the burden of establishing that the subject's consent to a search by law enforcement officers was specific, unequivocal, and voluntary, especially where the subject was in police custody at the time. Coerced consent is not voluntary consent and a show of force, such as the brandishing of a service revolver, may be enough to support a claim of coercion or duress.

A federal trial court in New York has developed at least a partial list of factors that shed light on the voluntariness of a consent to search:

> Among the factors that may be considered in determining the effectiveness and validity of a consent to search are whether at the time when it was given the defendant was under arrest . . .; whether he was overpowered by arresting officers, handcuffed, or similarly subject to physical restrictions . . .; whether the keys to the premises searched had already been seized by the police from the defendant . . .; whether the defendant employed evasive conduct or attempted to mislead the police . . .; and whether he denied guilt or the presence of any incriminatory objects in his premises. . . .
>
> The presence of some or all of the aforementioned facts is not controlling, since . . . each case "must stand or fall on its own special facts." . . . Although the defendant need not express a "positive desire" to have the search conducted in order to render his consent a voluntary waiver, . . . it must amount to more than mere submission or acquiescence in the nature of resignation to constitute a valid waiver. (*United States* v. *Lewis,* 274 F. Supp. 184 (S.D.N.Y. 1967).)

In mid-1973 the Supreme Court decided, in *Schneckloth* v. *Bustamonte,* 412 U.S. 218, that a police officer does not have to warn a person of his/her right to refuse to consent to a search as a necessary preliminary to obtaining a valid consent, at least where the consenting person is not in custody. Applying as it does to persons not in police custody, *Schneckloth* is consistent with most of the decided cases and with the basic policies underlying *Miranda* v. *Arizona.*

The Necessity for Prompt Action

If consent to a search is given, the search should be conducted as soon as possible, preferably immediately. Consent to a search at a particular time does not remain valid indefinitely.

Consent Given by Others

There are some situations in which a person other than the subject can give valid consent to search. This ordinarily involves a co-owner of the premises or a person—such as a spouse or parent—who has an equal right to make use of the premises. Today, however, with the emphasis on a right of privacy as the cornerstone of the Fourth Amendment, there may be a trend toward holding that only the person whose privacy is invaded by a search can effectively consent to that search. And this much is clear: one who has a legal interest in the premises but no immediate right to possession has no authority to give consent to a search. Thus a hotel clerk cannot give a valid consent to search a hotel room unless he has been specifically authorized by the hotel guest to do so. And this rule has peculiar application to landlords. To permit a tenant's home to be searched at the discretion of his landlord would make a very large hole in the Fourth Amendment; even a rented house can be a man's castle.

EXAMPLE:
In *Chapman* v. *United States*, 365 U.S. 610 (1961), it was held that a nonresident landlord could not validly consent to a search of leased premises despite the fact that he had retained the right to enter the premises for inspection, repair, and the like. His right of entry was too limited to support a power to consent to a search. Valid consent could only come from the lessee (tenant).

But a person who exercises *joint* control, along with the accused, over an area or an object can give the requisite consent. (*United States* v. *Matlock*, 415 U.S. 164 (1979).) One who gives his property to someone else for some reason runs the risk that the person will consent to a search of it. A good example of this is *Frazier* v. *Cupp*, 394 U.S. 731 (1969), in which Frazier left clothing in a duffel bag that he shared with a cousin, Rawls. The duffel bag was left at Rawls's home. Rawls was arrested at his home and gave his consent to a search of the bag, during which Frazier's clothing was seized. The Supreme Court said, "[Frazier], in allowing Rawls to use the bag and in leaving it in his house must be taken to have assumed the risk that Rawls would allow someone else to look inside." What the Court was really saying was that Frazier must not have put a premium on privacy, and a desire for privacy lies at the heart of the Fourth Amendment.

The Effect of Misrepresentations by the Investigating Officer

Some special problems arise when a search pursuant to consent has followed misrepresentations by the investigating officers. Misleading representations by the police can invalidate the consent apparently given by a subject.

A case that sets the background is *Gouled* v. *United States*, 255 U.S. 298 (1921). A business associate of the subject was acting as a police agent. He got into Gouled's office on the pretense of making a social visit. As soon as Gouled left his office, the associate searched it. He obtained certain documents which he turned over to law enforcement authorities. Although Gouled had concededly consented to the entry, the Supreme Court held that his papers had been seized in violation of the Fourth Amendment's guarantees. Gouled had agreed to a social call, not a search and seizure. But sometimes there is consent to a search and seizure, induced by deception. A different result will follow when the government agent deceives the subject regarding his purpose or identity but searches no further than the subject, in reliance on the deception, permits. Here the most illustrative case is *Hoffa* v. *United States,* 385 U.S. 293 (1966). *Hoffa* involved an associate of the labor leader who concealed the fact that he had turned government informer. The Supreme Court said that no interest shielded by the Fourth Amendment had been violated by this deception. The Court adopted a cynical but sensible view: "The risk of being . . . deceived as to the identity of one with whom one deals is probably inherent in the conditions of human society. It is the kind of risk we necessarily assume whenever we speak."

The *Hoffa* case strongly suggests that deception does not invalidate a consent to search. About the only relevance of deception is that it will lead courts to limit the scope of the search strictly; any search going beyond the terms of the subject's consent will be considered unlawful.

EXAMPLE:
In *Graves* v. *Beto,* 424 F.2d 525 (5th Cir. 1970), police obtained a blood sample from a subject by representing that it would only be tested for alcohol content. In actuality, it was tested for type and matched with a blood sample discovered at the scene of a rape. The consent was held inoperative with respect to the test for blood type. The subject's consent was limited to a test for alcohol content.

In 1980 the Supreme Court gave broad consideration to the consent exception. In *United States* v. *Mendenhall,* 446 U.S. 544 (1980), plainclothes Drug Enforcement Administration agents had approached a suspect in an airport and asked for identification. Mendenhall's airline ticket and her driver's license had been issued in different names, and she was briefly questioned about this discrepancy. One of the agents then identified himself and requested that Mendenhall go with him to his office in the airport. There Mendenhall agreed to a strip search after twice being informed of her right to refuse. The Court concluded that Mendenhall had voluntarily consented to the search even though it was against her interest to do so. Since Mendenhall had voluntarily accompanied the agent "there was little or no evidence that she was coerced." (Compare *Florida* v. *Royer,* 460 U.S 491 (1983), accused's consent tainted by unlawfulness of his arrest.)

L. Statutory Provision for Warrantless Searches

Some regulatory statutes provide for searches without warrant. For example, Arizona Revised Statutes §3-710(G) and (H) empower an inspector to "enter and inspect" any place that handles eggs and to "take for inspection representative samples of . . . invoices, eggs, and cases or containers" to determine whether regulations covering the production and distribution of eggs have been observed. Such statutory programs for regulating commercial enterprises have consistently been held to be reasonable and not violative of the Fourth Amendment. The Supreme Court so far has not questioned "such accepted regulatory techniques as licensing programs which require inspections prior to operating a business or marketing a product." It was careful in *See* v. *Seattle,* 387 U.S. 541 (1967), however, to point out that "Any constitutional challenges to such programs can only be resolved . . . on a case-by-case basis under the general Fourth Amendment standard of reasonableness."

M. Electronic Surveillance

The State of the Art

The law frequently experiences difficulty in keeping up with scientific advances. Nowhere is this more true than in connection with the increasing sophistication of electronic surveillance techniques, the use of which by law enforcement agents in their fight against crime has posed issues that are not readily susceptible of solution under the traditional approach to the Fourth Amendment.

As Professor Alan F. Westin, an authority on the law of privacy, has said, "The investigator's dream is to make his subject a walking radio transmitter, enabling the investigator to hear everything the subject says to someone else. . . ." This dream is by no means an impossible one. It can be done by wiring the subject's clothing, putting the microphone in one button, a sub-miniature transmitter in another button, and batteries in a third button. The thread used on the buttons is conductive wire, forming the antenna. Although access to the subject's clothing can sometimes be obtained at such places as his dry-cleaner's or a restaurant checkroom, wiring the subject is not always feasible.

Consequently, the most common electronic surveillance method involves wiring—"bugging"—premises frequented by the subject. Bugging devices are now of ultraminiature size, making it possible to hide them almost anywhere. A high-sensitivity microphone the size of a match-head or smaller can be attached to the underside of furniture or hidden inside telephones, clocks, picture frames, lamps, flower pots, and an unending list of other places.

Development of the laser beam has added a new weapon to the arsenal of electronic surveillance. The portable laser microphone emits an invisible infrared beam which is capable of remaining focused over long distances. It can travel for miles from the point of transmission to the targeted premises, where it hits a mirrored modulator which a criminal investigator has previously planted there. The modulator sends the laser beam back to its source. This returning beam has been modulated by the sound waves produced by conversations in the room being surveilled. A photo-amplifier at the listening post permits the investigator to transform the returning beam of light into comprehensible sound.

Where entry upon the premises to plant a listening device is impossible, a contact microphone can be employed as a sensitive ear to the wall. Since speech generates sound waves that set up measurable vibrations when they hit the walls of a room, a vibration-sensitive transducer attached to the opposite side of the wall will pick up the vibrations, thus making it possible for an investigator in the next room to listen and record accurately. Where the wall is exceptionally thick, a so-called spike-mike can be used. Directional parabolic microphones with a range of hundreds of feet can be used if the room to be observed has an open window. A radar microphone can beam its signal to window panes and get a returning beam, modulated by speech-generated vibrations, a mile or more away. Even more sophisticated than these mechanisms is the microwave beam. A tiny mechanism using a reflector and a microwave antenna is involved. When a microwave beam is transmitted into the observed room from as much as a city block away, the device is activated so that it sends an acoustical signal back to the listening post.

Then, of course, there is the telephone tap. It is almost impossible to carry on criminal activity without using the telephone. Any of the eavesdropping methods described above can be used to intercept speech that goes into a telephone receiver. Two-way wiretapping is possible. Requiring entry into the telephone circuit, two-way tapping lets the investigator overhear both ends of a telephone conversation. The most common technique in wiretapping still involves use of the induction coil. The coil is placed a few feet from the telephone or near its connecting wires at some point before they are commingled with other telephone wires. The induction coil is in the magnetic field that carries the subject's voice signal and picks up enough of it to permit listening and recording.

Not all electronic surveillance is aimed at the spoken word. For example, Zoomar television cameras permit investigators to look through windows into rooms. (Powerful binoculars and long-range telephoto cameras can be used for the same purpose.)

The law's question regarding all of these devices and others not mentioned is whether evidence secured through their use and without court approval is admissible at trial. In times past the answer was put in terms of *trespass.* The most important judicial opinion taking this tack was in *Olmstead* v. *United States,* 277 U.S. 438 (1928). In that opinion the Supreme Court said that the Fourth Amendment's prohibition against unreasonable searches and seizures did not foreclose wiretapping unless it was accomplished by means of an illegal trespass on the subject's premises. It was thought that the Fourth Amendment protected only tangible things. Since spoken words are intangible, there could be no violation of the Fourth

Amendment unless there was a trespass on property—property being something tangible.

Use of *Olmstead's* trespass test meant that there was no Fourth Amendment violation when a law enforcement agent, who was himself wired, was invited into the subject's presence and transmitted or recorded the subject's words without his knowledge. It also meant that there was no constitutional violation when a Detecta-phone was placed against the wall of an adjoining office. But use of the aforementioned spike-mike, which must be driven into the wall, was an "unauthorized physical penetration into the premises" which violated the Fourth Amendment.

Wiretapping was and is governed by a federal statute. The 1934 Federal Communications Act made it unlawful to intercept and disclose telephone conversations. The Supreme Court, basing its decision on this statute and not on the Fourth Amendment, held in 1937 that conversations intercepted in violation of the act were inadmissible in federal prosecutions (*Nardone* v. *United States*, 302 U.S. 379). In *Rathbun* v. *United States*, 355 U.S. 107 (1957), the Court held that there is no interception within the Communication Act's meaning where one party to a telephone conversation has consented to eavesdropping by some third person.

Katz *v.* United States: *A New Rationale*

Olmstead's trespass theory was not a very satisfactory one. It was slowly but surely undermined by the courts. Its total demise came in 1967 with the case of *Katz* v. *United States*, 398 U.S. 347. FBI agents had attached an electronic surveillance device to the outside of a public pay telephone booth and then listened in on and recorded telephone calls made by the accused. It could not be said that the agents had illegally trespassed on any premises of the accused. But the Supreme Court said that *Olmstead's* trespass doctrine had been badly riddled by the courts and was no longer to be relied upon. The FBI agents' action "violated the privacy upon which [the accused] justifiably relied while using the telephone booth and thus constituted a 'search and seizure' within the meaning of the Fourth Amendment." By reverting to the privacy concept underlying the Fourth Amendment, the Court reached the conclusion that intangible words could, after all, be susceptible to seizure. The agents' failure to get court authorization for the electronic surveillance activities made those activities unreasonable. The exclusionary rule would be applied.

The Two Branches of the Katz *Rule*

The *Katz* test has two branches: (1) The surveillance subject must have *relied* on the apparent circumstances to provide him with privacy in his activities, and (2) his reliance must have been *justified.*

In *United States* v. *White,* 401 U.S. 745 (1971), the Supreme Court took up the impact of *Katz* on the situation of the "bugged agent," who is wired to pick up and perhaps also record the words of a surveillance subject with whom he talks. With four dissents, the Court held that "if the conduct and revelations of an agent without electronic equipment do not invade the defendant's constitutionally justifiable expectations of privacy, neither does a simultaneous recording of the same conversations made by the agent or by others from transmissions received from the agent to whom the defendant is talking and whose trustworthiness the defendant necessarily risks." This commonsense decision leaves intact the holding in two earlier cases: *On Lee* v. *United States,* 343 U.S. 747 (1952) (law enforcement agent could properly carry electronic device which transmitted conversations to agents located elsewhere) and *Lopez* v. *United States,* 373 U.S. 427 (1963) (agent could properly use equipment concealed on his person to record conversations with subject. (See also *United States* v. *Karo,* 468 U.S. 705 (1984) (approving admission of evidence resulting from monitoring of beeper planted by government agents in can of ether to be sold to defendants because this form of surveillance "revealed . . . no information that could not have been obtained through visual surveillance.").)

The Relationship between Electronic Surveillance and the Prosecution's Case

Ordinarily it would be difficult for an accused to demonstrate a direct relationship between the use of electronic surveillance and the prosecution's case where the surveillance guided law enforcement agents to evidence that is offered at trial. Much of this difficulty was eased by the opinion in *Alderman* v. *United States,* 394 U.S. 165 (1969), which held that the accused is entitled to see the records of any electronic surveillance which he or she has standing to challenge. The accused and his lawyer can, however, be ordered by a judge not to make unnecessary disclosures of the records.

Electronic Surveillance and the General Requirement of a Search Warrant

It will by now be evident that searches conducted by means of electronic surveillance are subject to the warrant requirements of the Fourth Amendment. Of course, electronic surveillance is unlike other searches and the warrant requirement must be modified to take account of this fact.

The warrant requirement in the context of electronic monitoring was considered by the Supreme Court in *Berger* v. *New York,* 388 U.S. 41 (1967), a case involving the placing of a recording device in a suspect's office pursuant to a state court's authorization. The order issued by the court was held to be improperly drawn. There were four reasons that it did not meet

Fourth Amendment requirements: (1) It was not sufficiently specific, since it did not state, and no one had been required to show, what crimes had been or were being committed, whose conversations were to be monitored, or what specific conversations were to be overheard. (2) It authorized a whole series of electronic surveillances. (3) It included no direction that the surveillance be halted as soon as described conversations were overheard. (4) The order contained no provision for notice to the suspect or any excuse for the omission of notice.

One year later the Congress took a look at the warrant procedure in the context of electronic surveillance. The 1968 Omnibus Crime Control and Safe Streets Act, 18 U.S.C.A. §2510 *et seq.*, prohibits any person from intercepting or attempting to intercept by electronic, mechanical, or other device any oral or wire communication except under court authority. Oral communication is defined in the statute as being "any oral communication uttered by a person exhibiting an expectation that such communication is not subject to interception under circumstances justifying such expectation." Obviously, this section of the Act was modeled after the Supreme Court's opinion in *Katz*.

The Omnibus Crime Control and Safe Streets Act sets up a procedure for federal prosecutors to follow in applying for the issuance of electronic surveillance orders by federal judges. Provision is also made for state prosecutors to follow the same procedure in state courts. This means that a state court judge can grant an order that conforms both to an applicable state statute and the federal procedure, with the consequence that evidence obtained under his order will be admissible in both judicial systems.

There are eight key procedural provisions of the federal statute:

1. The prosecutor's application for a surveillance order must include detailed information concerning any prior applications involving the same persons, facilities, or places.
2. An application can be made only in connection with an investigation of relatively serious crimes.
3. The trial judge, before issuing an order, must determine (a) that there exists probable cause for believing that the named person is committing, has committed, or is about to commit a specified offense; (b) that there exists probable cause for believing that particular communications relating to that offense will be obtained by means of the requested interception; (c) that normal investigative methods have either been tried and were unsuccessful or are likely to be highly dangerous if attempted; and (d) that there exists probable cause for believing that the place or facilities to be monitored are to be used in connection with the designated crime or leased by or listed in the name of or commonly used by the named suspect.

4. The authorizing order must be specific about the nature, location, and owner of the facilities to be monitored. It must give a detailed description of the communications sought to be intercepted and it must state the period during which interception is authorized.
5. The order's duration can be for only that period of time which is necessary to gain the objective of the interception, and in no event can it be for more than thirty days. Under the statute there can be, in effect, no extensions, only new applications.
6. The order must provide that the surveillance be conducted in such a way as to minimize the interception of communications which are irrelevant to the investigation.
7. If possible, intercepted communications are to be recorded rather than simply overheard. Written records of interrogations are to be sealed up and retained for a minimum of ten years.
8. Within at least ninety days of the interception's termination, the persons named in the prosecutor's application are to be notified of the application and whether or not communications were intercepted. Ten days before use of intercepted evidence in court the parties in the case must be provided with information about the manner in which the authorizing order was obtained.
9. The contents of even a validly intercepted communication remain privileged from disclosure unless some degree of disclosure is specifically authorized by a court. Knowledge of the contents, and evidence derived from such knowledge, can be used by a law enforcement officer "to the extent such use is appropriate to the proper performance of his official duties" and can be disclosed only to other law enforcement officers and only if, again, the disclosure is within the disclosing officer's performance of official duties. Disclosure is authorized during sworn testimony before grand juries and in criminal cases.

These portions of the Omnibus Crime Control and Safe Streets Act are subject to constitutional testing before the Supreme Court. The act's requirement that only "type" of conversation be specified may be too broad to meet the requirements of the *Berger* opinion. And the act seems not to face up to *Berger's* requirement of advance notice in the absence of an excuse. Furthermore, the act applies only to electronic eavesdropping, not to other methods of surveillance. For example, the act has no application to devices that record the telephone numbers dialed from a particular instrument (pen registers) or that trace the source of telephone calls made to a particular number (tracers). The use of pen registers is not even limited by the Fourth Amendment, since telephone users have no reasonable expectation that the numbers they dial are private. They must realize that the telephone company often keeps records of such numbers. (*Smith* v. *Maryland,* 442 U.S. 735 (1979).) The rule, however, may prove to be different in connection with *incoming* calls since telephone companies are not understood by the public routinely to record incoming calls. This lingering question was noted but not decided in *In re* Application for an Order Authorizing the Installation of a Pen Register or Touch Tone Decoder and a Terminating Tap, 610 F.2d 1149, 1154 n. 3 (3d Cir. 1979). In that case the Third Circuit ruled that a hearing must be held to determine whether the burden on telephone companies is reasonable before law enforcement personnel can require them to assist in tracing calls. This cumbersome procedure may discourage future reliance on tracer devices by law enforcement agencies.

The Kahn *Decision: "Others as Yet Unknown"*

A significant interpretation of the permissible breadth of wiretap orders came down in 1974. The facts of *United States* v. *Kahn,* 415 U.S. 144 (1974), were these: A Justice Department attorney applied to a federal District Court judge to issue a wiretap order under the authority of the 1970 Omnibus Crime Control and Safe Streets Act. The affidavit accompanying the application stated that Irving Kahn was a bookmaker who operated from his residence with the aid of two home telephones.

The affidavit further stated that government informants refused to testify against Kahn; that telephone company records alone would not be sufficient to support a criminal conviction; and that physical surveillance or normal search and seizure techniques would not be likely to produce useful evidence. The wiretap application concluded that "normal investigative procedures . . . appear unlikely to succeed" and requested authorization to intercept communications by Irving Kahn and "others as yet unknown" over the two home telephone lines.

The judge entered an order authorizing government agents to "intercept wire communications of Irving Kahn and others as yet unknown" to and from the two described telephones. Shortly thereafter, Irving Kahn made two telephone calls from Arizona to his Chicago home and related gambling information to his wife, Minnie. On the same date, Minnie Kahn made two calls on the tapped telephones to a "known gambling figure" and related gambling information.

Indicted for using a facility in interstate commerce to promote gambling, Irving and Minnie Kahn filed a motion to suppress their intercepted telephone conversations and a federal judge granted it.

The U.S. Court of Appeals affirmed the trial judge's suppression of the tapped conversations, but the Supreme Court reversed the lower court. The top court rejected the lower courts' view that only intercepted conversations in which Irving Kahn took part were admissible. The wiretap order had not mentioned conversations *between* Irving Kahn and others; it had spoken about conversations *of* Irving Kahn *and* others. The Supreme Court recognized that the purpose of the wiretap was "to reveal the identities of

[Kahn's] confederates, their places of operation, and the nature of the conspiracy involved." These purposes could well be served by interception of conversations to which Irving Kahn was not a party. The Supreme Court also held that the Court of Appeals had erred in interpreting the phrase "others as yet unknown" to exclude Minnie Kahn's conversations.

Dalia *v.* United States: *Covert Entry to Emplace Bugging Devices*

The text of the 1970 Omnibus Crime Control and Safe Streets Act does not refer explicitly to covert entry. But the Supreme Court, in *Dalia* v. *United States,* 441 U.S. 238 (1979), found that "Congress meant to authorize courts . . . to approve electronic surveillance without limitation on the means necessary to its accomplishment." The means, however, must be reasonable under the circumstances. In *Dalia,* the Court validated what amounted to a breaking and entering on the part of FBI agents, because the agents saw no other way to position the listening device. A second holding in the case concluded the Fourth Amendment does not require that an electronic surveillance order include a specific authorization to enter covertly the premises described in the order. Law enforcement officials are given wide discretion.

Minimization Requirement

A telephone tap or other listening device almost inevitably reveals communications not relevant to the investigation. These matters are not properly subject to interception, and the statute requires that effort be made to minimize their interception. Frequently it is possible for officers in good faith to turn off the monitor when an irrelevant conversation begins. If they are uncertain about a communication's relevance, they can spot-check every few minutes and turn the recorder back on if the discussion becomes relevant to the investigation. Some law enforcement departments utilize a dual recorder system. While officers monitor one recorder, using their good-faith discretion, a second machine records *all* communications. If something is missed on the first recorder, a search warrant may be obtained to reveal the full communication, recorded by the second device.

The Supreme Court, in *Scott* v. *United States,* 436 U.S. 128 (1978), significantly weakened the minimization requirement. The Court concluded that compliance with the minimization requirement will not be evaluated solely on the basis of the officer's good faith. Rather, the courts will objectively assess the officer's actions in light of the facts and circumstances confronting him at the time. If, for example, the investigation is focusing on a widespread conspiracy, extensive surveillance might be justified. Under the *Scott* decision a court could draw this conclusion even where the investigation agents knowingly disregarded the minimization requirement.

N. The "Fruit of the Poisonous Tree" Doctrine

Not all improper investigatory activities result in the offering at trial of evidence that is the direct product of the improper conduct. There can be an indirect connection, as when improperly seized evidence provides leads to other incriminating evidence. The Supreme Court has had to consider whether the exclusionary rule should be applied to this other, indirect evidence.

The Silverthorne *Decision*

A hard line against the use of indirect evidence was taken by the Court in *Silverthorne Lumber Co.* v. *United States,* 251 U.S. 385 (1920). In that case federal agents had improperly seized some books and records. The accused got a court order directing that they be returned to him but the agents had already photographed them. At trial the prosecutor made use of the photographs to get from the court a subpoena requiring production of the documents. This use of the photographs—the indirect evidence—was disapproved by the Supreme Court. It declared that "The essence of a provision forbidding the acquisition of evidence in a certain way is that not merely evidence so acquired shall not be used before the Court *but that it shall not be used at all*" (italics added).

In *Silverthorne* the Court said that if knowledge of the facts is obtained from a source *independent* of the improper investigative activity, the facts can be proved.

EXAMPLE:

Had the prosecution in *Silverthorne* been able to establish the existence of the books and records by some means other than the photographs taken of them, the knowledge of their existence would have had an independent source and would be admissible.

The hard line of *Silverthorne* was softened slightly in *Nardone* v. *United States,* 308 U.S. 338 (1939). In *Nardone* the Court said that sometimes the connection between the "poisonous tree" (that is, the original improper activity) and the evidence offered at trial "may have become so attenuated as to dissipate the taint." In *Wong Sun* v. *United States,* 371 U.S. 471 (1963), the Court tried to define what degree of attenuation (lessening of force or strength) would be enough to avoid the taint of the original illegality. The Court said:

> We need not hold that all evidence is "fruit of the poisonous tree" simply because it would not have come to light but for the illegal actions of the police. Rather, the more apt question in such a case is "whether, granting establishment of the primary illegality, the evidence to which instant objection is made

has been come at by exploitation of that illegality or instead by means sufficiently distinguishable to be purged of the primary taint."

Since *Wong Sun* the Court has spoken on several occasions about the meaning of attenuation. The most important of these decisions is *Brown* v. *Illinois,* 422 U.S. 590 (1975), a case in which the Court considered whether the administration of *Miranda* warnings (essentially the right to remain silent and to have an attorney present during questioning) after a Fourth Amendment violation can remove the taint of illegality from a subsequent confession. The facts in *Brown* were these: Two Chicago police officers arrested Brown for murder without a warrant or probable cause. This made the arrest illegal. The officers then took Brown to the station, where he was placed in an interrogation room. After some minutes, the officers returned with a file on the investigation. They read Brown his *Miranda* rights and proceeded to question him. This questioning produced a two-page statement in which Brown admitted that he and a man named Jimmy Claggett had murdered the appropriately named Roger Corpus. The Supreme Court held that "*Miranda* warnings, *alone* and *per se*, cannot always make the act sufficiently a product of free will to break, for Fourth Amendment purposes, the causal connection between the illegality and the confession." Rather, *Miranda* warnings are but one important factor to be considered. The Court suggested several other relevant considerations: the temporal proximity of the arrest and the confession, the presence of intervening circumstances, and particularly, the purpose and flagrancy of the official misconduct. Of course, once an accused shows the initial Fourth Amendment violation, it is incumbent upon the prosecution to show that evidence obtained as a result of the illegality is distanced sufficiently, by one or more of the *Brown* criteria, from the illegality. (See also *Segura* v. *United States,* 468 U.S. 796 (1984).)

Of growing importance in the Court's approach to attenuation is an idea raised by Justice Byron White in dissent in *Harrison* v. *United States,* 392 U.S. 219 (1968). He thought a finding of insufficient attenuation should be made only if doing so would advance the underlying purpose of the exclusionary rule, which is the deterrence of unlawful investigative conduct. Under the facts in *Brown* it is plain the Court correctly excluded the confession. To allow police officers to cure a Fourth Amendment violation merely by reading *Miranda* rights to a suspect would hardly deter police misconduct.

Lower courts have experienced some difficulty in trying to apply the "fruit of the poisonous tree" doctrine. At the very least, they have insisted upon a factual causal relationship between the illegal investigatory activity and the evidence that is ultimately offered by the prosecution. Consequently, evidence obtained *before* the police engaged in any illegal conduct will not be subject to exclusion. But hard questions are posed where it is contended that the accused made an incriminating statement because of prior unlawful investigative activity. Some courts have been willing to assume a causal link between any confession following illegal activity that was known to the accused at the time of his statement.

Another difficult question is presented when it is argued that unlawful police conduct led not to specific items of subsequently discovered evidence but to an entire investigative effort which, in turn, led to the offered items. It has been said by a distinguished federal trial judge that if unlawfully obtained evidence "leads the government to substantially intensify an investigation," all evidence discovered later is fatally tainted by the original unlawfulness (Judge Jack B. Weinstein, in *United States* v. *Schipani,* 289 F.Supp. 43 (E.D.N.Y. 1968), *aff'd,* 414 F.2d 1962 (2d Cir. 1969)).

Often, of course, a later police investigation would have been conducted without regard to what may have been turned up by earlier illegal activity. In this situation the courts will refuse to find a causal relation between the initial illegality and the subsequent investigation. Furthermore, even the finding of a clear-cut causal relationship is not invariably fatal. An undeniably causal relationship will be considered legally insignificant where the asserted "fruits of the poisonous tree" would have been discovered sooner or later without the initial unlawful investigative activity.

EXAMPLE:
A witness's courtroom testimony is objected to on the ground that the witness was located as a result of illegally obtained evidence. On the assumption that the witness might have been discovered through further routine investigative activities or might have come forward voluntarily, many courts would overrule the objection. (But compare the attitude of the Illinois Supreme Court, which has held that a witness who was discovered during an unlawful search cannot give testimony for the prosecution. *People* v. *Albea,* 118 N.E.2d 277 (S. Ct. Ill. 1954).)

There is a second possible exception even where a causal link has been established between unlawful conduct and an item of evidence. If that item of evidence is of minimal significance in the case, it may be received despite the causal link. Thus if illegal methods, such as an unauthorized wiretap, are employed not to establish probable cause for arrest but simply to locate the arrestee, evidence found as an incident of the arrest will not be considered the tainted product of the original illegality.

If the causal link is present and the evidence is important, there is still the possibility that the relationship is so attenuated, stretched so thin, as to avoid the fatal taint. Lower courts, seeking guidance in such cases as *Wong Sun* v. *United States,* 371 U.S. 471 (1963), have adopted the attenuation theory whenever some significant independent act has intervened to weaken or break the causal chain.

Wong Sun had been unlawfully arrested. He had been released from custody and several days later voluntarily returned for questioning. During his interrogation he made incriminating statements. The Supreme Court held that Wong Sun's voluntary submission to interrogation was a significantly independent, intervening act to break the causal chain. The possible impact of his unlawful arrest on his incriminatory statements was blunted by Wong Sun's voluntary appearance for questioning.

O. Erosion of the Exclusionary Rule

Although the exclusionary rule, as originally conceived, flatly prohibited the use at trial of illegally seized evidence for any purpose, the Supreme Court has been cautiously backtracking and this process is certain to accelerate as the horrendous problems posed by international terrorism and illegal narcotics sales and use increase. It has been clear since 1954 that illegally seized evidence can be used to impeach an accused's contradictory direct testimony (*Walder* v. *United States,* 347 U.S. 62 (1954)). In *United States* v. *Havens,* 446 U.S. 620 (1980), the Supreme Court held that such evidence can also be employed to undercut an accused's responses to proper cross-examination questions that were "reasonably suggested" to the prosecutor by the accused's response to the direct examination of his own lawyer.

In *United States* v. *Payner,* 447 U.S. 727 (1980), the Court held that the supervisory powers of the federal courts do not authorize them to suppress otherwise admissible material on the ground that it had been illegally obtained from a third person not before the trial court. In *Payner* law enforcement agents had discovered an incriminating document during their unlawful search of a third person's briefcase.

In 1984 the Supreme Court accepted a case, *United States* v. *Leon,* 468 U.S. 897, that provided it with an opportunity further to loosen the exclusionary rule. In this California drug case a state court judge had issued a search warrant based on the affidavit of police officers who had acted on the tip of an informant "of unproven reliability." The warrant was technically valid on its face and the defendants were subsequently arrested and indicted. The trial judge, however, concluded that the warrant had been based on stale information and therefore had not been issued on a showing of probable cause. He suppressed the evidence, consisting mainly of illicit drugs, that had been seized under the warrant. The Supreme Court reversed, holding that the Fourth Amendment exclusionary rule should not be applied to bar the use of evidence obtained by law enforcement officers who acted in reasonable, good faith reliance on a search warrant issued by a detached and neutral magistrate even though the warrant was ultimately found to be invalid. The Court was careful to add that its ruling would be inapplicable, and evidence suppression would result, "if the officers were dishonest or reckless in preparing their affidavit or could not have harbored an objectively reasonable belief in the existence of probable cause." In short, law enforcement agents who have deliberately or recklessly misled a magistrate will not later be heard to say that they relied in good faith on the warrant that he or she was improperly induced to issue.

In an era during which terrorism and trafficking in illegal drugs are problems of staggering proportions, it is likely that the exclusionary rule will be further relaxed.

P. Standing to Object to Unlawfully Obtained Evidence

Extent of an Accused's Standing to Object

It is sometimes thought that every criminal accused has the right (standing) to invoke the exclusionary rule against unlawfully obtained evidence. This would certainly further the law's policy of drying up any incentive on the part of law enforcement officers to use illegal investigative methods. However, it is not the rule. In the leading case of *Rakas* v. *Illinois*, 439 U.S. 129 (1978), the Supreme Court announced that an accused can have relevant but illegally obtained evidence suppressed only if he can demonstrate a legitimate expectation of privacy in the place searched. The facts in *Rakas* sharply illustrate the implications of this rule: A short time after receiving a robbery report Illinois police stopped an automobile matching the description of the getaway car. They ordered the occupants—the woman driver and owner, Rakas and two others—to get out. Then, without a warrant, the officers searched the car, discovering a sawed-off shotgun and a box of shells. This evidence was admitted over Rakas' objection at trial, and he was convicted of the robbery. When the case rose to the Supreme Court, Justice Rehnquist, writing for the majority, noted that Rakas' claim failed because he asserted neither a property or possessory interest in the car or the items seized, nor did he assert some other "normal expectation of privacy." He was "merely aggrieved by the introduction of damaging evidence." It should be noted that the standing inquiry under *Rakas* is the same as the substantive Fourth Amendment question: Did the accused have a reasonable expectation of privacy in the place searched? Most courts, however, still consider standing a separate though related issue.

The Salvucci *Case*

Until recently, a defendant was granted "automatic standing" to raise Fourth Amendment challenges if the same possession needed to establish standing was an essential element of the offense charged. The Supreme Court had created the "automatic standing" rule in *Jones* v. *United States,* 362 U.S. 257 (1960). The accused had been charged with two narcotics offenses, both of which could be established by proof of possession. Jones moved to suppress the seized narcotics. However, the standing requirement trapped him in a Catch-22. If Jones, in order to establish standing, testified to an interest in either the premises or the narcotics at the hearing on his motion to suppress, his admission might rise to haunt him at his trial; if at trial he denied any interest in the premises or the narcotics he might be charged with perjury. And if he failed to allege such an interest, the trial court would not grant him standing to invoke the exclusionary rule. Hence the Supreme Court devised the "automatic standing" rule.

In *United States* v. *Salvucci,* 448 U.S. 83 (1980), however, the Supreme Court expressly overruled *Jones.* Justice Rehnquist, writing for the majority as he did in the *Rakas* case, concluded that a defendant charged with a crime of possession may invoke the exclusionary rule only if his own Fourth Amendment rights have been violated. In connection with the *Jones*-type dilemma, Justice Rehnquist pointed out that under the earlier decision in *Simmons* v. *United States,* 390 U.S. 377 (1968), if "a defendant testifies in support of a motion to suppress evidence on Fourth Amendment grounds, his testimony may not thereafter be admitted against him at trial on the issue of guilt, unless he makes no objection." It should be noted that the *Simmons* decision is limited to the use of such evidence to prove guilt. Under *Salvucci* a defendant may still be threatened by the prospect of his suppression hearing testimony being used to impeach his testimony at trial. For this reason many experts think the *Jones*-type dilemma will prevent many from raising Fourth Amendment issues at trial.

Establishing That the Accused Was the Victim of Unlawful Investigative Activity

Because of the *Jones-Alderman* rule, a criminal accused has the burden of establishing that he was the victim of improper investigatory conduct. This can be a difficult burden to discharge. There are three principal situations in which the accused can usually show that he qualifies as a victim:

1. *Possession of Rights Respecting the Seized Items.* Standing to contest a search and seizure can be based on the accused's ownership or right to possession of the items seized.

EXAMPLE A:

Ownership of books and papers gave standing to move to quash subpoena for their production directed to a third person who was in possession of them. (*Schwimmer* v. *United States,* 232 F.2d 855 (8th Cir.), *cert. denied,* 352 U.S. 833 (1956).)

EXAMPLE B:

Owner of car has standing to challenge a search of it even though he had loaned the car to a third person who had it at the time of the search. (*United States* v. *Eldridge,* 302 F.2d 463 (4th Cir. 1962).) (Of course, a person to whom the owner has relinquished possession may have the authority to *consent* to a search.)

2. *Interest in the Searched Premises.* An accused may have a legal interest in the searched premises which gives him standing to object to the search. Thus in *Alderman* v. *United States,* discussed above, the Supreme Court held that a homeowner has standing to challenge an illegal search of his or her house.

Ownership is not the only interest in premises that will give rise to standing to object. A renter has a sufficient interest in his leased apartment or rented motel room to challenge a warrantless search. Indeed, in *Jones* v. *United States,* discussed above, it was held that mere presence on the searched premises with the permission of the owner or lessee confirms standing to object to the fruits of an illegal search and seizure.

3. *Standing Based on the Right of Privacy.* Although, as was pointed out earlier, the Supreme Court has seemed to adhere to the restrictive standing rule laid down in *Jones v. United States,* a hint of revision can be found in the later case of *Mancusi* v. *DeForte,* 392 U.S. 364 (1968). In that case the Court downgraded the significance of any property right in the searched area or the seized materials. DeForte, who was a union official, shared office space with several other union officials. State authorities conducted a warrantless search of the office over DeForte's protest and took union records which were received in evidence at DeForte's trial. DeForte, who had been in the office legitimately at the time of the search, would have appeared to have had standing under *Jones* to object to the evidence. The Supreme Court, however, shifted its ground slightly. Pointing to *Katz* v. *United States,* 389 U.S. 347 (1967), the public telephone booth bugging case discussed in the earlier section on electronic surveillance, the Court said that the Fourth Amendment's protection "depends not upon a property right in the invaded place but upon whether the area was one in which there was a reasonable expectation of freedom from governmental intrusion." In other words, the Court again emphasized the right-of-privacy policy underlying the Fourth Amendment. DeForte, the Court thought, had good reason to believe that only the other union officers and their business visitors would enter his office and that the union's records would be examined only by union officials. He therefore had standing under the reasonable-expectations-of-privacy standard enunciated in *Katz.* Looking back at *Jones,* the Court insisted that this was also the rationale behind that decision.

The Time for Objection

As a general proposition, objections to the admissibility of evidence need not be voiced until the evidence has been offered (see chapter 3). However, most jurisdictions now provide that objections based on the way in which evidence was obtained should be made before trial whenever this is practicable. This allows the trial court to clear up what may be complicated and time-consuming evidentiary problems in advance of the trial, thus avoiding what to the jurors may be confusing and annoying interruptions.

Typical of these procedural provisions is Rule 41(e) of the Federal Rules of Criminal Procedure. It applies specifically to evidence obtained by means of allegedly unlawful searches and seizures, and by judicial decision (*Smith* v. *Katzenbach,* 351 F.2d 810 (D.C. Cir. 1965)) it has been extended to confessions. Rule 41(e) requires that a motion to suppress be made prior to trial unless the accused was unaware of the basis for the motion or for some reason had no opportunity to present the motion. (Of course, a trial judge can in his or her discretion excuse the lateness of a motion to suppress.)

CHAPTER ELEVEN

Confessions

A. Definitions

Confessions Distinguished from Admissions

It is possible, but not particularly worthwhile, to draw definitional distinctions between full-scale confessions and lesser admissions. A confession is an across-the-boards acknowledgement by a person of his guilt of a crime. An admission is a more circumscribed, narrower thing. It is an acknowledgement of some subsidiary fact or set of facts from which the ultimate issue of guilt can be inferred. An admission is one part of a larger picture; a confession is the whole picture. Thus it may be accurate to say that every confession is an admission, or is made up of a number of admissions, but not every admission constitutes a full confession.

EXAMPLE A:
"I thought about it for six days, night and day. I hated her guts. I bought a cheap gun and last night when she came home from work I shot her three times in the head. She's dead and I'm glad."

This is a *confession* of murder. It is a rather comprehensive one, being made up of a number of lesser admissions.

EXAMPLE B:
"It's true that I went out and bought a cheap gun."

This is an *admission*. Taken together with other established facts, it may give rise to an inference of guilt. If enough additional facts are supplied by the speaker's own admissions, the totality may be a full *confession*, as in Example A above.

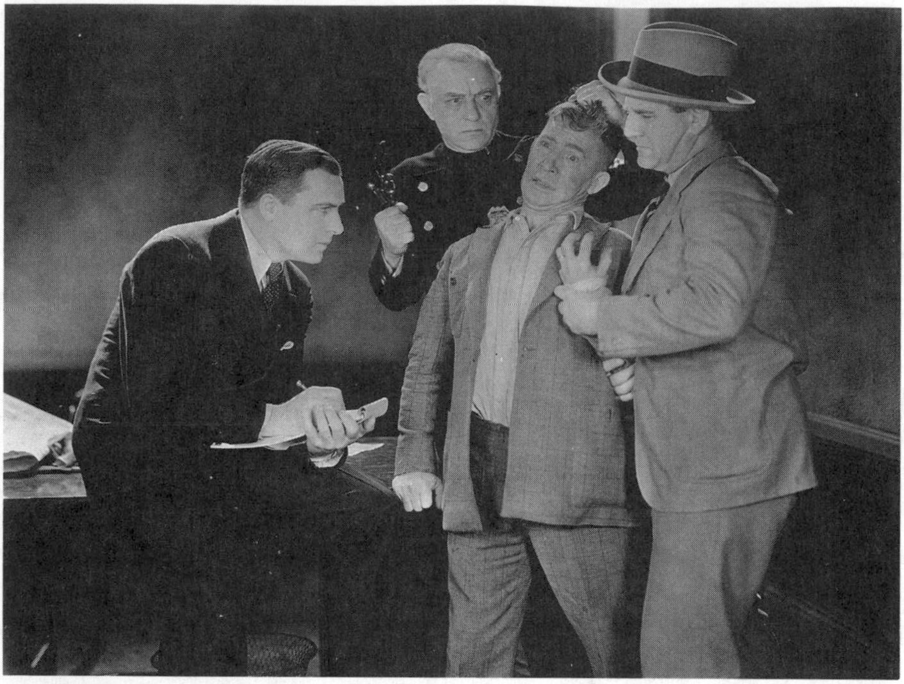

A confession, to be admissible in evidence, must be voluntary, a requirement based on the Fourteenth Amendment. The approach depicted in this scene from Roland West's film *Alibi,* is not permissible.

The legal rules regarding the admissibility of confessions and admissions are today, to all intents and purposes, identical. The distinction between a confession and an admission may contribute to a clearer understanding of the different types of evidence, but it is no longer legally significant.

B. The Common Law and Constitutional Background

The Due Process Clause

It should be evident from our earlier discussion of the hearsay rule and the exception to it dealing with party-admissions that the rule against hearsay does not prevent the prosecution from offering an accused's confession or admissions against him at trial. However, other rules drawn from constitutional doctrine may come into play. Very likely the most important of these is the rule that a confession, to be admissible in evidence, must be *voluntary*—the product of a free will and a rational mind.

The voluntariness requirement is drawn from the Fourteenth Amendment to the U.S. Constitution, which prohibits the states and their law enforcement agents from depriving "any person of life, liberty, or property without due process of law." This means, among other things, that a coerced confession will be excluded from evidence against the accused in a criminal case. Hammering a suspect over the head until he blurts out a confession, threatening to inflict bodily harm, making glowing promises of leniency, are not examples of the due process of law.

The fact that a confession was involuntary did not always result in its exclusion from evidence. Before the middle of the eighteenth century, confessions were allowable in evidence without regard to the techniques used to extract them from criminal suspects. Gradually, however, judges developed a common law rule against the receipt of statements extracted by means of violence, threats of violence, or promises of leniency or other special treatment. Today this common law rule is considerably less important than the federal constitutional requirement of voluntariness founded upon the Fourteenth Amendment's wording.

C. The Emergence of the Voluntariness Requirement

The First Important Case

The key case is *Brown* v. *Mississippi,* 297 U.S. 278 (1936). With the Supreme Court's opinion in this case, voluntariness emerged as a due process requirement dictated by the Fourteenth Amendment. The requirement is applicable in state and federal jurisdiction alike.

In *Brown* it was held that a conviction based *solely* on a brutally coerced confession could not stand. In subsequent cases the Court went further, holding that the receipt in evidence of a forced confession will result in the reversal of a conviction even though there was *other* evidence in the case sufficient to support the finding of guilt. In other words, appellate courts are prohibited from ruling that the admission of a coerced confession was "harmless error." Thus the Supreme Court in *Chapman* v. *California,* 386 U.S. 18 (1967), declared that the voluntariness of confessions is "so basic to a fair trial" that no violation of the voluntariness rule could be overlooked by a reviewing court.

The Automatic Reversal Rule

The voluntariness rule has become a rule of automatic reversal. If the proffered and received confession was coerced, the conviction must be reversed even though there is no showing that the accused was actually prejudiced by receipt of the statement.

In the *Brown* case, mentioned above, the Supreme Court said that the Fifth Amendment's privilege against compulsory self-incrimination was not behind the voluntariness rule. In a later case, however, the Court described the voluntariness standard which it had read into the Fourteenth Amendment's Due Process Clause as "the same general standard which [is] applied in federal prosecutions—a standard grounded in the policies of the privilege against self-incrimination."

The Values Underlying the Voluntariness Rule

In another significant case, *Blackburn* v. *Alabama,* 361 U.S. 199 (1960), the Supreme Court suggested that a whole "complex of values" was behind the voluntariness rule.

1. The values involved in the privilege against compulsory self-incrimination are at work here. Although police officers have no legally enforceable right to require a suspect to answer questions, less sophisticated suspects may believe that they do. Thus the values that give meaning to the Fifth Amendment would be undermined by coercive pretrial questioning.

2. A second important value underlying the voluntariness requirement is encouragement of decent police practices. It is thought that even a person rightly suspected of criminal conduct is deserving of reasonably civilized treatment and that employment of improper interrogation techniques is not consistent with civilized treatment.

3. The voluntariness requirement helps to maintain proper balance in a criminal case. Jurors are likely to accord great weight to a confession, causing all other aspects of the case to shrink in importance. And yet the prosecution is supposed to have a heavy burden of proof. Insisting that only voluntary confessions be available for use in evidence by the State helps to make a criminal trial a truly adversary and reasonably balanced process.

4. Shielding jurors, not to mention defendants, from unreliable confessions is another value that supports the voluntariness rule. For a long time the law has been intensely suspicious of forced confessions because of the possibility that a confession made to avoid physical brutality or to get some promised favor, and not out of a consciousness of guilt, is untrustworthy. This has not been considered a very important value, however, and a coerced confession will not be rendered inadmissible by a showing, however strong, that it was a truthful one. It follows from this that a trial judge cannot tell the jurors that they are free to consider an involuntary confession if they find that it is corroborated by other evidence in the case.

*The Post-*Brown *Cases*

The Supreme Court has elaborated on the voluntariness requirement laid down in *Brown,* but it has not modified it in any significant way.

The cases coming immediately after *Brown* involved extreme physical brutality. It is clear, however, that physical coercion is not the only improper police conduct prohibited by the voluntariness standard. In 1944 the Supreme

Court, in *Ashcraft* v. *Tennessee,* 322 U.S. 143, held that the psychological impact of questioning techniques could render a statement involuntary even though no physical violence was involved.

In 1961 the late Mr. Justice Frankfurter of the Supreme Court summed up the voluntariness requirement:

> The ultimate test . . . [is] voluntariness. Is the confession the product of an essentially free and unconstrained choice by its maker? If it is, if he has willed to confess, it may be used against him. If it is not, if his will has been overborne and his capacity for self-determination critically impaired, the use of his confession offends due process.
>
> . . . The line of distinction is that at which governing self direction is lost and compulsion, of whatever nature or however infused, propels or helps to propel the confession.

In *Clewis* v. *Texas,* 386 U.S. 707 (1967), the Court said that voluntariness depends on the "totality of the circumstances" under which a confession was obtained.

D. Inherently Coercive Circumstances

In some cases the "totality of the circumstances" surrounding a confession will be ruled *inherently coercive* without any subjective inquiry about whether the particular suspect's will had in fact been "overborne."

The inherently coercive approach was first adopted by the Court in *Ashcroft* v. *Tennessee,* mentioned above. The accused, Ashcroft, had been held incommunicado for thirty-six hours. During this period he got no sleep or rest. He was questioned by relays of "officers, experienced investigators, and highly trained lawyers." The Court said that this situation was "so inherently coercive that its very existence is irreconcilable with the position of mental freedom by a lone suspect against whom its full coercive force is brought to bear." In a number of later cases the Supreme Court held that lengthy periods of incommunicado interrogation were inherently coercive. Even an express *threat* of continued incommunicado detention may be sufficient to make a resulting confession inadmissible in evidence.

EXAMPLE:

The accused in *Haynes* v. *Washington,* 373 U.S. 503 (1963), was arrested at 9:00 p.m. for a service station robbery. On the way to the station house he orally admitted the crime. He was questioned from about 10:00 to 10:30 p.m. and was required to take part in a lineup. He was also told that he could call his wife only if he confessed. On the following morning he was questioned from 9:30 a.m. until 11:00 a.m. and a statement was taken which he later signed. He was not taken before a magistrate until 4:00 p.m. The Supreme Court held that the totality of the circumstances surrounding the statement were inherently coercive.

From the decided cases, the following eight characteristics of inherently coercive police conduct stand out in sharp relief:

1. Physical violence or abuse, or the threat of it;
2. The length of the questioning;
3. The failure of law enforcement officers to take the suspect before a magistrate or other judicial officer within an appropriate period of time;
4. The unwillingness of law enforcement agents to let the suspect contact legal counsel, family, or friends, especially where contact has been expressly requested either by the suspect or his/her lawyer, members of his family, or friends;
5. The failure of the police investigators to advise the suspect of his or her legal rights;
6. The coercive physical conditions under which the interrogation in conducted or the suspect is confined;
7. The obvious desire of the police interrogators to obtain a confession consistent with a preconceived police version of the offense being investigated; and
8. The lack of apparent justification for belief by the police investigators that the particular suspect was the perpetrator of the offense.

Subjective Considerations

The inherently coercive approach taken in such cases as *Ashcraft* v. *Tennessee,* above, is an essentially objective one; it pays scant attention to the subjective reaction of the suspect to interrogation techniques. In a second group of judicial decisions the crucial issue has been whether the suspect's confession was in fact the product of "free and unconstrained choice" rather than of overbearing interrogation techniques that swamped the suspect's free will.

In these cases, not involving inherently coercive situations, the Supreme Court has added two subjective characteristics to its list:

1. The individual's understanding of his or her constitutional right to remain silent; and
2. The suspect's ability to resist pressures upon him to abandon his right to remain silent.

Numerous factors will be taken into consideration in evaluating these two subjective characteristics. They include the suspect's age, physical and mental condition, educational level, and prior experience with police investigative procedures.

Age, Race, Sex

The courts have occasionally found evidence of a suspect's inability to combat external pressure to confess in the fact that the suspect was youthful and thus probably unsophisticated and impressionable.

> EXAMPLE:
> In *Gallegos* v. *Colorado,* 370 U.S. 49 (1962), the Supreme Court insisted that a fourteen-year-old boy could not be compared with an adult in full possession of his or her senses and knowledgeable about the consequences of confessions.

The Court has also suggested that the fact that the suspect is a member of a minority group or of the female sex should be considered.

> EXAMPLE A:
> *Beecher* v. *Alabama,* 389 U.S. 35 (1967) (black man suspected of murdering a white woman after raping her).

> EXAMPLE B:
> *Lynumn* v. *Illinois,* 372 U.S. 528 (1963) (female lacking any experience with criminal investigations; sexist overtones).

Youth alone is not enough to exclude a suspect's confession. By way of example, in *State* v. *Lloyd,* 212 S.W. 2d 671 (S. Ct. Minn. 1973), the court ruled that a confession given by a juvenile before the juvenile court that had waived its jurisdiction and referred him to be prosecuted as an adult is admissible in his criminal prosecution if the juvenile was apprised of his constitutional rights and knowingly waived them. The court emphasized that the confession would be scrutinized carefully to assure that the juvenile court atmosphere did not encourage the child to confess when, had he known that criminal prosecution as an adult could result, he might have exercised his right to remain silent.

Physical Condition

Courts have been sensitive to any injury or illness of the suspect, the assumption being that the pain or discomfort of illness or injury reduces resistance to interrogation to avoid extended questioning and not because of consciousness of guilt.

EXAMPLE A:
Beecher v. *Alabama,* above (the suspect had been shot in the leg at the time of his arrest).

EXAMPLE B:
Greenwald v. *Wisconsin,* 390 U.S. 519 (1968) (the suspect suffered from high blood pressure).

Mental Condition

The courts have also been alert to the abnormal mental condition of interrogation subjects. It is obviously thought that a subject suffering from mental illness or retardation is less capable than others of resisting a forceful police interrogation.

Psychological abnormality resulting from medication will be considered in connection with the issue of a confession's voluntariness, despite the fact that the police investigators were unaware of the medication's effect.

EXAMPLE:
In *Townsend* v. *Sain,* 372 U.S. 293 (1963), "truth serum" had been given a suspect to ease narcotic withdrawal symptoms. He was accorded an evidentiary hearing in a *habeas corpus* proceeding on his claim that his confession was the result of the "truth serum," despite the fact that his interrogators were unaware of the drug's qualities.

In contrast to the medication example given above, voluntary intoxication by a suspect has usually been considered only for its possible impact on the trustworthiness of his inculpatory statement unless, at the time of it, the suspect was so drunk that he could not understand the meaning of his own words. However, a few lower federal courts have concluded that voluntary intoxication is a factor in the "totality of circumstances" that must be considered in employing the voluntariness standard of the Fourteenth Amendment.

EXAMPLE:
In *Logner* v. *North Carolina,* 270 F.Supp. 970 (N.D.N.C. 1966), the suspect was so drunk at the time of his confession that his capacity to resist interrogation was "critically impaired" although he probably understood the significance of his words. The use of his confession was held to violate the due process standard.

Some courts still suggest that a drunken suspect's confession will be inadmissible only if he was intoxicated to a state of "mania."

EXAMPLE:
State v. *Williams,* 208 So. 2d 172 (S. Ct. Miss. 1968), the court held a confession inadmissible because the accused had been "in an acute, rampant state of intoxication equivalent to mania."

Reliance by police investigators on cases employing the extreme "mania" standard would be ill-advised, however.

Level of Education

Courts will consider the suspect's educational level since an educated person is likely to have a greater comprehension of his or her legal rights and the way in which they can be invoked.

EXAMPLE:
Greenwald v. *Wisconsin,* 390 U.S. 519 (1968), involved the confession of a suspect with a ninth-grade education. It was held to be involuntary (the accused also suffered from a physical disability, high blood pressure).

Sophistication Regarding Police Procedures

It is thought that a person with no prior experience with police investigation and interrogation techniques will be more likely to surrender to the pressures of police questioning than a more sophisticated subject. Apparently the theory is that past experience with police methods enhances one's knowledge of relevant legal rights.

Advice Concerning Legal Rights

In applying the voluntariness standard the courts will ask whether the suspect was advised of his or her legal rights by police questioners. That is to say, judges will inquire whether the suspect was advised by the police of his right to remain silent and his right to counsel. What is basically involved here is the *Miranda* warning, analyzed in chapter 8.

E. Indirect Coercive Influences

The Subtle Approach

Thus far the discussion has centered on direct or threatened compulsion; the more subtle modes of coercive interrogation have not been considered. But the voluntariness requirement does not stop with the two most obvious forms of coercion. The Supreme Court has said that an incriminating statement "must not be extracted by any sort of threats of violence, nor obtained by any direct or implied promises, however slight, nor by the exertion of any improper influence."

Admonitions about indirect pressures on a suspect are easy to phrase; proof that they were brought to bear on a suspect and they induced a confession comes harder.

Demanding That the Suspect Tell the Truth

Certainly it is not improper for a police interrogator to exhort a suspect to tell the truth, to "come clean."

EXAMPLE:
"Bushmat, you'll feel a lot better if you quit covering up and just tell us the truth. We'll find out, anyway. Give us the story." This is nothing more than a request for the truth and cannot be considered coercive.

Promising Not to Prosecute or to Drop Pending Charges

Although there is nothing wrong with asking a suspect to tell the truth, quite a few courts have said that a resulting confession will be excluded from evidence when the interrogator has gone a long step further and suggested that the suspect will not be prosecuted if he or she confesses. Similarly, it has repeatedly been held violative of the voluntariness standard to promise a suspect that charges will be reduced or dropped altogether if he talks.

EXAMPLE A:
"Bushmat, things will go a lot better for you if you admit you did it." A step into the danger zone has now been taken by the interrogator. References to "things going better for you" sound too much like a veiled promise of leniency or some other form of favorable treatment.

EXAMPLE B:
"Clyde, we just want to clear this complaint. We don't care who slugged the guy. He probably deserved it. I'll tell you what, you admit you punched him and I guarantee you there'll be no prosecution." The forbidden step has now been taken by the interrogator. A confession traceable to a promise not to prosecute is vitiated; it will not be receivable in evidence against the suspect.

EXAMPLE C:
"Clyde, we just want to get this thing off the books. It's just a nickel-dime thing. Nobody cares about it. You admit your part in it and we'll

drop the charges against you." This, too, represents the forbidden step. A promise to drop a prosecution already commenced is just as bad as a promise not to initiate a prosecution.

EXAMPLE D:
"Look, Bushmat, we're not after your blood. You admit that you cut the guy after he called you a bad name and we'll reduce the charge to involuntary manslaughter." Again, the forbidden step, this time an offer to reduce the charges against the suspect.

EXAMPLE E:
"Clyde, these judges always go easy on the guy who has confessed. The guy who confesses can expect probation." This is another form of the forbidden step.

EXAMPLE F:
"Clyde, make a clean breast of it now and it'll help you get out on bail pending trial." Several federal courts have indicated that this is not a sufficiently powerful inducement to render a subsequent confession inadmissible.

Confessions Obtained During Periods of Wrongful Detention

In 1942 the Supreme Court, in the case of *McNabb* v. *United States,* 318 U.S. 332, held that a statement obtained by federal agents during a period of "unnecessary delay" before taking the prisoner before a magistrate was to be excluded from evidence in a federal trial. In 1957, in *Mallory* v. *United States,* the Court specifically ruled that a delay for purposes of questioning a suspect was unreasonable. By and large, only "the ordinary administrative steps"—booking—could properly be undertaken prior to producing an arrestee before a magistrate (who would probably admit the arrestee to bail, thereby making in-custody interrogation a practical impossibility). This became known as the *McNabb-Mallory* Rule and it was intensely unpopular in federal law enforcement circles.

Federal authorities were not opposed to the principle of prompt presentation before a magistrate. They simply thought that an exclusionary rule was too costly a method of enforcing adherence to the principle. A statement might meet traditional voluntariness requirements and yet be excluded under the *McNabb-Mallory* Rule; a laudable principle—prompt presentation—was being enforced at the cost of losing reliable evidence of guilt.

The *McNabb-Mallory* Rule was not grounded upon the Constitution's Due Process Clause or any other provision of the Bill of Rights. The rule was an exercise of the Supreme Court's supervisory power over lower federal courts. Consequently, the rule was not binding on state courts. Only the Supreme Courts of Delaware and Michigan flirted with a comparable rule and they soon abandoned it in favor of the traditional voluntariness test. And in 1968, in the Omnibus Crime Control and Safe Streets Act, 18 U.S.C.A. §3501(c), the Congress significantly modified the federal rule.

Under the terms of the 1968 legislation, a statement is not inadmissible solely because of a delay in presenting the arrestee before a magistrate if (1) the statement has been found by the trial judge to have been voluntary, (2) its evidentiary weight is left to the jury's determination, and (3) it was made within six hours of arrest or other detention. Furthermore, even the six-hour limitation is inapplicable where a longer delay is found "reasonable considering the means of transportation and the distance traveled to the nearest available magistrate."

Heavy reliance on this aspect of the Omnibus Crime Control and Safe Streets Act may be unwise. The Supreme Court might hold that this part of the act is unconstitutional. To reach this conclusion the Court would have only to decide that prompt presentation before a magistrate or other judicial officer is a constitutionally protected right. It could base such a decision on the Due Process Clause or it could declare that a delay in presentation is an unreasonable seizure of the arrestee under the Fourth Amendment ("The right of the people to be secure in their *persons* . . . against unreasonable searches and seizures, shall not be violated . . . [emphasis added]"). Certainly it can be said that in-custody interrogation prior to presentation to a magistrate should not exceed six hours in duration unless extraordinary circumstances are present.

What if an inculpatory statement has been secured during a period of detention following an unlawful arrest? Up until 1963 it had not been thought that such a statement would be subject to an exclusionary rule. In 1963, however, the Supreme Court suggested that the Fourth Amendment's requirement that seizure of a person be "reasonable" would support the exclusion of statements gotten after an illegal arrest.

In *Wong Sun* v. *United States,* 371 U.S. 471 (1963), some federal narcotics agents had approached James Way Toy's laundry at six o'clock in the morning. They broke down the door and followed Toy as he ran to his living quarters in back of the laundry. There Toy was observed reaching into a drawer. One of the narcotics agents drew a gun, arrested Toy and handcuffed him. Toy, told that he had been implicated as a narcotics source, admitted that he possessed some narcotics and stated that he had gotten them from one Yee. Later, Toy also named Wong Sun. Both Yee and Wong Sun were arrested. The three men were released on their own recognizances.

Several days later Wong Sun appeared voluntarily at the office of the Bureau of Narcotics for questioning. He made some incriminating statements. Those statements, along with Toy's original statements, were admitted into evidence against the makers of them.

On appeal, the Supreme Court held that both Toy's arrest and Wong Sun's had been without probable cause and were therefore contrary to the Fourth Amendment. Toy's statements were held to be inadmissible because "verbal evidence which derives so immediately from an unlawful entry and an unauthorized arrest . . . is no less the 'fruit' of official illegality than the more common tangible fruits of the unwarranted intrusion." The Court said that an inference that Toy's statements were an exercise of free will would be unreasonable and in a footnote it suggested that his statements would be inadmissible even if such an inference were proper: "Even in the absence of such oppressive circumstances, and where an exclusionary rule rests principally on nonconstitutional grounds, we have sometimes refused to differentiate between voluntary and involuntary declarations." On the other hand, Wong Sun's incriminating statement was admissible against him, since "the connection between the arrest and the statement 'became so attenuated as to dissipate the taint.' "

Lower courts have had difficulty grasping the meaning of *Wong Sun.* Does the opinion in that case mean that any statement made during custody secured without probable cause must be excluded from evidence automatically? Or does *Wong Sun* merely confirm the traditional voluntariness requirement? Probably the answer can be found in the opinion of Connecticut's top court in *State* v. *Traub,* 196 A.2d 755 (S. Ct. of Errors Conn. 1963). In that case the Connecticut court said that where an arrest and subsequent detention are unlawful, an inculpatory statement made during the period of detention will be excluded from evidence unless the State established that it was voluntary. Any element of coercion stemming from the unlawful arrest and detention will be considered in answering the voluntariness question. "But even though . . . a confession made during an illegal detention is properly found to have been truly voluntary, nevertheless, if the illegal detention was an operative factor in causing or bringing about the confession, then the confession will be considered as the fruit of the illegal detention and will be inadmissible." The Connecticut court said that it was this causation factor that *Wong Sun* added to the traditional voluntariness requirement. The court went on to say that "if the confession is truly voluntary and the causation factor of the illegal detention is so weak, or has been so attenuated, as not to have been an operative factor in causing or bringing about the confession, then the connection between any illegality of detention and the confession may be found so lacking in force or intensity that the confession would not be the fruit of the illegal detention." In other words, the arrestee's decision to talk must be free of any element of coercion stemming from his unlawful arrest and detention.

The Admissibility of Evidence Obtained Through the Use of an Inadmissible Confession

The older cases held that the inadmissibility of a statement had no impact on the admissibility of other evidence turned up by investigators through the use of the inadmissible confession. In other words, the fruits of an inadmissible confession were not necessarily to be excluded from evidence.

Today, however, the rule is different. The policies behind the rules requiring the exclusion of confessions are approximately the same as those underlying the rules requiring exclusion of unreasonably seized evidence. It follows that the question of whether the fruits of an inadmissible statement are receivable in evidence is to be resolved in the same way one resolves the question of whether the fruits of unlawfully seized evidence are so tainted as to be inadmissible. This "fruit of the poisonous tree " doctrine is discussed in detail in chapter 10.

One special problem should be taken up at this point, however. It has to do with the relationship of an inadmissible confession to ***subsequent*** statements obtained from the suspect. Do the factual circumstances that make the first statement inadmissible also infect later statements? To a degree they do. The U.S. Supreme Court has several times made it clear that the existence of an earlier involuntary confession is a significant factor in determining whether later statements by the same person were voluntarily given. Federal courts must inquire whether there was a cessation of coercive forces and a restoration of the suspect's ability to decide of his own free will whether or not to make any additional statements.

The mere passage of time may not be enough to insulate a later confession from attack. By way of example, the accused in *Beecher* v. *Alabama,* 389 U.S. 35 (1967), had confessed at gunpoint when he was arrested. This was a significant factor in the Court's determination that a second statement, given five days after a *Miranda* warning, was nonetheless involuntary.

Many state courts are even more stringent than the U.S. Supreme Court where the first statement was involuntary. They often enforce a *presumption* that the coercive forces carry over to the later statements, tainting them and rendering them inadmissible.

Neither the federal nor the state courts are as demanding where the first confession was made inadmissible not because of illegal duress but because some required warning was omitted. Courts are likely to discount the influence of an earlier confession, obtained without a *Miranda* warning, if the subsequent statements were preceded by the required *Miranda* ritual.

F. Adoptive or Implied Confessions

Not all confessions and admissions are verbal and explicit. They do not always come out, "I did it and I'm glad!" Sometimes the criminal investigator encounters, and must be able to recognize, the adoptive or implied confession or admission.

Reaction to Accusation

An adoptive or implied confession may occur when an unmistakably accusatory statement is made in the suspect's hearing and he either remains silent, which creates an inference that he adopts the accusation as true, or makes an equivocal response instead of the strong denial that would normally be expected from an innocent person. It may also occur when the suspect engages in affirmative conduct from which his admission of the accusation's truth can be inferred.

EXAMPLE A:
"This man raped me!" The man stares at the ground sheepishly and says nothing. His silence constitutes an implied or adoptive confession.

EXAMPLE B:
"This man raped me!" The man replies, "Now wait a minute. That's not exactly true. It takes two to tango, you know." This equivocal response gives rise to an implied admission.

EXAMPLE C:
"You have sexually molested our daughter!" After his wife makes this accusation the suspect consults a psychiatrist. There is an implied admission in this conduct.

The Impact of Miranda

Of course, when a person is in police custody his silence may reflect a desire not to make a statement. In *Miranda* the Supreme Court said, "[I]t is impermissible to penalize an individual for exercising his Fifth Amendment privilege when he is under police custodial interrogation. The prosecution may not, therefore, use at trial the fact that he stood mute or claimed his privilege in the face of accusation." In short, silence or an express claim of the Fifth Amendment during custodial interrogation is not admissible against an accused. Neither is his reaction, or lack of one, to an accusation made during a judicial proceeding, such as a preliminary hearing. Courts take the common sense approach that such charges do not naturally call out for a denial. For that matter, some judges can be expected to rule that nothing can properly be read into pre-arrest silence in the face of an accusation.

However, the prosecution is free to introduce evidence of an accused's post-arrest silence to challenge his insistence at trial that he cooperated with the authorities at the scene of his arrest. (*Doyle* v. *Ohio,* 426 U.S. 610 (1976).) And notice that evidence of pre-arrest silence is admissible if that silence is inconsistent with an exculpating statement offered by the accused for the first time during his trial. Thus in *Jenkins* v. *Anderson,* 447 U.S. 231 (1980), the Supreme Court held that evidence of the accused's pre-arrest silence was proper to cast doubt on his in-trial self defense claim since "no governmental action induced [the accused] to remain silent before arrest."

Of course, an accused can waive—knowingly and voluntarily surrender—his or her *Miranda* rights. Obviously, a signed *Miranda* waiver is potent evidence. (*North Carolina* v. *Butler,* 441 U.S. 369 (1979).) But the waiver need not be so explicit; courts will look to surrounding circumstances for signs of a valid waiver. (*Ibid.*) These will include assessment of the accused's mental and physical characteristics. (*Tague* v. *Louisiana,* 444 U.S. 469 (1980).) Factors to be considered will include the accused's background and experience (*White* v. *Finkbeiner,* 611 F.2d 186 (7th Cir. 1979)), his I.Q. (*United States* v. *Glover,* 596 F.2d 857 (9th Cir.), *cert. denied,* 444 U.S. 860 (1979)), education (*Government of Canal Zone* v. *Peach,* 602 F.2d 101 (5th Cir.), *cert. denied,* 444 U.S. 952 (1979)), and the possible influence of alcohol or drugs (*United States* v. *Smith,* 608 F.2d 1011 (4th Cir. 1979)).

Finally, it should be held in mind that *voluntary* statements obtained in violation of *Miranda's* dictates are nonetheless admissible to contradict (impeach) the accused's later testimony if he takes the stand, although of course *involuntary* statements of the accused are useless for this or any other purpose. (See *Mincey* v. *Arizona,* 437 U.S. 385 (1978).)

A voluntary statement that is *Miranda*-bad may lead law enforcement agents to a person who can give important testimony. Although a *Miranda*-bad statement provided the useful lead, the resulting testimony is not considered the tainted "fruit" of the *Miranda* violation and can be offered in evidence to establish the accused's guilt. (*Michigan* v. *Tucker,* 417 U.S. 433 (1974).)

In *Rhode Island* v. *Innis,* 446 U.S. 291 (1980), the Supreme Court spoke of the meaning of the term "interrogation" in a *Miranda* context. Innis had been arrested for the armed robbery of a taxi driver. The accused expressed a desire for legal counsel. The police put Innis in a cruiser where he overheard them expressing concern for the safety of children playing in the area where the police thought the accused's sawed-off shotgun might be found. Innis interrupted the officers and directed them to the weapon's location. The Supreme Court held that the accused had not been subjected to an interrogation violative of his *Miranda* rights. Although the point seems distinctly debatable, the Court held that the policeman's overheard conversation did not amount to "words or actions . . . that the police should know are reasonably likely to elicit an incriminating response from the suspect." This holding can be expected to lead to some artfully contrived conversations between law enforcement agents, calculated to play on the sensitivities, if any, of their suspect.

G. Statements Obtained by Private Persons

The Inapplicability of Miranda

For fairly obvious reasons, incriminating statements made to private persons, rather than to law enforcement agents, are given different treatment. A private individual who is not acting on behalf of a law enforcement agency has no obligation to warn an accused of his constitutional rights. Accordingly, an inculpatory statement made to a private person is admissible against its maker even though it was not preceded by the *Miranda* ritual.

The Voluntariness Test

The only test applicable to statements given to private individuals is the basic voluntariness test. A statement given as a direct result of coercion or inducements by a private individual is just as inadmissible as if it had been extracted by someone in a position of authority.

EXAMPLE A:
In *Schaumburg* v. *State,* 432 P. 2d 500 (S. Ct. Nev. 1967), admissions made by a casino employee to two supervisors while he was in a room guarded by private security personnel were admissible against him at trial.

EXAMPLE B:
In *State* v. *Little,* 439 P. 2d 387 (S. Ct. Kan. 1968), a shop owner asked the accused, in the presence of a policeman, whether she had passed a forged check. The accused's inculpatory response was admissible in evidence against her.

EXAMPLE C:
In *Agee* v. *State,* 185 So. 2d 671 (S. Ct. Miss. 1966), a teacher told the accused that "it would be lighter on him if he told the truth." This suggestion of leniency was enough to render the accused's statement inadmissible.

H. Procedural Safeguards

Corroboration

The trustworthiness of confessions as proof of guilt has always been subject to a healthy skepticism by courts. This has inspired some procedural safeguards. From the standpoint of the criminal investigator, the most important of these safeguards is the one requiring some kind of corroboration of an accused's confession.

Two Types of Corroboration

Corroboration of a confession can come in two different forms. Some courts simply say that the prosecution must come up with independent evidence that tends to confirm the trustworthiness, the evidentiary reliability of a proffered confession. But the majority of courts have gone further, holding that prosecution must introduce independent proof of the *corpus delicti,* which is a way of saying that there must be some evidence, independent of the accused's self-incriminating statements, that tends to establish that the offense charged was actually committed.

Meaning of Corpus Delicti

Literally translated from the Latin, *corpus delicti* means "body of the crime." As a practical matter, the *corpus delicti* consists of the first two elements of a successful criminal prosecution. A successful criminal prosecution has a total of three elements. The prosecution must prove (1) that the harm or injury specified in the offense actually was inflicted, (2) that this harm or injury was inflicted by some person's criminal conduct, and (3) that the accused was that person. *Corpus delicti,* as that phrase is employed in the rule requiring independent corroboration of confessions, encompasses only elements (1) and (2); the prosecution must offer independent proof that injury was inflicted by someone's criminal activity, but it need not, as an aspect of corroboration, introduce independent evidence linking the accused to the crime.

The independent proof of the *corpus delicti* need not establish the two essential elements beyond a reasonable doubt, although some courts have emphasized that the corroborating evidence should be substantial.

Once the required corroboration has been developed in the evidence, both the accused's confession and the corroborating proof can be considered by the jury in deciding whether all three elements of the crime have been proved beyond a reasonable doubt.

Two Illinois cases are illustrative of the confession-corroboration rule:

EXAMPLE A:

In *People* v. *Hubbard,* 230 N.E. 2d 220 (S. Ct. Ill. 1967), the defendant was charged with rape. However, the inherently incredible testimony of the two alleged victims, who made no attempt to escape, to summon the police, or to make "fresh complaint" despite ample opportunity to do so, was *insufficient* to corroborate the defendant's confession.

EXAMPLE B:
People v. *Perfecto,* 186 N.E. 2d 258 (S. Ct. Ill 1962), was also a rape case. The defendant's confession was offered in evidence. The following evidence was held *sufficient* to corroborate it: A witness testified that the defendant left his hotel room and returned later, holding a handkerchief over his face. Still later the witness observed scratches and a bite on the defendant's shoulder. There was testimony that there was a "red smear" on the wall of the hotel room in which the offense had occurred and papers all over the floor. The defendant's seventy-five-year-old victim was bleeding, bruised, and had a broken collarbone and had to be removed from the hotel on a stretcher.

Evidence Confirming a Confession's Trustworthiness

The federal courts adhere to the minority approach to confession-corroboration. Instead of demanding independent proof of the *corpus delicti,* the federal courts require only that there be "substantial independent evidence which would tend to establish the trustworthiness of the statement." (*Opper v. United States,* 348 U.S. 147, 156 (1954).) In practical effect, however, independent proof of the *corpus delicti* tends also to confirm the reliability of a confession. Thus the federal courts' wording of the corroboration requirement probably amounts to a distinction without a difference.

Separate, Preliminary Determination of a Confession's Admissibility

A second safeguard surrounding the receipt into evidence of an accused's confession involves the procedure for determining the voluntariness of the confession. Over the years, three different procedures have emerged, but one of them has been held to be unconstitutional.

1. Under the procedure that once pertained in New York, the trial judge made a preliminary determination of voluntariness. The judge would exclude the accused's statement only if its involuntariness was clear. If the voluntariness of the confession was a disputed issue of fact, the judge would submit the confession to the jury, instructing the jurors that they were to determine its voluntariness and give it evidentiary weight only if they found it was voluntary. This approach was held to be constitutionally inadequate in *Jackson* v. *Denno,* 378 U.S. 368 (1964).

In the *Jackson* case the New York procedure was held to violate the Due Process Clause of the Fourteenth Amendment. The New York approach posed three risks. First, the jury might believe that the accused's confession was true, and this belief might cause the jurors to make a distorted assessment of the evidence bearing on the voluntariness question. Second, the jurors' belief in the truth of the confession might lead them to reject the policies underlying the voluntariness requirement. Third, even if the jurors found the confession to have been involuntary, its content might nevertheless influence their decision on the issue of guilt or innocence.

2. Under the procedure followed in Massachusetts, the trial judge makes a voluntariness determination and submits the accused's confession to the jury only if he or she has found the confession voluntary. This procedure was held to be constitutionally satisfactory in *Jackson* v. *Denno, supra.*

3. The usual procedure permits the trial judge to resolve any factual disputes relating to the voluntariness issue. Under this procedure the trial judge, and not the jury, makes the only formal determination of voluntariness.

As a constitutional proposition, the voluntariness of a confession need only be established by a *preponderance* of the evidence; it need not be proved beyond a reasonable doubt.

CHAPTER TWELVE

Common Law and Statutory Testimonial Privileges

A. Reasons for the Testimonial Privileges

We have discussed the constitutional privilege against compulsory self-incrimination. We have also considered the impact of the Constitution's Due Process Clause on coerced confessions and have described how the Constitution's search and seizure provisions shield people from improper invasions of privacy. We now leave the constitutional area and take up some of the testimonial privileges that have their origins in the common law or in legislative enactments. These include the attorney-client privilege, the physician-patient privilege, and the marital privileges.

Testimonial privileges, which permit a person to refuse to disclose and to stop others from disclosing in judicial proceedings certain sorts of confidential information, have one basic reason for their existence, which is society's desire to encourage certain relationships by ensuring their confidentiality. Society values some relationships sufficiently that it is willing to guard their confidential nature even at the expense of the loss of information that is highly relevant to the issues in a case. (For example, it is difficult to imagine anything more truth-frustrating than the attorney-client privilege.)

It is thought that these special relationships—accused and counsel, patient and physician, husband and wife, and so on—will be encouraged if confidentiality, when desired, is guaranteed. To put it another way, and more specifically, it is thought that persons might forego needed medical attention or be less than honest when talking with legal counsel were there no guarantee that communications made during the physician-patient and attorney-client relationships would be given confidential status in legal proceedings.

It should be added that some of the testimonial privileges are quite frankly based on hardheaded practicality. Some types of disclosure could not be obtained, as a practical matter, even if there were no protective testimonial privilege. A good example would be efforts to obtain disclosure of confidences made in the confessional. No priest, even when confronted by a contempt of court citation, would breach the priest-penitent relationship. And so the law, accepting reality, has designed a clergy-penitent privilege.

Despite the easily identified policy of confidentiality underlying the privileges, the pattern of testimonial privileges in the United States has been oddly hit-or-miss. In many states some quite significant relationships are not protected by a privilege. For example, social workers and accountants are the subject of no privilege in a number of states. Not all jurisdictions have a physician-patient privilege and not all have enacted a privilege shielding a journalist's information sources from disclosure. Perhaps strangest of all, while all jurisdictions have some form of husband-wife privilege, almost none has a parent-child privilege.

B. The Attorney-Client Privilege

A Common Law Privilege

Lawyers and judges take care of themselves; the first testimonial privilege ever established was the attorney-client privilege. Every American jurisdiction has one. It is a common law privilege, although in some jurisdictions it has now been codified by statute. It carries with it fewer exceptions than any other testimonial privilege.

Rationale of the Lawyer-Client Privilege

The lawyer-client privilege can be traced back to Roman times, when it was thought that a lawyer's loyalty to his client precluded him from being a witness against his client. It would not be an honorable thing for a lawyer to give damaging evidence against the very person who had retained his professional services. In later years the rationale shifted. Ever since the eighteenth century the ethical underpinnings of the privilege have been less important than the practical considerations. Trials are most efficiently handled by trained lawyers. And lawyers function most effectively when their clients inform them fully of the facts. The idea is that this desired full disclosure will be encouraged if clients know that their discussions with their lawyers will not become public knowledge. A client, presumably, will be more open and frank with his or her attorney if he or she comprehends that the attorney cannot be required, over the client's objection, to divulge the content of the client's disclosures.

Dean Wigmore, the master scholar of evidence law, said that the lawyer-client privilege's "benefits are all indirect and speculative; its obstruction is plain and concrete." Certainly Wigmore was correct that the lawyer-client privilege is truth-frustrating. There would be many more criminal convictions than there currently are if a prosecuting attorney were free to place defense counsel on the witness stand and ask him to disclose to the jury everything his client told him about the case. Often the defense lawyer, if he or she were truthful, would have to reply, "He told me that he did it." The lawyer-client privilege blocks prosecutors from taking this easy route.

Scope of the Privilege

Essentially, communications between lawyer and client made during professional consultation are privileged from disclosure. In other words, a client has a privilege to refuse to disclose, and to prohibit others from disclosing, confidential communications between himself or his representative and his lawyer or his lawyer's representative. All of the terms used in this description of the attorney-client privilege require careful definition.

1. *Definition of "client."* A client, in the context of a typical attorney-client privilege, can be an individual private citizen. It can also be a public officer, a corporation, or any other organization, public or private, to which professional legal services are provided.
2. *Definition of "lawyer" or "attorney."* A lawyer or attorney is any person who is authorized, or, in many jurisdictions, who is *reasonably believed* by the client to be authorized, to practice law in any state or nation.
3. *Definition of "representative of a client."* A representative of a client is anyone who has the authority to obtain legal services on behalf of the client; in other words, an agent or go-between.
4. *Definition of "representative of a lawyer."* A representative of a lawyer is one employed by the lawyer to assist in the giving of professional services; for example, a secretary or law clerk or paralegal aide.
5. *Definition of "confidentiality."* A communication is confidential if it was not intended to be disclosed to persons other than those to whom disclosure would be in furtherance of the giving of legal services to the client or those, such as a messenger, who are necessary for the transmission of the communication.

It is not enough merely to show that there was a communication between an attorney and his client. Surrounding circumstances indicating a desire for confidentiality—secrecy—must be shown by way of foundation. The element of secrecy is missing where the client's expressed intent was that the information conveyed to his or her lawyer would be made public or disclosed to third persons.

EXAMPLE A:
A client provides her lawyer with information to be used by the lawyer in preparing the client's income tax returns for transmittal to the Internal Revenue Service. The information is not privileged, since it was to be forwarded to third persons (the IRS).

EXAMPLE B:
An accused instructs his lawyer that he should ask certain questions of a witness at an impending preliminary hearing. The suggested questions are not privileged, since they were intended to be revealed at the preliminary hearing.

The presence during a lawyer-client consultation of third persons is often significant. If the lawyer-client conversations are had in the presence and hearing of total strangers, it would seem clear that confidentiality was not uppermost in the client's mind. On the other hand, the necessary presence of the lawyer's secretary, who is making notes on the conference, does not suggest a lack of interest in secrecy. Even the presence of a relative or friend of the client, especially when there was some good reason for it, would not breach the privilege.

EXAMPLE:
Prosecution for seducing a female under the age of eighteen. The girl's statements at a conference with a lawyer in connection with possible bastardy proceedings against the accused are privileged even though made in the presence of her mother, who accompanies her to the conference to lend moral support.

Today it is widely accepted that attorney-client privilege is not lost where the third person overhearing the consultation was an unknown eavesdropper.

EXAMPLE A:
Fred Stitz shoots his wife, Irene, and promptly telephones his lawyer. Unbeknownst to Stitz, a telephone operator listens in on the telephone. The operator's eavesdropping does not destroy the confidential nature of Stitz's call and the attorney-client privilege will be applicable.

EXAMPLE B:
Stitz's lawyer consults with his client in a room set aside for the purpose at the county jail. The room is bugged. Electronic eavesdropping is no different than any other kind. The privilege will be applicable. (Indeed, as will be mentioned again later, this sort of conduct on the part of law enforcement agents may result in a mistrial

or even the dismissal of charges against an accused whose right to consult with a lawyer has been compromised.)

When two or more people consult one lawyer, their disclosures are not confidential, quite obviously, as amongst themselves. This means that in a lawsuit between themselves the lawyer-client privilege would be inapplicable. On the other hand, the clients may have desired confidentiality as against the outside world. In a litigation involving an outsider the privilege will be applicable.

EXAMPLE:
Bushmat and Lishniss, while still friendly, jointly consult the same lawyer about a business venture. Later they have an argument about the conduct of the business and Bushmat punches Lishniss in the nose. In a civil suit between Lishniss and Bushmat the attorney-client privilege would *not* be applicable to their joint conference with their lawyer. However, in a prosecution of Bushmat for assault and battery the privilege could be invoked to bar the prosecuting attorney from questioning the lawyer. The prosecuting attorney represents the outside world, as to which Bushmat and Lishniss may well have desired confidentiality.

Existence of an Attorney-Client Relationship

It is, in the main, essential to a claim of attorney-client privilege that the relationship of attorney and client actually existed at the crucial time.

EXAMPLE A:
Bushmat runs into Martin Lex, a lawyer, at a cocktail party and makes factual disclosures to him in an effort to get some free advice from him. The attorney-client relationship is not present and there will be no privilege as to the disclosures made.

EXAMPLE B:
Bushmat runs into the same Martin Lex at a party and tells him that he has some money, which he obtained in a bank robbery, that he would like to invest in a legitimate business. Lex discusses various investment possibilities with Bushmat. Since Lex was not acting in his professional capacity as a lawyer, the lawyer-client relationship was not involved and there will be no privilege.

There is one exception to the general rule that the existence of a lawyer-client relationship is vital to the claim of the lawyer-client privilege. Disclosures made before the lawyer has decided to accept or decline a case are covered by the privilege if all other requirements are present.

> EXAMPLE:
> Bushmat, charged with burglary, goes to Martin Lex and, in the course of trying to get Lex to represent him, makes some damaging disclosures. In the end Lex refuses to take Bushmat's case because Bushmat is unwilling to pay the fee demanded by Lex. The lawyer-client privilege is nonetheless applicable to disclosures made by Bushman during these fee or retainer negotiations.

Exceptions to the Attorney-Client Privilege

There are a number of exceptions to the application of the attorney-client privilege, but only one of them is likely to crop up in criminal cases.

Legal Advice in Aid of Wrongdoing; The Crime-Fraud Exception

There is no testimonial privilege if the services of the lawyer were sought or obtained as an aid in the planning or actual commission of something that the client knew or should have known was a crime or a fraud.

In re Ryder, 263 F. Supp. 360 (E.D. Va. 1967), is an illustrative case. Attorney Ryder's client told him that he had come into possession of a large sum of money and had put it in a safe-deposit box. Ryder knew that the FBI, investigating the bank robbery with which his client was charged, would soon discover the safe-deposit box and obtain authority to open it. The lawyer removed the money and a sawed-off shotgun from his client's safe-deposit box and placed these items in his own box. He apparently intended to withhold the evidence until after the client's trial and then make restitution of the money. The attorney-client privilege was held not to be applicable to protect the incriminating evidence and the U.S. District Court suspended Ryder from the practice of law for a year and a half.

Standing in contrast to *In re* Ryder, above, is the case of *State* v. *Olwell,* 394 P. 2d 681 (S. Ct. Wash. 1964). There a lawyer was subpoenaed to produce all knives in his possession "relating to" three named persons, one of whom he was defending against a murder charge. The subpoena did not simply require attorney Olwell to produce *all* knives in his possession, it stipulated the names of persons to whom the knives were supposedly *relevant*. As a consequence of the loaded wording of the subpoena, the lawyer could not produce the knives without betraying privileged communications.

Even if the subpoena in *Olwell* had simply required the lawyer to surrender all knives in his possession, without naming the persons to whom the evidence supposedly related, the lawyer probably could have refused to do so, at least for a period of time. The court in *Olwell* said that a lawyer is entitled to hold for a reasonable period of time evidence given him by a client or coming into his custody through information given him by the client. The court did not reach the question of how *long* a lawyer could retain control of such evidence. It suggested that he could keep it at least long enough to conduct tests and otherwise examine it. Presumably he would be required to turn it over well enough in advance of trial to give the prosecution a chance to examine it.

Another case illustrating the operation of the attorney-client privilege and the exception for legal advice in aid of wrongdoing is *Tillotson* v. *Boughner,* 350 F. 2d 663 (7th Cir. 1965). The defendant attorney was held in contempt of court when he refused to obey a court order requiring him to divulge the name of a client on whose behalf he had anonymously paid a large sum of money to the Internal Revenue Service. The U.S. Court of Appeals reversed the lower court, holding that the name of the client fell within the attorney-client privilege. It said, "The disclosure of the identity of the client . . . would lead ultimately to disclosure of the taxpayer's motive for seeking legal advice."

Schulze v. *Rayunec,* 350 F. 2d 666 (7th Cir. 1965), was a companion case to *Tillotson,* above. There the court ordered Rayunec, the auditor of the bank on which the cashier's check to the Internal Revenue Service was drawn, to produce the bank records that would show the source of the funds covering the check. The Seventh Circuit held that there is no common law or statutory privilege against the release of such information by a bank. (All of which means that in the future the unethical lawyer will buy cashier's checks with untraceable cash.)

C. The Physician-Patient Privilege

The Nature and Significance of the Privilege

The physician-patient privilege is a statutory privilege rather than a judge-made one. Furthermore, it has not been adopted in all jurisdictions.

In more than half the states a physician is prohibited from divulging in judicial proceedings, against a patient's wishes, information that he or she acquired while attending the patient in a professional capacity, if the information was necessary to enable the physician to act in his or her professional capacity.

Exceptions to the Privilege

There are such huge exceptions to the application of the physician-patient privilege that it is no longer of much importance. The largest of the exceptions are these:

1. *Inapplicable Where Patient Puts Physical Condition in Issue.* The physician-patient privilege is not applicable in those situations creating the

largest number of lawsuits, since a person cannot claim the privilege where the person has put his or her physical condition in issue.

EXAMPLE:
The plaintiff sues the driver of an automobile for personal injuries sustained in a vehicular collision. In his formal complaint the plaintiff alleges that he suffered injuries to his head and back which required extensive medical treatment and hospitalization. He further alleges that he has suffered pain, disability, and other ill effects that will continue to necessitate medical treatment. Having put his physical condition in issue in the lawsuit, the plaintiff will not be permitted to invoke the physician-patient privilege when the defendant seeks to discover the true medical facts from plaintiff's treating physicians.

2. *Inapplicable in Criminal Proceedings.* It is commonly held that the physician-patient privilege cannot be invoked in criminal proceedings.

EXAMPLE:
The victim of an alleged crime of violence, unwilling to get "involved," seeks to claim the physician-patient privilege during the accused's trial to block testimony by the victim's treating doctor. The claim of the privilege will not be sustained.

3. *Inapplicable in Proceedings to Recover Damages for Criminal Conduct.* Under such provisions as Section 999 of the California Evidence Code, there is no physician-patient testimonial privilege in a proceeding to recover damages on account of conduct of the patient that constitutes a crime. Provisions of this type make disclosure of information possible in negligence suits based on conduct that is also criminal without the necessity of trying the criminal case first.

4. *Inapplicable Where Physician's Services Sought in Aid of Criminal Conduct.* There is no physician-patient testimonial privilege if the physician's services were sought or obtained in aid of the planning or actual commission of a crime. Similarly, there is no privilege if the physician's services were sought or obtained to escape detection or apprehension after the commission of a crime.

EXAMPLE A:
The accused went to a plastic surgeon *prior* to the commission of a crime and sought to have his appearance surgically altered in order to avoid recognition. He cannot successfully invoke the physician-patient privilege to block testimony against him by the plastic surgeon.

EXAMPLE B:
The accused goes to a plastic surgeon *after* the commission of a crime to have his appearance surgically altered to avoid identification. Again, the privilege cannot successfully be claimed by the accused.

D. Psychotherapist-Patient Privilege

Nature and Scope of the Privilege

In many jurisdictions a patient has a privilege to refuse to disclose, and to prohibit others from disclosing, confidential communications between himself and his psychotherapist or persons who are participating in his diagnosis or treatment under the direction of the psychotherapist.

Definitions

Under this privilege, a *patient* is a person who consults or is examined or interviewed by a psychotherapist for purposes of diagnosis or treatment of his mental or emotional condition.

A *psychotherapist,* akin with a physician under the physician-patient privilege, is a person authorized to practice medicine in any state or nation. Beyond that, he is one who devotes a substantial portion of his time to the practice of psychiatry or is reasonably *believed* to do so by the patient. A psychotherapist can also be a person licensed or certified as a psychotherapist who devotes a substantial portion of his or her time to the practice of clinical psychology.

Exceptions to the Privilege

There are exceptions to the psychotherapist-patient privilege which are similar to those outlined in connection with the general physician-patient privilege, above.

E. Marital Privileges

Background of the Marital Privileges

The marriage relationship, obviously one worthy of encouragement and protection, has given rise over the years to principles of evidence in four categories: (1) the total incompetency of one spouse not to give testimony against the other; (2) the privilege of one spouse not to give testimony against the other; (3) the privilege of one spouse not to have the other testify against him or her; and (4) a privilege against disclosure of confidential communications between spouses. Today the marital privileges are largely governed by statutes.

Incompetency

Parties and other interested persons are no longer incompetent to give testimony (see chapter 15). By the same token, a spouse is no longer incompetent in this country to testify on behalf of his or her marriage partner. Either by statute or judicial decision, spousal incompetency, the first category mentioned in the previous paragraph, has been abolished.

The Privilege Not to Testify against a Spouse

About ten states recognize a privilege not to testify against one's spouse in a criminal case. In other words, the privilege belongs to the witness spouse, not to the defendant spouse. The trend may be in this direction since this is now the rule in the federal courts as a result of the Supreme Court's decision in *Trammel* v. *United States,* 445 U.S. 40 (1980). However, this form of the marital privilege has been criticized by some commentators on the ground that it may inspire prosecutors to put undue pressure on witnesses to testify against their spouses, thereby undermining the marriage relationship. (See, for example, Lempert, *A Right to Every Woman's Testimony,* 66 Iowa Law Rev. 725 (1981).

The Privilege to Prevent a Spouse from Testifying

More than half of the states recognize a privilege on the part of an accused in a criminal case to prevent his or her spouse from testifying. This is often referred to as the *spousal incapacity privilege.* It has vitality only if the marriage is still in existence.

> EXAMPLE:
> In *Wyatt* v. *United States,* 362 U.S. 525 (1960), the defendant was charged with violating the Mann Act, which prohibits what is quaintly referred to as "white slavery" (*i.e.,* pimping). Between the time of the alleged violation and the trial, the defendant married the woman he was charged with having transported in interstate commerce for purposes of prostitution. The prosecution called the wife as a witness for the Government.
>
> The Supreme Court in *Wyatt* held that neither spouse could invoke the marital privilege under the circumstances of that case. In an earlier case the Court had said that a party has a right to exclude adverse testimony of a spouse. In *Wyatt,* however, the Court said that the defen-

dant should not be permitted to claim a privilege the purpose of which is to foster and protect the marital relationship since the crime with which he was charged was a "shameful offense against wifehood." (The Court's reasoning is somewhat circular here, since the denial of the privilege occurs before the defendant stands convicted of the charge whose evil nature justifies the demand of the privilege.)

The Confidential Communications Privilege

This marital privilege, a widely recognized one, is closely related to the other testimonial privileges—for example, the attorney-client privilege already discussed—in that it protects *confidential* communications between members of the marital relationship. Confidentiality is the key ingredient.

EXAMPLE:
In *People* v. *Melski*, 217 N.Y.S. 2d 65 (Ct. App. N.Y. 1961), the accused was charged with taking part in a gun theft. After the alleged theft he and his alleged accomplices returned to the accused's home where, at a later hour, they were discovered by his wife. At trial the wife was allowed to testify to "the incriminating fact that accomplices were present in the home completing the crime."

Was there any communication here at all? The New York Court of Appeals held that acts or conduct—the accused's disclosure of his accomplices to his wife—can amount to a communication.

The court held that the presence of the accomplices rendered the accused's communication nonconfidential. It thus was not subject to the confidential marital communications privilege.

The confidential communications privilege is held by both marital partners. Unlike the spousal incapacity privilege, the confidential communications privilege can be claimed by either ex-spouse after the marriage has come to an end so long as the communication in question took place *during* the marriage.

In all jurisdictions this privilege is subject to a number of exceptions. For example, under Section 981 of the California Evidence Code, the confidential communications privilege is inapplicable to a communication "made, in whole or in part, to enable or aid anyone to commit or plan to commit a crime or fraud." Under Section 987 of the California Evidence Code a nondefendant spouse cannot claim this privilege to prevent a defendant spouse in a criminal case from introducing the contents of a confidential marital communication as a part of his or her defense.

F. Clergy-Penitent Privilege

Reasons for the Privilege

The same considerations that require recognition of testimonial privileges generally give strong support for a privilege shielding confidential communications to members of the clergy. The law wishes to encourage resort to spiritual advisors, who in this day and age give valuable counseling in a variety of areas, including marital advice. There was never a clear-cut common law privilege protecting confidential communications to members of the clergy, but today about two-thirds of the states recognize such a privilege, usually by statute.

Scope and Nature of the Privilege

In those jurisdictions recognizing this privilege, a person has a privilege to refuse to divulge, and to prevent other persons from divulging, a confidential communication by the person to a member of the clergy acting in the capacity of spiritual advisor.

Definitions

The term *clergy* is usually defined broadly, although not broadly enough to include all manner of self-styled "ministers," gurus, and the like. The lack of absolute precision in definition stems from the lack of licensing regulations for men or women of the cloth. However, it is clear enough that clergy can be a minister, priest, rabbi, or other similar member of a religious organization. He (or she) can also be someone *reasonably believed* to be clergy by the person consulting him, even though he in fact turns out to be a charlatan and a fraud. (This is consistent with the general principle that marriages performed by unauthorized persons are nonetheless valid if the parties [or party] intended to be fooled or defrauded reasonably believed the person performing the marriage ceremony to be a genuine clergyman.)

All confidential communications to the clergy, and not just confessory or penitential ones, are covered by this privilege. This aspect of the privilege takes into account the circumstance that many members of the clergy now have training in marriage counseling and in the handling of personality problems.

It is unlikely that the term *confidential* would ever be construed so as to remove this privilege's protection where both spouses visit a clergyman for marital advice. It is true that when a husband and wife jointly consult a clergyman for marriage counseling, for each spouse the presence of the other would negate the confidentiality of any disclosures. This is akin to the situation in which several persons jointly consult the same attorney. In the marriage counseling situation the courts are likely to hold that a communication remains confidential for purposes of this privilege even if it is disclosed to third persons (the other spouse and perhaps the couple's children or parents) where the presence of those third persons is necessary to the rendition of the service offered by the primary person—here the clergy—to whom the disclosure is made.

G. Journalist's Source Privilege

Scope of the Privilege

Although not constitutionally obligated to do so, some jurisdictions provide for a more or less restricted journalist's information source privilege. Thus Section 1070 of the California Evidence Code provides that a journalist cannot be cited for contempt of court for a refusal to divulge his or her sources of information before, for example, a grand jury investigating crimes about which the journalist has published newspaper accounts.

This limited privilege is of no help to journalists in proceedings other than those involving a contempt citation. For example, it does not protect the journalist from a libel action based on what he or she wrote.

The Fear of Fabrication

Although the legislatures may now be in a mood to grant a broader privilege to newspeople, there has been a cynical attitude lurking behind their previous reluctance to do so. It is inspired by the fear that members of the press will simply invent newsworthy stories if they are assured that their falsity cannot be revealed by checking with the writers' asserted sources.

H. Political Vote

Nature and Scope of the Privilege

A majority of jurisdictions provide that every person has a privilege to refuse to disclose his or her vote in a political election conducted by secret ballot, unless the vote was cast illegally. The rationale behind this privilege, of course, is that in order to effectuate the policy of the secret ballot, a fundamental tenet of participatory democracy, its secrecy must be maintained after the ballot has been cast.

It is not absolutely clear whether this privilege would apply where a person has voted with the assistance of another or where a snooper has ascertained the tenor of a person's vote. There is a lack of confidentiality in both of these situations. However, it is reasonable to assume that the privilege will be interpreted so as to permit the voter to prevent disclosure of how he or she voted in either situation, unless the vote was cast illegally.

Classified documents relating to national security.

I. Military and State Secrets

Nature and Scope of the Privilege

The federal government has a privilege to refuse to give evidence, and to prevent any persons from giving evidence, upon a showing of reasonable likelihood of danger that disclosure of the evidence would be injurious to the national defense or the international relations of the United States. In *United States* v. *Reynolds,* 345 U.S. 1 (1953), the Supreme Court said that the privilege for military and state secrets was "well established in the law of evidence" and Dean Wigmore, the leading authority in the field of evidence, said that the privilege is one "the existence of which has never been doubted."

Holder of the Privilege

The privilege is lodged with the government. The right to invoke it rests with the chief officer of the governmental department concerned with the matter involved, although the actual assertion of the privilege can be by the government's legal counsel. It is the department chief who comes up with the required showing, that is, who demonstrates that there would be a reasonable likelihood of danger to national security or international relations if disclosure were allowed. It has been thought that the privilege will not be indiscriminately invoked if the decision to invoke it must be considered and made by a high-level official.

Illustrative Case

The most influential case involving the military and state secrets privilege is *United States* v. *Reynolds,* 345 U.S. 1 (1953). The widows of three civilian observers who had been killed in the crash of an Air Force plane sued the federal government under the provisions of the Federal Tort Claims Act. The Tort Claims Act waives the government's traditional sovereign immunity to suit and makes the federal government "liable in the same manner as a private individual" for the wrongs it does.

The plaintiffs in *Reynolds* tried to obtain the Air Force's official accident report, containing data concerning the electronic equipment with which the Air Force had been experimenting. The government resisted this pretrial discovery effort, contending that the data was privileged. The trial judge ordered disclosure, stating that the Tort Claims Act worked a waiver of any privilege based on executive control over government documents. The secretary of the Air Force then dispatched a letter to the judge, advising him that production of the requested documents would be against the public interest. The judge then ordered a rehearing, at which the government entered a formal claim of privilege by the secretary. In it the secretary said that the documents in question contained military secrets. The trial judge ordered the government to produce the documents for his inspection, so that he could see for himself whether they contained any privileged matter. The government announced that even inspection by a federal judge would be too risky. The judge then ordered a finding in favor of the three plaintiff widows on the issue of the defendant United States' negligence. (This was done pursuant to Rule 37 of the Federal Rules of Civil Procedure, which provides that a party refusing to abide by a discovery order will suffer a finding against him on all factual issues to which the unproduced information is relevant.) In effect, the three widows won because the government would not abandon its asserted privilege.

A Court of Appeals upheld the trial judge's action in *Reynolds* but the Supreme Court reversed the lower courts. It held that the Federal Rule of Civil Procedure could be employed to force discovery only if the requested materials were not privileged. It added that the secretary of the Air Force had entered a valid claim of privilege.

The real problem confronted by the Supreme Court in *Reynolds* was how to go about testing the validity of a claim of governmental privilege. Chief Justice Vinson conceded that "Judicial control over the evidence in a case cannot be abdicated to the caprice of executive officers." The Court came up with a compromise by which the trial judge was to allow the claim of privilege after the government had shown that "there is reasonable danger that compulsion of the evidence will expose military matters which . . . should not be divulged." The *Reynolds* opinion required that a claim of privilege must be formally submitted to the trial judge by the head of the governmental department involved. The department head must have given the matter his personal attention.

In *Reynolds* the good faith of the Secretary of the Air Force was reasonably evident. Both the circumstance that the requested data was quite conceivably a proper subject of military secrecy and that the amount of money at stake in the lawsuit was piddling in comparison with the Air Force's budget would indicate that the secretary's withholding of the information was not inspired by a simple desire to win a lawsuit. Furthermore, the secretary's opinion about whether an item of information should be considered a sensitive military secret is bound to be a more informed opinion than one generated by a trial judge. The department chief is more familiar with the field involved and is better equipped to assess the importance of secrecy. Furthermore, even if the trial judge were given complete access to the information, his probable lack of expertise in the abstruse field involved might make his inspection of the data next to useless.

The Supreme Court in *Reynolds* concluded that the plaintiffs did not really need the unproduced documents to make out their negligence case. It therefore held that the government's claim of privilege could be granted on a less powerful showing than would otherwise be required.

Effect of a Claim of the Privilege in Criminal Cases

The *Reynolds* case, described above, was a civil negligence case, not a criminal case. The effect of a claim of military or state secrets privilege in a criminal case can be more potent. In criminal prosecutions where the government is called on to produce relevant information that it considers privileged, it must provide the information or dismiss the prosecution. The majority justices in the *Reynolds* case explained this more radical approach by saying that in criminal cases the government has a responsibility to assure that justice is done. The justices added that the government has *commenced* the criminal case, while it is a passive party which is itself hauled into court against its will in the civil situation that was directly involved in *Reynolds.*

There are, in truth, two fundamental reasons for refusing to let the government invoke these privileges in a criminal case. In the first place, the law tries to adhere to an especially elevated standard in shielding defendants from wrongful conviction in criminal proceedings. Secondly, the number of cases in which a criminal accused can defeat his own prosecution by demanding the production of information which he knows the government will refuse to supply is probably small.

J. Identity of an Informer

The Rule of Privilege

The federal government or a state or subdivision of a state, such as a city, has a privilege to refuse to disclose the identity of a person who has supplied to a law enforcement agent information purporting to reveal a violation of law. This privilege reflects a recognition that anonymity is essential to the effective use of informants in law enforcement. As the Supreme Court said in *Roviaro* v. *United States,* 353 U.S. 53 (1957), the privilege is one that is "well established at common law." It applies to the concerned citizen who comes forward with information and it applies to police undercover agents, such as narcotics agents.

Who May Claim the Privilege

In times past it has been said that this privilege could be invoked by the prosecution, by the trial judge, or by the informer. Today, however, the tendency is to hold that the privilege belongs exclusively to the government since it is the flow of information to law enforcement agents that is sought to be protected.

The privilege can be invoked by an appropriate representative of the government, regardless of whether the information was supplied to an officer of the government. Usually the appropriate representative of the government will be legal counsel in the case, but this will not invariably be true since the United States, a state, or a subdivision may not be a party to the litigation.

> EXAMPLE:
> *Bocchicchio* v. *Curtis Publishing Co.,* 203 F. Supp. 403 (E.D. Pa. 1962), was a civil libel action. A police officer, who was not represented by counsel, successfully invoked the privilege to conceal the identity of an informant.

Exceptions

Three fundamental exceptions to the rule of privilege pertaining to the identity of a police informant are emerging in the law. One of them involves voluntary disclosure of the informant's identity; another involves the situation in which the informant probably could give testimony helpful to the accused were his identity made known; a third involves situations in which an informer's statements were relied on to provide probable cause for an arrest.

1. *Voluntary Disclosure.* No privilege exists if an informer's identity or his interest in the subject matter of his communication has been disclosed

to those who would have cause to resent the communication, or if the informant actually appears in court as a witness on behalf of the prosecution.

Obviously, if the informant's identity is revealed, nothing further is to be gained by efforts to suppress it. Disclosure of his identity can be direct or it can result from actions plainly revealing the informant's interest in the subject matter of the prosecution or civil suit.

If the informant becomes a witness in the case, the interests of justice favor disclosing his status since it might be a source of bias upon which the opposing side could impeach his veracity. The interests of justice are thought to outweigh any interest in nondisclosure that might remain after the informant has taken the stand.

It is usually held that waiver of the privilege does not occur unless the informer's identity, or his interest in the subject matter, is revealed to those whose interests are adversely affected by his communication.

2. *Testimony Helpful to an Accused.* The informer privilege cannot be employed where society's interest in the flow of information to law enforcement agents is outweighed by the right of the accused to prepare his or her defense. Sometimes, as the saying goes, the prosecution must "fish or cut bait." If it appears from the evidence in the case that an informant might be able to give testimony necessary to a fair determination of guilt or innocence (or, for that matter, of a material issue in a civil case), and the government asserts the privilege, the trial judge will accord the government an opportunity to show facts, in a hearing that is usually closed to all but the trial judge, the government's representative, and a court reporter, that are relevant to deciding whether the informant can give such testimony. This showing is usually made by means of sworn statements (affidavits), but the trial judge may direct that witnesses be called and testimony taken if he determines that the matter cannot be resolved satisfactorily on the basis of written statements alone.

If the judge decides that there is a reasonable probability that the informant can give testimony helpful to the defendant and the prosecution elects not to disclose his identity, the judge on motion of the accused in a criminal case will dismiss any charges to which the informant's testimony would relate. A judge can also dismiss the case, or parts of it, on his or her *own* motion. (In civil cases, the trial court can enter any order that the best interests of justice dictate. For example, it might enter a finding against the government on an issue to which the informer's testimony would be relevant.)

Evidence submitted to the trial judge at a hearing of the sort described above is sealed and carefully preserved so that it will be available to reviewing courts in the event of an appeal. The contents of the evidence will not be disclosed to anyone else without the prosecution's consent.

3. *Legality of Securing Evidence.* Occasionally information from a police informant is relied upon to establish the legality of the means by which evidence was obtained. If a judge is not satisfied that this sort of informa-

tion was received from an informant whom the police reasonably believed to be reliable or credible, he can direct that the identity of the informer be disclosed to him. If the prosecution requests it, this disclosure can be made in a hearing at which no legal counsel or party will be allowed to be present. In the absence of such a request by the prosecution, all counsel and any parties concerned with the issue of legality will be permitted to be present at the hearing. If disclosure of the informant's identity is made at a closed session, the record of the hearing will be sealed and preserved for possible use by reviewing courts and the contents, again, will not in any other way be revealed without the prosecution's approval.

Illustrative Cases

The leading case involving the informer privilege is *Roviaro* v. *United States,* 353 U.S. 53 (1957). Roviaro was charged with the transportation and sale of a quantity of heroin to a government informer who was under surveillance. No other evidence against him was ever found. At his trial, narcotics agents testified to the sale. The accused then demanded the name of the informer, insisting that he had no way to counter the evidence of the sale without knowing the identity of the person to whom he was charged with selling the heroin.

Before the United States Supreme Court the Government conceded that refusal to disclose the informer's name was legally erroneous with respect to the *sale* charge. However, it argued that there was no error with regard to the *transportation* count. The Supreme Court held that refusing to reveal the informer's name was reversible error as to *both* counts.

The Court in *Roviaro* made it clear that the prosecution's privilege to suppress the identity of informants is a restricted one. One of the limitations on the privilege arises from "the fundamental requirements of fairness." As a matter of fact, the only evidence of transportation was the alleged fact of the subsequent *sale.* Consequently, the accused, in the Court's view, should have been given the chance to refute the sale by summoning the informant to the stand, something which he could not do without knowing the informant's identity. He then could hope that the informant's testimony would contradict that of the narcotics agents.

In narcotics cases, informers are typically used in the following way: A person, usually one against whom a law enforcement agent has incriminating evidence to use as leverage, is pressed into the service of narcotics agents. Before the informant parts company with the agents, they search him to make certain that he has no narcotics on his person. The agents provide him with money (the serial numbers of which have been recorded and which is usually marked) and direct him to a suspect with orders to offer to purchase narcotics from him. The agents watch the informant until he has a transaction with the suspect and returns to the agents.

They then search the informant, who now has narcotics in his possession and no money.

The suspect is then arrested. Often he is charged with transportation or concealment rather than with a sale since evidence of the sale embraces evidence of the other offenses as well.

The procedure just described does not constitute unlawful entrapment of the suspect because the informant is instructed to avoid playing on the emotions of the suspect. Entrapment would consist of imploring the suspect to sell narcotics on numerous occasions and in the face of his repeated refusals. The procedure outlined here envisions a willing buyer-willing seller situation.

Law enforcement agencies are not usually concerned with the question of whether evidence procured in this manner is adequate to support a conviction. Usually they will have found other evidence of the sale to provide probable cause for the arrest. Often the seller will have additional narcotics in his possession at the time of his arrest. Furthermore, the money paid to him by the informer-purchaser will have been marked. And after the suspect's arrest, criminal investigators can continue to dig up information attesting his involvement in the narcotics traffic.

In *Roviaro,* however, the only evidence the prosecution had was evidence of the transaction between the accused and "John Doe," the informant. The government's agents, having observed the informant prior to and during the alleged sale, testified to the transaction in court. It is altogether likely that these agents were telling the truth; certainly reasonable jurors could have concluded that they were. On any rational basis, the agents' testimony alone ought to have been sufficient to support a conviction. It included an identification of the accused and appeared to be probative of every element of the crime charged. The only disturbing thing about this sort of evidence is that the accused's ability to meet it is diminished by the prosecution's refusal to reveal the informant's identity.

On the other hand, an accused in Roviaro's situation has an opportunity to cross-examine the narcotics agents themselves. But this does not satisfy the accused; as was earlier suggested, the accused hopes that the informant, were he on the stand, would contradict the agents' testimony. This hardly is very likely, however. In the first place, in the scheme of things the agents' testimony is probably truthful. For another thing, the informant probably believes himself to be at the mercy of the narcotics agents and will struggle manfully to corroborate their testimony. Finally, jurors are unlikely to believe an informer even if his testimony *does* contradict that of law enforcement agents. In light of the foregoing, it seems reasonable to suggest that a defendant's access to an informer's identity and testimony ordinarily has little practical value. Nonetheless, the Supreme Court in *Roviaro* decreed that the accused must be given a fighting chance to refute that portion of the case against him which rests on the evidence of an informer.

In *McCray* v. *Illinois,* 386 U.S. 300 (1967), the accused was arrested and searched without a warrant. Heroin was found on him and he was charged with possession of narcotics. At a hearing on the accused's motion to suppress the evidence obtained by means of the search, the arresting Chicago police officers explained that an informer "of known reliability" had tipped off the police to McCray. The officers advised the court that this same informer had provided them in the past with fifteen or sixteen tips culminating in the arrest or conviction of a number of persons for narcotic law violations.

On cross-examination, defense counsel asked one of the police officers for the informer's name. The prosecuting attorney objected and the trial judge ruled that the witness did not have to disclose the name.

The Supreme Court affirmed McCray's conviction, holding that an informer's identity need not be disclosed to the defense where his or her communication to arresting officers bears only upon the existence of probable cause for the arrest.

There are some good reasons for distinguishing between evidence secured from an informer that goes to the issue of *guilt or innocence* (as in *Roviaro*) and that which goes only to *probable cause* (as in *McCray*). First of all, testimony of the informer at trial could in no way assist the accused in defeating, on its merits, the charge against him. This is true because the evidence on which the charge rests is not the product of the information given by the informer; the informer's information simply led to the accused's arrest; *then* the evidence of his guilt—additional dope, marked bills—was obtained from him. Still and all, had the accused been arrested without probable cause, his conviction could not stand even though a great deal of evidence against him was seized incident to his arrest. In this sense, the accused's interest in litigating the probable cause issue is as strong as his interest in litigating the issue of his guilt or innocence. However, an informer's testimony on the probable cause issue is not likely to prove significant. It would have utility to the defense only if the informer were to contradict the arresting officer's testimony on the issue of his own reliability as an informer or on the question of exactly what information he gave to the police. The possibility of the informer's giving contradictory testimony is minute. To the extent that it exists at all, it is weakened by the circumstance that jurors are decidedly inclined to believe the police in preference to their underworld contacts. Even if the informer had testified that he was lying to the Chicago police about McCray, probable cause would still have existed so long as the arresting officers were not *aware* that the informer was lying. The fact that the police may have been skillfully fooled by their informer does not detract from their probable cause for acting on the information given them.

In *Smith* v. *Illinois,* 390 U.S. 129 (1968), a police informant testified for the prosecution at trial but refused to disclose his real name or his address to the defense. Without making any reference to *Roviaro,* the Supreme Court further restricted the informer privilege by holding that the right of confrontation requires disclosure of the informer's true name and address whenever his credibility is a key issue. In *Smith* the defendant had been convicted of selling narcotics. The police informant, calling himself "James Jordan," bought a bag of heroin from the defendant with marked money. At trial he testified as the State's principal witness, using his fictitious name. Because the testimony lacked corroboration and the descriptions of the transaction by him and by the defendant differed substantially, the comparative credibility of the informer and the defendant was an important issue. The defense moved for disclosure of "James Jordan's" true identity.

The Supreme Court in *Smith* reversed the defendant's conviction, holding that he had been deprived of his right of confrontation of the most important witness against him. Justice Potter Stewart, writing the *Smith* opinion for the Court, said that whenever the credibility of a witness is in dispute, "the very starting point in exposing falsehood and bringing out the truth through cross-examination must necessarily be to ask the witness who he is and where he lives." Observing that "The witness' name and address open countless avenues of in-court examination and out-of-court investigation," Justice Stewart concluded that "To forbid this most rudimentary inquiry at the threshold is effectively to emasculate the right of cross-examination itself."

The reason that the informer was called to the stand in this last case was probably that the narcotics agents had lost track of him between their separating from him and their searching of him after his transaction with the accused seller. If every moment of that interim period were not adequately accounted for by the prosecution's evidence, the defense could argue that the informer had obtained the narcotics from someone other than the accused while he was out of the narcotic agents' view. Ordinarily, however, the testimony of informers is not used unless absolutely essential to the making of the prosecution's case. Informers are almost always undesirable types and the prosecution does not wish to afford the defense an opportunity for credibility impeachment; this might hurt the prosecution more than the informer's testimony could possibly help it.

Current Trends

For a time it seemed evident that the *Smith* decision does not require that an informer-witness's identity must invariably be divulged. For example, in *United States* v. *Alston,* 460 F. 2d 51 (5th Cir. 1972), the court affirmed a conviction for the illegal sale of heroin, ruling that the trial judge had properly refused a defense request for disclosure of a government agent-witness's current address where his life and his family's safety might have been jeopardized. Another example is *People* v. *Abbott,* 249 N.E. 2d 675

(Ill. App. 1969), *cert. denied,* 398 U.S. 940 (1970). The accused in this narcotics case had been introduced by the informer, a known addict, to "Danny," who was a plainclothes policeman. "Danny" thereafter made three controlled substance purchases from the accused and was the State's main witness at trial. Defense counsel contended that disclosure of the informer's true identity and address was essential to its entrapment defense since the prosecution and defense accounts of the transaction differed and the informer's testimony was thus subject to impeachment. But the reviewing court held that the defense was already sufficiently informed about the informer's background of addiction and crime, and it also upheld the trial judge's determination that the informer's life was in danger. *Abbott* differs from *Smith,* of course, in that the *Abbott* informer was not the State's principal witness, his credibility was not sharply in issue, and his testimony was corroborated.

Despite such decisions as *Alston* and *Abbott,* the Federal Rules of Evidence and the codes of some states require disclosure of an informer's identity if he testifies at trial. This may be the trend of the future. If it is, it makes it imperative that law enforcement agents and prosecutors be in a position to make every link in their cases without having to place an informant on the witness stand.

K. Waiver of Testimonial Privileges

How Waiver Is Accomplished

A person holding a privilege against disclosure of a confidential matter loses the protection of that privilege—waives it—if he or she voluntarily discloses or consents to disclosure of any significant part of the privileged matter. Waiver was discussed in detail in chapter 8, dealing with the constitutional privilege against compelled self-incrimination.

It is enough here to remind the reader that the main purpose of most of the privileges discussed in this chapter is the promotion or encouragement of some favored relationship by endowing it with confidentiality. It is therefore understandable that a privilege will end when the holder of it voluntarily breaches this secrecy.

It has sometimes been said that waiver is the intentional surrendering of a known right. (*Johnson* v. *Zerbst,* 304 U.S. 458 (1938).) However, in connection with the confidential privileges considered in this chapter, no later claim of privilege can restore its vitality once confidentiality has been voluntarily abandoned and knowledge or lack of knowledge of the existence of the particular privilege by the holder of it is beside the point.

Waiver Must Be Voluntary

The privileges discussed in this chapter are usually invoked in order to *prevent* disclosure of confidential information and a favorable ruling means that the information will not come out. Occasionally, however, it is necessary to consider the status of a disclosure of information that has already been made. In other words, one must consider the effect of a disclosure made under compulsion or without any opportunity to claim the applicable privilege.

Once secrecy has been breached, it cannot as a practical matter be restored: "the horse is out of the barn." Even so, some satisfaction can be taken in the application of an exclusionary rule. And most jurisdictions make the remedy of exclusion available where the antecedent disclosure was (1) erroneously compelled or (2) required without giving an opportunity to claim privilege. In self-incrimination cases it is agreed that erroneously compelled disclosures are not admissible in a later criminal action against the holder of the constitutional privilege. This rule is considered equally valid when applied to the privileges described in this chapter.

In connection with erroneously compelled disclosure—a judge, making a legal mistake, compels the witness to answer—it is occasionally contended that the holder of the privilege ought to be required in the first instance to invoke the applicable privilege, stand his ground in the face of a judicial order to answer the question, incur a contempt of court citation, and then employ appeals to vindicate his conduct. However, as the drafters of the Federal Rules of Evidence pointed out, "This exacts of the holder [of the privilege] greater fortitude in the face of authority than ordinary individuals are likely to possess, and assumes unrealistically that a judicial remedy is always available." The general rule, therefore, is that the holder can bow to judicial authority, give the commanded response, and later call for its exclusion from evidence on the ground that it was erroneously extracted.

L. Comment on or Inference from Invocation of a Testimonial Privilege

The No-Comment Rule

As was pointed out in chapter 8, in criminal cases a prosecutor cannot comment to the jury on the defendant's assertion of the privilege against compulsory self-incrimination. However, there has been a serious conflict among the judicial opinions as to whether this no-comment rule applies to *all* of the testimonial privileges, that is, to the privileges discussed in this chapter.

Today many courts would extend the no-comment rule to all of the privileges discussed in this chapter and this is probably the current trend. Thus a prosecutor's references, during his closing argument to a jury, to the accused's assertion of a common law or statutory privilege will nowadays result in a swiftly sustained objection and perhaps a sharp rebuke from the bench. In the case of several of the more sacred nonconstitutional privileges, most notably the attorney-client privilege, such references would probably lead to the ordering of a mistrial.

EXAMPLE A:

BY THE PROSECUTING ATTORNEY: Ladies and gentlemen of the jury, you will recall that shortly after this hideous offense the accused visited a physician who maintained offices in the Appletree Building on North Clark Street. And when we asked the accused what went on in that doctor's office, what was said, what treatment was given to him, the defense lawyer jumped to his feet and objected. He took the privilege, so to speak. He claimed a doctor-patient privilege and cut off the accused's testimony. Now, don't you wish you knew what happened in that office?

BY DEFENSE COUNSEL: Just a minute, please. I hate to interrupt any lawyer's closing argument, but this is highly improper, Your Honor. Mr. Burger knows better than that. He's commenting on a testimonial privilege which the law gives to us. We object and we ask for a mistrial.

THE COURT: The objection is sustained. Mr. Prosecutor, the defense lawyer is right—you surely know better than to get into this. Let's hear no more about it. Among other things, you are disregarding my ruling excluding the testimony that you improperly sought.

Ladies and gentlemen of the jury, you will totally disregard the prosecutor's last remarks. They were improper.

EXAMPLE B:

BY THE PROSECUTING ATTORNEY: Ladies and gentlemen of the jury, you heard me ask the accused what he told his lawyer—I won't call her his mouthpiece, that would be improper—about this whole affair when he first consulted her. That would be a good way to get at the truth, wouldn't it? What did he tell the lawyer about his involvement in this mess? But they objected.

BY DEFENSE COUNSEL: And we strenuously object now, Your Honor. This is outrageous!

THE COURT: Yes, it is. You should have objected even sooner, or perhaps I was remiss in not injecting myself earlier even in the absence of an objection from you.

This case has gone on for two weeks and I am therefore extremely reluctant to see it go down the drain. I assume you have a motion, however.

BY DEFENSE COUNSEL: We do, Your Honor. We move for a mistrial.

THE COURT: Well, I'm inclined to grant it, but we will take a recess and I'll listen to the arguments of counsel on the motion. Incidentally, Mr. Prosecutor, I'm about as much concerned about your snide reference to a "mouthpiece" as by your improper references to the assertion of a testimonial privilege.

CHAPTER THIRTEEN

Burden of Proof and Presumptions

A. Burden of Proof

Definitions

The term *burden of proof* has inspired some confusing definitional attempts by courts and legal writers. They have injected two additional phrases: *burden of persuasion* and *burden of producing evidence* (sometimes called the *burden of going forward*). Some legal writers treat the term burden of proof as a general term that has two subdivisions: burden of persuasion and burden of producing evidence. Others treat the three phases—burden of proof, burden of producing evidence, and burden of persuasion—as three separate and distinct phenomena. This latter approach is the most easily understandable.

1. *Burden of Proof.* Burden of proof means the obligation to establish a particular issue by the required degree or level of proof. The side making a charge or setting up a defense has the burden of proving it.

2. *Burden of Producing Evidence.* This term—burden of producing evidence—refers to the obligation to make, or to meet, a *prima facie* showing as to a particular issue; that is, a showing that is sufficiently weighty to warrant submitting the issue to the jurors. The burden of producing evidence lies with the side that would *lose* if no further evidence on the particular issue were received. It is for this reason that the burden of producing evidence is occasionally called the burden of going forward, which simply refers to the burden of going forward at trial with the production of evidence.

EXAMPLE:

If, in a murder prosecution, the state's attorney fails to prove that anyone was killed, he has failed to carry the state's burden of proof and, at the same time, he has failed to carry the burden of producing evidence.

On the other hand, if the prosecution shows that the accused shot someone to death, the accused will have the burden of producing evidence that he did not do so or that he was legally justified in doing so.

3. *Burden of Persuasion.* Burden of persuasion refers to the forensic burden of persuading the fact-finder of the *truth* of issues as to which evidence has been produced. The burden of persuasion, in other words, calls for the art of advocacy by trial lawyers, largely in closing arguments to the jury.

Allocation of Burden of Proof in Criminal Cases

The prosecution is obligated to prove beyond a reasonable doubt all of the material elements of the offense charged. The accused, as the saying goes, can "put the prosecution to its proof" by pleading not guilty and admitting nothing.

Most judges refuse to give jurors a definition of reasonable doubt, considering this standard of proof to be self-explanatory. As one court put it, "There is no more lucid definition of the term 'reasonable doubt' than the term itself." The term has always been thought to suggest that measure of doubt which would stop a reasonable and just person from arriving at a determination of guilt.

If evidence of an affirmative defense (for example, self-defense) is introduced, during either the prosecution's or the defendant's case, then the prosecution must carry the burden of disproving it beyond a reasonable doubt. Two standards of proof are at work here, since an affirmative defense can be raised by a mere *preponderance* of the evidence but must be disproved *beyond a reasonable doubt.* A rough way of making these two standards of proof understandable is to say that *beyond a reasonable doubt,* on a scale of 1 to 10, is a 9; *preponderance,* on the same scale, is a 6. (See *Brown* v. *Bowen,* 847 F. 2d 342 (7th Cir. 1988).)

Allocation of Burden of Persuasion

The jurors must be persuaded that *all* of the material elements of the offense have been proved beyond a reasonable doubt in order for them to find the defendant guilty as charged. If any element is not thus established to the jury's satisfaction, or if any defense is not thus disproved by the prosecution, the defendant must be acquitted.

B. Presumptions

General Definitions

A *presumption* is an inference of the existence or nonexistence of a fact that arises from proof of other basic, underlying facts. Presumptions are usually said to be either *conclusive* or *rebuttable.*

1. *Conclusive Presumptions.* Some presumptions (or inferences) are *conclusive* in civil but not in criminal cases. When a statute renders a presumption or inference irrebuttable, it cannot be overcome by any evidence except evidence that the basic facts underlying and giving rise to the asserted presumption are not true.
2. *Rebuttable Presumptions.* A rebuttable (i.e., disputable) presumption is an inference, drawn from circumstantial evidence, that can be overcome by other evidence. It is evidence that a factfinder, such as a jury, can accept and act on when there is no direct evidence in support of the particular issue in dispute. It is this type of presumption that is encountered in criminal cases.

The law speaks also of *presumptions of fact* and *presumptions of law.*

1. *Presumptions of Fact.* A presumption of *fact* is one deriving from the mental process by which the existence of one unknown fact is inferred from proof of other known, basic facts because common sense and experience teach that the known, basic facts usually go hand-in-hand with the unknown fact. This is the sort of presumption that sometimes arises in criminal litigation.
2. *Presumptions of Law.* A presumption of *law* is an inference that the law *requires* the fact-finder to draw once certain basic facts have been established, assuming, of course, that there has been no *direct* evidence on the particular subject. This type of presumption is encountered only in noncriminal litigation.

Probative Force

A rebuttable presumption *substitutes* for direct evidence and will support a finding by the trier of the facts unless and until it is rebutted by other evidence.

Some Commonly Encountered Rebuttable Presumptions of Fact

Presumptions play a much larger role in civil litigation than they do in criminal matters. A lengthy catalogue of rebuttable presumptions of fact applicable in civil cases can be developed. The following are representative. Only a few of them would have application to criminal matters.

1. *Chastity.* There is a presumption that a person is chaste and virtuous.
2. *Continuation of a Condition.* Proof that a fact of a continuous nature (such as human life) existed at a given point in time gives rise to a presumption that the fact also existed at a given later time (there is a presumption of continuing life).
3. *Knowledge of the Law.* Persons are presumed to know the law of the state and country in which they reside.
4. *Letters.* A letter properly mailed is presumed to have been received in due course by its addressee.
5. *Name of Vehicle.* The inscription on a vehicle—"United Parcel Co."—is presumed to be its owner's name.
6. *Validity of Marriage.* There is a presumption in favor of the validity of a marriage.
7. *Suicide.* There is a presumption against suicide.
8. *Solvency.* All persons are presumed to be solvent.
9. *Official and Corporate Regularity.* Government and corporate officials, when they act, are presumed to have acted in the normal, regular way.

Rebuttable Presumptions of Fact in Criminal Cases

So far we have been speaking generally about presumptions; now we focus specifically on the criminal law.

The accused in a criminal matter is presumptively innocent until the prosecution proves every element of the offense beyond a reasonable doubt. Accordingly, it is clear that in criminal cases presumptions do not shift to the accused the burden of producing evidence or of persuading the fact-finder. A presumption in a criminal case is truly nothing more than a permissible inference. Thus the trial judge in a criminal case is not free to charge the jury that it *must* find a "presumed" fact against the accused. When the existence of a presumed fact is submitted to the jury, the judge will instruct the jurors that they *may* regard the basic, underlying facts as sufficient evidence of the presumed fact but that they are not *required* to do so. If the presumed fact establishes guilt, is an element of the offense charged, or negates a defense, its existence must be proved beyond a reasonable doubt.

A commonly confronted presumption in the criminal law is that recent, conscious, and exclusive possession of the fruits of a crime, unexplained or explained feebly, permits an inference of guilt. A specific application of this sort of presumption was involved in the case of *Barnes* v. *United States,* now to be discussed.

"I trust, counselor, that all this is adding up to something."

Presumptions and the Barnes *Decision*

The current status of presumptions in the criminal law is sharply mirrored in the Supreme Court's opinion in *Barnes* v. *United States,* 412 U.S. 837 (1973). Barnes was charged with two counts of possessing U.S. Treasury checks, knowing them to have been stolen from the mails, with two counts of forging the checks, and with two counts of uttering (i.e., passing) the checks, knowing the endorsements to be forgeries. The evidence at trial was fairly typical for this sort of prosecution. It was established that Barnes opened a checking account on July 2, 1971, using the unimaginative pseudonym of "Clarence Smith." On July 1 and July 3, 1971, the U.S. Disbursing Office at San Francisco had mailed four Treasury checks in the amounts of $269.02, $154.70, $184.00, and $268.80 to Nettie Lewis, Albert Young, Arthur Salazar, and Mary Hernandez, respectively. On July 8, 1971, the accused Barnes deposited these same four checks in his "Clarence Smith" account. Each check bore the apparent endorsement of the payee and a second endorsement by "Clarence Smith."

At Barnes's trial the four payees testified that they had never received, endorsed, or authorized endorsement of the checks. A government questioned documents examiner testified that Barnes had made the "Clarence Smith" endorsement on all four checks and that he had signed the payees' names on the Hernandez and Lewis checks; his findings were inconclusive as to who had signed as payee on the Salazar and Young checks.

Barnes did not take the stand at his trial but a postal inspector testified to statements made by the accused at a post-arrest interview. Barnes had explained that he got the checks in question from people who sold furniture for him door-to-door and that the checks had been signed in the payees' names when he received them. Barnes also said that he could not name or identify any of the salespeople and he could not substantiate the existence of any furniture orders because the salespeople assertedly wrote their orders on scraps of scratch paper that had not been kept. Barnes admitted making the "Clarence Smith" endorsements but denied having made the payees' endorsements.

The trial judge instructed the jury that "[p]ossession of recently stolen property, if not satisfactorily explained, is ordinarily a circumstance from which you may reasonably draw the inference and find, in the light of the surrounding circumstances shown by the evidence in the case, that the person in possession knew the property had been stolen." The jury convicted Barnes on all counts.

Mr. Justice Powell, writing for the majority of the Supreme Court, measured the challenged jury instruction against four earlier decisions. The first was *United States* v. *Gainey,* 380 U.S. 63 (1965), in which the Court had sustained the constitutionality of an instruction which authorized a jury to infer from the accused's unexplained presence at an illegal still that he was carrying on "the business of a distiller or rectifier without having given bond as required by law." Recognizing that there must be a "rational connection between the fact proved and the ultimate fact presumed," the Court in *Gainey* upheld the challenged inference on the basis, primarily, of the common knowledge that "illegal stills are secluded, secret operations."

In its next term, however, the Supreme Court in *United States* v. *Romano,* 382 U.S. 136 (1965), decided that presence at an illegal still could not support an inference that the accused was in possession, custody, or control of the still, a much narrower offence. The Court said, "Presence is relevant and admissible evidence in a trial on a possession charge; but absent some showing of the defendant's function at the still, its connection with possession is too tenuous to permit a reasonable inference of guilt—'the inference of the one from proof of the other is arbitrary'. . . ."

Three and a half years after *Romano,* the Court in *Leary* v. *United States,* 395 U.S. 6 (1969), considered a challenge to a statutory presumption that possession of marijuana, unless satisfactorily explained, established that the accused knew it had been imported into the United States illegally. Since there is a significant possibility of domestic growth, coupled with the improbability that a user would have known whether his marijuana was of foreign or domestic origin, the Supreme Court concluded that the *Leary* inference did not meet the "rational connection" test of *Gainey* and *Romano.* Referring to those cases, the *Leary* Court said that an inference is "irrational" and hence unconstitutional "unless it can at least be said with substantial assurance that the presumed fact is more likely than not to flow from the proved fact on which it is made to depend." The Court stated the challenged inference failed to satisfy this more-likely-than-not standard.

In *Turner* v. *United States,* 396 U.S. 398 (1970), the Supreme Court addressed the constitutionality of instructing the jury that it could infer from possession of heroin and cocaine that the accused knew the drugs had been imported. For reasons having to do with the likelihood of domestic origin, the Court upheld the inference with respect to heroin but held that the more-likely-than-not standard was left unsatisfied in connection with cocaine, which could be of domestic origin.

In *Barnes* the Court, referring to the four cases just discussed, said, "What has been established by the cases . . . is at least this: that if a statutory inference submitted to the jury as sufficient to support conviction satisfies the reasonable doubt standard (that is, the evidence necessary to invoke the inference is sufficient for a rational juror to find the inferred fact beyond a reasonable doubt) as well as the more-likely-than-not standard, then it clearly accords with due process." In *Barnes* the challenged instruction only permitted the inference of guilt from *unexplained* possession of recently stolen property. On the basis of the prosecution's evidence, "common sense and experience tell us that [the accused] must have known or been aware of the high probability that the checks were stolen." Thus evidence was sufficient to enable the jury to find *beyond a reasonable doubt* that the accused knew the checks were stolen. Since the inference satisfied the most stringent standard the Supreme Court ever applies in assessing permissive criminal law inferences, the Court in *Barnes* concluded that the demands of due process of law were satisfied.

Finally, in *County Court of Ulster County, New York* v. *Allen,* 442 U.S. 140 (1979), the Supreme Court, speaking through Justice John Paul Stevens, made clear the application of *Leary's* more-likely-than-not test in cases involving permissive, as distinguished from mandatory, presumptions. In *Allen* the four defendants had been tried for unlawful possession of two loaded handguns found in an automobile in which the four had been riding when they were stopped for speeding. At their trial the accused objected to introduction of the guns, contending that the prosecution had failed to prove a connection between the guns and each of the accused. The trial court overruled this objection, relying on a New York statutory presumption: the presence of a firearm in an automobile is presumptive evidence of its illegal possession by all persons then occupying the vehicle, unless in fact the weapon was in the possession of a particular occupant. The guns in *Allen* had been in the open handbag of "Jane Doe," a sixteen-year-old girl, on either the front seat or the front floor of the passenger side of the car where she was sitting.

The defendants were convicted. The Supreme Court concluded that "As applied to the facts of this case, the presumption of possession is entirely rational." Although the handguns were in Doe's purse, several circumstances made it improbable that she was their sole custodian: the guns were too large to be concealed in the handbag, and so the bag was open and the guns were in plain view, within easy reach of the driver and perhaps even of the passengers in the rear seats. Of the four in the car, the young girl was the least likely to be the owner of two heavy guns. It was more likely that when the car was halted for speeding the other three occupants, anticipating a search, had tried to hide the guns in the girl's purse. It was rational to infer that all four occupants were aware of the guns' presence and had both the ability and the intent to exercise control over them. The "rational connection" between basic facts *proved* and ultimate fact *presumed* was present.

And the test, as indicated in *Leary,* is a more-likely-than-not test. In other words, the evidence necessary to invoke the presumption need not necessarily be sufficient, standing alone, for a jury to find the inferred (presumed) fact *beyond a reasonable doubt.*

It must be reemphasized that a *mandatory* presumption, as distinguished from a merely permissible one, would relieve the prosecution of its obligation to present evidence proving, beyond a reasonable doubt, every element of the charged offense. This would violate the accused's due process rights: it would undermine the presumption of innocence and invade the truth-determining function that is exclusively the jury's in criminal matters.

EXAMPLE:

Jury instructions, given at trial for grand larceny based on an accused's failure to return a rental car, *required* jury—among other things—to presume accused's criminal intent upon a finding by it that the car was not returned within twenty days of written demand by owner after expiration of lease agreement. The Supreme Court held that this instruction created a constitutionally impermissible mandatory presumption. (*Carella* v. *California,* ______ U.S. ______ 109 S. Ct. 1738 (1989); see also *Francis* v. *Franklin,* 471 U.S. 307 (1985).)

CHAPTER FOURTEEN

Judicial Notice

A. Judicial Notice of Adjudicative Facts

Definition

Adjudicative facts are the facts of the particular case being tried. They are distinguished from *legislative facts*, to be discussed later in this chapter, which have broad relevance to legal reasoning and the law-making process.

Reasons for Judicial Notice of Adjudicative Facts

The existence of some facts is thought to be so self-evident that no formal proof of them is necessary during a trial. Thus no witnesses need be called and no tangible evidence need be offered to establish these widely accepted facts. A trial court will simply take notice of them and instruct the jurors that they are to be taken, or can be taken, as established without formal proof.

Types of Facts Subject to Judicial Notice

Courts can take judicial notice of two types of adjudicative facts: (1) those facts which are subject to *common knowledge*, and (2) those that are subject to *certain verification*.

1. A court can take judicial notice of those facts that are common knowledge in the jurors' community.

EXAMPLE A:
A trial court could take judicial notice that the city and county where the victim testified that an attack on her took place were located within the state in which the trial court was sitting. (*McDonald* v. *State,* 477 S.W. 2d 759 (S. Ct. Tenn. 1972).)

EXAMPLE B:
A court can take judicial notice that contraband is often smuggled into prisons. (*Mathis* v. *Superior Court for Sacramento County,* 105 Cal. Rptr. 126 (Cal. App. 1972).)

EXAMPLE C:
A trial court can take judicial notice that knives and other small weapons can be hidden in wallets or billfolds and that cards and addresses found in wallets may disclose the names of those who may have conspired with the person searched. (*United States* v. *Simpson,* 453 F. 2d 1028 (10th Cir. 1972).)

EXAMPLE D:
A trial court can take judicial notice that, under normal circumstances, the reading of approximately forty pages of transcribed testimony would take considerable less than an hour. (*United States* v. *Rabb,* 453 F. 2d 1012 (3d Cir. 1971).)

EXAMPLE E:
A trial court could take judicial notice that 7:30 p.m. in July is daytime in Dallas, Texas, during daylight saving time. (*United States* v. *Wilson,* 451 F. 2d 209 (5th Cir. 1971).)

EXAMPLE F:
A trial court could take judicial notice that while most establishments engaged in repairing vehicles and dismantling or selling used vehicles are honestly conducted, this type of business is frequently utilized as a front by persons engaged in illegal activities such as stealing automobiles, stripping them, exchanging parts, repainting them, etc., leading ultimately to the sale of stolen cars or their parts. (*People* v. *Gray,* 100 Cal. Rptr. 245 (Cal. App. 1972).)

EXAMPLE G:
A trial court can take judicial notice that a loaded revolver in the hands of two fighting combatants becomes a dangerous instrumentality which is capable of bringing about, and is likely to bring about, disastrous results. (*People* v. *Brown,* 195 N.W. 2d 60 (Mich. App. 1972).)

EXAMPLE H:
It is a matter subject to judicial notice that receiving and dispensing information and wagers in connection with sporting events is not limited to such specific hours of the day that an electronic interception order can define precisely the period during which interception can be conducted. (*United States* v. *Becker,* 334 F. Supp. 546 (S.D.N.Y. 1971).)

EXAMPLE I:
A trial court can take judicial notice that tape decks are frequently stolen from parked automobiles. (*Jones* v. *United States,* 285 A. 2d 861 (D.C. App. 1972).)

EXAMPLE J:
It can be judicially noticed that a person may exhibit symptoms of having consumed alcohol without necessarily losing the capacity to form an intent to do a criminal act. (*State* v. *Zamora,* 491 P. 2d 1342 (Wash. App. 1972).)

EXAMPLE K:
A court can take judicial notice that fingerprinting is a common method of identification used by many employers and in the issuing of licenses and permits, as well as by individuals to assure positive identification in case of sudden death or accident. (*State* v. *Emrick,* 282 A. 2d 821 (S. Ct. Vt. 1971).)

EXAMPLE L:
It is common knowledge, and so subject to judicial notice, that sellers and users of illicit narcotics frequently attempt to destroy incriminating evidence by placing it in their mouths and swallowing it. (*People* v. *Jones,* 97 Cal. Rptr. 492 (Cal. App. 1971).)

EXAMPLE M:
The terms "reds," "red devils," and "Christmas trees" are in such widespread and common usage as to justify judicial notice that they refer to secobarbital. (*People* v. *Davis,* 286 N.E. 2d 8 (Ill. App. 1972).)

2. A court can take judicial notice of those facts which, although not specifically known by all persons, are susceptible to accurate and ready determination—in other words, certain verification—by recourse to sources the accuracy of which cannot reasonably be disputed.

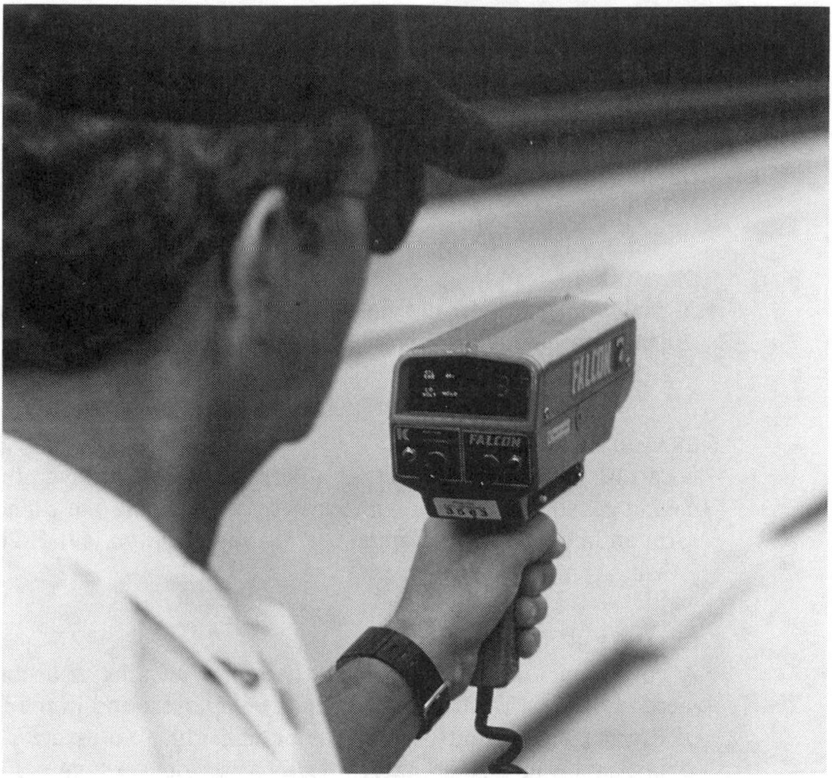

A radar speed gun. If the radar device is properly used and calibrated, judicial notice will be taken of the validity of its findings as scientifically provable facts.

EXAMPLE A:

Courts can take judicial notice of the underlying principles and reliability of properly tested and operated radar devices for determining the speed of motor vehicles without hearing expert testimony on the theory and mechanics of a particular device. (*State* v. *Gerdes,* 191 N.W. 2d (S. Ct. Minn. 1971).)

EXAMPLE B:

A trial court will take judicial notice of the scientific principles that justify the use of blood tests to evidence nonpaternity and intoxication. (*Houghton* v. *Houghton,* 137 N.W. 2d 861 (S. Ct. Neb. 1965) (non-paternity); *State* v. *Miller,* 165 A. 2d 829 (N.J. Super. 1960) (intoxication).)

EXAMPLE C:

Judicial notice will be taken of the validity of techniques for identifying questioned handwriting and typewriting. (*Fenelon* v. *State,* 217 N.W.

711 (S. Ct. Wis. 1928)(handwriting); *United States* v. *Hiss,* 107 F. Supp. 128 (S.D.N.Y. 1952)(typewriting).)

EXAMPLE D:
The validity of expert firearms identification testimony will be judicially noticed. (*People* v. *Fisher,* 172 N.E. 743 (S. Ct. Ill. 1930).)

EXAMPLE E:
So far, courts have been largely unwilling to take judicial notice of the scientific validity of the Polygraph ("lie detector"), on the ground that the results of Polygraph tests depend more on the operator's skill than on the inherent reliability of the device. (*State* v. *Brown,* 177 So. 2d 532 (S. Ct. Fla. 1965).)

The reasoning behind the judicial noticing of facts of this sort is that "It brings discredit upon the legal profession and it makes a mockery of a court of justice to permit a jury to accept or reject in accordance with their prejudices a fact capable of exact scientific determination." (Keefe, Landis & Shaad, *Sense and Nonsense About Judicial Notice,* 2 Stanford Law Rev. 664 (1950).)

This branch of judicial notice expands as humankind's scientific knowledge expands. At one time firearms identification evidence was considered worthless, even, as one court put it, "preposterous." Today, its reliability is subject to judicial notice. A few years ago no court would take judicial notice of the trustworthiness of a so-called voiceprint; today some courts are cautiously moving toward a more affirmative stance. Perhaps someday all courts will develop sufficient faith in some form of Polygraph testing to take judicial notice of its worth. (See chapter 18 on various types of scientific evidence in criminal cases.)

Discretionary Judicial Notice of Adjudicative Facts

A trial or appellate court *may,* in its discretion, take judicial notice of adjudicative facts, whether requested by counsel to do so or not.

Mandatory Judicial Notice of Adjudicative Facts

A court or judge *must* take judicial notice of adjudicative facts if requested by a party to do so and if the necessary information supporting the taking of judicial notice is provided. Since not all trial judges are noted for their independent research efforts, judicial notice is most commonly taken only after counsel for one side or the other has done the research necessary to back up a formal request for the judicial noticing of a particular fact.

EXAMPLE A:

BY THE PROSECUTING ATTORNEY: Your Honor, we ask that the court take judicial notice that May 9, 1987, fell on a Wednesday. I have here a ten-year calendar put out by the Chicago Title and Trust Company which Your Honor can consult. It shows May 9, 1987, was a Wednesday.

THE COURT: Yes, I see it did fall on a Wednesday. Ladies and gentlemen of the jury, you will take it as established in this case, without any further proof, that May 9, 1987, was a Wednesday.

EXAMPLE B:

BY THE PROSECUTING ATTORNEY: Your Honor, we'll request that the court judicially take notice that all acts of war between the United States and Germany in World War II terminated on May 8, 1945. We have a number of history texts here if Your Honor would care to check them. Let me hand up to you Flatt's *The Second Great War.* You'll see the discussion on page 369 bears me out on the date.

THE COURT: Yes. The jurors are instructed to take it as proven, without any additional evidence, that the armed hostilities between the United States and Germany came to an end on May 8, 1945.

Opportunity to Be Heard

A party is entitled, on timely request, to have a chance to be heard—to have a hearing—on the propriety of taking judicial notice and on the nature of the matter proposed to be judicially noticed. If, following this hearing, the court rules that judicial notice is appropriate, the jury will be instructed to accept the judicially noticed fact as fully established. The opposing side will not be permitted to dispute the noticed fact in open court; its only recourse is an appeal to a higher court.

Use of Judicial Notice in Criminal Case

Some courts are reluctant to permit the use of judicial notice when it would establish an *element* of a criminal offense. An example of this reluctance can be found in the case of *State* v. *Lawrence,* 234 P. 2d 600 (S. Ct. Utah 1951). The accused was charged with grand larceny involving the theft of a three-year-old automobile. Under Utah's law, grand larceny is defined as the theft of property worth $50 or more. In *Lawrence* the prosecution failed to prove the value of the automobile and defense counsel moved for his client's acquittal.

Instead of reopening the case and introducing evidence of the car's value, the prosecuting attorney in *Lawrence* requested the trial judge to take judicial notice that its value exceeded $50. The judge agreed to do so and then denied the accused's acquittal motion. On appeal, Lawrence's conviction was reversed. Underlying the reversal was the notion that in criminal cases a jury should be allowed to be arbitrary, even irrational, in the defendant's favor. In *Lawrence* and cases similar to it this policy of giving the accused every possible break is thought to outweigh the policy behind judicial notice. Thus some courts hold that judicial notice can be employed in a criminal defendant's *favor* but not to his *disadvantage* in connection with an element of the crime charged.

> EXAMPLE:
> The defendant is charged with grand larceny in the theft of a pair of work pants. A trial court could properly take judicial notice that a pair of work pants is worth *less* than $50, even though in a case such as *Lawrence*, above, it would not take judicial notice against the accused that a stolen article is worth *more* than the statutory amount.

Reliance on Judicial Notice of Adjudicative Facts

As the reader may have detected by now, a request for the taking of judicial notice is often a desperation attempt by a lawyer who suddenly realizes that he has failed to prove something vital to his case. Having neglected at trial to prove that the Breathalyzer is a scientifically reliable device for measuring blood-alcohol rations, the prosecutor tries to get an appellate court to plug the gaping hole in his case by taking judicial notice.

Competent trial lawyers do not rely heavily on judicial notice to build their cases. In all but the most obvious situations (the sun rises in the East and sets in the West), counsel will put on the best possible evidentiary proof of all issues in the case.

By the same token, a competent criminal investigator, no matter how well versed in the law of evidence, will not place much reliance on concepts of judicial notice. Uninterested in dangerous shortcuts, he or she will go out and get the hard evidence so that the prosecutor will not have to fall back on judicial notice at trial.

B. Judicial Notice of Legislative Facts

Judicial Legislation

In reality, appellate court judges legislate, rather than adhere to longstanding and unchanging legal principles, in the sense that they make "new" law when they consider the constitutional validity of statutes or interpret statutes and when they enlarge or restrict some established common law principle. Appellate judges—and this has been especially true of the justices of the Supreme Court of the United States, at least during some periods of history—often make policy judgments on the basis of their comprehension of widely known facts; what might be termed "the facts of life." In other words, upper court judges make use of *legislative facts* and this is a second type of judicial notice.

One of the most talked-about examples of judicial notice of legislative facts was observable in *Brown* v. *Board of Education of Topeka,* 347 U.S. 483 (1954). In this landmark school desegregation case the opinion of the Supreme Court included a conclusion that segregation instilled a sense of inferiority in black school children and that it caused other ill effects, all of which tended to retard "educational and mental development of Negro children." Chief Justice Earl Warren said that "this finding is amply supported by modern authority" and referred the reader of the opinion to the published works of a number of psychologists and social commentators, including Gunnar Myrdal.

However debatable might be the legislative facts relied on by the Court in *Brown,* the Court's reliance on them constituted a form of judicial notice since the psychologists and sociologists had not testified in court. Such commentators as the late Edmond Cahn of the New York University Law School have been apprehensive about judicial notice of legislative facts gleaned from such "young, imprecise, and changeful" disciplines as the behavioral sciences.

In *Dennis* v. *United States,* 341 U.S. 494 (1951), judicial notice of legislative facts led the Supreme Court into deep water. Dennis and ten other officers of the United States Communist party were charged with conspiracy to effect the violent overthrow of the United States government. The alleged conspiracy was conducted by means of talk—advocacy. The Supreme Court concluded that the old "clear and present danger" test, originally formulated by Justice Oliver Wendell Holmes, was outmoded. In a day when Communist takeovers of entire nations was a common occurrence, the Court thought the era of soapbox oratory was past. In formulating a new test—"whether the gravity of the evil, discounted by its improbability, justifies such invasion of free speech as is necessary to avoid the danger"—the Court was taking judicial notice of the existence of "the Communist menace." Justice Felix Frankfurter argued that in doing so the Court was engaging in fact-finding of a sort more appropriately left to the Congress.

C. Judicial Notice of Law

Domestic Law

State and federal courts take judicial notice of domestic law. In other words, in locating and interpreting the law applicable to the issues in a case, a court will take judicial notice of federal law and of the law of the state in which the court is located. State and national administrative regulations having the force of law are also subject to judicial notice if they are published in such a way as to be readily available. For example, when an agency regulation is published in the Federal Register it is statutorily provided that its contents shall then be subject to judicial notice.

Municipal ordinances, except in the municipal courts of the particular municipality, are not ordinarily held to be subject to judicial notice. Their language must be proved, often by a certified copy.

Judicial Notice of the Law of Sister States

Courts in more than half of the states will take judicial notice of the common law and statutes of every other state. This is the consequence of their having adopted the Uniform Judicial Notice of Foreign Law Act of 1936.

Judicial Notice of the Law of Foreign Countries

Few American courts will take judicial notice of the law of other nations. Foreign law must be proved with sworn testimony by an expert or by officially certified copies.

CHAPTER FIFTEEN

Competency of Witnesses

A. The Meaning of Witness Competency

Testimonial Attributes; The Trend Toward Witness Competency

The term *competency,* in the context of a trial's conduct, refers to a witness's testimonial abilities.

Long ago, at common law, there were numerous inflexible rules of witness competency. By way of a few examples, *parties* to a case could not take the witness stand in it, because they were interested in its outcome and so were presumed to be prejudiced; *convicted felons* could not give testimony, because they were presumed to be beyond belief; and one *spouse* could not testify in a litigation to which the other spouse was a party, since he or she was at least indirectly interested in the outcome and thus might be biased. In modern times, for the most part, these rigid rules have been swept away.

It once was thought that the mentally ill person was incapable of giving trustworthy courtroom testimony. We now know that a person can be insane only at certain times or in connection with certain subjects. Furthermore, the most deeply psychotic person can experience periods of lucidity. A curious example is found in an old English case. An insane asylum attendant was under prosecution for killing an inmate. The prosecution called another inmate as one of its witnesses. There was not the slightest question that he was and had been insane. He said in court that he was possessed by twenty thousand spirits who talked to him. But he seemed to grasp the meaning of the testimonial oath and the consequences of perjury. Moreover, he gave a rational account of the events in question, which he stated he had witnessed. His testimony was admitted into evidence.

It is everywhere the rule today that an insane person can be a competent witness if he or she passes two tests: (1) appreciation of the obligation of a testimonial oath and the consequences of giving false testimony (in this respect the insane witness is comparable to the infant witness), and (2) the ability to give an intelligent account of what he or she perceived. The same tests apply to the witness who was intoxicated or under the influence of narcotics at the time of the events about which he is to testify.

Long ago a person who had been convicted of a crime was rendered "infamous" and lost all the rights of citizenship, including the right to testify in court. This rule of incompetency has gradually been abolished in most American jurisdictions, except that by statute a number of states have made conviction of perjury and of subornation of perjury a continuing ground of witness incompetency.

A witness who violates an order excluding him from the courtroom prior to his testimony may be disqualified by his conduct from giving testimony. Courts are disturbed by the possibility that a witness has tailored his testimony to take account of the testimony of others which he has overheard.

Today, almost all persons are assumed to be competent to testify unless the contrary is affirmatively demonstrated. Thus, for example, Section 700 of the California Evidence Code provides: "Except as otherwise provided by statute, every person is qualified to be a witness and no person is disqualified to testify to any matter."

The Requirement of Personal Knowledge

Personal knowledge is ordinarily a crucial testimonial attribute. As a general rule, it must be shown that the witness on the stand has personal—that is, firsthand—knowledge concerning the matters about which he or she is going to testify. This essential showing can consist of the witness's own testimony that he or she does in fact have personal knowledge of the matters about which he or she is going to give testimony.

An important exception to the general rule requiring firsthand knowledge involves opinion testimony by expert witnesses, discussed in chapter 17.

B. General Standards of Competency

Testimonial Attributes

As was indicated at the beginning of this chapter, competency to testify involves a witness's testimonial attributes.

Essentially, this means that trial witnesses must have three testimonial attributes or capacities:

1. *Ability to Perceive.* A witness must, at the crucial time, have had the ability to perceive, by means of one or more of the senses, that which he is going to testify about. For example, was the witness's vision defective? Was he too intoxicated to observe accurately? Was he under the influence of narcotics at the time?
2. *Ability to Recall.* A witness's memory must be intact. Questions that may arise are whether a particular witness is senile or a victim of amnesia.
3. *Communicative Ability.* A witness must have both the ability and the willingness to communicate honestly and understandably so that the fact-finder will not be misled. In this connection, a trial witness must testify under oath or solemn affirmation.

C. Effect of Diminution of Capacity

Affects Testimony's Weight

A diminution, or lessening, of any of the three testimonial attributes or capacities usually goes only to the weight that the fact-finder will attach to a witness's testimony; it does not render the testimony absolutely incompetent (inadmissible).

However, a witness could be so deficient in testimonial capacity as to be wholly incompetent to testify.

EXAMPLE:
An eyewitness to a crime is able to communicate only by lifting his knee to indicate "Yes." The witness is incompetent because cross-examination would be too drastically impaired.

The competency of an infant witness is left largely to the trial court's discretion after a hearing. At this hearing the judge and counsel will pose questions to the child aimed at determining whether the child has sufficient testimonial capacity, including a realization of the necessity to tell the truth. The child's competency is gauged as of the time its testimony is offered in evidence, not as of the time of the event or occurrence in question.

In no American jurisdiction is religiosity—the existence of religious beliefs—a test of a witness's competency to give trial testimony. Evidence of the state of a witness's religious beliefs or opinions is not admissible to impair or, for that matter, to enhance his credibility. The law long ago recognized that some people who profess to be deeply religious can lie like troopers, and that an atheist may be the most truthful of witnesses.

D. Procedural Aspects

Objecting on Grounds of Incompetence

An objection to the competency of a witness must be made by trial counsel at the earliest possible point or it is waived. This means that objection must be made as soon as the incompetency of the witness becomes apparent.

If grounds for attacking a witness's competency are known at the time he takes the stand, he must be challenged immediately. If the basis for disqualification of the witness is not known when he first takes the stand but comes out during his direct testimony, the challenge to his competency must then be made.

A witness is not competent to testify as an expert witness, giving opinions on specialized matters such as ballistics, unless and until his or her qualifications have been developed as a preliminary aspect of direct examination. If opposing counsel thinks the witness has not been shown to be sufficiently qualified, or if cross-examination brings this out, the competency of the witness to testify can then be challenged. On the other hand, if the challenge to a proffered witness relates to some general type of incompetency, such as mental incapacity, the burden is on the objecting side to demonstrate the incompetency, either through cross-examination of the witness or by independent evidence.

CHAPTER SIXTEEN

Writings

The need to authenticate tangible evidence in general, and the techniques for doing so, were discussed in chapter 3. At that point it was mentioned that one type of tangible evidence, *written* evidence, poses some special evidentiary problems. Those specialized problems are taken up in the present chapter.

A. The Best Evidence Rule

Definition of the Rule

The name of this evidentiary rule, the best evidence rule, is needlessly confusing. Its title makes it sound as though it set up a general requirement that in all cases the best available evidence, in the sense of the strongest or weightiest, must be produced by the lawyers. In truth, the rule might more accurately be dubbed "The Original Writing Rule." It is simply a rule that expresses a preference for the *original* of any *writing* that is offered in evidence.

Application of the Rule

The best evidence rule is usually said to apply only to writings, such as letters, telegrams, and the like. However, modern cases and codes usually make it clear that the rule is also applicable to recordings and photographs, including motion picture film and X-rays.

The rule expresses a preference for the original of a writing (however broadly the term "writing" may be defined) as distinguished from a copy (secondary evidence) of it or verbalized recollection of its contents. As was said in *Herzig* v. *Swift & Co.,* 146 F. 2d 444 (2d Cir. 1945), "In its modern application, the best evidence rule amounts to little more than the requirement that the contents of a writing must be proved by the introduction of the writing itself, unless its absence can be satisfactorily accounted for."

Of course, not all writings appear on paper. In other words, a writing, within the meaning of this rule, can be something other than a document. It could, for example, be a police officer's badge with its number; it could be a tombstone with an inscription on it, or an inscribed engagement ring. It could be an engine block with its serial number. However, because the rule does apply only to writings, a photograph of powdered fingerprints is admissible in evidence; the prosecution need not physically produce in court the surface on which the fingerprints were impressed.

The best evidence rule does not apply to writings that are merely collateral or peripheral. To put it another way, the rule applies only to writings that are the subject of a significant issue in the case.

> EXAMPLE:
> A witness to a confession by the accused testifies that the date of the confession was the day following the commission of the crime. He says he is certain about this date because he read about the crime in his local newspaper for that day. The witness's reference to the newspaper is merely incidental or peripheral; the newspaper itself need not be produced in court, let alone the original of the reporter's news story about the crime.

In seeking to determine whether a writing is collateral, courts consider (1) whether the writing appears to be central to the main issues in the case; (2) the complexity of the relevant parts of the document; and (3) whether or not there is any real dispute about the writing's contents.

Requirements of the Rule

The so-called best evidence rule requires the proponent (that is, the offerer), of a writing, the terms of which are material in the case, to produce the original of it, or a true duplicate such as a photocopy, or provide an adequate explanation of his or her inability to do so.

The "original" is the thing the parties *intended* to be considered as such. Therefore, and despite some confusion in the cases, the rule does *not* apply to recorded prior testimony or to a confession that has been reduced to writing. One who heard the oral testimony or statement can repeat it in court, since he is giving evidence of the oral testimony or statement, not the transcription of it. Despite what has just been said, however, some courts, mildly confused as to the proper application of the best evidence rule, hold that the transcription must be produced because it "speaks for itself" and is the "best" evidence of its contents. These courts are simply requiring, in an isolated instance, that the strongest and most reliable form of evidence be offered.

Laying the Foundation for Receipt of Secondary Evidence of a Writing

If the original of a crucial writing, such as the ribbon copy of a letter or a duplicate, is unavailable to be offered into evidence at trial, the necessary foundation for the introduction of secondary evidence has three parts:

1. Proof that the original *existed* at one time;
2. Proof that the original was *genuine;* and
3. An *excuse* for not producing the original.

Legitimate Excuses for Failure to Produce the Original

The excuse for failure to produce the original of a writing can be one of many:

1. The original writing was lost by the side offering secondary evidence of it and diligent search for it was made, with no success.
2. The original of the writing was destroyed, in good faith, by the proponent of the secondary evidence.
3. The original of the writing is in the possession of the offering side's adversary and production of it has not been made by the opposing side despite the proponent's request.
4. The writing is in the possession of some third person and production by that person has been refused despite the issuance of a subpoena for it by the offering side (if the third person is within the court's jurisdiction) or the making of a reasonable effort to secure it (if the third person is beyond the jurisdiction).
5. The physical inconvenience of producing numerous and bulky writings may justify the use of a so-called summary witness, often an accountant, to summarize the records (for example, numerous canceled checks in a "net worth" tax evasion case). The originals must be made available to the opposing side for its inspection. Sometimes a photograph will be permitted to substitute for a solitary but nonetheless bulky writing (for example, a photograph of the serial numbers on an engine block).

Ranks of Secondary Evidence

Many jurisdictions recognize *gradations* or *ranks* of secondary evidence.

EXAMPLE:
A carbon copy or photographic copy is preferred to a witness's testimonial recollection of the contents of a writing. (And see Fed. R. Evid. 1001(4), 1003.)

Thus, in *Baroda State Bank* v. *Peck,* 209 N.W. 827 (S. Ct. Mich. 1926), the court observed that "The current authority in this country [as distinguished from the rule in England], as shown by adjudications in a majority of states, has adopted what is known as the American rule, which holds that a copy of a lost paper is the next best evidence, and, if it is available, oral evidence is inadmissible."

B. Authentification of Writings

Basic Principles

The evidentiary significance of writings frequently depends on their *authorship.* If the alleged ransom note was written by the accused, it will be one of the most important items of evidence in a kidnapping case; if its authorship is not established, it will be useless. Accordingly, it frequently is necessary to develop proof on the question of authorship for use at trial. Is the writing actually what it seems to be on its face, a ransom note composed and written by the accused?

A writing, in other words, is not admissible in evidence until it has been *authenticated.* Its genuineness must be demonstrated to the trial judge, as a preliminary matter, before the jury can properly consider it. It cannot be read or shown to the jurors until the necessary authenticating foundation has been laid by trial counsel and the writing has been formally received in evidence by the judge.

Methods of Authenticating Writings

A writing can be authenticated in a variety of ways:

1. By *direct* evidence that proves the handwriting in question. This may be either the identifying testimony of the author of the writing, or the testimony of anyone who observed the writing being made.
2. By proving the handwriting through *circumstantial* evidence, which can be accomplished:
   a. By the identifying testimony of some person who is familiar with the handwriting of the person in question and recognizes it;
   b. By the testimony of a handwriting expert (an examiner of questioned documents) who compares the questioned handwriting with one or more demonstrably genuine specimens or exemplars (see chapter 18); or

   c. By letting the members of the jury themselves compare the questioned handwriting with genuine specimens. (This, however, is a most unsatisfactory method and is rarely relied upon.)

3. By reliance on common law or statutory or rules provisions that make some writings self-authenticating or that set up presumptions of authenticity, as is true in connection with many kinds of public records.

   EXAMPLE:
   A copy of a judgment of conviction, certified as such by the clerk of the court involved, is admissible without the necessity of placing an authenticating witness on the stand.

The Reply Doctrine

"A" sends a properly addressed letter through the regular mails to "B" and requests a reply. A responsive letter, received by "A" in due time through the mails and purporting to be from "B," is presumed to be from "B."

Authenticity as Distinguished from Truth

It will be realized that a showing of authenticity (genuineness) is not necessarily a showing of the *truth* of the assertions contained in the writing. For example, a letter may be fully authenticated as having been written by a particular party, but its assertions may all be falsehoods.

CHAPTER SEVENTEEN

Opinion, Expertise, and Experts

A. The Opinion Rule

Opinion Testimony by a Layman

The law of evidence includes a well-known general rule against testimony by laymen in the form of an *opinion* or *conclusion.* (In lawyer series on television one is forever hearing counsel say, "Object, Your Honor, calls for a conclusion!") Generally speaking, it is true that a layman, called to the stand to give testimony, must restrict himself to describing material facts about which he has firsthand knowledge. He cannot ordinarily unburden himself of opinions and conclusions which he has drawn from his firsthand observations. This is true for one of two reasons: either the lay witness is technically unqualified, for lack of some essential skill, training, or experience, to draw such a conclusion; or the jurors themselves are fully capable of drawing the right conclusion from the recited facts—and if they are, the witness's opinion testimony would invade the rightful province of the jury.

Not all jurisdictions enforce the opinion rule with equal force. Judges will be quick to exclude apparently baseless opinions on ultimate issues—for example, "In my opinion the defendant is guilty of this crime"—but may be slower to react to conclusory statements that do not go to the very heart of the case.

Furthermore, there are numerous realistic exceptions to the rule against opinion testimony. Most of them involve lay "shorthand" testimony where it is next to impossible to express the matter in any other way.

EXAMPLES:
a. *Matters of taste and smell*—"It smelled like gunpowder."
b. *Another's emotions*—"He seemed very nervous."

c. *Vehicular speed*—"He was going very, very fast."
d. *Voice Identification*—"I've known Clyde Bushmat for fifteen years and I'd recognize his voice anywhere. It was Bushmat's voice on the telephone."
e. *A witness's own intent, where relevant*—"I was planning on crossing the street."
f. *Genuineness of another's handwriting*—"That's my wife's signature."
g. *Another's irrational conduct*—"He was acting like a crazy man."
h. *Intoxication*—"The man was drunk."

Reasoning Behind the Rule Against Lay Opinion Testimony

A fundamental aspect of the reasoning underlying the opinion rule is that factual conclusions that are within the grasp or comprehension of the average layperson should be left to the jury, which is supposedly made up of just such average laypersons. If a juror can just as well arrive at his or her own conclusions by adding together the factual components provided by the witnesses, there is no need for the witnesses to inject their own conclusions.

EXAMPLE A:
In *State* v. *Thorp,* 72 N.C. 186 (1875), the defendant was charged with drowning her son Robert. The prosecution offered a witness who had known Robert. He testified that he was too far away from the defendant and the child she was holding to be certain that the child was Robert. He did testify, however, that it was "his best impression" that the child was Robert. The defendant's conviction was overturned on appeal because the witness had given prohibited opinion testimony.

EXAMPLE B:
In *Commonwealth* v. *Holden,* 134 A.2d 868 (Pa. 1957), the accused was convicted of murder. While he was in custody he gave the police an alibi to the effect that he had been with one Ralph Jones at the crucial time. Jones, questioned by the police, denied this. During the questioning of Jones, the accused, who was present, had winked at him. At trial Jones testified about the wink and stated that he interpreted it as a signal to him to supply the defendant with an alibi. Although the accused's conviction was affirmed without consideration of the opinion rule problem in any detail, one justice of the Pennsylvania Supreme Court noted that Jones's testimony reflected an opinion.

EXAMPLE C:
In *United States* v. *Schneiderman,* 105 F. Supp. 892 (S.D. Cal. 1952), the defendants were charged with Smith Act violations. The Govern-

ment offered the testimony of former members of the Communist party that the defendants, by their actions, appeared to be members of the party. The trial court held that this was permissible since there was no other way the witnesses could convey to the jury what they had observed. (This was a questionable ruling, made during the hysterically anti-Communist era of Senator Joseph R. McCarthy.)

The Federal Approach

Rule 701 of the Federal Rules of Evidence takes a practical approach: "If the witness is not testifying as an expert, the witness's testimony in the form of opinions or inferences is limited to those opinions or inferences which are (a) rationally based on the perception of the witness and (b) helpful to a clear understanding of his testimony or the determination of a fact in issue."

B. Experts and Expertise

An Exception to the Opinion Rule

Opinion testimony by *expert* witnesses comes in through an important exception to the general rule against opinion testimony.

The Definition of "Expert"

There are those who have the mistaken notion that the title of "expert" can properly be bestowed only on a few members of professional groups who have a cluster of postgraduate degrees after their names. Some people think that only a scientist of one sort or another and perhaps a few engineers can rightly be called experts. But the term "expert," at least in the law and common sense, is far broader in meaning than this. Anyone who has ever tried to repair his own automobile or television set knows that some people are experts at these kinds of work and some are not. The proficient garage mechanic is an expert in his field even though a Ph.D. may be the last thing he ever hoped to acquire; the trained and experienced television repairer is just as surely an expert as is the most renowned neurosurgeon. The same sort of thing can be said of the brick mason, the sheet metal worker, the plumber, the carpenter, and the electrician, just to name a few more genuine experts.

Getting closer to the immediate point, the label "expert" applies to the firearms identification technician and those who are proficient at fingerprint or handwriting comparison. And it applies to the policeman or policewoman who knows how to use, interpret, and explain special equipment, such as radar vehicular speed measuring devices and equipment for measuring blood-alcohol ratios. Thus a basic law dictionary, Black's, sweepingly defines experts as "Men [and women] of science educated in the art, or persons possessing special or peculiar knowledge *acquired from practical experience*" (italics added).

The Four Basic Conditions of Expert Testimony

An expert witness, such as a pathologist or ballistics technician, can testify to an opinion or conclusion if four basic conditions are met:

1. The opinions, inferences, or conclusions depend on special knowledge, skill, or training not within the ordinary experience of lay jurors;
2. The witness must be shown to be qualified as a true expert in the particular field of expertise;
3. The witness must testify to a reasonable degree of certainty (probability) regarding his or her opinion, inference, or conclusion; and
4. Although this fourth condition is currently in the process of modification, at least in times past it has generally been true that an expert witness must first describe the data (facts) on which his or her opinion, inference, or conclusion is based or, in the alternative, the witness must testify in response to a hypothetical question that sets forth the underlying data.

Rationale Behind the Expert Witness Exception to the Rule Against Opinion Testimony

The reasoning behind letting expert witnesses give testimony in the form of opinions or conclusions is that experts have special training, knowledge, and skill in drawing conclusions from certain sorts of data that lay jurors do not have. Expert witnesses and their opinions are permissible only in areas in which lay jurors cannot draw conclusions unassisted or would find it difficult to do so.

The point has been made by Dean Wigmore: "We are dealing merely with a broad principle that, whenever the point is reached at which the tribunal is being told that which it is itself entirely equipped to determine without the witness's aid on this point, his testimony is superfluous and is to be dispensed with."

An illustration can be drawn from a Canadian case, *Regina* v. *Kuzmack,* 14 W.W.R. (N.S.) 595 (Alta. Ct. App. 1954). The accused had been charged with murder. His defense was accident and a physician testified that the wounds on the deceased's neck and hands were inflicted with a knife. He went further, however, stating that "I should think that the hand was at the base of the neck when the knife was put into the neck." The Canadian court ruled that the physician could not properly express an opinion on this aspect of the matter:

> [B]ecause it was merely conjecture and not on a subject requiring any special study or experience. It was a mere guess which anyone might have made. . . .
>
> The [accused], in giving his testimony that the wound was the result of an accident, testified that he had the deceased's right arm pinned to her side with his right arm around her shoulder at the time the knife, in his story, entered the flesh. The doctor's testimony that her right hand was up by her throat endeavoring to stave off a knife blow is a contradiction of the [accused's] explanation, calculated, in my opinion, to lead the jury to disbelieve the [accused's] explanation. . . .

Life nowadays is sufficiently complicated that lay jurors may need expert assistance in myriad situations. The technical aspects of many criminal cases will usually be far beyond the competence of the jurors who are to assess the issue of guilt or innocence. (Consider, by way of support for this statement, the number of sections in the next chapter, which deals with scientific evidence in criminal cases.)

"Your Honor, the defense concedes that the prosecution witness is an expert in his field!"

There is nothing unique about the requirement of expert testimony in criminal cases involving technical matters beyond the unguided comprehension of lay jurors. Just as a successful criminal prosecution may depend on the testimony of a firearms identification expert, a fingerprint comparison expert, a handwriting expert, a pathologist, and a psychiatrist, many types of civil suits may call forth an array of essential experts: aeronautical or mechanical engineers and metallurgists in a case involving an airplane that allegedly crashed as a result of metal fatigue in the wing structure; pathologists in a product liability case against a food processor or distributor (was the corn borer that crept into the defendant's canned corn really poisonous?); handwriting experts in a will contest; entomologists, civil engineers—the catalogue of potentially crucial witnesses in both criminal and civil cases stretches on and on. It is so lengthy a list because both criminal and civil cases so frequently involve esoteric issues which a jury, unaided, could not possibly resolve on any basis other than guesswork. To the extent that it can, the American system of justice prohibits verdicts having baseless speculation as their only support. The requirement of expert testimony on technical issues, and the exception to the opinion rule that permits it, is designed to avoid guesswork verdicts.

In short, lay jurors may have a reasonable basis in their own life experience for deciding that it is reckless to drive an automobile down the wrong side of the highway at ninety miles an hour while heavily intoxicated; on the other hand, their life experience may not give them any basis for assessing, for example, the precise cause of death in some homicide cases.

Qualifying the Witness as an Expert

From what has been said thus far it follows that the exception for expert testimony is available only when the witness is shown to be a true expert in the field that is involved. Before a witness can testify to an expert opinion, examining counsel must lay the necessary foundation by bringing out the witness's training, experience, and special skills. Trial lawyers call this process "qualifying the witness."

At the conclusion of the direct questions aimed at qualifying the witness as an expert, and before examining counsel gets into the meat of the witness's testimony, opposing counsel is entitled to interrupt and engage in cross-examination as to the witness's expertise. This examination will be limited strictly to probing the witness's credentials as an expert.

EXAMPLE A:

BY THE PROSECUTING ATTORNEY: Give your full name if you would, please.

A: Fred Stitz.

Q: Where do you live, Mr. Stitz?

A: In Chicago, Illinois. 373 West Pavon Street.
Q: What is your occupation or profession?
A: I'm an examiner of questioned documents.
Q: What does your work consist of?
A: I examine disputed documents and make reports as to their genuineness. I examine typewriting and matters of disputed interlineations, erasures, and deal with matters of papers, pens, and inks.
Q: How long have you had this profession?
A: I have been doing this work since 1965.
Q: Do you devote all of your time to this work?
A: Yes, I do.
Q: Have you ever testified before in a court regarding questioned documents?
A: I have testified in forty-two of the states and in Canada.
Q: Have you had any special study to prepare yourself to be an examiner of questioned documents?
A: Oh, yes. I have read all of the texts on the subject of questioned documents and on the related subjects that I mentioned. I have studied microscopy, inks and their manufacture, paper and paper manufacturing, and photography. I have all the necessary equipment. I have an office and a laboratory for my work and I exchange ideas constantly with other experts in this field.
Q: Where is your office and lab?
A: 662 North Pennell Street, Chicago.
Q: You are able, I take it, to compare handwriting of known origin with handwriting of unknown origin and form a conclusion or opinion as to whether they were written by the same person?
A: That's right.
Q: Then I will show you what has been marked Prosecution Exhibit Number 3 for Identification.
BY DEFENSE COUNSEL: Just a moment, if you please. May I ask this witness a few questions, Your Honor?
THE COURT: With respect to his qualifications?
BY DEFENSE COUNSEL: Yes.
THE COURT: You may proceed.
BY DEFENSE COUNSEL: Mr. Stitz, have you attended any special schools that teach one how to become a handwriting expert?
A: No, I don't think there are any.
Q: So you have had no special degrees or certificates that reflect special study in a college or university?
A: No, I do not.
Q: Your supposed expertise is simply based on your own experience in examining documents, is that it?
A: That's right, and my reading and so on.

BY DEFENSE COUNSEL: Well, we have no strong objection to this witness testifying, Your Honor.
THE COURT: If that is supposed to be some kind of objection, counsel, it is overruled.

EXAMPLE B:
Q: What is your name, sir?
A: John V. DeMarco.
Q: Where do you live?
A: At the Belmont Hotel here in the city.
Q: What is your occupation or profession, sir?
A: I am a physician and toxicologist.
Q: Of what medical school are you a graduate, Doctor?
A: The Northwestern University Medical School in Chicago.
Q: When did you graduate?
A: In 1954.
Q: What was your undergraduate school?
A: The University of Michigan.
Q: What was your major field of study at Michigan?
A: Chemistry.
Q: After your graduation from medical school, what did you do?
A: I was with the Health Department in Chicago for three years and then in 1957 I became the toxicologist for the Coroner's Office in Chicago.
Q: Do you hold that position today?
A: Yes, I have held it continuously since 1957.
Q: What have your duties been as a toxicologist?
A: My duties involve the examination of organs for the presence of poisons and research concerning poisons. I have concluded many post-mortems.
Q: About how many since 1957?
A: Probably around ten thousand. And I examined the organs of many people on whom I did not do a post-mortem.
Q: Do you hold any teaching positions at the present time?
A: Yes, I am Professor of Toxicology at Rush Medical College in Chicago.
Q: How long have you had this professorship, Doctor DeMarco?
A: Since 1970.
Q: Have you ever written anything on the subject of toxicology?
A: Yes, I've written a number of articles on poisons and their detection. I have written chapters that were included in texts on toxicology and I have delivered papers at professional seminars.
Q: Would you describe toxicology for us, Doctor?
A: It is the science that deals with toxic substances, poisons, their origin, and their detection by chemical or other means.

Q: When you speak of poison, what precisely do you mean?
THE COURT: Just a moment, counsel. Are you now going to get into this witness's substantive testimony?
BY EXAMINING COUNSEL: That was my intention, Your Honor.
THE COURT: Let me inquire of opposing counsel whether she desires at this point to examine further into the witness's qualifications.
BY OPPOSING COUNSEL: We reserve the right to cross-examine Doctor DeMarco on the substance of his testimony, Your Honor, but we do not dispute his qualifications as an expert in the field of toxicology.
THE COURT: Very well. You may proceed, counsel.
BY EXAMINING COUNSEL: What is it that you mean when you talk of a poison, Doctor?
A: A poison is a substance which, when taken into the system, is capable of seriously affecting health adversely or of causing death, and that's its principal action.

Stipulating to the Witness's Expertise

Sometimes counsel, realizing that the opposing side's witness has impressive credentials that will probably awe the jurors, will try to prevent the jury from hearing them described. Counsel does this by offering to stipulate (agree) that the witness is qualified to testify as an expert, thereby magnanimously saving opposing counsel from having to elicit the witness's full catalogue of credentials through the questioning process. This gambit is not usually successful. Opposing counsel is not obligated to accept an offered stipulation unless it gives everything that he or she would be entitled to prove with evidence. And counsel is entitled to prove his or her expert witness's qualifications in some detail; a mere stipulation that the witness is qualified to testify does not give the side offering the witness everything to which it is entitled. Experienced counsel will know that it is important to show the details of his or her expert's training and experience in any case in which there is to be a battle of experts. This is so because jurors must decide what weight to attach to the testimony of each side's experts. They can rationally apportion evidentiary weight only if they are in a position to compare the witnesses' relative qualifications.

EXAMPLE:
Q: Doctor, will you give the jury your full name?
A: Jeffrey Eddy.
Q: Where do you reside?
A: 820 West Addison Street, Chicago, Illinois.
Q: What is your profession?
A: Physician and surgeon.

Q: What specialty, if any, have you made in your medical practice?
A: I specialize in neurosurgery.
Q: We'll come back to that, Doctor Eddy. How long have you practiced medicine?
A: Thirteen years this coming April.
Q: Of what medical school are you a graduate?
A: Northwestern University Medical School in Chicago.
Q: Have you done any postgraduate work?
BY OPPOSING COUNSEL: Pardon me just a moment. We would be willing to stipulate that Doctor Eddy is a qualified neurosurgeon and can testify here.
BY EXAMINING COUNSEL: We would rather make our proof on this, Your Honor. The jurors are entitled to hear his training and his experience in medicine and neurosurgery. They have to decide what weight to give his testimony, possibly in comparison with the testimony of an expert called by the other side, and they can't very well make that decision without hearing his qualifications in full.
THE COURT: It might speed things up a little if you accepted the stipulation, counsel, but I can't force you to do so. You may proceed to establish the witness's qualifications. Just don't get into the most minute details.
BY EXAMINING COUNSEL: Very well, Your Honor. We'll limit ourselves to the most important things. Doctor Eddy, have you had some postgraduate training?
BY OPPOSING COUNSEL: In view of our offer to stipulate, we object to counsel's going into this, Your Honor.
THE COURT: Overruled.

Sources of the Expert Witness's Data

Four sources of information are open to the expert witness in the formation of his or her opinions.

1. The expert witness can express an opinion or conclusion based on facts personally observed by him, as occurs in the case of a medical examiner who renders a conclusion concerning cause of death on the basis of data clinically observed. (Such an expert can take into account facts communicated to him by another expert. For example, the medical examiner can base his opinion in part on the report of an X-ray technician. If the data upon which the expert bases his opinion or inference are of a type reasonably relied on by experts in the field when forming opinions or inferences on the subject in question, the data need not themselves be admissible in evidence through the expert.)

2. An expert witness who has been present in the courtroom can base an opinion on the evidence adduced if that evidence is not in conflict. (An

expert will not be permitted to weigh conflicting evidence since, unbeknownst to anyone, he or she might accord it a weight different from that given it by the jurors.)

3. In some jurisdictions, notably the federal and those state jurisdictions that have adopted Rule 703 of the Federal Rules of Evidence, an expert witness can base his or her opinion on data made known to him/her in *advance* of the trial or hearing. Furthermore, the data thus conveyed to the expert need not itself be received in evidence and, even beyond that, need not necessarily be legally admissible. All that is required under rules such as Federal Rule of Evidence 703 is that the inadmissible evidence relied on by the expert have been of "a type reasonably relied upon by experts in the particular field in forming opinions or inferences upon the subject." Thus an expert witness would be entitled to rely at least in part on hearsay, as when the prosecution's psychiatrist gives an opinion as to the defendant's sanity based on such materials as hospital staff notes, the report of a consulting psychiatrist, and reports of other professionals who had observed the defendant. (*United States* v. *Phillips*, 515 F. Supp. 758 (E.D. Ky. 1981).) It has been suggested, however, that there may be a serious constitutional confrontation problem if the prosecution's expert bases his opinion *entirely* on hearsay information, thereby precluding the accused from effective cross-examination of the expert's sources. (*United States* v. *Lawson,* 653 F.2d 299 (7th Cir. 1981).) And it is clear that an expert will not be permitted to base an opinion on data that is inadmissible because of its lack of trustworthiness. (*Zenith Radio Corp.* v. *Matsushita Elec. Ind. Co.,* 505 F. Supp. 1313 (E.D. Pa. 1980).)

EXAMPLE A:
A Drug Enforcement Administration agent was permitted to base an opinion concerning the value of narcotics in various cities upon information supplied to him by other DEA agents. (*United States* v. *Golden,* 532 F.2d 1244 (9th Cir. 1976), *cert. denied,* 429 U.S. 842 (1977).)

EXAMPLE B:
A government expert's opinion that a substance was heroin, based on laboratory comparison with a substance represented to him to be heroin, was reasonable. (*United States* v. *Hollman,* 541 F.2d 196 (8th Cir. 1976).)

EXAMPLE C:
The opinion of a vehicle "accidentologist" concerning the point of impact, based entirely on comments from bystanders, would be impermissible. (See WALTZ, THE NEW FEDERAL RULES OF EVIDENCE: AN ANALYSIS 111 (2d ed. 1975).)

4. An expert witness can base an opinion on data conveyed to him or her by means of a hypothetical question that is drawn from the evidence introduced during the trial.

EXAMPLE:

Q: Please give us your name and place of residence.

A: Stephen Mendoza. I live here in Chicago and also have my office here.

Q: What is your profession, your educational background, and what licenses, if any, have you held?

A: I am a mechanical engineer. I graduated from the Massachusetts Institute of Technology in 1959. I hold professional engineer's licenses in Illinois, Ohio, and New York. I've been in the engineering profession ever since my graduation from MIT. I am a member of the American Association of Mechanical Engineers, the National Association of Professional Engineers, and the American Society of Safety Engineers.

Q: Have you ever held any teaching posts?

A: I have been teaching at Purdue for thirteen years, in the field of industrial safety.

Q: Does this course that you give at Purdue require you to give instruction on situations involving analyses of time, space, speed, distance, and safety factors, and on the evaluation of them?

A: Yes, it does.

Q: Have you ever been consulted by industrial concerns and by legal counsel in connection with the sorts of things that I just mentioned?

A: Yes, many times.

Q: Has your work required you to give opinions concerning the causes of vehicular accidents, and to reconstruct such accidents by scientific analysis of the physical facts?

A: Yes, sir.

Q: Are you able to make automobile accident reconstruction evaluations, without actually observing the accident, the road surface, or the vehicle involved?

A: Yes, I can do that if I'm given the various physical factors such as a description of the type of roadway, the type of vehicles that are involved, the nature and dimensions of the various markings on the road, and that sort of thing. Photographs are helpful. Charts, too.

Q: Are there definite mathematical and scientific formulae, and recognized terminology, which are accepted as reliable by safety engineers and by the engineering profession in general which are applicable to such situations?

A: Yes.

Q: Do your evaluations include reliance on the laws of physics and mathematics?
A: Yes, they do.
Q: In making accident reconstruction evaluations, have you in the past studied roadway and damage markings left by various vehicles that have been involved in accidents?
A: Yes.
Q: In making scientific automobile accident analyses, is there a term "rotation markings" and if there is, please tell us what it means.
A: There is such a term. When two vehicles come into collision, after both of them have been traveling at a pretty rapid speed, one or both of the cars will generally bounce off. This usually leaves certain marks on the road surface and we call them "rotation markings." The impact itself ordinarily also leaves distinctive markings which help to pinpoint the actual point of impact.
Q: Is "reaction time distance" also a factor in the type of analysis that you do? If so, tell us what it is.
A: "Reaction time" is the period it takes a driver to apply his brakes after seeing something. The average reaction time of a driver is three-fourths of a second, although it may take a driver from half of a second to two seconds. The "reaction time distance," then, is the distance the vehicle will travel from the time the driver sees something, such as an obstacle, until he reacts by applying the brakes.
Q: How does that differ from the braking distance factor?
A: The braking distance factor doesn't begin to apply until the reaction time period is over. Braking distance represents the distance the vehicle travels from the time the brakes are applied until the car stops.
Q: Is there also a term known as "stopping distance"?
A: Yes. That is the "reaction time distance" plus the "braking distance."
Q: Mr. Mendoza, let me ask you, for the benefit of the jury, to define and distinguish the two terms: "scuff marks," from "skid marks."
A: A "scuff mark" is a distinctive mark left on a roadway by the tires, or even by some other part of a vehicle, when it makes contact, or is being pushed, generally not in the original direction of travel. A "skid mark," on the other hand, is a mark that is caused by the abrasion of the tires on a roadway due to the application of brakes, and it follows the direction of travel.
Q: Are the positions of the vehicles, following an automobile accident, and the presence, type and length of "skid," "scuff," "rotation" or other marks on a highway among the significant factors which must be considered in professional accident analysis of motor vehicle accidents?
A: Yes.

Q: For example, what can be determined from "skid marks"?
A: The length of the "skid marks" is important in determining the speed of the vehicle, as of the time the brakes were applied.
Q: Is there a recognized scientific formula for determining speed from skid marks?
A: There is.
Q: What is it?
A: V = the square root of 30fS. The capital "V" is the velocity of the moving object expressed in miles per hour. The small letter "f" is the "coefficient of friction" of the roadway. The capital "S" is the length of the skid mark expressed in feet.
Q: Does this formula take into consideration the things we discussed before, namely: "reaction time," distance, the "drag" or "braking" distance factors, and the sum total of both, known as the "speed distance" factor?
A: This formula, as derived, covers only the "braking distance," but from the "braking distance" we then calculate the speed; and this enables us to also then calculate the distance covered by the vehicle during the "reaction time" period. In this way we can compute the total of both.
Q: Would the type and condition of the road surface have any effect on the drag or braking distance of the vehicle?
A: Yes.
Q: Would you explain that?
A: If the road surface is wet, slippery or ice-covered, this of course increases the distance required to bring the vehicle to a halt. Formulae have been developed in scientifically published studies, recognized by the profession, which indicate the drag factor of various different types of road surfaces.
Q: Is the "drag factor" of the various roadway surfaces determined by a particular "coefficient of friction" formula—one which is also recognized by the engineering profession?
A: Yes.
Q: Will you tell us what the term and formula are and explain their significance in greater detail?
A: A "coefficient of friction" relates to the weight of the vehicle, and the type of road surface on which the vehicle is traveling. If the coefficient of friction were the number "one," which is the absolute maximum, then the "speed (or braking) distance" is the "coefficient of the friction" of the road surface. We determine this factor by taking into consideration the "coefficient of friction" of the roadways, which we call "f." Then we take the velocity of the vehicle, in feet per second, which we call the small letter "v," and then we obtain the length of the skid marks expressed in feet, which we call

the capital letter "S." The formula, which I mentioned above, may also be expressed in v = 8.02 times the square root of fS. We also have formulae in which "W" is the weight (in pounds) of the moving object and the capital letter "V" is its velocity, in miles per hour. We know that

$$\frac{Mv^2}{2} = \frac{WV^2}{30}$$

and

$$f = \frac{V^2}{30S.}$$

Thus, with any two of the three quantities known, the other can be calculated.

Q: Is kinetic energy a factor in this evaluation of time, speed and distance in accident reconstruction cases?

A: It is.

Q: What is kinetic energy, and what is the formula for determining it?

A: Kinetic energy is the energy given off by a moving object, and the applicable formula is Mv2. The capital letter "M" represents the "mass" of the moving object; the small letter "v" is the velocity at which the object travels, in feet per second; and by applying the formula, we are able to translate mass into pounds of weight and velocity from feet per second into miles per hour.

Q: Are these your own formulae, or are they recognized by the profession?

A: These are basic scientific formulae, derived from elementary physics, and are recognized by the entire profession.

Q: Assume that a trailer-tractor, such as is shown on the photograph in evidence (exhibit A), weighs thirty tons, and that it was involved in a collision with the Dodge sedan shown. The truck driver has claimed he was traveling no more than forty miles per hour on an asphalt pavement highway prior to the accident, well within the 45 miles per hour speed limit. This was a dry, clean and straight roadway. This testimony, given at an examination before trial, was that he saw the Dodge sedan ahead of him for a distance of about 20 seconds prior to the collision. If he were traveling at 40 miles per hour, as he testified, would you be able to tell me, with a reasonable degree of certainty, how far away he was from the sedan when he saw it?

A: He would have had to be at least 600 or more feet away. The average coefficient of friction of such a road surface is about .78. Since your statement of facts asks me to assume that the roadway was dry, clean and straight, I am justified in accepting .78 as the average coefficient of friction of such a road surface.

Q: If we were to assume that the trailer-tractor was traveling about 40 miles per hour, and its truck driver was reasonably alert, and allow for average reaction time—if the trailer-truck had brakes in proper working order, would you be able to express an opinion, with reasonable certainty, as to what distance the trailer-tractor would travel before it would come to a halt, following application of its brakes, assuming the truck driver saw the Dodge sedan ahead of him about 20 seconds prior to the collision?

A: Yes. Allowing for a reasonably alert driver, for the known average reaction time, and for the average braking distance of such a vehicle, assuming its brakes were in proper working order, the trailer-tractor should have been able to come to a halt within 125 feet from the time its driver saw the sedan—well within the 600 feet available.

Q: Assume also that the driver of the trailer-tractor has testified, in his examination before trial, that the sedan came from an intersecting road to the right, and proceeded at a fast rate of speed across the front of the trailer-tractor, and that he testified that the sedan was trying to make a left turn northbound at a fast rate of speed when the collision occurred. Would this photograph (exhibit B), taken shortly following the accident, be of any assistance to you in determining, with reasonable certainty, whether the sedan had indeed been traveling at a fast rate of speed, at the time the collision occurred?

A: Yes. This photograph shows no "rotation markings" on the roadway following the collision, such as one would have expected to find had the sedan been traveling at a fast rate of speed at the moment of impact. Also there were no skid marks left by the sedan at all. On the other hand, the same photograph shows that the truck clearly left skid marks. These physical facts are significant in enabling me to conclude, with reasonable certainty, that the sedan was not traveling at a fast rate of speed at the time of the collision. On the contrary, the facts you have asked me to assume, and these photographs taken that very night, indicate that the sedan was either standing still, or moving very slowly across the road, at the time it was struck by the trailer-tractor. This is further corroborated by the crushing type of damage which was inflicted on the sedan.

Q: Assume also that the trailer-tractor left the type of skid marks shown in the photo, and that the testimony of a state trooper has indicated that they were 90 feet long, and that the Dodge sedan was pushed another 87 feet from the point of impact, would you be able to compute, with reasonable certainty, the speed at which the truck was traveling prior to impact?

A: Yes. My computations would indicate that it was traveling at least 65 miles per hour at the time the brakes were applied, not 40 miles per hour, as testified.

Q: How did you make your computations?

A: By applying the formulae which I referred to previously. Indeed the truck may have been traveling at an even faster rate of speed, for I do not have sufficient data to calculate the additional kinetic energy which it took to push the sedan ahead so many additional feet, following the impact.

Q: I show you another photograph, Plaintiff's Exhibit C, which has been identified by the trooper as fairly representing the appearance presented by the sedan shortly following the collision. Is the type of damage shown thereon significant to you, and if so, why?

A: Yes. It indicates the "crushing" type of damage sustained by the sedan to which I have referred, as distinct from "rotation" type of damage. This corroborates the opinion I previously gave, for this crushing type of damage shown here would be expected if a fast moving trailer-tractor were to strike a slow-moving, or stationary, sedan.

Efforts to Eliminate the Hypothetical Question

Obviously, the hypothetical question is often awkward and hypertechnical. It is fraught with possibilities of reversible error. Hypothetical questions can be extremely time-consuming and they are frequently confusing to jurors. More often than not they are used by counsel to make an extra summation in the middle of the case. Although counsel may think there is some advantage in getting this opportunity to summarize the evidence far in advance of closing arguments, it is more likely that he is putting the jurors to sleep. Still, there are lawyers who believe that the hypothetical question represents the best method yet devised for extracting helpful opinions from an expert witness who is not directly familiar with the facts of the case.

Efforts are occasionally made to do away with the necessity for using hypothetical questions. For example, Rule 705 of the Federal Rules of Evidence provides that an expert can testify in terms of opinion "without prior disclosure of the underlying facts or data." The major change intended to be accomplished by this language is the elimination of the necessity for the hypothetical question in eliciting expert testimony. Under Rule 705 examining counsel does not have to disclose underlying facts to his or her expert witness by means of a hypothetical question posed in open court as a preliminary to his or her opinion. The necessary data can be conveyed to the expert prior to his direct examination and it need not be disclosed during that examination. Of course, opposing counsel can cross-examine the expert about the data on which his opinion testimony is based.

Although elimination of the requirement of preliminary disclosure at trial of underlying data has a long history of support, abandonment of the requirement of a hypothetical question is not entirely uncontroversial. Under Federal Rule of Evidence 705 an expert might base his opinion on unreliable data. Examining counsel could avoid revealing the weakness of this data during his direct examination of the expert. The remedy of cross-examination to bring out the weakness of the expert's information sources might occasionally leave the adverse party at a tactical disadvantage, forcing him to engage in a blind cross-examination in those jurisdictions that do not permit extensive pretrial discovery of the other side's evidence in criminal cases.

Expert Witnesses and the Insanity Defense

In times past an expert witness would not be allowed to render an opinion on the ultimate issues in a case (e.g., whether a person's conduct was "negligent") because this would usurp the role of the jury. The modern trend is to repudiate this ambiguous limitation. "Testimony in the form of an expert opinion is not objectionable because it embraces the ultimate issue or issues to be decided by the trier of fact." (*United States* v. *Scavo,* 593 F.2d 837 (8th Cir. 1979).)

However, there remains one exception to the modern trend toward permitting expert opinion testimony on the core issues in a case. In the aftermath of John Hinckley's controversial acquittal, by reason of insanity, for the attempted assassination of former President Ronald Reagan, the Congress enacted a statute which provides that an expert witness *cannot* state an opinion or inference as to whether the accused had the mental state or condition constituting an element of the crime charged or of a defense to the charge. (Fed. R. Evid. 704(b), added in 1984.) Under this rule, an expert can testify that the accused suffered from a mental disease or defect and can describe the characteristics of such a condition, but cannot offer a conclusion as to whether the condition rendered the accused incapable of appreciating the nature and quality or wrongfulness of his or her acts. That is left to the jury.

Court-Appointed Experts

Ever since 1946 there has been a comprehensive federal procedure for court-appointed experts and many states have similar procedures. A federal trial judge can order the accused or the Government, or both, to show cause why expert witnesses should not be appointed and can request the parties to submit the names of possible witnesses. The judge can either appoint experts agreed upon by the parties or can appoint experts of his or her own selection. A court-appointed expert is informed of his or her duties by the judge, either in writing or at a conference at which the parties have an opportunity to take part. A court-appointed expert will inform the parties of his or her findings and can thereafter be called to the stand by the trial judge or any party to give testimony. Court-appointed experts are subject to full cross-examination by all parties.

Experts appointed by the trial court are most commonly encountered in cases in which it is suggested either that the accused was legally insane at the time of the offense charged or that the accused is presently incompetent to stand trial because of his inability to comprehend the proceedings and cooperate with his defense counsel. In such situations the trial court may appoint one or more psychiatrists to examine the accused and report.

The use of court-appointed experts occasionally avoids the frustrating phenomenon known as the battle of experts. Both sides in criminal and civil cases alike will shop for experts who are receptive to the position being taken by the side retaining them. Furthermore, some experts are in fact venal; one often hears remarks about "the best expert witness money can buy." And many reputable experts are unwilling to involve themselves in litigation. So, although the suggestion is occasionally made that court-appointed experts take on an aura of infallibility which they may not deserve, the trend is increasingly to provide for their use. The very availability of this appointment procedure reduces the need for resorting to it. This is because the mere possibility that the trial judge *might* appoint an objective, disinterested expert in a given case exerts a sobering influence on a party's expert and on the lawyer who is making use of his services.

Impeachment of an Expert Witness

Aside from attacking his qualifications and disinterestedness or the thoroughness and competence of his investigation, there are two commonly encountered methods of attacking or impeaching an expert witness's opinion. They involve (1) contradictory material in authoritative publications in the field and (2) alteration of the facts of a hypothetical question put to the witness during his direct examination.

1. An expert witness can be confronted, on cross-examination, with contradictory material from authoritative published works in the pertinent field of expertise. In most jurisdictions it is not essential that the witness relied on the particular treatise or other items of literature in forming the conclusions given in his direct examination, although this was once a common requirement.

EXAMPLE:

BY THE PROSECUTING ATTORNEY: Dr. Faust, you insisted in your direct testimony earlier this afternoon that a person who is a manic depressive may have a propensity for committing murder or assault to murder, didn't you?

A: Well, "insist" is a pretty strong word but that's what I said.
Q: And you believe your statement to be correct? You think it is medically and physically sound?
A: Certainly I do.
Q: Dr. Faust, at any given time a manic depressive can be in either the manic or exhilarated phase or the depressive, the subdued or depressed phase of the psychosis, can he not?
A: That's true.
Q: Would your statement about a propensity to commit violent acts be as true of a person in the depressive state as it would be of a person who was in a manic state?
A: I think so, yes.
Q: Do other psychiatrists agree with your position in this respect?
A: I don't know specifically but I would presume so. My position is the correct one.
Q: I see. Do you know Dr. Carl S. Milcher's work entitled *The Murderer's Mind?*
A: I know of it. Everyone does.
Q: Is Dr. Milcher a recognized authority on the psychic condition of persons who have committed murder?
A: I would say so. He is a distinguished psychiatrist.
Q: And has done a great deal of work in this area?
A: Yes.
Q: Did you in any way rely on Dr. Milcher's work in forming your opinions regarding the accused in this case? [This question, although not required in a number of jurisdictions, is usually asked anyway.]
A: I may have unconsciously. His work is part of the fund of knowledge that I carry around in my head.
Q: Dr. Faust, I hand you a copy of Dr. Milcher's book, *The Murderer's Mind,* published in 1988, which I have opened to page 492. On that page Dr. Milcher is discussing the manic depressive state, is he not? Take your time and look at it, Dr. Faust, and then you can answer.
A: Yes, he describes the state here.
Q: He mentions there that a person in the manic phase may have a propensity for murder or assault to murder, doesn't he?
A: Yes, he does.
Q: And Dr. Milcher is a widely recognized expert, is he not?
A: I said so.
Q: Yes, you did. Now look at the last full sentence on page 492 of Dr. Milcher's book. I want you to read that sentence to the court and jury. You can read it over to yourself first, if you want to, but then read it to the members of the jury, loud and clear.
A: [Reading.] "The depressive aspect of the illness manifests itself more commonly in suicide."

BY THE PROSECUTING ATTORNEY: Thank you sir. That will be all.

2. Examining counsel will frequently omit certain facts from a hypothetical question put to his expert witness on direct examination. It is entirely permissible for opposing counsel to inquire whether consideration of the omitted facts would have an impact on the witness's opinion.

EXAMPLE:

BY THE PROSECUTING ATTORNEY: Doctor Faust, if you were requested to assume these additional facts, which were not mentioned by defense counsel in his hypothetical question to you, namely [the omitted facts are recounted], would your opinion remain the same?

A: No, it wouldn't.

Q: What would your opinion be if we include those facts, Doctor?

A: [The witness gives his revised opinion.]

Sometimes facts included in a hypothetical question are later disproved by the evidence. In this situation the expert witness will be asked on cross-examination whether his conclusion would remain the same if those facts were eliminated from the hypothetical question.

EXAMPLE:

BY THE PROSECUTING ATTORNEY: Doctor Faust, would your response to the hypothetical question have been different if in putting the question to you defense counsel had left out of consideration the statement that the blood found under the left shoulder was clotted?

A: My answer would have been different, yes.

Expert Witnesses and Scientific Evidence

The topic of expert witnesses is inevitably bound up with the whole subject of scientific evidence, which is considered in the next chapter. The proper functions of experts cannot fully be understood until the purposes of scientific evidence in criminal cases are spelled out.

CHAPTER EIGHTEEN

Scientific Evidence

A. General Considerations

Advances in Scientific Knowledge

As humankind's knowledge increases, new scientific and experimental techniques for obtaining or verifying data achieve acceptance among experts and are determined, as a general proposition, to be admissible evidence if the proper foundation is laid by trial counsel. For example, as was noted in the discussion of relevance in chapter 4, there was a time when firearms identification evidence was considered irrelevant, even preposterous. Today it is so highly regarded that judicial notice of its general worth will be taken. Fingerprint and handwriting comparison evidence is now fully acceptable in criminal courts. So are various chemical intoxication tests and tests, such as the Nalline test, for drugs. Microanalysis, used for identifying the source of small objects and particles and for comparison purposes, often plays a key role in criminal litigation. Neutron activation analysis for the identification and comparison of physical evidence has been gaining in usefulness as has DNA fingerprinting ("genetic marking"). Spectrographic voice identification—the so-called voiceprint—has taken on some respectability. All manner of photographic evidence—X-ray photography, infrared, photomicrography, photomacrography, microphotography—is encountered in the criminal courts today. Law enforcement officers concerned with traffic control have become experts in the scientific detection of vehicular speed, using VASCAR principles (VASCAR stands for Visual Average Speed Computer and Record), radar equipment, or laser "guns."

Of course, some assertedly scientific techniques have been accorded little or no judicial recognition. For example, testimony about hypnotically refreshed memory has been rejected by a majority of courts. In the late 19th century, a California court put it bluntly: "The law of the United States does not recognize hypnotism" (*People* v. *Banks,* 49 P. 1050 (Cal. 1897).) More recently a few courts have admitted testimony concerning hypnotically enhanced memory if certain procedural safeguards were scrupulously followed. (E.g., *United States* v. *Valdez,* 722 F. 2d 1196 (5th Cir. 1984).) And in 1987 the U.S. Supreme Court held that a blanket rule excluding the hypnotically induced testimony of a criminal defendant violated his constitutional right to testify in his own defense (*Rock* v. *Arkansas,* 483 U.S. 44 1987). However, the Court emphasized that its decision was a narrow one: "This case does not involve the admissibility of testimony of previously hypnotized witnesses other than criminal defendants and we express no opinion on that issue."

In the middle ground, but probably moving toward judicial acceptance, is the Polygraph or lie detector method of testing the truthfulness of a person's statements. Until recently, results of Polygraph tests have not been ruled admissible unless they were the subject of express agreement (stipulation) between the prosecution and the defense. Judicial attitudes are in the process of thawing, however, and the day may not be far off that Polygraph results will be more freely received in evidence.

Methods of Establishing Acceptance and Reliability of Scientific Evidence

The acceptance of the scientific validity, that is, the general reliability, of a particular scientific method of testing or conducting an experiment can be attested by witnesses who are experts in the field that is involved. As was indicated above, the reliability of a scientific technique may even be so firmly settled as to be subject to judicial notice.

At one time it was thought that the opinion in an early Polygraph case, *Frye* v. *United States,* 293 Fed. 1013 (D.C. Cir. 1923), accurately stated the test for admissibility of scientific evidence. The *Frye* Court had said:

> Just when a scientific principle or discovery crosses the line between the experimental and demonstrative stages is difficult to define. Somewhere in this twilight zone the evidential force of the principle must be recognized, and while courts will go a long way in admitting expert testimony deduced from a well-recognized scientific principle or discovery, the thing from which the deduction is made must be sufficiently established to have gained *general acceptance* in the particular field in which it belongs. (Italics added.)

But the quoted language of *Frye* is no longer precisely accurate. Stress is no longer laid on *general* acceptance; it is often enough if specialists within a general scientific field recognize the worth of a technique, even though the technique may not be known to experts in other branches of the same field. Today the true touchstones may be demonstrated reliability (even of novel methodologies) and helpfulness to the fact-finder. In short, in many jurisdictions the test is now said to be one of simple relevance. (See, e.g., *Andrews* v. *State,* 533 So. 2d 841 (Fla. App. 1988) (rejecting *Frye* test, adopting relevance test, and approving admission of DNA genetic matching tests, a procedure discussed later in this chapter).)

EXAMPLE A:

In *People v. Williams,* 331 P. 2d 251 (Cal. App. 1958), the accused, charged with using opiates, challenged the admission of the results of a Nalline test administered to him. On cross-examination the prosecution's medical experts conceded that the medical profession *generally* was not familiar with the use of Nalline and that it therefore could not accurately be said that the Nalline test had met with general acceptance by the medical profession as a whole.

However, the California court held that the prosecution's medical testimony was strongly supportive of reliability. Familiarity with the testing method by the entire medical profession was not considered essential.

EXAMPLE B:

In *Coppolino* v. *State,* 223 So. 2d 68 (Fla. App.), *cert. denied,* 399 U.S. 927 (1968), there was evidence of some scientific tests that had been specifically developed by a pathologist to identify the presence in body tissue of a particular chemical. His test had not previously been known to pathologists. Experts for the defense testified that the test was not of proven reliability. The test results were received in evidence, however. The court held that novel tests, designed to solve a special problem, are not rendered inadmissible simply because the entire profession is not yet familiar with them. The true touchstone is demonstrated reliability.

In *Daubert* v. *Merrell Dow Pharmaceuticals, Inc.,* ____ U.S. ____, 113 S. Ct. 2786 (1993), the U.S. Supreme Court rejected the *Frye* "general acceptance" test in favor of a looser relevance test. Under *Daubert's* test, applicable to federal trial courts, general acceptance in the scientific community is only one factor. The other factors include whether the theory or methodology in question can be and has been tested, whether it has been subjected to publication and attendant peer review, its known or potential error rate, and the existence and implementation of standards controlling its operation.

Although *Daubert* was a civil case, the term "error rate" suggests that the Supreme Court had in mind DNA testing and other forensic science evidence employed to identify criminal perpetrators.

It should be held in mind that *Daubert*'s test applies to scientific evidence and not to other types of technical or specialized expert knowledge that are more practical than they are scientific. Thus the theories of an expert automobile mechanic or an examiner of questioned documents are undoubtedly admissible without a showing that they have been tested scientifically or subjected to peer review.

Sources and Purposes of Expert Scientific Evidence

The prosecution's experts are often salaried employees of federal, state, or local government. As MOENSSENS, STARRS, HENDERSON & INBAU have pointed out in their important book, SCIENTIFIC EVIDENCE IN CIVIL AND CRIMINAL CASES (4th ed. 1995), the testimony of prosecution experts in a criminal case usually has one of four fundamental aims:

1. The identification, through such techniques as document examination, microbiological matching of blood and semen, or toxicological analysis of drugs, of items of incriminating evidence that can be traced to the accused;
2. Proof, through psychiatric evidence concerning sanity, toxicological evidence of blood-alcohol ratio, and the like, that the accused at a given time was in a particular mental or physical condition;
3. Proof of the criminality of unobserved or suspicious death by means of post-mortem examination (autopsy); and
4. The impeachment or rehabilitation of a witness's testimonial credibility.

This is not the place to present a definitive discussion of every scientific crime detection technique. For one reason, this is a text on evidentiary rules, not on technical scientific principles or criminalities. A second reason is that a number of specialized treatises address this subject, preeminent among them the work of Moenssens, Starrs, Henderson and Inbau, mentioned above. Their treatise provides in-depth coverage of the thirteen principal areas of scientific proof: (1) psychiatry and psychology; (2) toxicology and the chemical sciences; (3) forensic pathology; (4) photography, motion pictures, and videotape; (5) microanalysis; (6) neutron activation analysis; (7) fingerprint identification; (8) firearms evidence and comparative micrography; (9) spectrographic voice identification; (10) questioned documents; (11) the Polygraph technique; (12) scientific detection of vehicular speed; and (13) narcoanalysis and hypnosis. The authors also take up the use of certain types of demonstrative evidence, such as casts, models, maps, and drawings.

This chapter's discussion will be limited to reasonably condensed references to the significance of the most basic areas of scientific proof. Often the focus will be on the application of any special evidentiary principles controlling the admissibility of such evidence and not on technical scientific details. Emphasis will be placed on those modes of scientific proof in which the typical law enforcement agent can be expected to play an active part.

B. Psychiatry and Psychology

Insanity

The psychiatric condition broadly called *insanity* can provide a defense to a criminal charge, either because the accused was unable, because of his mental condition, to form the essential criminal intent or because his mental condition made it impossible for him to exercise a free will.

The M'Naughten *Rule*

Different jurisdictions apply different tests of legal insanity but humankind has recognized from the beginning of recorded history that insanity is a fact of life. It was settled as early as 1327 in England that complete madness was a good defense to a criminal prosecution. However, it was necessary that the accused's insanity be so gross that he was "not greatly removed from beasts [which] lacked reasoning." Slowly but surely it was understood that a person could be more rational than a wild animal and yet be so severely crippled mentally as not to be justly responsible for one's conduct. The landmark decision was in *The Queen* v. *Daniel M'Naughten;* the following description of that case is taken from KAPLAN & WALTZ, THE TRIAL OF JACK RUBY.

On January 20, 1843, in London, Daniel M'Naughten (whose name in various accounts is also spelled MacNaughten, MacNaghten, M'Naghten, and Macnaughton) shot and fatally wounded Edward Drummond, private secretary to Sir Robert Peel, prime minister of Great Britain. M'Naughten had apparently mistaken Drummond for Sir Robert. On March 3 and 4, 1843, M'Naughten was tried for murder at London's Central Criminal Court.

The prosecution established without opposition that M'Naughten had fired the fatal shot. It contended that the accused appeared sane and had exhibited no outward symptoms of a diseased mind. To demonstrate premeditation, the prosecution established that M'Naughten had been seen loitering around the neighborhood of the Treasury and Admiralty Houses, the scene of the killing, for several days prior to the murder.

The defense contended that there was no motive for the slaying. M'Naughten had never exhibited animosity toward either Drummond or the prime minister and it was argued that no sane murderer would slay his victim in an area where capture was inevitable. Defense counsel then delved deeply into M'Naughten's background to produce evidence of his history of instability.

M'Naughten was a woodturner from Glasgow, Scotland. He had been in business with his father as an apprentice and journeyman and when his father had refused him a partnership, M'Naughten opened his own workshop. By 1841 M'Naughten had sold his business, which had become profitable, and moved to London. After returning to Glasgow for a few months, he had gone briefly to France, finally returning to London in July of 1842, where he remained until the shooting of Drummond six months later. During his second stay in London M'Naughten lodged at a succession of homes but was not allowed to remain long at any of them because of what his landlords described as his "peculiar" behavior.

M'Naughten appeared to be a gloomy, reserved, and unsocial man. Witnesses at his trial testified that he would never speak until spoken to and then would gaze ashamedly at the floor while talking. Testimony was offered by several witnesses that the accused frequently complained of being followed by police and spies for the Catholic church and the Tory party. They related conversations with the accused during which he had told them the reason for his travels—to escape the persecution of the Tories and the Church of Rome. In M'Naughten's mind the trips had been to no avail; he confided that on returning to England the spies were still with him, watching his every movement. M'Naughten had once gone so far as to approach a member of Parliament, seeking relief from his persecution. When brought before a magistrate after the shooting of Drummond, M'Naughten claimed that the Tories had driven him to despair and had afflicted him with consumption. He announced that the newspapers of London had begun attacks on his character. When asked by officials to point out such articles or identify the spies, M'Naughten would only reply that it would be a waste of time to do so.

At the trial an employee of M'Naughten told the court that the accused had complained of head pains and had exhibited isolated episodes of overexcitement. Owners of lodgings where the accused had boarded revealed that M'Naughten walked in his sleep, broke into unexplainable fits of laughter, and frequently talked incoherently. Medical testimony was unanimous that although he appeared normal, M'Naughten had been laboring under a disease of the mind in that he was unable to control himself against passions and impulses that could, and did, compel him to kill. A physician testified that the accused had been experiencing delusions for nearly two years and that the killing of Drummond was a direct consequence of these delusions.

Daniel M'Naughten was acquitted by a jury. He was removed to a hospital and thereafter transferred to Broadmoor Asylum where, still haunted by his delusions, he died some twenty years after his attack on Drummond.

The acquittal of M'Naughten caused an immediate outcry in England. It was suggested by the newspapers that he was "profitably insane" and that he had induced soft-headed physicians and jurors into letting him cheat the gallows. In the face of this storm of controversy the House of Lords invited the judges of England to advise them on the proper law regarding the level of mental impairment that would excuse a defendant from criminal responsibility. The opinion of the judges stated a concise and seemingly simple rule. The accused was not criminally responsible for his act if he was laboring "under such a defect of reason from a disease of the mind, as not to know the nature and quality of the act he was doing, or if he did know it, that he did not know that he was doing what was wrong."

The *M'Naughten* rule was imported into America and is still widely followed here. Almost everyone agrees that the *M'Naughten* rule is a strict one. M'Naughten himself probably could not have met the *M'Naughten* test. Although he suffered from ungovernable delusions of persecution, he probably realized that he was killing another man and that in some sense his act was wrong.

The rule in M'Naughten's case has been a subject of intense debate ever since it was handed down by the English judges. The psychiatrists are in general far more vehement than the lawyers in their objections to the *M'Naughten* rule, denouncing it on a host of grounds. They complain that the test forces them to testify in legal rather than in psychiatric terms and thereby hamstrings them. Psychiatrists, they claim, are able to diagnose and classify the symptoms of the mentally ill, but their ability to ascertain whether a given subject knew the difference between "right" and "wrong" is severely limited. Moreover, the psychiatrists object to the *M'Naughten* test on another and entirely different ground—that it does not go far enough. Psychiatrists point out with increasing force that many persons who are, by an appropriate psychiatric definition, mentally ill can nevertheless differentiate, at least in a sense, between right and wrong even as their illness compels them to engage in the "wrong" conduct. In other words, the *M'Naughten* rule operates on the incorrect assumption that so long as a mentally ill person knows what is right and what is wrong, he can control his actions sufficiently to obey the law. By turning knowledge of right and wrong into a touchstone, the *M'Naughten* rule arguably puts too much emphasis on just one of the many symptoms that determine whether a person is mentally ill. Finally, most psychiatrists object to the all-or-nothing quality of the insanity defense. Wherever the line is drawn, it will fail to recognize that many of the mentally ill suffer from varying degrees of impairment of their ability to distinguish and appreciate the difference between right and wrong, ranging all the way from almost full appreciation to a total lack of knowledge. (On the permitted scope of expert testimony, see the preceding chapter and Fed. R. Evid. 704 (b).)

The *M'Naughten* rule has been resistant to these and other attacks. During the nineteenth century the right-wrong test was accepted by every American jurisdiction except New Hampshire. However, many states modified the rule in one respect, exculpating the accused who knew that his act was wrong but who was subject to an irresistible impulse and therefore was unable to stop himself from committing it.

The Durham *Test*

Then in 1954 the Court of Appeals for the District of Columbia focused renewed attention on the relation between insanity and the criminal law. In a case involving an obviously mentally ill burglar named Monty Durham, the Court of Appeals resurrected the old New Hampshire rule and held that the defendant was not criminally responsible "if his unlawful act was the product of a mental disease or mental defect." At first the flexible-sounding *Durham* rule was thought by most psychiatrists and many lawyers to be the solution to the insanity problem. Later, psychiatrists began to object to the *Durham* standard on the ground that it misconstrued the nature of mental illness. Psychiatrists contend that the personality of even the mentally ill is an integrated whole and that to ask whether a crime was a "product" of the accused's mental illness is like asking whether it was caused by the fact that he was what he was. The crimes of the mentally ill, like all their acts, many psychiatrists say, are always the product of their illness. Lawyers, meanwhile, attacked the *Durham* rule on other grounds, contending that it is an abject surrender to the psychiatrists, placing the answers to essentially legal and moral questions in the hands of medical experts who are not trained to provide them. Lawyers and other law enforcement experts have said that the psychiatrists have been so much impressed by the discovery that a high percentage of our criminals are seriously mentally disturbed that they have neglected the evident fact that many noncriminals are apparently equally mentally disturbed and yet manage to lead useful, law-abiding lives.

The *Durham* rule, despite all the bright hopes for it, has been rejected by almost every court that has considered it. Ironically, in 1972 the Court of Appeals for the District of Columbia itself abandoned the *Durham* test (see *United States* v. *Brawner,* 471 F. 2d 969 (D.C. Cir. 1972)).

The American Law Institute Test

A much more popular test is the one drawn up by the American Law Institute in its Model Penal Code. It exculpates the accused in that situation where the law could not deter him anyway: if "at the time of such conduct as a result of mental illness or defect he lacks substantial capacity either to appreciate the criminality of his conduct or to conform his conduct to the requirements of the law." Some lawyers, regarding deterrence as the basis of the criminal law, argue that this ALI standard is adequate, the only problem being that the psychiatrists do not yet know enough about the human mind to tell in a given case whether a defendant *meets* this standard. Others say the question is much more difficult, that the real question is the moral one: how should we define for the jury the type of mental disability which makes an accused not morally responsible for his acts? If this is so the insanity problem may be an impossible one. It also may be that the verbal standard we use in defining insanity is not very important. Many lawyers insist that jurors will convict or acquit on the basis of their feelings about whether the accused is morally responsible, regardless of the technical standard which they are supposed to apply. In any event, the ALI test, with or without minor modifications, has been adopted in a number of states and by numerous federal courts, including the federal court that originally devised the *Durham* rule (see *United States* v. *Brawner,* cited above).

The Concept of Diminished Responsibility

A number of courts have also accepted the concept of *diminished responsibility* or *partial insanity.* In these jurisdictions the fact-finder (judge or jury) is permitted to consider the accused's impaired mental condition to reduce the degree of the offense charged or in mitigation of punishment even though the impairment does not rise to the level of legal insanity under the pertinent test.

The XYY Chromosome Defect

In recent times it has been suggested that the XYY chromosome defect might provide a defense to a criminal charge. The normal human cell has forty-six chromosomes arranged in twenty-three pairs. The normal chromosome pair for a female is XX; for a male it is XY. Some scientists believe that the X chromosome is responsible for the passive aspect of one's personality and the Y chromosome controls one's potential for aggressiveness. If a male has an extra Y chromosome, giving him an XYY chromosomal defect, the theory is that he may become extremely aggressive and antisocial and have a comparatively low intelligence. Beyond this, it is theorized that the XYY male may be unable to control his behavior.

Due to insufficient research, the XYY theory has not yet achieved significant acceptance, although it may eventually be accorded some evidentiary weight.

Psychiatric Reports

Relevant evidence on the insanity question will usually consist of the testimony of a forensic psychiatrist or allied specialist, such as a clinical psychologist. The expert's testimony, if it is to have much force, will be based on a physical and mental examination of the accused which is later developed into a written report. Ideally, the accused will not have been under any type of sedation at the time of the examination.

A properly prepared psychiatric report will include *general clinical observations:* (1) The circumstances surrounding the examination (date and time, location, presence or absence of third persons, the reason for making the examination); (2) the accused's appearance (age, sex, race, demeanor, clothing, skin, eyes, etc.); (3) the accused's behavior (intelligence, orientation, perception, speed of thought, vocabulary, memory, judgment, etc.); and (4) the accused's emotional condition (depressed, elated, angry, hallucinating, etc.). Many of the psychiatrist's clinical observations will be achieved through fairly simple testing procedures; for example, the accused's memory may be tested by telling him a story and then requesting him to repeat it.

A useful psychiatric report will contain the accused's *past and current family and personal history.* Family history will include any prior instances of mental illness. The accused's personal history will include the details of his birth; medical history; marital status; work and military record; criminal record; sex development; general health (including his symptoms and complaints); previous attacks of mental illness, and the like.

The report will often contain the results of a *physical examination, lab tests* (urine, blood, spinal fluid), and possible *neurological and/or psychological examinations.*

Finally, the examining psychiatrist's report will contain the author's *diagnosis* of the accused's mental condition, a prognosis (prediction of future condition), and perhaps *recommendations* for future disposition.

The Evidentiary Problems

When psychiatrists and allied specialists are called as witnesses at the accused's trial, the evidentiary problems will be of the kind discussed in the preceding chapter on the use of expert witnesses. A few special problems may arise, however.

If an insanity defense to a criminal charge is raised, or if the competency of the accused to go to trial is questioned, psychiatrists and associated experts may be permitted, at the suggestion of the trial court or the prosecutor, to examine the accused. Later on they may be called to testify regarding the accused's mental condition. Three special sorts of evidentiary problems can arise at this time: (1) Is a diagnosis that is based at least in part on hearsay material to be received in evidence? (2) Is it proper for the prosecution to inquire about incriminating statements made by the accused to the examining psychiatrist or other expert? (3) On cross-examination is it proper for defense counsel to elicit any self-serving, exculpating statements that may have been made by the accused to the prosecution's psychiatrist or to others?

Diagnosis Based on Hearsay

A psychiatric opinion or other expert opinion that is based wholly or in part on the findings of people other than the witness might seem to raise serious hearsay problems. (See chapter 5 on the rule against hearsay evidence.) A psychiatrist will often rely heavily on medical records and other sources that constitute "out-of-court declarations" within the sense of the hearsay rule. Confronted by defense counsel's hearsay objection, the prosecutor might be well advised to convey this outside information to the expert witness in a hypothetical question of the type described in the last chapter. But this is awkward and time-consuming.

Today, some enlightened judges hold that the hearsay rule is *inapplicable* to psychiatric opinions since the out-of-court data is not itself being offered into evidence to establish the truth of the data but instead is merely being employed as part of the basis for the expert witness's own opinion. This is the approach taken by Rule 703 of the Federal Rules of Evidence:

"The facts or data in the particular case upon which an expert bases an opinion or inference may be those perceived by or *made known* to the witness at or before the hearing. If of a type reasonably relied upon by experts in the particular field in forming opinions or inferences upon the subject, the facts or data need not [themselves] be admissible in evidence" (italics added).

Some courts have simply said that there is an *exception* to the rule against hearsay for this type of expert testimony. They point to Supreme Court Justice Benjamin Cardozo's somewhat lofty remark that "It is for ordinary minds and not for psychoanalysts that our rules of evidence are framed." In other words, psychiatrists can be trusted to accord proper weight to hearsay evidence even if "ordinary" mortals cannot.

Incriminating Statements by the Accused

Any effort to offer incriminating statements made by the accused to a prosecution expert while the accused was in a custodial situation will raise voluntariness, *Miranda,* and self-incrimination issues. Essentially, courts will take the approach, in the absence of an effective waiver of rights, that the accused's incriminating statements are admissible on the question of his mental condition but *not* on the issue of guilt or innocence, another of those fine-line distinctions that a fact-finder may consider baffling.

Self-Serving Statements by the Accused

Transparently self-serving statements to an examining psychiatrist or allied expert, obviously intended as such by an accused, cannot properly be brought out by defense counsel in cross-examination of the expert. On the other hand, spontaneous descriptions of present physical and mental condition and verbal facts ("I am the Pope!") or other circumstantial evidence of incompetency or insanity may be admissible on the issue of mental condition even though they are in a sense self-serving.

C. Toxicology and the Chemical Sciences

Their Role in Criminalistics

Toxicology and the chemical sciences loom larger and larger in modern-day efforts to detect and combat crime. Chemical tests for intoxication identify the drunk driver, separating him from the innocent person whose symptoms stem from a diabetic condition, carbon monoxide poisoning, or head injuries. The forensic serologist can use blood found at a crime scene as a source of proof linking a suspect to the offense. Other biochemical procedures are available to identify saliva, semen, fecal matter, vomitus, even perspiration. The forensic toxicologist can identify poisonous (toxic) substances and describe their effects. Other toxicological experts can analyze seized substances to determine whether they are illegal drugs.

The Need for Expertise

Except in connection with intoxication tests, criminal investigators are rarely qualified as experts in clinical toxicological-chemical testing, where practical experience must ordinarily be combined with fairly formal training in such fields as chemistry, biochemistry, and hematology.

> EXAMPLE:
> In *Scott* v. *State,* So. 357 (S. Ct. Ala. 1904), the witness who was held qualified to testify that death was caused by morphine in the stomach was a university professor of chemistry who also had for years been a state chemist and toxicologist. (It made no difference that he was neither a pathologist nor a pharmacist.)

Of course, law enforcement agents can occasionally give an opinion that is based not on clinical testing of a type requiring special expertise but on their own eyewitness observation of physical phenomena. Thus some courts would permit a police officer to testify to his opinion that a person was under the influence of drugs, based on his experience in dealing with persons later established to have been narcotics addicts. Even a lay citizen is sometimes allowed to give this sort of testimony.

> EXAMPLE:
> In *Pointer* v. *State,* 467 S.W. 2d 426 (Tex. Crim. App. 1971), a layperson who had been robbed was allowed to give his opinion that the accused was under the influence of narcotics at the time of the offense. The witness's opinion was based on his observations of the physical condition of narcotics addicts while he was in the Air Force.

It has sometimes been said that a narcotics addict is a qualified expert on the addictive properties of substances.

> EXAMPLE:
> In *Howard* v. *State,* 496 P. 2d 657 (S. Ct. Alaska 1972), it was held that a drug addict could testify to the narcotic quality of the substance in question, and in *State* v. *Johnson,* 196 N.W. 2d 717 (S. Ct. Wis. 1972), a user of LSD was permitted to express an opinion that a substance was LSD.

While holding it in mind that toxicological-chemical procedures are used by trained experts in the investigation of blood and a wide range of other biological matter, we will focus this discussion on intoxication tests since law enforcement officers are frequently directly involved in this type of testing. Identification of narcotic substances is also discussed briefly.

Chemical Intoxication Testing

The scientific validity of chemical intoxication tests is now so firmly established that most states make the results of them admissible under express statutory provisions. Thus in 1967 McIntyre and Chabraia could report in their article *The Intensive Search of a Suspect's Body and Clothing* in 58 Journal of Criminal Law, Criminology & Police Science 18, that forty states then had chemical test laws which provided that 0.15 percent of alcohol in a suspect's blood, as determined by chemical testing, is *prima facie* evidence of intoxication.

Because, among other things, tolerance for alcohol varies from person to person, it is not possible accurately to measure the degree to which a person is intoxicated on the basis of the *amount* of alcohol he or she has consumed. Intoxication can, however, be reliably demonstrated by scientific measure of the amount of alcohol that has reached the subject's brain, since the brain's alcohol content is the cause of most of the effects of alcohol.

The alcohol in liquor is ethyl alcohol. It has a low boiling point, is volatile, almost odorless (the "odor" of liquor comes from added flavoring matter), colorless, and toxic in that an overdose can be fatal. Ethyl alcohol is produced by the enzymatic breakdown of sugar, the process known as fermentation.

Alcohol is not digested when it goes into the stomach. Approximately 10 to 20 percent of any alcohol in the stomach is absorbed through the stomach's membranes into the bloodstream, the remainder being absorbed in the small intestine. A number of factors control the speed and amount of absorption of alcohol from the stomach into the bloodstream, such as (1) the amount of alcohol the person has consumed, (2) the nature and amount of coating in the stomach, and (3) the concentration of alcohol in the beverage consumed.

Other conditions being equal, alcohol consumption after a substantial meal has a slower absorption rate than alcohol drunk on an empty stomach. It has been reported that straight whiskey taken on an empty stomach attains maximum concentration in the bloodstream within half an hour. In contrast, alcohol consumed along with or after the ingestion of food may reach maximum concentration as much as an hour and a half after consumption. Sugar, fatty foods, and milk retard alcohol absorption somewhat.

Alcohol absorbed into the bloodstream does not undergo significant transformation; it is still alcohol. After it has been absorbed into the bloodstream, it is distributed throughout the body in a constant proportional relationship to the water content of the various body tissues. It is eliminated from the tissues by being oxidized to energy, water and carbon dioxide. A great deal of alcohol's metabolism (assimilation) takes place in the liver. A smaller percentage is excreted unchanged in the urine, breath, and perspiration.

Needless to say, the higher the concentration of alcohol in the bloodstream, the higher will be the relative proportion of alcohol that is excreted. The percentage of alcohol excreted in the breath or as urine varies proportionately with the concentration of alcohol in the blood. While blood-alcohol concentration is decreasing, the urine-alcohol concentration may be as much as one and one-half that of blood alcohol. Blood alcohol concentration is about twenty-one hundred times that of the same unit volume in the deep alveolar breath. While varying somewhat from person to person, the rate of elimination is fairly constant in relation to body size. The average person weighing 150 pounds can eliminate one-third of an ounce of pure alcohol per hour. This equals two-thirds of an ounce of 100-proof whiskey per hour.

The quantity of alcohol ingested does not dictate the degree of mental and physical impairment; the level of impairment is governed by the quantity of alcohol that has been absorbed into the bloodstream and carried to the central nervous system. Alcohol is not a stimulant; it depresses the central nervous system's responses (brain, spinal cord, spinal nerves). Alcohol-laden blood entering the brain through the vascular system has a depressing effect until the alcohol is eliminated. Its main depressant effect occurs in the brain's cerebral areas, which control the human body's higher functions. It is in this way that the ingestion of alcohol causes diminution of judgment, self-restraint, and responses to stimuli. At elevated concentrations, blood-alcohol ratio produces loss of muscular control, lengthened reaction time, diminished sensitivity to pain, disturbances of sensory perception (vision, hearing), confusion, thick or slurred speech and unsteady gait. If the blood alcohol concentration is even higher, a state of stupor approaching paralysis results. If the concentration is sub-lethal, the person will pass from stupor into unconsciousness.

Many jurisdictions have enacted statutory standards describing the smallest percentage of blood alcohol necessary to create a rebuttable presumption of intoxication. Since no presumption in a criminal case is ever absolutely conclusive, test results can be weighed and accepted or rejected by the fact-finder.

In the absence of a statute, the prosecution must place its reliance entirely on the testimony of expert witnesses.

1. *Chemical Testing; Blood Analysis.* There are a number of chemical tests for intoxication. The most reliable of them involves direct analysis of brain tissue. This method is not used on a large scale since it is confined to corpses, just as is spinal fluid analysis. The tests most commonly used on living persons involve analysis of the blood, urine, and breath. Direct analysis of the blood is thought to be the most reliable of these three methods, but there is a practical problem in that direct analysis of the blood requires that a physician or qualified medical technician secure a blood sample under proper conditions. It also generates evidentiary chain-of-custody requirements. For these reasons, blood analysis is not used as widely as breath testing.

2. *Breath Tests.* Breath testing for intoxication operates on the assumption that a breath sample is saturated with alcoholic vapor at normal respiratory tract temperature. In other words, alcohol breath testing is an indirect means of detecting blood alcohol levels. As was suggested earlier, the validity of this type of testing is based on the circumstance that blood will contain about twenty-one hundred times as much alcohol as alveolar air.

The first device for breath analysis of blood alcohol ratio was graphically named the Drunkometer by its inventor, Dr. R. N. Harger of the University of Indiana Medical School. The Drunkometer, perfected in 1931, was rapidly followed by the Intoximeter, D.P.C. Intoximeter, Photo-Electric Intoximeter, Alcometer, Infrared Intoxograph, the Kitagawa-Wright device, and the Breathalyzer, and this is not a complete list of such equipment. Today the Drunkometer, Breathalyzer, and the Intoximeter are the most commonly used. All three of them function in accordance with the principles worked out by Harger.

Harger's Drunkometer operates on the principle that the alcohol present in breath will cause discoloration of permanganate, a salt of permanganic acid. The alcohol concentration is determined from the amount of breath that is necessary to cause the chemical reaction, which is evidenced by the discoloration of a measured amount of permanganate. The last step is a mathematical conversion from the reading on the Drunkometer to blood-alcohol ratio. Any police officer can operate a Drunkometer and provide essential courtroom testimony about test results after a short period of training.

The Intoximeter lacks certain of the Drunkometer's advantages. It uses magnesium perchlorate rather than permanganate, and foundation testimony regarding the pretest condition of the device and any changes caused by the breathtesting process is essential. Police officers do not ordinarily develop the level of expertise required by the Intoximeter process.

The Breathalyzer was perfected by a member of the Indiana State Police, Captain R. F. Borkenstein. The theory behind it is that the normal yellow color of a solution of potassium dichromate and liquid sulfuric acid will turn green if alcohol is present in breath that passes through the solution. When a person suspected of being intoxicated blows his or her breath forcefully through a mouthpiece into a heated plastic tube in the Breathalyzer, it raises a piston in a metal cylinder. The suspect's breath fills the cylinder and the piston then drops down to seal it. When a valve is rotated, a measured quantity of the breath is forced through 3 milliliters of 50 percent (by volume) sulfuric acid in water, which contains 0.25 milligrams of potassium dichromate per milliliter, and a catalytic agent. The breath bubbles through this test solution in approximately thirty seconds. Before the Breathalyzer test is commenced the solution in the test ampul (a glass vessel) is photometrically balanced against a reference ampul until a meter marked "Null" centers. This indicates that each of two photocells is receiving the same amount of light through the two ampuls. After the suspect has blown into the mouthpiece, the photometric reading light is again turned on. More light will be received by the righthand photo cell and the "Null"

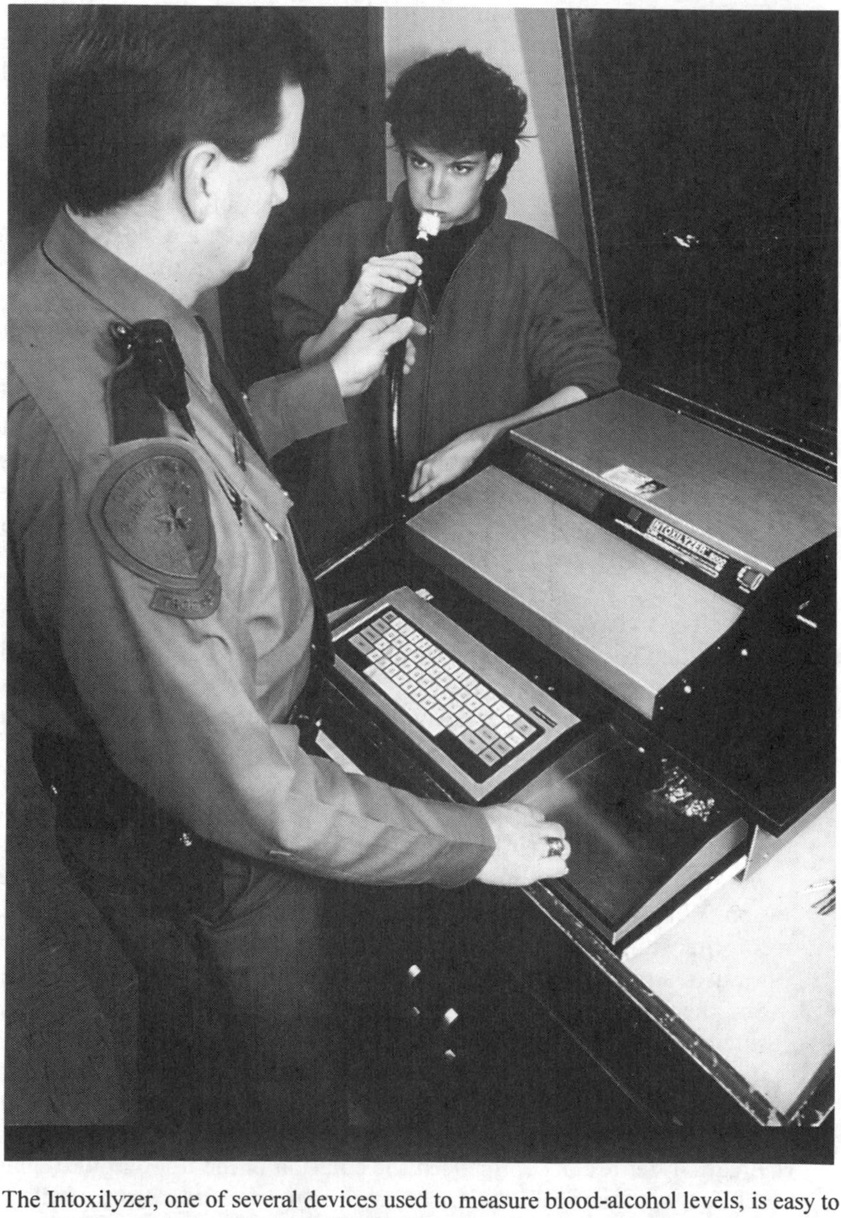

The Intoxilyzer, one of several devices used to measure blood-alcohol levels, is easy to operate because it does not need chemicals.

meter will no longer be centered if some of the potassium dichromate in the test ampul has been consumed by alcohol. By means of a thumb wheel the light is moved until the "Null" meter is again centered. The distance which the light has to be moved is directly related to the quantity of alcohol in the suspect's breath. The light scale is calibrated to show blood-alcohol percent or ratio.

Another device known as an Intoxilyzer has been developed. It relies on infrared absorption of energy by ethyl alcohol vapors in breath samples. It provides a direct and rapid means of measuring breath alcohol quantitatively. The Intoxilyzer is easy to operate because it uses no chemicals; it may eventually supplant the older equipment described in the preceding paragraph. A more detailed description of the Intoxilyzer can be found in Harte, *An Instrument for the Determination of Ethanol in Breath,* 16 Journal of Forensic Science 493 (1971).

Breath testing will lack accuracy if the chemical reagents are not fresh (e.g., permanganate is unstable and will decompose quickly, producing a falsely high breath alcohol reading). Improper operator conduct can lead to error—so can a failure to employ the equilibration and standardization tests recommended by the manufacturers of the equipment. Essential test procedures, aimed at assuring accuracy, are described in Hall, *The Equilibrator—An Answer for Improving Breathalyzer Techniques and Field Testing Suspect Alcohol Solutions,* 1 Police Law Quarterly 11 (1971).

A breath test will not produce an accurate picture if more than fifteen minutes have passed between the ingestion of the alcohol and the taking of the breath sample. Recent use of breath fresheners and mouthwashes that have an alcoholic content can throw off the results of breath testing. Alcohol remaining in the subject's throat and mouth can produce a falsely high reading; this can happen when the subject has regurgitated.

Preliminary Breath Testing

A new tool for detecting drunken drivers has gained approval in California. In 1989 that state's attorney general upheld the use by Highway Patrol officers of a flashlight-size device that checks the air exhaled by a motorist for traces of alcohol. The device, called a Preliminary Breath Tester, can be aimed toward a driver from outside his or her vehicle and will detect the presence of alcohol vapors when the vehicle's window is opened. "It's like an extension of the officer's nose," explained a spokeswoman for the California Highway Patrol.

The PBT measures only the presence, not the concentration, of alcohol in a driver's breath. This may save it from successful court challenges based on the prohibition against unreasonable searches and seizures. It will be used at random sobriety checkpoints. A positive read-out will prompt full-scale blood-alcohol ratio testing.

Evidentiary Aspects

Not surprisingly, the results of blood-alcohol tests are not considered conclusive of intoxication in the eyes of the law. This means that juries can accept or reject test results when considering the evidence of intoxication in totality. State chemical test statutes usually call for some corroboration of test results.

> EXAMPLE:
> The Wisconsin Statute, Wis. Stats. Ann., §325.235(1), reads: "The fact that the analysis shows that there was fifteen-hundredths of one per cent or more by weight of alcohol in the person's blood is prima facie evidence that he was under the influence of an intoxicant, but shall not, without corroborating physical evidence thereof, be sufficient upon which to find the person guilty of being under the influence of intoxicants."

The corroborating physical evidence referred to in statutes of the sort quoted above usually consists of the testimony of police officers who administered or observed coordination tests in which the subject engaged in nose-touching, name-writing, line-walking, and the like. (Actually, coordination test results alone are enough to sustain a driving-while-intoxicated conviction: there is no absolute requirement that the prosecution produce scientific evidence in intoxication cases.)

If scientific tests are to be relied upon, the prosecution must lay a preliminary foundation. Usually this foundation has three principal components: (1) testimony that there was periodic inspection of the test equipment and supervision of the operator by a person having a clear understanding of the scientific principles on which the test method is based; (2) testimony that the chemicals utilized in the test procedure were fresh and properly compounded; and (3) proof that the witness who will testify to the test results is qualified to do so. The third foundation requirement dictates the use of a witness who possesses enough knowledge to convert the breath-analysis reading to blood alcohol without exclusive reliance on a chart provided by the manufacturer of the testing equipment, since this would inject a hearsay element.

Whenever chemical testing of body fluids, such as blood or urine, or other substances, such as compounds thought to be illegal drugs, is conducted, special care must be taken to preserve a provable chain of custody.

The Supreme Court has held that the police have a right to require a person to undergo a reasonably conducted blood-alcohol test. (*Schmerber* v. *California,* 384 U.S. 757 (1966); see also *United States* v. *Jackson,* 886 F. 2d 838 (7th Cir. 1989).) Under the provisions of many state statutes, however, one is allowed to refuse such a test, but at the price of losing one's license to drive. Furthermore, the Court has held that evidence of a person's refusal to submit to a blood-alcohol test can be offered against him or her at trial, since the right of refusal is not based on any constitutional ground. (*South Dakota* v. *Neville,* 459 U.S. 553 (1983); see also *United States* v. *Jacobowitz,* 877 F. 2d 162 (2d Cir. 1989)(since a handwriting exemplar can properly be compelled, a defendant's refusal to comply may constitute circumstantial evidence of guilt); compare *Griffin* v. *California,* 380 U.S. 609 (1965)(prosecution cannot comment on defendant's refusal to take the witness stand, since this is a defendant's constitutional right under the Fifth Amendment).)

Drug-Testing Methodology

A vital element in any prosecution for the possession or sale of an illegal drug is proof that the substance which the accused allegedly possessed or sold was an unlawful drug. Law enforcement officers are not directly involved in the development of this proof since this element of the prosecution's case is established by laboratory analysis. At trial the prosecuting attorney will find it necessary, in the absence of a stipulation by defense counsel, to produce a forensic analyst who can accurately describe the methodology leading to his or her identification of the substance in question as an illicit drug.

A number of testing methods are available in the drug field. The most basic are:

1. Color Tests
   a. Spot tests
      i. Single color tests (cobalt thiocynate test, p-Dimethylamino-benzaldehyde test [oddly enough, this is usually referred to simply as the p-DMAB test!]; and Zwikker's alkaline cobalt test)
      ii. Multiple color tests (Frohde Test; Marquis Test; Mecke Test)
   b. Duquenois-Levine Test (a color test for hashish and marijuana)
2. Chromatography
   a. Thin-layer chromatography (TLC)
   b. Gas chromatography
3. Spectrophotometric Methods of Measurement and Identification
   a. Visible spectrophotometry
   b. Ultraviolet spectrophotometry
   c. Infrared spectroscopy
   d. Fluorescence analysis
   e. Nuclear magnetic resonance spectroscopy
   f. Mass spectrometry
4. The Microcrystal Test
5. The Melting-Point and Mixed Melting-Point Tests
6. Immunoassay Techniques

This is not the place to describe in detail the methodology involved in all of the testing procedures named above. (For a full but understandable description of how these tests function, see Stein, Laessig and Indriksons, *An Evaluation of Drug Testing Procedures Used by Forensic Laboratories and the Qualifications of Their Analysts,* 1973 Wisconsin Law Rev. 727 (1973).) A few commonly used techniques will be described here.

Amphetamines, such as Methedrine (stimulants, "uppers"), can be identified through microscopy. One or two milligrams of a concentrated solution are placed on a slide with a drop of 5 percent aqueous gold chloride. The slide is examined under 100-power magnification. Amphetamine crystals will appear as square, yellow forms.

The most common test for barbiturates ("downers") is the Koppanyi test, which is a color test. Cocaine is quite easily recognized in its crystal form. Its characteristic crystalline configurations appear as a series of fine projections at right angles on one side of the long axis. Color tests, using chemical reagents, are also available, as are animal reaction tests (placing a drop of cocaine solution in a cat's eye will cause rapid dilation). A peppermint odor produced by sulfuric acid testing provides confirmation.

A not altogether satisfactory color test is standard procedure for classifying lysergic acid diethylamide (LSD). Most experts consider the test inconclusive. A more highly regarded test for LSD involves infrared spectrophotometry. The suspect sample and a standard sample are both put in individual alcohol solutions and are then evaporated. The residues are treated with a few milliliters of heptane-chloroform mixture. When both solutions are evaporated the residues are transferred to a sodium chloride disk. The infrared spectra produced are then measured and compared. If the suspect sample has a spectrum virtually identical to the standard LSD spectra, the sample is concluded to be LSD.

Federal narcotics authorities use the Duquenois-Levine method for identifying marijuana. This, again, is a color test. Microscopic tests are also available for marijuana.

There are many widely accepted tests for identifying the opiates, such as heroin and morphine; for example, the so-called Marquis test, another color test. The color reaction to heroin of a solution of 40 drops of formaldehyde and 60 cubic centimeters of concentrated sulfuric acid is a purplish-red to red-violet. These tests are not entirely satisfactory; microscopic identification is considered preferable. At the time of arrest, saliva and urine tests can supply circumstantial proof of opiate use. The saliva or urine is injected under the skin of a laboratory rat; if an opiate is present, the rat's tail will take on an "S" shape.

However, this test cannot distinguish between the different opiates; the same "S" shape will be caused by morphine, heroin, or any other alkaloidal narcotic.

The Nalline test is frequently used by the prosecution in opiate drug cases. A physician uses Nalline, which is a synthetic, nonaddictive drug, to detect opiate use by examining the pupils of the suspect's eyes. The suspect is placed in a special type of chair and the examining physician employs a card with a series of dots on it (the "pupillometer") to measure the size of the pupil. Then three milligrams of Nalline are injected under the skin. In half an hour the subject's pupils are again measured. If the defendant has not been using an opiate, the diameter of his pupils will be smaller than before. If he has used opiates occasionally, his pupils will still be approximately the same size as before. If he is an addict, his pupils will enlarge from 0.5 to 2 millimeters, depending on the level of his addiction.

In *People* v. *Williams,* 331 P. 2d 251 (Cal. App. 1958), the accused, charged with using opiates, challenged the admission of the results of a Nalline test administered to him. On cross-examination the prosecution's medical experts conceded that the medical profession generally was not familiar with the use of Nalline and that it therefore could not accurately be said that the Nalline test had met with general acceptance by the medical profession as a whole. However, the California court held that the prosecution's medical testimony was strongly supportive of reliability. Familiarity with the testing method by the entire medical profession was not considered essential by the court. Furthermore, a section of the California Health and Safety Code had expressly given evidentiary value to the Nalline test.

Expert Testimony in Narcotics Cases

Scientific evidence is ordinarily introduced through the testimony of expert witnesses. (See chapter 17, *Opinion, Expertise, and Experts*). Narcotics cases are typical.

EXAMPLE A:
[The preliminary questioning, establishing the witness's qualifications as an expert, is omitted here. See chapter 17.]
BY THE PROSECUTING ATTORNEY: Doctor Faust, would you tell the court and jury the correct chemical name for what we call heroin?
A: Yes, it is acetomorphine or diacetylmorphine.
Q: Is there an established method of testing for it?
A: Yes, there is. It is called the Marquis test.
Q: Would you describe it please?
A: The Marquis test uses a chemical reagent . . .
Q: Excuse me, Doctor, but would you explain what a reagent is?
A: A reagent is a substance that is useful in detecting the presence of some other substance—in this case, heroin—because it reacts chemically to it.

Q: Thank you. Go ahead, please.

A: In the Marquis test that I mentioned the reagent is 16 milliliters of formaldehyde and 984 milliliters of sulfuric acid. You put a small amount of the suspected material, the suspected heroin, on a porcelain spot plate. Then you add a drop of the Marquis reagent that I've described. You observe the color that is first formed and then you watch the changing of this first color to another color.

Q: What colors do you get?

A: Heroin gives a purplish-red or a red-violet color.

Q: Do other compounds give off this color?

A: Oh, yes, quite a few.

Q: What tests, if any, are used to distinguish between heroin and other compounds?

A: Well, there are so-called spot tests, ultraviolet spectrometry, gas chromatography, thin-layer chromatography. These are non-specific tests but they are used to make tentative identification. Then positive identification of heroin can be accomplished by comparing the purified suspicious material with a known standard or sample. This involves a variety of tests, which I can explain if you want me to.

Q: Just give us their names, Doctor.

A: Mixed melting-point plus matched nuclear magnetic resonance spectra, or mixed melting-point plus superimposable infrared spectra, or mixed melting-point plus a mass spectrum, or you can have a combination of these tests and others.

EXAMPLE B:

[Again the preliminary questioning is omitted.]

BY THE PROSECUTING ATTORNEY: Doctor Faust, are you familiar with the compound known as LSD?

A: I am.

Q: It is technically known as lysergic acid diethylamide?

A: That is correct.

Q: And also commonly known as "acid"?

A: Yes.

Q: Doctor, what is an isomer?

A: The term applies to the phenomena in which two or more chemical compounds have the same molecular formula but differ in their atomic structure, with the result that they have different properties.

Q: How many isomers of LSD are there?

A: Four.

Q: What are we concerned with in this case?

A: Dextro-LSD.

Q: How do you distinguish this isomer or compound from others?

A: With the ORD test, which stands for optical rotary dispersion, or infrared analysis. Infrared analysis is definitive.

Cross-examination of an expert witness in a narcotics case might proceed in the following fashion:

BY DEFENSE COUNSEL: Doctor Faust, I understand that the police gave you four bags of material to test, is that right?
A: Yes, it is.
Q: Did you test the entire contents of those four bags?
A: Just samples from each one.
Q: And then what did you do with the bags?
A: Gave them back to the police.
Q: Ever see them again?
A: No.
Q: Do you still have the samples that you took from them?
A: No, I don't.
Q: Did you have any left over after your testing?
A: Probably.
Q: Well, what happened to it?
A: I would have destroyed it.
Q: So there is no way that an expert engaged by the defendant in this case could duplicate the tests that you performed?
A: That's right, I suppose.
Q: In doing your testing did you have to rely on any published sources?
A: Yes, I use *Methods of Analysis for Alkaloids, Opiates, Marijuana, Barbiturates, and Miscellaneous Drugs.*
Q: Who puts that out?
A: The Internal Revenue Service.
Q: Can you give us the name of the author?
A: No, I can't.
Q: So you wouldn't know what kind of training the author had, if any?
A: No.
Q: On your direct examination you spoke of running a spectrophotometer, did you not?
A: Yes, sir.
Q: Do you have the results of the testing procedure with you?
A: Yes, sir.
Q: You are handing me some graphs, is that right?
A: Yes, graphics.
Q: What do they do for you?
A: See the peaks? By seeing where the peak is, we can tell whether what we've got is morphine or heroin or whatever.

Q: But these graphs show different peaks, don't they?
A: Of course. The heroin content differed from bag to bag.
Q: I see. You would have to have special training to read these graphs then?
A: Surely.
Q: If I show you some different graphs could you read them for the court and jury?
A: I'd have to have something to compare them with or I couldn't.
Q: So these graphs, by themselves, tell you nothing?
A: Standing alone, that's right.
Q: And you threw away the samples?
A: Yes, I did.

The Necessity of a Comparative Testing Process in Narcotics Cases

Positive identification of a questioned substance can be made only by comparing the results of a given test on the unknown sample with the results obtained from the same test on a known sample. In other words, the testing procedures which are catalogued earlier in this section, a few of them thereafter being briefly described, do not produce conclusive results when applied only to an unknown substance; a comparative process is essential.

Specific Versus Nonspecific Narcotics Tests

Some of the tests listed earlier are *specific:* that is to say, they measure properties of chemical compounds that are unique to each compound. While it is perhaps going too far to say that these tests are conclusive, it is fair to suggest that they are highly reliable indicators of a particular unknown substance's identity as an illicit drug. (Specific tests include infrared spectroscopy, nuclear magnetic resonance spectroscopy, mass spectroscopy, and mixed melting-point.)

Other tests listed above are *nonspecific.* They cannot be considered as conclusive proof of the identity of an unknown substance since numerous innocent substances can produce indistinguishable results. (Nonspecific tests include spot tests, thin-layer chromatography, gas chromatography, ultraviolet spectroscopy, melting-point, and fluorescence spectroscopy.)

It will be observed that none of the procedures described in this section is suitable for on-scene testing. As the problem of drug use by the drivers of vehicles increases, as it plainly is, the need for new testing techniques will become acute.

D. Forensic Pathology

The Forensic Pathologist's Role in Criminal Matters; In General

Pathology, once restricted to a study of the effects of disease, today encompasses not only the structural changes brought about by disease but also bacteriology and laboratory examination of samples (blood, spinal fluid, etc.) which have been removed from the body.

A pathologist will have had at least five years of specialized training on top of his or her medical school education and licensure as a medical doctor. Certification in the field of forensic pathology is granted, after an examination, by the American Board of Pathology. A prerequisite of certification is at least one year of active experience in the official investigation of violent and suspicious deaths.

Forensic pathology has played a significant role in criminal prosecutions for many years. Expert pathological investigation can illuminate half a dozen cause-and-effect issues:

1. Cause of death (violent or natural causes?)
2. Suicide or homicide
3. Estimated time of death
4. Type of weapon
5. Deceased's identity
6. The possible complicating involvement of disease or trauma

Post-mortem Determinations (Autopsies)

Often a key function of the pathologist, whether he or she is a medical examiner or a member of the coroner's staff, is the performance of post-mortem determinations—autopsies.

An autopsy is a comprehensive study of a dead body, performed by a trained physician employing recognized dissection procedures and techniques. Although nonofficial autopsies are authorized in a number of situations, our concern here is with official autopsies, the most common purpose of which is determination of the cause or causes of death. In cases of death by violence or poisoning, obviously, such a determination may be crucial to a question of possible criminal conduct.

It is a general but not unvarying rule that a surviving spouse or the next of kin has the legal power to grant or deny authority for an autopsy. Like all general precepts, however, this one has its exceptions. As one court has remarked, "The right to have a dead body remain unmolested is not an absolute one; it must yield where it conflicts with the public good or where the demands of justice require such subordination." (*Stasny* v. *Tachovsky,* 132 N.W. 2d 317 (S. Ct. Nebr. 1964).) The demands of justice—that there be as few "perfect" (that is, undetected) criminal homicides as possible—have inspired the enactment in every state of statutes permitting a coroner or medical examiner to perform an autopsy when death was caused by casualty or violence or when there exist reasonable grounds for concluding that one of these contributive factors was present. Statutory authorization to conduct an autopsy carries with it an implied power to remove from the cadaver anything that is essential for purposes of examination; blood samples, for example.

In some states the coroner or medical examiner is required to convene an inquest before autopsy will be proper; in others he is free to act on his own initiative. His or her role in criminal matters can be of the greatest importance. A discouraging case in point occurred following the assassination of President John F. Kennedy. It is possible that some of the more fantastic theories surrounding that event would have been obviated had the staff of the local Dallas, Texas, medical examiner been permitted to conduct a prompt and careful autopsy prior to the return of the deceased president's body to Washington, D.C.

The Physician Untrained in Forensic Pathology

Sometimes the physician who examines a dead body is not specially trained in forensic pathology. All too often a physician without this special training is requested to look at a dead body and tell the police how long it has been dead, or how long the person lived after sustaining injury. This is a risky process.

Any physician who ventures to answer such questions after merely viewing the body or making a cursory examination of it risks the possibility of a subsequent disclosure of gross error. Moreover, an inaccurate time-of-death estimate can have a seriously misleading effect on a police investigation. For example, if a physician gives an opinion that the body has been dead for twelve hours, or three days, or for some other explicit period of time, or that the cause of death (stabbing, shooting, etc.) occurred at a specific time prior to death, police investigators may erroneously eliminate from suspect consideration a guilty person who was nowhere near the deceased at the incorrectly estimated time of death or injury.

Even the most highly qualified forensic pathologist will avoid guesswork of the sort mentioned in the last paragraph. The forensic pathologist also understands that in many instances an estimate is impermissible and would be ruled inadmissible at a trial, even though a complete autopsy and various laboratory tests were conducted.

A reliable estimate of post-mortem interval, or of the elapsed time between injury and death, can seldom be made on medical evidence alone. Ordinarily required is the existence of a number of factors, both medical and circumstantial. This has been called the *association method.* For example, in attempting to estimate post-mortem interval, or the elapsed time between physical incapacitation and death, where time in terms of days is involved, the medical examiner or other investigator must take into account such nonmedical and unspectacular events as the date when the last newspaper or milk bottle was delivered at the deceased person's residence. This information can then be correlated with the time-of-death indications revealed by a medical determination of the state of digestion of stomach contents, the stage of body deterioration, and the like.

It is worth mentioning here that a body condition which can be seriously misinterpreted by a physician untrained in forensic pathology is the presence or absence of *rigor mortis*. The onset and disappearance of *rigor mortis* are dependent upon a number of factors; for example, environmental and internal body temperatures (heat will accentuate both onset and disappearance); the presence or absence of physical activity at the time of death (activity increases the onset); and muscular condition of the deceased (onset is delayed in a muscular person).

For an extensive bibliography dealing with estimation of time of death and of the interval between occurrence of injury and death, consult WALTZ & INBAU, MEDICAL JURISPRUDENCE 356-360 (1971).

Autopsy Reports

Autopsy reports are often generated at the very time the pathologist is conducting the autopsy; the pathologist dictates a description of findings as he or she proceeds and often calls for the taking of photographs of noteworthy aspects of the body being examined. Later the dictated notes are worked into a formal report.

A standard autopsy report will at minimum contain the following supportive data:

1. *A general description of the deceased*
   a. Sex
   b. Age
   c. Race
   d. Frame (including stature, musculature, nutrition)
   e. Distinguishing characteristics (including hair distribution, scars, tattoos, and the like)
2. *Signs of death*
   a. *Rigor Mortis*
   b. Lividity
   c. Heat loss
   d. Decomposition
3. *External examination* of head, trunk, extremities, and genitalia (including an examination of any external wounds and a charting of the internal course of such wounds)
4. *Internal examination* of the organ systems, the stomach and its contents, rectum, small intestines, genitalia, spinal cord, neck, head, heart and major vessels

It is on the foregoing types of data that the pathologic diagnoses, often spelled out on the covering page of the autopsy report, are based.

The Medical Practitioner and Physical Evidence in Criminal Cases

It will be helpful for agents of law enforcement to have a reasonably clear understanding of the medical practitioner's role in criminal matters, and especially the physician's contact with physical evidence. There will be occasions when the trained criminal investigator has a better appreciation than most physicians of the way physical evidence should be handled by the medical practitioner. There may even be times when those in charge of a criminal investigation can diplomatically impress upon the physician, if he is known to be inexperienced in dealing with criminal matters or untrained in forensic pathology, the need for special care in the handling of any physical evidence that he may encounter during his ministrations or post-mortem examination. It should be emphasized that, in handling tangible evidence, criminal investigators should themselves emulate the procedures recommended for medical practitioners in so far as the opportunity presents itself.

The following discussion of the medical practitioner's obligations relating to physical evidence in criminal cases is drawn in large part from WALTZ & INBAU, MEDICAL JURISPRUDENCE 329-353 (1971).

The traditional role of most physicians involves diagnosis, treatment, and prognosis. The physician is comfortable in this role and tends to view any unrelated responsibility as an unjustified encroachment on his or her time and energy. Nevertheless, the physician will occasionally find himself in a professional situation that is not of an exclusively medical nature. This will happen whenever he is the physician attending the victim of a criminal offense or of an accident that has possible criminal implications.

There are occasions when a physician will be the only person who can adequately observe the fresh, unaltered wounds caused by firearms, knives, or other objects. Police investigators will have to rely on the physician for accurate observation and documentation of the nature and characteristics of such wounds and the proper collection and preservation of tangible criminal evidence. It is therefore relevant here to mention some of the evidentiary problems that may be encountered by police investigators when a physician lacking special training in the handling of criminal matters has examined a wound.

A proper examination and documentation of a wound may reveal the nature of the wound-inflicting object, the direction of force, the approximate time lapse between the infliction of the wound and the physician's observations, and other matters significant to criminal investigators. The proper collection and preservation of any physical evidence the physician can obtain may be vital in a later prosecution of the person responsible for the injury. Criminal investigators realize that in all of this the physician's cooperation is crucial.

The medical practitioner often fails to record what he sees at the time of an examination of a patient. He is usually preoccupied with diagnosis and treatment and may feel that written or other documentation is of secondary importance. In this he is quite correct; documentation must come second to the saving of the patient's life and to prompt and efficient treatment of his traumatic problems. But frequently a physician, after his completion of therapeutic efforts, will either deliberately or inadvertently neglect to document what he has seen. He may harbor a concern about "getting involved" in a police matter, especially one that may culminate in a trial. As a consequence, he may deliberately avoid recording observations of vital significance to criminal investigators. At other times a physician who is not attached to a police department may simply neglect even to consider the importance of documentation and either omit it completely or else perform it inadequately.

In cases involving patients who have been wounded by someone else, the physician has a moral and social obligation, and also sometimes a legal duty, to document the nature and extent of the wound to the best of his or her ability. The doctor should note, sketch, diagram, or perhaps even have a photograph made of the wound so long as such efforts will not adversely affect diagnosis, therapy, or the outcome of the patient's traumatic disability. Whenever the welfare of the patient is no longer a pressing consideration, there can be no justification for omitting proper documentation and a failure to do so is a breach of the physician's obligation to the patient and to the public. Occasionally spokespersons for law enforcement agencies have an opportunity to impress this fact on medical groups.

Although documentation is imperative, a risk is incurred any time the physician exceeds that responsibility and ventures into the area of interpretation of his own recorded observation. If he lacks the benefit of special training in such matters, or has no opportunity for a visual internal examination of the wounded patient, he may reach an erroneous conclusion. The physician's job is documentation, not interpretation. The latter must be left to the expert in traumatic injuries, such as a pathologist. Nothing is more disconcerting to law enforcement officers, and occasionally to the courts, than having to contend with an inadequate or improper interpretation by a physician who is not adequately qualified for the task.

EXAMPLE:
The difficulty of distinguishing between an entrance and an exit bullet wound is often great. Accurately distinguishing between the two is a hazardous task for the unqualified observer.

The need for documentation of an external wound prior to any alteration by therapeutic efforts arose at the time of President John F. Kennedy's assassination. If proper notation had been made of the exit (outshoot) bullet wound in the front of the president's neck prior to the making of a tracheotomy incision, much subsequent confusion concerning the course of the bullet would have been avoided.

EXAMPLE:
Scrubbing the skin surface around a bullet wound can destroy the only means of later establishing facts such as the approximate distance from which a bullet wound was inflicted. A reliable conclusion of suicide or murder may depend on a proper documentation of physical evidence of this type.

It is not enough for the examining and treating medical practitioner merely to make note of, or in some other way document, the nature and area of the wound itself. Other parts of the body should also be scrutinized and appropriate documentation made of anything out of the ordinary.

EXAMPLE:
Clyde Bushmat committed suicide by holding a pistol against his right temple with his left hand and pulling the trigger with a finger on his right hand. Documentation of the blood on Bushman's left hand will be important in establishing the fact of suicide.

Whenever it is necessary for a physician to extract a bullet from a patient's body, he or she should exercise caution to avoid a mutilation of the bullet or bullet fragments, since the gun barrel impressions on a bullet or bullet fragment may serve to identify the weapon from which it was fired. (See section J of this chapter on firearms identification.)

EXAMPLE:
Surgeons use instruments as extensions of their fingers and most surgical procedures are performed without the surgeon's fingers ever touching the body tissues in any significant measure. It is, therefore, a natural action for the surgeon to remove bullets with forceps and surgical clamps. But, in general, bullets fired from rifled arms are composed of a soft lead alloy and surgical forceps or clamps may damage the bullet to such an extent as to destroy its value as a means of firearms identification. This kind of bullet mutilation may deprive the police and prosecution of an indispensable item of evidence establishing the guilt of the assailant or killer.

It follows that physicians should be advised that whenever possible, under conditions that will not impair the patient's welfare, bullets should be removed with the fingers or by the use of a clamp having jaws that are covered with rubber tubing. (For a good illustration of the damage that a surgical removal process can cause to the surface of a bullet, see WALTZ & INBAU, MEDICAL JURISPRUDENCE 335, Fig. 5 (1971).)

Subsequent to the proper removal of a bullet from a gunshot victim, the bullet should be placed on a piece of gauze and left within sight of the surgeon or other assistant or staff member who may later arrange for its preservation as evidence. Then, when circumstances permit, the bullet should be labeled and stored in a secure place. A removed bullet should be marked with an identifying set of letters and, in some instances, with numbers as well. The surgeon, preferably, should do this himself. However, any assistant, staff member, or criminal investigator who witnessed its removal would be a satisfactory substitute. The important thing is that the markings be placed on the removed bullet by someone who can later tell the police (if they were not present at the removal) and perhaps a judge and jury that, on the basis of his identifying markings, the bullet is the one he saw removed from the victim's body.

In some instances it may be of importance also to state from which part of the body, or from which internal organ, the bullet was extracted. This is one reason that the surgeon or an assisting physician is the preferred person for identification purposes whenever there is any indication that such details may be of some future value. Ordinarily, however, where the precise cause of death is not an issue and the only fact that need be proved is that "this is the bullet that was removed from the body," any witness to the bullet's removal will suffice. Perhaps the most cautious procedure is to have the surgeon place his marking on the bullet while one or two other persons witness his markings and make their own records of what those markings were, the date and place of removal, the victim's name, and the like. In this way a prosecuting attorney will not have to rely on one person alone as an identifying witness; he or she can summon the one on whom a courtroom appearance would impose the least inconvenience.

The experienced criminal investigator knows, and perhaps can advise the medical practitioner, that a removed bullet should be marked with an identifying set of numbers or letters at the bullet's base, or perhaps its nose, but never on the circular surface bearing the gun barrel impressions. Then the bullet should be placed in a suitable envelope and sealed by the individual referred to in the last paragraph or by some other witness to the removal and marking. The person sealing the envelope should write his or her name or initials across the sealed flap of the envelope.

If more than one bullet (or, for that matter, any other foreign object) has been removed from a victim's body or found in or about his or her clothing, each one should be marked and placed in a separate envelope. On the outside of each envelope should be noted the location where its contents were found, either inside or outside the body. The location should be indicated by a number on the base or nose of the bullet, and then this location-identifying number can be noted in a record book kept by the physician or some other witness to its removal. At a later time the matter of location may become crucial, especially when it is necessary to determine whether the particular bullet was the actual cause of death.

Bullets preserved as suggested above should be placed in a locked container by the same person who handled the evidence from the very beginning.

By confining these various procedures to one person, the need for the courtroom appearance of other chain-of-custody or tracing-the-evidence witnesses can be avoided.

In addition to bullets, other foreign objects removed from a patient can be significant in the investigation of criminal cases.

EXAMPLE A:
Three shotgun wads, several pellets, and the inner lining of a shotgun shell were recovered from a debridement of the shoulder of a shotgun blast victim. From the wads the gauge of the shotgun was determined; from the inner lining of the shell, blown into the shoulder muscles, the police were able to ascertain the specific type of ammunition involved. This information enabled the investigating officers to determine which of two possible assailants, each armed with a shotgun, actually fired the shot in question.

EXAMPLE B:
A piece of plastic tablecloth was removed from the depths of an abdominal wound. Criminal investigators were able to establish from this evidence that an assault victim had fallen across a glass-topped table, shattering it and injuring himself.

When the time comes for a physician or other person to turn over bullets or other small foreign objects to the police, an outer and larger envelope should be used as the container for all of the small ones. The large envelope, too, should be sealed, with the sealer's name or initials written by him across the sealed flap. When evidence of this sort is relinquished to the police, a receipt can be supplied to the witness with instructions that he or she preserve it in the files along with other records in the case.

The clothing worn by victims of accidents, criminal homicides, and suicides may be of utmost importance in the investigation of criminal cases and in criminal trials. It would be ideal if clothing worn by accident and crime victims could be gently removed without tearing or cutting. However, it is recognized that in many circumstances speedy removal is required in order to expose body areas involved by trauma. Consequently, cutting or tearing away of the clothing is considered an acceptable practice by physicians. Nevertheless, whenever it is possible to do so without impinging upon the physician's primary responsibility to the patient, the clothing should be cut or torn in an area *away* from any bullet hole or any wound caused by knives or other instrumentalities or objects. A preferred area is along a seam in the garment.

Clothing removed from the victim of a possible crime should not be thrown on the ground or floor or otherwise discarded or destroyed. A simple example of the inadvisability of this is the victim of a hit-and-run automobile accident. A torn piece of clothing lodged in the undercarriage of a suspected vehicle may be matched with a torn area in the clothing of the victim.

Removed articles of clothing should be handled as little as possible and without any deliberate shaking or dusting. They should be placed in *clean* plastic bags or other suitable *clean* containers. Separate bags or containers should be used for each article, and all the bags or containers must be properly labeled.

Gastric washings and specimens of blood, urine, or other substances removed from a patient require the same careful attention for criminal case investigation purposes as was previously recommended with respect to bullets and other objects. Their handling, labeling, and preservation can be crucial.

In suspected poisoning cases, vomitus and gastric washings should be preserved. Nothing should be discarded. All too frequently, multiple stomach washings collected from a patient who has ingested a poison are thrown together and a sample of this mixed washing is all that the toxicologist receives for analysis. Even when several washings are preserved separately, if they are not labeled to establish sequence it will be impossible to determine which was obtained first and, therefore, which has the greatest potential for recovery of the toxic material.

Blood specimens taken in suspected poisoning cases also require special attention if the physician is to aid rather than hinder the police investigation. Frequently the first specimen of blood obtained in an emergency situation is one for typing of the patient for possible blood transfusion. After several hours of observation, the subject is now thought to be the victim of an overdose of a toxic substance and blood is obtained at this time for toxicological examination. The several hours that elapsed between the time the first sample of blood was drawn for blood typing and the time that poisoning was suspected and a sample of blood drawn for toxicological analysis may have given the body sufficient time to metabolize (absorb) the toxic substance. The first sample of blood would be much more likely to contain a measurable quantity of the poison than the second sample, but this is frequently overlooked by the physician and the opportunity for toxicological proof of the poisoning is lost.

There are occasions when the police may wish to have blood samples taken from an injured person for the purpose of chemical tests for alcoholic intoxication. Many physicians are reluctant to comply, out of concern that they may not legally do so. In almost all cases, however, there is a legal justification for the extraction of blood for medical purposes—for example, blood typing for possible transfusions—and there is no sound reason that some of the blood sample should not be turned over to the police for the auxiliary purpose of chemical testing for alcoholic intoxication and for blood grouping tests in effecting comparisons with blood on weapons or on a suspect's clothing or on other objects.

In certain sorts of criminal cases, especially sex crimes, the police investigators will be interested in vaginal smears as well as oral and rectal smears from the victim for crime laboratory examination purposes. They may also want to have specimens of pubic as well as head hair for possible comparison with loose hair found on a suspect. Fingernail clippings will also be desired for examination of blood, body tissue, or other material that the victim may have picked up in the process of resisting the attacker. As to all of this the physician should be requested to give his or her full cooperation. When the specimens are obtained, they should be labeled and preserved.

The same documentation procedures should be employed with respect to crime victims who are already dead when the physician first sees them and when no medical examiner or coroner facilities are available and the procurement and the preservation of evidence rest solely upon the medical practitioner. Where medical examiner or coroner facilities are available, the body should be left undisturbed until the arrival of members of the staff of either office.

X-rays taken on an emergency basis (and an emergency is involved in most of the types of cases that are the subject of this discussion) are usually not labeled properly; indeed, they may not even be identified or dated in any way. Many are the instances when X-rays taken under emergency conditions have been lost, mislaid, misfiled, or otherwise made unavailable for future use simply because they were not properly labeled. The crucial evidence needed in a subsequent court trial may have been lost forever. A physician can render a valuable public service, therefore, by suggesting to the X-ray technician that a proper documentation be made in order to preserve the value of the X-ray as evidence. Criminal investigators can properly suggest to the physician, if there is an opportunity to do so, that he or she make this suggestion to the X-ray technician.

Whenever a physician indulges in therapeutic efforts on a shotgun or stabbing victim that leave markings which may be confused later on with the effects of the criminally inflicted injuries, he should be advised to be particularly careful to document that fact. For instance, if a surgical "stab wound" is made in the thoracic area for the purpose of draining the pleural cavities, that wound may be externally indistinguishable from one made with criminal intent.

Large trocars used for the purpose of therapy might leave skin defects that could be mistaken for gunshot wounds, so far as external appearances are concerned. If surgical wounds are made, adequate documentation of their location and nature must be made by the physician in his own records or on the hospital chart so as to prevent confusion if the patient should expire and an autopsy be undertaken by a physician unfamiliar with the particular case.

A careless manipulation of a patient's body, or the body of a person killed by bullet wounding, may result in the loss of crucial evidence. The reader may recall that one of the bullets fired by President John F. Kennedy's assassin was found on a hospital stretcher without anyone having observed how it got there. Had his assassin been brought to trial, considerable difficulty might have been encountered in authenticating the exhibit for courtroom use.

It is important for medical-legal purposes that the physician guard against rough handling of a patient who has been the victim of a shooting, stabbing, or other such wound infliction. In addition, it would be well to have a covering sheet or plastic cloth placed under and about the victim's body at all times, particularly during any movement of the body. Moreover, the sheet or plastic cloth itself should be preserved for the police investigators, in order that they may recover whatever evidence may have been deposited upon it. This will afford protection against the loss of valuable evidence.

There is an adage in homicide investigation that states: "If the visible wounds do not seem to account for death, look in other areas where a wound may be hidden." This holds true in clinical medicine also. The medical practitioner should be reminded that wounds may be present in hard-to-examine areas such as the scalp, axilla, and perineal regions and that wounds in these regions may be responsible for the patient's problem. If the physician fails to recognize this, treatment may be directed only toward the less severe wounds found in areas most likely to be examined by the physician.

When death occurs to a crime victim or to a victim of an accident with possible criminal implications, particular care should be taken to leave endotracheal tubes, drains, and other paraphernalia attached to or within the several orifices of the body. It may be of utmost importance, for example, to know where the distal end of the endotracheal tube is in relation to the carinas of the main-stem bronchi. Of equal importance is the placement of nasogastric tubes and nasal catheters. Tubing and other apparatus left in place will be of great significance in the interpretation of the death when the autopsy is commenced.

Once death has occurred there should be no probing of gunshot or stab wounds. Probing will not clearly establish the wound track, and it may easily create false and misleading passages. It is also highly *inadvisable* for an attending physician to perform a "mini-autopsy" for the purpose of ascertaining the cause of death. First of all, in the particular state where he is practicing he may lack legal authorization to do so, either with or without the consent of relatives of the deceased. In any event, the autopsy function should be left for the medical-legal expert in the office of the medical examiner or coroner.

Among the many difficulties encountered by the forensic pathologist in his or her efforts to arrive at a satisfactory diagnosis as to the precise cause of a crime victim's death is the interpretation of the written records made by physicians and hospital staff following hospitalization or the death of the patient.

Probably the single most neglected item in the hospital chart is the dating and timing of notes made by the physician. As if this were not confusing enough, frequently the notes are found on several pages in the record and these are not arranged in any orderly, chronological fashion.

The time and energy required to insert the date and time of the note entry constitute a very slight burden, whereas the time and energy required to interpret undated and untimed notes may be considerable. Moreover, in many instances a determination of date and time may be impossible, particularly in view of the rapid changeover in hospital physician populations. Physicians can sometimes be diplomatically advised of this problem.

A second problem that is frequently encountered with hospital records is that there are no notes dealing with the therapy rendered the patient. If the hospital is one that requires notes to be made by the nursing staff, it may be possible to rectify this omission by examination of the nurses' notes. When such nursing notes are not provided, however, it is an impossible task to reconstruct properly the therapeutic endeavors of the physician unless he himself provides written notes regarding them.

Whenever possible, consistent with the welfare of the patient, a physician should cooperate with the police in their need to talk to the patient. All too often a physician either will flatly refuse police permission to do so, or else will be overly cautious about the time when he will authorize the patient-police contact. Most law enforcement officials recognize that the patient must not be exposed to early or too intense interrogation. They would be the first not to want to endanger the patient's recovery by virtue of prolonged questioning. Indeed, it is not in the best interest of law enforcement officers to push the patient farther than his or her physical stamina will allow. In the long run, the interests of justice would only be jeopardized by doing so. The overprotectiveness sometimes exhibited by physicians and the apparent guarding of their patients to prevent police questioning is genuinely reprehensible.

Physicians should realize that ultimately the police will have access to the patient anyway, and they should endeavor to cooperate with law enforcement officials as soon as it appears that questioning will not adversely affect the condition of the patient. The earlier the police can talk to a crime victim, the sooner they can embark upon a search for the offender and for the required evidence of guilt.

Pathological Findings and Opinions as Evidence

Evidence of pathological findings and their significance must come from witnesses who are expert in the field, since lay jurors lack the ability to comprehend pathological data. This does not necessarily mean that the witness must be a specializing pathologist, however. It has frequently been held that a general physician can testify to the cause of death. But many authorities disagree with the approach taken by these courts and suggest that in this age of specialization the minimum requirement to qualify as an expert witness on pathological findings should be nothing less than board certification as a pathologist when these findings are strictly within the pathologist's—as opposed to another medical specialist's field.

E. Photographic Evidence, Motion Pictures, and Videotape

The History and Uses of Photographic Evidence in Criminal Cases

This is not the sort of book in which to describe in exhaustive detail the theory and practice of photography, but it is not a bad place to reiterate the remark that in criminal litigation, as elsewhere, one picture is often worth ten thousand words. Over the years the importance of photography in making the facts of criminal cases comprehensible to lay jurors has increased dramatically.

Today the use of photographic techniques, from the simple to the sophisticated, is a commonplace criminal courtroom occurrence. Still photographs, both black and white and color, are used for identification purposes, to depict crime scenes and accident sites, to show firearm and tool markings, fingerprints, handwriting, typewriting, and the like. Still photographs are also employed to portray medical-legal subjects: blood, urine, semen, toxic substances, and so on. Highly sophisticated applications of photography include infrared photography, ultraviolet, stereoscopic, photocopying, aerial photography, and motion picture photography.

Nearly every police department in the nation has some photographic equipment on hand and personnel who are qualified to make use of it; large metropolitan departments will have fully equipped and staffed photographic laboratories. These larger departments will boast patrol vehicles that include cameras among their equipment, special accident-investigation vehicles, and trucks or station wagons fitted out as field crime investigation laboratories. A well-trained police photographer can authenticate his or her photographs in court and generally is an impressive prosecution witness.

It was in 1839 that a French painter named Jacques Daguerre revealed his invention of a photographic process that came to be known as daguerreotypy. It had its flaws, but many of them were rapidly overcome. In 1839 a husband obtained a divorce on the bases of a compromising photograph of his wife. Within less than a year a German medical student, Albrecht Breyer, was able to copy the pages of medical books by putting them in contact with light-sensitive materials. By 1843 post-arrest identification photographs of the sort we now call mug shots were being taken in Belgium.

The American beginnings of legal photography probably start with *Luco* v. *United States,* 64 U.S. 515 (1859). The case involved a claim based on a land grant. The Government contended that the title document was a forgery. Although originals had been used at the trial level, before the Supreme Court the Government presented photographs, saying "By the employment of the beautiful art of photography, this tribunal can examine the assailed title, and contrast it with papers of undoubted genuineness, with the same certainty as if all the originals were present, and with even more convenience and satisfaction. . . ." The Court accepted the Government's invitation. Mr. Justice Grier wrote, "We have ourselves been able to compare these signatures by means of photographic copies, and fully concur . . . that the seal and the signatures . . . on this instrument are forgeries."

Fresh impetus came a year later, on the eve of the war between the states. In *Marcy* v. *Barnes,* 82 Mass. 161 (Sup. Jud. Ct. Mass. 1860), photomicrographs (the court called them "magnified photographic copies") of the signature on a questioned note were admitted in evidence for comparison with concededly genuine exemplars. By 1865 photographs were being affixed to German passports. In 1866 a photograph was presented in evidence to show damage done by trespass to real property.

A case important to the criminal law was decided in 1871. In *Ruloff* v. *People,* 45 N.Y. 213 (Ct. App. N.Y. 1871), photographs of two male bodies had been taken after their recovery from a river. Trial witnesses were allowed to identify the deceased men from these photographs.

Judicial notice of the value of photography was first taken in the 1874 case of *Udderzook* v. *Commonwealth,* 76 Pa. 340 (S. Ct. Pa.), a murder case in which the victim's identity was in dispute. A photograph of the alleged victim, taken while he was alive, was allowed in evidence for identification purposes. The Pennsylvania Supreme Court said, "The process [of photography] has become one in general use, so common that we cannot refuse to take judicial cognizance of it as a proper means of producing correct likenesses."

One year after *Udderzook* a photograph of an accident site was for the first time received in evidence in an American court. Traffic in 1875 was a less complicated affair than it is today: the photograph in *Blair* v. *Inhabitants of Pelham,* 118 Mass. 420 (Sup. Jud. Ct. Mass. 1875), was one of the site of an accident in which the plaintiff, driving a horse and buggy, had been injured when he went over an unguarded embankment while trying to avoid a mud hole in the roadway. A photograph of a railroad wreck was admitted in an 1877 Iowa case; a photograph showing the victim's injuries was received in an 1879 Iowa assault case. By 1887 some banks in this country were equipped with flashlight cameras to photograph robbers.

In 1891 Thomas A. Edison revealed his invention of the kinetescope; the motion picture had arrived. In 1895 Roentgen's discoveries concerning X-rays were revealed. Firearms identification photography was used with judicial approval in 1902 (see *Commonwealth* v. *Best,* 62 N.E. 748 (Sup. Jud. Ct. Mass. 1902)). By 1907 police in Denver were photographing all persons arrested for crimes involving intoxication. Photographic speed recorders were catching violators of speed laws by 1910, the year in which the Photostat machine was invented. In 1911 the Illinois Supreme Court approved the use of fingerprinting identification photographs in *People* v. *Jennings,* 97 N.E. 1077 (S. Ct. Ill. 1911). The use of motion picture photography received the judicial stamp of approval in *Duncan* v. *Kiger,* 6 Ohio App. 57 (1916), a personal injury case in which the defendant successfully offered a motion picture of the plaintiff using his left foot more effectively than he claimed was possible.

Aerial photography from balloons was undertaken as early as 1856 in France, but the first mention of it in an American appellate court decision came in 1928 when, in *In re United New Jersey Railway & Canal Co.* v. *Golden,* 140 A. 450 (S. Ct. N.J. 1928), the exclusion of an aerial photograph was upheld for want of adequate authentication. The court in no way disapproved of the photographic technique, and today the courtroom use of aerial photographs is not unusual.

It was in 1930 that a sound motion picture of an accused's confession was first held admissible in evidence (see *Commonwealth* v. *Roller,* 100 Pa. Super. 125 (1930)). In *State* v. *Thorp,* 171 A. 633 (S. Ct. N.H. 1934), the court approved the use of infrared photographs showing footprints in blood on a linoleum floor. The photographs revealed distinctive markings on the soles of the accused's shoes. Infrared photography was also involved in *Kauffman* v. *Meyberg,* 140 P. 2d 210 (Cal. App. 1943). In that case it was employed to bring up erased handwriting on the stub of a stock certificate. In 1938, in *United States* v. *Manton,* 107 F. 2d 834 (2d Cir. 1938), involving a corrupt federal judge, the admissibility of microfilm facsimiles of checks was upheld.

Although the history of color photography can be traced back to 1861, when J. Clark Maxwell developed the three-color photographic process, the first appellate court ruling on its use came in 1943 in the case of *Green* v. *City and County of Denver,* 142 P. 2d 277 (S. Ct. Colo. 1943). In 1961 the use of a Polaroid camera, utilizing a diffusion-transfer photographic process that provides a finished photograph in less than a minute, was favorably mentioned in *Vavra* v. *State,* 343 S.W. 2d 709 (Tex. Crim. App. 1961). Two years later Polacolor film came on the market, making it possible to get a color Polaroid picture in less than a minute.

In 1965 the fully automatic electronic flash unit was introduced. It was now possible to take properly exposed strobe photographs at distances of from two to twenty feet without the necessity of changing the camera's shutter speed or lens opening. By 1967 the police of Miami, Florida, had begun making videotapes of every arrested suspect. In that same year, in Topeka, Kansas, a videotape was introduced in evidence showing the accused reliving a murder under the influence of a drug.

In the current era it is possible for one of the important authorities on legal evidence, Charles C. Scott, to say, "The wildest predictions of

Daguerre and other photographic pioneers did not foresee the important part photography would eventually play in the trial of lawsuits" (see SCOTT, PHOTOGRAPHIC EVIDENCE, 3 vols. (2d ed. 1969)). As Scott points out, "Virtually anything that can be seen and many subjects that cannot be seen can be photographed for use as evidence." Furthermore, "Astounding developments are just around the corner that are sure to lead to even greater use of photographic evidence."

The Admissibility of Photographic Evidence, in General

It is firmly established, as a general proposition, that photographic evidence (still or motion; black and white or color) is admissible in evidence if three basic conditions have been satisfactorily met:

1. The relevance of whatever the photographic evidence depicts must be demonstrated;
2. The evidence must be shown to constitute a true and accurate representation of what it depicts; and
3. The probative worth of the photographic evidence must not be outweighed by a potential for unfair prejudice stemming from its gruesome or inflammatory nature.

The authentication of photographic evidence need not be by the person who made the evidence; for example, the "sponsoring" witness for a still photograph need not be the cameraman who took the photograph. The sponsoring witness need not even have been present when the photograph was taken, so long as he or she has a basis for testifying to the accuracy of the depiction. On the other hand, the photographer may be available and, if so, can serve as a verifying witness.

EXAMPLE A:

BY THE PROSECUTING ATTORNEY: Would you give us your full name, please?

A: Irene Stitz.

[Additional preliminary questions omitted.]

. . .

Q: And how long have you lived at the Pavon Parkway exit of the Finitzo Freeway?

A: Nineteen years, ever since it was built. In fact, we were there first.

Q: Do you drive a car?

A: Yes, sir.

Q: Have you ever had occasion to drive off of the Finitzo Freeway, making use of the Pavon Parkway exit?

A: Oh, yes, often.

Q: How often, would you say, over the past nineteen years?
A: That would be hard to say. I don't know how to estimate.
Q: How many times per day, for example?
A: Once or twice.
Q: Once or twice a day for nineteen years?
A: Yes, sir.
Q: So you have used that exit thousands of times, have you not?
A: That's the way it would come out, yes.
Q: Are you or are you not familiar with the way that exit has looked over the years?
A: I am very familiar with it. I know it like the back of my hand.
Q: Good. And were you familiar with the appearance of the Pavon Parkway exit on and about the date involved in this case, which was April 1, 1989?
A: Certainly.
Q: Thank you, Ms. Stitz. I will now ask the court reporter to mark this Prosecution Exhibit Number 14, which I believe is the number we have reached. [Court reporter complies.]
Handing to you what has been marked Prosecution Exhibit Number 14, Ms. Stitz, I will ask you what it is.
A: It's a photograph of the exit we've been talking about.
Q: The Pavon Parkway exit off the Finitzo Freeway?
A: Yes, sir.
Q: Ms. Stitz, is Prosecution Exhibit 14 a true, fair, and accurate representation of what it portrays?
A: Yes, it is.
Q: And would Prosecution's 14 be a true, fair, and accurate representation of the way the Pavon Parkway exit looked to you on or about April 1, 1989?
A: Yes, sir.
Q: To your knowledge, have there been any noticeable changes or alterations to the exit since April 1, 1989?
A: There haven't been any changes at all.
BY THE PROSECUTING ATTORNEY: Thank you. Your Honor, we offer into evidence what has been marked Prosecution Exhibit Number 14, a photograph of the site.
THE COURT: It is received.

EXAMPLE B:
BY THE PROSECUTING ATTORNEY: Please give the Court and jury your name, sir.
A: Richard Kaseguma.
[Additional preliminary questions omitted.]

. . .

Q: What is your business or occupation, Mr. Kaseguma?
A: I'm a professional photographer assigned to the photo lab of the Belvedere Police Department.
Q: How long have you been a photographer for the Police Department?
A: It's nineteen years now.
Q: You have had training and experience with the use of various types of cameras and other photographic equipment?
A: Yes, indeed.
BY DEFENSE COUNSEL: We will stipulate that he's a qualified photographer.
BY THE PROSECUTING ATTORNEY: Thank you. Now, Mr. Kaseguma, on April 19, 1989, did you have occasion to go to 421 Olson Avenue in Belvedere?
A: I did.
Q: What is located at that address?
A: A single-family dwellinghouse.
Q: What did you do at that address?
A: I took a photograph of a stationwagon that was parked in the driveway there.
BY THE PROSECUTING ATTORNEY: [to the court reporter]: Miss Nixon, would you be good enough to mark this photograph Prosecution Exhibit Number 15? [Court reporter complies.]
Now then, Mr. Kaseguma, I hand you Prosecution Exhibit 15 for identification and inquire whether or not it is a true, fair, and accurate representation of the stationwagon to which you have referred as you saw it standing in the driveway at 421 Olson Avenue, Belvedere?
A: Yes, sir, it is.
Q: Is it a clear and accurate picture of the vehicle as you observed it?
A: Yes, sir.
Q: Who developed this picture that is marked Prosecution Exhibit 15?
A: I did, at the lab.
[The exhibit is now offered in evidence and received.]

Surveillance Photography

Business and public institutions, especially banks and supermarkets, have turned increasingly to the use of surveillance photography to fight robberies, burglaries, and thefts.

One type of surveillance camera, frequently used in banks, is activated from a remote position only when the need for a photograph arises. For example, during an attempted robbery a bank teller triggers the remote camera by means of a concealed switch. The resulting type of surveillance photograph has been ruled admissible in evidence in a number of reported cases (see, e.g., *United States* v. *Hobbs,* 403 F. 2d 977 (6th Cir. 1968); *Commonwealth* v. *Balukonis,* 260 N.E. 2d 167 (Sup. Jud. Ct. Mass. 1970)).

The second basic type of surveillance camera photographs a particular area every few seconds. The motion picture film used in this type of surveillance photography is developed only if a theft or unlawful intrusion is suspected.

Although the two types of surveillance cameras described above are currently the most commonly encountered, a few other types also exist. One type that is being used with increasing frequency takes a photograph of any person who seeks to cash a check at a currency exchange or supermarket and of the check itself when triggered by a cashier. Regrettably, one demonstrably misguided appellate decision holds that photographs of this kind are inadmissible in evidence unless the cashier can make an independent identification of the check-passer and the check (see *Sisk* v. *State,* 192 A. 2d 108 (S. Ct. Md. 1963)). Since the cashier often triggers hundreds of these photographs in a day without any particular reason to suspect the presenter of each check, a photographic memory would be needed to satisfy this requirement.

The law ought not demand the impossible unless there exists good reason to do so. Photographs of the sort described in the foregoing paragraph should be admitted into evidence whenever a typical three-part foundation has been developed by offering counsel, demonstrating that:

1. The camera equipment was in proper working condition when the photograph in question was taken;
2. The film was developed and printed in the usual manner; and
3. No alterations of the negative or print were made.

X-Ray Photography; Photomicrography; Photomacrography; Other Special Photographic Techniques

A variety of special photographic techniques have been approved by the courts.

For example, X-ray photographs are treated much like any other photographs. The essential foundation involves a four-step demonstration that:

1. The X-ray equipment used was of an acceptable type;
2. The equipment was in working order when the X-ray picture in question was taken;
3. The technician who operated the equipment was adequately qualified to do so; and
4. The offered X-ray picture is of the person whose condition is in issue.

Finally, of course, it will be necessary for a qualified witness to *interpret* the X-ray picture for the court and jury. An X-ray technician can be used to lay the four-part foundation outlined above, but a physician is needed to provide the interpretation of X-ray plates.

Photomicrographs (photographs taken through a microscope) and photomacrographs (using special lenses to obtain a detailed view) were held admissible in evidence as far back as 1887. All that need be demonstrated is that the fact-finder would be aided by viewing the item in question with a microscope or a magnifying glass.

Identification Photographs: "Mug" Shots

As would be anticipated, it is generally held that photographs are admissible to identify the accused in a criminal matter.

A recurring example of identification photographs is the so-called mug shot—the identification photograph taken post-arrest at a police station or prison (from chest up, full face and profile, and sometimes also full length, black and white or in color, often taking in a plaque bearing an identifying number and the name of the police department or other agency). These "mug" photographs go into the department's individual criminal history files. They also are usually attached to the reverse of the arrestee's fingerprint card. Of course, they also show up on fugitive posters in post office branches.

Since the proper identification of the accused is almost invariably an issue in criminal cases, courts have been free in admitting mug shots into evidence, even when they carry legends identifying them as coming from police files. (See, e.g., *Dirring* v. *United States,* 328 F. 2d 512 (1st Cir.), *cert. denied,* 377 U.S. 1003 (1964).) However, a few courts have concluded that identification photographs showing a police department plaque are of questionable admissibility if the plaque indicates prior arrests (see e.g., *Matters* v. *Commonwealth,* 245 S.W. 2d 913 (S. Ct. Ky. 1952)). This problem can be resolved by masking out objectionable portions of the photograph.

When a complainant has made a pretrial identification from photographs displayed by the investigating police officers, the photographs will be admissible in evidence at trial so long as the identification procedure was conducted in a fair manner. (See chapter 9 on identification confrontations.)

Motion Pictures

American courts have not been reluctant to receive motion pictures in evidence where they have a "sponsoring" witness whose testimony they help to explain. Sound films are admissible if the sound portion is relevant, but the sound factor necessitates a second level of authentication. The sponsoring witness will have to identify the sounds (voices, etc.) on the track. Magnetic sound tracks are easy to alter and therefore are often excluded from evidence, while optic sound recording, which is far less susceptible to improper alteration, is usually ruled admissible.

Motion pictures are frequently used in driving-while-intoxicated (DWI) cases to show the arrestee's appearance, demeanor, and physical mannerisms (see, e.g., *Lanford* v. *People,* 409 P. 2d 829 (S. Ct. Colo. 1966)). Films of this sort do not extract evidence of a testimonial nature from the arrestee and consequently do not impinge upon Fifth Amendment rights (see chapter 11).

Videotapes

Although there has thus far been little case law on the subject, there is every reason to believe that videotapes will be considered admissible in evidence on the same foundational bases as are still photographs and motion pictures. Already several jurisdictions have upheld the receipt in evidence of videotaped confessions and statements (see, e.g., *Paramore* v. *State,* 229 So. 2d 855 (S. Ct. Fla. 1969); *State* v. *Lusk,* 452 S.W. 2d 219 (S. Ct. Mo. 1970)).

Videotapes of a line-up and of a crime reenactment have received judicial sanction (State v. Kidwell, P. 2d 316 (S. Ct. Kan. 1967); *People* v. *Heading,* 196 N.W. 2d 325 (Mich. App. 1972)).

Unquestionably, videotaping is a techniques for which law enforcement agencies will find ever-expanding uses. The courts can be expected to facilitate the proper evidentiary uses of this versatile technique.

Photographs as Demonstrative Evidence

Photographs generally fall into the category of demonstrative evidence—an evidentiary classification that poses some special problems. Some of the pitfalls involved in the use of photographs as demonstrative evidence are considered in chapter 19.

F. Fingerprinting

The Beginning

The first written work on the value of fingerprinting for identification purposes was entitled ON THE SKIN-FURROW OF THE HAND. It was published by a Scottish physician in 1880. The first full-scale treatise on fingerprinting was published twelve years later in England. It was not until about 1910 that fingerprinting came into its own in America. Now, of course, most law enforcement agencies have access to fingerprinting identification bureaus, the largest being that of the Federal Bureau of Investigation in Washington, D.C.

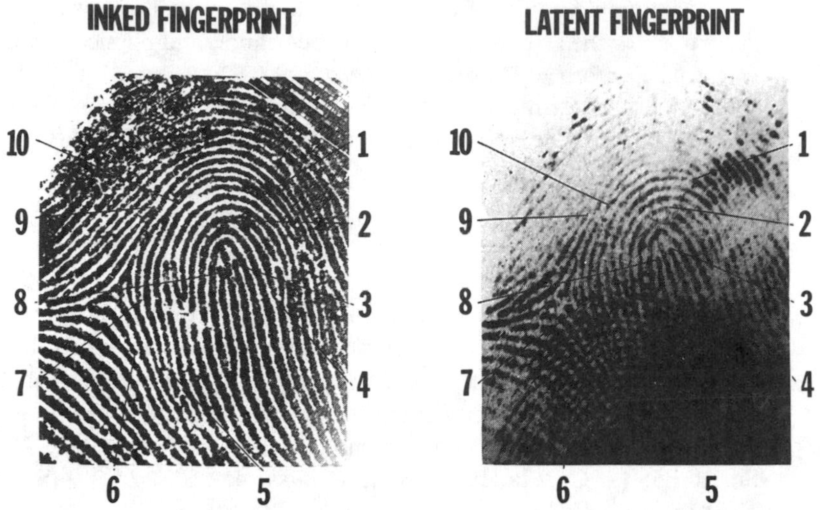

A fingerprint inked for clarity and in its original state.

Fingerprint Identification

Fingerprint identification involves the comparison of the ridge characteristics of fingerprints. Ridge characteristics include bifurcations (branching into two parts), trifurcations, ridge dots, ridge endings, and ridge crossings. All fingerprints fall within one of three general classes of patterns—arches, loops, and whorls—but to establish identity through fingerprint comparison it is necessary to go further and demonstrate an adequate number of ridge characteristics appearing in the same position with the same frequency in the same area of the compared prints.

Everyone knows that a fingerprint is an impression of the picture created by the skin ridges on the palmar side of an individual's fingers and thumbs. (The same sort of skin ridge design is also found on the palms of the hands and the soles of the feet.) There are rows of perspiration pores on the skin ridges. The perspiration exuded by these pores and also other body oils coat the skin of the fingers. As a result of this coating, a finger that presses against a smooth surface will leave an impression of its skin ridge pattern. An impression of this type is referred to as a *latent fingerprint.* There are three kinds of latent prints:

1. *Visible prints.* This is a visible, accidental fingerprint impression in soot, dust, blood, powder, etc. Visible prints are easily obliterated.
2. *Invisible prints.* This is an invisible, accidental fingerprint impression resulting when the perspiration-oil-dirt coating of the skin ridges comes

in contact with a smooth, hard surface. Invisible prints are also easily obliterated.

3. *Plastic prints.* A plastic print is a visible accidental fingerprint that is more durable than other chance fingerprint impressions because it has been made in such substances as putty, candle wax, clay, tar, grease, oily film, and the like.

Latent fingerprints are usually invisible but are rendered distinct with lasers, dyes, powders and chemicals.

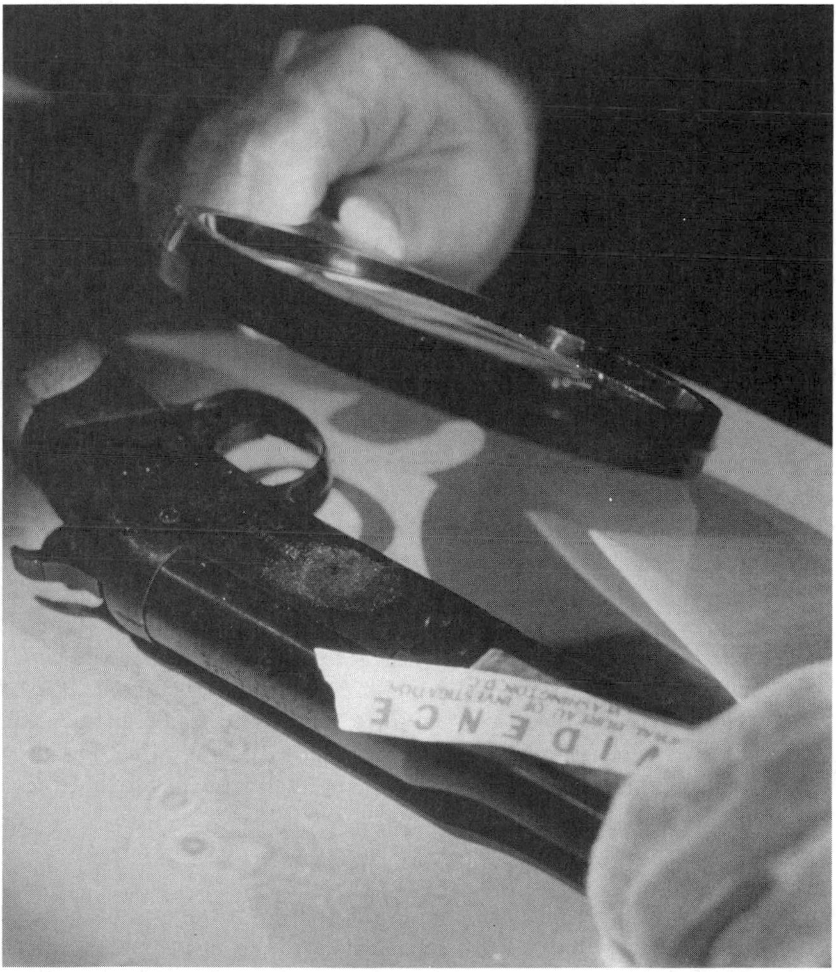

A laser is used to reveal fingerprints on the breech of this gun.

A recently devised technique for raising fingerprints involves the use of cyanoacrylate ester fumes from what is commonly known by the tradename SuperGlue. To ascertain whether an object bears latent prints, it is first exposed to a laser beam. If this fails to render any prints visible, SuperGlue is used as an enhancer. The object is placed in a sealed chamber. SuperGlue is spread at the base of the chamber and heat is introduced to accelerate the fuming process. The SuperGlue acts on the moisture that is secreted from one's fingerprints. The object will again be subjected to a laser and the enhanced print can then be photographed. The technique must be implemented with care; if too much glue is used, part or all of any fingerprint may be destroyed. When properly conducted, the technique can have dramatic results. For example, in a Chicago murder case the accused's truck was successfully subjected to this process.

Law enforcement agencies make inked fingerprints on fingerprint record cards. These prints, to be distinguished from chance (accidental) latent prints, are used for two principal purposes: identification of wrongdoers by means of comparison with latent prints, and proof of prior criminal convictions (usable, if serious enough, to impeach the accused's veracity and to shed light on the appropriate penalty if he is convicted of the current charge against him).

Our fingerprint identification system is based on three premises: (1) that the skin ridge patterns start developing during the fetal stage and continue unchanged throughout one's life and even subsequent to death (until decomposition sets in); (2) that the skin ridge patterns vary from person to person, perhaps even from finger to finger, and in their minute details are never duplicated; and (3) that the overall appearance of skin ridge patterns has certain similarities that can be used to develop a systematic classification of fingerprint impressions.

When a suspect is arrested, inked fingerprints are recorded on standard fingerprint record cards. These cards have spaces for rolled impressions of the inked fingers and also for impressions made by pressing the fingers against the card without any rolling motion. The record card is then marked with a classification formula. The police can compare latent prints, left at a crime scene, with recorded prints and make an identification. Moreover, a person who seeks to avoid apprehension by altering his appearance or using an alias can be foiled by the inked fingerprint file.

The Work of the Fingerprint Technician

Fingerprint identification requires the skills of a fingerprint technician. In comparing an unidentified latent print with an identifiable inked impression, the technician searches for four elements: (1) the similarity of the *general pattern type,* or at least for likeness in the configuration of the skin ridges; (2) *quantitative* similarity in the skin ridge characteristics; (3) (*qualitative* similarities in the skin ridge characteristics (i.e., are the ridge endings, bifurcations, ridge dots, etc., the same in both impressions?); and (4) similarity in the *location* of these characteristics. There is no hard and fast rule regarding the minimum number of matching characteristics that should exist between the latent impression and the comparison print before an identification can properly be made. The figure eight as a minimum is often mentioned, but most technicians would prefer ten to twelve matching characteristics or "concordances."

Judicial Acceptance of Fingerprints as Evidence

Today most courts are sufficiently satisfied of the reliability of fingerprint comparison evidence that they will take judicial notice of it as a valuable method of positive identification. Professor Andre Moenssens, in his definitive work entitled FINGERPRINTS AND THE LAW, published in 1969, pulls together a long list of opinions recognizing the validity of fingerprint identification evidence. Fingerprints have been called "unforgettable signatures," and a number of courts have announced that they constitute the strongest possible evidence of an individual's identity. (But see the discussion of DNA profiling in the next section.) In *Grice* v. *State*, 151 S.W. 2d 211 (Tex. Crim. App. 1941), the court concluded that the reliability of fingerprint comparison evidence was so well settled in the courts that in the future prosecutors would not be required to offer proof that no two fingerprints are alike. The burden of disproving the force of fingerprint evidence would henceforth rest on the accused.

Fingerprint Identification Testimony at Trial

Lay testimony about fingerprint comparison is not admissible at trial. It can be given only by qualified experts. As is usual in connection with proposed expert testimony, the qualifications of the witness as an expert must be established as part of the preliminary foundation unless the defense offers an acceptable stipulation (agreement) that he or she is adequately qualified.

Most fingerprint expertise is garnered from practical experience and reading of the literature rather than from formal study, although it is increasingly true that law enforcement agencies at federal and state levels and some private institutions are offering training courses covering the rudiments of fingerprint identification.

Fingerprint Records; Photographic Evidence; In-Court Experiments

Fingerprint records can be introduced in evidence so long as they have been adequately authenticated. Their admission is for purposes of fingerprint identification, not to convey to the jurors prejudicial extraneous information on the record cards regarding an accused's previous criminal record. (If fingerprint records are offered in evidence, any references on them to the accused's past criminal activities and convictions should be masked from the juror's view; to do otherwise might constitute reversible error.)

Objects that bear latent prints are themselves admissible in evidence like any other real evidence if they are relevant and are not subject to exclusion on the basis of some constitutional claim. Properly authenticated fingerprint photographs, enlarged or not, are likewise receivable.

Trial judges often permit fingerprint experts to use demonstrative evidence (e.g., photographic enlargements of prints) in the courtroom to illustrate to the jurors that all fingers have distinctive characteristics. There is no longer much need to engage in demonstrative *experiments* in the courtroom in order to establish the efficacy of fingerprint evidence. Few courts today would take time for the sort of thing that was done in the 1921 case of *Moon* v. *State*, 198 Pac. 288, in which each member of the jury was allowed to place his fingertips on sheets of paper while the fingerprint expert was out of the courtroom. The expert then developed the jurors' latent fingerprints, using powder. He obtained inked comparison prints from the fascinated jurors and then accurately paired up the inked and latent prints.

Constitutional Considerations

The Supreme Court, in *Schmerber* v. *California,* 384 U.S. 757 (1966), which was discussed in detail in chapter 8, made it clear that compulsory fingerprinting does not violate a suspect's Fifth Amendment rights against forced self-incrimination. The Court has also indicated that a suspect is not constitutionally entitled to have counsel present or available for consultation prior to or during a fingerprinting session (see *United States* v. *Wade,* 388 U.S. 218 (1967)).

Of course, prints that have been obtained illegally are subject to suppression. In *Davis* v. *Mississippi,* 394 U.S. 721 (1969), the Supreme Court held that an accused's prints, obtained as an incident of an illegal arrest procedure, were inadmissible at his trial. The point is that fingerprints are subject to the same exclusionary rule as all other unlawfully seized evidence. And it is possible that the problem cannot be avoided by the use of a different set of fingerprints unrelated to the illegal arrest or unlawful search and seizure. If it it can be said that the fingerprint identification of the accused was tainted by the antecedent illegal arrest, any comparison prints taken thereafter are likely to be held inadmissible under the "fruits of the poisonous tree" doctrine enunciated by Justice Frankfurter in the wiretap case, *Nardone* v. *United States*, 308 U.S. 338 (1939), discussed in chapter 10.

Tracing the Chain of Custody

A gap in the chain of custody may result in the exclusion of fingerprint evidence. An illustrative case is *People* v. *Rice,* 10 N.W.2d 912 (S. Ct. Mich. 1943). The defendant was charged with breaking and entering. The state's case depended heavily on fingerprint evidence. On the second day after the offense was committed, a police officer discovered the latent prints of two fingers (the middle finger and ring finger of a right hand) on the sill of the window through which entry into the dwelling had been made. These prints were photographed and the developed negative was Exhibit B at the defendant's trial. Exhibit D at that trial was an enlargement of Exhibit B.

Almost a year after the offense, imprints of all of the defendant's fingers were taken while she was being held in the county jail. This fingerprint card was Exhibit C at the trial.

A photographer attached to the Michigan State Police testified as follows:

> A: . . . Exhibit F is the negative from which this enlarged photograph [i.e., Exhibit E] was made. It is taken from the fingerprint made of a rolled impression.
>
> BY THE PROSECUTING ATTORNEY: I will hand you People's Exhibit C and ask you whether or not that [Exhibit F] is a negative of the picture taken of the fingerprint card?
>
> A: Yes, sir.
>
> Q: Now, it is a picture taken from what parts of that card?
>
> A: The right middle finger and right ring finger. I made the negative myself.
>
> BY THE PROSECUTING ATTORNEY: I will offer in evidence People's Exhibits E and F.
>
> BY DEFENSE COUNSEL: The exhibits are objected to as not being properly identified.
>
> THE COURT: Overruled. They are received.

Following the foregoing testimony, a fingerprint expert testified that he had made a comparison between Exhibit F and Exhibit B and had concluded that they were made "by one and the same person." Negatives of the fingerprints and the enlargements of them were then presented to the jury and the witness indicated the points of similarity. The defendant was convicted.

On appeal, the reviewing court noted that although the fingerprint expert had testified that Exhibit F was a negative taken from Exhibit C, such was not the fact. Instead, Exhibit F must have been taken from some fingerprint card other than Exhibit C, and this other fingerprint card was not in evidence. There could be no doubt about this because a comparison of Exhibit F with Exhibit C disclosed that two check marks found in Exhibit F were not on Exhibit C, from which Exhibit F was supposedly taken, and there were other discrepancies as well. It followed that the use of Exhibit F in establishing the defendant's identity with that of the person whose latent prints were found on the window sill was improper. The defendant's conviction was reversed.

The Sufficiency of Fingerprint Evidence

A criminal conviction cannot be founded exclusively or largely on fingerprint evidence unless the prosecution shows that the accused's prints were discovered under circumstances that would be inconsistent with innocence. This does not mean, however, that the prosecution must exclude every conceivable possibility that the accused was at the crime scene at some time other than the time of the commission of the alleged offense. As was said in *Lawless* v. *State,* 241 A. 2d 155 (Md. App. 1968), "The fingerprint evidence . . . need be coupled only with evidence of other circumstances tending to reasonably exclude the hypothesis that the print was impressed at a time other than that of the crime." The court stressed that "The rule does not require under all circumstances in every case that the State affirmatively and conclusively prove that the defendant could *not* have been there other than a time when the crime was committed" (court's italics). The general rule was accurately described in *Brown* v. *United States,* 380 F. 2d 595 (D.C. Cir. 1967): The prosecution must demonstrate that the surfaces on which the latent prints were found were generally not accessible to the accused; otherwise the fingerprint evidence will be excluded.

Of course, the prosecution will have a difficult row to hoe if the accused can be shown to have had access to the crime scene before or after the crime's commission. Since it is difficult to assess the age of latent prints, the prosecution might have trouble proving the exact time that the latent prints were impressed. Still, circumstantial evidence may come to the State's aid.

> EXAMPLE:
> Clyde Bushmat, the nephew of Irene Stitz, is charged with murdering her husband, Fred Stitz. Bushmat made a social call to the Stitz home on Friday afternoon; Stitz was killed late Friday night. It might seem impossible for the prosecution to prove that Bushmat had deposited a particular latent print on a glass-topped coffee table in the Stitzes' living room at the time of the murder, rather than at the time of his social visit. But this proof becomes less difficult if the Stitzes' housecleaner can testify that on the evening before the murder, just after Bushmat left following his social visit, she had thoroughly cleaned the top of the coffee table with soap and water.

Places of forced entry are often inaccessible to people carrying on normal activities. The presence of a suspect's prints at a place of forced entry gives rise to a circumstantial inference that they were deposited at the time of the entry.

EXAMPLE:
People v. *Rodis,* 301 P.2d 886 (Cal. App. 1956) (defendant's latent prints were found on the outside of a window that was 9 feet above ground level and covered by a screen; conviction upheld).

Sometimes fingerprints, while not direct evidence of the perpetration of an offense, serve to tie the accused to the crime. A typical example is provided by *Debinski* v. *State,* 71 A. 2d 460 (Ct. App. Md. 1950), in which the court said that the presence of a codefendant's latent print on a flashlight found at a burglary scene was potent evidence linking the defendant to the crime.

Fingerprint evidence is not invariably conclusive. A variety of circumstances can lead equally competent technicians to different conclusions. Scars on the fingers may make comparison with earlier unscarred impressions difficult; variations in pressure can cause confusing differences between prints; the presence of dirt in the skin ridges can confuse a ridge count; the powder used to develop latent prints may adhere between ridges, creating a false ridge characteristic; excessive finger pressure during the taking of an inked print may force several skin ridges together, creating the appearance of a single ridge.

Soleprints and Palmprints

The skin ridges that create fingerprints can also be found on the palms of the hands and soles of the feet. Accordingly, courts agree that palmprint identification evidence is admissible. Barefoot impressions are understandably rare, but there is no rational reason for excluding them from evidence since they can be identified by an expert in the same way fingerprints and palmprints are identified. A substantial number of trial courts have allowed toeprint identification, but to date there has been no published higher court opinion upholding the use of toeprint comparisons.

Pretrial Discovery of Print Evidence

The refusal of police to let the defense examine fingerprint evidence has been held to be improper and a ground for the reversal of a criminal conviction.

EXAMPLE A:
People v. *Wilson,* 345 P. 2d 535 (Cal. App. 1959)(rights of accused violated by refusal of defense counsel's request that an official identification expert compare witness's prints—which were on file in sheriff's office—with prints of jail inmates in order to identify witness).

EXAMPLE B:
United States v. *Rich,* 6 Alaska 670 (S. Ct. Alaska 1922)(prosecution should have given defense a photograph of fingerprints allegedly defendant's).

G. DNA Profiling

On August 26, 1988, a sleeping University of Illinois student was sexually assaulted in her darkened apartment. She could not identify her attacker because she was not wearing her contact lenses and the intruder had placed a pillow over her face.

On February 16, 1990, it took a jury only 75 minutes to convict Vincent Lipscomb on two counts of aggravated criminal sexual assault. The only identification evidence in the case against him was a so-called DNA test demonstrating that genetic material taken from a sample of the defendant's blood matched samples of semen taken from the victim. One of the prosecution's expert witnesses had testified that the odds against the occurrence of two identical DNA patterns were 1 in 6.8 billion. Since the world's population is only about 5 billion, the jury obviously thought it was on firm ground in finding Lipscomb guilty after hearing two weeks of expert testimony about deoxyribonucleic acid, non-polymorphous probes, band sizings, and autoradiograms. The jury based its verdict on the results of a new procedure that, in the years to come, is likely to revolutionize criminal investigation and proof. And yet it is disturbing to see a conviction for serious crime that is based entirely on the result of a testing methodology that in some respects is still in its infancy. Courts are rushing to accept DNA matching despite warnings from some segments of the scientific community that standards ensuring reliability are sorely lacking.

DNA profiling is a laboratory identification process. The term DNA profiling is a generic one, referring to two versions of what is known as Restriction Fragment Length Polymorphism (RFLP), which is a technique for analyzing the chromosomes forming the strand of the DNA molecule found in virtually every human cell. As a method of identifying perpetrators of violent crimes, DNA profiling will revolutionize law enforcement.

In a 1989 interview, Kenneth Nemmich, special agent in the FBI's Laboratory Division, said, "We're now doing DNA profiling routinely. It's the biological equivalent of fingerprinting, the closest to a positive personal identification." Agent Nimmich was referring to one of the most recent scientific techniques to come to the aid of law enforcement.

Prior to 1990, DNA profiling had been used in only a small number of cases and involved the work of a few private laboratories, although it had been used in Great Britain for a number of years. In late 1988, following a year of testing, the FBI initiated widespread American implementation of the technique. The process is now available not only to the FBI's own agents but also to any local police department. Under proper circumstances, DNA profiling permits positive identification of a suspect as the crime perpetrator, or excludes that person from further suspicion, based on the unique genetic material in a small specimen of blood, semen, or other body fluids or tissues. It is especially helpful in connection with sex crimes, historically the most difficult to solve. (On the civil side, the DNA technique is likely to become dispositive in most paternity actions, replacing blood typing; see, e.g., *Matter of Adoption of "Baby Girl S,"* 532 N.Y.S. 2d 634 (N.Y. 1988).)

DNA testing reconstructs a descriptive physical profile, including eye and hair color, by unlocking the genetic codes that can be extracted from specimens as small as a hair, a drop of blood (even when drawn from a dead body), a skin scraping, or a dime-size spot of semen. Any description of this genetic "marking" process is likely to be mind-boggling to anyone who is not a molecular biologist; it is an extremely complicated and tedious process.

A sense of the technique can be conveyed simply by observing that DNA, which is short for deoxyribonucleic acid, is found in every human cell. It forms the genes and carries the code for heredity. And that genetic code is different in every person, with the exception of identical twins. Through a laborious testing process, the laboratory scientist, using specimens of the sort mentioned above that have been forwarded by criminal investigators or defense counsel, can extract this code and render it graphic. There follows a simplified but nonetheless formidable description of the process.

The original test, known in the United States by the trade name DNA Fingerprinting, was developed in England in the early 1980s at the University of Leicester by geneticist Alex Jeffreys. His technique involves subjecting the DNA molecule to an enzyme that cuts the molecule into fragments. These fragments are then propelled through a gel by means of an electrical charge in a process called electrophoresis. The fragments will be of varying lengths. Since short fragments will be propelled through the gel more rapidly than long ones, the electrophoresis process sorts them by length, creating a pattern. To "fix" (stabilize) this pattern so that it can be analyzed, radioactive probes are introduced into the sample. These probes bind to a sequence of points or bases on the DNA fragments. The sample is then blotted on photographic film, which is exposed by the radioactivity. A pattern of bands emerges, looking very much like the bar code on supermarket items. (For a fuller description of DNA testing, see *People* v. *Wesley*. 533 N.Y.S. 2d 643 (N.Y. 1988), and the secondary sources listed in the Additional Reading section at the end of this book.)

Because every person's DNA pattern is unique (except, as mentioned, for those of identical twins), the pattern created by the sorted fragments is unique to the test subject's DNA. Cellmark Diagnostics, which markets DNA Fingerprinting in this country, represents that the technique is 99.9 percent accurate. Jeffreys puts it as a statistical proposition: he says that there is only a 1 in 1 quadrillion chance that two unrelated persons will exhibit the same DNA "fingerprint." His assertion is supported by a computerized database that tracks the occurrence of gene frequencies within specific ethnic groups. This database draws on blood samples that have been obtained, in the main, from blood banks. (California is considering the establishment of a statewide database, to be created from blood and saliva samples extracted from persons convicted of murder, assault, rape, and other sexual offenses.) Another private testing laboratory, Lifecodes Corporation, performs what it calls DNA-Print. Its process is substantially similar to Cellmark's. Cetus Corporation uses a variant of the RFLP technique. It is less specific but can work with smaller samples.

With the entry of the FBI into DNA profiling, these private laboratories will be used primarily by private individuals such as criminal defendants. The fees charged by the private laboratories may be prohibitive in some cases (perpetrators of violent crimes tend to be poor people), which will give yet another advantage to the prosecution. (As of 1990, for example, Cellmark Diagnostics charged between $1,500 and $2,000 per DNA test and between $750 and $1,000 a day for an expert witness.)

As is often true of scientific techniques, the problem may be not so much with methodology as with its human implementation. Standards will have to be developed; the FBI has already gone a long way toward generating them. For example, the proper preservation of evidence samples is crucial and this poses some difficulties. One of these difficulties is traceable to the fear of AIDS. Those who treat rape victims are concerned that the victim may contract AIDS from her attacker if potentially AIDS-contaminated bodily fluids are not quickly removed. Thus the victim will immediately be cleansed of semen and blood, resulting in the loss of critical evidence. The FBI has recommended that rape victims first be swabbed with a sterile tissue in order to preserve DNA samples. At an even more basic level, there must be assurances that the preserved sample is neither contaminated nor too degraded to be useful.

Another problem is that DNA patterns, if not handled with great care, can stretch or shift, making them difficult or impossible to interpret.

A relatively recent Supreme Court decision—one that has been widely criticized—may also pose a threat. *Arizona* v. *Youngblood,* ______ U.S. ______, 109 S. Ct. 333 (1988), was a child molesting case involving the sodomizing of a boy who had been abducted from a carnival. A standard sexual assault kit was used to test the victim. Thereafter, the boy identified Youngblood as his assailant. At trial, in 1985, the defendant claimed mistaken identity. The police had permitted the semen samples to become degraded; they could no longer be tested to confirm or exclude Youngblood as possessing the assailant's blood type. The Arizona Court of Appeals reversed Youngblood's conviction, holding that due process is violated when identity is at issue and the police have permitted the destruction of evidence that could exclude the accused as the perpetrator.

The U.S. Supreme Court reversed the state court, saying "We . . . hold that unless a criminal defendant can show bad faith on the part of the police, failure to preserve potential useful evidence does not constitute a denial of due process of law." The threat posed by this ruling was addressed, in dissent, by Justice Blackmun: "As technology develops, the potential for this type of evidence to provide conclusive results on any number of questions will increase." Referring specifically to DNA testing, the Justice continued, "Current genetic testing measures . . . are already extraordinarily precise. . . . The importance of these types of evidence is indisputable, and requiring police to recognize their importance is not unreasonable."

By mid-1989 the FBI laboratory at Quantico, Virginia, had received over 200 specimens from its agents and from various police departments. Final reports in the first 80 of these cases demonstrate the efficacy of the DNA technique in identifying the innocent along with the guilty. In 50 cases the DNA profile positively tied the suspect to the crime under investigation, which was usually either rape or murder. In 20 cases the profiling process exonerated the original suspect. (In 10 cases the biological specimen was too tiny or too decayed to be testable.)

By mid-1989 the DNA testing technique had been involved in some 80 reported court cases. Its reliability went virtually unchallenged, the only question being (a) whether the test was properly conducted (b) on an appropriate biological specimen. As the DNA technique's utilization becomes increasingly widespread its impact on the disposition of criminal cases is likely to be dramatic, particularly in view of the fact that biological evidence—blood, hair, skin, semen—is much more commonly found at crime scenes than are usable fingerprints. The impact of DNA profiling will undoubtedly be most evident at the plea-bargaining stage of the criminal justice process. Lifecodes has reported that a majority of the criminal defendants tested by its laboratory changed their plea to "Guilty" after receiving adverse test results.

H. Firearms Evidence

The Role of the Firearms Examiner

The function of the firearms examiner is to make identifications of firearms and ammunition. He or she draws on knowledge of firearms manufacturing methods. Four types of firearms are commonly involved in criminal conduct: (1) the revolver, (2) the semiautomatic pistol, (3) the rifle, and (4) the shotgun. Revolvers, semiautomatic pistols, and rifles have rifled barrels and their size is indicated by *caliber.* The bore of a shotgun is not rifled; its size is indicated by *gauge.*

The barrel of any rifled firearm bears markings caused by the rifling process in which a cylindrical tool cuts out the twisting grooves—the "rifling"—that impart a rotational (twisting) velocity to a bullet fired from the weapon. These markings will not be the same in any two barrels, not even in barrels manufactured one after the other in uninterrupted sequence. These barrel markings are transmitted from the barrel to the fired bullet.

Bullet Identification

There is no feasible way to make a direct comparison between the irregularities and imperfections inside a gun barrel and the reverse impression of those markings on a fired bullet. The firearms examiner must fire a sequence of test bullets from the questioned firearm into a box filled with cotton waste or into a container of water. He recovers the bullets and uses them, not the weapon's barrel, for comparison purposes. After preliminary visual examination establishing the similarity of the test bullets and the evidence bullet, the firearms technician makes use of a binocular comparison microscope, which in actuality is two separate microscopes mounted in tandem. The test bullet is placed under one microscope, the evidence bullet under the other. In a typical comparison process, the technician then examines the entire surface of the rotating evidence bullet. He or she uses low magnification while picking out the most prominent group of markings (striations). After these markings have been found, the evidence bullet is held in a stationary position and the test bullet is rotated as the technician searches its surface for a corresponding area that reveals matching characteristics. This process, if carefully conducted, supplies the basis for a conclusion that the evidence bullet and the test bullets were or were not fired from the same gun barrel.

Damaged bullets pose a special problem. However, smashed or otherwise distorted evidence bullets and even bullet fragments may be subject to accurate identification. Cartridge case and primer identification is also possible on the same principles that permit bullet identification; indeed, in many instances cartridge case identification is even stronger than bullet identification.

Bullet comparison. These two photographs show the grooves on a pair of bullets made when they were fired from the same gun.

The firearms expert can do more than identify bullets, cartridges, and the like. He/she frequently can determine muzzle-to-target distance, which can be significant in almost any shooting case. (Was the shooting an unlawful homicide, an accident, suicide, or a case of self-defense?) By studying gunshot residue tests, the expert can detect whether a suspect recently fired a weapon. By means of chemical tests, he may be able to restore a firearm serial number that has been filed off or otherwise obliterated or obscured.

Judicial Acceptance of Firearms Evidence

The first American judicial decision approving comparison testimony regarding test bullets and an evidence bullet was *Dean* v. *Commonwealth,* 32 Gratt 912 (S. Ct. Va. 1879). The evidence was equivocal—there was testimony that two or three other weapons found in the community "might have" carried the same type of ball as the fatal one—but it was received in a first degree murder prosecution.

The first judicial opinion to stand on a solid footing was *Commonwealth* v. *Best,* 62 N.E. 748 (Sup. Jud. Ct. Mass. 1902). A test bullet had been forced through the barrel of the accused's rifle. Photographs of this test bullet and the evidence bullets were made. At trial the accused objected to testimony comparing the photographs, arguing that "the conditions of the experiment did not correspond accurately with those at the date of the shooting, that the forces impelling the different bullets were different in kind, that the rifle barrel might be supposed to have rusted in the little more than a fortnight that had intervened. . . ." In an opinion by Oliver Wendell Holmes, then the chief justice of Massachusetts' highest court and destined to become a justice of the United States Supreme Court, it was held that "the sources of error suggested [by the accused] were trifling." "We see," said Chief Justice Holmes, "no other way in which the jury could have learned so intelligently how that gun barrel would have marked a lead bullet fired through it."

The Holmes decision did not have immediate impact. One court even suggested that ballistics evidence was "preposterous." (*People* v. *Berkman,* 139 N.E. 91 (S. Ct. Ill. 1923).) But by the late twenties firearms identification evidence was being given serious consideration. In 1928 and 1929 the Supreme Court of Kentucky published lengthy opinions supporting the scientific validity of ballistics evidence. By 1930 the Supreme Court of Illinois had reversed its opinion that such evidence was "preposterous." (*People* v. *Fisher,* 172 N.E. 555 (S. Ct. Ill. 1930).)

Today trial courts will take judicial notice of the reliability of firearms identification evidence when it is offered through qualified witnesses. Furthermore, courts have upheld the receipt of expert testimony culminating in the identification of shells through comparison of firing pin impressions, breechface imprints, and extractor and ejector markings.

EXAMPLE:
State v. *Clark,* 196 Pac. 360 (S. Ct. Ore. 1921) (identification testimony based on "A peculiar mark on the brass part of the primer" was upheld).

In fact, shell casing identification evidence is often used to corroborate the identification of bullets. In a number of cases where an evidence bullet is unavailable or too badly mutilated for comparison purposes, cartridge identification has supplied the only link to a particular firearm.

EXAMPLE:
Edwards v. *State,* 81 A. 2d 631 (S. Ct. Med. 1951) (accused had removed barrel rifling with steel wool to prevent bullet comparison; identification by breechface marking upheld).

The ballistics expert can also be utilized for purposes other than bullet or cartridge identification.

EXAMPLE:
Brown v. *Commonwealth,* 275 S.W. 2d 928 (S. Ct. Ky. 1955)(shotgun wadding found in deceased's head admitted into evidence after comparison with wadding from shells found in the house of the accused's father).

Courts have approved of expert testimony concerning firing distance determination (muzzle-to-target distance). Since shotgun pellet penetration will be deeper if the muzzle is close to the target, penetration tests are admissible if they were carried out under conditions sufficiently similar to those surrounding the actual shooting. Because shot patterns will be more widely dispersed the farther the muzzle is from the target, properly conducted shot dispersal experiments have been upheld.

EXAMPLE:
Williams v. *State,* 179 S.W.2d 297 (Tex. Crim. App. 1944) (prosecution showed that shot dispersal test was standard one, involving comparison of shot dispersed in wound with patterns obtained by firing cartridges and loads similar to those discovered in accused's shotgun, which had been found at the crime scene).

Powderburn tests may prove helpful to show muzzle-to-target distance. Powderburn evidence is received if buttressed by experiments that show what muzzle-to-target distance would result in the depositing of similar burns and powder residue. Similarity of conditions has been stressed by the courts.

EXAMPLE A:
State v. *Atwood,* 108 S.E. 2d 219 (S. Ct. N.C. 1959)(experiments conducted with same firearm and similar ammunition; blotting paper utilized in experiment admitted into evidence).

EXAMPLE B:
Miller v. *State,* 236 N.E. 2d 585 (S. Ct. Ind. 1968)(condition of weapons, ammunition type, bullet weight, and atmospheric conditions differed from those involved in alleged crime; test evidence excluded).

Chain of Custody: Time Lapse

Tracing an unbroken chain of custody can be crucial to the effective use of firearms identification evidence. This does not mean, however, that changes in the condition of firearms evidence or the passage of a substantial period of time between the shooting and the recovery of the firearms evidence will foreclose admissibility at trial. Such considerations usually go only to the amount of weight the fact-finder will give to evidence.

EXAMPLE A:
Ignacio v. *People of the Territory of Guam,* 413 F. 2d (9th Cir. 1969), *cert. denied,* 397 US. 943 (1970)(bullet recovered two days after discovery of victim; held admissible).

EXAMPLE B:
State v. *Lanes,* 233 P. 2d 437 (S. Ct. Ariz. 1951)(cartridges had been dropped in river months before recovery; held admissible).

Of course, it is important that, to the extent possible, all law enforcement agencies provide for the safe storage of vital evidence prior to trial. Police departments are well advised to maintain a locked evidence room manned by an officer who keeps detailed records not only of its contents but of the disposition of items of evidence and the names of persons entering the room for any purpose.

I. Voiceprints

The Need for Scientific Voice Identification

Courts have long permitted the identification of one person by another on the basis of the former's voice. The identifying witness can be termed an "ear-witness," as distinguished from an eyewitness who identifies another individual on the basis of observed physical characteristics. Unfortunately, this sort of voice identification is probably even less reliable than eyewitness identification testimony. It is therefore natural that law enforcement authorities have hoped for the development of scientific instrumentation for the identification of persons by their voices. Such instrumentation would be of substantial assistance in cases involving recorded telephone threats (e.g., bomb threats), ransom demands, extortion attempts, and the like.

Development of the Sound Spectrograph

The sound spectrograph, an electromagnetic instrument which can produce a graphic picture of human speech, was developed in the early 1940s by the Bell Telephone Laboratories. It could "read" the frequencies of a speech sample recorded on a loop of magnetic tape. A Bell employee,

Dr. Lawrence Kersta and his voiceprint analyzer. Although the device is not universally accepted by courts, it has been valuable in a number of cases.

Lawrence G. Kersta, adapted the sound spectrograph for voice identification purposes by means of the so-called voiceprint method. Kersta's idea was that a person's voice, like fingerprints, has unique characteristics. If these characteristics could be demonstrated by spectrographic analysis, an important new identification technique could be made available to law enforcement agencies.

Voiceprint Identification

Spectrographic devices adapted for voiceprint analysis make use of (1) a recording of the questioned voice, and (2) a comparison voice recording of known origin. The parallel between questioned voice identification techniques and questioned documents analysis is superficially obvious. Kersta's theory of voice uniqueness has two sources: (I) the process by which a person learns to talk, and (2) the physiological manner in which persons produce speech. In other words, the uniqueness of a voice is based on the *mechanism* of speech. This involves an understanding of those aspects of the vocal tract that make for the individuality of one's voice: the vocal cavities and the articulators.

The vocal cavities (nasal, oral, and pharyngeal) act as resonators. The contribution of the vocal cavities to voice individuality comes from their size and relationship to each other. It is said to be unlikely that any two people will have vocal cavities of identical size and relationship.

The manipulation of the articulators to vary the vocal cavities is of even greater significance in Kersta's theory of voice identification. The articulators are the tongue, teeth, lips, soft palate, and jaw muscles. By manipulating these articulators we produce understandable speech. Implicit in Kersta's theory is the notion that no two people are likely to use their articulators in precisely the same way, producing identical use patterns. Different people learn to talk in different ways. The improbability of identical articulator use patterns, taken together with the improbability of identical vocal cavity structure, makes for positive and accurate voice identification, according to Kersta.

Kersta originally made use of two different types of voice spectrograms. There was the *bar spectrogram* and the *contour spectrogram.* The bar spectrogram showed the resonance bars of a human voice in terms of loudness, frequency, and time dimensions. Contour spectrograms measure levels of loudness, frequency, and time as shapes which look much like a topographical map or the whorls of a fingerprint (thus the designation, *voiceprint*). Contour spectrograms are employed in the computerized classification of voiceprints; bar spectrograms are used in the comparison (matching) of known and unknown voice samples.

The Kersta voiceprint technique requires the comparison of questioned speech with a known speech sample recorded from a suspect. The spectrographic impressions of eight frequently used cue words found in the questioned speech are compared with the spectrographic impressions of the same eight cue words in the known speech specimen. The cue words are *a, and, I, is, it, the, to,* and *you.* If the spectrographic impressions of these word-sounds substantially match, Kersta would conclude that the samples had each been produced by the same speaker.

From time to time, Kersta, on the basis of experiments conducted by him, has claimed a high degree of accuracy for his voiceprint technique. In 1962 he stated that more than fifty thousand tests produced an accuracy record greater than 99 percent. Some years later Dr. Oscar Tosi of Michigan State University's Audiology Department conducted tests that failed to produce the level of accuracy which Kersta had announced. Kersta, Tosi, and other experts are carrying on continuing experimentation, and increasing scientific acceptance of the voiceprint technique is to be expected.

Two Legal Hurdles to the Use of Voiceprints

In dealing with voiceprints, courts have confronted two major legal hurdles. First, they have had to assess the reliability of the voiceprint technique from a scientific vantage point. Second, the courts have had to address such important constitutional issues as the privilege against self-incrimination, the right to legal counsel, and unlawful search and seizure.

Scientific Validity

Judicial opinions dealing with voiceprint technique demonstrate an evolution from the early judicial stance against their use to the contemporary viewpoint which, despite the scientific community's reservations, generally accepts the reliability of voiceprint evidence.

In one of the first criminal litigations involving a voiceprint, the New Jersey Supreme Court returned the case to the trial court for a determination of whether the voiceprint technique and the spectrographic equipment that had been utilized in the case were sufficiently reliable and accurate to produce admissible results. In this case the police desired to obtain a suspect's voiceprint in order to compare it with a taped anonymous telephone call concerning a homicide. The lower court concluded that a comparison of the taped voice with a voiceprint would not be admissible in evidence. This ruling was upheld on appeal because the state failed to produce sufficient expert testimony to support the validity of the voiceprint technique. (See *State* v. *Cary,* 264 A. 2d 209 (S. Ct. N.J., 1970).) Similarly, California's first reported voiceprint identification decision held that the admission into evidence of voiceprint identification testimony constituted reversible error. *People* v. *King,* 72 Cal. Rptr. 478 (Cal. App. 1968), grew out of a television interview in which an unidentifiable criminal defendant made inculpatory statements about his involvement in a riot in the Watts community of Los Angeles. Lawrence Kersta, the developer of the voiceprint technique, testified at the accused's trial in an effort to prove that the voice on the televised interview was the accused's. However, Kersta's admission that his process had not gained general acceptance in the scientific community prompted the California court to rule that his opinion testimony was inadmissible.

In two early cases Kersta's theories were vindicated. In *United States* v. *Wright,* 17 U.S.C.M.A. 183 (U.S. Ct. Mil. App. 1967), a military case, the defendant had been accused of making obscene telephone calls, one of which had been recorded by law enforcement agents. Kersta testified as an expert witness and was permitted to make a voiceprint identification of the accused. Kersta was also found qualified as an expert witness in *People* v. *Straehle,* 279 N.Y.S. 2d 115 (S. Ct. N.Y. 1967), *reversed on other grounds,* 294 N.Y.S. 2d 42 (App. Div. N.Y. 1968). The defendant in *Straehle* was a police officer who had allegedly warned a gambler, by telephone, of an impending police raid. Before a grand jury the police officer denied making such a telephone call; he was indicted for perjury. Lawrence Kersta, on the basis of spectrographic comparison, was permitted to testify that the defendant was the maker of the taped telephone call.

More recent opinions have uniformly concluded that voiceprints are the product of a valid scientific method and are, therefore, admissible in evidence where the technique has been properly used.

EXAMPLE A:
State ex re. Trimble v. *Hedman,* 192 N.W. 2d 432 (S. Ct. Minn. 1971)(voiceprint testimony admissible on probable cause for issuance of arrest and search warrants).

EXAMPLE B:
United States v. *Raymond,* 337 F. Supp. 641 (D.D.C. 1971)(defendants convicted on the basis of voice exemplars; the jurors had been instructed to accord voiceprint evidence as much or as little credence as they felt it deserved).

EXAMPLE C:
Worley v. *State,* 263 So. 2d 613 (S. Ct. Fla. 1972)(voiceprint received to corroborate police officer's testimony identifying the accused as the person who made a false bomb threat by telephone).

Even opinions purporting to perpetuate the *Frye* general acceptance standard reveal a subtle shift in focus. They go to the heart of the matter: demonstrated reliability. *Frye* general acceptance is strong evidence, if not proof positive, that a technique is considered reliable by those who ought to know but there are other, more specific ways of showing the trustworthiness of a scientific technique. (See, e.g., *United States* v. *Smith,* 869 F. 2d 348 (7th Cir. 1989)(Which twin sister telephoned banks to make fictitious wire transfers of nonexistent funds?; spectrographic voice identification evidence accepted); *United States* v. *Williams,* 583 F. 2d 1194 (2d Cir. 1978), *cert. denied,* 439 U.S. 1117 (1979)(technique need not be shown to be "infallible").)

Attitude of the Scientific Community

While courts now seem generally receptive to voiceprint evidence, the scientific community remains less than completely converted. In an article published in 1971 and grounded upon extensive research, James J. Hennessey and Clarence Romig concluded that Kersta's theory of invariant speech had not yet been solidly established. (Hennessey & Romig, *Sound, Speech, Phonetics and Voiceprint Identification,* 16 Journal of Forensic Science 438 (1971).) A year earlier the Acoustical Society of America's Committee on Speech Communication arrived at a similar conclusion and recommended substantial additional research.

The scientific community's negative attitude is likely to be a greater impediment to future evidentiary use of the voiceprint than are any constitutional principles.

Constitutional Requirements

Once a court is willing to conclude that the voiceprint technique is scientifically supportable, it must face a few constitutional questions relating to the privilege against compelled self-incrimination, illegal search and seizure, right to legal counsel, and due process of law.

The privilege against self-incrimination was specifically addressed in *State* v. *Vice,* 190 S.E. 2d 510 (S. Ct. N.C. 1972), *United States* v. *Askins,* 351 F. Supp. 408 (D. Md. 1972) and *United States* v. *Dionisio,* 410 U.S. 1 (1973). In *Vice,* the court ruled that requiring the defendant to make a voice tape for identification purposes did not violate the privilege against self-incrimination or deny him due process of law. The defendant's taped exemplar was compared with a taped anonymous telephone call to the police about a stabbing; the defendant was convicted of voluntary manslaughter.

In *Askins* the defendant's Fourth and Fifth Amendment objections to the required giving of voice exemplars to establish the identity of voices recorded on the wiretapped telephones of a gambling house were denied.

More importantly, the U.S. Supreme Court decided in *Dionisio* that a grand jury could compel the giving of voice exemplars without violating the defendant's Fourth or Fifth Amendment rights. The ruling applied to the use of the exemplars for identification purposes; their use in evidence for their communicative *content*—for example, admissions made while giving the exemplars—would be constitutionally impermissible.

In *Gilbert* v. *United States,* 388 U.S. 263 (1967), it was held that an accused was not entitled to have legal counsel present at the taking of handwriting exemplars since this was not a "critical stage" in the process of criminal prosecution. It seems clear that this ruling is equally applicable to a voiceprint procedure.

J. Questioned Document Evidence

In chapter 3, dealing with the making of the trial record, and again in chapter 16, on written evidence, it was stressed that often it is necessary in criminal litigation to prove the authenticity—the genuineness—of writings, be they the product of the human hand holding a pen or of a typewriter. This is obviously true in forgery cases, but it can be true in a wide variety of criminal matters. Two of the most famous examples of the use of handwriting comparison techniques involved not typical forgery charges but treason (the Dreyfus case in France, in which Alphonse Bertillon, chief of the French Identification Service, gave a mistaken opinion which resulted in one of the most dramatic *causes celebres* in all history, "l'affaire Dreyfus," described in Zola's J'ACCUSE) and kidnapping (the Lindbergh case, in which the prosecution built its case on the opinion of handwriting experts that the ransom notes received by the Lindberghs were in Bruno Hauptmann's hand). A notorious case involving typewritten documents was the espionage prosecution of Alger Hiss in which the prosecution made a convincing showing that the "Baltimore letters," conveying American military secrets to the Soviet Union, had been composed on Hiss's worn Woodstock machine.

The Document Examiner's Functions

The role of the handwriting expert, who today is more accurately referred to as a *document examiner,* is not restricted to determining the authorship of questioned documents. Today's document examiner carries out many tasks that are far more complex than the simple comparison of handwriting specimens. Operating in a modern laboratory with sophisticated equipment, he or she can decipher and restore writings that have been burned, water-damaged, lightfaded, or deliberately erased. He can detect alterations and substitution of pages; he can date writings and put them in proper sequence. He studies not only handwriting but paper, including watermarks, printing, duplicating processes, and typewriting and rubber stamp impressions. His equipment includes stereoscopic microscopes and other special optical instruments, measuring and calibrating apparatus, and special photographic equipment.

In the typical case involving a forgery, a worthless check, or an anonymous letter, the questioned documents examiner will address three principal questions: (1) Did the person who assertedly wrote a questioned document (with pen, pencil, typewriter, etc) in fact do so? (2) When was the questioned document made? (3) Does the questioned document bear any erasures, alterations, or the like?

The Meaning of the Term "Questioned Document"

By "questioned document" we mean any surface, be it paper or any other, on which there appears handwriting, typewriting, printing, or other communicative symbols, the genuineness of which is in dispute. The word "document" is not narrowly defined. The questioned document expert examines telegrams, business record entries, wills, passports, motel and hotel registration cards, gambling slips, driver's licenses, writings on interior and exterior walls and even, occasionally, writings on the bodies of homicide victims.

A document is taken to be "questioned" whenever there exists a dispute or doubt as to its genuineness in whole or in part. The dispute or doubt may go not just to authorship but may involve possible alterations of portions of the document or possible erasures.

The Handling of Questioned Documents

The competent criminal investigator employs great care in the handling of evidentiary documents prior to their submission to an expert document examiner. The investigator is careful to avoid any damage to the document but, over and beyond this, he or she realizes that the document may bear fingerprints which might be obscured or even obliterated with careless handling. A realization that the trained document examiner usually handles questioned writings with tweezers underscores this point.

Handwriting Comparison Methods

The questioned document examiner compares the questioned writing with other writings of known genuineness, which are called the *standards* or *exemplars.* The origin and authenticity of a standard must be affirmatively shown before it can be used for comparison purposes. (It would not be productive to compare one questioned document with another document of equally questionable origin.) This can be accomplished through the giving of samples by the suspected author in the examiner's presence or the writer may admit authorship of older documents. It can also be accomplished through the testimony of witnesses who observed the writing being made or of persons, such as a secretary, who are familiar with the suspected author's handwriting. The standards or exemplars should be of approximately the same age as the questioned writing is supposed to be.

The Criminalistics Division of the Chicago Police Department has developed a printed form which the suspected writer fills out. The form is designed to produce usable specimens of every letter in the alphabet (upper case and lower, longhand and in handprinting) and numbers 1 through 10.

Testimony by the Documents Examiner

The opinion testimony of a qualified documents examiner is almost invariably held to be admissible on the authenticity of a questioned document. He can deliver an opinion as to genuineness and explain the reasons underlying his findings.

At one time many courts felt that the testimony of handwriting experts was not of substantial weight. For example, in the early thirties the Iowa Supreme Court, in *Keeney* v. *Arp De La Gardee,* 235 N.W. 745 (S. Ct. Iowa 1931), directed that jurors could be instructed by a trial judge that the opinion of a documents examiner is "most unsatisfactory" and "of the lowest order." Nowadays, however, most courts concede that expert handwriting testimony is of substantial value in both criminal and civil litigation. Much, of course, depends on the training and the breadth of experience of the particular witness.

To give added clarity to his or her testimony, the handwriting expert will often make use of demonstrative evidence, such as photographic enlargements of the questioned document and the standards with which it is to be compared. Few courts have refused to permit use of such demonstrative evidence as an aid to understanding.

Compelled Production of Handwriting Exemplars

In *United States* v. *Mara,* 410 U.S. 9 (1973), Mara had been subpoenaed before a grand jury investigating thefts from interstate shipments. He was requested to submit specimens of his handwriting to the grand jury but refused to comply. The Government then petitioned the District Court to compel compliance, arguing that the handwriting exemplars were "essential and necessary" to the grand jury's efforts. The District Court rejected Mara's contention that the request added up to an unlawful search and seizure and ordered compliance. When Mara persisted in his refusal, he was held in contempt of court. The Court of Appeals for the Seventh Circuit reversed the trial court, holding that a showing by the Government of reasonableness was an essential precondition.

The Supreme Court, in turn, reversed the Seventh Circuit. It held that the constitutionality of compulsory production of exemplars is to be gauged by a two-part test: (1) Was the initial compulsion of the witness to appear before the grand jury itself valid? and (2) Was the subsequent demand to produce tangible evidence by itself an unreasonable search within the meaning of the Fourth Amendment?

The Supreme Court concluded that since there is a historical obligation to appear before a grand jury and since such juries have broad investigatory powers, a "subpoena to appear before a grand jury is not a 'seizure' in the Fourth Amendment sense, even though that summons may be inconvenient or burdensome." In other words, a grand jury subpoena to testify is not the sort of governmental breach of privacy that is barred by the Fourth Amendment.

The Court also held that the later demand to produce handwriting exemplars was reasonable. The Fourth Amendment only protects against reasonable expectations of privacy. Since a person reveals his handwriting every day of his life, he can have no reasonable expectation of privacy surrounding the physical characteristics of his writing. Therefore, a demand for handwriting specimens does not cut through the privacy concept that lies at the heart of the Fourth Amendment unless the person involved is being unlawfully detained. (See also the companion case of *United States* v. *Dionisio,* 410 U.S. 1 (1973), resulting in an identical ruling with respect to voice exemplars. This case is mentioned in J., above.)

A Note on Typewriting Comparison

The method for proving the identity of typewriting, like that of handwriting, is based on comparison of the questioned typewriting and one or more standards or exemplars. Jurors are entitled to the expert guidance of a qualified documents examiner in this process; indeed, the admissibility of typewriting identification expertise was first recognized as long ago as 1886 in the Canadian case of *Scott* v. *Crerar,* 14 Ont. App. Rep. 152. The first opinion in the United States to accept typewriting identification evidence was *Levy* v. *Rust,* 49 Atl. 1017, rendered by the Supreme Court of New Jersey in 1893. Again, the weight to be given a typewriting expert's testimony depends in large measure on his or her training and experience.

Sources Of Questioned Documents Expertise

Expertise as a questioned documents examiner is obtained through apprenticeship with a seasoned examiner, through study of technical literature, and through experience.

Qualified documents examiners can be obtained through their professional organizations, the American Society of Questioned Document Examiners, the Questioned Documents Section of the American Academy of Forensic Sciences, and the International Association for Identification.

K. Polygraph Testing

The Polygraph Technique, Equipment, and Examiner

Polygraph ("lie detector") testing is a diagnostic procedure that requires both specialized equipment and a qualified examiner. The premise underlying Polygraph testing is that the natural human tendency is to tell the truth and that the telling of a falsehood causes psychological conflict which in turn produces involuntary physiological responses measurable as indicia of the anxiety caused by lying.

The most commonly used Polygraph equipment consists of two basic components: (1) a recorder of changes in *blood pressure* and *pulse,* and (2) a recorder of changes in *respiration.* (There is also a type of unit that records *electrodermal response*—galvanic skin reflex—which is said to be the result of alterations in the activity of the sweat pores in the subject's hands. Another type of unit records *muscular pressure and movements.*)

Body attachments are employed to record blood pressure, pulse, and respiration: (1) a flexible pneumograph tube is fastened around the chest or abdomen of the test subject and (2) a blood pressure cuff, of the sort commonly used by physicians, is wrapped around the subject's upper arm. For recording electrodermal response, electrodes are fastened to the fingers or hand. No body attachments are used to record muscle pressure and movement; this is accomplished by means of inflated bladders fastened to the chair in which the test subject sits.

Training to be a Polygraph examiner is gained through individualized training and internship. It has been said by such experts in the field as Professor Fred E. Inbau that a Polygraph examiner should be a college graduate who has studied both psychology and physiology. The examiner must also have certain personality traits that permit him to work easily with test subjects. Internship training involves individualized training given by a competent and thoroughly experienced examiner who has enough cases to afford the trainee an opportunity to observe a substantial number of actual Polygraph examinations.

Polygraph Test Procedure

A competent Polygraph examiner will conduct a pretest interview with the subject, during which the nature and purpose of the examination will be explained. The examiner will often impress upon the subject, in a scrupulously objective way, the effectiveness of the technique since this serves to precondition both the honest and the lying subject.

Three types of questions are used in a Polygraph test: (1) relevant questions, (2) control questions, and (3) irrelevant questions. *Relevant questions,* quite obviously, are those relating to the very matter under investigation. *Control questions* are questions that are not directly related to the matter under investigation but which are of a similar, though less serious, nature. For example, the robbery suspect will be asked, "Have you ever robbed anyone?" The recorded physiological response (or lack of one) to this question will then be compared with the responses obtained to relevant questions. *Irrelevant questions* are used in order to determine the subject's norm under test conditions. For example, he may be asked, "Are you twenty-one years of age?"

The following is a run of Polygraph test questions in a moderately complicated case:

1. Are you called Charlie? [The examiner learned during the pretest interview that the subject is generally called "Charlie."]
2. Are you over twenty-one years of age?
3. Did you rob Clyde Bushmat last Saturday night?
4. Are you in Chicago now?
5. Did you knife Clyde Bushmat last Saturday night?
6. Have you ever stolen anything?
7. Did you ever go to high school?
8. Do you know who knifed Clyde Bushmat?
9. Were those your footprints next to Bushmat's body?
10. Have you ever stolen anything from an employer?

One such run of questions does not constitute a complete Polygraph examination, however; at least three more runs of similar makeup—usually more—will be conducted before a diagnosis is attempted. The time interval between the questions is fifteen or twenty seconds and the entire examination will last about an hour. Surprise has nothing to do with the Polygraph technique. The subject is told, ahead of the examination, precisely what the questions will be.

It is an oversimplification, but it is nonetheless generally true that a subject is considered to be telling the truth if his Polygraph responses are greater in connection with the control questions. If the subject's reactions to the relevant questions are greater, deception is suggested.

Even the Polygraph's stoutest defenders recognize that it is not invariably a conclusive diagnostic tool. It has been said that truthfulness or deception will be sharply indicated in about 25 percent of all Polygraph examinations. In about 65 percent of the examinations, the indications will be much more subtle, making it difficult for the examiner to explain them adequately to a fact finder. In the remaining 10 percent of examinations, diagnosis will be completely impossible because of the subject's peculiar psychological or physiological attributes or other special factors beyond the examiner's control.

Despite increasing reliance upon the Polygraph test over the last decades on the part of businesses and employers as well as police investigators, there remain substantial judicial hurdles to the admissibility of such evidence in courts of law, to be discussed below.

The Frye *Case and the General Rule of Inadmissibility*

The first judicial consideration of the Polygraph technique came in *Frye v. United States,* 293 F. 1013 (D.C. Cir. 1923). In 1923 the Polygraph test was referred to by the *Frye* court as "the systolic blood pressure deception test." In *Frye* the trial court was affirmed in its refusal of both the offer of the defendant's expert testimony as to the results of the test and the defense's offer to conduct a test in the presence of the jury. The court said that the test had "not yet gained such standing and scientific recognition among physiological and psychological authorities as would justify the courts in admitting expert testimony deduced from the discovery, development, and experiments thus far made."

The *Frye* standard was interpreted as requiring acceptance within the relevant scientific field and, generally, the rule has continued to be that results of Polygraph testing are inadmissible in courts of law. There are some exceptions to this general proposition, however.

Evidence of "Willingness"

Polygraph evidence being inadmissible, courts generally hold it to be error for either side in a criminal case to make reference to the willingness or unwillingness of a party or witness to subject himself to testing. The reasoning is that if Polygraph evidence is incompetent, willingness or unwilling ness to undergo such testing must also be considered inadmissible; on the one hand it would encourage the jury to draw the same inferences that would be drawn if the actual test results were presented to it, while on the other hand it avoids the normal requirement of laying of a proper foundation for scientific evidence and expert testimony, all the while effectively foreclosing opposing counsel from vital cross-examination.

Courts have rejected the argument that "unwillingness" evidence should be received as evidence of consciousness of guilt, and consider it reversible error in some instances.

(But a number of courts have considered the error harmless, curable by appropriate instruction to the jury, or simply not prejudicial where the defendant did not object or where a motion for a mistrial was untimely.)

Confessions During Polygraph Testing

As for confessions obtained as an incident to Polygraph testing, the rule generally is that the testing does not render a confession inadmissible. It is, however, a factor that is considered by many courts in their determination of the voluntariness of confessions. In addition, at least one author has contested the general rule on the ground that the examinee's bodily responses are by definition involuntary and therefore barred by the Fifth Amendment privilege against self-incrimination. The argument is that no matter how eager a party is to take the test, his responses cannot be said to have been freely given and so confessions given as a result of the Polygraph testing should be barred in later trial proceedings. (See Radeck, *The Admissibility of Polygraph Results in Criminal Trials: A Case for the Status Quo,* 3 Loyola Univ. Law Jour. 289 (1972).)

Stipulation: A Key Exception to the General Rule of Inadmissibility

Like many other evidentiary standards, the rule against the admissibility of Polygraph test results has its exceptions. The largest breach in the barrier to admissibility occurs where there has been a stipulation (agreement) by both parties to the admission of the evidence. Though there is a split among the various courts, Polygraph evidence has been found admissible in criminal cases upon stipulation if certain safeguards are observed.

The most likely reason behind this halfway acceptance of Polygraph test results is increased evidence of the reliability of the Polygraph technique. For example, in *State* v. *Valdez* 371 P. 2d 894 (S. Ct. Ariz. 1962), the Arizona Supreme Court based its holding of admissibility, subsequent to proper stipulation, on recognized advances in the state of the Polygraph art: "Although much remains to be done to perfect the lie-detector as a means of determining credibility, we think it has been developed to a state in which its results are probative enough to warrant admissibility upon stipulation." A later opinion is even more outspoken. *State* v. *McDavitt,* 297 A.2d 849 (S. Ct. N.J. 1972), was a breaking and entering case. The accused, convicted, claimed on appeal that the trial court had erred in admitting into evidence the results of a Polygraph test taken by the accused during trial. The test had been administered, and the results received in evidence, under a stipulation between the accused and the State. In holding that the admission into evidence of the test results was not error, the Supreme Court of New Jersey said, "[P]olygraph testing has been developed to such a point of reliability that in a criminal case when the State and defendant enter into a stipulation to have defendant submit to a Polygraph test, and have the results introduced in evidence, such stipulation should be given effect." The court took judicial notice "that Polygraph testing is used extensively by police and law enforcement agencies and private industry for investigative purposes." It declared that Polygraph testing's "growing use as a scientific tool cannot be doubted."

The rationales of other courts permitting receipt of stipulated Polygraph evidence vary from fair play notions to concepts of contractual agree ment. Demonstrative of the former is the court in *People* v. *Houser,* 193 P. 2d 937 (Cal. App. 1948), where it was remarked that "It would be difficult to hold that defendant should now be permitted on this appeal to take advantage of a claim . . . that as to the results of the test such evidence was inadmissible, merely because it happened to indicate that he was not telling the truth. . . ." Examples of the latter type of reasoning are found in numerous opinions emphasizing the status of a stipulation as a binding agreement.

Courts that refuse to accept stipulations usually point out that a stipulation in no way increases the reliability of Polygraph test results and therefore creates no justification for deviation from a strict exclusionary policy. For example, in *People* v. *Potts,* 220 N.E. 2d 251 (Ill. App. 1966), it was held that stipulation does not foreclose appellate review of the admissibility of Polygraph evidence. The court found that there had not been proper inquiry into the qualifications of the examiner and test conditions, thus affirming the general notion of many courts that stipulation in the case of Polygraph evidence must be accompanied by a variety of safeguards. The court in *Potts* summarized these safeguards:

1. The stipulation must be in writing, signed by both defendant and his/her counsel.
2. It remains within the trial court's discretion to refuse admission based on the examiner's inadequate qualifications and poor test conditions.
3. Each party has the right to cross-examine the examiner regarding:
   a. his or her training;
   b. the test conditions;

c. possible errors in technique; and
d. any other matters considered pertinent.

4. An instruction should be given to the jurors to the effect that they can give *corroborative* weight to the testimony, but that it should not be taken to *establish* (prove) any element of the crime and that the test evidence can indicate truth-telling only as of the time of the exami nation, not before or after.

Accuracy and Reliability

As most courts have interpreted the rule of the *Frye* case, accuracy and reliability have been perceived as the major barriers to acceptance of the Polygraph in courts of law. Most courts feel that the level of accuracy attainable is not sufficient to warrant "general acceptance in the particular field." (*United States* v. *Valdez,* 371 P. 2d 894 (S. Ct. Ariz. 1962).)

Leading proponents of the Polygraph claim that development of the method has achieved a level of accuracy more than equal to that of other scientific evidence presently being admitted in courts. Reid and Inbau claim that a level of known errors of less than 1 percent is obtainable by a trained, competent examiner. (This does not include the 5 percent of cases in which no diagnosis at all is attempted due to psychological or physiological impairment of the subject.)

A study published in 1971 concluded that experienced examiners, viewing only the graph results—that is, the graphic recordings of the various physiological responses made during the examination—could reach a level of accuracy of 86.2 percent. (See Horvath & Reid, *The Reliability of Polygraph Examiner Diagnosis of Truth and Deception,* 62 Jour. of Criminal Law 276 (1971).)

A large part of the Polygraph technique is the examiner's observation of the subject during test preparation and the actual response session. The important Reid and Inbau work on the Polygraph technique, TRUTH AND DECEPTION (1966), is full of commentary on the importance of the examiner's observation of the subject. The following is an example of the methods Reid and Inbau recommend:

> During all of the pretest interview, the examiner should continue to make notes regarding the subject's comments and behavior. Particular attention should be paid to the matter of whether or not he is coughing or sniffing during the pretest interview. If no such activities occur during the interview but they do occur during the test, the fact is indicative of a possible attempt to distort the Polygraph tracings, which in turn may be indicative of deception. . . . A subject who has given such evidence of probable lying . . . will probably continue to do so thereafter, even though cautioned to refrain from such activities prior to his fourth test; or he may resort to some other kind of effort to distort the Polygraph tracings. His continued indulgence in this kind of

> activity . . . can be pointed out to him at the conclusion of the examination, as attention is called to the fact that the examiner's notes reveal that no activities of this sort occurred during the pretest interview . . . No final conclusion could be drawn from the subject's answers or reactions which we have pointed out as indications of probable deception or truthfulness. Nevertheless, they are very helpful as factors to be considered in the ultimate decision to be made of truthfulness or deception. At the very least, they may place the examiner on guard against a positive opinion based upon the test results alone whenever these various pretest answers and reactions point to an opposite indication. (See REID & INBAU at p. 15.)

With so much reliance being placed on the examiner's expertise, it is no wonder that the lack of uniformity of examiner qualifications has supplied a vital area of criticism of the Polygraph technique. Even such staunch supporters of the Polygraph as Reid and Inbau conceded this to be an area of vital concern "basic to . . . the utility and accuracy of the Polygraph technique." They have suggested some specific qualifications:

> Before permitting the results to be admitted as evidence in any case . . . the courts should require the following: (1) That the examiner possess a college degree. (2) That he has received at least six months of internship training under an experienced, competent examiner or examiners with sufficient volume of case work to afford frequent supervised testing in actual case situations. (3) That the examiner have at least five years' experience as a specialist in the field of Polygraph examinations. (4) That the examiner's testimony must be based upon Polygraph records that he produces in court and which are available for cross-examination purposes. (See REID & INBAU at p. 257.)

They also concede that "many persons now functioning as Polygraph examiners do not possess these basic qualifications." Professor Inbau has been quoted as saying: "Eighty percent of the people who administer tests do not measure up to standards we feel are required."

Accuracy figures given by Polygraph technique proponents have been attacked on statistical grounds. Basically, the argument is that in spite of a claim of 99 percent accuracy (on an absolute basis), the resultant level of false positives (i.e., subjects incorrectly diagnosed as liars), when compared with the "actual" number of liars, can result in a figure of accuracy far lower than that touted by Polygraph technique advocates. Skolnick explains why this figure is crucial in his statistical analysis. If the "actual" number of liars at trial is less than 50 percent, then the final accuracy figure is less than the absolute figure that is proposed by Polygraph technique proponents.

EXAMPLE:
Population of 1000 persons, including 10 liars; accuracy of the technique = 90 percent. Test results reveal 9 liars correctly. But of the 990

truthful subjects, *99* will be *incorrectly labeled as liars.* Even at 99 percent accuracy roughly 10 truthtellers will be incorrectly diagnosed as liars.

It is sometimes argued that the basic premises underlying the working of the Polygraph technique have not been generally accepted by physiologists and psychologists. These premises are that there is:

1. A direct and consistent relationship between lying and distinct emotional response, and
2. A high correlation between emotional response and physiological reaction.

Reid and Inbau themselves list a variety of factors affecting test results: lack of concern over the possibility of detection, nervousness, overanxiety, anger, physical discomfort during the test, involvement in other similar acts or offenses, excessive interrogation prior to the test, rationalization and self-deceit, inadequacy of the phraseology of the questions, inadequate control questions, and physiological and mental abnormalities.

There have always been enthusiastic proponents of the Polygraph machine and its methods and some authors have recently expressed optimism about a possible trend moving toward admissibility of such evidence. Scientific and technological arguments aside, it is essential to consider the legal and policy considerations involved in the use of Polygraph evidence.

Lie Detection and the Fifth Amendment Privilege Against Self-Incrimination

It has been suggested that the admissibility of Polygraph results can be successfully contested on the grounds of the Fifth Amendment privilege to refrain from testifying against one's self. (See chapter 8.) But this privilege has been limited to protection against compulsory *testimonial* disclosures. Thus in *U.S.* v. *Wade,* 388 U.S. 218 (1966), a police lineup identification was contested as a violation of this privilege. The Court had no doubt as to the legality of compelling a person to display his/her person for observation by a prosecution witness. And compelling Wade to speak words allegedly spoken by a robber was held not to be testimonial in nature, the purpose being identification, not that of requiring a suspect to speak his own guilt.

The Supreme Court in *Wade* repeated some *dicta* from *United States* v. *Schmerber,* 384 U.S. 751 (1965), explaining that the distinction to be drawn for Fifth Amendment purposes was between "communication," in whatever form (vocal or physical) and "compulsion which makes a suspect or accused the source of 'real or physical evidence.'"

Such language discourages use of Polygraph evidence on a compulsory basis because of its "real" or "physical" nature. However, following a change in Supreme Court personnel during the Nixon administration, this strong *dicta* from *Schmerber* was subjected to erosion by two cases decided together in January 1973.

In *United States* v. *Dionisio*, 410 U.S. 1 (1973), witnesses were found guilty of contempt in refusing to provide voice exemplars to a grand jury that was investigating gambling activities. The witnesses were then required to read transcripts of telephone conversations. This is not barred by the Fifth Amendment because "the voice recordings were to be used solely to measure the physical properties of the witnesses' voices, not for the testimonial or communicative content of what was said." Similarly, in *United States* v. *Mara*, 410 U.S. 19 (1973), a witness was ordered by the grand jury to produce writing exemplars to help in determining whether he was the author of a certain writing. On the face of these decisions it appears clear that physical data can be obtained from the accused in order to link him to a crime. Is there a possibility that the Supreme Court would allow physiological data, obtained with the aid of the Polygraph technique, to be used to link an accused to a crime? In *Dionisio* the Court pointed out that the evidence was not used for the testimonial or communicative content of the words spoken; the same may be said of Polygraph results and testimony by Polygraph experts. Compulsion to display an identifiable physical characteristic has not been considered an infringement on the Fifth Amendment privilege; in *Schmerber* it was said that involuntary blood sampling was not barred by the Fifth Amendment privilege because it was "neither testimony nor evidence relating to some communicative acts." Of course, it will be vigorously argued that Polygraphic responses (physiological measurements) are in fact the product of communicative acts and therefore are to be excluded.

Even if Polygraph evidence were barred because of a relationship to some communicative act, it may be possible to design a Polygraph technique similar to the "peak of tension" test currently in use as part of the Reid and Inbau technique during which the subject would not be required to respond verbally; the physiological responses would be monitored, and so fall within *Schmerber's* definition of real or physical rather than testimonial evidence.

Finally, it may yet develop that debate over the admissibility of forced Polygraph examination is academic because valid testing cannot take place when there is coercion of the subject.

The Hearsay Objection

In *United States* v. *Ridling*, 350 F. Supp. 90 (E.D. Mich. 1972), the court overruled a hearsay objection to Polygraph evidence, comparing the expert testimony to that of "a physician who examines a patient and is permitted to express his opinion of the physiological condition of the patient." "This," the court said, "has nothing to do with hearsay."

The Polygraph's Future

There have been few recent cases allowing presentation of expert testimony revealing the results of Polygraph tests. For example, the court in *United States* v. *DeBetham,* 348 F. Supp. 1377 (S.D. Calif. 1972), though finding that the defendant, in proffering as evidence results of Polygraph examinations, had satisfied the court that significant impairment of the technique's reliability could be precluded through reliance on a truly qualified examiner, held that the defendant had "failed to demonstrate the Polygraph's compliance with the 'general acceptance' test as set forth in *Frye* v. *United States* . . . and interpreted by subsequent case law." (The *DeBetham* opinion contains one of the best judicial reviews of the law and literature in the area of Polygraph evidence.)

Two other cases were at the federal trial level: *United States* v. *Ridling,* 350 S. Supp. 90 (E.D. Mich. 1972), and *United States* v. *Zeiger,* 350 F. Supp. 685 (D.C.D.C. 1972). The *Ridling* case involved a perjury prosecution. The trial court agreed to allow the defendant's Polygraph evidence if the defendant would submit himself to one of three Polygraph experts (designated by the court). The court was careful to limit its ruling to admissibility contingent on use of a court-appointed expert and only in perjury cases. The court said that a perjury case is "the best case for testing the admissibility of the Polygraph evidence. . . . The Polygraph test is aimed at the aspect of truth in issue. . . . [I]t is direct evidence on this point and may be offered by either side regardless of whether the accused takes the stand or puts his character in issue."

In dealing with the various legal grounds for objection, the *Ridling* court said that waiver of the self-incrimination privilege is possible. The court answered a hearsay objection with an analogy to the testimony of a physician who examines a patient and then expresses an opinion as to his physiological state.

In terms of public policy and benefits to the judicial system, the *Ridling* court felt that more defendants would be summarily discharged, decreasing the overburdening of our criminal courts. The court felt that the sophistication of the American jury would be more than adequate to prevent any undue emphasis on such testimony.

But *Ridling* was essentially rejected in a Court of Appeals case, *United States* v. *Frogge,* 476 F. 2d 969 (5th Cir. 1973). The appellate court gave no explanation of its "feeling" that "nothing in *Ridling* persuades us to abandon the traditional view" as expressed in the *Frye* case, *supra.*

Another case, citing *Ridling,* was *United States* v. *Zeiger,* 350 F. Supp. 685 (D.C.D.C. 1972). The trial court made a valiant attempt to show that the *Frye* standards had been met by the defendant's submission of evidence of the technological advances in the field, as demonstrated by various studies of the Polygraph test's accuracy.

As to the danger of overreliance by the jury on such testimony, the *Zeiger* court answered that the problem could be overcome by education, cross-examination, and proper instruction by the judge. However this decision suffered an even worse fate than *Ridling:* it was specifically reversed by the federal Court of Appeals (475 F. 2d 1280 (D.C. Cir. 1972)).

Conclusions

The Polygraph technique has undoubted potential. It seems likely that its admissibility will gradually come to be recognized under carefully controlled conditions. Recent Supreme Court opinions avoid the open hostility displayed by some writers on the subject, and recent lower court federal cases indicate that at least some judges are willing to accept Polygraph evidence under certain circumstances.

The most important of these lower court cases is *United States* v. *Piccinonna,* 885 F. 2d 1529 (llth Cir. 1989). The defendant had been charged with committing perjury before a grand jury investigating antitrust violations. Prior to trial the US. Attorney turned down the defendant's requested stipulation to the admissibility of the results of a proposed Polygraph examination. Undaunted, the defendant took the test and offered the results in evidence. The trial judge, citing the 11th Circuit's absolute rule against admitting lie detector results, excluded the evidence.

The Court of Appeals reversed. It observed that the traditional bar against Polygraph evidence, *Frye's* general acceptance standard, has come under increasing criticism. The "tremendous advances" in instrumentation, technique, and training, along with extensive use of Polygraph by federal agencies, were said to warrant reexamination of the court's absolutist position. Declaring that "the science of polygraphy has progressed to a level of acceptance sufficient to allow the use of polygraph evidence in limited circumstances where the danger of unfair prejudice is minimized." The *Piccinonna* opinion defined two situations in which a trial court could receive Polygraph evidence. The first is one that we discussed above: where both parties have stipulated in advance to the circumstances of the testing and the scope of the admissibility of the results. Second, the courts would be free to admit Polygraph evidence either to impeach or to corroborate the testimony of an impeached witness, provided the opposing party had adequate notice and an opportunity to have its own expert give an examination involving the same questions. A dissenting judge insisted that the court's majority overstated the reliability of lie detector evidence.

Improvements in the Polygraph technique itself may soon undercut the standard objections of unreliability and inaccuracy; defense lawyers will have to turn to other issues, such as those in constitutional realms (Fifth Amendment) or involving statistical interpretation.

L. Speed Detection

Detection of Vehicle Speed

For many years police got along without such scientific methods for detecting vehicular speed as radar and the *Visual Average Speed Computer and Record* (VASCAR) technique. Traffic officers have always been permitted to testify that they were able to "check" or "clock" the arrestee by reference to a police vehicle's speedometer. For that matter, a police officer can simply testify to his or her own observation that the accused was driving at a speed in excess of the posted limit. And a few simple devices, such as a tube connected to a mechanism that measures the time lapse between the passage of the front wheels and the rear wheels over the tube, antedated reliance on more sophisticated equipment. Today, however, many police departments rely heavily on the two scientific speed detection methods mentioned above.

Radar: What It Means and How It Works

The term *radar* stands for *radio detection and ranging*. The radar speedometer used by many police departments is similar in theory and operation to the military radar that was developed during World War II. The basic components of a police radar speedometer are a transmitter and a receiver of radio waves. These two basic components are linked to a voltmeter calibrated in mile-per-hour equivalents. Sometimes there is also a graph recorder on the equipment.

The radio wave transmitter sends out a continuous and constant stream of radio waves in the direction in which the speedometer has been aimed. When this beam hits an object, such as a passenger car, part of the beam is bounced back to the receiver component of the radar device; this is called an *echo*.

When the object struck by the radio wave beam is at a standstill, the frequency of the echo will be the same as the frequency of the outward beam, but if the object is coming toward or going away from the radar transmitter the echo will have a different frequency. The change in frequency varies in direct relationship to the speed of the moving object off which the echo has bounced. This is the so-called Doppler Effect, named after its discoverer, Christian J. Doppler.

A calculation made automatically inside the radar equipment determines the difference in frequencies between the outgoing and incoming waves; the speed (velocity) of the vehicle is recorded in mile-per-hour equivalents on the face of the voltmeter. A traffic control officer in the radar car radios registered speed, license number (if possible), and a description of the offending driver and his vehicle to a "catch" car located down the road from the radar car. It is the traffic control of ficer in the radar car who records the offender's speed and issues the summons. (Only the officer in the control car can properly testify to the offender's speed; the officer in the "catch" car would be subject to a hearsay objection were he to recount the speed registration relayed to him by the officer in the radar car.)

Police officers using radar equipment must know how to operate it properly and must be prepared to testify in court that they did so on the occasion in question. Furthermore, most jurisdictions have laid down requirements for the testing of radar equipment prior to and after its use. Testing can be accomplished with one or more tuning forks but the road test is probably the most common testing method: a police car with a calibrated speedometer is driven past the radar device and the speedometer reading in the car is compared with the reading on the radar unit.

VASCAR

The VASCAR device has three components: an odometer module, a control module, and a computer module. It operates on the indisputable formula that an object's average velocity equals the distance traveled divided by the time taken to travel that distance. The odometer module measures time and distance. The control module activates the distance- and time-measuring device. Its readout feature gives a digital reading of speed.

When a vehicle reaches a reference point on the roadway, the time switch is turned on, activating the time circuitry in the computer module. When the police car reaches the reference point, the distance switch is turned on; this activates the distance circuitry, which will record the distance being measured by the police car. As the violator reaches a second fixed point, the time switch will be turned off. The period of time taken by the violator's vehicle to travel between the two reference points has been measured and fed into the computer module. When the police vehicle reaches the second reference point, the distance switch is shut off. Now the distance between the two reference points has been measured and fed into the computer module. The violator's speed is electronically computed and shows on the readout in miles per hour. The offender's speed will continue to show on the readout until a reset button is pushed.

Judicial Acceptance of Scientific Speed Detection

The admissibility of radar evidence of speed is guaranteed by statute in some states, so that expert testimony concerning the scientific validity of the radar principle is unnecessary. In many other states the courts will now take judicial notice of its worth. All that is required is proof of proper testing and operation of the equipment. The foundation for receipt of radar evidence will thus usually involve four steps:

1. Proof that the operator of the radar equipment had the necessary training;
2. Proof that the equipment had been properly calibrated, checked, and tested *after* being put in position;
3. Testimony by the operator that he or she observed the speed of the violator's vehicle on the radar apparatus as the vehicle broke the radar beam; and
4. Testimony by the operator that he or she could identify the defendant's vehicle as being the one responsible for the speed reading about which the operator is testifying.

Although VASCAR is a relatively new technique, at least one lower court has recognized its scientific validity (see *State* v. *Schmiede,* 289 A. 2d 281 (N.J. Super. 1972)). It is likely that VASCAR will be as widely and fully recognized as radar.

Lasers

In part because of the favorable publicity it received during the Gulf War, it is possible that laser technology will someday supplant radar and Vascar in the field of speed detection. ("Laser" is an acronym: Light Amplification by Simulated Emission of Radiations.") A laser "gun" produces a straight, narrow, intense beam of light that can be focused—and "lock" on—a narrow target, unlike radar. This makes for ease and precision in target selection, a speeding vehicle. It also has the advantage of being immune to the sort of countermeasures sometimes employed by motorists to disrupt radar.

Although the use of laser guns is on the increase, several problems remain. More police officers will have to be trained in their use. Lasers do not function effectively under poor weather conditions: the laser's light waves are reflected or dispersed by snow, rain, or hail. There is a lingering question whether a laser beam, striking a person in the eyes, may be seriously injurious. And, finally, laser units are currently almost twice as expensive as radar devices.

CHAPTER NINETEEN

Demonstrative Evidence

A. Historical Background

It is pointed out in chapter 3 that demonstrative evidence is to be distinguished from real evidence in that demonstrative evidence consists of tangible materials that are used for illustrative or explanatory purposes only and do not purport to be "the real thing"—the murder weapon, the burglary tools actually used by the accused, the heroin seized by the narcotics agents when they arrested the defendant. It was also mentioned in chapter 3 that there are two basic types of demonstrative evidence: (1) *selected* demonstrative evidence, such as handwriting exemplars, and (2) *prepared* or *reproduced* demonstrative evidence, such as a sketch or diagram. The sort of evidentiary foundation that must be laid by counsel preliminarily to an offer of demonstrative evidence was described in chapter 3, which deals generally with the making of the trial record. In this chapter we go into somewhat greater depth in describing types of demonstrative evidence and the range of possible objections to its use.

There has been a resurgence of interest in the imaginative use of demonstrative evidence, after a lengthy period during which trial lawyers were reluctant to rely on it for fear of causing an adverse reaction by jurors who might draw the implication that an essentially weak case was being overproved by means of unsubstantial gimmickry. Unquestionably, the use of demonstrative evidence has had its ups and downs, as the following commentary—made almost a hundred years ago—attests:

> In the early and rude ages there was a strong leaning toward the adoption of demonstrative and practical tests upon disputed questions. Doubting Thomases demanded the satisfaction of their senses. . . . As society grew civilized and refined, it seemed disposed to despise these demonstrative methods,

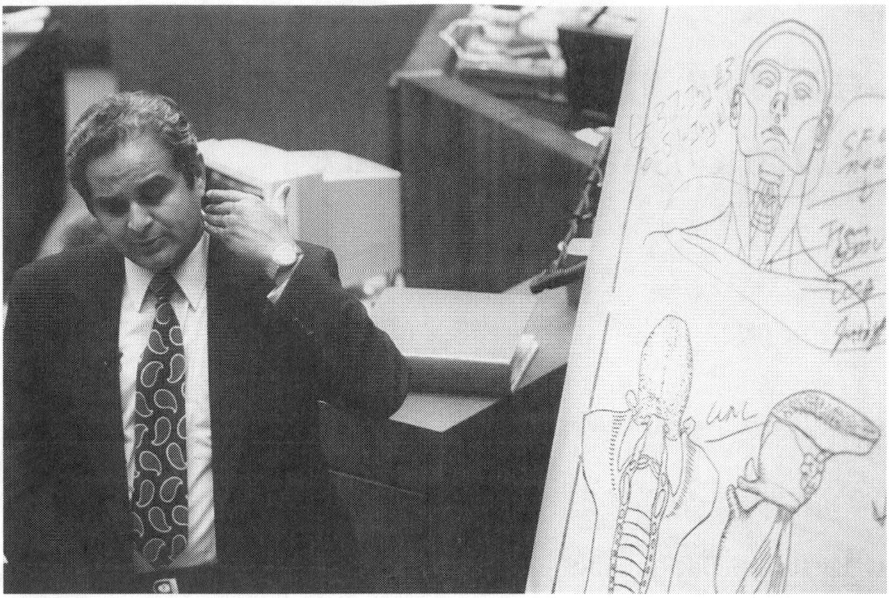

The Los Angeles County Coroner presents evidence showing injuries sustained by victim Ronald Goldman. He testified during the O. J. Simpson murder trial in 1995.

> and inclined more to the preference of a narration, at second-hand, by eye and ear witnesses. But in this busy century there seems to have been a relapse toward the earlier experimental spirit, and a disposition to make assurance doubly sure by any practical method addressed to the senses. (Browne, *Practical Tests in Evidence,* 4 Green Bag 510 (1892).)

Of course, there is nothing inherently wrong with evidence which is addressed to some sense other than that of hearing. One character in the musical *My Fair Lady* may have unwittingly summed up the attitude of many jury members when she said, "Words, words, words—I'm sick of words. Is that all you [lawyers] can do? *Show me!*"

For a number of years now, trial lawyers have paid increasing attention to demonstrative evidence as a means of *showing* the elements of a case to the fact-finder.

Perhaps the earliest reported use of demonstrative evidence was in the case of *James Watson, the elder, Surgeon, on an Indictment charging him with High Treason,* 32 Howard State Trials 1 (1817). There was offered into evidence in that case a sketch of a flag that allegedly had been used to whip up a "treasonous assemblage" in England. Defense counsel objected, arguing that the flag "was a matter of verbal description, not of description by drawing." The trial judge sneered and overruled the objection: "Can there be any objection to the production of a drawing, or a model, as illustrative of evidence? Surely there is nothing in the objection."

Another leading case, this time arising in America but not many years after the Watson trial, is *Commonwealth* v. *Webster,* 5 Cush. 295 (Sup. Jud. Ct. Mass. 1850). Professor Webster had been charged with murdering Doctor Parkman and burning his body in a furnace. A mold of Doctor Parkman's jaw, made several years previously when he had been fitted for dentures, taken together with some teeth that had survived the furnace fire, was credited with securing Webster's conviction.

Today the propriety, in fact the wisdom, of using demonstrative evidence to help jurors follow the trial evidence goes pretty much without question in many cases, both criminal and civil. Objections to demonstrative evidence are frequently voiced, however.

B. Bases for Objection to Demonstrative Evidence

Misguided Objections

Some objections to demonstrative evidence are misguided and will be swiftly overruled. Occasionally a lawyer will become confused about the proper application of the best evidence rule, discussed in chapter 16, and contend that the "original," and not "a mere example," must be produced in court. Thus one hears about the Texas judge who prohibited the use of a skeletal model because it did not consist of the very bones of the complaining witness (who was not dead). This judge had forgotten, if he ever knew, that the best evidence rule applies only to written documents.

Then, too, one sometimes encounters a misguided hearsay objection to demonstrative evidence. Defense counsel leaps up to object to the prosecution's offer of a witness's freehand sketch of a crime scene, asking, "How can we cross-examine a sketch, Your Honor?" What this objection misses, of course, is the fact that the sketch is being offered as part of the testimony of a witness on the stand who is fully subject to confrontation and cross-examination.

Objections Grounded on Lack of Verity or Accuracy

As was suggested in chapter 3, dealing with the perfecting of the trial record, a proper foundation or predicate must be laid before an item of demonstrative evidence can successfully be offered. The witness who is in a position to "sponsor" (authenticate) the exhibit must identify it and verify the accuracy of whatever it portrays. This does not mean that the sponsoring witness must be the person who took the photograph or prepared the drawing, chart, or map.

EXAMPLE:

BY THE PROSECUTING ATTORNEY: Officer Ham, you have testified that you were present, in your investigative capacity, at the scene of the murders, isn't that correct?

A: That's right, I was in the room for maybe three hours.

Q: And you have testified to its general layout and appearance, have you not?

A: Yes, our photographer took a number of shots of the place.

Q: Officer Ham, I now hand you what previously has been marked Prosecution Exhibit 12 for Identification, being a photographic print, and ask you whether or not it is a fair and accurate representation of the room at 421 Melrose Street on the day in question?

A: Yes, sir, it is. That's exactly the way it looked.

BY THE PROSECUTING ATTORNEY: Your Honor, we offer prosecution's 12 into evidence.

BY DEFENSE COUNSEL: We have no objection.

THE COURT: The exhibit will be received.

There can be no stronger an objection to demonstrative evidence than that it is not a fair representation of what it supposedly depicts. If, for example, a photograph or a map significantly distorts relevant aspects of the scene depicted, it will be subject to successful objection, or at least to an instruction that the jury is to disregard the distorted parts.

Occasionally photographs can be obtained only after autopsy procedures have in a sense distorted the picture of a deceased: the head has been shaved; large incisions have been made; sutures may be visible. Still, the tendency is to admit such photographs if they add to the case anything of real probative value. Thus in *Young* v. *State,* 299 P. 682 (S. Ct. Ariz. 1931), the court, commenting on the receipt in evidence of post-autopsy photographs, said, "[T]he fact of the ghastly appearance of the wounds, even though such appearance was heightened by the shaving of the head and the use of mercurochrome . . . did not make [the photographs] inadmissible."

So long as the color has not been artificially and misleadingly heightened, there is a trend toward preferring natural color to black-and-white photographs. Some years ago Professor Conrad, an authority on photographic evidence, wrote "[W]e have used black and white photographs for so long that we accept them as the real thing. Actually, black and white photography is considered an abstract medium and does not represent reality as such. . . . The inherent realism of color photography has been urged [as preferable to black and white]. . . ." (Conrad, *Evidential Aspects of Color Photography,* 4 Jour. of Forensic Science 176, 178 (1959).)

The fact that a photograph or other item of demonstrative evidence has been retouched or marked will not, in and of itself, result in inadmissibility. For example, in *State* v. *Weston,* 64 P. 2d 536 (S. Ct. Ore. 1937), plaster casts of a body containing gunshot wounds had been prepared prior to autopsy. Many small blue dots had been placed on the casts by a witness who compared the casts with the body in order to distinguish the bullet wounds from air bubbles in the plaster cast. When the casts were offered in evidence to exemplify the location of the bullet wounds, defense counsel objected that "after the blue dots which indicate the wounds had been placed upon the cast it was no longer . . . a true representation of deceased's forearm and hand." The Oregon Supreme Court laid down the applicable principles:

> The jury was amply informed that the sole purpose of the blue dots was to indicate the presence of the wounds. Since the jurors could rightfully look at the indications of the wounds, we cannot understand how the help which these small dots gave them in locating the wounds would have prejudiced any interest properly claimed by the defendant. . . .
>
> [W]e deduce the rule that maps, photographs, et cetera, containing markings, are not inadmissible if they are otherwise relevant and if the individual who made the mark or wrote the legend was familiar with the facts and so testifies, or if some other witness, familiar with the facts, adopts the mark or legend as his own. (See also Busch, *Photographic Evidence,* 4 DePaul Law Rev. 195 (1955).)

Models are sometimes rejected by trial courts because they may be misleading or confusing due to difference in scale.

EXAMPLE A:
San Mateo County v. *Christian,* 71 P. 2d 88 (Cal. App. 1937) ("While models may frequently be of great assistance to a court and jury, it is common knowledge that even when constructed to scale, they may frequently, because of the great disparity in size between the model and the original, also be very misleading. . . .").

EXAMPLE B:
Martingdale v. *City of Mountain View,* 25 Cal. Rptr. 148 (Cal. App. 1962) (in assault and battery case, testimony was that victim had been beaten with 2′ stick; offer in evidence of axe handle 3′ long rejected).

Courts are suspicious of filmed reenactments and posed photographs, lest they be misleading. A leading case, *Richardson* v. *Missouri-K.T.R. Co. of Texas,* 205 S.W. 2d 819 (Tex. Civ. App. 1947), arose on the civil side. To establish that the plaintiff himself had been negligent, the defendant introduced a color film showing plaintiff's shop foreman demonstrating how plaintiff's hand "*could* be caught and run through the blades" of a shaping machine (italics added). The foreman testified that "he did not know how the fingers of [plaintiff] were caught in the machine and therefore his experiments did not undertake to show how [plaintiff] was operating it at the time."

The Texas court brushed aside the plaintiff's objections to this filmed reenactment. "In the final analysis," the court said, "the increased danger of fraud peculiar to posed photographs must be weighed against their communicative value. Only the additional danger of fraud or suggestion separates this question from that of the admissibility of ordinary photographs."

In line with the *Richardson* decision, posed and photographed reenactments of a crime are sometimes admitted in evidence after a careful foundation, which manifests the accuracy of the reenactment, has been laid by the prosecuting attorney.

Computer technology, although commonplace in certain sorts of civil cases, has not yet had much impact on the trial of criminal matters. Until recently there was only one reported appellate case involving the use of this technology to produce demonstrative evidence in a criminal matter. (*People* v. *McHugh,* 476 N.Y.S.2d 721 (1984).) Its use, however, is likely to increase as both prosecutors and defense counsel become fully familiar with its potential and as its cost gradually comes down. It is enough to mention here the two current uses of the computer to generate demonstrative evidence. First there is computer *animation.* This involves a series of still images produced on a computer. These images, when viewed frame-by-frame at playback speed, produce a moving picture, an animation.

The second form of computer-generated demonstrative evidence is the computer *simulation.* It combines the computer's animation capability with its computation capabilities. A simulation is a projection of possible outcomes—such as the trajectories of vehicles following impact—mathematically predicted by a computer program. The simulation is converted to an animation that can be stored on a videotape or a laser disc.

It is the animation that most readily lends itself to demonstrative use. Simulations are more frequently used as part of the basis for an opinion by an expert and this may bring either the *Frye* or *Daubert* test into play.

Gruesome Films and Photographs

As was intimated earlier, another prime basis of objections to demonstrative evidence is that the motion picture or still photograph is gruesome and inflammatory; in other words, that its potential for prejudice to the accused's right to a fair trial outweighs whatever probative worth it may have. An objection of this sort is directed to the trial judge's discretion.

A photograph or motion picture is not admissible simply because it is gruesome. That has been understood ever since the opinion in *Franklin* v. *State,* 69 Ga. 36 (S. Ct. Ga. 1882), involving some gruesome photographs:

> The throat of the deceased was cut; the character of the wound was important . . .; the man was killed and buried . . .; we cannot conceive of a more impartial and truthful witness than the sun, as its light stamps and seals the similitude of the wound on the photograph put before the jury; it would be more accurate than the memory of witnesses, and as the object of all evidence is to show the truth, why should not this dumb [in the sense of mute] witness show it?

Ever since *Franklin* it has been the rule that photographs and films are not rendered inadmissible simply because they depict in a graphic way the details of a shocking or revolting crime. They will be deemed inadmissible only if they are irrelevant to the issues in the case or where their probative worth is outweighed by their potential for unfair prejudice.

EXAMPLE A:
Johnson v. *Commonwealth,* 445 S.W. 2d 704 (S. Ct. Ky. 1970) (hideous photographs showing mangled body in morgue, *held,* admissible to support autopsy surgeon's explanatory testimony).

EXAMPLE B:
Henninger v. *State,* 251 So. 2d 862 (S. Ct. Fla. 1971) (three gruesome photographs showing knife wounds in back, partially severed head, and pantyhose wrapped around neck, *held,* admissible to establish identity of accused, cause of death, and to rebut claim of self-defense).

Appellate courts will conclude that it was an abuse of judicial discretion to receive gruesome photographs only when they were unnecessary, cumulative to the narrative testimony of witnesses, or where, although of minimal evidentiary value, they have been overemphasized to the jury. Thus it may be error to admit gruesome photographs when the testimony of an available pathologist would do just as well (see, e.g., *State* v. *Bischert,* 308 P. 2d 969 (S. Ct. Mont. 1957)). In an early California case, *Thrall* v. *Smiley,* 9 Cal. Rep. 529 (S. Ct. Cal. 1858), the court rejected drawings of the defendant's damaged teeth, noting that the sketches were not "necessary to illustrate the fact asserted [since] the extent of the injury could be as well understood from the statement of the dentist who repaired them." And projecting color slides of the deceased's wounds for a full half day during a four and one-half day trial has led to reversal. (*Commonwealth* v. *Johnson,* 167 A. 2d 511 (S. Ct. Pa. 1961).) Some additional examples are given below:

EXAMPLE A:
Commonwealth v. *Dankel,* 301 A. 2d 365 (S. Ct. Pa. 1973) (where only factual dispute was whether accused aided in burglary during which

a homicide occurred, introduction by prosecution of four gruesome photographs of victim, showing face eroded by ammonia burns, was reversible error).

EXAMPLE B:
Terry v. *State,* 491 S.W. 2d 161 (Tex. Crim. App. 1973) (where bruises and other injuries sustained by infant homicide victim had already been shown with pre-autopsy photographs, it was prejudicial error to receive four post-autopsy photographs depicting massive mutilation to child caused by autopsy procedures).

EXAMPLE C:
Beagles v. *State,* 273 So. 2d 796 (Fla. App. 1973) (where defense in first degree murder case admitted victim's death, the cause of death, and her identity, the admission of numerous gruesome color photographs of the victim was error: "Photographs should be received in evidence with great caution and photographs which show nothing more than a gory or gruesome portrayal should not be admitted.").

Trial judges will protect an accused against the use of demonstrative evidence the primary purpose of which is to whip jurors into a vindictive mood. But demonstrative evidence has a firmly settled place in criminal litigation. If it is used sparingly, with scrupulous accuracy, and only when it holds out genuine promise of making the case more readily understandable by judge and jurors, courts can be expected to be liberal in their rulings on the admissibility question.

APPENDIX

Federal Rules of Evidence for United States Courts and Magistrates

As amended to December 1, 1994

Table of Rules

Article I. General Provisions

Article II. Judicial Notice

Article VI. Witnesses

601. General rule of complacency.
602. Lack of personal knowledge.
603. Oath or affirmation.
604. Interpreters.
605. Competency of judge as witness.
606. Competency of juror as witness:
    (a) At the trial.
    (b) Inquiry into validity of verdict or indictment.
607. Who may impeach.
608. Evidence of character and conduct of witness:
    (a) Opinion and reputation evidence of character.
    (b) Specific instances of conduct.
609. Impeachment by evidence of conviction of crime:
    (a) General rule.
    (b) Time limit.
    (c) Effect of pardon, annulment, or certificate of rehabilitation.
    (d) Juvenile adjudications.
    (e) Pendency of appeal.
610. Religious beliefs or opinions.
611. Mode and order of interrogation and presentation:
    (a) Control by court.
    (b) Scope of cross-examination.
    (c) Leading questions.
612. Writing used to refresh memory.
613. Prior statements of witnesses:
    (a) Examining witnesses concerning prior statement.
    (b) Extrinsic evidence of prior inconsistent statement of witness.
614. Calling and interrogation of witnesses by court.:
    (a) Calling by court.
    (b) Interrogation by court.
    (c) Objections.
615. Exclusion of witnesses.

Article VII. Opinions and Expert Testimony

701. Opinion testimony by lay witnesses.
702. Testimony by experts.
703. Bases of opinion testimony by experts.
704. Opinion on ultimate issue.
705. Disclosure of facts or data underlying expert opinion.
706. Court appointed experts:
    (a) Appointment.

(b) Compensation.
(c) Disclosure of appointment.
(d) Parties' experts of own selection.

Article VIII. Hearsay

801. Definitions:
   (a) Statement.
   (b) Declarant.
   (c) Hearsay.
   (d) Statements which are not hearsay:
      (1) Prior statement by witness.
      (2) Admission by party-opponent.
802. Hearsay rule.
803. Hearsay exceptions; availability of declarant immaterial:
   (1) Present sense impression.
   (2) Excited utterance.
   (3) Then existing mental, emotional, or physical condition.
   (4) Statements for purposes of medical diagnosis or treatment.
   (5) Recorded recollection.
   (6) Records of regularly conducted activity.
   (7) Absence of entry in records kept in accordance with the provisions of paragraph (6).
   (8) Public records and reports.
   (9) Records of vital statistics.
   (10) Absence of public record or entry.
   (11) Records of religious organizations.
   (12) Marriage, baptismal, and similar certificates.
   (13) Family records.
   (14) Records of documents affecting an interest in property.
   (15) Statements in documents affecting an interest in property.
   (16) Statements in ancient documents.
   (17) Market reports, commercial publications.
   (18) Learned treatises.
   (19) Reputation concerning personal or family history.
   (20) Reputation concerning boundaries or general history.
   (21) Reputation as to character.
   (22) Judgment of previous conviction.
   (23) Judgment as to personal, family, or general history, or boundaries.
   (24) Other exceptions.
804. Hearsay exceptions; declarant unavailable:
   (a) Definition of unavailability.
   (b) Hearsay exceptions:

(1) Former testimony.
(2) Statement under belief of impending death.
(3) Statement against interest.
(4) Statement of personal or family history.
(5) Other exceptions.

805. Hearsay within hearsay.
806. Attacking and supporting credibility of declarant.

Article IX. Authentication and Identification

901. Requirement of authentication or identification:
    (a) General provision.
    (b) Illustrations:
        (1) Testimony of witness with knowledge.
        (2) Nonexpert opinion on handwriting.
        (3) Comparison by trier or expert witness.
        (4) Distinctive characteristics and the like.
        (5) Voice identification.
        (6) Telephone conversation.
        (7) Public records or reports.
        (8) Ancient documents or data compilation.
        (9) Process or system.
        (10) Methods provided by statute or rule.
902. Self-authentication:
    (1) Domestic public documents under seal.
    (2) Domestic public documents not under seal.
    (3) Foreign public documents.
    (4) Certified copies of public records.
    (5) Official publications.
    (6) Newspapers and periodicals.
    (7) Trade inscriptions and the like.
    (8) Acknowledged documents.
    (9) Commercial paper and related documents.
    (10) Presumptions under Acts of Congress.
903. Subscribing witness' testimony unnecessary.

Article X. Contents of Writings, Recordings, and Photographs

1001. Definitions:
    (1) Writings and recordings.
    (2) Photographs.
    (3) Original.
    (4) Duplicate.
1002. Requirement of original.

Article I. General Provisions

Rule 101. Scope

These rules govern proceedings in the courts of the United States and before United States bankruptcy judges and United States magistrate judges, to the extent and with the exceptions stated in rule 1101.

Rule 102. Purpose and Construction

These rules shall be construed to secure fairness in administration, elimination of unjustifiable expense and delay, and promotion of growth and development of the law of evidence to the end that the truth may be ascertained and proceedings justly determined.

Rule 103. Rulings on Evidence

(a) Effect of Erroneous Ruling. Error may not be predicated upon a ruling which admits or excludes evidence unless a substantial right of the party is affected, and

(1) *Objection.* In case the ruling is one admitting evidence, a timely objection or motion to strike appears of record, stating the specific ground of objection, if the specific ground was not apparent from the context; or

(2) *Offer of Proof.* In case the ruling is one excluding evidence, the substance of the evidence was made known to the court by offer or was apparent from the context within which questions were asked.

(b) Record of Offer and Ruling. The court may add any other or further statement which shows the character of the evidence, the form in which it was offered, the objection made, and the ruling thereon. It may direct the making of an offer in question and answer form.

(c) Hearing of Jury. In jury cases, proceedings shall be conducted, to the extent practicable, so as to prevent inadmissible evidence from being suggested to the jury by any means, such as making statements or offers of proof or asking questions in the hearing of the jury.

(d) Plain Error. Nothing in this rule precludes taking notice of plain errors affecting substantial rights although they were not brought to the attention of the court.

Rule 104. Preliminary Questions

(a) Questions of Admissibility Generally. Preliminary questions concerning the qualification of a person to be a witness, the existence of a privilege, or the admissibility of evidence shall be determined by the court, subject to the provisions of subdivision (b). In making its determination it is not bound by the rules of evidence except those with respect to privileges.

(b) Relevancy Conditioned on Fact. When the relevancy of evidence depends upon the fulfillment of a condition of fact, the court shall admit it upon, or subject to, the introduction of evidence sufficient to support a finding of the fulfillment of the condition.

(c) Hearing of Jury. Hearings on the admissibility of confessions shall in all cases be conducted out of the hearing of the jury. Hearings on other preliminary matters shall be so conducted when the interests of justice require, or when an accused is a witness and so requests.

(d) Testimony by Accused. The accused does not, by testifying upon a preliminary matter, become subject to cross-examination as to other issues in the case.

(e) Weight and Credibility. This rule does not limit the right of a party to introduce before the jury evidence relevant to weight or credibility.

Rule 105. Limited Admissibility

When evidence which is admissible as to one party or for one purpose but not admissible as to another party or for another purpose is admitted, the court, upon request, shall restrict the evidence to its proper scope and instruct the jury accordingly.

Rule 106. Remainder of or Related Writings or Recorded Statements

When a writing or recorded statement or part thereof is introduced by a party, an adverse party may require the introduction at that time of any other part or any other writing or recorded statement which ought in fairness to be considered contemporaneously with it.

Article II. Judicial Notice

Rule 201. Judicial Notice of Adjudicative Facts

(a) Scope of Rule. This rule governs only judicial notice of adjudicative facts.

(b) Kinds of Facts. A judicially noticed fact must be one not subject to reasonable dispute in that it is either (1) generally known within the territorial jurisdiction of the trial court or (2) capable of accurate and ready determination by resort to sources whose accuracy cannot reasonably be questioned.

(c) When Discretionary. A court may take judicial notice, whether requested or not.

(d) When Mandatory. A court shall take judicial notice if requested by a party and supplied with the necessary information.

(e) Opportunity to Be Heard. A party is entitled upon timely request to an opportunity to be heard as to the propriety of taking judicial notice and the tenor of the matter noticed. In the absence of prior notification, the request may be made after judicial notice has been taken.

(f) Time of Taking Notice. Judicial notice may be taken at any stage of the proceeding.

(g) Instructing Jury. In a civil action or proceeding, the court shall instruct the jury to accept as conclusive any fact judicially noticed. In a criminal case, the court shall instruct the jury that it may, but is not required to, accept as conclusive any fact judicially noticed.

Article III. Presumptions in Civil Actions and Proceedings

Rule 301. Presumptions in General in Civil Actions and Proceedings

In all civil actions and proceedings not otherwise provided for by Act of Congress or by these rules, a presumption imposes on the party against whom it is directed the burden of going forward with evidence to rebut or meet the presumption, but does not shift to such party the burden of proof in the sense of the risk of nonpersuasion, which remains throughout the trial upon the party on whom it was originally cast.

Rule 302. Applicability of State Law in Civil Actions and Proceedings

In civil actions and proceedings, the effect of a presumption respecting a fact which is an element of a claim or defense as to which State law supplies the rule of decision is determined in accordance with State law.

Article IV. Relevancy and Its Limits

Rule 401. Definition of "Relevant Evidence"

"Relevant evidence" means evidence having any tendency to make the existence of any fact that is of consequence to the determination of the action more probable or less probable than it would be without the evidence.

Rule 402. Relevant Evidence Generally Admissible; Irrelevant Evidence Inadmissible

All relevant evidence is admissible, except as otherwise provided by the Constitution of the United States, by Act of Congress, by these rules, or by other rules prescribed by the Supreme Court pursuant to statutory authority. Evidence which is not relevant is not admissible.

Rule 403. Exclusion of Relevant Evidence on Grounds of Prejudice, Confusion, or Waste of Time

Although relevant, evidence may be excluded if its probative value is substantially outweighed by the danger of unfair prejudice, confusion of the issues, or misleading the jury, or by considerations of undue delay, waste of time, or needless presentation of cumulative evidence.

Rule 404. Character Evidence Not Admissible to Prove Conduct; Exceptions; Other Crimes

(a) Character Evidence Generally. Evidence of a person's character or a trait of character is not admissible for the purpose of proving action in conformity therewith on a particular occasion, except:

(1) *Character of Accused.* Evidence of a pertinent trait of character offered by an accused, or by the prosecution to rebut the same;

(2) *Character of Victim.* Evidence of a pertinent trait of character of the victim of the crime offered by an accused, or by the prosecution to rebut the same, or evidence of a character trait of peacefulness of the victim offered by the prosecution in a homicide case to rebut evidence that the victim was the first aggressor;

(3) *Character of Witness.* Evidence of the character of a witness, as provided in rules 607, 608, and 609.

(b) Other Crimes, Wrongs, or Acts. Evidence of other crimes, wrongs, or acts is not admissible to prove the character of a person in order to show action in conformity therewith. It may, however, be admissible for other purposes, such as proof of motive, opportunity, intent, preparation, plan, knowledge, identity, or absence of mistake or accident, provided that upon request by the accused, the prosecution in a criminal case shall provide reasonable notice in advance of trial, or during trial if the court excuses pretrial notice on good cause shown, of the general nature of any such evidence it intends to introduce at trial.

Rule 405. Methods of Proving Character

(a) Reputation or Opinion. In all cases in which evidence of character or a trait of character of a person is admissible, proof may be made by testimony as to reputation or by testimony in the form of an opinion. On cross-examination, inquiry is allowable into relevant specific instances of conduct.

(b) Specific Instances of Conduct In cases in which character or a trait of character of a person is an essential element of a charge, claim, or defense, proof may also be made of specific instances of that person's conduct.

Rule 406. Habit; Routine Practice

Evidence of the habit of a person or of the routine practice of an organization, whether corroborated or not and regardless of the presence of eyewitnesses, is relevant to prove that the conduct of the person or organization on a particular occasion was in conformity with the habit or routine practice.

Rule 407. Subsequent Remedial Measures

When, after an event, measures are taken which, if taken previously, would have made the event less likely to occur, evidence of the subsequent measures is not admissible to prove negligence or culpable conduct in connection with the event. This rule does not require the exclusion of evidence of subsequent measures when offered for another purpose, such as proving ownership, control, or feasibility of precautionary measures, if controverted, or impeachment.

Rule 408. Compromise and Offers to Compromise

Evidence of (1) furnishing or offering or promising to furnish, or (2) accepting or offering or promising to accept, a valuable consideration in compromising or attempting to compromise a claim which was disputed as to either validity or amount, is not admissible to prove liability for or invalidity of the claim or its amount. Evidence of conduct or statements made in compromise negotiations is likewise not admissible. This rule does not require the exclusion of any evidence otherwise discoverable merely because it is presented in the course of compromise negotiations. This rule also does not require exclusion when the evidence is offered for another purpose, such as proving bias or prejudice of a witness, negativing a contention of undue delay, or proving an effort to obstruct a criminal investigation or prosecution.

Rule 409. Payment of Medical and Similar Expenses

Evidence of furnishing or offering or promising to pay medical, hospital, or similar expenses occasioned by an injury is not admissible to prove liability for the injury.

Rule 410. Inadmissibility of Pleas, Plea Discussions, and Related Statements

Except as otherwise provided in this rule, evidence of the following is not, in any civil or criminal proceeding, admissible against the defendant who made the plea or was a participant in the plea discussions:

(1) a plea of guilty which was later withdrawn;

(2) a plea of nolo contendere;

(3) any statement made in the course of any proceedings under Rule 11 of the Federal Rules of Criminal Procedure or comparable state procedure regarding either of the foregoing pleas; or

(4) any statement made in the course of plea discussions with an attorney for the prosecuting authority which do not result in a plea of guilty or which result in a plea of guilty later withdrawn.

However, such a statement is admissible (i) in any proceeding wherein another statement made in the course of the same plea or plea discussions has been introduced and the statement ought in fairness be considered contemporaneously with it, or (ii) in a criminal proceeding for perjury or false statement if the statement was made by the defendant under oath, on the record and in the presence of counsel.

Rule 411. Liability Insurance

Evidence that a person was or was not insured against liability is not admissible upon the issue whether the person acted negligently or otherwise wrongfully. This rule does not require the exclusion of evidence of insurance against liability when offered for another purpose, such as proof of agency, ownership, or control, or bias or prejudice of a witness.

Rule 412. Sex Offense Cases; Relevance of Alleged Victim's Past Sexual Behavior or Alleged Sexual Predisposition

(a) Evidence Generally Inadmissible. The following evidence is not admissible in any civil or criminal proceeding involving alleged sexual misconduct except as provided in subdivisions (b) and (c);

(1) Evidence offered to prove that any alleged victim engaged in other sexual behavior.

(2) Evidence offered to prove any alleged victim's sexual predisposition.

(b) Exceptions.

(1) In a criminal case, the following evidence is admissible, if otherwise admissible under these rules:

(A) evidence of specific instances of sexual behavior by the alleged victim offered to prove that a person other than the accused was the source of semen, injury or other physical evidence;

(B) evidence of specific instances of sexual behavior by the alleged victim with respect to the person accused of the sexual misconduct offered by the accused to prove consent or by the prosecution; and

(C) evidence the exclusion of which would violate the constitutional rights of the defendant.

(2) In a civil case, evidence offered to prove the sexual behavior or sexual predisposition of any alleged victim is admissible if it is otherwise admissible under these rules and its probative value substantially outweighs the danger of harm to any victim and of unfair prejudice to any party. Evidence of an alleged victim's reputation is admissible only if it has been placed in controversy by the alleged victim.

(c) Procedure to Determine Admissibility.

(1) A party intending to offer evidence under subdivision (b) must

(A) file a written motion at least 14 days before trial specifically describing the evidence and stating the purpose for which it is offered unless the court, for good cause requires a different time for filing or permits filing during trial; and

(B) serve the motion on all parties and notify the alleged victim or, when appropriate, the alleged victim's guardian or representative.

(2) Before admitting evidence under this rule the court must conduct a hearing in camera and afford the victim and parties a right to attend and be heard. The motion, related papers, and the record of the hearing must be sealed and remain under seal unless the court orders otherwise.

Rule 413. Evidence of Similar Crimes in Sexual Assault Cases

(a) In a criminal case in which the defendant is accused of an offense of sexual assault, evidence of the defendant's commission of another offense or offenses of sexual assault is admissible, and may be considered for its bearing on any matter to which it is relevant.

(b) In a case in which the Government intends to offer evidence under this rule, the attorney for the Government shall disclose the evidence to the defendant, including statements of witnesses or a summary of the substance of any testimony that is expected to be offered, at least fifteen days before the scheduled date of trial or at such later time as the court may allow for good cause.

(c) This rule shall not be construed to limit the admission or consideration of evidence under any other rule.

(d) For purposes of this rule and Rule 415, 'offense of sexual assault' means a crime under Federal law or the law of a State (as defined in section 513 of title 18, United States Code) that involved—

(1) any conduct proscribed by chapter 109A of title 18, United States Code.

(2) contact, without consent, between any part of the defendant's body or an object and the genitals or anus of another person;

(3) contact, without consent, between the genitals or anus of the defendant and any part of another person's body;

(4) deriving sexual pleasure or gratification from the infliction of death, bodily injury, or physical pain on another person; or

(5) an attempt or conspiracy to engage in conduct described in paragraph (1)-(4).

Rule 414. Evidence of Similar Crimes in Child Molestation Cases

(a) In a criminal case in which the defendant is accused of an offense of child molestation, evidence of the defendant's commission of another offense or offenses of child molestation is admissible, and may be considered for its bearing on any matter to which it is relevant.

(b) In a case in which the Government intends to offer evidence under this rule, the attorney for the Government shall disclose the evidence to the defendant, including statements of witnesses or a summary of the substance of any testimony that is expected to be offered, at least fifteen days before the scheduled date of trial or at such later time as the court may allow for good cause.

(c) This rule shall not be construed to limit the admission or consideration of evidence under any other rule.

(d) For purposes of this rule and Rule 415, 'child' means a person below the age of fourteen, and 'offense of child molestation' means a crime under Federal law or the law of a State (as defined in section 513 of title 18, United States Code) that involved—

(1) any conduct proscribed by chapter 109A of title 18, United States Code, that was committed in relation to a child;

(2) any conduct proscribed by chapter 110 of title 18, United States Code;

(3) contact between any part of the defendant's body or an object and the genitals or anus of a child;

(4) contact between the genitals or anus of the defendant and any part of the body of a child;

(5) deriving sexual pleasure or gratification from the infliction of death, bodily injury, or physical pain on a child; or

(6) an attempt or conspiracy to engage in conduct described in paragraphs (1)–(5).

Rule 415. Evidence of Similar Acts in Civil Cases Concerning Sexual Assault or Child Molestation

(a) In a civil case in which a claim for damages or other relief is predicated on a party's alleged commission of conduct constituting an offense of sexual assault or child molestation, evidence of that party's commission of another offense or offenses of sexual assault or child molestation is admissible and may be considered as provided in Rule 413 and Rule 414 of these rules.

(b) A party who intends to offer evidence under this Rule shall disclose the evidence to the party against whom it will be offered, including statements of witnesses or a summary of the substance of any testimony that is expected to be offered, at least fifteen days before the scheduled date of trial or at such later time as the court may allow for good cause.

(c) This rule shall not be construed to limit the admission or consideration of evidence under any other rule.

Article V. Privileges

Rule 501. General Rule

Except as otherwise required by the Constitution of the United States or provided by Act of Congress or in rules prescribed by the Supreme Court pursuant to statutory authority, the privilege of a witness, person, government, State, or political subdivision thereof shall be governed by the principles of the common law as they may be interpreted by the courts of the United States in the light of reason and experience. However, in civil actions and proceedings, with respect to an element of a claim or defense as to which State law supplies the rule of decision, the privilege of a witness, person, government, State or political subdivision thereof shall be determined in accordance with State law.

Article VI. Witnesses

Rule 601. General Rule of Competency

Every person is competent to be a witness except as otherwise provided in these rules. However, in civil actions and proceedings, with respect to an element of a claim or defense as to which State law supplies the rule of decision, the competency of a witness shall be determined in accordance with State law.

Rule 602. Lack of Personal Knowledge

A witness may not testify to a matter unless evidence is introduced sufficient to support a finding that the witness has personal knowledge of the matter. Evidence to prove personal knowledge may, but need not, consist of the witness' own testimony. This rule is subject to the provisions of rule 703, relating to opinion testimony by expert witnesses.

Rule 603. Oath or Affirmation

Before testifying, every witness shall be required to declare that the witness will testify truthfully, by oath or affirmation administered in a form calculated to awaken the witness' conscience and impress the witness' mind with the duty to do so.

Rule 604. Interpreters

An interpreter is subject to the provisions of these rules relating to qualification as an expert and the administration of an oath or affirmation to make a true translation.

Rule 605. Competency of Judge as Witness

The judge presiding at the trial may not testify in that trial as a witness. No objection need be made in order to preserve the point.

Rule 606. Competency of Juror as Witness

(a) At the Trial. A member of the jury may not testify as a witness before that jury in the trial of the case in which the juror is sitting. If the juror is called so to testify, the opposing party shall be afforded an opportunity to object out of the presence of the jury.

(b) Inquiry into Validity of Verdict or Indictment Upon an inquiry into the validity of a verdict or indictment, a juror may not testify as to any matter or statement occurring during the course of the jury's deliberations or to the effect of anything upon that or any other juror's mind or emotions as influencing the juror to assent to or dissent from the verdict or indictment or concerning the juror's mental processes in connection therewith, except that a juror may testify on the question whether extraneous prejudicial information was improperly brought to the jury's attention or whether any outside influence was improperly brought to bear upon any juror. Nor may a juror's affidavit or evidence of any statement by the juror concerning a matter about which the juror would be precluded from testifying be received for these purposes.

Rule 607. Who May Impeach

The credibility of a witness may be attacked by any party, including the party calling the witness.

Rule 608. Evidence of Character and Conduct of Witness

(a) Opinion and Reputation Evidence of Character. The credibility of a witness may be attacked or supported by evidence in the form of opinion or reputation, but subject to these limitations: (1) the evidence may refer only to character for truthfulness or untruthfulness, and (2) evidence of truthful character is admissible only after the character of the witness for truthfulness has been attacked by opinion or reputation evidence or otherwise.

(b) Specific Instances of Conduct. Specific instances of the conduct of a witness, for the purpose of attacking or supporting the witness' credibility, other than conviction of crime as provided in rule 609, may not be proved by extrinsic evidence. They may, however, in the discretion of the court, if probative of truthfulness or untruthfulness, be inquired into on cross-examination of the witness (1) concerning the witness' character for truthfulness or untruthfulness, or (2) concerning the character for truthfulness or untruthfulness of another witness as to which character the witness being cross-examined has testified.

The giving of testimony, whether by an accused or by any other witness does not operate as a waiver of the accused's or the witness' privilege against self-incrimination when examined with respect to matters which relate only to credibility.

Rule 609. Impeachment by Evidence of Conviction of Crime

(a) General Rule. For the purpose of attacking the credibility of a witness,

(1) evidence that a witness other than an accused has been convicted of a crime shall be admitted, subject to Rule 403, if the crime was punishable by death or imprisonment in excess of one year under the law under which the witness was convicted, and evidence that an accused has been convicted of such a crime shall be admitted if the court determines that the probative value of admitting this evidence outweighs its prejudicial effect to the accused, and

(2) evidence that any witness has been convicted of a crime shall be admitted if it involved dishonesty or false statement, regardless of the punishment.

(b) Time Limit. Evidence of a conviction under this rule is not admissible if a period of more than ten years has elapsed since the date of the conviction or of the release of the witness from the confinement imposed for that conviction, whichever is the later date, unless the court determines, in the interests of justice, that the probative value of the conviction supported by specific facts and circumstances substantially outweighs its prejudicial effect. However, evidence of a conviction more than 10 years old as calculated herein, is not admissible unless the proponent gives to the adverse party sufficient advance written notice of intent to use such evidence to provide the adverse party with a fair opportunity to contest the use of such evidence.

(c) Effect of Pardon, Annulment, or Certificate of Rehabilitation. Evidence of a conviction is not admissible under this rule if (1) the conviction has been the subject of a pardon, annulment, certificate of rehabilitation, or other equivalent procedure based on a finding of the rehabilitation of the person convicted, and that person has not been convicted of a subsequent crime which was punishable by death or imprisonment in excess of one year, or (2) the conviction has been the subject of a pardon, annulment, or other equivalent procedure based on a finding of innocence.

(d) Juvenile Adjudications. Evidence of juvenile adjudications is generally not admissible under this rule. The court may, however, in a criminal case allow evidence of a juvenile adjudication of a witness other than the accused if conviction of the offense would be admissible to attack the credibility of an adult and the court is satisfied that admission in evidence is necessary for a fair determination of the issue of guilt or innocence.

(e) Pendency of Appeal. The pendency of an appeal therefrom does not render evidence of a conviction inadmissible. Evidence of the pendency of an appeal is admissible.

Rule 610. Religious Beliefs or Opinions

Evidence of the beliefs or opinions of a witness on matters of religion is not admissible for the purpose of showing that by reason of their nature the witness' credibility is impaired or enhanced.

Rule 611. Mode and Order of Interrogation and Presentation

(a) Control by Court. The court shall exercise reasonable control over the mode and order of interrogating witnesses and presenting evidence so as to (1) make the interrogation and presentation effective for the ascertainment of the truth, (2) avoid needless consumption of time, and (3) protect witnesses from harassment or undue embarrassment.

(b) Scope of Cross-Examination. Cross-examination should be limited to the subject matter of the direct examination and matters affecting the credibility of the witness. The court may, in the exercise of discretion, permit inquiry into additional matters as if on direct examination.

(c) Leading Questions. Leading questions should not be used on the direct examination of a witness except as may be necessary to develop the witness' testimony. Ordinarily leading questions should be permitted on cross-examination. When a party calls a hostile witness, an adverse party, or a witness identified with an adverse party, interrogation may be by leading questions.

Rule 612. Writing Used to Refresh Memory

Except as otherwise provided in criminal proceedings by section 3500 of title 18, United States Code, if a witness uses a writing to refresh memory for the purpose of testifying, either—

(1) while testifying, or

(2) before testifying, if the court in its discretion determines it is necessary in the interests of justice,

an adverse party is entitled to have the writing produced at the hearing, to inspect it, to cross-examine the witness thereon, and to introduce in evidence those portions which relate to the testimony of the witness. If it is claimed that the writing contains matters not related to the subject matter of the testimony the court shall examine the writing in camera, excise any portions not so related, and order delivery of the remainder to the party entitled thereto. Any portion withheld over objections shall be preserved and made available to the appellate court in the event of an appeal. If a writing is not produced or delivered pursuant to order under this rule, the court shall make any order justice requires, except that in criminal cases when the prosecution elects not to comply, the order shall be one striking the testimony or, if the court in its discretion determines that the interests of justice so require, declaring a mistrial.

Rule 613. Prior Statements of Witnesses

(a) Examining Witness Concerning Prior Statement. In examining a witness concerning a prior statement made by the witness, whether written or not, the statement need not be shown nor its contents disclosed to the witness at that time, but on request the same shall be shown or disclosed to opposing counsel.

(b) Extrinsic Evidence of Prior Inconsistent Statement of Witness. Extrinsic evidence of a prior inconsistent statement by a witness is not admissible unless the witness is afforded an opportunity to explain or deny the same and the opposite party is afforded an opportunity to interrogate the witness thereon, or the interests of justice otherwise require. This provision does not apply to admissions of a party-opponent as defined in rule 801(d)(2).

Rule 614. Calling and Interrogation of Witnesses by Court

(a) Calling by Court. The court may, on its own motion or at the suggestion of a party, call witnesses, and all parties are entitled to cross-examine witnesses thus called.

(b) Interrogation by Court. The court may interrogate witnesses, whether called by itself or by a party.

(c) Objections. Objections to the calling of witnesses by the court or to interrogation by it may be made at the time or at the next available opportunity when the jury is not present.

Rule 615. Exclusion of Witnesses

At the request of a party the court shall order witnesses excluded so that they cannot hear the testimony of other witnesses, and it may make the order of its own motion. This rule does not authorize exclusion of (1) a party who is a natural person, or (2) an officer or employee of a party which is not a natural person designated as its representative by its attorney, or (3) a person whose presence is shown by a party to be essential to the presentation of thc party's causc.

Article VII. Opinions and Expert Testimony

Rule 701. Opinion Testimony by Lay Witnesses

If the witness is not testifying as an expert, the witness' testimony in the form of opinions or inferences is limited to those opinions or inferences which are (a) rationally based on the perception of the witness and (b) helpful to a clear understanding of the witness' testimony or the determination of a fact in issue.

Rule 702. Testimony by Experts

If scientific, technical, or other specialized knowledge will assist the trier of fact to understand the evidence or to determine a fact in issue, a witness qualified as an expert by knowledge, skill, experience, training, or education, may testify thereto in the form of an opinion or otherwise.

Rule 703. Bases of Opinion Testimony by Experts

The facts or data in the particular case upon which an expert bases an opinion or inference may be those perceived by or made known to the expert at or before the hearing. If of a type reasonably relied upon by experts in the particular field in forming opinions or inferences upon the subject, the facts or data need not be admissible in evidence.

Rule 704. Opinion on Ultimate Issue

(a) Except as provided in subdivision (b), testimony in the form of an opinion or inference otherwise admissible is not objectionable because it embraces an ultimate issue to be decided by the trier of fact.

(b) No expert witness testifying with respect to the mental state or condition of a defendant in a criminal case may state an opinion or inference as to whether the defendant did or did not have the mental state or condition constituting an element of the crime charged or of a defense thereto. Such ultimate issues are matters for the trier of fact alone.

Rule 705. Disclosure of Facts or Data Underlying Expert Opinion

The expert may testify in terms of opinion or inference and give reasons therefor without first testifying to the underlying facts or data, unless the court requires otherwise. The expert may in any event be required to disclose the underlying facts or data on cross-examination.

Rule 706. Court Appointed Experts

(a) Appointment. The court may on its own motion or on the motion of any party enter an order to show cause why expert witnesses should not be appointed, and may request the parties to submit nominations. The court may appoint any expert witnesses agreed upon by the parties, and may appoint expert witnesses of its own selection. An expert witness shall not be appointed by the court unless the witness consents to act. A witness so appointed shall be informed of the witness' duties by the court in writing, a copy of which shall be filed with the clerk, or at a conference in which the parties shall have opportunity to participate. A witness so appointed shall advise the parties of the witness' findings, if any; the witness' deposition may be taken by any party; and the witness may be called to testify by the court or any party. The witness shall be subject to cross-examination by each party, including a party calling the witness.

(b) Compensation. Expert witnesses so appointed are entitled to reasonable compensation in whatever sum the court may allow. The compensation thus fixed is payable from funds which may be provided by law in criminal cases and civil actions and proceedings involving just compensation under the fifth amendment. In other civil actions and proceedings the compensation shall be paid by the parties in such proportion and at such times as the court directs, and thereafter charged in like manner as other costs.

(c) Disclosure of Appointment. In the exercise of its discretion, the court may authorize disclosure to the jury of the fact that the court appointed the expert witness.

(d) Parties' Experts of Own Selection. Nothing in this rule limits the parties in calling expert witnesses of their own selection.

Article VIII. Hearsay

Rule 801. Definitions

The following definitions apply under this article:

(a) Statement. A "statement" is (1) an oral or written assertion or (2) nonverbal conduct of a person, if it is intended by the person as an assertion.

(b) Declarant. A "declarant" is a person who makes a statement.

(c) Hearsay. "Hearsay" is a statement, other than one made by the declarant while testifying at the trial or hearing, offered in evidence to prove the truth of the matter asserted.

(d) Statements Which Are Not Hearsay. A statement is not hearsay if—

(1) *Prior Statement by Witness.* The declarant testifies at the trial or hearing and is subject to cross-examination concerning the statement, and the statement if (A) inconsistent with the declarant's testimony, and was given under oath subject to the penalty of perjury at a trial, hearing, or the proceeding, or in a deposition, or (B) consistent with the declarant's testimony and is offered to rebut an express or implied charge against the declarant of recent fabrication or improper influence or motive, or (C) one of identification of a person made after perceiving the person; or

(2) *Admission by Party-Opponent.* The statement is offered against a party and is (A) the party's own statement in either an individual or a representative capacity or (B) a statement of which the party has manifested an adoption of belief in its truth, or (C) a statement by a person authorized by the party to make a statement concerning the subject, or (D) a statement by the party's agent or servant concerning a matter within the scope of the agency or employment, made during the existence of the relationship, or (E) a statement by a coconspirator of a party during the course and in furtherance of the conspiracy.

Rule 802. Hearsay Rule

Hearsay is not admissible except as provided by these rules or by other rules prescribed by the Supreme Court pursuant to statutory authority or by Act of Congress.

Rule 803. Hearsay Exceptions; Availability of Declarant Immaterial

The following are not excluded by the hearsay rule, even though the declarant is available as a witness:

(1) Present Sense Impression. A statement describing or explaining an event or condition made while the declarant was perceiving the event or condition, or immediately thereafter.

(2) Excited Utterance. A statement relating to a startling event or condition made while the declarant was under the stress of excitement caused by the event or condition.

(3) Then Existing Mental, Emotional, or Physical Condition. A statement of the declarant's then existing state of mind, emotion, sensation, or physical condition (such as intent, plan, motive, design, mental feeling, pain, and bodily health), but not including a statement of memory or belief to prove the fact remembered or believed unless it relates to the execution, revocation, identification, or terms of declarant's will.

(4) Statements for Purposes of Medical Diagnosis or Treatment. Statements made for purposes of medical diagnosis or treatment and describing medical history, or past or present symptoms, pain, or sensations, or the inception or general character of the cause or external source thereof insofar as reasonably pertinent to diagnosis or treatment.

(5) Recorded Recollection. A memorandum or record concerning a matter about which a witness once had knowledge but now has insufficient recollection to enable the witness to testify fully and accurately, shown to have been made or adopted by the witness when the matter was fresh in the witness' memory and to reflect that knowledge correctly. If admitted, the memorandum or record may be read into evidence but may not itself be received as an exhibit unless offered by an adverse party.

(6) Records of Regularly Conducted Activity. A memorandum, report, record, or data compilation, in any form, of acts, events, conditions, opinions, or diagnoses, made at or near the time by, or from information transmitted by, a person with knowledge, if kept in the course of a regularly conducted business activity, and if it was the regular practice of that business activity to make the memorandum, report, record, or data compilation, all as shown by the testimony of the custodian or other qualified witness, unless the source of information or the method or circumstances of preparation indicate lack of trustworthiness. The term "business" as used in this paragraph includes business, institution, association, profession, occupation, and calling of every kind, whether or not conducted for profit.

(7) Absence of Entry in Records Kept in Accordance With the Provisions of Paragraph (6). Evidence that a matter is not included in the memoranda reports, records, or data compilations, in any form, kept in accordance with the provisions of paragraph (6), to prove the nonoccurrence or nonexistence of the matter, if the matter was of a kind of which a memorandum, report, record, or data compilation was regularly made and preserved, unless the sources of information or other circumstances indicate lack of trustworthiness.

(8) Public Records and Reports. Records, reports, statements, or data compilations, in any form, of public offices or agencies, setting forth (A) the activities of the office or agency, or (B) matters observed pursuant to duty imposed by law as to which matters there was a duty to report, excluding, however, in criminal cases matters observed by police officers and other law enforcement personnel, or (C) in civil actions and proceedings and against the Government in criminal cases, factual findings resulting from an investigation made pursuant to authority granted by law, unless the sources of information or other circumstances indicate lack of trustworthiness.

(9) Records of Vital Statistics. Records or data compilations, in any form, of births, fetal deaths, deaths, or marriages, if the report thereof was made to a public office pursuant to requirements of law.

(10) Absence of Public Record or Entry. To prove the absence of a record, report, statement, or data compilation, in any form, or the nonoccurrence or nonexistence of a matter of which a record, report, statement, or data compilation, in any form, was regularly made and preserved by a public office or agency, evidence in the form of a certification in accordance with rule 902, or testimony, that diligent search failed to disclose the record, report, statement, or data compilation, or entry.

(11) Records of Religious Organizations. Statements of births, marriages, divorces, deaths, legitimacy, ancestry, relationship by blood or marriage, or other similar facts of personal or family history, contained in a regularly kept record of a religious organization.

(12) Marriage, Baptismal, and Similar Certificates. Statements of fact contained in a certificate that the maker performed a marriage or other ceremony or administered a sacrament, made by a clergyman, public official, or other person authorized by the rules or practices of a religious organization or by law to perform the act certified, and purporting to have been issued at the time of the act or within a reasonable time thereafter.

(13) Family Records. Statements of fact concerning personal or family history contained in family Bibles, genealogies, charts, engravings on rings, inscriptions on family portraits, engravings on urns, crypts, or tombstones, or the like.

(14) Records of Documents Affecting an Interest in Property. The record of a document purporting to establish or affect an interest in property, as proof of the content of the original recorded document and its execution and delivery by each person by whom it purports to have been executed, if the record of a public office and an applicable statute authorizes the recording of documents of that kind in that office.

(15) Statements in Documents Affecting an Interest in Property. A statement contained in a document purporting to establish or affect an interest in property if the matter stated was relevant to the purpose of the document, unless dealings with the property since the document was made have been inconsistent with the truth of the statement or the purport of the document.

(16) Statements in Ancient Documents. Statements in a document in existence twenty years or more the authenticity of which is established.

(17) Market Reports, Commercial Publications. Market quotations, tabulations, lists, directories, or other published compilations, generally used and relied upon by the public or by persons in particular occupations.

(18) Learned Treatises. To the extent called to the attention of an expert witness upon cross-examination or relied upon by the expert witness in direct examination, statements contained in published treatises, periodicals, or pamphlets on a subject of history, medicine, or other science or art, established as a reliable authority by the testimony or admission of the witness or by other expert testimony or by judicial notice. If admitted, the statements may be read into evidence but may not be received as exhibits.

(19) Reputation Concerning Personal or Family History. Reputation among members of a person's family by blood, adoption, or marriage, or among a person's associates, or in the community, concerning a person's birth, adoption, marriage, divorce, death, legitimacy, relationship by blood, adoption, or marriage, ancestry, or other similar fact of personal or family history.

(20) Reputation Concerning Boundaries or General History. Reputation in a community, arising before the controversy, as to boundaries of or customs affecting lands in the community, and reputation as to events of general history important to the community or State or nation in which located.

(21) Reputation as to Character. Reputation of a person's character among associates or in the community.

(22) Judgment of Previous Conviction. Evidence of a final judgment, entered after a trial or upon a plea of guilty (but not upon a plea of nolo contendere), adjuding a person guilty of a crime punishable by death or imprisonment in excess of one year, to prove any fact essential to sustain the judgment, but not including, when offered by the Government in a criminal prosecution for purposes other than impeachment, judgments against persons other than the accused. The pendency of an appeal may be shown but does not affect admissibility.

(23) Judgment as to Personal, Family, or General History, or Boundaries. Judgments as proof of matters of personal, family, or general history, or boundaries, essential to the judgment, if the same would be provable by evidence of reputation.

(24) Other Exceptions. A statement not specifically covered by any of the foregoing exceptions but having equivalent circumstantial guarantees of truthworthiness, if the court determines that (A) the statement is offered as evidence of a material fact; (B) the statement is more probative on the point for which it is offered than any other evidence which the proponent can procure through reasonable efforts; and (C) the general purposes of these rules and the interests of justice will best be served by admission of the statement into evidence. However, a statement may not be admitted under this exception unless the proponent of it makes known to the adverse party sufficiently in advance of the trial or hearing to provide the adverse party with a fair opportunity to prepare to meet it, the proponent's intention to offer the statement and the particulars of it, including the name and address of the declarant.

Rule 804. Hearsay Exceptions; Declarant Unavailable

(a) Definition of Unavailability. "Unavailability as a witness" includes situations in which the declarant—

(1) is exempted by ruling of the court on the ground of privilege from testifying concerning the subject matter of the declarant's statement; or

(2) persists in refusing to testify concerning the subject matter of the declarant's statement despite an order of the court to do so; or

(3) testifies to a lack of memory of the subject matter of the declarant's statement; or

(4) is unable to be present or to testify at the hearing because of death or then existing physical or mental illness or infirmity; or

(5) is absent from the hearing and the proponent of a statement has been unable to procure the declarant's attendance (or in the case of a hearsay exception under subdivision (b)(2), (3), or (4), the declarant's attendance or testimony) by process or other reasonable means.

A declarant is not unavailable as a witness if exemption, refusal, claim of lack of memory, inability, or absence is due to the procurement or wrongdoing of the proponent of a statement for the purpose of preventing the witness from attending or testifying.

(b) Hearsay Exceptions. The following are not excluded by the hearsay rule if the declarant is unavailable as a witness:

(1) *Former Testimony.* Testimony given as a witness at another hearing of the same or a different proceeding, or in a deposition taken in compliance with the law in the course of the same or another proceeding, if the party against whom the testimony is now offered, or, in a civil action or proceeding, a predecessor in interest, had an opportunity and similar motive to develop the testimony by direct, cross, or redirect examination.

(2) *Statement Under Belief of Impending Death.* In a prosecution for homicide or in a civil action or proceeding, a statement made by a declarant while believing that the declarant's death was imminent, concerning the cause or circumstances of what the declarant believed to be impending death.

(3) *Statement Against Interest.* A statement which was at the time of its making so far contrary to the declarant's pecuniary or proprietary interest, or so far tended to subject the declarant to civil or criminal liability, or to render invalid a claim by the declarant against another, that a reasonable person in the declarant's position would not have made the statement unless believing it to be true. A statement tending to expose the declarant to criminal liability and offered to exculpate the accused is not admissible unless corroborating circumstances clearly indicate the trustworthiness of the statement.

(4) *Statement of Personal or Family History.* (A) A statement concerning the declarant's own birth, adoption, marriage, divorce, legitimacy, relationship by blood, adoption, or marriage, ancestry, or other similar fact

of personal or family history, even though declarant had no means of acquiring personal knowledge of the matter stated; or (B) a statement concerning the foregoing matters, and death also, of another person, if the declarant was related to the other by blood, adoption, or marriage or was so intimately associated with the other's family as to be likely to have accurate information concerning the matter declared.

(5) *Other Exceptions.* A statement not specifically covered by any of the foregoing exceptions but having equivalent circumstantial guarantees of trustworthiness, if the court determines that (A) the statement is offered as evidence of a material fact; (B) the statement is more probative on the point for which it is offered than any other evidence which the proponent can procure through reasonable efforts; and (C) the general purposes of these rules and the interests of justice will best be served by admission of the statement into evidence. However, a statement may not be admitted under this exception unless the proponent of it makes known to the adverse party sufficiently in advance of the trial or hearing to provide the adverse party with a fair opportunity to prepare to meet it, the proponent's intention to offer the statement and the particulars of it, including the name and address of the declarant.

Rule 805. Hearsay within Hearsay

Hearsay included within hearsay is not excluded under the hearsay rule if each part of the combined statements conforms with an exception to the hearsay rule provided in these rules.

Rule 806. Attacking and Supporting Credibility of Declarant

When a hearsay statement, or a statement defined in Rule 801(d)(2), (C), (D), or (E), has been admitted in evidence, the credibility of the declarant may be attacked, and if attacked may be supported, by any evidence which would be admissible for those purposes if declarant had testified as a witness. Evidence of a statement or conduct by the declarant at any time, inconsistent with the declarant's hearsay statement, is not subject to any requirement that the declarant may have been afforded an opportunity to deny or explain. If the party against whom a hearsay statement has been admitted calls the declarant as a witness, the party is entitled to examine the declarant on the statement as if under cross-examination.

Article IX. Authentication and Identification

Rule 901. Requirement of Authentication or Identification

(a) General Provision. The requirement of authentication or identification as a condition precedent to admissibility is satisfied by evidence sufficient to support a finding that the matter in question is what its proponent claims.

(b) Illustrations. By way of illustration only, and not by way of limitation, the following are examples of authentication or identification conforming with the requirements of this rule.

(1) *Testimony of Witness With Knowledge.* Testimony that a matter is what it is claimed to be.

(2) *Nonexpert Opinion on Handwriting.* Nonexpert opinion as to the genuineness of handwriting, based upon familiarity not acquired for purposes of the litigation.

(3) *Comparison by Trier or Expert Witnesses.* Comparison by the trier of fact or by expert witnesses with specimens which have been authenticated.

(4) *Distinctive Characteristics and the Like.* Appearance, contents, substance, internal patterns, or other distinctive characteristics, taken in conjunction with circumstances.

(5) *Voice Identification.* Identification of a voice, whether heard firsthand or through mechanical or electronic transmission or recording, by opinion based upon hearing the voice at any time under circumstances connecting it with the alleged speaker.

(6) *Telephone Conversations.* Telephone conversations, by evidence that a call was made to the number assigned at the time by the telephone company to a particular person or business, if (A) in the case of a person, circumstances, including self-identification, show the person answering to be the one called, or (B) in the case of a business, the call was made to a place of business and the conversation related to business reasonably transacted over the telephone.

(7) *Public Records or Reports.* Evidence that a writing authorized by law to be recorded or filed and in fact recorded or filed in a public office, or a purported public record, report, statement, or data compilation, in any form, is from the public office where items of this nature are kept.

(8) *Ancient Documents or Data Compilation.* Evidence that a document or data compilation, in any form, (A) is in such condition as to create no suspicion concerning its authenticity, (B) was in a place where it, if authentic, would likely be, and (C) has been in existence 20 years or more at the time it is offered.

(9) *Process or System.* Evidence describing a process or system used to produce a result and showing that the process or system produces an accurate result.

(10) *Methods Provided by Statute or Rule.* Any method of authentication or identification provided by Act of Congress or by other rules prescribed by the Supreme Court pursuant to statutory authority.

Rule 902. Self-Authentication

Extrinsic evidence of authenticity as a condition precedent to admissibility is not required with respect to the following:

(1) Domestic Public Documents Under Seal. A document bearing a seal purporting to be that of the United States, or of any State, district, Commonwealth, territory, or insular possession thereof, or the Panama Canal Zone, or the Trust Territory of the Pacific Islands, or of a political subdivision, department, officer, or agency thereof, and a signature purporting to be an attestation or execution.

(2) Domestic Public Documents Not Under Seal. A document purporting to bear the signature in the official capacity of an officer or employee of any entity included in paragraph (1) hereof, having no seal, if a public officer having a seal and having official duties in the district or political subdivision of the officer or employee certifies under seal that the signer has the official capacity and that the signature is genuine.

(3) Foreign Public Documents. A document purporting to be executed or attested in an official capacity by a person authorized by the laws of a foreign country to make the execution or attestation, and accompanied by a final certification as to the genuineness of the signature and official position (A) of the executing or attesting person, or (B) of any foreign official whose certificate of genuineness of signature and official position relates to the execution or attestation or is in a chain of certificates of genuineness of signature and official position relating to the execution or attestation. A final certification may be made by a secretary of an embassy or legation, consul general, consul, vice consul, or consular agent of the United States, or a diplomatic or consular official of the foreign country assigned or accredited to the United States. If reasonable opportunity has been given to all parties to investigate the authenticity and accuracy of official documents, the court may, for good cause shown, order that they be treated as presumptively authentic without final certification or permit them to be evidenced by an attested summary with or without final certification.

(4) Certified Copies of Public Records. A copy of an official record or report or entry therein, or of a document authorized by law to be recorded or filed and actually recorded or filed in a public office, including data compilations in any form, certified as correct by the custodian or other person authorized to make the certification, by certificate complying with paragraph (1), (2), (3) of this rule or complying with any Act of Congress or rule prescribed by the Supreme Court pursuant to statutory authority.

(5) Official Publications. Books, pamphlets, or other publications purporting to be issued by public authority.

(6) Newspapers and Periodicals. Printed materials purporting to be newspapers or periodicals.

(7) Trade Inscriptions and the Like. Inscriptions, signs, tags, or labels purporting to have been affixed in the course of business and indicating ownership, control, or origin.

(8) Acknowledged Documents. Documents accompanied by a certificate of acknowledgment executed in the manner provided by law by a notary public or other officer authorized by law to take acknowledgments.

(9) Commercial Paper and Related Documents. Commercial paper, signatures thereon, and documents relating thereto to the extent provided by general commercial law.

(10) Presumptions Under Acts of Congress. Any signature, document, or other matter declared by Act of Congress to be presumptively or prima facie genuine or authentic.

Rule 903. Subscribing Witness' Testimony Unnecessary

The testimony of a subscribing witness is not necessary to authenticate a writing unless required by the laws of the jurisdiction whose laws govern the validity of the writing.

Article X. Contents of Writings, Recordings, and Photographs

Rule 1001. Definitions

For purposes of this article the following definitions are applicable:

(1) Writings and Recordings. "Writings" and "recordings" consist of letters, words, or numbers, or their equivalent, set down by handwriting, typewriting, printing, photostating, photographing, magnetic impulse, mechanical or electronic recording, or other form of data compilation.

(2) Photographs. "Photographs" include still photographs, X-ray films, video tapes, and motion pictures.

(3) Original. An "original" of a writing or recording is the writing or recording itself or any counterpart intended to have the same effect by a person executing or issuing it. An "original" of a photograph includes the negative or any print therefrom. If data are stored in a computer or similar device, any printout or other output readable by sight, shown to reflect the data accurately, is an "original."

(4) Duplicate. A "duplicate" is a counterpart produced by the same impression as the original, or from the same matrix, or by means of photography, including enlargements and miniatures, or by mechanical or electronic re-recording, or by chemical reproduction, or by other equivalent techniques which accurately reproduces the original.

Rule 1002. Requirement of Original

To prove the content of a writing, recording, or photograph, the original writing, recording, or photograph is required, except as otherwise provided in these rules or by Act of Congress.

Rule 1003. Admissibility of Duplicates

A duplicate is admissible to the same extent as an original unless (1) a genuine question is raised as to the authenticity of the original or (2) in the circumstances it would be unfair to admit the duplicate in lieu of the original.

Rule 1004. Admissibility of Other Evidence of Contents

The original is not required, and other evidence of the contents of a writing, recording, or photograph is admissible if—

(1) Originals Lost or Destroyed. All originals are lost or have been destroyed, unless the proponent lost or destroyed them in bad faith; or

(2) Original Not Obtainable. No original can be obtained by any available judicial process or procedure; or

(3) Original in Possession of Opponent. At a time when an original was under the control of the party against whom offered, that party was put on notice, by the pleadings or otherwise, that the contents would be a subject of proof at the hearing, and that party does not produce the original at the hearing; or

(4) Collateral Matters. The writing, recording, or photograph is not closely related to a controlling issue.

Rule 1005. Public Records

The contents of an official record, or of a document authorized to be recorded or filed and actually recorded or filed, including data compilations in any form, if otherwise admissible, may be proved by copy, certified as correct in accordance with rule 902 or testified to be correct by a witness who has compared it with the original. If a copy which complies with the foregoing cannot be obtained by the exercise of reasonable diligence, then other evidence of the contents may be given.

Rule 1006. Summaries

The contents of voluminous writings, recordings, or photographs which cannot conveniently be examined in court may be presented in the form of a chart, summary, or calculation. The originals, or duplicates, shall be made available for examination or copying, or both, by other parties at a reasonable time and place. The court may order that they be produced in court.

Rule 1007. Testimony or Written Admission of Party

Contents of writings, recordings, or photographs may be proved by the testimony or deposition of the party against whom offered or by that party's written admission, without accounting for the nonproduction of the original.

Rule 1008. Functions of Court and Jury

When the admissibility of other evidence of contents of writings, recordings, or photographs under these rules depends upon the fulfillment of a condition of fact, the question whether the condition has been fulfilled is ordinarily for the court to determine in accordance with the provisions of rule 104. However, when an issue is raised (a) whether the asserted writing ever existed, or (b) whether another writing, recording, or photograph produced at the trial is the original, or (c) whether other evidence of contents correctly reflects the contents, the issue is for the trier of fact to determine as in the case of other issues of fact.

Article XI. Miscellaneous Rules

Rule 1101. Applicability of Rules

(a) Courts and Judges. These rules apply to the United States district courts, the District Court of Guam, the District Court of the Virgin Islands, the District Court for the Northern Mariana Islands, the United States courts of appeals, the United States Claims Court, and to United States bankruptcy judges and United States magistrate judges, in the actions, cases, and proceedings and to the extent hereinafter set forth. The terms "judge" and "court" in these rules include United States bankruptcy judges and United States magistrate judges.

(b) Proceedings Generally. These rules apply generally to civil actions and proceedings, including admiralty and maritime cases, to criminal cases and proceedings, to contempt proceedings except those in which the court may act summarily, and to proceedings and cases under title 11, United States Code.

(c) Rule of Privilege. The rule with respect to privileges applies at all stages of all actions, cases, and proceedings.

(d) Rules Inapplicable. The rules (other than with respect to privileges) do not apply in the following situations:

(1) *Preliminary Questions of Fact.* The determination of questions of fact preliminary to admissibility of evidence when the issue is to be determined by the court under rule 104.

(2) *Grand Jury.* Proceedings before grand juries.

(3) *Miscellaneous Proceedings.* Proceedings for extradition or rendition; preliminary examinations in criminal cases; sentencing, or granting or revoking probation; issuance of warrants for arrest, criminal summonses, and search warrants; and proceedings with respect to release on bail or otherwise.

(e) Rules Applicable in Part. In the following proceedings these rules apply to the extent that matters of evidence are not provided for in the statutes which govern procedure therein or in other rules prescribed by the Supreme Court pursuant to statutory authority: the trial of misdemeanors and other petty offenses before United States magistrate judges; review of agency actions when the facts are subject to trial de novo under section 706(2)(F) of title 5, United States Code; review of orders of the Secretary of Agriculture under section 2 of the Act entitled "An Act to authorize association of producers of agricultural products" approved February 18, 1922 (7 U.S.C. 292), and under sections 6 and 7(c) of the Perishable Agricultural Commodities Act, 1930 (7 U.S.C. 499f, 499g(c)); naturalization and revocation of naturalization under sections 310–318 of the Immigration and Nationality Act (8 U.S.C. 1421–1429); prize proceedings in admiralty under sections 7651–7681 of title 10, United States Code; review of orders of the Secretary of the Interior under section 2 of the Act entitled "An Act authorizing associations of producers of aquatic products" approved June 25, 1934 (15 U.S.C. 522); review of orders of petroleum control boards under section 5 of the Act entitled "An Act to regulate interstate and foreign commerce in petroleum and its products by prohibiting the shipment in such commerce of petroleum and its products produced in violation of State law, and for other purposes", approved February 22, 1935 (15 U.S.C. 715d); actions for fines, penalties, or forfeitures under part V of title IV of the Tariff Act of 1930 (19 U.S.C. 1581–1624), or under the Anti-Smuggling Act (19 U.S.C. 1701–1711); criminal libel for condemnation, exclusion of imports, or other proceedings under the Federal Food, Drug, and Cosmetic Act (21 U.S.C. 301–392); disputes between seamen under sections 4079, 4080, and 4081 of the Revised Statutes (22 U.S.C. 256–258); habeas corpus under sections 2241–2254 of title 28, United States Code; motions to vacate, set aside or correct sentence under section 2255 of title 28, United States Code; actions for penalties for refusal to transport destitute seamen under section 4578 of the Revised Statutes (46 U.S.C. 679); actions against the United States under the Act entitled "An Act authorizing suits against the United States in admiralty for damage caused by and salvage service rendered to public vessels belonging to the United States, and for other purposes", approved March 3, 1925 (46 U.S.C. 781–790), as implemented by section 7730 of title 10, United States Code.

Rule 1102. Amendments

Amendments to the Federal Rules of Evidence may be made as provided in section 2072 of title 28 of the United States Code.

Rule 1103. Title

These rules may be known and cited as the Federal Rules of Evidence.

Additional Reading

Chapter Three: The Trial Record

Books

BERGMAN, TRIAL ADVOCACY (NUTSHELL SERIES) (1979).
GOLDSTEIN, TRIAL TECHNIQUE (1935).
JEANS, TRIAL ADVOCACY (1975).
JOINER, TRIALS AND APPEALS (1957).
KEETON, TRIAL TACTICS AND METHODS (2d ed. 1973).
WALTZ & KAPLAN, EVIDENCE: MAKING THE RECORD (1982).

Articles

Berg, *Refine Your Record-Making Skills,* 95 Case & Comment 9 (1990).
Burger, *Counsel for the Prosecution and Defense—Their Roles Under the Minimum Standards,* 8 Amer. Criminal Law Quarterly 2 (1969).
Finer, *Ineffective Assistance of Counsel,* 58 Cornell Law Quarterly 1077 (1973).
Waltz, *Inadequacy of Trial Defense Representation as a Ground for Post-Conviction Relief in Criminal Cases,* 59 Northwestern Univ. Law Rev. 289 (1964).
Waltz, *Making the Record,* in LOUISELL, KAPLAN & WALTZ, CASES AND MATERIALS ON EVIDENCE 1 (6th ed. 1987).

Chapter Four: A Return to Relevance

Articles

James, *Relevancy, Probability and the Law,* 29 California Law Rev. 689 (1941).
Slough, *Relevancy Unraveled*, 5 Kansas Law Rev. 1 (1956).

Trautman, *Logical or Legal Relevancy—A Conflict in Theory,* 5 Vanderbilt Law Rev. 385 (1953).

Weinstein & Berger, *Basic Rules of Relevancy in the Proposed Federal Rules of Evidence,* 4 Georgia Law Rev. 43 (1969).

Chapters Five and Six: The Rule and Exceptions to the Rule Against Hearsay

Books

McCormick, Evidence 724-918 (3d ed. 1984).

Weinstein & Berger, Weinstein's Evidence 801-51 to 801-87 (1975).

Articles

Alexander, *Hearsay Exception for Public Records in Federal Criminal Trials,* 47 Albany Law Rev. 699 (1983).

Bocchino, *Rape Victim Shield Laws and the Sixth Amendment,* 128 Univ. of Pennsylvania Law Rev. 544 (1980).

Burns, *Bright Lines and Hard Edges: Anatomy of a Criminal Evidence Decision,* 85 J. of Crim. L. and Criminology 843 (1995).

Callen, *Hearsay and Informal Reasoning,* 47 Vand. L. Rev. 43 (1994).

Cole, *Residual Exceptions to the Hearsay Rule,* 16 Litigation 26 (1989).

Falknor, *Hearsay,* (1969) Law & Social Order 591.

Falknor, *The Hearsay Rule and its Exceptions,* 2 Univ. of California, Los Angeles, Law Rev. 43 (1954).

Finman, *Implied Assertions as Hearsay,* 14 Stanford Law Rev. 682 (1962).

Galvin, *Shielding Rape Victims in the State and Federal Courts: A Proposal for the Second Decade,* 70 Univ. of Minnesota Law Rev. 763 (1986).

Garland, *The Co-Conspirator's Exception to the Hearsay Rule,* 63 Jour. of Criminal Law, Criminology & Police Science 1 (1972).

Griswold, *The Due Process Revolution and Confrontation,* 119 Univ. of Pennsylvania Law Rev. 711 (1971).

Jefferson, *Declarations Against Interest: An Exception to the Hearsay Rule,* 58 Harvard Law Rev. 1 (1944).

Marcus, *Co-Conspirator Declarations: The Federal Rules of Evidence and Other Recent Developments from a Criminal Law Perspective,* 7 Amer. Jour. of Crim. Law 287 (1979).

McCormick, *The Borderland of Hearsay,* 39 Yale Law Jour. 489 (1930).

Miller, *Evidence of Conviction in Criminal Proceedings,* 121 New Law Jour. 573 (1971).

Morgan, *Admissions,* 1 UCLA Law Rev. 18 (1953).

Morgan, *Declarations Against Interest,* 5 Vanderbilt Law Rev. 451 (1952).

Morgan, *Hearsay,* 25 Mississippi Law Jour. 1 (1953).

Morgan. *Hearsay Dangers and the Application of the Hearsay Concept,* 62 Harvard Law Rev. 177 (1948).

Slough, *Spontaneous Statements and State of Mind,* 46 Iowa Law Rev. 224 (1961).

Smith, *Dying Declarations,* 3 Wisconsin Law Rev. 193 (1925).

Swift, *A Foundation Fact Approach to Hearsay,* 75 Cal. L. Rev. 1339 (1987).
Tracy, *The Introduction of Documentary Evidence—Business Records,* 24 Iowa Law Rev. 436 (1939).
Tuerkheimer, *Convictions Through Hearsay in Child Abuse Cases: A Logical Progression Back to Square One,* 72 Marquette Law Rev. 47 (1988).
Waltz, *The Present Sense Impression Exception to the Rule Against Hearsay: Origins and Attributes,* 66 Iowa Law Rev. 869 (1981).
Weinstein, *The Probative Force of Hearsay,* 46 Iowa Law Rev. 331 (1961).
Williamson, *The Prior Recorded Testimony Exception to the Hearsay Rule in Criminal Cases in State and Federal Courts,* 6 Criminal Law Bulletin 179 (1970).

Law Review Comments and Notes

Comment, *The Admissibility of Computer-Kept Business Records,* 55 Cornell Law Quarterly 1033 (1970).
Comment, *The Admissibility of Dying Declarations,* 38 Fordham Law Rev. 509 (1970).
Comment, *Admissibility of Suicide Note Inculpating the Defendant as a Declaration Against Interest,* 98 Univ. of Pennsylvania Law Review 755 (1950).
Comment, *Constitutional Law—The Right of Confrontation—Admissibility of Hearsay,* 22 Case Western Reserve Law Rev. 575 (1971).
Comment, *Proof of Former Convictions,* 24 Oklahoma Law Rev. 372 (1971).
Comment, *Use of Prior Recorded Testimony and the Right of Confrontation,* 54 Iowa Law Rev. 360 (1968).
Note, *Business Entry Statutes,* 48 Columbia Law Rev. 920 (1948).
Note, *Evidentiary Use of Constitutionally Defective Prior Convictions,* 68 Columbia Law Rev. 1168 (1968).

Chapter Seven: Impeachment of Witnesses' Credibility

Books

GOLDSTEIN, TRIAL TECHNIQUE 487-592 (1935).
KAPLAN & WALTZ, BASIC MATERIALS ON CRIMINAL EVIDENCE 235-293 (1980).
KAPLAN & WALTZ, THE TRIAL OF JACK RUBY 120-21 (1965).
MCCORMICK, EVIDENCE 72-115 (3d ed. 1984).

Articles

Blumenthal, *A Wipe of the Hands, a Click of the Lips: the Validity of Demeanor Evidence in Assessing Witness Credibility,* 72 Neb. L. Rev. 1157 (1993).
Bogart, *Criminal Procedure: Jencks Act: Right of Defense to Criminal Investigators' Notes for Impeachment Purposes,* 27 Judge Advocate General Jour. 427 (1973).
Davis, *Impeachment by Prior Inconsistent Statement: Disputing a Witness' Credibility,* 25 Trial 64 (1989).
Merritt, *Psychiatric Testimony as to Credibility in Criminal Cases,* 13 Criminal Law Quarterly 79 (1970).

Thomas, *Rehabilitating the Impeached Witness with Consistent Statements,* 32 Missouri Law Rev. 472 (1967).

Law Review Comments and Notes

Comment, *Conviction Upon Plea of Nolo Contendere as Impeaching Evidence,* 21 Arkansas Law Rev. 124 (1967).

Comment, *Impeaching One's Own Witness With a Prior Inconsistent Statement: Ohio and Federal Rules 607 and Hearsay Considerations,* 50 U. of Cincinnati L. Rev. (1981).

Comment, *Impeachment, Use Immunity and the Perjurious Defendant,* 77 Dickinson Law Rev. 23 (1973).

Comment, *Use of Grand Jury Testimony to Impeach Credibility at Trial,* 18 Loyola Law Rev. 468 (1972).

Note, *Statements Inadmissible Against a Defendant as Substantive Evidence May Be Used to Impeach Credibility of Defendant's Trial Testimony,* 39 Geo. Washington Law Rev. 1241 (1971).

Chapter Eight: The Constitutional Privilege Against Self-Incrimination

Books

HARDING, FUNDAMENTAL LAW IN CRIMINAL PROSECUTIONS, § 4 (1959).

HOOK, COMMON SENSE AND THE FIFTH AMENDMENT (1959).

LEVY, ORIGINS OF THE FIFTH AMENDMENT: THE RIGHT AGAINST SELF-INCRIMINATION, § 2 (1960).

MAGUIRE, EVIDENCE OF GUILT—RESTRICTIONS UPON ITS DISCOVERY OR COMPULSORY DISCLOSURE, § 2 (1959).

MAYERS, SHALL WE AMEND THE FIFTH AMENDMENT? (1954).

MCCORMICK, EVIDENCE 278-360 (3d ed. 1984).

ROGGE, THE FIRST AND FIFTH, WITH SOME INCURSIONS INTO OTHERS, § 2 (1960).

Articles

Alito, *Documents and the Privilege Against Self-Incrimination,* 48 Univ. of Pittsburgh Law Rev. 27 (1986).

Clapp, *Privilege Against Self-Incrimination,* 10 Rutgers Law Rev. 541 (1956).

Eli, *Confessions: The Problem and Practical Solution—The Case for an Absolute Fifth Amendment,* 7 Lincoln Law Rev. 225 (1972).

Hechtkopf, *Sufficiency of Use and Derivative-Use Immunity to Compel Testimony of a Witness Over a Claim of the Privilege Against Self-Incrimination,* 27 Judge Advocate General Jour. 401 (1973).

Holtz, *Miranda in a Juvenile Setting: A Child's Right to Silence,* 78 Jour. of Criminal Law & Criminology 534 (1987).

Meltzer, *Privileges Against Self-Incrimination and the Hit-and-Run Opinions,* 1971 Supreme Court Rev. 1 (1971).

Zupancic, *The Privilege Against Self-Incrimination,* 1981 Arizona State Law Rev. 1.

Law Review Comments and Notes

Comment, *Fear of Foreign Prosecution and the Fifth Amendment,* 58 Iowa Law Rev. 1304 (1973).

Comment, *Interrogation of Juveniles: The Right to a Parent's Presence,* 77 Dickinson Law Rev. 543 (1973).

Comment, *Miranda and Minor Offenses,* 14 Arizona Law Rev. 766 (1972).

Note, *The Fifth Amendment Does Not Protect Federal Grand Jury Witnesses From Being Compelled to Give Testimony Which Would Incriminate Them in a Foreign Jurisdiction,* 8 Texas Internat'l Law Jour. 262 (1973).

Note, *Minor's Request to See Parent Made Before or During Custodial Investigation Invokes Fifth Amendment Privilege,* 1972 Univ. of Illinois Law Forum 628 (1972).

Note, *Scope of Testimonial Immunity Under the Fifth Amendment,* 67 Northwestern Univ. Law Rev. 106 (1972).

Note, *Seizure of Personal Records Violates the Fifth Amendment,* 46 Tulane Law Rev. 545 (1972).

Note, *Statement Admissible to Impeach Defendant Even Though Miranda Warnings Were Not Given,* 40 Fordham Law Rev. 394 (1971).

Note, *Use of Information Provided Without Objection on Income Tax Return Prohibited in Prosecution for Nontax Offense,* 86 Harvard Law Rev. 914 (1973).

Chapter Nine: Exclusion of Identification Evidence

Books

AMSTERDAM, SEGAL, & MILLER, TRIAL MANUAL FOR THE DEFENSE OF CRIMINAL CASES, § 36 (1977).

FISHMAN & LOFTUS, EXPERT PSYCHOLOGICAL TESTIMONY ON EYEWITNESS IDENTIFICATION (1978).

WALL, EYE-WITNESS IDENTIFICATION IN CRIMINAL CASES (1968).

Articles

Mayer, *Due Process Challenges to Eyewitness Identification Based on Pretrial Photographic Arrays,* 13 Pace L. Rev. 815 (1994).

McGowan, *Constitutional Interpretation and Criminal Identification,* 12 Wm. & Mary Law Rev. 735 (1970).

Sobel, *Assailing the Impermissible Suggestion: Evolving Limitations on the Abuse of Pre-Trial Criminal Identification Methods,* 38 Brooklyn Law Rev. 261 (1971).

Young, *Due Process Considerations in Police Showup Practices,* 6 Crim. Law Bull. 373 (1970).

Law Review Comments and Notes

Comment, *Erroneous Eyewitness Identification at Lineups—The Problem and its Cure,* 5 Univ. of San Francisco Law Rev. 85 (1970).

Comment, *Mandatory Exclusion of Identifications Resulting from Suggestive Confrontations: A Conceptual Alternative to the Independent Basis Test,* 53 Boston Univ. Law Rev. 433 (1973).
Comment, *Right to Counsel at Scene-of-the-Crime Identification,* 117 Univ. of Penna. Law Rev. 916 (1969).
Note, *Counsel's Presence Is Not Required at Pre-Indictment Identification Confrontation,* 18 Villanova Law Rev. 501 (1973).
Note, *The Lineup's Lament,* 22 DePaul Law Rev. 660 (1973).
Note, *Post-Indictment Photographic Lineup Requires Presence of Defendant's Counsel,* 41 Fordham Law Rev. 149 (1972).

Chapter Ten: Unreasonable Searches and Seizures of Evidence

Books

BERRY, ARREST, SEARCH, AND SEIZURE (1973).
DAVID, FEDERAL SEARCHES AND SEIZURES (1964).
FISHER, SEARCH AND SEIZURE (1970).
RINGEL, SEARCHES AND SEIZURES, ARRESTS AND CONFESSIONS (1972).
SILBERMAN, CRIMINAL VIOLENCE, CRIMINAL JUSTICE 262-264 (1978).
TOBIAS, PRE-TRIAL CRIMINAL PROCEDURE: A SURVEY OF CONSTITUTIONAL RIGHTS (1972).

Articles

Bevan & Lidstone, *The New Law of Search and Seizure: Castles Built with Air?,* 1985 Public Law 423.
Bogacz, *Bright Lines and Opaque Containers: Searching for Reasonable Rules in Automobile Cases,* 10 Touro L. Rev. 679 (1994).
Bogdanos, *Search and Seizure. A Reasoned Approach,* 6 Pace Law Rev. 543 (1986).
Carden, *Federal Power to Seize and Search Without Warrant,* 18 Vanderbilt Law Rev. 1 (1964).
Claerhout, *Pen Register,* 20 Drake Law Rev. 108 (1970).
Clark, *Wiretapping and the Constitution,* 5 California Western Law Rev. 1 (1968).
Cook, *The Art of Frisking,* 40 Fordham Law Rev. 789 (19782).
Cook, *Requisite Particularity in Search Warrant Authorizations,* 38 Tennessee Law Rev. 496 (1971).
Cook, *Varieties of Detention and the Fourth Amendment,* 23 Alabama Law Rev. 287 (1971).
Eckhardt, *Intrusion into the Body,* 52 Military Law Jour. 141 (1971).
Evans, *Search and Seizure Incident to Lawful Arrest,* 4 William & Mary Law Rev. 121 (1963).
Fishman, *Pen Registers and Privacy: Risks, Expectations, and the Nullification of Congressional Intent,* 29 Catholic U Law Rev. 557 (1980).
Graham, *Police Eavesdropping: Law Enforcement Revolution,* 7 Criminal Law Bulletin 445 (1971).
Grano, *Dilemma for Defense Counsel: Spinelli-Harris Search Warrants and the Possibility of Police Perjury,* 1971 Univ. of Illinois Law Forum 405 (1971).

Henzi, *Electronic Eavesdropping,* 56 Illinois Bar Jour. 938 (1968).

Holladay, *Boundaries of the Warrantless Search,* 8 Air Force Judge Advocate General Law Rev. 44 (1971).

Hufstedler, *Invisible Searches for Intangible Things: Regulation of Governmental Information Gathering,* 127 U of Pennsylvania Law Rev. 1483 (1979).

Kaczynski, *The Admissibility of Illegally Obtained Evidence: American and Foreign Approaches Compared,* 101 Military Law Rev. 83 (1983).

Kaplan, *The Limits of the Exclusionary Rule,* 26 Stanford Law Rev. (1974).

Kipperman, *Inaccurate Search Warrant Affidavits as a Ground for Suppressing Evidence,* 84 Harvard Law Rev. 825 (1971).

Kitch, *Katz v. United States: The Limits of the Fourth Amendment,* 1968 Supreme Court Rev. 133 (1968).

Kuh, *In-Field Interrogation: Stop, Question, Detention and Frisk,* Criminal Law Bulletin, 597 (1967).

Kuipers, *Suspicious Objects, Probable Cause, and the Law of Search and Seizure,* 21 Drake Law Rev. 252 (1972).

LaFave, *Administrative Searches and Seizures and the Fourth Amendment: The Camera and See Cases,* 1967 Supreme Court Rev. 1 (1967).

LaFave, *"Street Encounters" and the Constitution: Terry, Sibron, Peters and Beyond* 67 Michigan Law Rev. 40 (1968).

Leonard, *Good Faith Exception to the Exclusionary Rule: A Reasonable Approach for Criminal Justice,* 4 Whittier Law Rev. 33 (1981).

Levinson, *The Employment of Informants' Statements in Establishing Probable Cause for Issuance of a Search Warrant,* 4 John Marshall Law Jour. 38 (1970).

Lipton, *The Search Warrant in Tax Fraud Investigations,* 56 Amer. Bar Assoc Jour. 941 (1970).

Loewy, *Police-Obtained Evidence and the Constitution: Distinguishing Unconstitutionally Obtained Evidence from Unconstitutionally Used Evidence,* 87 Michigan Law Rev. 907 (1989).

Mascolo, *The Emergency Doctrine Exception to the Warrant Requirement of the Fourth Amendment,* 22 Buffalo Law Rev. 419 (1973).

Mascolo, *Specificity Requirements for Warrants Under the Fourth Amendment: Defining the Zone of Privacy,* 73 Dickinson Law Rev. 1 (1968).

McCormick, *Search Warrants: The Requisites of Validity,* 3 St. Mary's Law Jour. 55 (1971).

McIntyre & Chabraja, *Intensive Search of a Suspect's Body and Clothing*, 58 Jour. of Criminal Law 18 (1967).

Mintz, *Searches of Premises by Consent,* 73 Dickinson Law Rev. 44 (1968).

Nelson, *The Paradox of the Exclusionary Rule,* 96 Public Interest 117 (1989).

Oaks, *Studying the Exclusionary Rule in Search and Seizure,* 37 Univ. of Chicago Law Rev. 665 (1970).

Pilcher, *The Law and Practice of Field Interrogation,* 58 Jour. of Criminal Law 465 (1967).

Player, *Warrantless Searches and Seizures,* 5 Georgia Law Rev. 269 (1971).

Power, *Technology and the Fourth Amendment: A Proposed Formulation for Visual Searches,* 80 Jour. of Criminal Law & Criminology 1 (1989).

Rebell, *The Undisclosed Informant and the Fourth Amendment: A Search for Meaningful Standards,* 81 Yale Law Jour. 703 (1972).

Scott, *Wiretapping and Organized Crime,* 14 Howard Law Jour. 1 (1968).
Slobogin, *Capacity to Contest a Search and Seizure: The Passing of Old Rules and Some Suggestions for New Ones,* 18 Amer. Criminal Law Rev. 387 (1981).
Stroud, *The Inventory Search and the Fourth Amendment,* 4 Indiana Legal Forum 471 (1971).
Tiffany, *The Fourth Amendment and Police-Citizen Confrontations,* 60 Jour. of Criminal Law 442 (1969).
Wingo, *The Growing Disillusionment with the Exclusionary Rule,* 25 Southwestern Law Jour. 573 (1971).
Wright, *Must the Criminal Go Free if the Constable Blunders?* 50 Texas Law Rev. 736 (1972).

Law Review Comments and Notes

Comment, *Airport Security Searches and the Fourth Amendment,* 71 Columbia Law Review 1039 (1971).
Comment, *Arson Investigations and the Fourth Amendment,* 30 Washington & Lee Law Rev. 133 (1973).
Comment, *Automobile Searches and the Fourth Amendment,* 47 Chicago-Kent Law Rev. 232 (1970).
Comment, *Border Searches and the Fourth Amendment,* 77 Yale Law Jour. 1007 (1968).
Comment, *Breaking and Entering into Private Premises to Effect Electronic Surveillance,* 39 Maryland L. Rev. 754 (1980).
Comment, *The Collateral Use Doctrine: From Walder to Miranda*, 62 Northwestern Univ. Law Rev. 912 (1968).
Comment, *Consent Search Waiver of Fourth Amendment Rights,* 12 St. Louis Univ. Law Jour. 297 (1967).
Comment, *Effective Consent to Search and Seizure,* 113 Univ. of Pennsylvania Law Rev. 260 (1964).
Comment, *Electronic Surveillance and the Fourth Amendment,* 2 Chicago-Kent Police Law Reporter 12 (1969).
Comment, *Electronic Surveillance and the Right to Privacy,* 52 Boston Univ. Law Rev. 831 (1972).
Comment, *Electronic Visual Surveillance and the Right of Privacy: When Is Electronic Observation Reasonable?,* 35 Wash. & Lee L. Rev. 1043 (1978).
Comment, *The Federal Rules of Criminal Procedure and Joint Searches,* 28 Washington & Lee Law Rev. 501 (1971).
Comment, *Field Interrogations: Court Rule and Police Response,* 49 Jour. of Urban Law 767 (1972).
Comment, *From Private Places to Personal Privacy: A Post-Katz Study of the Fourth Amendment Protection,* 43 New York Univ. Law Rev. 968 (1968).
Comment, *Illegality of Eavesdrop-Related Break-ins,* 92 Harvard Law Rev. 919 (1979).
Comment, *Inadmissibility of Wiretap Evidence in State Courts,* 1968 Duke Law Jour. 1008 (1968).
Comment, *Judicial Control of Secret Agents,* 76 Yale Law Jour. 994 (1967).
Comment, *The Neglected Fourth Amendment Problem in Arrest Entries,* 23 Stanford Law Rev. 995 (1971).

Comment, *One Party's Consent to Electronic Surveillance,* 24 Univ. of Miami Law Rev. 194 (1969).

Comment, *Permissible Eavesdropping Under the Berger and Katz Standards,* 1969 Univ. of Toledo Law Rev. 419 (1969).

Comment, *Permissible Search of Premises Incidental to a Lawful Arrest,* 43 Temple Law Quarterly 180 (1970).

Comment, *Police Bulletins and Private Searches,* 119 Univ. of Pennsylvania Law Rev. 63 (1970).

Comment, *Police Inventories of the Contents of Vehicles and the Exclusionary Rule,* 29 Washington & Lee Law Rev. 197 (1972).

Comment, *Police Power to Stop, Frisk, and Question Suspicious Persons,* 65 Columbia Law Rev. 848 (1965).

Comment, *Police Practices and the Threatened Destruction of Tangible Evidence,* 84 Harvard Law Rev. 1465 (1971).

Comment, *Police Use of Remote Camera Systems for Surveillance of Public Streets,* 4 Columbia Human Rights Law Rev. 143 (1972).

Comment, *Probable Cause and the First-Time Informer,* 43 Univ. of Colorado Law Rev. 357 (1972).

Comment, *Scope Limitations for Searches Incident to a Lawful Arrest,* 78 Yale Law Jour. 433 (1969).

Comment, *The Scope of Searches Incident to Arrest,* 43 Univ. of Colorado Law Rev. 63 (1971).

Comment, *Search and Seizure and the Law Regarding Trespass,* 22 Baylor Law Rev. 561 (1970).

Comment, *Search and Seizure by Private Parties: An Exception to the Exclusionary Rule,* 5 Land & Water Law Rev. 653 (1970).

Comment, *Search and Seizure—The Inventory Search of an Automobile,* 7 Univ. of Richmond Law Rev. 151 (1972).

Comment, *Search and Seizure Incident to Traffic Violations,* 4 Willamette Law Jour. 247 (1966).

Comment, *Searches of the Person Incident to Lawful Arrest,* 69 Columbia Law Rev. 866 (1969).

Comment, *Seizures by Private Parties: Exclusion in Criminal Cases,* 19 Stanford Law Rev. 608 (1967).

Comment, *Sneaking Through the Castle Gates: Covert Entries by Police to Plant Bugging Devices,* 67 Georgetown Law Jour. 1429 (1979).

Comment, *Testing the Factual Basis for a Search Warrant,* 67 Columbia Law Rev. 1529 (1967).

Comment, *Third Party Consent to Search and Seizure: A Reexamination,* 20 Jour. of Public Law 313 (1971).

Comment, *Third Party Destruction of Evidence and the Warrantless Search of Premises,* 1971 Univ. of Illinois Law Forum 111 (1971).

Comment, *Unreasonable Private Searches and Seizures and the Exclusionary Rule,* 16 American Univ. Law Rev. 403 (1967).

Comment, *Unrevealed Informants and the Fourth Amendment,* 40 Tennessee Law Rev. 75 (1972).

Comment, *Waiver of Fourth Amendment Rights by the Accused,* 31 Montana Law Rev. 57 (1969).

Comment, *Waiver of Rights in Police Interrogation: Miranda in the Lower Courts,* 36 Univ. of Chicago Law Rev. 413 (1969).
Comment, *Warrantless Searches Incident to Arrest,* 24 Alabama Law Rev. 607 (1971).
Note, *Announcement in Police Entries,* 80 Yale Law Jour. 139 (1970).
Note, *Eavesdropping and the Constitution: A Reappriasal of the Fourth Amendment Framework,* 50 Minnesota Law Rev. 378 (1969).
Note, *Eavesdropping Orders and the Fourth Amendment,* 66 Columbia Law Rev. 355 (1967).

Chapter Eleven: Confessions

Articles

Andrews, *Involuntary Confessions and Illegally Obtained Evidence in Criminal Cases,* 1963 Criminal Law Rev. 15 (1963).
Corns, *The Admissibility of Confession Evidence,* 58 Law Institute Jour. 1316 (1984).
Corr, *A Law Enforcement Primer on Custodial Interrogation,* 15 Whittier L. Rev. 723 (1994).
Cray, *Criminal Interrogations and Confessions: The Ethical Imperative,* 1968 Wisconsin Law Rev. 173 (1968).
Eisen & Rosett, *Protection for the Suspect Under Miranda v. Arizona,* 67 Columbia Law Rev. 645 (1967).
Glen, *Interrogation of Children: When Are Their Admissions Admissible?* 2 Family Law Quarterly 280 (1968).
Koessler, *Admission of Confessions Obtained by Trickery,* 50 Amer. Bar Assoc. Jour. 648 (1964).
Martin, *Admissibility of Confessions and Statements,* 5 Criminal Law Quarterly 35 (1962).
Ogletree, *Are Confessions Really Good for the Soul?: A Proposal to Mirandize Miranda,* 100 Harvard Law Rev. 1826 (1987).
Robinson, *Police and Prosecutor Practices and Attitudes Relating to Interrogation as Revealed by Pre- and Post-Miranda Questionnaires: A Construct of Police Capacity to Comply,* 1968 Duke Law Jour. 425 (1968).
Saltzburg, *Miranda v. Arizona Revisited: Constitutional Law or Judicial Fiat?,* 26 Washburn Law Rev. 1 (1986).
Southerland, *Crime and Confession,* 79 Harvard Law Rev. 21 (1965).
Sterling, *Police Interrogation and the Psychology of Confession,* 14 Jour. of Public Law 25 (1965).
Weiss, *Confessions Under the Influence of Alcohol or the Case of the Shrunken Drunken Man,* 2 Texas Southern Univ. Law Rev. 1 (1971).
White, *Confessions Induced by Broken Government Promises,* 43 Duke L.J. 947 (1994).

Law Review Comments and Note

Comment, *Confessions of Juveniles,* 5 Willamette Law Jour. 66 (1968).
Comment, *Confessions Obtained Through Interrogations Conducted by Private Persons, Investigators and Security Agents,* 4 Willamette Law Jour. 262 (1966).

Comment, *Criminal Interrogation,* 35 Tennessee Law Rev. 604 (1968).
Comment, *Custodial Statements of Criminal Suspects,* 4 Willamette Law Jour. 189 (1966).
Comment, *Examination of the Right to a Voluntariness Hearing,* 53 Jour. of Criminal Law 30 (1972).
Comment, *Intoxicated Confessions: A New Haven in Miranda,* 20 Stanford Law Rev. 1269 (1968).
Comment, *The Right to Non-Legal Counsel During Police Interrogation,* 70 Columbia Law Rev. 757 (1970).
Comment, *The Rights of the Criminal Defendant: Arrest to Preliminary Hearing,* 34 Tennessee Law Rev. 482 (1967).
Comment, *Self-Corroborating Confessions,* 17 Baylor Law Rev. 434 (1965).
Comment, *Six-Hour Delay: A Confession Killer,* 33 Univ. of Pittsburgh Law Rev. 341 (1971).
Comment, *Tacit Admissions and Miranda,* 36 Tennessee Law Rev. 566 (1969).
Note, *Miranda Interrogations—Interrogation Defined as Express Questioning or Its Functional Equivalent,* 85 Dickinson L. Rev. 361 (1981).

Chapter Twelve: Common Law and Statutory Testimonial Privileges

Articles

Baldwin, *Confidentiality Between Physician and Patient,* 22 Maryland Law Rev. 181 (1962).
Ball, *Waiver of the Attorney-Client and Physician-Patient Privileges,* 14 Ohio State Law Jour. 432 (1953).
Beaver, *The Newsman's Code, the Claim of Privilege and Everyman's Right to Evidence,* 47 Oregon Law Rev. 243 (1968).
Chafee, *Privileged Communications: Is Justice Served or Obstructed by Closing the Doctor's Mouth on the Witness Stand?* 52 Yale Law Jour. 607 (1943).
Coburn, *Child-Parent Communications: Spare the Privilege and Spoil the Child,* 74 Dickinson Law Rev. 599 (1970).
Davidson, *Waiver of the Attorney-Client Privilege,* 64 Oregon Law Rev. 637 (1986).
Fox, *Psychotherapy and Legal Privilege,* 54 Massachusetts Law Quarterly 307 (1968).
Gutterman, *The Informer Privilege,* 58 Jour. of Criminal Law 32 (1967).
Guttmacher & Weihofen, *Privileged Communications Between Psychiatrist and Patient,* 12 Indiana Law Jour. 32 (1952).
Kuhlman, *Communications to Clergymen—When Are They Privileged?,* 52 Valparaiso Univ. Law Rev. 265 (1968).
Louisell & Crippin, *Evidentiary Privileges,* 30 Minnesota Law Rev. 413 (1956).
Orfield, *Privileges in Federal Criminal Evidence,* 40 Univ. of Detroit Law Jour. 403 (1963).
Peterson, *The Attorney-Client Privilege in Internal Revenue Investigations,* 54 Minnesota Law Rev. 67 (1969).
Radin, *The Privilege of Confidential Communication Between Lawyer and Client,* 16 California Law Rev. 487 (1928).
Rappeport, *The Psychiatrist-Patient Privilege,* 23 Maryland Law Rev. 39 (1963).

Rosenheim, *Privilege, Confidentiality, and Juvenile Offenders,* 11 Wayne Law Rev. 660 (1965).

Saltzburg, *Communications Falling Within the Attorney-Client Privilege,* 66 Iowa Law Rev. 811 (1981).

Sawyer, *The Physician-Patient Privilege: Some Reflections,* 14 Drake Law Rev. 83 (1965).

Waltz, *The Attorney-Client Privilege in the Criminal Practice, in 4* CRIMINAL DEFENSE TECHNIQUES 77A-1 (1983).

White, *Evidentiary Privileges and the Defendant's Constitutional Right to Introduce Evidence,* 80 Jour. of Criminal Law 377 (1989).

Whitford, *The Physician, the Law, and the Drug Abuser,* 119 Univ. of Pennsylvania Law Rev. 933 (1971).

Zagel, *The State Secrets Privilege,* 50 Minnesota Law Rev. 875 (1966).

Law Review Comments

Comment, *Adverse Spousal Testimony: A New Rule for the Federal Courts,* 32 U. of Florida Law Rev. 784 (1980).

Comment, *Attorney-Client Communications: The Right to Uncensored Mail,* 1 Amer. Jour. of Criminal Law 28 (1972).

Comment, *The Attorney-Corporate Client Privilege,* 38 Tennessee Law Rev. 271 (1971).

Comment, *The Attorney in Possession of Evidence Incriminating His Client,* 25 Washington & Lee Law Rev. 133 (1968).

Comment, *The Defendant's Right to Inspect Investigative Files of Law Enforcement Agencies,* 25 Washington & Lee Law Rev. 70 (1968).

Comment, *Evidentiary Privileges in the Federal Courts,* 52 California Law Rev. 640 (1964).

Comment, *The Federal Rules of Evidence and the Law of Privileges,* 15 Wayne Law Rev. 1287 (1969).

Comment, *Fruits of the Attorney-Client Privilege: Incriminating Evidence and Conflicting Duties,* 3 Duquesne Univ. Law Rev. 239 (1965).

Comment, *The Future Crime and Tort Exception to Communications Privileges,* 77 Harvard Law Rev. 730 (1964).

Comment, *Impeachment by Unconstitutionally Obtained Evidence: The Rule of Harris v. New York,* 1971 Washington Univ. Law Quarterly 441 (1971).

Comment, *The Informer's Privilege in Criminal Cases,* 1967 Univ. of Illinois Law Forum 665 (1967).

Comment, *The Informer Privilege. What's in a Name?* 64 Jour. of Criminal Law 56 (1973).

Comment, *The Privilege of Withholding the Identity of an Informer,* 28 Univ. of Pittsburgh Law Rev. 477 (1967).

Comment, *The Right of a Criminal Defense Lawyer to Withhold Physical Evidence Received From His Client,* 38 Univ. of Chicago Law Rev. 211 (1970).

Comment, *The Social Worker-Client Relationship and Privileged Communications,* 1965 Washington Univ. Law Quarterly 362 (1965).

Chapter Thirteen: Burden of Proof and Presumptions

Book

McCormick, Evidence, Chap. 12 (3d ed. 1984).

Articles

Allen, *Rationality and Accuracy in the Criminal Process: A Discordant Note on the Harmonizing of the Justices' Views on Burdens of Persuasion in Criminal Cases,* 74 Jour. of Criminal Law & Criminology 1147 (1983).

Bell, *Decision Theory and Due Process: A Critique of the Supreme Court's Lawmaking for Burdens of Proof* 78 Jour. of Criminal Law & Criminology 557 (1987).

Christic & Pye, *Presumptions and Assumptions in the Criminal Law: Another View,* 1970 Drake Law Jour. 919 (1970).

Falknor, *Notes on Presumptions,* 15 Washington Law Rev. 71 (1940).

Harris, *Constitutional Limitations on Criminal Presumptions as an Expression of Changing Concepts of Fundamental Fairness,* 77 Jour. of Criminal Law & Criminology 308 (1986).

McBaine, *Burden of Proof: Degrees of Belief,* 32 Calif. L. Rev. 242 (1944).

Morgan, *Further Observations on Presumptions,* 16 So. California Law Rev. 245 (1943).

Nesson, *Rationality, Presumptions, and Judicial Comment: A Response to Professor Allen,* 94 Harvard Law Rev. 1574 (1981).

Law Review Notes

Note, *Abrogation of Criminal Statutory Presumptions,* 5 Suffolk Univ. Law Rev. 161 (1970).

Note, *Criminal Presumption and Inference Instructions,* 6 Willamette Law Jour. 497 (1971).

Note, *Presumptions According to Purpose: A Functional Approach,* 45 Albany Law Rev. 1079 (1981).

Chapter Fourteen: Judicial Notice

Books

Maguire, Evidence—Common Sense and Common Law 166-175 (1947).

McCormick, Evidence Chap. 11 (3d ed. 1984).

Articles

David, *Judicial Notice,* 55 Columbia Law Rev. 945 (1955).

Davis, *Judicial Notice, Law & Social Order* 513 (1969).
Keefe, Landis & Shaad, *Sense and Nonsense about Judicial Notice,* 2 Stanford Law Rev. 664 (1950).
Kleri, *Judicial Notice of Scientific Facts,* 15 Cleveland-Marshall Law Rev. 140 (1966).
Morgan, *Judicial Notice,* 57 Harvard Law Rev. 269 (1944).
Roberts, *Preliminary Notes Toward a Study of Judicial Notice,* 52 Cornell Law Quarterly 210 (1967).
Weinstein, *Judicial Notice and the Duty to Disclose Adverse Information,* 51 Iowa Law Rev. 807 (1966).

Law Review Comments

Comment, *Binding Effect of Judicial Notice Under the Common Knowledge Test,* 21 Baylor Law Rev. 208 (1969).
Comment, *The Presently Expanding Concept of Judicial Notice,* 13 Villanova Law Rev. 528 (1968).

Chapter Fifteen: Competency of Witnesses

Articles

Bigelow, *Witnesses of Tender Years,* 9 Criminal Law Quarterly 298 (1967).
Cartwright, *The Prospective Child Witness,* 6 Criminal Law Quarterly 196 (1963).
Corboy, *Proof of Distance Objects Can Be Seen,* 9 Trial Lawyer's Guide 57 (1965).
Grosman, *Testing Witness Reliability,* 5 Criminal Law Quarterly 318 (1962).
Henkel, *Competency, Compellability and Coroners' Courts,* 12 Criminal Law Quarterly 166 (1970).
Kingston, *The Law of Probabilities and the Credibility of Witnesses and Evidence,* 15 Jour. of Forensic Science 18 (1970).
Low, *Police Officer as a Witness in a Motor Vehicle Case,* 16 Practical Lawyer 15 (1970).
Nahstoll, *Observation and Memory of Witnesses,* 48 Amer. Bar Assoc. Jour. 68 (1962).
Saxe, *Psychiatry, Psychoanalysis and the Credibility of Witnesses,* 45 Notre Dame Lawyer 238 (1970).
Stafford, *The Child as a Witness,* 37 Washington Law Rev. 303 (1962).

Chapter Sixteen: Writings

Articles

Alexander, *Authentication of Documents Requirement: Barrier to Falsehood or to Truth?,* 10 San Diego Law Rev. 266 (1973).
Broun, *Authentication and Contents of Writings,* 1969 Law & Social Order 611 (1969).
Conrad, *Magnetic Recordings in Court,* 40 Virginia Law Rev. 23 (1954).
Purves, *The Policeman's Notebook,* 1971 Criminal Law Rev. 212 (1971).
Rogers, *The Best Evidence Rule,* 1945 Wisconsin Law Rev. 278 (1945).

Strong, *Liberalizing the Authentication of Private Writings,* 52 Cornell Law Quarterly 284 (1967).

Law Review Comments

Comment, *Critical Appraisal of the Application of the Best Evidence Rule,* 21 Rutgers Law Rev. 526 (1967).
Comment, *Photostatic Copies and the Best Evidence Rule: Time for a Change,* 40 Tennessee Law Rev. 709 (1973).
[See also bibliographical listings on questioned document evidence, following Chap. 18.]

Chapter Seventeen: Opinion, Expertise, and Experts

Books

KAPLAN & WALTZ, THE TRIAL OF JACK RUBY 21, 32, 50-52, 189-192, 253, 270-271, 286-287 (1965).
WALTZ & INBAU, MEDICAL JURISPRUDENCE, 54-56, 59-107 (1971).

Articles

Beuscher, *The Use of Experts by the Courts,* 54 Harvard Law Rev. 1105 (1941).
Clendenning, *Expert Testimony,* 9 Criminal Law Quarterly 415 (1967).
Diamond, *The Fallacy of the Impartial Expert,* 3 Archives of Criminal Psychodynamics 221 (1959).
Dieden & Gasparich, *Psychiatric Evidence and Full Disclosure in the Criminal Trial,* 52 California Law Rev. 543 (1964).
Elson & Schatz, *Using the Expert Witness,* 46 Nebraska Law Rev. 457 (1967).
Feeney, *Expert Psychological Testimony on Credibility Issues,* 115 Military Law Rev. 121 (1987).
Frank, *Obscenity: Some Problems of Values and the Use of Experts,* 41 Washington Law Rev. 631 (1966).
Gee, *The Expert Witness in the Criminal Trial,* 307 Criminal Law Rev. 14 (1987).
Handberg, *Expert Testimony on Eyewitness Identification: A New Pair of Glasses for the Jury.* 32 Am. Crim. L. Rev. 1013 (1995).
Imwinkelried, *The Daubert Decision on the Admissibility of Scientific Evidence: The Supreme Court Chooses the Right Piece for All the Evidentiary Puzzles,* 9 St. John's J. of Legal Commentary 5 (1993).
Kaplan & Miller, *Courtroom Psychiatrists. Expertise at the Cost of Wisdom?,* 9 Int'l Jour. of Law & Psychiatry 451 (1986).
Maguire & Hahsey, *Requisite Proof of Basis for Expert Opinion,* 5 Vanderbilt Law Rev. 42 (1952)
Martindale, *Intoxication and Opinion Evidence,* 8 Trial Lawyer's Quarterly 102 (1964).
Schuck, *Techniques for Proof of Complicated Scientific and Economic Facts,* 40 Fed. Rules Decisions 33 (1966).

Vann & Morganroth, *Psychiatrists and the Competence to Stand Trial,* 42 Univ. of Detroit Law Jour. 75 (1964).
Wolff, *Direct Examination of Experts,* 24 Trial 97 (1988).

Law Review Comments

Comment, *Accident Reconstruction by Expert Testimony,* 10 So. Dakota Law Rev. 161 (1965).
Comment, *Expert Testimony in Obscenity Cases,* 18 Hastings Law Jour. 161 (1966).
Comment, *The Expert Witness: Hearsay vs. Opinion,* 24 Baylor Law Rev. 108 (1972).
Comment, *The Use of Expert Testimony in Obscenity Litigation,* 1965 Wisconsin Law Rev. 113 (1965).

Chapter Eighteen: Scientific Evidence

General Article

Allen, *Expertise and the Daubert Decision,* 84 J. Crim. L. & Criminology 1157 (1994).
Coleman & Walls, *Evaluation of Scientific Evidence,* 1974 Criminal Law Rev. 276.
Faigman, *Mapping the Labyrinth of Scientific Evidence,* 46 Hastings L.J. 555 (1995).
Gianelli, *The Admissibility of Laboratory Reports in Criminal Trials: The Reliability of Scientific Proof,* 49 Oh. St. L.J. 671 (1988).
Taslitz, *Daubert's Guide to the Federal Rules of Evidence: A Not-So-Plain-Meaning Jurisprudence,* 32 Harv. J. on Legis. 3 (1995).

Psychiatry and Psychology

Books

Arieti, American Handbook of Psychiatry, 4 vols. (1959).
Cronbach, Essentials of Psychological Testing (2d ed. 1960).
Fish, An Outline of Psychiatry (1964).
Irvine & Breije, Law, Psychiatry and the Mentally Disordered Offender, 2 vols. (1972).
Kaplan & Waltz, The Trial of Jack Ruby (1965).
Overholser, The Psychiatrist and the Law (1953).
Roche, The Criminal Mind (1958).
Weihofen, Insanity as a Defense in Criminal Law (1933).
Whitlock, Criminal Responsibility and Mental Illness (1963).

Articles

Bartholomew, *Some Problems of the Psychiatrist in Relation to Sentencing,* 15 Criminal Law Quarterly 325 (1973).
Bauer, *Legal Responsibility and Mental Illness,* 57 Northwestern Univ. Law Rev 12 (1962).

Cooper, *Fitness to Proceed: A Brief Look at Some Aspects of the Medico-Legal Problem Under the New York Criminal Procedure Law,* 52 Nebraska Law Rev. 44 (1972).
Curran, *Expert Psychiatric Evidence of Personality Traits,* 103 Univ. of Penna. Law Rev. 999 (1955).
Diamond, *Criminal Responsibility of the Mentally Ill,* 14 Stanford Law Rev. 59 (1961).
Goldstein, *The Indigent Accused, the Psychiatrist and the Insanity Defense,* 110 Univ. of Penna. Law Rev. 1061 (1963).
Nelson, *The Clinical Psychologist in Juvenile Court,* 23 Juvenile Justice 26 (1972).
Reinhardt, *Incidence of Mental Disorder,* 18 Catholic Lawyer 195 (1972).
Suarez & Hunt, *The Scope of Legal Psychiatry,* 18 Jour. of Forensic Science 60 (1972).

Law Review Notes

Note, *The Durham Court Changes the Insanity Rule,* 8 New England Law Rev. 328 (1973).
Note, *Pretrial Psychiatric Examination: A Conflict With the Privilege Against Self-Incrimination,* 20 Syracuse Law Rev. 738 (1969).
Note, *The Psychologist in Court,* 33 Chicago-Kent Law Rev. 230 (1955).

Toxicology and the Chemical Sciences

1. In General

Books

ARENA, POISONING (2d ed. 1970).
CURRY, ADVANCES IN FORENSIC AND CLINICAL TOXICOLOGY (1972).
CURRY, POISON DETECTION IN HUMAN ORGANS (1963).
SUNSHINE, HANDBOOK OF ANALYTICAL TOXICOLOGY (1969).

2. Chemical Intoxication Tests

Books

DONIGAN, CHEMICAL TESTS AND THE LAW (1967).
FORRESTER, THE USE OF CHEMICAL TESTS FOR ALCOHOL IN TRAFFIC LAW ENFORCEMENT (1950).
GARZA, MULTI-UNIT, NARCOTICS MANUAL (1976).
REEDER, INTERPRETATION OF IMPLIED CONSENT LAWS BY THE COURTS (1972).

Articles

Borkenstein, *The Evolution of Modern Instruments for Breath Alcohol Analysis,* 5 Jour. of Forensic Science 395 (1960).
Greenberg, *Physiological Factors Affecting Breath Samples,* 5 Jour. of Forensic Science 11 (1960).

Newman, *Proof of Alcoholic Intoxication,* 34 Kentucky Law Forum 250 (1946).
Smith, *The Avoidance of Biologic Variables in Breath Tests for Alcohol in Blood,* 32 Amer. Jour. of Clinical Pathology 34 (1959).

3. Drugs

Books

Bailey & Rothblatt, Handling Narcotic & Drug Cases (1972).
Clarke, Isolation and Identification of Drugs (2d ed. 1986).
Eldridge, Narcotics and the Law (1967).
Pace & Styles, Handbook of Narcotics Control (1972).
Williams, ed., Narcotics and Hallucinogens—A Handbook (1967).

Articles

de Silva & D'Arconte, *The Use of Spectrophofluorometry in the Analysis of Drugs in Biological Materials,* 14 Jour. of Forensic Science 184 (1969).
Fales, *et al., Identification of Barbiturates by Chemical Ionization Mass Spectrometry,* 42 Analytical Chemistry 1430 (1970).
Finestone, *Narcotics and Criminality,* 22 Law & Contemporary Problems 69 (1956).
Turk, *et al., A Simple Chemical Method to Identify Marihuana,* 14 Jour. of Forensic Science 289 (1969).

Forensic Pathology

Books

Anderson, Pathology (5th ed. 1966).
Gonzalles, Vance, Helpern & Umberger, Legal Medicine, Pathology & Toxicology (1954).
Gradwohl, Legal Medicine (2d ed. 1968).
Gray, Attorney's Textbook of Medicine (3d ed. 1961).
Hendrix, Investigation of Violent and Sudden Death: A Manual for Medical Examiners (1972).
Merkeley, The Investigation of Death (1957).
Moenssens, Inbau & Starrs, Scientific Evidence in Criminal Cases, Chap. 5 (3d ed. 1986).
Moritz & Statler, Handbook of Legal Medicine (2d ed. 1964).
Morland, Science in Crime Detection (1958).
Muir, Muir's Textbook of Pathology (8th ed. 1965).
O'Hara, Fundamentals of Criminal Investigation (1956).
Simpson, Forensic Medicine (5th ed. 1964).
Snyder, Homicide Investigation (2d ed. 1972).
Spitz & Fisher, Medicolegal Investigation of Death (1972).
Waltz & Inbau, Medical Jurisprudence 329-333 (1971).

Articles

Marshall & Hoare, *Estimating the Time of Death,* 7 Jour. of Forensic Science 56 (1962).
Taylor, *Scientific Findings on Death and Coroner's Inquest,* 20 Rocky Mountain Law Rev. 199 (1948).
Wecht, *The Role of the Forensic Pathologist in Criminal Cases,* 37 Tennessee Law Rev. 669 (1970).

Photographic Evidence, Motion Pictures, and Videotape

Books

ANONYMOUS, BASIC POLICE PHOTOGRAPHY (2d ed. 1964)
ANONYMOUS, ENCYCLOPEDIA OF PHOTOGRAPHY (1964).
COX, PHOTOGRAPHIC OPTICS (13th ed. 1966).
NEWHALL, THE HISTORY OF PHOTOGRAPHY (rev. ed. 1964).
SANSONE, MODERN PHOTOGRAPHY FOR POLICE AND FIREMEN (1971).
SCOTT, PHOTOGRAPHIC EVIDENCE, 3 vols. (2d ed. 1969).

Articles

Busch, *Photographs—Still, Motion and X-ray,* 44 Illinois Bar Jour. 168 (1955).
Fischnaller, *Technical Preparation and Exclusion of Photographic Evidence,* 8 Gonzaga Law Rev. 292 (1973).
Paradis, *The Celluloid Witness,* 37 Univ. of Colorado Law Rev. 235 (1965).
Rouse, *Are We in Focus on Photo Identification?,* 7 Univ. of San Francisco Law Rev. 419 (1973).
Sweeny, *Sound Motion Pictures as Evidence of Intoxication in Drunken Driving Prosecutions: Constitutional Standards,* 52 Cornell Law Rev. 323 (1967).
Tuttle & Conrad, *Motion Pictures of Intoxicated Drivers,* Fingerprint & Ident. Mag., Apr., 1963, p. 3: Sept., 1965, p. 3.
Warton, *Litigators Byte the Apple: Utilizing Computer-Generated Evidence at Trial,* 41 Baylor L. Rev. 731 (1989).

Law Review Comment

Comment, *The Admissibility of Photographs of the Corpse in Homicide Cases,* 7 William & Mary Law Rev. 137 (1966).

Fingerprinting

Books

BRIDGES, PRACTICAL FINGERPRINTING (2d ed. 1964).
CUMMINS & MIDLO, FINGER PRINTS, PALMS AND SOLES (2d ed. 1964).

F.B.I. MANUAL, SCIENCE OF FINGER PRINTS: CLASSIFICATION & USES (1979).
GALTON, FINGER PRINTS (2d ed. 1965).
MOENSSENS, FINGERPRINT TECHNIQUES (1971).
SCOTT, FINGERPRINT MECHANICS (1951).

Articles

Almog & Gabay, *A Modified Super Glue Technique—The Use of Polycyanoacrylate for Fingerprint Development,* 31 Jour. of Forensic Science 250 (1986).
Brooks, *Techniques for Finding Latent Prints,* Fingerprint & Ident. Mag., Nov., 1972, p. 3.
Moenssens, *The Fingerprint Witness in Court,* Fingerprint & Ident. Mag. Apr. 1973, p. 3.
Moenssens, *Testifying As A Fingerprint Witness,* Fingerprint & Ident. Mag., Dec., 1972, p. 3.

DNA Profiling

Articles

Beeler & Wiebe, *DNA Identification Tests and the Courts,* 63 Washington Law Rev. 903 (1988).
Koehler, *DNA Matches and Statistics: Important Questions, Surprising Answers,* 76 Judicature 222 (1993).
Schornhorst, *Don't be Cowed by Scientific Evidence: A Primer for Prosecutors and Defense Attorneys,* 3 Criminal Justice 18 (1988).
Smith, *The Precarious Implications of DNA Profiling,* 55 U. Pitt. L. Rev. 653 865 (1994).
Thompson & Ford, *Acceptance and Weight of the New Genetic Identification Tests,* 75 Virginia Law Rev. 45 (1989).
Williams, *Conviction by Chromosome,* 18 Student Lawyer 26 (1989).
Williams, *DNA Fingerprinting: A Revolutionary Technique in Forensic Science and Its Probable Effects on Criminal Evidentiary Law,* 37 Drake Law Rev. 1 (1987).

Law Review Note

The Dark Side of DNA Profiling: Unreliable Scientific Evidence Meets the Criminal Defendant, Stanford Law Rev. 465 (1990).

Firearms Evidence

Books

BRADY, COLT AUTOMATIC PISTOLS (1956).
BRAVERMAN, THE FIREARMS ENCYCLOPEDIA (1960).
BURRARD, THE IDENTIFICATION OF FIREARMS AND FORENSIC BALLISTICS (1951).

CUMMINGS, EVERYDAY BALLISTICS (1950).
DAVIS, AN INTRODUCTION TO TOOL MARKS, FIREARMS AND THE STRIAGRAPH (1958).
DE HASS, SINGLE SHOT RIFLES AND ACTIONS (1969).
HATCHER, FIREARMS INVESTIGATION, IDENTIFICATION, AND EVIDENCE (1946).
HATCHER, JURY & WELLER, FIREARMS INVESTIGATION, IDENTIFICATION AND EVIDENCE (1957).
KRCMA, THE IDENTIFICATION AND REGISTRATION OF FIREARMS (1971).
MATHEWS, FIREARMS IDENTIFICATION, 2 vols. (1962).
SCHMIDT-ORNDORFF, ET AL., PECULIARITIES OF CERTAIN .22 CALIBER REVOLVERS (SATURDAY NIGHT SPECIALS), 19 Jour. of Forensic Science 48 (1974).
SMITH, THE BOOK OF RULES (1965).
SMITH, SMALL ARMS OF THE WORLD (1962).
STEBBINS, PISTOLS—A MODERN ENCYCLOPEDIA (1961).

Articles

Bellemore, *Ammunition: Manufacturing vs. Identification,* 5 Jour. of Forensic Science 148 (1960).
Biasotti, *The Principles of Evidence Evaluation as Applied to Firearms and Tool Mark Identification,* 9 Jour. of Forensic Science 428 (1964).
Goddard, *Scientific Identification of Firearms and Bullets,* 17 Jour. of Criminal Law & Criminology 254 (1926).
Harrison, *Rifling Twist,* American Rifleman, Nov., 1965, P. 52.
Howe, *Cartridge Case Marking,* American Rifleman, NOV., 1965, P. 12.
Jauhari, *et al., Statistical Treatment of Pellet Dispersion Data for Estimating Range of Firing,* 17 Jour. of Forensic Science 141 (1972).
Koffler, *Zip Guns and Crude Conversions—Identifying Characteristics and Problems,* 61 Jour. of Criminal Law, Criminology & Police Science 115 (1970).
Sinha & Kshettry, *Pellet Identification,* 63 Jour. of Criminal Law, Criminology & Police Science 134 (1972).
Sojat, *Organization, Study and Use of Fired Standards,* 10 Jour. of Forensic Science 442 (1968).
Van Amburgh, *Common Sources of Error in the Examination and Interpretation of Ballistics Evidence,* 26 Boston Univ. Law Rev. 207 (1946).
Wilson, *The Identification of Extractor Marks on Fired Shells,* 29 Jour. of Criminal Law & Criminology 724 (1939).

Voiceprints

Articles

Bolt, *et al., Speaker Identification by Speech Spectrograms: A Scientist's View of its Reliability for Legal Purposes,* 47 Jour. of the Acoustical Society of Amer. 597 (1970).
Cedarbaums, *Voiceprint Identification: A Scientific and Legal Dilemma,* 5 Criminal Law Bulletin 323 (1969).
Hennessy & Romig, *A Review of the Experiments Involving Voiceprint Identification,* 16 Jour. of Forensic Science 183 (1971).

Questioned Document Evidence

Books

BRUNELLE & REED, FORENSIC EXAMINATION OF INK AND PAPER (1984).
HILTON, SCIENTIFIC EXAMINATION OF QUESTIONED DOCUMENTS (1981).

Articles

Masson, *Felt Tip Pen Writing: Problems of Identification,* 30 Jour. of Forensic Science 172 (1985).
Miller, *An Analysis of the Identification Value of Defects in IBM Selectric Typewriters,* 29 Jour. of Forensic Science 624 (1984).
Risinger, Denbeaux & Saks, *Exorcism of Ignorance as a Proxy for Rational Knowledge: The Lessons of Handwriting Identification "Expertise,"* 137 Univ. of Pennsylvania Law Rev. 731 (1989).

Polygraph Testing

Book

REID & INBAU, TRUTH AND DECEPTION: THE POLYGRAPH ("LIE DETECTOR") (2d ed., 1977).

Speed Detection

Articles

Kopper, *The Scientific Reliability of Radar Speedmeters,* 33 North Carolina Law Rev. 343 (1955).
Woodbridge, *Radar in the Courts,* 40 Virginia Law Rev. 809 (1954).

Index

Jim Ziv, Northwestern University

Jon R. Waltz

About the Author

Jon R. Waltz is the Edna B. and Ednyfed H. Williams Memorial Professor of Law at Northwestern University School of Law and a lecturer at Northwestern's Medical School. Previously he was a member of the trial department of the law firm of Squire, Sanders & Dempsey of Cleveland, and chief prosecuting attorney in Willowick, Ohio. He also served in the Judge Advocate General's Corps of the U.S. Army.

Professor Waltz has been a member of the advisory committee of the U.S. Commission on Civil Rights and of the National Association of Criminal Defense Lawyers and Public Defenders. He has served as a consultant to the Federal Law Enforcement Training Center at Brunswick, Georgia, and as a member of the Illinois Criminal Justice Information System Policy Review Committee. He is a former member of the Board of Governors of the Society of American Law Teachers and former Chairman of the Section on Evidence of the Association of American Law Schools. He has been a member of the Illinois Judicial Inquiry Board and the American Medical Association's Committee on Medical Education.

Professor Waltz is the author or co-author of *The Trial of Jack Ruby; Principles of Evidence and Proof; Cases and Materials on Evidence; The Federal Rules of Evidence: An Analysis; Medical Jurisprudence; Cases and Materials on Criminal Evidence; Cases and Materials on Law and Medicine;* and *Evidence: Making the Record.* He has written on legal subjects in various law reviews, including those published by the law schools of the University of Michigan, New York University, Northwestern University, Stanford, the University of Pennsylvania, and Yale. In a more popular vein, he has published in the *Chicago Tribune Magazine, The Nation, The New York Times Magazine, Playboy,* and *Saturday Review.* He is a regular commentator on legal books in the Book World columns of the *Washington Post.*

Recently Professor Waltz received the Distinguished Service Award of the Society of Midland Authors for his published work on medical-legal problems. He received the 1987 Distinguished Alumni Award of the College of Wooster.

Photo Credits

Page 2: David Bentley
Page 9: Joel Gordon
Page 16: UPI/Corbis-Bettmann
Page 19: UPI/Corbis-Bettmann
Page 32: UPI/Corbis-Bettmann
Page 149: AP/Wide World Photos
Page 166: Corbis-Bettmann
Page 203: Susan Kuklin, Photo Researchers
Page 206: Spencer Grant, Photo Researchers
Page 228: Photofest
Page 260: AP/Wide World Photos
Page 284: Camerique/H. Armstrong Roberts
Page 338: Daemmrich/Stock Boston
Page 368: Illinois State Police, Division of Forensic Services
Page 369: Illinois State Police, Division of Forensic Services
Page 381: Illinois State Police, Division of Forensic Services
Page 385: AP/Wide World Photos